National Intelligencer Newspaper Abstracts 1856

Joan M. Dixon

HERITAGE BOOKS
2008

HERITAGE BOOKS
AN IMPRINT OF HERITAGE BOOKS, INC.

Books, CDs, and more—Worldwide

For our listing of thousands of titles see our website
at
www.HeritageBooks.com

Published 2008 by
HERITAGE BOOKS, INC.
Publishing Division
100 Railroad Ave. #104
Westminster, Maryland 21157

Copyright © 2008 Joan M. Dixon

All rights reserved. No part of this book may be reproduced or transmitted in any form or by any means, electronic or mechanical, including photocopying, recording or by any information storage and retrieval system without written permission from the author, except for the inclusion of brief quotations in a review.

International Standard Book Numbers
Paperbound: 978-0-7884-4772-3
Clothbound: 978-0-7884-7475-0

NATIONAL INTELLIGENCER NEWSPAPER
WASHINGTON, D C
1856

TABLE OF CONTENTS

Daily National Intelligencer, Washington, D C, 1856: pg 1

Acting Midshipmen: 353
Appointments by the President: 26; 29; 30
Appropriations made during the 34th Congress: 410-414
Artic explorer, Dr Elisha Kent Kane: 424
Attack by Seminole Indians: 37
Autobiography of Daniel Webster: 434

Balt & Ohio railroad accident: 251
Bellona Arsenal: 331; 430
Birthplace of George Washington: 53
Business Directory, Balt, Md: 142-147
Cadets appointed by the President: 184
Charter Oak tree: 317
Church directory: 193-195
Commencement at Academy of Visitation, Gtwn: 258-259
Congressional Cemetery: 155-156
Dayton, Wm Lewis-ancestors: 248

Death of Cmdor Charles Morris: 31
Death of Gen James Bankhead: 385
Death of Gen James Thompson: 364
Death of Hon Ogden Hoffman: 169
Death of Revolutionary Soldiers: 12-13
Death of Wm Goodloe, sr: 387
Death of Wm H Maxwell: 34-35

Deserters massacred: 352
Disaster at Last Island-New Orleans: 314
Don Jose Dario Arguello family: 130
Earliest newspaper: 400
Election, Balt, Md: 357
Fall of the Alamo: 406
Fighting at Walla Walla: 54

Fire on the propeller Tinto: 270
Frederic VII: 233
Gen O'Donnell: 312
Georgetown, D C, election: 73
Grave of Madison: 38
Herndon, Edward-kin: 100
House of Rothschild: 2; 28
Indian fight in Oregon-casualties: 16-17
John Hancock: 158
Jury-Wash, D C: 223; 319; 406-407
Indian war in Florida-U S Troops: 173; 255
Ladies-Drs of Medicine: 213
Life of Gen Arthur St Clair: 283-284
Maine, N Y, and Md history: 378
Maury, John W-monument: 138
Memoir of Col Fred'k Baron de Weisenfels: 138
Military movements-New Orleans: 417
Mount of Olives: 231

Officers of the: Jamestown: 181
                    Plymouth: 247
                    Portsmouth: 95
                    Savannah: 405

Ohio Fair Ground tragedy: 356
Oldest Church in Phil, Pa: 376
Panama railroad accident-casualties: 206
Pay of Army Ofcrs: 86
Philadelphia railroad accident: 264; 274
Police Ofcrs-Wash, D C: 97; 319
Poughkeepsie, N Y, railroad accident: 11-12
Printer's Ball: 47-48
Prisoners at Santa Rosa: 166
Promotions in the Navy: 271-274
Public School Teachers-Wash City: 304-305
Reminiscences-British fleet in the Potomac river: 328
Sale of real estate of Agnes M Easby: 241-242
Schooner A Levering capsized: 33; 40
Schooner Bancroft fire: 6
Ship Germania disaster: 112
Ship St Denis disaster: 21
Soldiers of the War of 1812: 8-9
Steamboat Metropolis disaster: 120
Steamer Nautilus disaster: 323
Steamer Monmouth collision in Chesapeake Bay: 364

Steamer Niagara lost: 345
Steamer Northern Indiana disaster: 266
Steamer Pacific lost-passengers: 48
Thomas Keating killed in the Willard Hotel: 178; 179
Thos Norsworth-almost 100 years old: 432
Yellow Fever victims: 5
Vigilance Cmte, Calif: 262; 322-323
Virginia and Florida history: 380
West Point graduates: 226
Whig Convention, Balt, Md: 339-340
Whigs of Lexington, Ky: 154

Index: pg 442

Dedicated to the memory of my uncle:
Alfred Neff b.1893 Wash, D C d. 1974, Md.
Married. Aug, 1918
Caroline Rosalie Sweeney
b. 1894, Wash, D C d. 1962, PG Co, Md

PREFACE
Daily National Intelligencer Newspaper Abstracts
1856
Joan M Dixon

The National Intelligencer & Washington Advertiser is hereafter the Daily National Intelligencer. It was the first newspaper printed in Washington, D C; Samuel H Smith, the originator. The same was transferred to Jos Gales, jr on Aug 31, 1810; on Nov 1, 1812, the paper was under the firm of Jos Gales, sr, & Wm W Seaton. The Library of Congress has microfilm of the paper from the first issue of Oct 31, 1800 thru Jan 8, 1870, the final paper. The Evening Star Newspaper of Jan 10, 1870 reports: The Intelligencer is discontinued: the proprietor, Mr Alex Delmar, says that having lost several thousand dollars, & being in poor health, he has resolved to discontinue its publication.

Included in the abstracts are advertisements; appointments by the President; Hse o/Rep petitions; passed Acts; legal notices; marriages; deaths; mscl notices; social events; military promotions; court cases; deaths by accident; prisoners; & maritime information-officers-crews. Items or events which might be a clue as to the location, age or relationship of an individual are copied.

No attempt has been made to correct the spelling. Due to the length of some articles, it was necessary to present only the highlights of same. Chancery and Equity records are copied as written.

The index contains all surnames and *tracts of lands/places*. **Maritime vessels** are found under barge, boat, brig, frig, schn'r, ship, sloop, steamboat, tugboat, yacht or vessel.

ABBREVIATIONS:

AA CO	ANNE ARUNDEL COUNTY
CMDER	COMMANDER
CMDOR	COMMODOR
ELIZ	ELIZABETH
ELIZA	ELIZA
MONTG CO	MONTGOMERY COUNTY
PG CO	PRINCE GEORGES CO
WASH	WASHINGTON
WASH, D C	WASHINGTON, DISTRICT OF COLUMBIA

BOOKS IN THE NATIONAL INTELLIGENCER NEWSPAPER SERIES: 1800-1805/1806-1810/1811-1813/1814-1817/1818-1820/1821-1823/1824-1826/1827-1829/1830-1831/1832-1833/1834-1835/1836-1837/1838-1839/1840/1841/1842/1843/1844/1845/1846/1847/ 1848/1849/ 1850/1851/1852/1853/1854/1855/1856. SPECIAL: CIVIL WAR 2 VOLS, 1861-1865

NATIONAL INTELLIGENCER NEWSPAPER ABSTRACTS
1856

TUE JAN 1, 1856
Senate: 1-Memorial from Wm H De Forrest & others, asking remuneration for property destroyed by the bombardment of San Juan or Greytown, in Central America. The memorialists set forth their property was unjustly & unnecessarily destroyed by the bombardment & fire of that town on Jul 1, 1854, by Capt Hollins, in virtue of written instructions from the present Gov't of the U S. As citizens, faithful to their allegiance, are entitled to protection in property as well as in life & liberty. 2-Additional documents presented in relation to the memorial of Thos Ewbank, respecting improvements on propelling blades for steamers. 3-Ptn from Wm R Combs, asking a pension for disability incurred while in the U S military service. 4-Ptn from T L Elliott, late chaplain in the army, asking to be allowed bounty land. 5-Ptn from Wm Allen Pierce, asking to be allowed a quantity of land equal to that of which he was deprived by an error of the U S surveyor, & which was converted to the use of the Gov't.

Died: on Dec 25, at the NavyYard, William Henry, eldest son of Chas H & Eliz E Gordon, aged 14 months, 6 months & 19 days.

Private sale: the one undivided half of the Miners' Journal, formerly the Cumberland Civilian, established over 25 years, & one of the oldest newspapers in Western Md, is now offered at private sale by the subscriber on reasonable terms. He will sell the one-half of the stock & the good-will at $1,500-one-half payable on day of sale; the balance by note, with approved security, the time to be arranged hereafter.
-Thos B Price, Editor Miners' Journal, Box 41, Post Ofc, Cumberland, Md.

Dissolution of partnership existing between E A Eliason & Clayton Cherry, under the firm of Eliason & Cherry, this day, Dec 31, 1855, by mutual consent. The Currying & Leather business will be continued by said Cherry & John Eliason, under the style of J Eliason & Cherry.

WED JAN 2, 1856
Accident at Shelbyville, Ky, on Sat last, as Mr McCormack, with Miss Scearce & Miss Linsey were approaching Shelbyville in a carriage or buggy, the horse took fright & ran off the side of a bridge some 20 or 30 feet high. Miss Scearce was killed instantly, Miss Linsey slightly wounded, & Mr McCormack's leg broken. Miss Searce was about 13 years old.

Household & kitchen furniture at auction on Jan 7, at the residence of Mrs Trippe, 6 4½ st, between C & D sts. -A Green, auct

Advices received of the death of the eldest brother of the house of Rothschild, at Frankfort, on Dec 6. Baron Anslem Von Rothschild is the 3rd of the brothers Rothschild who has departed this life in 1855, the head of the house in Naples, Carl, & the head of the house in Vienna, Solomon, having already died this year. Of the five brothers there remains now only James, the head of the house in Paris. Baron Anslem was looked on as the founder of the great financial Rothschild power, & though possessed of less cultivation & education than his brother, was a decided genius in money matters. He died childless, & has left to the house a fortune of 30,000,000 gulden.

I have this day associated with me my son, Henry C Noyes, & will continue the wholesale & commission Boot & Shoe business under the firm of Wm Noyes & Co. -Wm Noyes

Dissolution of copartnership, by mutual consent. -Wm S Butt, Wm M S Hopkins. Having bought out Mr Butt's entire interest, I shall always be on hand with fashionable styles of Hats, Caps, Furs, & Gents' Furnishing Goods. -Wm M S Hopkins, 6 & Pa ave.

Died: on Dec 31, at his residence, Nathl Frye, aged 77 years. He was one of our oldest & most respected citizens, having been in the employ of the Gov't since 1798. Removing with it to this city in 1800, he had become identified with its interests, &, like a faithful sentinel, has died at his post of duty. In each relation of husband, parent, & friend, he was faithful, affectionate, & true. His funeral will be tomorrow at 11 o'clock, from his late residence, 35 K st.

Died: on Jan 1, after a protracted illness, Miss Ann Eliz Danforth, in her 41st year. Her funeral will be from the residence of her father, in Wash Co, D C, at 2 o'clock, or Methodist Episcopal Church, Navy Yard, at 3 o'clock.

THU JAN 3, 1856
Telegraphic advices from Savannah, Ga, announce the death, at his residence, in that city, on Jan 1, of Hon John MacPherson Berrien, known to the country as Pres Jackson's first Atty Gen. We believe he had reached the ripe age of 75 or 76 years.

Indian war in Oregon. Col A Benton Moses, the U S Surveyor of Customs, was killed by a party of Indians about Nov 1st. He was at the time attached to an escort accompanying an express from Capt Malonny, of the U S army, into the Indian country. Dr Burns, of Steilacoom, was killed on the same day.

Savannah, Jan 1. Hon J Macpherson Berrien died here this morning, after an illness of only 12 days.

Andrew McGuire died at Boston on Dec 20th. He burnt his hand a week previously while finishing up a hat for his employer; on Thu he was a work on a lot of furs; on Fri his hand was a lot worse & the physician pronounced it a case of poison. Furs are preserved by the use of arsenic & other deadly poisons.

From the Stockholm Aftonblad of Nov 15, 1855. The first Russian newspaper was published in 1703. Peter the Great took part personally in its editorial composition. There are 2 complete copies of the first year's edition of this newspaper in the Imperial Library of St Petersburgh. One of the oldest newspapers of Northern Europe is the official Gazette of Sweden, the Post och Inrikes Jidning; founded in 1644, during the reign of Queen Christina, the daughter of Gustavus Adolphus the Great, & the present year is, without interruption, its 211th anniversary.

Mrd: on Dec 27, in Wash City, by Rev Jas B Donelan, Jas M Freeman, jr, to Miss M Augusta, daughter of De E C Robinson, all of Norfolk, Va.

Mrd: on Jan 1, in Wash City, by Rev Mr Hodges, Wm H Harmer, of N Y, to Miss Sarah Leana Henning, of Wash City.

Mrd: on Dec 23, in Wash City, by Rev T O'Toole, Dr R H Steele, of Saginaw, Mich, to Kate, eldest daughter of S Masi, of Wash City.

Mrd: on Jan 1, in Wash City, by Rev L J Gilliss, Isaac Hobart Kilby, of Eastport, Maine, to Maria Gilliss, daughter of A B Waller, of Wash City.

Mrd: on Dec 27, in Wilmington, N C, by Rev Dr Drane, Dr W W Anderson, U S A, to Mary Virginia, daughter of the late Gen Thos Childs, U S A.

Mrd: on Dec 11 last, at Malone, Franklin Co, N Y, by Rev Amos C Treadway, Hon Geo A Adams to Sydney M, daughter of the officiating minister.

Died: on Jan 1, Mrs Ann W Richey, wife of John Richey, in her 46th year. Her funeral is at 10 o'clock this morning, from her late residence, 316 C st, between 6th & 7th sts.

C Miller: Cupper, Leecher, & Bleeder. A fresh & good supply of Swedish & Russian leeches always on hand. Will attend to calls at any hour, day or night. Ofc 427 6th st west, between F & G.

FRI JAN 4, 1856
Senate: 1-Ptn from Chas Taylor, asking compensation for services & supplies furnished during the Black Hawk war. 2-Ptn from Saml V Niles, asking compensation for clerical services in the Gen Land Ofc. 3-Ptn from Cyprian F Jenkins, asking to be allowed to locate a quarter section of land in Fla under the armed occupation act. 4-Ptn from citizens of the U S asking that Cmder J J Nicholas, who was placed on the furlough list, may be restored to his position on the navy list.

The Balt Patriot: this old journal has enlarged its means by the accession of Messrs W H Carpenter & John Wills as associate editors & proprietors with Mr John F McJilton, the former proprietor.

U S Patent Ofc, Wash, Jan 2, 1856. Ptn of Zephaniah Bosworth, of Harmer, Ohio, praying for the extension of a patent granted to him on Apr 6,1842, for an improvement in constructing heating-stoves, for 7 years from the expiration of said patent, which takes place on Apr 6,1856. -Chas Mason, Com'r of patents.

U S Patent Ofc, Wash, Jan 2, 1856. Ptn of S W Bullock, of N Y, praying for the extension of a patent granted to him on Mar 23,1842, for an improvement in presses for pressing hay, for 7 years from the expiration of said patent, which takes place on Mar 23, 1856. -Chas Mason, Com'r of patents.

U S Patent Ofc, Wash, Jan 3, 1856. Ptn of L W & G W Blake, of Pepperville, Mass, praying for the extension of a patent granted to them on Apr 20,1842, for an improvement in water wheels, for 7 years from the expiration of said patent, which takes place on Apr 21, 1856. -Chas Mason, Com'r of patents.

The Winchester Virginian notices the death of John Bruce, a prominent citizen of that town, & father of the editor. Mr Bruce was at one time Pres of the Winchester & Potomac Railroad Co, & for many years a member of the Town Council, as well as an efficient magistrate.

The Richmond Examiner announces the death of Wm M Overton, on Jan 1, in Wmsburg, in the prime of life. Some time since he was connected with the Washington Union, but recently one of the editors of the Washington Sentinel.

On Jan 1st two murders were committed in Woodbridge, Conn, by Chas Sanford, an insane man, about 26 years old. He killed Mr Enoch Sperry, who was riding in his sleigh, & then went to the house of Ichabod Umberfield, a farmer, & killed him with an axe. Sanford is in jail, a raving maniac. He is the nephew of Sanford, who was one of the Wakemanites, arrested on suspicion of connexion with the recent murder of Justus Matthews.

Odd Fellows' Funeral Obsequies in Portsmouth, Va, on Sunday last: paid the last sad tribute of respect to the following members, who fell victims to the yellow fever:

Rev Vernon Eskridge	Saml Brewer	Jas Hineman
Wilson W Williams	Chas Cassell	Wm Brittingham
Dr John W H Trugien	John W Forrest	Wm Jones
Richd Wilson	Geo Chambers	Jas Mayo
Isaac Anderton	Geo Hope	Robt Nelms
R M C Young	D P Daughtrey	Jas H Finch
Robt Balentine	Harrison Ferribee	John Nash
Wm F Snead	Jas Henrahan	Robt A Graves
John D Cooper	Nathan Brittingham	Robt T Scott

Mrd: on Jan 2, in Wash City, at E st Baptist Church, by Rev G W Samson, Mr A C Richards, of Kirkland Co, Ohio, to Mary A, 2nd daughter of Andrew Rothwell, of Wash City.

U S Patent Ofc, Wash, Jan 3, 1856. Ptn of Jonathan Read, of Alton, Ill, praying for the extension of a patent granted to him on Mar 12, 1842, for an improvement in reaping machines, for 7 years from the expiration of said patent, which takes place on Mar 12, 1856. -Chas Mason, Com'r of patents.

At a meeting of the veterans of the war of 1812, in Norfolk, Thu, upon calling the roll it was found that 21 of those brave men had fallen since the last meeting. Mr Chas H Shield having resigned the Presidency of the Society, Thos G Broughton, filled the vacancy.

SAT JAN 5, 1856
Mrd: on Dec 27, in Wash City, by Rev Gideon H Day, Mr Caleb Pennington to Mary L Sutton.

Mrd: on Jan 3, by Rev Gideon H Day, Mr Geo P Harris to Miss Martha Ann Bowens, all of Wash City.

Died: on Jan 3, Geo Lamb, in his 66th year. For the last 30 years he has been a resident of Wash City. He was formerly of Balt, & was one of the gallant defenders of that city in 1814. His funeral will be on Jan 6, at 2 o'clock, from his late residence, opposite Willard's Hotel.

Died: yesterday, in Wash City, after a protracted illness, Catharine, wife of Henry Walker, in her 36th year. Her funeral will be from her late residence, 402 16th st, on Sunday evening at 3 o'clock.

James River land at Public Auction, on Feb 3 next: 2,300 acres, that valuable estate known as *Hog Island & the Main*. *Hog Island* is located in Surry Co, Va. A plat of the land may be seen at the counting-room of Messrs T Branch & Sons, of Petersburg, &, will be explained by Mr S S Griscom, the late Surveyor of same place. The land itself will be shown by Mr Doyle, residing on the place. -T B Robertson, exc of Wm Robertson, deceased.

Letters testamentary on the last will & testament of Col Saml Miller, late of Phil city, deceased, having been granted to the subscribers, all persons indebted to the estate are to make payment, & those having claims to make known the same without delay. -M L M Peters, Francis Peters, 196 Spruce st, Phil.

Wash City Ordinances: 1-Act for the relief of W W DeMaine: Mayor to have adjusted the claim of W W DeMaine, late assist surveyor of Wash City, so that he may be compensated for his services at the rate of compensation or salary of the Surveyor from the death of the late Surveyor, Henry W Ball, until the period when the present Surveyor, R F Hunt, entered upon his duties. 2-Act for the relief of Wm Guinand: refund to him so much of a wagon license as shall have accrued from Jul 6, 1855, to the end of the term for which said license was taken out.

To the humane public. Left the house of his parents, on 8th st, Wash, on Dec 28, Wm Faherty, aged 15 years. When last seen in Wash City he was with another lad about 18 years of age, with whom it is supposed he now is. As all exertions on the part of his parents to find his whereabouts have failed, it is earnestly hoped that any person who may see this notice & have it in his power to give information whereby he may be found will confer an obligation & relieve the anxiety of his parents by addressing a note or telegraphing W P Faherty, Dept of State, Wash. When spoken to it will be discovered that instead of pronouncing the letter G he pronounces it D.

MON JAN 7, 1856
Beaufort [S C] Dec 23, 1855. We, the citizens of Beaufort, desire of expressing out thanks to Lt Dan L Braine, U S Navy, & the ofcrs & crew of the schnr *Bancroft*, one of the vessels under your command, who assisted in arresting the flames that at one time threatened, on Dec 22, to consume a large portion of our town. Our sincere appreciation for the valuable service rendered. To Lt Com'g J N Maffitt, U S Navy, Com'g Coast Survey Party, Port Royal Sound.

E Rhett	E J Durban	W B Sherman
J J Porter	J B Porter	A L Aimun
D L Thompson	J C Cole	F F Sams
John E Talbird	W B Means	H McKel
F Fallard	R B Fuller	J J Bell
W C Dana	C E Bell	J W Bond
John A Bell	John Bell	

Dr Wm H Harding, a member of the House of Delegates of Va, aged about 35 years, died at Richmond on Fri last. He had been laboring for some 5 or 6 days under a severe attack of pneumonia. A prescription was prepared for magnesia & for some morphine-the latter to be used externally upon a blister which was painful. A servant obtained the medicine, & instead of taking it to the attending physician, as he was directed, he took it to the room of the patient, who emptied the powder into the bottle & then drank half of it. The paper contained 30 grains of morphine. The stomach pump was used, & everything to revive the patient was used, but in vain.

Orphans Court of Wash Co, D C. Letters testamentary on the personal estate of Thos J Johnston, late of Wash Co, deceased. -Isabella Johnston, admx

Naval: on Jan 1 Cmdor Gregory, the late commandant of the Boston naval station, reported himself in person to take charge of the new frig **Merrimac**, & many of the ofcrs ordered to her also reported to him. The frig will not be ready for sailing for some weeks.

The venerable John Sneed, of Boyle Co, Ky, died on Dec 21, at the great age of 101 years. He was born in Albemarle Co, Va, on Feb 2, 1755; was for some years the Sec of Thos Jefferson, then volunteered in an expedition against the Cherokee Indians, & after that became a soldier in the Revolutionary struggle. He was with Washington at Valley Forge; was detailed with a number of picked men to the command of Col Morgan, finally went to the South with Gen Greene, until the end of the war. He then emigrated from Va to Ky, & lived there until he died.

Noah Edminster, a soldier of the Revolutionary war, died at Dixmont, Me, on Dec 24, in his 93rd year. He was born in Malden, Mass, in 1758, & at an early age volunteered in the American army, at the commencement of the war at Bunker Hill. He witnessed the surrender of Burgoyne's army, & was with the army, under the immediate command of Washington, through one whole campaign.

On Sat, as Mr & Mrs Dean & another lady of Lawrence, were riding a sleigh, a bolt broke which allowed the cross-bar to fall against the horse's heels & caused him to run away & throw the whole party out. Mrs Dean struck her head upon a rock so violently as to cause her death in 2 hours. -Boston Journal

Desirable property for sale: the house now occupied by the subscriber, & for many years the residence of Mr Thos Blagden, on N J ave, south of the Capitol. The bldg is of brick 50 feet front by 46 feet deep, 3 stories, with a back bldg 18 by 28 feet; with 3 acres around it; & numerous out-bldgs. Apply to Wm H Ward, Atty at Law, or to the subscriber, at his residence, 716 N J ave, & at his Lumber Yard, Blagden's Wharf. -Theodore Mosher

Annual meeting of the Wash City Protestant Orphan Asylum will be held in Trinity Church on Jan 8 at 12 o'clock. -Susan R Coxe, sec

Cumberland, Jan 5. Miller, the murderer of Dr Hadel & Fred'k Graff, a few months since, was hung here yesterday. He died protesting his innocence. About 8,000 persons witnessed the execution.

TUE JAN 8, 1855
Mrd: on Jan 2, at Springfield, Mass, by Rev Bishop Fitzpatrick, M Edw De Stoeckl, the Charge d'Affaires of Russia, resident in Wash City, to Miss Eliza W Howard, youngest daughter of the late Hon John Howard, of Springfield, Mass.

Mrd: on Jan 6, in Wash City, by Rev F S Evans, Mr Wm W Reigle to Miss Mary H McDaniel.

Assistant teacher wanted in a Female Seminary in St Mary's Co, Md. -Robt Crane, St Inigoes P O, St Mary's Co, Md.

Dress-making: Miss A E Davidson: residence at 457 6th st, between D & E sts.

Orphans Court of Wash Co, D C. In the case of Gustavus Waters, adm of John H Thompson, deceased, the administrator & Court have appointed Jan 19 next, for the settlement of the personal estate of the deceased, with the assets in hand.
-Ed N Roach, Reg/o wills

Soldiers-1812. The soldiers of the war of 1812 will form a procession on Jan 8, to proceed to the Pres' mansion to pay their respects to his Excellency the Pres of the U S. Military escort of District volunteers, Col Wm Hickey, commanding. Color guard, under command of Maj Geo McNeir, Assist Marshal:

Gen G W P Custis	Col Jno F Hamtranck
Maj Geo Peter	Thos G Broughton
Gen Leslie Combs	Chas A Grice
Gen J S Van Rensselaer	Jno S Gallaher
Hon Jas M Porter	Jacob Gideon
Gen Jos Ritner	Col W W Seaton
Gen Jacob Markle	Col John S Williams
Col Harvey Baldwin	Col Jas L Edwards
Capt Thos Brunell	Dr Wm Jones
Col L C Judson	Gen Geo Biscoe
Gen Hugh Ely	Capt Saml George, Onnondaga chief
Gen Benj C Howard	Capt Peter Wilson, a sachem of the Oneidas
Hon Thos Franklin	

Aids to the Marshal in Chief:
Gen St John B L Skinner; Gen Anthony Miltenberger; Col John T Manning.

Assist Marshals:

Gen Geo Petre
Gen G W Biscoe
Maj Isaac Clarke
Col Wm McNeir
Jacob Gideon
G C Grammer
Christopher Hall
Capt Jas Jarvis
Gen W H Richardson
Col r G Saunders
Col Jas L Ranson
Capt Geo F de la Roche
-Wm P Young, Chief Marshal

Wm G Ridgley
Col Richd Burgess
Sterling Thomas
Capt Levin Jones
Capt Jas Wilson
Maj C R Johnson
John G Wilson
Wm Sumner
Jas A Williams
Jas A Kennedy
Capt Jas W Ashby

Senate: 1-Memorial of John A Ragan, setting forth that he has discovered a plan to prevent the overflowing of the Mississippi river & to reclaim inundated lands, & asking a grant of every alternate section he may so reclaim, in order to enable him to carry his plan into execution. 2-Ptn from H H Rhodes, late a lt in the U S Navy, & dropped by the Naval Board, asking to be restored to his original position; & also from Cmders Jos Myers & Wm M Armstrong, placed on the retired list by the Naval Board, asking that they be restored to the active list. 3-Additional documents presented in the case of Saml Lockwood, asking to be restored to the position occupied by him in the navy prior to the action of the naval board. 4-Ptn from Catharine Jacobs, widow of a waiter in the military household of Gen Washington, asking to be allowed a pension. 5-Ptn from Wm Marvin, asking confirmation to his title to certain lands in Florida claimed under
a Spanish grant.

WED JAN 9, 1855

The papers of the day recorded the death of Dr Tobias Watkins, at his residence in Wash City, on Nov 14 last. He came of an old & respectable Md family, whose branches extend throughout the State. He was born in Anne Arundel Co on Dec 12, 1780; the only child of Thos Watkins, & was yet a boy when his father died. Entered at an early age at St John's College, Annapolis, & graduated in 1798. In May, 1802, he married the eldest daughter of Geo Simpson, of Phil, cashier of the Bank of the U S; shortly after that commenced practice at Havre-de-Grace, Md. In a few years he removed to Balt & received the appointment of physician to the Marine Hospital. He was in active service during the war with England, having been, in May, 1813, appointed surgeon in the 38th regt of infty, commanded by Col Peter Little. He died at age 75 years, in the communion of the Catholic Church, & in favor with God.

Household & kitchen furniture at auction on: Jan 14, at the residence of Mr Daggy, 151 south B st; also a fine Chickering Piano Forte. -A Green, auct

Mrd: on Jan 8, in Wash City, by Rev R L Dashiell, Mr Wm H Falconer to Mary Ann, daughter of C W Boteler, sr.

Died: on Dec 27, at Richmond Hill, Yadkin Co, N C, Mrs Mgt Pearson, aged 42, wife of Hon R M Pearson, of the Supreme Court, & daughter of the late Col John Williams, of Tenn. She was for many years a member of the Presbyterian Church. Besides her husband, she left a family of 8 children.

The number of <u>Revolutionary pensioners</u> is now reduced to 726. The number of <u>Revolutionary widows</u> receiving pensions is 5,552.

New house & store for rent: on 7th st, between G & H. Apply to F W Geisecking, Gtwn, or V Harbaugh, druggist, near the premises.

For rent: large double brick house on E st, between 8th & 9th sts, lately occupied by Maj Potter, & more recently by Hon John Slidell, of the U S Senate. Apply to Dr Brown, 378 E st, between 10th & 11th sts, or at room 12, General Land Ofc.

THU JAN 10, 1856
Trustee's sale of lot 29 in square 468, on the Island, by deed of trust from S John Thompson, dated May 27, 1854, duly recorded: public auction on Jan 24, in the auction rooms of J C McGuire. -Wm B Webb, trustee -J C McGuire, auct

Died: on Jan 9, John McCutchen, in his 62nd year. His funeral is this day at 2:30 o'clock P M, from his late residence on Jefferson st, Gtwn.

Rooms to rent: 409 G st. Apply on the premises to Mrs Geiger.

FRI JAN 11, 1856
Chief Justice Taney's health has so far improved as to enable him to make the journey to the seat of gov't, where he arrived on Tue evening, & expects to take his place on the Bench in a few days.

Rev John Overton Choules, D D, one of the most eminent Ministers of the Baptist Church, died suddenly at N Y on Sat last. He arrived there from his residence at Newport, R I, on New Year's day upon a holyday visit, but a severe cold from which he was suffering caused congestion of the lungs, & on Sat, while quietly sitting in his chair, he expired without a murmur. His age was about 55 years.

Senate: 1-Ptn from Levy Robinson, asking to be allowed fishing bounty for the schnr **Mary Jane**, & compensation for preserving & taking care of public property. 2-Ptn from Jas Butler, to be allowed arrears of pension. 3-Ptn from Capt R A Wainright, asking to be relieved from the payment of certain amount of public money stolen from his possession in the city of Boston. 4-Ptn from Eliza & Abby E Peck, of Providence, R I, heirs at law of Wm Peck, of the R I line of the continental army, asking the half-pay granted by the resolution of Oct 21, 1780, after deducting the commutation at one-eighth of its nominal value. 5-Memorial of Thos Brownell, late a lt in the U S Navy, but dropped from the rolls in accordance with a decision of the late Naval Board, asking to be restored to his former position. 6-Memorial of Wm S Ogden, late a cmder in the U S Navy, asking an opportunity to rebut any charges upon which he may have been dropped from the navy, & asking Congress to grant such redress as his case demands. 7-Memorial of Howard Marsh, late a passed midshipman in the navy, complaining of having been dropped from the service, & asking that the action of said Board may be investigated. 8-Memorial of T D Shaw, a cmder in the navy, who was placed on the retired list in consequence of the proceedings of the late Board, together with some documents in relation to the case of the memorialist.

House of Reps: 1-<u>One hundred & sixth ballot</u> was had for <u>Speaker</u>: no choice having been effected.

Mrs Sata Payson Eldredge, better known as Fanny Fern, was married at N Y on Sunday to Mr Jas Parton, a member of the literary fraternity in that city.

Mrd: on Thu, in Wash City, by Rev John C Smith, Ezekiel Young, jr, to Miss Clara Lewis, all of Wash City.

Mrd: on Jan 10, in Wash City, by Rev Mr Boyle, Wm Locke to Miss Catharine Redmon, all of Wash City.

Mrd: on Jan 10, in Wash City, at Wesley Chapel Parsonage, by Rev R L Dashiell, Mr Thos G Wheeler, of Balt Co, Md, to Miss Grace R Moore, of Montg Co, Md.

Mrd: on Jan 1, at Richmond, at the First Baptist Church, by Rev Dr J Lansing Burrows, Mr Matthew Hobson to Miss Adrienne Grantland, all of Richmond.

Poughkeepsie, N Y, Jan 9. The express from Albany for N Y stopped just below here this afternoon, on account of a defect in the track, when it was run into with great force by another train from Poughkeepsie bound in the same direction. Killed: Mrs Green, of Utica, & a young man & woman, names unknown. Among the injured: Mr & Mrs Roberts, & 3 children, of Albany; Mrs Campbell, of Utica, slightly; H Emmon, of Vernon, Oneida Co, slightly; Mrs Oscar Hull, of New Haven, slightly; Capt Schuyler, of Albany, badly; Geo Klopp, of Madison Co, Ohio, seriously; Geo

Harrington, of Wash, D C, face scalded & otherwise hurt; Danl Lord, of N Y, slightly-face scalded & other injuries. [Jan 14th newspaper: Mr Isaac D Gott, was one of the passengers, a witness to what happened. Killed: Mrs Chas Green, of Utica; Mrs Henry Hurlburt, of Albany; a young man, not identified. Dangerously wounded: Mrs Campbell, of Utica; Geo Kios, of Ohio; Catharine Howell, of N Y; a young lady, about 25 years of age, not identified. The latter is deranged & has about $200 Canada money, a gold watch, a ring marked S C to M C G, & other valuables. Badly wounded, but doing well: Mr Bogert, of N Y; 2 children of G W Roberts, of Albany; Miss Gardiner, of Schoharie; & Mr Pond, of N Y.] [Jan 15th newspaper: the person killed & not identified was Jas Gordon, of Clinton, Canada West, & the lady injured & insensible was his wife. She is now partially sensible. Their friends have been telegraphed.]

SAT JAN 12, 1856
Maj Geo Deas, Assist Adj Gen of the U S Army, while walking on Pa ave on Thu, slipped upon the ice & fell, & broke a bone in his right leg near the ankle.

For sale, the large well arranged house now occupied by myself as a Tin Plate & Sheet iron manufactory, with dwlg above. The house is 4 stories high, & was built by Mr S G Morsell. On 7th st, between H & I sts, one of the best business stands in Wash City. -Jos F Hodgson

Death of <u>Revolutionary soldiers</u>: Amongst the statistics of the year 1855 we find gathered together the following obituary of Revolutionary soldiers. It is not probable that all who have died are included in this list.
Died, Jan 3, Rev Jonathan Smith & Harmon Utterbach; 7, Saml Eddy; 12, Stephen Dunham; 16, Jonathan Records & Nathl Chellis; 24, Simon Hicks; 27, Wm Shermhill; 20, Zenas Gage; 31, Elijah Barnes.
Feb 9, Jos Peck; 11, David Truax; 13, Robt Francis; 18, Hugh Harris; 19, Nathan Parmeter; 28, Abashal Eddy.
Mar 1, Abel Hawley; 4, Francis Otto; 8, Saml Dan; 9, Solomon Crittenden; 11, Capt Luther Pomeroy & Jepther Lee; 12, Stephen Brownell; 13, Marmaduke S Davis; 14, Jonathan Gillet; 19, Nathan Cook; 21, Saml Adams & Jas Dunham; 23, Wm Makepeace & Wm Holiday; 24, Saml Hinkle; 25, Elijah Page; 31, Ebenezer Whitney, Jos Ripley, Capt Robt Holmes, & Aaron Rogers.
Apr 3, John Kiger; 6, John Crightwell; 27, Lewis S Noble; 28, Chauncey Lewis.
May 2, Philip Blaisdell; 9, Rev Saml Mitchell; 27, Saml Rockwell.
Jun 5, Isaac Whitehead; 14, Nathan Smith; 15, Peter Cesanzon; 21, Jabez Leftwich; 22, Oliver Weeks; 28, John T Van Fleet.
Jul 3, Saml Redman; 4, Luther Ingals; 7, Jos Bassett; 12, Jas Ryan; 15, Josiah Hall & Jacob Diffenderfer; 17, Gen Geo S Nellis; 18, Francis Browning.
Aug 5, John Smith; 14, Saml Davis; 29, Henry Spohn; 31, Thos Dunbar.
Sep 13, Jos Crandell; 15, Stephen R Munn; 17, Jas Broadwell; 18, Mr Casler.

Oct 6, Elisha Bartlett; 11, Otis Ensign; 22, Danl Fitch.
Nov 2, Saml Maddox; 13, Jacob Lorman; 14, Seth Tucker.

Mrd: on Jan 3, at the Univ of Va, by Rev A D Pollock, Prof Wm J Martin, of Wash College, Pa, to Susan Agnes, daughter of Wm McCoy, of the former place.

Mrd: on Jan 10, by Rev Dr Norwood, Zachariah B Beall, of PG Co, Md, to Martha E Clagett, daughter of Henry Addison, Mayor of Gtwn, D C.

Mrd: on Jan 10, by Rev Mr Hilt, Miss Isabell, daughter of Resin Orme, of Fairfax Co, Va, to Benj C Lazenby, of Montg Co, Md.

Died: on Dec 18, 1855, at **Mulberry Grove**, near Port Tobacco, Md, of pneumonia, Danl Jenifer. A politician for more than 20 years, in the warmest contests most zealous & efficient, yet he was frank, true, & bold. As a private gentleman he was very extensively known in Europe & America. As a husband, father, master, neighbor & friend, he was truly & fervently loved & respected.

Local matters: 1-Geo Raglan, a mulatto, accused of killing a man in Wash City about a year since, was, upon his 2nd trial on Thu, convicted of manslaughter. 2-The trial of Wm W B Edwards, for shooting & killing Thornton Avery a few months ago, is now in progress.

Orphans Court of Wash Co, D C. Letters testamentary on the personal estate of Michl Dooley, late of Wash Co, deceased. -Jno C Fitzpatrick, exc

The Thirteenth St Baptist Church, Rev Mr Teasdale, pastor, is to be dedicated tomorrow. Rev Dr Fuller, of Balt, is to preach the opening sermon.

Died: on Jan 11, in Wash City, Mrs Harriette Curtis Langdon, in her 52nd year. Her funeral will be from the residence of her son, Wm Chauncy Langdon, on E st, near 3rd on Sunday afternoon, at 3 o'clock.

Died: on Jan 11, in Wash City, in a lingering illness, Richd L Spalding, in his 43rd year. His funeral will be on Sunday, at 2 o'clock, from his late residence, 318 5th st.

Anacostia Fire Co: ofcrs elected for the ensuing year:
Chas M Sanderson, Pres   Wm E Hutchinson, Treas
Wm H Harrison, V Pres   John M Mitchell, Steward
Jas R Cook, Sec

Rev Wm Arthur, of London, Sec of the Weslyan Missionary Society, will preach in the Hall of the House of Reps on Jan 13, at 11 o'clock.

Sig Severo Strini will commence Vocal Instruction in Wash City, on Feb 10. Apply to Mr Richd Davis' Music Store.

New Orleans, Jan 10: the steamer **Prometheus**, from San Juan, brings dates from San Francisco to be 10th ult. From Oregon: several battles had taken place between the whites & the Indians. In a battle near Wallawalla river Capt Penet & Lt Burrows & 3 privates were killed. In another battle, at Puget's Sound, Lt Slaughter & several others were killed.

MONDAY JAN 14, 1856
At Boston, on Jan 5, Miss Ida Morgan came to her death by chloroform, administered at her request by Dr Emery, a dentist in Broomfield st. One application did not produce insensibility, &, at the patient's request, the sponge was again placed to her nose. She then went into a spasm, breathed heavily, but soon her breathing became more easy. She never spoke after being removed from the chair. The chloroform, according to Dr Jackson, had changed the blood of the deceased to a substance as thin as water.

Dr Stephen W Taylor, Pres of the Madison Univ in N Y, died on Monday last, after a lingering illness.

Hon Francis E Rives, who had his arm broken several days ago by slipping down his steps while sleet was on the ground, underwent the painful operation of having the broken limb amputated on Sat last. He is doing very well under the circumstances. -Petersburg Intell of Jan 8.]

Disastrous fire occurred at Newport, R I, on Tue night last. The *Truro house*, a large & fashionable summer boarding establishment, owned by Mrs Sarah M Jeffroy, was burnt to the ground. The dwlg house on the west side, also owned by Mrs Jeffroy, & the cottage on the east side, owned by Mr Robt D Coggeshall, were pretty much destroyed. Whitfield House, opposite, owned & occupied by Stephen Slocum, was much injured.

Died: on Jan 13, in Wash City, Franck Boteler, infant son of John J & Ellen Willson, aged 15 months. His funeral will take place this afternoon at 2 o'clock.

The *Columbia Mills*. A Gtwn friend informs us that Col Lorenzo Thomas, U S Army, & Robt P Dodge, have each recently purchased an interest in these extensive flouring mills. The last Capt Boyce was, at the time of his death, the leading proprietor, & it is his portion which has been disposed of. Vincent Taylor, who was his only partner, remains in the concern, & Edw Boyce, takes the place of his father. The new firm is Boyce, Taylor & Co.

Mrs Bishop, [already the mother of 11 boys & 2 girls] gave birth on Wed to 3 boys- making a family of 16 children. They are in need of aid. Gifts can be left at the residence of Mrs Bishop, E st south, between 3rd & 4½ sts, north side, Wash.

After performing the most prominent part in "Ion" at the Worcester Museum, on Monday night, Mr Donald McGregor, actor, had an apoplectic fit in Taft's Hotel, which terminated fatally.

TUE JAN 15, 1856
Capt Roland Gardiner arrived at New Brunswick on Jan 9 from Nantucket, having left that place on Monday morning in the steamer **Island Home**. The train from Hyannis on the Cape Cod road having proceeded no further than Barnstable, being stopped by the heavy snow. Capt Gardiner walked to Wareham, 27 miles, which feat he accomplished in spite of the snow drifts, & then took a sleigh to Tremont reaching Boston over the Fall River road. -New Bedford Mercury

Winchester [Va] Republican. Mr C A B Coffroth, one of the proprietors for the last 6 years, retired, & Mr Geo E Sansenet is th sole editor & proprietor.

Two men, Dennis Hani & Morris Sweeney, were instantly killed last night in the wheel-house of the steamer **Elm City**. They were crushed between the A brace & guard-beam. The necks of both were broken. -New Haven Palladium of Fre.

Leverton Thomas, age 75 years, was convicted at Pittsburg recently upon the charge of forging a promissory note for $465. H is a man of wealth, & possessed much influence in Wash Co, Pa, where he resided.

Orphans Court of Wash Co, D C. Letters of administration on the personal estate of John T Neill, late of Wash Co, deceased. -Caesar A Brown, adm

The Glasgow [Scotland] Mail, per the last steamer: the case before the Court of Sessions last week, respecting the legality of a marriage with a deceased wife's sister, one of the counsel said it was a doubtful point whether such a marriage was prohibited in the Levitical Law; on which Lord Ardmillan remarked that he was surprised none of the counsel had referred to Jacob marrying two sisters, & to the fact that our **Saviour** was descended from one of them.

Stray cows came to my premise last winter, a Heifer; also, in the spring, two cows. The owner or owners are to come forward, prove property, pay charges, & take them away.
-Sarah Ann Nally, on Pa ave, near the Eastern Branch.

Com'r sale of a tract of land in Alexandria Co, Va: by decree of the Circuit Court of Alexandria Co, Va, rendered at the Nov term, 1855, in the writ of Hermann H Voss & Augustus H Voss, vs Lisette J Voss & others: public auction on Feb 22 of a tract of land in said county, lying on the county road, near the Gtwn Ferry; contains 33 acres, with a comfortable cottage house, kitchen, & stabling; the same being that tract of land of which Wm Voss, late of D C, died seized. -Andrew Wylie, Albert Stuart, Christopher Neale, Com'rs of sale.

Mrd: on Jan 10, in Wash City, by Rev Joshua Morsell, J Wm Woodward, of Wash City, to Miss Eliza H S Lowe, of Alexandria, Va.

Mrd: on Jan 9, in Wash City, by Rev G M Day, Wm Dyer to Miss Rachel Bixler, of Fairfax Co, Va.

Alton, Ill, Jan 11. A freight train on the Terre Haute & Alton Railroad ran off the track yesterday & five persons were killed: Mr King, engineer; Wesley Davis, fireman; John Morrison, of Dunkirk, & Messrs Bates & Drake, of Decatur, Ill.

WED JAN 16, 1856
Great Indian fight in Oregon: Headquarters, Left Column, 1st Regt O M V. Camp Wallawalla river, Dec 8, 1855. Yesterday, as my command was on the line of march from the mouth of the Do Shute river to Whitman's valley, we were attacked by about 400 Indians. This morning the battle was renewed & raged all day. The number of Indians fought are supposed to exceed 600. The noted Chief of the Wallawala valley, Peu-peu-mox-mox, was killed. He was taken prisoner by my command on Dec 5, & made an effort to escape. On doing so he was killed, with 4 other prisoners. -Jas K Kelly, Lt Col Reg O M V. To W H Farrar, adj.
List of killed & wounded. Killed:
Capt Bennett, Co F; 2nd Lt J M Barrows, Co H; Private Simon L Van Hageriman.
Mortally wounded-since dead: Privates Kelso, Co A; Henry Crow, Co H.
Mortally wounded-still alive: Casper Snook, Co H; Jos Sturdivant, Co V; Jesse Fleming, Co A.
Dangerously wounded: Co H: Capt Layton; Privates T J Payne, Nathan Fry, & Frank Crabtree; J B Gervais, Co K.
Severely wounded: Capt Wilson, Co A; Capt Munson, Co I; Sgt Maj Isaac Miller, Co H; Private G W Smith, Co B.
Slightly wounded: Private F Duval, Co A; A M Adington, Co H.
-Robt Thompson
+
We are informed by Mr McCarver that an express arrived at Roseburg on the 30th ult, from Little Meadows, on Rogue river, bringing news of a fight there a day or two before. A Mr Lewis, of Capt Kinney's company, was killed; one of Capt Kinney's, two of Capt Williams' & one of Capt Rice's companies were wounded.

+
News from Wash Territory to Dec 10. Express brought here by Mr Bradley, we have the intelligence from the command of Lt Slaughter, stationed near the forks of White & Green rivers, by which we are informed, that Lt Slaughter has been killed outright & others mortally wounded. Amongst the killed are Cpls Berry & Clarendon, [Capt Wallace's company,] & wounded privates Beck, Nolan, McMahan, & Grace; one man of Capt Key's company of artl, mortally wounded, now dead. -E D Keys, Capt 3rd Artl commanding. To Capt G Hays, commanding, Co V, Wash Territory Volunteers.

Wash Corp: 1-Cmte of Claims: act for the relief of Philip Aldroff: passed. 2-Ptn from Mrs S A Greeves, asking to be refunded certain money: referred to the Cmte on Finance.

Valuable land in Market: intending to remove to another state, I desire to sell one of the most desirable farms in Augusta Co, about 4 miles from Staunton: contains 470 acres, with a large & handsome brick mansion, stables, barn, & necessary outhouses. My purpose is to sell it speedily. My address is Staunton or *Cline's Mill*, Va. -Chesley Kinney

Mrd: on Dec 12, at Scott Hall, Eastern Shore, Va, by Rev Mr Cheevers, Thos R Joynes, jr, to Sallie Wise, eldest daughter of Thos P Bagwell, M D, all of Accomac Co, Va.
+
Mrd: on Dec 12, by Rev Mr Cheevers, Edw R Leatherbury, M D, to Bettie M, 2nd daughter of Dr Thos P Bagwell, all of Accomac Co, Va.

Mrd: on Jan 15, in Wash City, at the Foundry Parsonage, by Rev E P Phelps, Mr Albert W Ely to Miss Susannah B Triplette, all of Wash City.

Died: on Jan 10, at Bowling Green, Caroline Co, Va, in her 62nd year, Ann Hoomes Maury, wife of Wm G Maury, & mother of the late John W Maury, of Wash City.

Died: on Jan 10, at her residence in Alexandria, Mrs Harriet D P Baker, relict of the late John Martin Baker, formerly U S Consul in Europe & in South America, & daughter of the late Col Fred'k H Baron de Wiessenfels, of the Revolutionary army.

Extract from the Biography of late Senator Lewis F Linn, of Missouri, soon to be published. Both the grand-parents of Dr Linn, with 7 members of their family, fell victims to the merciless & bloody scalping-knife of the savages. His intrepid & chivalrous grandfather, Col Linn, espoused the cause of the colonies, & took up arms for their liberties at the dawn of the American Revolution. He lived to behold the independence for which he had striven, & some years after its establishment, fell overwhelmed by numbers in his last conflict, near Louisville, on the Ohio river.

The Phil American announced the death of a venerable citizen, Jasper Cope, suddenly, in the Friends' meeting-house on Sunday last, whilst at his devotions. He was born in 1775, thence was in his 81st year. Thos P Cope & Israel Cope were his elder brothers, & the lives of the three have ended almost in the same twelve months. They were all men of great integrity & uprightness. The name of Cope was not unknown to the country at large. It was always prominent when useful enterprises were on hand.

A Card. Mrs M A Dennison who advertises engravings for sale in this city is not Mrs Mary Andrews Denison, the author of Home Pictures, What Not, Mark, & The Sexton. She is residing at Boston with her husband, Rev C W Denison, as co-editor of the Olive Branch & editor of the Ladies' Enterprise.

Orphans Court of Wash Co, D C. Letters of administration on the personal estate of John McCutchen, late of Wash Co, deceased. -Jas McCutchen, adm

THU JAN 17, 1856
Mrs Hannah Bennett died at her residence, No 2 Vine st, Boston, on Friday, at age 100 years, 11 months & 16 days. She was a native of Roxbury, but passed most of her days in Boston. She was 20 years old when the American Revolution commenced. The colored woman, Mother Boston, is now the only centenarian known to be alive in Boston.

Died: on Jan 2, in Alexandria, Va, Edwin F Tatsapaugh, printer, in his 34th year, leaving a wife & 4 children to mourn their loss.

FRI JAN 18, 1856
Senate: 1-Memorial from Saml Lockwood, cmder in the U S Navy, setting forth that he entered the navy in 1820, & to the present time has faithfully performed all the duties required of him & protests against the action of the Naval Board, & earnestly pleads his claims to the position on the active list from which he says he was removed by the misjudgment of the Naval Board. 2-Memorial from E Carrington Bowers, Frank Ellery, Robt Handy, & Peter Turner, lts in the navy, complaining of the action of the Naval Board, & asking to be restored to the active duty list. Same for A K Long, a cmder in the Navy, asking to be restored to the active service list. 3-Ptn from Cmder B F Sands, asking to be compensated for the use of his method of ascertaining the character of the bottom in deep sea soundings. 4-Ptn from the widow of Brvt Maj O'Brien, late of the army, asking the payment of a balance due her husband as a captain of artl from Dec 31, 1849, to Mar 31, 1850. 5-Ptn from Saml Forrest, a purser in the navy, asking to be allowed a commission on a certain disbursements made by him, as special agent on board the U S ship **Ohio**, on the coast of Mexico

& Calif, in 1848. 6-Ptn from R St Clair Graham, one of the heirs of Gen Arthur St Clair, asking to be allowed the half-pay due his ancestor for services in the Revolutionary war. 7-Ptn from Leslie Combs, asking that the bounty land law may be extended to his regt of Ky volunteers, who served in the Seminole war, excluded by a decision of the Com'r of Pensions. 8-Ptn from Sarah Larabee, widow of a Revolutionary soldier, asking to be allowed bounty land. 9-Ptn from Danl Carr, asking that a pension may be granted him for services rendered in the war of 1812. 10-Ptn from the grand-daughter of Thos Diman, asking compensation for the services of her ancestor in the war of the Revolution. 11-Ptn from Zachariah Corlin, a soldier in the war of 1812, asking to be allowed a pension.

Lamentable accident on Tue in Jersey city, for 3 young women. While working for Messrs J G & J Edge, pyrotechnists, engaged in making fireworks at their residence in Prospect st, the works accidentally took fire & exploded. Mary Ann Blakemore managed to escape. Catharine Kelley & Catharine Haley died from suffocation.

Cmdor Stewart has addressed a long & earnest appeal to Congress against the action of the Naval Retiring Board.

A Naval Court Martial has been ordered to assemble today at the Phil Navy Yard for the trial of Cmder Robt Ritchie, for insulting language used to Capt Saml F Dupont, concerning the action of the late Naval Retiring Board, of which Capt Dupont was a member, & by which Com Ritchie was retired on full leave pay. Ofcrs who compose the court: Cmdors L Kearney, [Pres,] Geo W Storer, E A F Lavalette, Isaac Mayo, Captains Thos A Conover, Jas M McIntosh, John B Montgomery, Joshua R Sands, Wm C Nicholson, John Kelly, Thos A Dornin, Fred'k Engle, & John Rudd. Com H B W Kennedy will be Judge Advocate, & Hon Chas C Conrad, ex-Sec of War, counsel for the accused. [Jan 22nd newspaper: Mr Etheridge, late Chief Clerk of the Navy Dept, testified to an account of the transaction detailed by Cmder Ritchie, in which he boasted of having used the words liar, scoundrel, & coward. Examination not completed.]
[Mar 4th newspaper: The court-martial found Capt Ritchie guilty, & sentenced him to be reprimanded by the Sec of the Navy. The Sec decided that the action & verdict of the court-martial were dis-approved for the good of the service. In the decision the Pres concurred; & Capt Ritchie has been discharged from arrest & reinstated in his rank & position in the navy. -Star]

Col Doyle, U S Marshal of Nebraska Territory, met with a fatal accident on Dec 27th, which resulted in his death in a short time. He was coming out of his ofc in Omaha City, when he mis-steped & fell from the steps to the ground, so severely injured by the fall that he lived only about half an hour. He was from South Carolina.

U S Patent Ofc, Wash, Jan 17, 1856. Ptn of Alonzo C Arnold, of Norwalk, Conn, praying for the extension of a patent granted to him on Apr 23, 1842, for an improvement in punching machines for manufacture of covered buttons, for 7 years from the expiration of said patent, which takes place on Apr 23, 1856.
-Chas Mason, Com'r of Patents

U S Patent Ofc, Wash, Jan 16, 1856. Ptn of Saml Taylor, of Cambridge, Mass, praying for the extension of a patent granted to him on May 28, 1842, for an improvement in constructing brushes for dressing warps, for 7 years from the expiration of said patent, which takes place on May 28, 1856. -Chas S Mason, Com'r of Patents

The venerable Asa Andrews died at Ipswich, Mass, on Sunday last, in his 94th year. At the time of his death he was the oldest surviving graduate of Harvard College, & the oldest man in Ipswich. In 1796 he was appointed by Washington collector of the port of Ipswich, which ofc he held until 1829, when he was removed by Gen Jackson. He filled many ofcs of trust, & was a man of much ability.

Died: on Jan 16, in Wash City, Susannah Adelaide, aged 1 year, daughter of Geo & Mary E Seitz. Her funeral will be tomorrow at 2 o'clock P M.

Obit-died: on Nov 25, at **Pleasant Gardens**, McDowell Co, N C, Adolphus L Erwin, in his 67th year. He was born in Morganton, Burke Co, N C, where the greater portion of his life was spent in promoting the spiritual as well as temporal interest of his family, the church, & the community in which he lived. He was admitted to the bar in Jan, 1813. His marriage to Mary G Simianer took place in Nov, 1817, & in 1822, together with her, they united with the Presbyterian church of Morganton. About 10 years since he removed to McDowell Co.

Rooms, with or without board: s e corner of Pa ave & 4½ st. -Mrs Allen Thompson

SAT JAN 19, 1856
The trial of Manuel Echeveria in the U S District Court, at N Y, on a charge of fitting out a schnr for the African slave trade, was concluded on Wed-the jury returned a verdict of not guilty.

Mrd: on Jan 17, in Wash City, by Rev Andrew G Carothers, Mr Saml T Crown to Miss Mary Eliz Hutchins, both of Wash City.

Mrd: on Jan 17, in Wash City, by Rev Dr Sunderland, Mr John H Strain, of Arkansas, to Miss Cornelia W, daughter of John H Houston, of Wash City.

Mrd: on Jan 17, in Wash City, at Christ Church, by Rev Mr Morsell, A K Childs, of Georgia, to Susie, daughter of Jno P Ingle, of Wash City.

Mrd: on Jan 10, at **Woodland**, Sussex Co, Va, by Rev J W White, R C Barnard, of Wash Co, D C, to Fannie L, daughter of Capt Wm Briggs, of Sussex Co, Va.

Persons lost at sea on Jan 6 by the wreck of the ship **St Denis**, from N Y, bound for Havre: Passengers: in the cabin, Fred'k Weiss & wife, Geo Batenahl; in the steerage, Geo Bakefish, Jacob Heinhooldt, Paul Ludwig, J Jamoo, wife, mother & child, Philip Ludwig, John Graef, Gustav Schelenvecker. The Crew: Alonzo Follansbee, capt; Jas Coogan, 2nd mate; F Smith, carpenter; C S Davis, steward; Chas S Potter, cook; Richd Henry, 2nd cook; Jas Smith, Fred'k Lovett, Ephraim Simpkins, J B Petty, Wm Turner, John Connelly, John Luckauy, John Bodine, Thos Cummings, Geo Wilson, Duncan Logan, John Wilson, Jas Smith, Walter H Beach, seamen; Thos Lee, boy.

Edw Johnson, employed in a rolling mill at Niles, Mich, was mortally wounded in an explosion recently, & died after a few days of excruciating pain.

In the Lafayette [Indiana] Courier of Fri: this afternoon Stocking, Rice, & Driskill were duly executed, the first named for the murder of John Rose & the 2 latter for the murder of Cephas Fahrenbaugh. Neither of the miserable culprits had any confession to make; each protested his innocence to the last, even upon the scaffold.

Valuable farm for sale: 170 acres, at **Bayly's Cross Roads**; with a small frame house & stable. The title is unquestionable. Apply to F H Smith, at the House of Reps, or to J H Cleveland, on the premises.

Died: on Jan 2, at New Orleans, Nicholas D Rind, guager of liquors at that port. Mr Rind was a native of this District, but for the last 20 years a resident of New Orleans.

MON JAN 21, 1856

We are pleased to learn from Judge John F May, of this city, father-in-law of Gen Bayly, that the health of this gentleman is much improved. He went to Havana some time since on account of a pulmonary affection from which he was suffering.

A young man, Harry Grey, who is a watchman at the Ky Locomotive Works, recently had left him, conditionally, by a deceased uncle in England, $200,000. Mr Grey is 25 years o fage, already having inherited $45,000 from his father. His prudent old uncle, knowing his fast habits, in his youth, inserted a condition of the inheritance, that if said Harry was in debt at age of 30 $500, he should forfeit the inheritance. -Louisville Democrat

Letter to the Independence Belge, dated Madrid, Dec 28. The Duke of Sotomayor, former Pres of the Council of Ministers, committed suicide Dec 26 in a fit of despair caused by intense suffering from the gout. He was 60 years of age. Not many Americans thought that the subject of this notice was a Philadephian by birth, although he was also a nobleman of distinction in Spain. In 1796, while the seat of gov't of the U S was in Phil, Don Carlos Martinez, Marquis La Casa Yrujo, arrived here as ambassador from Spain. He was a young man & soon after his arrival here he married Sally McKean, daughter of Govn'r McKean, of Pa, a lady celebrated among the beauties of that time. The Marquis resided at 2nd & Pine sts, & there his son, the subject of this notice, was born. He inherited the estates & titles of his father, but on his marriage into the house of Sotomayor took the name of Duke of Sotomayor. Having resided in this country until he was 12 years of age, he received his early education here. He was in the full vigor of life, his intellect was unimpaired, & those who knew him of late years are shocked of the report of his death. -Phil Bulletin

Cincinnati papers announce the death of Hon Timothy Walker who died in that city on Jan 14. He was one of the most distinguished lawyers at the Western bar.

Obit-died: Mrs Swift, the estimable wife of Gen Jos G Swift, of Geneva, N Y. In severing an union of unchanging & unruffled affection of 50 years' duration, her death has inflicted upon her worthy husband, a deep & enduring sorrow, as well as an irreparable loss to all her domestic circle. [No death date given-recent.]

Died: Fanning Cobham Tucker, of N Y, [Major Tucker,] recently. He was a native of N Y; his father, a scholar of King's [now Columbia] College, became a surgeon in the British army. The family was related to the Tuckers of Bermuda & Va. The N Y family intermarried with the ancient Dutch family of Wolfendyke, & the Major himself with the family of Joshua Sands, formerly in Congress. [No death date given.]

Mrd: on Thu last, at Balt, by Rev Dr Wyatt, Alex'r Randall, of Annapolis, to Miss Eliz P Blanchard, daughter of the late John G Blanchard, all of Balt.

Orphans Court of Wash Co, D C. Letters of administration on the personal estate of John Mothershead, late of Wash Co, deceased. -Isabella Mothershead, adm

Orphans Court of Wash Co, D C. Letters of administration on the personal estate of Oliver Whittlesey, late of Wash Co, deceased. -Eliz Whittlesey, admx

TUE JAN 22, 1856
Ringwood Female School, Fauquier Co, Va, under the charge of the Misses Milligan, will commence on Feb 14 next.

Senate: 1-Memorial from Thos Petigru, late a cmder in the navy dropped from the list by the Naval Board, asking that he may be restored to his rank. Also, from Thos R Gedney, cmder in the navy, asking to be removed from the furlough & placed on the retired list. Also, from Capt Thos Paine, U S Navy, placed on the reserved list by the Naval Board, asking to be restored to his former position. 2-The Chamber of Commerce of Charleston, S C, complaining of the action of the Naval Board in placing Lt J N Maffit on the reserved list. 3-Memorial of Chas Gray, late a passed midshipman in the navy, dropped by the action of the Naval Board, asking to be returned to his former position. 4-Memorial from M L Maury, setting forth his services in the navy, & complaining of the action of the said board in his case. 5-Ptn from Washington Morse, asking to be placed on the pension list as an invalid from wounds & disabilities received in the war of 1812. 6-Paper in relation to the claim of Benj Berry, a Revolutionary soldier, asking to be placed on the pension list. 7-Ptn from the citizens of De Kalb Co, Ala, asking that the widow of Obadiah Benge, of the Revolutionary army, be placed on the pension roll. 8-Ptn from Capt Chas Boarman, asking to be restored to his former position in the navy, from which he had been retired by the action of the late Naval Board, setting forth that, without family or political influence, he had attained the highest rank known in the navy, without ever having been court martialed, arrested, or suspended; that he is in full & vigorous health, & as fit for duty as ever. 9-Memorial from Saml W LeCompte, late a cmder in the navy, complaining of being dropped by the action of the Naval Board. Also, from S Johnson, setting forth the hardships of his case in having been dropped from the list of lts by the action of the Naval Board, instead of having been placed at least on the reserved list.

Nashville [Tenn] Banner: the Supreme Court of Tenn now in session at the capital, has affirmed the judgment of death against Ben Herbert for murder in Montg Co; also, the judgment of imprisonment for life against John H Morgan, for murder in Stewart Co; & that of imprisonment for 10 years against Jos P Holt, Jesse B Williams, Thos H Williams, Henry Byford, & John Simmons, for murder in Cannon Co. [There existed a deadly feud between 2 clans in Cannon Co, know as the Holt & Cawthorn parties, daring & reckless men, under their respective leaders, Holt & Cawthorn. On Nov 4, 1854, both parties, armed & equipped, met in the public road. One of the Cawthorn clan was killed; 5 of the Holt clan, the parties named above, including the leader Jos P Holt, were arrested & convicted of murder & sentenced to 10 years' imprisonment at hard labor in the State Penitentiary.]

New Orleans Delta: a day or two since an old bachelor of our city, a German, John D Fink, died, & yesterday his last will & testament was probated in the second district court. He was reputed to be very wealthy. His will does not give any clue to the exact amount of his hoardings. He was born in the city of Wertemberg, Germany, a great many years since, & some 40 years ago emigrated to this city, where he continued to reside in a state of single-blessedness up to the hour of his death. He left the bulk of his property to some pseudo-charitable institution in preference to making his friends & relations happy. He makes Dedriich Buellerdeick, watchmaker in Commercial Place, his executor; gives to him his house & lot on Poydras st; to his daughter $3,000 & a slave girl; to his son $1,500. He then bequeaths to his nephew Schwartz, of this city, $2,000; to some other nephews residing here $2,000 each; to a nephew in Vera Cruz $2,000; to his sister Caroline & her 12 children, residing in Germany, $2,000 each; to the wife of his step-brother & her children, also residing in Germany, the sum of $2,000 each. He concludes by devoting the remainder of his large fortune to the purpose of erecting an asylum for destitute Protestant widows, to be called the Fink Asylum, & authorizes Mr Buellerdeick to appoint 3 trustees to carry the latter portion of the will into effect. He wills that his body be interred in the Protestant Cemetery on Girod st, & a marble monument erected over it, fenced in with an iron railing, the whole cost of which is not to exceed $2,000. Mr Fink has one consolation in the spirit-land-he has left no widow of his own to mourn his loss, but many destitute widows will probably be benefited by his demise.

In the Court of Chancery of the State of Delaware, for Sussex Co, Sept Term, A D 1855. Petition for partition. John P Hudson vs Henry T Hudson, Chas P Hudson, Martha Hudson, Wm L Hudson, Mary A Hudson, Jas B Prettyman, Burton Prettyman, John W Prettyman, Wm P Prettyman, Molton Prettyman, Paynter Prettyman, Nehemiah Dickerson & Amelia his wife, in right of said Amelia, Milton Hudson, & Kelita Hudson. Petition filed Sep 13, 1855, & summons awarded, Sept 15 summons issued, Sep 19 Sheriff returned non sunt. And now, to wit, this 19th day of Sep, 1855, it appearing to the Court that summons to appear & show cause why partition of the premises in said petition mentioned should not be made according to the prayer of the said petitioner, directed to the said dfndnts, which said summons hath been regularly issued, but that the said dfndnts have not caused their appearance to be entered upon such proceed within such time & manner, according to the rules of this Court, as the same ought to have been entered, in case such process had been duly served; & on motion of John R McFee, Solicitor for petitioner, & affadavit made to the satisfaction of this Court that the said dfndnts reside out of this State, it is ordered by the Chancellor that the said Henry T Hudson, Chas P Hudson, Martha Hudson, Wm L Hudson, Mary A Hudson, Jas B Prettyman, Burton Prettyman, John W Prettyman, Wm P Prettyman, Molton Prettyman, Paynter Prettyman, Nehemiah Dickerson & Amelia his wife, in right of said Amelia, Milton Hudson, & Kelita Hudson, do appear in this Court on Mar 11, 1856. -Jas Stuart, Reg-Crt of Chancery

Died: on Jan 16, in Balt, Jas R Hitaffer, in his 33rd year, formerly a resident of Wash City, where he leaves a wife & child to mourn his loss.

The Greatest Beverage of the Age. W Gillies & Brothers celebrated Dandelion Coffee is acknowledged to be equal to the finest old Mocha Coffee, & the most effectual remedy for dyspepsia, biliousness, derangement of the liver, & nervousness.

W Gillies & Bro, 235 & 237 Washington st, importers of the Dandelion Root, & sole manufacturers of the pure & unadulterated Dandelion Coffee, put up in tine cans, with a fac simile of our signature on each wrapper, as a protection against imposture. For sale by W H Gilman, Druggist, Pa ave & 4½ st.

WED JAN 23, 1856

The Georgia Historical Society, convened on Jan 7, at Savannah, & passed a resolution to the memory of their late Pres, Hon John Macpherson Berrien.

Trustees' sale of house & lot at auction: on Feb 25 next, in front of the premises, by deed of trust from John Trueman & wife to the subscribers, dated Jun 25, 1850, recorded in Liber J A S No 15, folios 406 to 408, of the land records for Wash Co, D C: sale of part of lot 6 in square 449, in Wash City, fronting on L st, between 6th & 7th sts. -Walter Lenox, Henry Naylor, trustees -A Green, auct

Hon Thos Corwin fell on ice in the street in Cincinnati, a few days ago, & fractured his thigh bone.

Trustees' sale of house & lot at auction: on Feb 22 next, in front of the premises, by deed of trust from Geo E Kirk & wife to the subscribers, dated Apr 1, 1849, recorded in Liber J A S No 4, folios 81 to 86, of the land records for Wash Co, D C: sale of part of lot 9 in square 437, fronting on south F st, between 7th & 8th sts, in Wash City. -Walter Lenox, Henry Naylor, trustees -A Green, auct

Law Notice. John S Tyson has removed his ofc to F st, two doors east of Chubb Brothers& attends to cases in the court of Claims & courts generally.

Chas Goodyear, jr, now residing in Paris, has obtained a patent for constructing the plates of artificial teeth of a hard compound of India rubber & gutta percha mixed with sulphur, & submitted to a degree of heat-a vulcanized compound of India rubber & gutta percha. This invention will greatly tend to reduce the cost of sets of artificial teeth.

U S Patent Ofc, Wash, Jan 22, 1856. Ptn of Jos H Burrows, of Cincinnati, Ohio, praying for the extension of a patent granted to him on Apr 23, 1842, for an improvement in mill stones, for 7 years from the date of expiration of said patent, which takes place on Apr 23, 1856. -Chas Mason, Com'r of Patents.

Died: on Jan 21, in Wash City, Mary Jane, wife of Louis L Brunett, in her 30th year. Her funeral will take place this afternoon at 2 o'clock, from the residence of Mr Grubb, on Mass ave, between 4th & 5th sts.

Ball of the Wash Highlanders, for the benefit of the poor of Wash City, will take place at Munder's Assembly Rooms, on Jan 28: tickets $1.00. Managers on behalf of the Company: Capt J Bain, Lt Reynolds, Sgt A Bain; Lt Campbell, Lt McCloud, & Private Harrover. Managers on behalf of the citizens: Hon John T Towers, Richd Wallach, Wm H Winter, & Columbus Monroe. All hats & capt [except worn by the military] must be left in the hat room. -Capt John Bain, treasurer, 480 Mass ave.

THU JAN 24, 1856
Household & kitchen furniture at auction on: Jan 31, at the residence of Thos P Watson, 540 L st, between 8th & 9th sts, all his household effects.
-Jas C McGuire, auct

Public sale of the *Columbia Foundry*, near Gtwn, in D C: by deed of trust, dated Jun 14, 1854, executed by Spencer B Root to the subscriber as trustee: sale on Feb 16 next, that well known property called the *Columbia Foundry*, on the Potomac river, with all the lands, bldgs, & mills belonging thereto. -Wm Selden, trustee

Trustee's sale of valuable bldg lots: on Feb 11 next, by deed of trust from Wm H Parker & wife to the subscriber, dated Jun 8, 1854, recorded in Liber J A S No 78, folios 226, of the land records for Wash Co, D C: sale of all of lot 2 in square 515; & south part of lot 28 in square 515. Lots 23 thru 26 in square 512-with improvements. The first named lots front on north K, between 4th & 5th sts; the last named lots front on 4th st, between N & O sts north. -Hugh B Sweeny, trustee
-A Green, auct

The partnership existing between the subscribers, in the coal & wood business, has this day been dissolved by mutual consent. -W E Waters, Mary L Waters: Jan 21, 1856.

Appointments by the Pres, by & with the advice & consent of the Senate.
Robt R Reid Surveyor of Customs at Palatka, Fla.
Robt Edgar Collector of Custons, Shieldsborough, district of Pearl River, vice David W Johnston, removed.
Land Ofcrs:
Alex'r D Anderson, of Iowa, to be register of the land ofc at Dubuque, Iowa, vice Geo McHenry, removed.
John H Crease, of Ark, to be register of the land ofc at Little Rock, Ark, vice Robt A Watkins, removed.
Wm A Bevins, of Ark, to be receiver of public moneys at Batesville, Ark, vice John C Claiborne, removed.
Alex'r W Rush to be register of the land ofc at Palmyra, Missouri, vice Wm P Harrison, resigned.

Wash City Ordinances: 1-That if any person shall feed, water, clean, or wash a horse, or feed or water a cow, or wash a carriage or other vehicle upon the paved or graveled foot-walks of any street or avenue, or water a horse within 15 feet of any public hydrant or pump, the person so offending in any of these particulars, or the owner of such horse, cow, carriage, or other vehicle, shall pay a fine of not less than $1 nor more than $5 for each offence. 2-It shall not be lawful for any person whatsoever to raise or keep geese, except in enclosures, within any part of Wash City; & if any geese shall be found running at large it shall be the duty of several police ofcrs & others to seize & take up such geese & carry them to the Intendant of the Asylum, for the use of the poor at the Infirmary. The rate of .25 will be given for each & every goose so delivered. 3-It shall not be lawful for any animal of the goat kind to run at large in Wash City, & the owner of every goat so found running at large shall pay no less than $3 nor more than $5 for every time such goat may be found at large; & it shall be the duty of the police constables to kill any such animals when found running at large. 4-Every person residing on any street or avenue in Wash City shall, within 6 hours daylight after any fall of snow, have the same removed from the pavement in front of his or her house, under a penalty of .50 for every hour the same shall remain after the said 6 hours. -A McD Davis, Pres of the Board of Common Council. Robt Clarke, Pres of the Board of Aldermen. Approved, Jan 17, 1855. -Jno T Towers, Mayor

The partnership existing between the subscribers, in the coal & wood business, has this day been dissolved by mutual consent. -W E Waters, Mary L Waters: Jan 21, 1856.

FRI JAN 25, 1856
Mr J A Noolan, postmaster at Milwaukee, has been indicted by the Grand Jury for having paid a mail contractor a post-ofc draft in other currency than that required by act of Congress.

Senate: 1-Memorial from Thos Ap Catesby Jones, of the navy, complaining of the action of the Naval board in placing him on the retired list. 2-Memorial of Lt Jas T McDonough, late a lt in the navy, dropped by the action of the Naval Board; asked to be restored to his former rank & placed on the retired list. 3-Memorial of Capt Jos Smoot, complaining of having been retired by the Naval Board.

Miss Mary Campbell, an interesting lady of 17 years, met with a shocking death in Augusta Co, Va, a few days ago. She attempted to step across the shaft of a threshing machine, when her dress was caught in the machinery, & she was drawn under the shaft & horribly mangled. She was dead when extricated.

Died: on Jan 23, Mr Wm Jewell, of Gtwn, in his 71st year. His funeral is this afternoon at 3 o'clock, from his late residence on Gay st.

Wanted, a lady to reside in the family, competent to teach the English & French language, together with music on the piano, to 3 girls respectively aged from 10 to 13, for which a salary of $250 will be paid, exclusive of board & washing. A member of the Episcopalian Church preferred. Address Thos Clagett, Upper Marlboro, Md.

A True wife. Petition introduced into the N Y Senate from Mrs Mary R Pell, praying for a divorce from her husband. Early in life she married a young gentleman every way suited to her. In a few years too close application to business on his part produced insanity, & for 23 years he had been an inmate of the Insane Asylum. From the income bequeathed her by her father she has set apart $10,000 to provide for his maintenance; but being advised that property which she may acquire cannot be sold without her husband's consent, which of course can never be obtained, she has reluctantly petitioned for a divorce in obedience to the advice of her friends

SAT JAN 26, 1856
Letter received at the Dept of State from Franckfort sur Maine, dated Dec 13 There died in this city, on Dec 6, at the age of 82 years, 5 months & 24 days, Baron Amshcel Mayer von Rothschild, Privy Counsellor of the Duke of Hesse Darmstadt, chief & senior of the celebrated banking firm of M A Rothschild & Sons, of Franckfort-on-the-Maine. Baron Rothschild was popular with all classes. He was a rigid observer of all the requirements of his faith, & at the sumptuous feast to which he was invited or which he gave, he was never known to touch any meat not prepared according to the Jewish mode, & neither sickness nor inclemency of the weather was able to restrain him from the performance of his religious duties & ceremonies. He belonged to the orthodox fraction of the Jewish community, but his benefits extended to all alike. He was married for more than 50 years, but had no children. His wife died in 1848, & his affections have been devoted to his sisters & brethren & to their numerous progeny. He was the eldest of 5 brothers, & outlived them all, with the exception of one, Baron Jas Rothschild, of Paris. Two of them, Chas & Solomon, died in the course of last year. The fortune left by Baron Amschel Mayer Von Rothschild is estimated at over sixty millions of florins; that left by Baron Chas at seventeen millions, & by Baron Solomon at forty-eight millions of florins. The will of Baron Rothschild was made in 1849. Among items of the will are: To found a majorat in favor of his nephew Anselm, son of Solomon: 4,000,000 florins. To his nephew Maria Chas, son of Chas: 1,000,000 florins. To a second son of Chas Wm, he gave his large house & gardens. The funeral of Baron Rothschild took place on Sunday last, according to the simple & modest custom of the Jewish religion.

Mrd: on Jan 3, at ***Argyle Plantation***, the residence of Mrs Wm R Campbell, Wash Co, Miss, by Rev Wm Wadsworth, Spencer M Ball, M D, of Bolivar Co, Miss, formerly of Wash City, to Miss Lavinia D Batemen.

Mrd: on Jan 23, by Rev J G Butler, Abner W Law to Rosamond, 2nd daughter of J B Brown, of Alexandria, Va.

Mrd: on Jan 9, at Savannah, Ga, Thos Pember, of Boston, Mass, to Miss Phebe Y, 4th daughter of J C Levy, of the former place.

Appointments by the Pres:
O Jennings Wise, of Va, to be Sec of the Legation at Paris, vice Don Piatt, resigned.
Edw G W Butler, jr, of Louisiana, to be Sec of the Legation at Berlin, vice O J Wise, transferred to Paris.
John N Garesche, of Delaware, to be Consul at Matansas, Cuba, vice Edw Worrell, removed.
Robt H Seese, of N Y, to be Consul at Spezzia, in Sardinia.
Jonathan S Jenkins, of Calif, to be Consul at Apia, Navigators' Islands.
Geo V Brown, of N Y, to be Consul at Tangier, Morocco, vice P Collins, deceased.

Putney, Vt, Jan, 1856. Died: in Putney, Jan 10, Hon Theophilus Crawford, aged 91 years, 8 months & 15 days. As a husband & parent the deceased was devoted & kind; at age 5 years he, with his parents, emigrated from Conn to Westminster, Vt, then almost an unbroken wilderness. He was a constant reader of the Nat'l Intelligencer from 1812 until near the close of his life. In his declining years he was an example of Christian resignation & patience under disease & suffering.

For rent: 3 story brick house, 506 E st, near 3rd containing 8 rooms; lit with gas, for rent, furnished, to a small family without children. Apply to Wm Chauncy Langdon, U S Patent Ofc.

From Calif: 1-Mr Silsbee, the Yankee comedian, died at San Francisco on Dec 22.
2-Geo M Chase, American Consul at Lahaina, is dead.

MON JAN 28, 1856
On Wed morning the new & beautiful cottage residence of ex-Lt Govn'r Leake, at Madison Court-house, was destroyed by fire. The family-all ladies & girls, barely escaped in their night dresses, & were forced to walk in bare feet through snow 20 inches deep to a neighbor's house. Nothing of value was saved from the burning bldg. Loss, $5,000. -Richmond Dispatch

I have just received from the North, & will open this morning, a beautiful assortment of fancy Head Dresses, Flowers, Sash Ribands, Glove Tops, Bretelles, Sylphides, & Berthas. -Mrs B E Gittings' 14 Pa ave, between 8th & 9th sts.

Appointments by the Pres: 1-Jas M Morrison, surveyor of the customs at New Albany, Indiana, vice John B Norman, resigned. 2-Chas K Loomis, collector of the customs at Sackett's harbor, N Y, vice Thos S Hall, removed.

Mail robbers sentenced. W H Lewis has been sentenced to 2 years' imprisonment for robbing the U S mail at Cahawba, Ala. Danl H Smith had been sentenced to 10 years' imprisonment for a like offence in Monroe Co, Ala.

Outrage in Fla: On Jan 6, Peter Johnson, with 2 men, while engaged in their work, were attacked by a band of Indians, who killed Johnson & one other. On Jan 8, 70 men started out, arriving at the scene of the murder found the two bodies, one of which had been scalped. A party from **Fort Dallas**, Fla, explored the country, but did not find the Indians.

Hong Kong Register of Nov 15. Courts Martial. Since the arrival of the squadron in this harbor four important courts-martial have been held. The first took place on Oct 29 for the trial of Francis Hogan, musician of the ship **H M S Pique**, for offering to strike Mr Oxenham, the carpenter. He was sentenced t o receive 50 lashes, be dismissed the service, & mulct of all pay & allowances. The second trial was that of Lt Geo Hope Mansell, of the same ship, for being drunk. He was sentenced to be dismissed the ship & placed at the bottom of the list. The third trial was on Mr Thos Wilson, Assist Surgeon of the ship **Rattler**, for acting in an ungentlemanly manner. He was sentenced to be dismissed the service, to lose all pay & prize-money, & to be imprisoned for one year. The sentence is generally thought to be too harsh a one. The fourth was on 1st Lt W H Phipps, of the ship **H M S Nankin**, for disrespect to his captain. He was reprimanded & cautioned to be more careful in the future.

Phil, Jan 27. Mrs Albright, the widow of Col Peter Albright, & her only daughter, aged 23, were drowned in the Delaware today.

Mrd: on Jan 17, in Gtwn, by Rev Benj F Brook, Mr Wm T Hines to Miss Kate L Thompson, both of Wash City.

Mrd: on Jan 24, in Annapolis, by Rev Mr Graff, G D Blackford, of the U S Navy, to Miss Susan Cox, daughter of Mr Jos Cox, of the U S Navy.

Died: on Jan 27, after a protracted & painful illness, Ninian Beall, in his 76th year. His funeral is this afternoon at 3 o'clock, from the residence of his son, corner of Market & 2nd sts, Gtwn.

Died: on Jan 19, in Balt, after a short but severe illness, Mr Stephen Culverwell, in his 78th year.

Died: on Jan 23, in Gtwn, D C, Wm Jewell, in his 71st year. Mr Jewell has long been among the prominent citizens of Gtwn, filling various public posts under the Corp, & being at the time of this death City Collector & Assessor. He had a well cultivated mind. -Advocate

Dissolution of copartnership under the firm of Baldwin & Nenning, by mutual consent. -W H Baldwin, P Nenning

Miss Brooke's English & French Boarding & Day School, 138 Pa ave, will commence on Feb 4.

TUE JAN 29, 1856
Navy Dept, Jan 28, 1856. The Navy Dept announces the death of Cmdor Chas Morris, who died on Jan 27, at his residence in Wash City, in his 72nd year.
-J C Dobbin, Sec of the Navy.
+
His funeral will take place from his late residence on H st, this day, at 2½ o'clock.
+
[Jan 30th newspaper: The remains of the lamented Cmdor Morris were yesterday consigned to the grave in the ***Georgetown Cemetery***. The Pres of the U S, the Sec of the Navy, & other members of the Cabinet, ofcrs of the Army & Navy & other distinguished personages, attended his funeral.] [Feb 6th newspaper: Cmdor Morris was born in Conn in 1784; was therefore in his 72nd year; nearly 57 of which he had passed in the service of his country, as he entered the navy on Jul 1, 1799, at aged 15; he died the senior ofcr on the active list. Two days previous to his death he requested a member of his family to take pen & paper & note down some directions he wished to give regarding his funeral. He wished no military parade at his funeral; the customary number of guns due to his rank to be fired at the navy yard when his body was interred was all he desired. He designated his pall-bearers, Cmdors Shubrick, Smith, & Perry, Gen Henderson, of the Marines, Gen Totten, of the Engineers, & Col Cooper, of the Army, all old & valued friends, & if Com Perry, [the only absent one,] should not be in the city some other ofcr to be substituted. If any address is made he desired it to be very short. If the weather is inclement he did not wish any ladies to attend the funeral.]

The Rochester Democrat published the marriage of the well known advocate of Women's Rights, the Rev Antoinette L Brown, to Mr Saml C Blackwell, of Cincinnati. The wedding ceremony was performed by Jos Brown, the bride's father, at his residence in the town of Henrietta, Monroe Co, on Thu of last week. The Democrat supposed Mr Blackwell to be a brother of Lucy Stone's husband.

Died: on Jan 28, in Wash City, Edwin J McClery, youngest son of Jas McClery, aged 31 years. His funeral will be from Trinity Church this afternoon at 3½ o'clock.

Accident on the Delaware river, at Pittsburgh, on Sat: a sleigh containing a gentleman & 4 ladies broke through the ice, & before assistance could be rendered, the widow of Col Peter Albright & her only daughter, age 23 years, were drowned. The body of Mrs Albright was recovered. The body of Miss Albright was swept under the ice. The horses & sleigh were lost.

We learn that a lad named Jas Matthews, residing with his parents between Wash & Gtwn, was nearly burnt to death on Sat by accidentally falling into a lime kiln his father was engaged in burning.

Senate: 1-Memorial from John C Carter, a lt in the U S Navy, complaining that, after long service, from some unknown & unaccountable cause, he finds himself placed on the furlough list, & asking redress in the premises. 2-Same for A D Harrell, late lt in the navy, stating that he was dropped by the action of the Naval Board. 3-Capt Foxall A Parker, U S Navy, protesting against the action of the Naval Board in placing him upon the furlough list, & appealing to Congress for justice & redress. He says he had served 22 years at sea. 4-Wm H Noland, complaining that after a service of 32 years he finds himself dropped by the action of the late Naval Board. 5-From Henry Walke, a lt in the U S Navy, asking to be restored to his original position in the navy, & charging that the board transcended its authority in disregarding all the rules & precedents for the gov't of civil & military courts. 6-Also, from John Josey Hall, late master in the navy, complaining of the action of the late Naval Board in dropping him from the list, & asking to be restored to his former position. 7-Addition documents submitted in relation to the memorial of Cmder Shaw of the navy. 8-Resolutions of the Board of Underwriters of Phil in behalf of Cmder B F Sands, who invented means of ascertaining the character of the bottom in deep-sea soundings, asking that he may be compensated for his invention, & that its benefits may be extended to the mercantile marine. 9-Ptn from Geo H Fletcher, U S Consul at Aspinwall, setting forth that the salary at that port is wholly inadequate, & giving the reasons why it is so, & asking that a law may be passed increasing the same. 10-Ptn from Jos Mount, a volunteer in the Indian war in Alabama, asking to be allowed bounty land. 11-Ptn from Col Gates, of the U S army, asking indemnity for property destroyed in the steamship **San Francisco**. 12-Ptn from Ed H Harrison, late collector at San Francisco, asking to be relieved from liability for public money collected at that port & stolen while in his custody. 13-Ptn from Martin Fenwick, asking confirmation to a tract of land in the State of Md. 14-Ptn from Norwood McClelland, asking compensation for losses sustained in transporting Gov't stores from New Orleans to **Fort Smith**, in Arkansas. 15-Ptn from Thos Foster, asking that widows pensioned under the act of 1838, & the heirs of those who have deceased, may be allowed arrears of pension from Mar 3, 1841 to Mar 4, 1843.

For rent: 3 story house on the corner of E & 9th sts, now in the occupation of Mr Zantzinger. Possession about the middle of Feb. -Harriet Fischer

Circuit Court of Wash Co, D C-in Chancery. Geo Kirby, exc of John B Kirby, deceased, against Barbara S Young, a admx, & the heirs at law of Ignatius F Young, deceased. Sales made & reported by the trustee of this Court are hereby ratified & confirmed. The said sales were of the title of said Ignatius of & in one undivided fifth part of pieces of property in square 709; square 776, squares 932 & 933; & the gross amount produced by the undivided interest was $54.66. -Jno A Smith, clerk

Valuable mill property & woolen factory for sale: by decree of the Court of Chancery, sitting in Equity: sale of the real estate of Chs R Simpson, deceased: on Feb 12 next, in Howard Co, Md: contains 215 acres of land, improved by a large Stone Mill, 40 by 50 feet, 3 stories high. Also, I will offer another piece of land, 100 acres, about 1 mile from the mill. -Wm Simpson, trustee

WED JAN 30, 1856
Trustee's sale of 3 brick dwlg houses & unexpired term of Lease of Lots, with privilege of purchase, on the corner of 9th st west & M st north: by deed in trust, dated Sep 12, 1854: sale on Feb 25, on the premises, all the unexpired term of a certain lease from Ulysses Ward to Aloysius N Clements, dated Jun 1,1854, recorded on Jun 19, 1854, of lots 2 & 3, in Saml Norment's subdivision of square 399, with the privilege of purchase. -Chas S Wallach, trustee -Jas C McGuire, auct

Letter from Gustavus Ober, exc of the late Stephen J Ober: by the last will & testament of the said Stephen J Ober, there was donated to the poor of Wash City the sum of $500. -Jno T Towers, Mayor

The schnr **W Levering** was capsized a few days since in the Chesapeake Bay, off **Watt's Island**. Her crew consisted of 2 white & 2 black men, who, together with Mr Owens, his wife & 8 children, all perished. The vessel belonged to Messrs Byrd & Matthews, of Accomac, & was at the time removing Mr Owens & family, with their effects, from York river to Newtown, Md.

Ex-Govn'r Walker, of Louisiana, died in New Orleans on Jan 24.

The 60th anniversary of the marriage of Luther Wright & Sarah Lyman, of Easthampton, who were joined in wedlock at that place on Jan 13, 1796, by Rev Payson Williston, then in the 7th year of his ministry, & now alive, a vigorous old man of 92 years, was celebrated at the residence of their son, Luther Wright, jr, late Principal of Williston Seminary, on Jan 14. The company present on the commemorative occasion were Rev Dr Williston, four of the six persons yet alive who were of the great company at the wedding, all the children & grandchildren of the aged pair, except a son & his family living in Wisconsin. During the evening a poem, written for the occasion by Mrs Sigourney, was read.

Capt Clement Rothwell, conductor on the Petersburg [Va] railroad, died at Richmond on Fri from injuries received by his head coming in contact with a bridge on the road. He once before was badly injured by coming in contact with the same bridge.

Died: on Jan 29, in Wash City, at the residence of her grandfather, Thos Foster, Florence Eliza, infant daughter of Mr H W Dinkle, late of Winchester, Va.

Wash City Ordinance: 1-Act for the relief of Ann Laporte: to be paid $3.85, the sum overpaid by her [on property assessed to Bernard McGowan,] in consequence of an erroneous entry made by the copying clerk. 2-Act for the relief of Philip Aldorffer: fine imposed for selling matches in & about the market-house is remitted: said Aldorffer paying costs of prosecution.

Wm H Maxwell, one of our most popular citizens, died on Jan 24. He was a Scotchman & had resided with us many years; educated for the law, but of late years, having a fine property, confined himself chiefly to literary pursuits & published a history of Ireland. -N Y paper [Mar 17th newspaper: from the Home Journal: the late Col Wm Homer Maxwell was the son of Jas Homer Maxwell, & grandson of Wm Maxwell, the first vice president of the Bank of N Y, born in 1737. He was descended from that branch of a Scottish family called the Maxwells of Corruchan, descended from those of Carlaverock, ancestors of the Earls of Nighesdale, intermarried with the Herries of Terregles, & whose present representative is Sir Wm Maxwell, of Monteith, the sixth baronet. It is supposed that, for want of male descendants in the direct line, the baronetcy will pass into the collateral branch of the family of which Col Maxwell was the next oldest rep, the heirs being now living in Scotland, at an advanced age, without issue. The family was distinguished for its steady adhesion to the cause of the Stuarts, & it was upon the accession of the Hanoverian princes to the British throne that the grandfather of the colonel emigrated to America, bringing with him little else than the claymore which, in the hands of a near relative, had done service at Culloden, & which still remains a valued relic in the possession of a descendant. Sir Walter Scott, in his novel of Reg-gauntlet, has made one of this very family the principal character in that tale. Many emigrants left their native land upon the downfall of the Stuarts; & among them we can trace the cavaliers to Va & Scottish lairds & gentlemen to N Y. The mother of Col Maxwell, Miss Van Zandt, the wife of Jas Homer Maxwell, was a celebrated belle, admired for her beauty & accomplishments, & often selected by Gen Washington as his partner in the dance. The Van Zandt family were Whigs, & her father, Jacobus Van Zandt, was with Gen Washington in Jersey, & one of his personal friends. Of two brothers, one went to England to complete his education before the war, & never returned. On the resignation of Sir Elijah Impey as Chief Justice of the Supreme Court of Bengal, Sir Robt Chambers, who had been the second Judge of that Court, succeeded to the vacancy. This Sir Robt, in early life, had been the schoolfellow & friend of Lords Stowell & Eldon, was educated at Oxford, & by his eminent abilities succeeded Sir

Wm Blackstone as Vinerian Professor of the laws of England. In 1773, on his departure for India, he married a Miss Wilton, by whom he had several children, sons & a daughter. The eldest son, on his way home to England to complete his education, was lost in the Grosvenor East Indiaman, the narrative of whose fate is one of the most thrilling in the history of shipwrecks. The daughter of Sir Robt became the object of attachment on the part of a New Yorker, then in the company's service, & that was Col Van Zandt, the uncle of Col Maxwell. After many difficulties their marriage took place on board the ship which carried the lady & her father home from India. Mrs Van Zandt survived her father & her husband many years, & died in England in 1851. By her death, Col Maxwell became, under the will of her husband, the possessor of a valuable property, part of which was gained at Seringapatam. The deceased was prepared for college at a school in Morristown, conducted by a Mr Todd. Among the pupils was Mr Wm B Astor & a young man who afterwards entered the British army, & is known to be the identical Gen Williams now known as the hero of Kars. Col Maxwell graduated at Columbia College, leaving it with the honor of an oration. Col Maxwell left behind him a handsome fortune which he principally bequeathed to a favorite niece, Mrs Henry Cheeseboro, & his nephew, Lt Maxwell Woodhull, a distinguished ofcr of the U S Navy, the only survivors of his family.]

THU JAN 31, 1856
Closing out sale of Family Groceries: on Jan 31, at the Prime Family Groceries at Mr John H Johnson's store, 7th & E sts. -Jas C McGuire, auct

Architecture: ofc Pa ave, between 10th & 11th sts. -Chas Haskins, Architect

Pusuant to a Decree of the High Court of Chancery, in England, made in a cause wherein Alex'r Ingram, Geo Ingram, David Ganton, David Johnstone, John Maitland, & John Graham are plntfs, & Joshua Wadington & Jas Ford Vaughan, a person appointed to represent the estate of Adam Ingram for all the purposes of the suit, are dfndnts, bearing date Jul 22, 1854, Adam Ingram, who was formerly a laborer at Roxburgh, Scotland, & afterwards a soldier in her Britannic Majesty's Twenty-first Regt; of Royal Scotch Fusiliers, & supposed to have been taken prisoner at the siege of New Orleans in 1814, if living, or if dead, in case he died after Jas Ingram, of Santiago, in Chili, in South America, merchant, the intestate in the pleading mentioned, who died in or about Jun, 1847, then the legal personal rep or reps of the said Adam Ingram, is or are, by their solicitors, on or before Mar 10, 1856, to come in & prove his & their claims at the chambers of the Vice Chancellor Wood, No 11 New Square, Lincoln's Inn, Middlesex, in England, or in default thereof he or they will be peremptorily excluded from the benefit of the said decree. May 17, 1856, is appointed for hearing & adjudicating upon the claims. Dated 17th day of Dec, 1855. -Richd Bloxam, Chief Clerk. Edw Bannister, 13 John st, Bedford Row, London, Solicitor for the Plntfs.

T Galligan & Co, dealers in Fancy Goods, Perfumery, & Jewelry. 370 Pa av, under Brown's Hotel, Wash.

From Oregon: 1-By the arrival of the ship **Fashion**, on Jan 17, we received news of the death of the chief Pee Pee-Mox-Mox. His war steed, which had been considered the best animal in the country, was brought down by Capt Van Bergen as a trophy. 2-There is a painful rumor afloat here that the schnr **Matthew Vassar** has been lost down the coast, with all hands on board.

FRI FEB 1, 1856
Circuit Court of Wash Co, D C-in Chancery. U S A, plntf, vs Wm Selden, John Withers, Laurence P Bayne, Geo W C Whiting, & Robt W Latham, late partners, in Wash City, D C, trading & contracting in the name of Selden, Withers & Co, John A English & Wm Bayne, assignees & trustees of said firm, Saml T Shugert, A B Little, David J Brown, A G Allen, & all other creditors of said firm, dfndnts. The firm above named were at the time they ceased to do business & made an assignment of their assets to said John A English & Wm Bayne largely indebted to the U S for moneys deposited with them by sundry agents of the plntf, & that the assets of said firm are inadequate to the satisfaction of all their liabilities, which state of facts it is alleged entitle the plntf to a decree for priority of satisfaction of their claim out of said assets, in pursuance of the provisions of the act of Congress passed Mar 2, 1797, entitled "An act to provide more effectually for the settlement of accounts between the U S & the receiver of public moneys:" that the creditors of said firm interested in the said assets are unknown to the plntf & are very numerous; & it appearing to the Court that all the dfndnts above named, John Withers, L P Bayne, Geo W C Whiting, Robt W Latham, Wm Bayne, A G Allen, & all other creditors of said firm, reside beyond the limits of D C, therefore, the same are to appear in this Court, in person or by solicitor, on or before the first Monday in Jun, 1856. -Jno A Smith, clerk

Com'rs sale-by decree rendered in the suit of John P Dulany vs Selden, Withers & Co, in Alexandria Circuit Court on Jun 1, 1855, the undersigned will sell at public auction, in front of Saml Catts' tavern, at West End, on Mar 29 next, 6 negro men & 2 negro women, & 4 children. -Fairfax H Whiting, Thos M Monroe, David Funsten, Com'rs

Geo Lamb, mate of the ship **Chariot of Fame**, of Boston, was brought up at the police court at Liverpool on a charge of having 3 wives, having married one in Liverpool in 1845, another in N Y in 1848, & another in Liverpool in 1855. The three were in court & gave evidence against him. His defence for marrying the last was that he was drunk as a pig, & did not know what he was about.

SAT FEB 2, 1856
Mrd: on Jan 29, at Eliz, N J, by Rev J J Bowden, Capt J B Ricketts, U S Army, to Fanny, daughter of the late J Tharp Lawrence, of the Island of Jamaica.

Mrd: on Jan 31, in Wash City, at St Mathew's Church, by Rev Jas B Donelan, Richd J Clements to Miss Malvina R I Favier, daughter of the late Agricol Favier, all of Wash City.

Detroit Daily Advertiser publishes the following family letter from Lt Hartsuff, U S Army, giving the particulars of the recent attack made by the Seminole Indians upon a small detachment of U S troops. **Fort Myers**, [Florida,] Dec 29. Dear Father: I have just returned from an expedition into the Indian country; we are now in a state of war with them; war was opened by the Indians attacking my party, a reconnoitering party, consisted of only 10 men; the attack was made about daylight; the first shot was fired while I was getting up. I hastily dressed, & taking my pistol looked out of my tent; every tree near me had an Indian behind it, & they were firing & whooping terribly. I shot two of them & then left my tent & ran to the wagons, about 30 yards off. Here I found 2 of my men. The first fire had stretched five of my men on the ground, & 3 had most shamefully ran away. With my 2 men, both of whom were wounded, I made a stand behind the wagons & fired several times with a rifle & a musket. I had just fired at & I believe hit an Indian when I got shot myself. The ball went through my left arm above the elbow & into my side just under the arm; another ball hit me in the breast, but struck my pistol, which I had thrust into my coat. This finished the fighting. I could neither load nor fire; & the 2 men with me could hardly stand. I told the men to make their escape & I crawled into a little hammock & remained there about 2 hours. I managed to walk about a mile & laid there that night & the next day. I had gone about 3 miles when I saw a fire, which from its size, I knew to be that of friends. I got to it, & found 2 companies had been sent out to find me, accompanied by a doctor. This was Sunday night, & I was wounded at daylight on Thu. Four of my men were killed & the rest escaped. Your affectionate son, Geo L Hartsuff

Died: yesterday, in Wash City, after a long & painful illness, Mrs Hannah C Tate, wife of Andrew Tate, in her 29th year. Her funeral will take place today at 1 o'clock, from her late residence.

Letter from Col Thos M Benton to Cmdor Stewart, U S Navy. C st, Wash, Jan 31, 1856. Sir: The act under which you & the rest have been eliminated is a bad act, passed in a bad way, & made worse in its execution. Ofcrs of the navy have a profession, & that profession is the business of their lives, & when they entered it there were laws in force for the gov't of the navy which specified the offences for which they might lose their places, & gave them a right to a trial before they could be dismissed. It was passed in a bad way, being slammed & gagged through the House. It was made worse in its execution.

Died: on Jan 27, in Balt, in her 88th year, Mrs Harriet *Ghequierc, relict of Chas Ghequierc, formerly an extensive merchant of that city. This venerable lady, through her long life, enjoyed the love & affectionate regard of a large circle of friends. [Feb 4th newspaper: correction of the spelling of Ghequierc to Ghequiere.]

Wash Co, D C. Estray taken up trespassing on the premises of Wm Anderson, a dark bay horse. -Z K Offutt, J P [Owner will come forward, prove property, pay charges, & take him away. -Wm Anderson [colored] corner of 7th & Pa ave.]

MON FEB 4, 1856

The Sec of the Navy has dispatched the U S steamer **Fulton**, of the Home Squadron, to search for the missing barque **Amelia**, which has not been heard from for 2 or 3 months. Lts Worden, Maxwell, & Erben left N Y in the sloop-of-war **Saratoga**, with orders to proceed to Port au Prince & bring to the U S the **Amelia**, captured at that port some time since by the American consul as a fillibuster. The **Amelia** is now supposed to be lost, with these ofcrs on board.

The Boston Transcripr states that the new work, Ernest Linwood, by Mrs Caroline Lee Hentz, is now in press, & will be issued this month by J P Jewett & Co, of Boston.

The grave of Madison. A bill has been reported in the Senate of Va providing for the erection of a plain tomb, of granite or marble, to bear the following inscription: "James Madison, born March 5, 1751, [O S] died 28th June, 1836. Virginia marks with sincere affection the grave of her son, the author of the Federal Constitution, the patriot and statesman."

Rev Payson Williston, D D, died at his residence, in Easthampton, Mass, Wed last, in his 93rd year. His illness had continued one week. He was the oldest graduate of Yale College.

Mr R A Williamson, late superintendent of the Memphis & Ohio Railroad, was on a train as it passed a bridge over Griffin's Creek, Tenn, & looking out of the train, his head came in contact with a post on the bridge, killing him instantly. His body fell from the car into the water below.

Coroner Hill held an inquest at N Y on Thu upon the body of Bridget Ford, a native of Ireland, 36 years of age, who died on Wed. It appears a quantity of snow & ice slid from the roof & struck her upon the forehead, producing a very servere injury.

In Newport, on Sat, Jas Hennesey, being intoxicated, poured a tumbler of gin down the throat of John Shannahan, a sick man, who instantly expired. Hennesey has been committed to jail.

Two desperate counterfeiters, Andrew St Clair & Jas W Jolly, were arrested at Albany, on Thu, with a considerable amount of bad money about them. They were armed with pistols, but made no resistance.

On Jan 28, Mr Thos Bevington & wife, of Beaver Co, Pa, left their home to visit a neighbor, & on returning the same evening found their house in ashes. It is not known how the fire originated.

House of Reps: Hon Nathaniel P Banks, of Mass, is declared Speaker of the House for the 34th Congress. [After 132 votes for Speaker.]

David Sampson, on Wed, received a verdict of $1,500 damages, in Pittsburgh, Pa, against David A Greer for having had an excavation in front of his property, into which the plntf & his daughter were precipitated on the night of Mar 17, 1853, & seriously injured. A motion was made for a new trial.

Jos M Field, the actor, died at his residence in Mobil on Wed last. He leaves a wife & daughter to mourn his early death. -Boston Courier

Dr J C Merrill [or Dr Velplean, in French] has been arrested & locked up in N Y, on a charge of swindling. The charge is made by various soft individuals who paid the Doctor $2 each for certain powders by which they might win the affections of any woman that might be induced to swallow them. The powders won't operate, & the fools are indignant. The Doctor has been taking, by mail & otherwise, about $80 per day by his discovery, & contends that his business is as legitimate as many others that are tolerated.

Desirable lot of ground for sale: contains 42 acres, near Wash City, & adjoins the lands of the late H Keliess, W Madox, & others. Apply to the subscriber, Upper Marlboro, PG Co, Md, or to S Pumphrey, 4½ st, Wash. -Rector Pumphrey

Mrd: on Jan 23, in Wash City, by Rev Geo Hildt, Nathl Wells to Mary E Burns, all of Wash City.

Mrd: on Jan 29, in Wash City, by Rev Geo Hildt, Mr Danl D Clark to Mary L Jarboe, all of Wash City.

Mrd: on Jan 31, in Wash City, by Rev Geo Hildt, Mr Geo Spear, of Newark, Ohio, to Miss Mary Jane Davis, of Wash City.

Mrd: on Jan 10, by Rev Geo Hildt, Mr John W Sullivan to Miss Alice Knox, both of Montg Co, Md.

Died: on Feb 2, in Wash City, Mrs Mary Lydoc, in her 79th year. Her funeral is this afternoon at 2½ o'clock, from the residence of her daughter, Mrs John A Blake.

Died: on Jan 28, at Portsmouth, Va, in her 24th year, Mrs Emily, wife of Chas H Williamson, Passed Assist Surgeon U S Navy, & daughter of Maj Edelin, of the U S Marine Corps.

Died: on Jan 26, at his residence in Nansemond Co, Va, Gen John C Crump, in his 69th year. He had for many years represented the different counties in which he at various periods lived in both branches of the Legislature.

From the *Fort Gibson* [Miss] Herald. Died: on Jan 5, after a lingering illness of more than 3 years, Thos Freeland, in his 69th year. For well night half a century a resident of this county. [He was for nearly 40 years, & to the time of his death, a subscriber of the Nat'l Intell.]

TUE FEB 5, 1856
We have already mentioned the fact that the schnr **T W Levering** was lately capsized in the Chesapeake Bay & 14 persons drowned. On Jan 12 the vessel was found off Onancock creek. On board were found Mrs Jas B Owens, of Jas City Co, & 6 children, all frozen to death. Her husband & the crew had been washed off & drowned. Mr Owens was a brother of Rev Pitman Owens, of Nansemond Co, Va.

Circuit Court of Wash Co, D C-in Chancery. Anthony Holmead, against John F Ennis, adm, & Thos C Wells, Susan Sears, Gilbert D Keane & Harriet Keane his wife, heirs at law of Catharine E Dent, deceased. The sale reported by Richd H Laskey, trustee, for the sale of the real estate of Catharine E Dent, deceased, be ratified. The amount of sale reported to be $254.95. -Jno A Smith, clerk

House of Reps: 1-Resolved-Adam J Glossbrenner to be declared Sgt-at-Arms of the House for the 34th Congress.

Died: on Jan 31, at his residence in this District, Gen Geo W Bowie, aged 52 years. Possessing strong domestic attachments & distinguished for his hospitable disposition, his loss will be deeply deplored by a large family & felt by a wide circle of friends.

Died: on Feb 2, in Wash City, Henry Draper, eldest son of Josiah C & Martha Ann Truman, in his 3rd year.

WED FEB 6, 1856
Died: on Feb 3, in Wash City, in his 77th year, Jeremiah W Bronaugh, a native of Loudoun Co, Va, & for many years a resident of Gtwn & this place.

Appointments by the Pres: 1-Geo M Dallas, of Pa, to be Envoy Extraordinary & Minister Plenipotentiary of the U S to her Britannic Majesty, vice Jas Buchanan, recalled at his own request. 2-Jas W McDonald, as Collector of the Customs at Natchez, Miss, vice Edw Pickett, resigned.

Trustee's sale of houses & lot near *Franklin Row*: by deed of trust from Francis Selden, dated Dec 1, 1846, recorded in Liber W B No 130, folios 231 thru 233: public sale on Feb 20, of the west half of lot 2 in square 247, fronting 29 feet on north L st, between 13th & 14th sts west, by 120 feet deep, with the 2 frame houses thereon. -Walter Lenox, trustee -Jas C McGuire, auct

Key West, Jan 21, 1856. Disastrous news from the neighborhood of *Fort Dallas*, Miami river. The Indians have been hovering about the settlements for some weeks, & on Jan 7 a large party attacked some settlers living on the border of the Indian hunting grounds, & killed Peter Johnson & Edw Farrall. The bodies of the murdered men were found scalped, their huts ransacked, & every thing of value carried away.

Died: on Feb 2, in Wash City, of chronic croup, after a short but severe illness of one week, Mary Catharine, daughter of Alex & Sarah Anne Devers, aged 3 years & 3 months. She was buried at 3 P M on Feb 3.

THU FEB 7, 1856
Senate: 1-Memorial from John H Reily & others, heirs & reps of ofcrs of the old Md line, setting forth the services & sufferings of their ancestors during the Revolution, & invoking the justice of Congress to allow them the half-pay due under the resolve of Oct 21, 1780: the pay from the date of the treaty of peace to the respective periods of the decease of the several ofcrs may be made, deducting therefrom the commutation of one-eighth its nominal value, at which rate the certificates could only be sold. 2-Memorial from Lt Junius J Boyle, who was placed on the furlough list, setting forth his 32 years of service, asking to be restored to the active list. 3-Memorial of Sam Chase Barney, dropped from the navy list, asking to be restored to his former position. 4-Cmte on Commerce: asked to be discharged from the consideration of the memorial of Oswald Peters: was referred to the Cmte of Pensions. Same cmte: asked to be discharged from the consideration of the memorial of Wm Foster, on the ground that his services were rather those of a diplomatic character than commercial & that it be referred to the Cmte of Foreign Relations.

John Rickels, of Oglethorpe Co, Ga, died on Jan 30, at the advanced age of 104 years. He was originally of Va, but moved to Georgia many years ago. Last year he cultivatd a few acres in corn with the hoe only, & made good corn. When he was over 100 he would frequently walk to Lexington, about 9 miles, to transact his business, & walk back the same day. He was a poor man & lived on the plainest diet. His father, John Fred'k Rickels, died in the same county in 1825, at age 100 years.

Railroad accident: from the Phil Bulletin of Thu. The train left the depot at 11th & Market st last night & above Hestonville, the rail broke throwing the forward car off the track. Mr Abraham B Hart, of the firm of Wm B Hart & Son, merchants, of Cincinnati, Ohio, was killed. Mr T B Watson, merchant of St Louis, was badly hurt. He was also among the wounded at the recent accident at the Gasconade river & was just recovering from those injuries.

Information wanted. My little son, John White, in his 11th year, was engaged on the canal boat **Anna Woodward** as driver, which boat was plying to Alexandria in the coal trade. During his absence Mrs White obtained a situation as house servant in the country, & when he returned, about Jan 1 last, to Gtwn, where his mother was living when he left, he was unable to learn where she was, & left the house without any prospect of a home for himself. It is believed he is in Gtwn, Wash, or Alexandria. Any information relative to the little boy left at this ofc or the Star ofc will greatly oblige a truly distressed mother. -Agnis White, at Mr Hogan's, 1½ miles north of Wash, 7th st P R.

Died: on Feb 5, Mrs Eliz A Hyde, in her 29th year, eldest daughter of Mr Jas Tucker. Her funeral is this morning at 10 o'clock, from the residence of her husband, Augustus Hyde, on 8th st west, between M & N sts north.

Phil, Feb 6. The woolen carpet factory of Jos Garside, on Haydock st, in this city, was totally destroyed by fire early this morning. Loss about $80,000, partly insured.

Family School for Boys, near Alexandria, Va: will commence on Feb 17.
-Rev E R Lippitt, Alexandria, Va

Mrs Trippe, 29 4½ st, is prepared to accommodate a number of Members of Congress with good rooms, with or without board.

FRI FEB 8, 1856
Hon Andrew J Miller, a distinguished citizen of Augusta, Ga, died at his residence in that city on Sunday last. He was a lawyer of much ability, had for a series of years represented Richmond Co in the State Legislature, & for several years was the Pres of the State Senate.

Extensive preparations have been made at New Orleans for the inauguration there Feb 9 of Mr Clark Mills' equestrian statue of Gen Jackson. Oration will be by L J Sigur.

Extensive sale of wines, liquors, & cigars: by order of the Orphans Court of Wash Co, D C: at store 562 on 7th st, belonging to the estate of J T Neale, deceased.
-C A Brown, adm -C W Boteler, auct

Pews in Trinity Church, Nos 36 & 61, for sale at the Auction Rooms on Feb 7. By order of the vestry. -Jas C McGuire, auct

Died: on Jan 28, at her residence, Salem, Chas Co, Md, after a long & painful illness from cancer, Mrs Mary Ann T T Cox, relict of the late Col Hugh Cox, in her 70th year.

Senate: 1-Memorial from Lt Geo B Gray, placed on the reserved list by the Naval Board, asking to be restored to his former position. 2-Ptn from Danl Draper & others, owners of the barque **St Harlampy**, a foreign built vessel, asking to be allowed to take out a new register in the name of the **Monmouth**. 3-Ptn from Thos Hays & Wm Guinard, watchmen at the Naval Observatory, asking to be allowed the 20% given to other employes of the Gov't. 4-Ptn from Jno S Ormsbee, heir of John Spurr, of the Revolutionary army, asking to be allowed commutation pay. 5-Ptn from Eliz Penniger, heir of an ofcr of the Revolutionary army, asking to be allowed commutation pay.

Obit-died: on Dec 24 last, at N Y, Dr John Styles, formerly of Valpariaso, & more recently of Sagua La Grande.

A Card. The undersigned, intending to make a visit to Havana on Feb 15, for the purpose of consummating a co-partnership arrangement with J B Belt, formerly of this city, but now, & for the last 9 years, a resident of Havana, would request all those indebted to him to make settlement previous to that date. -Edw C Dyer, Pa ave, between 12th & 13th.

SAT FEB 9, 1856
Va State Ofcrs. The two Houses of the Legislature, on Wed last, elected the following:
Geo W Munford, Sec of the Commonwealth
John S Calvert, Treas of the Commonwealth
Geo W Clutter, Auditor of Public Accounts
Wm A Moncure, Second Auditor
Stafford H Parker, Register of Land Ofc
Wm F Ritchie, Public Printer
Chas S Morgan, Superintendent of the Penitentiary
Jas C Spotts, Genr'l Agent & Storekeeper of the Penitentiary.

Geo Bennett, alias Geo Huffnerr, convicted of murder, was hung at Louisville [Ky] on Feb 1. He denied to the last that he was guilty of the crime for which he suffered- the murder of a person named Mullen, whose body was thrown into the river-though he confessed that he had committed a highway robbery near that spot on the same night.

Orphans Court of Montgo Co, Md. Letters testamentary on the personal estate of Robt Y Brent, late of Montg Co, deceased. -Harriet Brent, excx

Local Matters: yesterday Gen Cass was descending from the eastern portico, of the Dept of Interior, on 7th st, when he fell down several of the steps to the midway landing, & sustained injuries thought at first to be alarming. He has considerably revived.

Wash, Feb 6, 1856. The undersigned claims no merit as a politician, but simply to be a son of one of the sons of the Revolution, who labored in the fields of Stillwater & Saratoga, & fought for his country; a father of dear & precious memory, both as a patriot, a citizen, & a soldier. He was a man & a Christian. He lived till about 9 years ago, to his 91st year. The writer, who bears his name, has been a minister of the Gospel till about 17 years ago, when, from broken & infirm health, he retired, & has since been teaching.
-John Sherer

Mrd: on Feb 6, in Wash City, by Rev B F Bittinger, Mr J W Bennett, of N Y, to Miss Sarah Crocker, of Fairfax Co, Va.

Mrd: on Feb 7, in Wash City, by Rev Dr B Sunderland, Col Robt H Shankland, of Ellicottsville, N Y, to Eliz Hope, daughter of the late Jeremiah W Bronaugh, of Wash City.

Mrd: on Feb 7, in Wash City, at the Church of the Epiphany, by Rev Mr French, Lt Robt Ransom, 1st Cavalry U S Army, to Minnie E, daughter of the late Dr Hunt, of Wash City.

Mrd: on Thu, in Wash City, by Rev John C Smith, Mr Chas H Tucker to Miss Eliz A Gittings, both of Montg Co, Md.

Mrd: on Feb 3, in Wash City, by Rev S A H Marks, Mr Geo Myers to Miss Catharine McFarland, both of Wash City.

Died: on Feb 8, at his residence, Peter Brady, in his 64th year. He was for 40 years a citizen of Wash, & his memory will be cherished by a wide circle to whom he was endeared by the purity of his character & his intregity of life. His funeral will move from St Matthew's Church on Monday morning next, at 9 o'clock.

Died: on Feb 8, Mr Wm Galligan, at the residence of his father, Jas Galligan, 1st st, Capitol Hill, between B & C sts. His funeral will be at 3 o'clock Sunday afternoon.

Died: on Feb 4, at Catonsville, Balt Co, Md, of congestion of the lungs, in her 33rd year, Mrs Anna Maria, wife of Mr Henry Perkins. The deceased was originally from Gtwn, but for the last 14 years a resident of the Eastern Shore of Md. She leaves a husband & 4 children to mourn their irreparable loss.

Died: on Jan 28, suddenly, at Portsmouth, Va, at the residence of her father-in-law, Dr Thos Williamson, Mrs Emily, consort of Dr Chas H Williamson, of the U S Navy, & daughter of Major Edelin, of the Marine Corps.

In Equity-636. A Manyett & wife against S Spencer & wife, T Burns & wife, Bennet Lucas, W Burns & wife, Emily Lucas, & David Lucas. By order of the Circuit Court of Wash Co, D C I am directed to state the trustee's account. I shall do so on Feb 20, at my ofc in the City Hall, Wash, at 10 o'clock. -W Redin, auditor

Chancery: 1,099. Henry Lawrence & Celia his wife, Caroline Lawrence, Jas Green & Mary Ann his wife, & Eliz Lawrence against David Rich & Eliz his wife, Rebecca Lawrence, & Geo W Lawrence. Part of lots 11 thru 13 in square 283, in Davidson's subdivision, in Wash City, 33 feet on 13th st west & about 70 feet deep, having descended upon the parties above named as heirs of Isaiah Lawrence. I have been directed by the Court to report whether the same be susceptible of partition among said heirs, &, if not, whether it will be to the advantage of the minor heirs that the same should be sold. I shall proceed with said inquiry, at my ofc in City Hall, on Mar 4 at 10 o'clock. -W Redin, aud

Equity-1,116. Thos R Bird against Jas C McGuire, adm, & Rebecca C Brown, widow, & Jos Brown, heir at law of John D Brown, & of Alice Brown. The parties above named & creditors of the late John D Brown are notified that on Mar 3 next, at my ofc in the City Hall, Wash, I shall state an account of the said personal estate of said deceased. -W Redin, aud

A young German, who speaks, reads, & writes the English language well, is desirous to get employment as Clerk or Salesman. References can be given. Employers will please call at or address A Schonbork, s w corner of East Capitol & 4th st.

MON FEB 11, 1856
A board of naval surgeons will be convened at the Naval Asylum, Phil, on Mar 1 next, for the examination of assist surgeons for promotion & of candidates for admission into the medical corps of the navy. The following ofcrs will compose the board: Pres, Surgeon Jas M Greene; members, Surgeons Saml Barrington & John M Foltz, & Passed Assist Surgeon Jos Wilson, jr.

Drs J & R Hunter, Physicians for Diseases of the Lungs. Ofc 52 North Chas st, Balt, Md.

Hon Ben C Eastman, late a member of Congress from the neighboring district of Wisconsin, died at his residence in Platteville on Feb 2. He had been sick for a number of months, & his decease will not be unexpected to his many devoted friends. Mr Eastman was a native of Maine, but had made Wisconsin his adopted State. -Galena Gaz

Hon Horatio Byington, one of the Justices of the Court of Common Pleas, died at his residence in Stockbridge, Mass, on Wed last. He was about 55 years of age. He was raised to the bench by Gov Briggs in 1847. -Boston Atlas

Jos C Cabel died at his residence, near Warminster, Nelson Co, Va, on Feb 5. He was an associate of Jefferson in founding the Univ of Md, with which noble institution he was connected, at the time of his death, as a member of the Board of Visiters. For a long period he was Pres of the James River & Kanawha Company.
-Richmond Whig

Gen Jacquelin B Harvie, an old & prominent citizen of Richmond, died in that city on Friday. He was for many years brig general of the militia of that district. In early life he was a midshipman in the U S Navy. For many years he represented the district in the Senate of Va with credit to himself & usefulness to his fellow citizens.
- Richmond Dispatch

Rev Robt Henry died at Columbia, S C, on Wed last. For many years he had been a distinguished professor in the S C College. He has gone down to the grave amid the deep regrets of his late pupils & of the entire community. -Columbia Times

John H Manny, the inventor & maker of Manny's Reapers, died at his residence in Rockford on Thu last of consumption. He was one of the most enterprising men of Ill, & built up a business that was a source of honor & profit to the State.
-Chicago Tribune

London Daily News of Jan 18th announces the death of John Ferguson, of Irvine, Scotland, in his 69th year. He died possessed of property over the value of $6,300,000, about one half of which he has bequeathed to the relatives, & the residue for educational & charitable purposes in Scotland, of which kingdom he was a native.

Wash City Ordinance: 1-Act for the relief of Geo G Wilson: the sum of $32.88 be paid to him for taking up & resetting the curb on the west front of square 466.

Masonic-meeting of Nat'l Lodge 12 this evening at 7 o'clock, at their Hall, corner of D & 9th sts. -S Bulow Erwin, sec

Printers' Anniversary Ball on Feb 22, at the Wash Assembly Rooms; tickets $2, admitting a gentleman & ladies, to be had at any cmte.

Managers at Large:

Hon J T Towers	E B Robinson
Hon W W Seaton	Lem Towers
Hon Peter Force	J L Smith
Hon R C Weightman	R J Pollard
A G Seaman	Jas Wimer
G S Gideon	R W Claxton
J S Gallaher	Jos W Davis
C W Dunnington	C Wendell
W W Moore	H Polkinhorn
John Dowling	C G Klopfer
J B Tate	J Cowen
Jas T Crossfield	M Caton
J F Halliday	J Sessford, jr
Wm Towers, sr	R A Waters
J S Cunningham	W G Moore
F McNerhany	Geo W Cochran
Geo Cochran	G Whittington
T W Howard	S Lamborn
W Woodward	E S Cropley
C Alexander	

Cmte on Invitation & Reception [White Rosette.]

F Glenroy	F M Detweiler
J Bowen	A J Robinson
F J Waters	Ed Griffin
John Larcombe	R S Middleton
Chas I Canfield	Chas E Orme
J H Cunningham	Geo W Schryver
John M Judge	Andrew Humes
Jesse Judge	Oscar Kepler
P Rodier	E J Klopfer
W H Dennesson	David Wiber
Wm Harvey	Chas Schell
Geo Caton	Alfred Shaw
C Leves	J H Dennesson
J Mattingly	Geo Rogerson
J Hurley	John Melson

Cmte on Refreshments [Tri-colored Rosette.]

Wm E Morcoe	Geo Duvall
B C Wright	Saml Robertson
C F Lowrey	

Floor Managers [Red Rosette.]
Wm L Jones
C C Phelps
F Dorsett
Executive Cmte [Blue Rosette.]
Wm Woodward
S Culverwell
Jesse Judge
J T Halleck
F Dorsett

J T Nicholson
Wm Towers, jr

J H Cunningham
Benj C Wright
Wm McLean
H Bowen
Chas D McPherson

TUE FEB 12, 1856
By virtue of a distrain against Hefflebower & Lovett for house rent due & in arrears to Jno Sinon, & to me directed, I have, Feb 9, 1856, levied & distrained upon the goods & chattels in the American Hotel, formerly known as the Empire House, on Pa ave, between 3rd & 4½ sts, & shall expose the same at public sale in Feb 18, on the premises. -A E L Keese, bailiff -Jas C McGuire, auct

The steamer **Pacific**, which sailed from Liverpool for N Y on the 23rd ult, has not since been heard from. List of her passengers:

J Fiuerias
Mr Wilson
H C Sheldon
Mr Lieden
A W Atwater
W Macdougal
Mr Pauchette & lady
G N Cutter
R Haight
H Getz
Mr Steere
Jas Glen
H Dunn
Wm Topling
Mr Kershaw
Mr Ridgway
A K Carteer
Mr Horf
Mr O'Reilly
Mr Charlesworth

M Charrinaud
Wm Topling
Miss Jordan
Wm Peel Reilly
H Trimmer
Misses Heck
R Espie
M Lappa
G Jordan
W Whittaker
Corcosa
Dorizano
Wilson
A Moore
Mr Le Grand Smith
S B Berridge, lady & child
W B Symmons & lady
A Erving & lady
J Barbour, lady, & child

Oliver M Hyde, Fusionist, was elected Mayor of Detroit on Monday of last week.

Nat'l Theatre: last appearance of Misses Susan & Kate Denin, on which occasion will be presented Bulwer's beautiful Play entitled "Lady of Lyons." Claude Melnot-Miss Susan Denin. Pauline-Miss Kate Denin. After which will be presented the intensely thrilling drama of the "Wandering Boys." Paul-Miss Susan Denin. Justin-Miss Kate Denin.

The Sec of the Navy has acceded to the request of Lt Hartstene, of the U S Navy, to permit him to sail with the brig **Arctic** in search of the steamer. The steamer **Alabama** was chartered by Mr Collins for a similar purpose, & commenced her cruise from N Y on Sunday in command of Capt Schenck. The Board of Underwriters provisioned her with 500 barrels of provisions for the relief of any vessels fallen in with. A store of clothing is also taken out for the same purpose, with extra spars, boats, & water. [Feb 13th newspaper: great anxiety is felt in regard to Collin's steamer **Pacific**, Capt Eldridge, which left Liverpool on the 23rd ult-3 days before the departure of the steamer **Persia**, & has not yet been seen or heard of. -N Y Com Adv] [Feb 19th newspaper: Halifax, Feb 18. A private letter by the Canada states that the **Pacific** is safe, having put back into the River Shannon.] [Mar 7th newspaper: N Y, Mar 5: the ofcrs & crew of the **Pacific** is published, & foots up 141 persons, making, with the 45 passengers, a total of 186 souls. Another of those malicious rumors that she was safe floated about the city today, & of course, when proved to be false, tended only to swell the increasing anxiety.]

Trial for murder at Huntsville, Ala, last month produced intense excitement in all that region. Abner Tate & John Gordon were accused of having murdered some years ago, several men who disappeared mysteriously & have never been heard of. The principal witness was a widow woman of excellent character, & her testimony was so explicit & minute, & fitted so perfectly to the known circumstances, that apprehensions began to be entertained that the accused were actually guilty, although their general character forbade any such supposition. The case was concluded when the woman was found not to be in her right mind, but thoroughly insane. The men were of course acquitted.

Lost, by Mrs Ann S Stephens, at the President's levee, Fri last, a large Diamond Cluster Pin. The finder will be suitably rewarded by returning it to Mrs Stephens at Willard's Hotel.

Caution. A painful duty obliges me to notify the public that my son, A Lammond,jr, has no interest in or connexion with my Store, & I warn all persons from letting him have money on my account. I also particularly request them not to loan him any on his own account, as he devotes it to an improper use & has no means of repaying them. -A Lammond, sr

A mason, searching for some obstruction that prevented a chimney from drawing, came upon the body of a man wedged into the flue. It was found to be Louis Miller, insane from intemperance, who had been missing since New Year's day.

Edw Tyrrel Channing, for 32 years Prof of Rhetoric & Oratory in Harvard College, Mass, died on Thursday of congestion of the lungs, aged 65 years.

Mrd: on Feb 10, in Wash City, by Rev G W Samson, Mr Maurice Tucker to Miss Sarah A Killmon, both of Wash City.

Died: on Feb 9, at Balt, Mrs Anne Pyne Bankhead, wife of Gen Jas Bankhead, U S A, & daughter of the late John Pyne, of S C.

Died: on Feb 8, Cornelius Deasy, in his 82nd year, a native of the Parish of Caragh, County Cork, Ireland, but for the last 9 years a resident of Wash City. May he rest in peace!

Senate: 1-Mail between Cairo & New Orleans: the Postmaster Gen states that he contracted with Isaac N Eastham, Wm Henry Gaines, & John Woodburn for a daily mail, at $329,000, on Dec 3 last. The postmaster at Cairo writes, under date of Jan 30, 1856, that the contractors have done every thing in their power in the prosecution of their contract, the floating ice from Cairo to Red river, 750 miles, prohibited boats with any degree of regularity. 2-Memorial from the Govn'r of N J, in regard to restoring Cmdor Chas Stewart to his late position of senior post captain of the navy. He was placed upon the retired list by the action of the Naval Board. 3-Ptn for A E Rolando, wife of Henry Rolando, complaining that her husband has been placed on the reserved list, while another, his subordinate in rank, is rendered eligible to futher promotion. She represents that a wrong has been inflicted on her husband. 4-Cmte on Indian Affairs: bill for the relief of Anson Dart: recommended its passage.

WED FEB 13, 1856
Heavy damages for slander: suit was brought by Miss Mary Doherty against John L Brown, in which she claimed $5,000 damages for alleged gross defamation of her character & reputation, & which has been decided this morning in the Superior Court. The jury found a verdict for the plntf for $3,666.66. The dfndnt has long been known as a keeper of a billiard saloon, is reputed to be wealthy, & has been married to two of the plntf's sisters. -Boston Transcript, Sat

Mr Jas G Cox, for many years a citizen of this parish, set out with his negroes in Dec for Western Texas, where he had determined to locate. We learn that while crossing a prairie 40 miles wide the cold northers attacked his party & 8 of his negroes froze to death, & 2 of his wagons were cut up & burnt as fuel to save the lives of himself & the balance of his negroes. -Shreveport [La] Gaz

Senate: 1-Memorial from Thos H Stephens, late a lt in the navy & dropped by the action of the Naval Board, asking redress. 2-Memorial from Abner Read, late a lt in the navy dropped by the action of the late Naval Board. 3-Memorial from Capt Wm Jameson, placed on the reserved list by the late Naval Board, asking to be restored to his former position. 4-Additional papers submitted in relation to the case of H H Rhodes, late a lt in the navy. 5-Ptn from Anton L C Portman, asking compensation for his services as an interpreter in the Japan expedition. 6-Ptn from the legal reps of Thos G Nelson, asking compensation for property destroyed during the Revolutionary war, & also to be allowed commutation pay. 7-Ptn from the widow of Marmaduke S Davies, a Revolutionary soldier, asking to be allowed bounty land. 8-Ptn from A E Donohoo, in behalf of the surviving heir of Robt Wilcox, of the Revolutionary war, asking compensation for his services. 9-Ptn from Jno Allen, asking to be allowed a pension or a grant of land for his gallantry in capturing an armed barge of the enemy in the last war with Great Britain, while master of a schooner engaged in the lumber trade. 10-Cmte on Military Affairs: asked to be discharged from the consideration of the memorial of Leslie Combs, & that it be referred to the Cmte on Public Lands: which was agreed to.

Appointments by the Pres: 1-Geo P Scarburgh, of Va, to be Judge of the Court of Claims, vice Jos H Lumpkin, declined. 2-A G Seaman, of D C, to be Superintendent of the Public Printing.

Trustee's sale of hardware & merchandise at auction: by deed of trust recorded in the Clerk's Ofc in Wash Co, D C: sale on Feb 15, in the storehouse 614 8th st east, near the Navy Yard gate, now used & occupied by J W Stevens in carrying on the Hardware & Cigar business, as a retail store, to satisfy two notes drawn by Keilholtz & Stevens, for $37.71 each, & one note drawn by J W Stevens for $160, all of which is now due. -Saml A H Marks, trustee -A Green, auct

The restaurant *Verandah*, on Pa ave, between 10th & 11th sts, offered for sale: the stock, fixtures, & furniture, with unexpired license & the good will of the establishment. Apply to H C Spalding, atty, 337 North D st, between 9th & 10th sts.

On Sat the house of Mr Phillips, 6 miles of Waukegan, was burnt, & himself & daughter perished in the flames. The family consisted of Mr Philips, two grown-up daughters, & a hired man. The fire took place while all were asleep, & only 1 daughter & the hired man escaped. She was badly burnt, & frozen afterward, & her recovery is doubtful, & she will be crippled for life if she survives. -Chicago Press, Feb 7

Died: on Feb 11, Wm Sutherland, in his 13th year, the eldest child of Wm A & Jane F Mulloy, after a long & protracted illness of several months. His funeral will be from the residence of his father, 3rd & East Capitol sts, this afternoon, at 3 o'clock.

On Jan 25, the house of Mr A McFarland, on Cayuga road, 8 miles below Jarvis, was destroyed by fire, & with it his whole family of 5 children were burnt to death. The eldest was about 9 years old, the two youngest were twins of 2 years. Their parents were on a visit to a sick neighbor at the time. The fire is supposed to have originated from a barrel of ashes standing near a corner of the house. -Long Point [C W] Advocate

Orphans Court of Wash Co, D C. Letters of administration on the personal estate of Ninian Beall, late of Wash Co, deceased. -Geo W Beall, adm

Mrs R A Wheeler, Pa ave, 3rd door below 3rd st, has several well-furnished Rooms vacant, which she would rent with or without board on most accommodating terms.

THU FEB 14, 1856

New Book: Extracts from the Diary & Correspondence of the late Amos Lawrence, with a brief Account of some Incidents in his Life. Edited by his son, Wm R Lawrence, M D. Boston, Guild & Lincoln, 1856. In a correspondence in 1843 he writes: My nephew by marriage, Franklin Pierce, seems to be prominent candidate for the White House for the next 4 years.

Senate: 1-Memorial of Lt Alex'r Murray, remonstrating against the action of the late Naval Board & requesting to be restored to the active list, from which he was removed for causes unknown to him. 2-Memorial from Maj Chas S Merchant, of the 3rd regt of U S artl, asking pecuniary relief for losses sustained in Dec, 1853, by the destruction of the provisions & stores on the steamship **San Francisco**. 3-Ptn from Wm L Briggs, a messenger connected with the marine corps, asking the same compensation as is allowed to other messengers of similar grade. 4-Ptn from Wm W Belden, asking remuneration for military stores & provisions furnished during the war of 1812, & lost by the destruction of **Fort Niagara** by the British. 5-Ptn from John Vreeland, asking a pension on account of the services of his father in the Revolutionary war. 6-Memorial from Capt John D Sloat, placed on the retired list, asking to be restored to the active service list. 7-Memorial from Lt John S Taylor, placed on the reserved list, asking to be restored to his former position. 8-Ptn from Lt Jas D Johnson, asking that his accounts as naval storekeeper at Valparaiso may be settled. 9-Cmte on Military Affairs: adverse report on the memorial of Col R A Wainwright to be relieved from the payment of public money stolen from him; also on the memorial of Denison E Seymour, asking for some remuneration for losses sustained & hardships suffered in consequence of having been induced to enlist in the corps of engineers in consequence of misrepresentations, accompanied by written reports in each case. Same cmte: asked to be discharged from the consideration of the memorial of B H Mooers, a lt in the war of 1812, asking that pensions may be granted to the survivors of the war, & that it be referred to the Cmte on Pensions: which was agreed to.

Birth-place of Geo Washington. Mr Lewis W Washington, of Jefferson Co, Va, son of the late Hon Geo C Washington, of Md, as heir of the estate, has tendered to the State of Va, through Gov Wise, the title to 60 acres of land in Westmoreland Co, the site of the birth-place of Geo Washington, & the house & graves of his progenitors in America. The condition of the gift is, that the State shall cause the premises to be permanently enclosed by an iron fence, based on a stone foundation, & shall mark the same by suitable & modest, though substantial tablets, to commemorate for the rising generation those notable spots. The Govn't recommends the acceptance of the gift on the terms proposed, & say an appropriation of $2,000 will be sufficient.

Pittsfield [Mass] Eagle: the 9 year old daughter of Dr Jennings died from a small bit of strychnine accidentally administered to her, when she was ill with some slight disorder. Her little brother had gotten hold of the fatal powder, which Mrs Jennings, supposing it to be one of the Dover's powders, gave it to her daughter. She died in a short time.

Ira Colby, of McHenry, Ill, had been engaged in slaughtering hogs & some blood remained upon his clothes, when he lead his bull to water; the bull sprung at him, tossed him, tearing out his bowels, & injuring him so that he is thought not able to survive.

Circuit Court of Wash Co, D C-in Equity. Jas Lynch, Jane Lynch his wife, Janet B Smallwood, & Jas Lynch, Lunatic trustee of Ann Philips, vs Henry May, Trustee, Jourdan Maury & others. Jane Lynch, Janet B Smallwood, & Ann Philips are sisters & heirs-at-law of Jas B Philips, deceased; that on Mar 30, 1848, said Philips conveyed certain lots in Washington to Henry May, in trust to secure said Philips' note to J & C Maury for $3,000, dated Mar 30, 1848, for 3 years; that after the death of said Philips & before the note was due, viz, in May, 1850, the said trustee sold said property, & subsequently conveyed most of it; that the debt then due from Philips did not exceed $1,387.83; that the sales produced about $3,000; & the surplus, after paying said debt, was applied to certain judgments against Philips in the hands of said J & C Maury, leaving a balance of $57.88. It claims that said sale was void; that the conveyances by the trustee only passed the legal title subject to the trust; that complnts are entitled to redeem all the property on payment of the balance due on the note aforesaid, or to have it resold, & the surplus, after paying said debt, paid over to them; & it asks this relief for them. It states that all the property was conveyed by the trustee to the purchasers, except lot 38 in square 462, & square 936, the legal title to which remains in the trustee. It further states the willingness of cmplnts, if the judgments aforesaid are equitable liens on the property, that they should be paid out of it; & it states that said Henry May & Jourdan May reside out of D C. Same to appear in this Court, in person or by solicitor, on or before the first Monday of Jul next. -Jas S Morsell, Asst Judge Cir Court, D C -Jno A Smith, clerk

House of Reps: 1-Cornelius Wendell elected Printer of the House for the 34th Congress.

Steam boiler explosion at Algonac, Mich, on Jan 31, killed Mr Bell, the miller, a son of Mr Beers, & an Indian, who were in the mill at the time.

Died: on Feb 12, in Wash City, after a severe illness of only 10 days' duration, Ida, only surviving child of Andrew & the late Hannah C Tate, aged 25 months. Thus within the brief space of 12 days, has the shading angel removed a happy wife & two lovely children from a home circle where they were honored & loved. The last link in love's golden chain has now been severed, & a lovely infant been called to join its mother & sister in that spirit-land where hopes are never blighted & sorrow is unknown. Her funeral will take place on Feb 15 at 1 o'clock, from the residence of her father.

Orphans Court of Wash Co, D C. Letters of administration on the personal estate of Andrew T Ball, late of the U S Navy, deceased. -Chas G Ball, adm

FRI FEB 15, 1856
Fighting at Walla-Walla: Jan 10: a few Indians presented themselves on the hill, filled up some of our trenches & dug new ones of their own. Wasco boys on the hill & Linn boys along the brush fought for 2 hours, when the Indians began to retreat. Maj Chinn ordered a charge, when Linn & Wasco pitched in & ran the devils past their upper camp; 3 Indians killed. Jan 11: 350 men under Col Kelly mounted on horseback & pursued the enemy. Followed about 40 miles, found considerable stock, but not one Indian. Jan 13: Col Kelly & company returned, brought with them 30 or 40 Indian horses; saw quite a number of cattle & horses, but due to the fog could not find them as they returned; found a valuable cache deposited by a settler. Houses nearly all burnt; grain etc destroyed by the Indians. The loss of our settlers is thus reported: Capt Wilson's Co: mortally wounded: E B Kelsey & Capt A V Wilson; slightly wounded, F Duval, J W Smith, & J Studivan.
Capt Humason's Co: Mortally wounded, Jesse Fleming
Capt Bennet's Co: Capt Chas Bennett, killed; B Miller, Ira Allen, & A Shepherd, wounded.
Capt Layton's Co: Killed, John M Burrows & Henry Crow; wounded, Capt Layton, I Miller, Franklin Crabtree, T J Payne, Casper Snooks, Nathan Fry, & A M Addington.
Capt Monson's Co: Wm Hagerman, killed at ***Fort Walla-Walla***, & Wm Andrews at ***Fort Henrietta***; wounded, Capt J B Monson & J B Smith.
Capt Cornoyer's Co: John Jarvaise, wounded

Mrd: on Feb 12, in Wash City, in St Mary's Church, by Rev Maathias Alig, Mr Albin Schell, of Wash, to Rosina Celler, of Balt.

Mrd: on Feb 12, in the Chapel of the Holy Trinity, by Rev Harvey Stanley, Wm T Duvall to Mgt E Duckett, all of PG Co, Md.

Mrd: on Feb 14, by Rev Mr Cummins, Mr J Presly Barthlow to Miss Isabella Phillips, all of Wash City.

Senate: 1-Mr Butler addressed the Senate at length, condemning the Naval Board law, but defending the members of the Board acting under it from any impurity of motive. He defended all the memorialists whose papers he had presented with much zeal, particularly Lts Rolando & Maffitt, Cmders Pettigru, Gedney, & others. 2-Ptn from Marthan Stanton, widow of a Revolutionary soldier, asking that her pension may be continued as at present, & not reduced, as contemplated by the decision of the present Com'r of Pensions. [Brief history: her husband during the war, & particularly in the defence of *Fort Griswold*, was desperately wounded there, contending that such men, & the widows of such men, were entitled to the grateful remembrance of the country. He invoked speedy action as the widow was now 88 years of age.] 3-Ptn from Geo Jones, a chaplain on board the steam frig **Mississippi** during the Japan expedition, asked to be allowed 500 copies of the volume of Com Perry's work comprising the obscuration of the zodiacal light. 6-Ptn from the heirs of Saml Miller, asking to be allowed the 7 years half-pay due said Miller as a captain in the Revolutionary war. 7-Ptn from Eugene Relliena, asking compensation for property destroyed during the bombardment of Greytown by the U S sloop-of-war **Cyane**. 8-Ptn from Lt J M Gilliss, complaining of the action of the Naval Board in placing him on the reserved list, & asking such redress as Congress may deem meet. 9-Ptn from D F Dulaney, late a lt in the navy, dropped by the action of the Naval Board, asking to be restored to his former position. 10-Ptn from Lt M C Perry, jr, placed on the reserved list, asking to be restored to his former position.

House of Reps: 1-After prayer by Rev H C Dean, Chaplain to the Senate, the Journal yesterday was read. 2-Mr Florence, of Pa, presented the memorial of Gov A H Reeder, contesting the seat of J W Whitfield as Delegate from the Territory of Kansas. In presenting this memorial Mr Florence thought it was due to himself to state that he had arrived at no conclusion in relation to the declarations which it contained: referred to the Cmte of Elections. 3-The memorial of Miguel A Otero, contesting the seat of Jose Manuel Gallegos as Delegate from the Territory of New Mexico: referred to the Cmte on Elections. 4-Memorial of Albert Fabre, contesting the seat of Geo Eustis as Rep from the first district of the State of Louisiana: referred to the Cmte on Elections.

U S Patent Ofc, Wash, Feb 13, 1856. Ptn of Michl B Dyott, of Phil, Pa, praying for the extension of a patent granted to him for an improvement in lamps for essential oils, for 7 years from the expiration of said patent, which takes place on May 30, 1856. -Chas Mason, Com'r of Patents

Trustee's sale of an undivided interest in the Nat'l Hotel, Wash, for sale at public auction: Trustee's sale. By deed of trust from Roger C Weightman, & by the direction of Mary E Barney, cest. Q. trust of the estate of Edw DeKraft, deceased, the subscribers will sell at auction, at the auction store of Jas C McGuire, Wash, on Mar 18, eight undivided three hundred & fifteen parts, the whole into three hundred & fifteen equal parts, being divided of & in all & singular lots of ground in Wash, C C, marked & known on the plat thereof as lots 8 thru 13 in square 491, adjoining said lot 13, fronting 20 feet on North C st, running back at right angles, with the establishment known as the Nat'l Hotel thereon, now in the occupancy of Wm Guy. -Richd Wallach, John H Saunders, trustees -J C McGuire, auct

Died: on Feb 13, after a painful illness, Mrs Ellen Burch, wife of the late Remigius Burch, aged 63 years. Her funeral will take place of Sat morning at 10 o'clock.

SAT FEB 16, 1856
Army intelligence. 1-Maj Wm H Chase, U S Engineers, ordered to the command of the U S Military Academy at West Point. He has been relieved of the command of **Fort Taylor** by Maj W H Frasier, U S Engineers. 2-Capt H G Wright, Engineer Corps, U S Army, ordered from the command of **Fort Jefferson** to Washington. Capt Woodbury has relieved him of the command of the works at the Dry Tortugas, & has entered upon the duties of his station.

Lost, on Feb 15, probably on H st, between the residence of W W Corcoran & 13th st, a wide gold bracelet, with blue enameled clasp, on the back is engraved Lucia King. Suitable reward on giving information to 328 N Y ave, near 9th st.

Died: on Feb 14, in Wash City, of whooping cough & congestion of the lungs, in his 8th year, John Thomas, only son of J C & the late Sophia A Baker, of Wash City. His funeral is this afternoon at 2 o'clock, from the residence of his grandmother, Mrs Perrin, on H, between 9th & 10th st.

Mrd: on Feb 14, by Rev Mr French, Mr Robt V Laskey to Miss Mary H White, of Wash City.

Wm T Smithson, Banker & Exchange Dealer, next door north to the Bank of Wash. Will attend promptly to the collection of bills of exchange & notes, & make returns at sight, on principal cities, at the current rates, without other charge.

Melle Manvers, Parisienne, removed to a more central location, will continue to give lessons in the French & Spanish languages, & also Italian singing, to ladies & gentlemen, private or in classes, at her own residence or that of scholars. 10th st, between E & F sts.

MON FEB 18, 1856
Rev Rowland Williams has been dismissed by the Bishow of Llandaff from his ofc of chaplain on account of the work entitled "Rational Godliness."

The U S steam-frig **Powhatan**, Capt Wm J McCluney, from Japan & the China seas, & last from Table Bay, Cape of Good Hope, arrived at Norfolk on Thu, after a pleasant passage from the Cape of 38 days, about half the distance from the Cape to the U S under canvass alone. The **Powhatan** was one of the East India & Japan squadron under Com Perry. She has been absent on this cruise 3 years & in commission 3½ years. Deaths during the cruise: by disease, Lt J H Adams, & 13 men; by accident, Boatswain Wm Whiting & 2 men; in action with pirates in Kulan Bay, 5 men. -Norfolk Herald

Mr Wirt Trimble, of Gtwn, D C, had invented a composition for Printers' Rollers which will be unaffected by temperature.

Massachusetts Supreme Court on Monday [says the Boston Post:] case involving custody of 2 children. Two years ago libels for divorce were entered by Ezra T Kidder against his wife Mary A Kidder, & by the wife against the husband. In Oct 1854, one of the cases came on for a hearing before Judge Bigelow, in which an attempt was made to show too great a familiarity of Mrs Kidder with Dr Patterson, a spiritual medium, who acted as a medical practitioner under spiritual influences, & as such was called at attend Mrs Kidder. The hearing was postponed before it concluded, & the parties arranged to live separate, the father taking the custody of the 2 children. Mr Kidder died in Florida 3 or 4 weeks since, leaving the children in charge of Jas Leach, of Northboro, [Mrs Leach being his sister,] & Saml Lovejoy, of Balt, another brother-in-law, as guardians. This case came before the court on a petition of Mrs Kidder for a writ of habeas corpus for the custody of her children, Caroline M, aged 12 years, & Dudley T, 10 years. The father having control of the children, gave him no power beyond his lifetime. By statute law the mother became the guardian, unless it were proved that she was incompetent for the trust.
The Court was satisfied that Mrs Kidder had fully established her claim, & decree that she should have the future custody of her children.

Doylestown, Pa, Feb 15. The execution of Jacob Armbruster, who was convicted of the murder of his wife, Catherine, took place in the jail yard today. He maintained his composure to the last, protesting his innocence. He ascended the scaffold accompanied by his son, who wept bitterly at the dreadful situation of his father.

Barnum in Bankruptcy. Meeting of the creditors of the Jerome Clock Co on Mon but about $136,000 of the indebtedness was represented. It was voted that the company should go into bankruptcy. B T Barnun has been put into bankruptcy here, & Fred'k Crowell, has been appointed trustee of his estate. -New Haven Courier

At Boston on Wed an avalanche of ice fell from the roof of John Ballard's bldg in Bromfield st. Mr Ezra R Tebbetts, of Lynn, who was passing at the time, was struck & prostrated by a piece of ice about 2 feet long & 1 foot thick. Drs Stedman & Cabot were called, & by their advice he was taken to the hospital, where he died later. He left home about three-quarters of an hour before the accident. Mr Tebbetts was about 50 years of age, & leaves a wife & several children. He was one of the Assessors of Lynn, & a very worthy citizen. -Boston Atlas

Another fire at Madison Court-house, Va. The handsome frame residence owned by Mrs H Barnes, opposite Eagle Tavern, was destroyed by fire on Feb 14. Mr Thomas' tinware manufactory was among the bldgs burnt-also owned by Mrs Barnes. The saddler shop of W T Fouchee was torn down in order to prevent the further spread of the flames. Not many days since the mansion of ex-Govn'r Leake was destroyed, & a few months before a new church, scarcely finished.

Murder in Missouri. Mr Basil H Gordon, Assist Engineer of the North Missouri railroad, was murdered near Warrenton, Mo, last week. His body was found near a ravine buried in snow. He was out collecting subscriptions for the construction of the road, & it is supposed he was murdered for the money in his possession. Mr Gordon was last seen in company with 2 men, one named May from Ky, about 30 years of age. Mr Gordon is represented to have been a gentleman of great worth. He was a native of Va & was about 40 years of age.

Michl Mahan, age 8, of 87 Baxter st, N Y, died on Thu from the effects of a large dram of liquor. Bridget Mahan, mother of the child, testified that her son has been intoxicated on other occasions & chewed tobacco freely.

Died: on Feb 8, at his residence, Shawanee Springs, Mercer Co, Ky, Col Geo C Thompson, in his 78th year.

Genr'l information: Mrs Columbus Munroe is the Treasurer of the Ladies' Benevolent & Employment Society. Mrs M E Gurley is the Sec.

Maj Ben Perley Poore consents to lecture for the Benefit of the Poor on Mar 18: Foreign Travel, from Paris to Palestine, by the way of Constantinople. [Reply to invitation from J P Pepper, W J C Duhamel, M D, Thos E Baden; Thos Berry, & A R Allen.]

To Members of Congress & others. Monsr D Fabronius, Lithographic Artist, from Paris & London, announces his arrival in Wash City, where he intends devoting a few months to the taking of Portraits from life direct on stone. Studio: Casaris' Hotel, Capitol Hill..

TUE FEB 19, 1856
Trustee's sale of hardware, cutlery, & fancy goods: on Feb 26, at the auction store of A Green, 526 7th st, by deed of trust from John W Stevens to B P Smith, dated Feb 14, 1856, filed for record in the clerk's ofc of Wash Co, D C, by five writs of fieri facias issued by Z K Offutt, at the suit of Harvey H Adams & J G Smith & Co, against the goods & chattels of said Stevens, a general assortment of goods. Terms cash. -Henry Yeatman, constable -A Green, auct

Trustee's sale of valuable bldg lots: on Mar 3 next, by deed of trust from Estwick Evans & wife to the subscriber, dated Aug 23, 1854, recorded in Liber J A S, folios 9 thru 12, of the land records of Wash Co, D C: sale of lot 7 in square 583, in Wash City, 45 feet & 9 inches on 3rd st, between south E & G sts. -Hugh B Sweeny, trustee -A Green, auct

Naval: Capt Pendergrast ordered to the command of the new U S steamer **Merrimac**, vice Capt Gregory, relieved at his own request. If the vessel is found to work as well as is anticipated, the trial trip will be continued to Europe.

Ballston, N Y, Feb 15. The trial of Kingsbury & Henderson, charged with burglary at Congress Hall, Saratoga Springs, on Aug 5 last, when Gen Robt Halsey, of Ithaca, was robbed of between fifteen & twenty thousand dollars worth of property, came before the Court of Sessions at this place on Feb 12. The burglars were detected when Mr Edw M Skidmore was at dinner at Congress Hall on Aug 5, & recognized the burglar Edding, who had been arrested in NY on a charge of entering the room of one of the guests at the Howard Hotel. Edding & Henderson had taken rooms at the hotel. Skidmore alerted the book-keeper of his suspicions. Previous to this Gen Halsey's room had been robbed of diamonds, jewelry, & railroad bonds. They were arrested & taken before Justice Pike. Edding was discharged with insufficient evidence, but Kingsbury & Henderson were committed for trial. Kingsbury is an inveterate villain, & has followed the business of hotel-thieving in this country & in Europe for the past 25 or 30 years. He had a alias, Horace D Champion.

Senate: 1-Ptn from Saml A Pugh, asking to be allowed to enter a certain tract of land in lieu of one improperly sold by the U S. 2-Ptn from Marie Rice, asking to be allowed a pension on account of the services of her husband during the war of 1812. 3-Ptn from the heirs of Manuel Gonzales Moro, asking to be allowed to enter certain lands in Mo. 4-Ptn from the heirs of Thos Van Buskirk, asking compensation for supplies furnished during the Revolutionary war. 5-Ptn from Eliz Foster, widow of an ofcr in the army who died in service, asking to be allowed a pension. 6-Ptn from Capt Thos M Newell, complaining of the action of the Naval board in placing him on the retired list, & asking redress.

The Louisville Courier learns that Mr John McMurty, of Lexington, Ky, carpenter, architect, & foundry-man, has failed for about $800,000, his assets not amounting to half that sum.

House of Reps: 1-Bill for the relief of the heirs of Louis & Basil Vasseurs: referred. 1-Bill for the relief of Robt Mitchell: referred. 3-Bill to amend an act for the relief of Nancy Weatherford, widow of Col Wm Weatherford, of the 1st Ill regt of volunteers in the Mexican war. 4-Resolved: the Pres of the U S is requested to communicate to the House the report of Capt E Boutwell, & all documents, relative to the operations of the U S sloop-of-war **John Adams**, under his command, at the Fejee Islands, in 1855. 5-Mr Hall, of Mass presented: Ptn of Saml Norris for pay for beef & flour furnished the Indians in Calif in 1851.

The **Brigantine House**, on Brigantine Beach, N J, occupied by Maj Nilis, was entirely washed away & carried out to sea during the recent heavy storm. It was not occupied at the time, & not a single article of furniture was saved. The house was put up by a company, & the loss, it is supposed, will not fall short of $50,000.

The Yazoo [Miss] Democrat says that the circuit court of that county recently adjourned. Six men, 3 black & 3 white, were found guilty of murder, & sentenced to be hung on Feb 16, & one sentenced to the penitentiary for 5 years. The condemned criminals are John Cotton, for the murder of Smith; Jack Lynch, for the murder of Wright; & Young C Boyard, for the murder of his wife; the negroes for the murder of their master, Theophilus Pritchard.

Lt Harrison, U S R M, who belongs to Wash City, has distinguished himself in the current Indian war on our Pacific coast. [Letter to Hon Jas Guthrie, Sec of Treasury. U S revenue cutter **Jefferson Davis**, Steilacoom, W T, Dec 12, 1855. The gallant conduct of Lt Harrison is deserving of great praise. He has been engaged in two encounters with the Indians, in both of which he has acted with great coolness & bravery. -Wm G Pease, Capt]

Sale of the Maysville & Lexington Railroad, with all its property & franchises, locomotives, & cars. Jas Pannett & others, plntfs, against the Maysville & Lexington Railroad Co & others, dfndnts. By judgment of the Fayette Circuit Court, I will sell at the public auction, on Apr 23 next, at the Public Square, in the city of Lexington, Ky, the M & L Railroad. -Eben Milton, Receiver & Com'r, Lexington, Ky

Teacher wanted: a gentleman qualified to teach English, Mathematics & Classical studies, to take charge of a school now in progress. -J Ravenscroft Jones, Lawrenceville, Brunswick Co, Va.

The Third Annual Cotillon Party of the President's Guards will take place on Feb 19 at the Armory, on La ave, between 6th & 7th sts. Managers:

Capt Jos Peck	W Sanderson	W Bosse
Lt C W Flint	W Sareter	R J Clements
Surg Dubamel	R Teale	A N Clements
Q Mas J T Evans	C Wise	D A Harrover
Serg J L Heise	J Yeabower	R Laskey
Serg Geo Seitz	J Hess	P Mackay
Serg Hamilton	J Ash	W Preston
Corp J H McCutchen	Lt John W Baden	A Schwartes
J Agustofer	Lt John Bohlayer	W Thoma
A Bohlayer	Ensign J C Peck	W Wilson
S Bien	Serg W H Hayward	H T L Wilson
J W Cruit	Serg S W Owen	E Jones
J T Essex	Q M Serg J A King	W H Topping
F A Lutz	Corp A Shucking	H Heard
John Murphy	Corp C J Noerr	
J Pedichord	W D Bell	

Died: on Feb 17, in Wash City, in his 34th year, Augustus C Gillett, of N Y, a clerk in the Dept of State. His funeral will take place from his late residence, 407 H st, between 12th & 13th sts, on Feb 19, at 2 o'clock.

Died: on Feb 18, in Wash City, Mr Alfred G Ridgely, in his 35th year. His funeral will be from his late residence on Pa ave, between 19th & 20th sts, on Feb 20, at 3 P M.

Died: on Feb 17, in Wash City, Miss Madeline Pierson, in her 17th year, daughter of the late Wm & Catherine Pierson, of Va.

Died: on Jan 19, at his residence, King & Queen Co, Va, after a brief illness, Saml Butler, in his 59th year. He was a native of King Wm Co, & leaves there, as well as every where known, many warm & sincere friends to deplore his loss. He was a soldier of the war of 1812, in the artl company commanded by Capt Andrew Stevenson, at *Camp Holly*.

Died: on Feb 18, in Wash City, Robt Keyworth, in his 61st year. His funeral will be from his late residence, on Pa ave, between 9th & 10th sts, on Feb 20 at 3½ P M.
+
Masonic: Grand Lodge of D C: members are to assemble on Wed with a view to attending the funeral of our deceased brother, M W Past Grand Master, Robt Keyworth. -Geo C Whiting, Grand Sec

Died: on Feb 17, in Wash City, in her 65th year, Mrs Lydia Allen, widow of the late Wm Allen, of Prince Wm Co, Va. The deceased was for near half a century an exemplary member of the Methodist Episcopal Church. Her funeral will take place from the residence of her son-in-law, C W C Dunnington, 298 south B st, Capitol Hill, at 3 o'clock this evening.

Valuable farm for sale: 170 acres, at **Bayly's Cross Roads**, 6½ miles s w of Wash City; bldgs consist of a small frame house & stable. Apply to F H Smith, at the House of Reps, or to J H Cleveland, on the premises.

WED FEB 20, 1856
Senate: 1-Memorial from Jno L Gilbert & others, asking that the direction of Delaware ave as laid down in the plat of Wash City may be changed. 2-Ptn from J E Martin, asking compensation for diplomatic services in Portugal from Jul 20, 1850 to Jun 15, 1851. 3-Ptn from Asa R Ford, adm of Augustus Ford, asking compensation for preparing a chart of Lake Ontario in the war of 1812, for the use of the squadron thereon. 4-Ptn from Wm K Latimer, complaining of being placed on the retired list, & asking to be restored to his former position. 5-Ptn from Lt Augustus H Kilty, making a like complaint, asking to be restored. 6-Ptn from Horatio J Perry, asking compensation for services as acting charge d'affaires to the U S at the Court of Madrid, & to be remunerated for certain expenses unavoidably incurred. 7-Ptn from Lts Wm D Porter & Saml R Knox, complaining of the action of the Naval Board in placing them on the retired list. 8-Ptn from Fred'k W Mooers, a master in the navy, making a like complaint, & stating that his pay is not adequate to the support of himself & family, & asking Congress to place the pay of masters of 20 years service on a footing with lts, as a reward for long & faithful service. 9-Ptn from Capt Chas W Skinner, placed on the reserved list by the Naval Board, asking to be restored to his former position. 10-Ptn from Eleazer Williams, asking that a sum intended to have been secured to him by the terms of a treaty between the U S & the St Regis Indians, in consideration of services in their behalf, but unjustly withheld from him through the interposition of others, may now be paid to him. 11-Ptn from the heirs of Thos W Corby, asking indemnity for spoliations committed by the French prior to 1800. 12-Ptn from Jos Nock, asking an extension of his patent. 13-Additional documents submitted in relation to the cases of Hall Neilson & of Lt Jno S Taylor. 14-Ptn from the widow of Wm Morris, a Revolutionary ofcr, asking to be allowed arrearages of pension & to be allowed bounty land. 15-Additional evidence in support of the claim of the heirs of Jas Hook, submitted. 16-Ptn from Geo L Browne & Wm Curry, asking remission of certain duties on a cargo of coal taken from a vessel wrecked on the Florida reef & brought by them into Key West. 17-Cmte on Revolutionary Claims: asked to be discharged from the consideration of the memorial of Benj Hathaway, & that it be referred to the Cmte on Public Lands: agreed to. Same cmte: asked to be discharged from the consideration of the ptn of the citizens of

De Kalb Co, Ala, in behalf of Sarah Beuge & John Vreeland, & also that of John Burkhalter, & they be referred to the Cmte on Pensions: agreed to.

House of Reps: 1-Memorial of Mrs Eliz A R Linn, of Missouri, for commutation & interest for the Revolutionary services of Col Wm Linn.

Mr H C Pratt, an eminent portrait painter of Boston, purposes returning to Wash City in a few days, & will remain several weeks, to fulfill professional engagements entered into during his last visit to Wash. One of his portraits is now at the Executive mansion, & is cherished by the Pres. It is the likeness of the Pres' father, Govn'r Pierce, of N H, painted shortly after his retirement, nearly 20 years ago.

528 Mormon emigrants, on their way to Great Sale Lake City, arrived at N Y on Sat, in the ship **John J Boyd**, Capt Austin, from Liverpool Dec 15. [Feb 21st newspaper: The Mormons are mostly Danes; but among them are several Norwegians, Italians from the Protestant valley of Piedmont, & two Icelanders. They are stout hearty looking people, with an expression of intelligence above that of the average European immigrants. It is estimated that about 2,000 converts will be landed at N Y this season, mostly from the sources above named. -Journal of Commerce]

Mr H B Hemingway, of Chicago, was on Sat robbed of $8,500 in the cars between Albany & Schenectady. The money was in a carpet-bag & $2,000 of it was in specie. Hemingway was asleep when the robbery was committed.

Wash Corp: 1-Bill for the relief of John N Lovejoy: passed. 2-Cmte of Claims: adverse report on the ptn of Wm A Barnes & asked to be discharged from its consideration: agreed to.

Capt Hartstene, in command of the brig **Arctic**, which vessel was sent from N Y by the Gov't to search for the steamer **Pacific**, has been compelled to put into Halifax in consequence of his vessel becoming disabled. He reports having heard or seen nothing of the missing steamer.

Mr & Mrs Rolf, of Cerro Gordo Co, Iowa, were frozen to death a few days ago. They had been to a neighboring town shopping, & on their way home got lost in a snow storm on the prairie. Mr Rolf, who was an invalid, could not leave his sled. His wife, wrapping her shawl around him, unhitched the oxen, & followed them as they trudged homewards for half a mile, when she sank down in a snow drift, & there died. On the arrival of the oxen at the house the neighbors turned out in search & found both of them frozen to death. -Detroit Free Press

Died: on Jan 31, at the **Academy of the Visitation**, Gtwn, Eliz Ellen, in her 12th year of her age, daughter & only child of Washington A Posey, of Chas Co, Md.

Died: on Jan 24, at his residence in Vermillionville, La, Dr Wm G Mills, formerly of Charleston, S C, aged 42 years, survived by an affectionate wife & a group of lovely children & a large circle of friends.

Died: on Feb 11, in Mariana, Fla, Mrs Caroline Lee Hentz. It is a sad coincidence that upon the day which introduces to the public by far the ablest production of the pen of this gifted authoress, her friends should announce to the work that it is the last. She was a true & noble woman, a devoted wife, a tender & faithful mother, an ardent friend, & a sincere trusting Christian. Mrs Hentz was a native of Lancaster, Mass, & a sister of the late Brig Gen Henry Whiting, of the U S Army. -W C L

THU FEB 21, 1856
Senate: 1-Memorial from Lt Simeon B Bissell, complaining of the action of the Naval Board in placing him on the reserved list, & asking to be restored. Same for Lt Jas M Watson: asking redress as Congress may deem proper. 2-Memorial from David Gordon, representing that the accounting ofcrs of the Treasury have refused to adjust his claims, for the settlement of which an act had passed at the last Congress, & asking that a further act may be passed for his relief. 3-Ptn from Jonas P Levy, asking to be allowed bounty land for military services rendered by him in the late war with Mexico. 4-Ptn from Edw A Stevens, asking an extension of his patent for a method of applying air to the furnaces of steam engines. 5-Cmte on Commerce: bill for the relief of Levi Robinson. 6-Cmte on Military Affairs: bill for the relief of Capt L C Easton, Assist Quartermaster U S Army. 7-Cmte on Commerce: asked to be discharged from the consideration of the memorial of Geo L Bowne & Wm Curry: referred to the Cmte on Finance. 8-Bill for the relief of Peyton G King, late receiver of public money at Monroe, La: submitted. 9-Bill for the relief of Abram S Emmett, of Knox Co, for gallant services in the war of 1812: submitted. 10-Bill granting 160 acres of land to Richd Smith, of Coshocton Co, Ohio, for military services in the war with the Rickaree Indians: submitted. 11-Bill granting a pension to Wm Davis, of Coshocton Co, Ohio, for injuries received while performing military duty in the war of 1812: submitted.

Trustee's sale of house & bldg lot at auction: on Mar 4, by deed of trust from Jas Muntz & wife to the subscriber, dated Feb 13, 1855, recorded in Liber J A S No 72, folios 484 thru 487, of the land records for Wash Co: sale of lots 1, 2, 9 thru 12, in square 751, Wash City, with a 2 story frame house: fronts on north H st east of the railroad. -John Y Donn, trustee -A Green, auct

Extensive sale of furniture, housekeeping articles, & superior Store fixtures, in the stock of Messrs Donn, Bro & Co: on Mar 5, at their establishment, 9th & D sts. -Jas C McGuire, auct

Household & kitchen furniture at auction on: Mar 3, at the residence of Gen Patten, 468 6th st; all his furniture. -Jas C McGuire, auct

Death of a Revolutionary Hero. Peter Bizen, aged 102 years & 7 days, the last of the Revolutionary band residing in Perry Co, Ohio, died at his residence in Hopewell township, Perry Co, on Jan 11th. He had been married 4 times, was the father of 25 children, & leaves a widow, 69 grandchildren, & 23 great-grandchildren.

Orphans Court of Wash Co, D C. Letters testamentary on the personal estate of Wm Jewell, late of Wash Co, deceased. -Eliz Jewell, Thos Jewell, Anne Jewell, excs

Died: on Feb 20, after a protracted illness, Philip Mohun, a native of Ireland, in his 74th year, formerly a resident of Md, but for the last 37 years of Wash City. His funeral will take place from his late residence, on 3rd, near G st, at 9 o'clock A M, tomorrow.

Died: on Feb 19, of consumption, at Loyola College, Rev Peter B O'Flanagan, S J, in his 49th year. R I P His remains will be received in Gtwn this morning for interment in the Catholic cemetery. The Young Catholic's Friend Societies of Wash & Gtwn, together with the congregations generally of the District, are requested to meet at the Wash depot at 11 o'clock, & join the procession to Trinity Church, Gtwn, where high mass will be celebrated & a funeral sermon preached by Rev B Maguire, Pres of Gtwn College. [Feb 22nd newspaper: the remains of Rev Peter B O'Flanagan, a priest of the Roman Catholic Church & member of the Society of Jesus, were yesterday received from Balt & conveyed to the burial place of Gtwn College by a large number of mourning friends.]

Wash City Ordinance: 1-Act for the relief of Lewis F Skidmore: fine imposed in occupying a stand in the Centre market with out having a license, is remitted. The said Skidmore paying the costs of prosecution.

<u>White Sulphur Springs</u> for sale: the death of Jas Calwell, the principal proprietor of this celebrated watering-place, having rendered it necessary for a settlement of his estate that the property should be sold, the owners have united in conferring on the undersigned full power to sell it. It is located in Greenbrier Co, on the western slope of the Alleghany mountains; contains 7,000 acres; bldgs are conveniently arranged; receipts of the establishment are now very large. -Wm H MacFarland, of Richmond, Va -Alex H H Stuart, of Staunton, Va

FRI FEB 22, 1856
Household & kitchen furniture at auction on: Feb 28, at the residence of Mrs Humphreys, on B st, between 2nd & 3rd sts. -C W Boteler, auct

Senate: 1-Memorial from Thos Gregory Smith, asking that some honorary testimonial be offered by Congress to the memory of Lt Mathew Smith, who fell at the battle of Germantown during the Revolutionary war. 2-Ptn from Josiah A Parker, trying to be reimbursed for certain expenditures made by him on public account while in command of the frig **Brandywine** in the China seas. 3-Additional papers presented in relation to the claim of Harriet L B Ruth; also in relation to the claim of Lucy Piatt. 4-Cmte on Public Lands: asked to be discharged from the consideration of the ptn of the heirs of Sam Miller: referred to the Cmte on Revolutionary Claims. 5-Resolved: that there be paid out of the contingent fund of the Senate to the widow of Michl Dooly, late superintendent of the folding-room, the sum of $159 for funeral expenses, & one quarter's salary, to be computed from the day of his death. 6-Passed: bills for the relief of Anson Dart; of John H Horne; & of Jacob Dodson.

House of Reps: 1-Rev Danl Waldo, having received a majority of the whole number of votes given, was declared duly elected chaplain to the House for the present session. 2-Senate bill directing payment to Geo P Marsh for judicial services rendered by him, while Minister Resident of the U S to the Ottoman Porte: referred to the Cmte on Foreign Affairs. 3-Bill for the relief of Benj Alvord, late of the U S army.

Household & kitchen furniture at auction on: Mar 14, at the residence of W Chauncey Langdon, 506 E st, near 3rd st. -Jas C McGuire, auct

Instructions of Frederick the Great to Maj Borcke: Potsdam, Sept 24, 1751. I entrust to you the education of my nephew, heir-presumptive to the Crown, &, as it is very different to bearing up a private person or one destined to govern States, I now give you instructions as to what you must observe. 1st-In regard to masters: My nephew must go through a course of ancient history, that he may know the succession of the different monarchies. I insist on the Catholic religion. It is widely enough spread in Silesia, in the Dutchies of Cleves, & elsewhere. It this child were to become a fantical Calvinist, all would be lost. Of course my nephew will learn to read, write, & reckon. He is too young to comprehend fortification; it will be time enough when he shall be 10 or 11 years old. Exercises, such as dancing, fencing, riding, can be learned in the afternoon, during digestion. This direction is only good until the age of from 10 to 12 years.

The Jerome Manufacturing Co has gone into insolvency. Isaac Anderson & Saml Rowland, of this city, are appointed trustees. Mr Fred Croswell was appointed assignee of Mr Barnum on petition of the County Bank of this city, & Mr Sanford on petition of the Farmer's Bank of Bridgeport. -New Haven Palladium

Fatal affair in Sussex Co, Va, on Feb 2, between Harrison Morris & Wm Ellis, when the former drew a knife & was about to strike, when the latter suddenly opened a knife & plunged it into the neck of Morris, inflicting a fatal wound.

Edw H Ruloff, a physician, was convicted in Tompkins Co, 10 years ago, of the abduction of his wife & child. They had disappeared. Every one believed he murdered them, but he was convicted only of the abduction. He was offered pardon if he would reveal his guilt, but he has refused to speak. It is said that a large estate has fallen to him in Europe. But, just as his term expires, he is again arrested & is to be tried for the abduction of his child. The sheriff of Tompkins arrested him on a bench warrant as soon as he was discharged. It is believed that the crime of murder can this time be brought home to him. -Albany Argus

Mrs Julia Dean Hayne will appear at the Nat'l Theatre this evening as Bianca, in the play of "Fazio," & as the Duchess, in the comedy of "Faint Heart Never Won Fair Lady."

Mrd: on Feb 20, in Wash City, by Rev Mr Marks, Robt W Fenton to Miss Sarah Ellen Mount, both of Wash City.

Mrd: on Feb 19, in Wash City, at Trinity Church, by Rev G D Cummins, Alex Strausz to Annie, daughter of Dr Noble Young, of Wash City.

Died: on Feb 21, in Wash City, Jas Sweeny, in his 26th year. His funeral will be Sunday afternoon, at 3 o'clock, from the residence of his mother, 5 south A st, Capitol Hill

Died: on Feb 21, in Wash City, after a lingering & painful illness, Walter Louis Shei, aged 74 years, of Sussex Co, N J. Mr Shei was son of the late Gen John Shei, of Phil. The remains were taken to Phil for interment. [See Feb 23rd newspaper: died-Walter Louis Shee, son of Gen John Shee, of Phil.]

Died: on Feb 21, in Wash City, George Hall, only child of R B & Annie Donaldson, aged 9 months & 6 days. His funeral will take place from 357 D st, at 11 o'clock this morning.

Died: at the Navy Yard, Elizabeth Ellen, infant daughter of Chas H & Eliz E Gordon. Her funeral will be today at 3 o'clock, from the residence of Mr Gordon, on 10th st, between M & Va ave. [No death date given.]

Obit: died: Maj Thos Harrison, on Jan 27, at his residence, Boston. A companion-in-arm of Gen Scott, he was ever a prized friend of that distinguished soldier. He received a wound in the war with Great Britain, having been at Lundy's Lane, Bridgewater, & in other battles. He leaves a widow, a Southern lady, but no children. For the past 13 years he was an ofcr in the Boston custom-house. -Boston Post

Phil, Feb 21. E D Worrell, charged with the murder of Mr Basil H Gordon, in Missouri, was arrested last night at Dover, Dela, by the ofcrs who tracked him there. He goes West with them voluntarily, without waiting for a requisiton. The prisoner had saddlebags, a watch, & a blanket, which Mr Gordon's brother-in-law recognized as belonging to the deceased. The arrest was made at the house of Worrell's father. [The report that the murderers of Mr Gordon were arrested in Ill has proved to be erroneous.] [Feb 25th newspaper: Worrell said he did not murder Gordon, but stood by & saw it, that his companion, now under arrest in the west, {referring to Stephen Greene, we presume,} was the man who fired the fatal shot. Worrell is age 26 years, of very gentlemanly appearance & deportment. His parents reside in Dover. Greene was arrested in Carthage where he was temporarily residing with his wife, Mary, & family. -Cincinnati Commercial of Feb 18.]

Wheeling, Feb 21. Railroad accident yesterday, 100 miles east of this city, the forward engine of a train broke one of its wheels & went down an embankment about 100 feet high, killing the fireman, Christian Zeigler, of Fred'k Co, Md, & seriously injuring the engineer, Thos McKinley, of Balt. The train was conveying the Law Greys on an excursion to this city, but fortunately none were injured.

SAT FEB 23, 1856
Trustee's sale of 2 frame houses & valuable lot at auction: on Feb 29, by deed of trust from John Powers, dated May 16, 1853, recorded in Liber J A S No 65, folios 360 thru 362, of the land records of Wash Co, D C: sale of part of lot 11 in square 514, 2,663 square feet, fronting on 5th st west, between L & M sts north, with 2 good frame houses. -R A Hyde, trustee -A Green, auct

In Judge Storer's Court, at Cincinnati, Mrs Henly made application to be allowed her dower from the estate of her husband, who had not been heard of within the last 12 years, & was therefore presumed to be dead. The Judge decided that the presumption was a fair one, & ordered the dower to be paid over to the presumed widow.

Judge Tyler, in the Circuit Court of Stafford Co, has decided the suit for Ebenezer Church in favor of the Methodist Episcopal Church South, & has appointed trustees to hold the church & lot of land. -Richmond Dispatch

South American Exploration. Letters have been received at the Navy Dept from Lt Thos J Page, in command of the U S steamer **Water-Witch**, dated Buenos Ayres, Dec 15, 1855, which gives additional information in relation to the exploration of the river Salado, upon which work Lt Page has been engaged for some time back.

Mules for sale: 60 head just arrived from Ky. Also, a number of fine horses. -Jas H Shreve, 7th st

City of Richmond, to wit: At a court of Hustings held for the said city, at the Courthouse, Feb 14, 1856. In the case of Wellington Goddin, adm, with the will annexed, of Wm D Talley, deceased, & who qualified as such administrator in this Court in 1851; on the motion of Wm D Talley, jr, who is the legatee under the will of the late Wm D Talley, & it appearing to the Court that more than 2 years have elapsed since the qualification of the administrator aforesaid, the Court doth order that the creditors of the deceased do appear here on Apr 16, 1856, & show cause, if any they can, against the payment & delivery of the estate of the said deceased to the said legatee. -Ro Howard, clerk

Fairfax land at public auction: on Mar 17, in front of the Court-House, 2 farms in said county; one tract contains 200 acres, the other 240 acres, adjoining, having originally been one farm. Mr J S J Bently, now occupying the premises, will show the land. Improvements moderate. -M C Klein, Charlestown, Va
-Jos J Love, Snickersville, Va

Mrs Wood, wife of Hon Mr Wood, of Maine, was robbed on Thu, of about $1,000 in money & $500 in jewelry, which were taken from her apartments, at Willard's Hotel, during her absence. On the same evening a number of visiters at the residence of Mr Merrick, on F st, were robbed of their overcoats & hats which had been left in the hall.

To Teachers: wanted in a private family, residing in Logan Co, Va, a lady or gentleman capable of teaching all the branches of English education, also Latin, French, & Music. An elderly lady would be preferred. Good references will be required as to qualifications. Apply to Wm Cooper, 121 D st south, near Ryland Chapel.

Died: on Feb 21, after a long & painful illness, Mrs Sarah Alice Gray, in the* _4th year of her age. He funeral is this afternoon at 2 o'clock, from the residence of her son-in-law, Robt J Roche, 415 12th st, near N Y ave. [*Could be 84-part of the first number is creased.]

Died: on Feb 21, in Wash City, after a painful illness, Walter Louis Shee, of Sussex Co, N J, son of the late Gen John Shee, of Phil. His remains will be taken to Phil.

Died: on Feb 7, at Erie, Pa, Thos H Sill, aged 72 years. He was a native of Conn, & son of Capt Richd H Sill, an ofcr of the Revolution. Having pursued legal studies with Jacob Burney, of Cincinnati, he selected Erie in 1813 as the place of his residence & scene of his labors. He was elected to Congress in 1826, & against in 1828.

Died: on Feb 22, David Walker, infant son of Moses & Mary W Kelly. His funeral will take place from the residence of Mrs Isabella Walker, [Missouri ave, near 4½ st,] this afternoon at 4 o'clock.

Died: on Feb 17, in Wash City, at the residence of his grandfather, Notley L Adams, Josias N, son of Mary Jane & the late Josias Clements, aged 2 years & 4 months.

Information wanted of Saml Weaver, a native of Gtwn, D C, Butcher by trade. He left his wife & children [Jun, 1854,] in Indianapolis, Indiana, in destitute circumstances, since which time he has not been heard from. Any information of him would be greatly received by his afflicted wife, who has been confined by sickness for months. Address Robt Cunningham, Gtwn, D C.

MON FEB 25, 1856

Late from Oregon: Mrs Harris, whose house was attacked by a large force of Indians, fought off the Indians who had killed her husband at first fire. She & her daughter, who also was wounded, barred the doors & fired their guns, preventing the Indians from getting close enough to set the cabin on fire. She killed several Indians, when she was relieved by the arrival of a friendly party.

Isaac H Rand, who, in connexion with his brother, John W Rand, was indicted for breaking into the Savings Bank in Concord, N H, on Aug 10th last, stealing about $1,000, has been convicted at the term of the Supreme Judicial Court now in session in Concord. Sentence has been suspended until some exceptions made by the counsel are decided.

The Chillicothe [Ohio] papers announce the death of the venerable Judge Thos Scott, who died at his residence there on Feb 15, in his 85th year. He was Sec of the first Constitutional Convention, which met at Chillicothe in 1802, & was the last survivor of that able body of men.

The sentence of the law was yesterday passed upon Sarah Haycraft, tried & found guilty of the murder of Thos Hudson, in this city, 2 or 3 months since. Judge Lackland sentenced her to be hung on Apr 11 next. -St Louis Republican, Feb 17.

I have this day [Feb 14] associated with me in copartnership John V Mitchell. The business will hereafter be the firm of Harper & Mitchell. -Walter Harper

Jas F Harvey, Undertaker, 410 7th st, east side, between G & H sts. All orders for Funerals promptly attended to at the shortest notice. [Apr 21st newspaper: The undertaking business carried on by the late Jas F Harvey will be continued by his widow. Mr Geo Harvey, [brother of the deceased husband] has been engaged to conduct & manage the business. -Maria E Harvey, 410 7th st west.]

Orphans Court of Wash Co, D C. Letters of administration on the personal estate of Nathl Frye, late of Wash Co, deceased. -C B M Frye, admx

Mr J Goldsborough Bruff, of Wash City, a graphic & designing artist, who made both pen & pencil sketches during an overland journey to Calif in 1849, has issued a prospectus of the publication of his writings & drawings, as they have recently perfected & prepared for the press. His work will comprise a daily record of the incidents, sufferings, & mortality on the route of over 2,000 miles.

Died: on Feb 24, in Wash City, Ella, daughter of Chas & Eliz Miller, aged 14 months & 13 days. Her funeral is this afternoon at 3:30 P M, 612 Garrison st.

TUE FEB 26, 1856
The celebrated temperance lecturer, John B Gough, is to deliver an address tonight at the Smithsonian Institution.

Letters received in Wash City, announcing the death of Mr Jos Armstrong, a son of the late Gen Robt Armstrong. His death was occasioned by a fall from his horse near Corpus Christi, Texas. He was a brother-in-law of Gen Persifer F Smith, U S Army, their wives being sisters. -Star

The young man who was killed on the railroad last Sat was John Murphy. He was traveling on foot in company with Geo Harrington, & when within a short distance of Laurel factory, they sat down upon the track to rest. Before they were aware of their danger the passenger train from Wash came upon them. Murphy was caught beneath the cow-catcher & maimed in a horrible manner. Harrington was pushed off the track, & escaped with slight bruises.

Hon Benj Seaver, Mayor of Boston in 1852 & 1853, died on Thu, at the residence of his son-in-law, Mr Wm Blanchard, of Roxbury, in which town Mr Seaver was born, Apr 12, 1795. He has long been known as a distinguished & successful merchant.

A monument of Christopher Columbus has been for a number of years in progress at Genoa. Bartolini, the sculptor, engaged to model the statue, received an advance payment of 9,000 francs, & died before the plaster model was completed. It was transferred to a young artist, Trocchia, who, after receiving 25,000 francs, failed, under a malancholy alienation of mind. The sculptors engaged proved defaulters or renounced their contracts. After these losses the ravages of the cholera in the city affected the resources of the company, & they have now appealed to the city authorities for aid.

Died: on Feb 24, in Wash City, Mary Alice, aged 5 months, infant child of Geo T & Sarah J Rogerson. Her funeral is this afternoon, at 3 o'clock, from 183 N Y ave.

On Feb 16, a bold attempt was made to assassinate Recorder Seuzeneau, of New Orleans, while he was passing from the Recorder's ofc to a private apartment, by an ex-watchman of the city named Nat McCann. McCann has been upon the Police at times for 3 or 4 years past, & repeatedly discharged for misconduct. He went to see Seuzeneau on being re-elected again as watchman. Receiving new encouragement, he shot Seuzeneau. The wound is serious, but not dangerous. -New Orleans Bulletin

Senate: 1-Cmte on Pensions: memorial of John T Sprague, of the U S army, asking that the widow of Maj Gen Worth may be allowed the pension her husband was entitled to for disability incurred during the last war with Great Britain, submitted an adverse report on the same, stating that the bill was before them at the last session, & after full consideration an adverse report had been made thereon. The cmte say they can find no reason upon a reinvestigation of the case, & are confirmed in the opinion that the claim has no foundation in law or equity.

U S Patent Ofc, Wash, Feb 25, 1856. Ptn of Elisha Foote, of Seneca Falls, N Y, praying for the extension of a patent granted to him on May 26, 1842, for an improvement in regulating the draught in stoves, for 7 years from the expiration of said patent, which takes place on May 26, 1856. -Chas Mason, Com'r of Patents

Died: on Feb 25, in Wash City, after a long & painful attack of liver disease & dropsy, Wm F S, eldest son of Isaac & Johanna Hill, aged 21 years. His funeral will be on Wed morning, at 8 o'clock, from his father's residence, 417 9th st, between G & H sts, whence his remains will be conveyed to St Patrick's Church, where mass will be offered for him. [Feb 28th newspaper: The funeral time is 9 o'clock.]

Died: on Feb 24, in Wash City, Mary Alice, aged 5 months, infant child of Geo T & Sarah J Rogerson. Her funeral is this afternoon, at 3 o'clock, from 183 N Y ave.

Orphans Court of Wash Co, D C. Letters of administration on the personal estate of Arthur Middleton, late of the State of South Carolina, deceased. -Rd Smith, adm, of Arthur Middleton.

Orphans Court of Wash Co, D C, Feb 23, 1856. In the case of Mary Corcoran, admx of John Corcoran, deceased, the admx & Court have appointed Mar 18 next, for the final settlement of the estate of said deceased, of the assets in hand.
-Ed N Roach, Reg/o wills

WED FEB 27, 1856
The European journals bring the intelligence of the death, at Warsaw, on Feb 1, of Ivan Feodorovitch Paskiewitch, Prince of Warsaw, Count of Erivau, & Viceroy of the Kingdom of Poland. He had suffered from a cancerous affection for a long time, & his death had been anticipated for many weeks. Paskiewitch was born at Pultawa, in the south of Russia, May 2, 1782. His successor in the viceroyalty of Poland is not named. The grand Duke Nicholas, brother of the Emperor, & Prince Gortschakoff, are both named for the ofc.

Senate: 1-Ptn from Wm G Mosely, deputy surveyor in Florida, asking compensation for losses sustained in consequence of a recent Indian outbreak in that country. 2-Memorial from the Board of Trade of Phil in favor of purchasing Cmder Sands' invention for obtaining specimens of the bottom in deep-sea soundings. 3-Memorial from Cmder Thos J Manning & Lt Rich Forrest, complaining of the action of the Naval Board, & asking to return to their original positions. 4-Ptn from T L Preston & others, asking that the times for holding the U S District Court for the Western District of Va may be changed. 5-Cmte on Pensions: bill for the relief of Benj Berry, a soldier of the Revolution, with a report: ordered to be printed. Same cmte: adverse reports on these ptns: of Rufus K Lane, of Isaac Carpenter; of Deborah Chaffee; & of Wm R Combs: ordered to be printed.

<u>Municipal Election in Gtwn yesterday, with the following results:</u>

Anti-Know-Nothing	Know-Nothing
For Alderman	For Alderman
Geo Waters: 330	Jas A Magruder: 305
Joshua Riley: 322	Wm H Edes: 307
Chas E Mix: 324	Philip T Berry: 293
Geo W Beall: 346	Francis Wheatley: 294
Robt P Dodge: 352	Jos Libbey: 369
Common Council	Common Council
David English: 343	W McK Osborn: 312
Grafton Tyler: 340	Wm H Godey: 299
Robt White: 334	Jos F Birch: 290
Henry Barron: 328	Jos L Simms: 318
Esau Pickrell: 338	Louis Mackall, jr: 305
Wm F Seymour: 320	John T Bangs: 296
Saml Cropley: 340	Chas V Welch: 304
R R Crawford: 326	A L Yerby: 286
Richd Jones: 328	John Cameron: 288
*Henry M Sweeny: 379	Chas Myers: 298
Jeremiah Orme: 351	

*Part of the day his name was on both tickets.

Wash Corp: 1-Ptn from Thos F Owens, for the remission of a fine: referred to the Cmte of Claims. 2-Ptn from Nicholas Acker & others for a foot pavement in front of square 685: referred to the Cmte on Improvements.

Administrator's sale of farming utensils, horses, wagons, cows, provender, & furniture at auction: on Mar 5, at the farm of the late Ninian Beall, deceased, near Tenally Town, on the river road, all personal effects thereon. -Geo W Beall, adm -Barnard & Buckey, aucts

House of Reps: 1-Memorial, with the accompanying papers, of Aurelius Miner, asking Congress that his accounts for defending Thos M Sullivan & John Platts, paupers, be allowed. 2-Ptn of Henry W Wharton, captain in the 6th Regt of Infty of the U S Army, stationed at *Fort Kearney*, praying that the troops may be placed upon the same footing in regard to extra pay as those stationed at *Fort Laramie*.

Valuable farm, 4 miles from Wash, a part of which is in D C, at auction: on Mar 12, a fine Farm containing 120 acres, part in D C & part in PG Co, Md, near the Navy Yard, adjoining the farms of Messrs Berry & Gleson. -W Tasker Weit
-A Green, auct

Mrd: in Wash City, by Rev Alfred Holmead, Jas M Dawson, jr, of Montg Co, Md, to Louisa Virginia, only daughter of David Hepburn, of Wash. [No marriage date given- current item.]

New Orleans, Feb 25. Mr Beverley C Sanders & Mr Richd P Hammond, both formerly Collectors of the port of San Francisco, have been indicted for embezzling funds. [Feb 29th newspaper: Maj Hammond charged with using for his own purposes, on Jun 28, 1855, about the time of his removal, $48,732; & on Aug 2, 1853, he is charged with having used $30,000 to purchase a part of the rancho called *San Antonio*. The charge against Sanders is, that in Jun, 1853, he used $48,665. It is alleged by some that this amount was paid over to Maj Hammond, who succeeded to the ofc about that time.]

THU FEB 28, 1856
Caleb B Atkins, the teller of the Wash Bank, Boston, was arrested on Sat on the charge of embezzling from that bank $7,000 in Jan last & an equal amount on Saturday. Atkins had loaned $7,000 to his brother with the expectation of getting it back & returning it to the bank before the April examination of accounts. [Mar 4th newspaper:Atkins, age 24 years, was arrested, & after being in custody 24 hours, confessed that he had been a defaulter to the bank to the amount of $7,298, which sum he had loaned to a brother, expecting to make it good before his accounts were examined in April. -Boston Atlas]

Senate: 1-Memorial from Amaral & Bartos, & from Manuel A T Barloza & Alexand'r J Da Cruz, Louis Vidal Ceran & Burtos Pacheco des Santos, asking indemnity for losses in consequence of seizures on the high seas by the U S brig **Perry** for an alleged participation in the African slave trade. 2-Memorial from Lt John M Brooks, of the navy, asking compensation for his invention of a method for obtaining specimens of the bottom in deep-sea sounding. 3-Cmte on Printing: adverse report on the memorial of Geo Jones, a chaplain in the navy, asking for a certain number of copies of Com Perry's report for his own use. 4-Bill for the relief of John S Pendleton: committed. 5-Resolved: that the ptn of Chas Wilkes & others, owners of real estate on north Capitol st, for damages occasioned by excavations, together with the accompanying papers: referred to the Court of Claims.

<u>**Behavior Book**</u>: avoid slang words:do not say "snooze" for nap: "pants" for pantaloons; or "polking" when engaged in a certain dance.

The Richmond Whig announces the death, on Feb 21, of Judge John B Christian, of the Genr'l Court of Va, a brother-in-law of Ex-Pres Tyler.

Mrd: on Feb 20, in Wash City, by Rev Mr French, D D, Alex Gau, Chancellor of the Prussian Legation, to Mgt, daughter of the late Jas Campbell, of N Y.

Died: on Feb 12, in Alamance Co, N C, Mr Jas Turner, sen, in his 98th year. He was a soldier of the Revolutionary war, fought at Briar Creek & Guilford Court-house, was taken prisoner, & for several months kept on board a prison ship.

FRI FEB 29, 1856
Senate: 1-Ptn from Saml A Lowe, asking to be compensated for preparing & superintending the printing of the laws of the Territory of Kansas. 2-Memorial from Capt Geo C Read, complaining of being placed on the reserve list, & asking to be restored to his former position. 3-Memorial from insurance companies of N Y C, asking the Cmder R Gedney may be placed on the reserved list instead of furlough. 4-Ptn from Peter Grover, asking remuneration for injuries sustained while employed on the works at **Fort Scammel**. 5-Memorial from Cmder R Ritchie, complaining of having been placed on the reserved list by the Naval Board, & asking to be restored to his original position. 6-Cmte of Claims: resolution for the relief of Hall Neilson: ordered to be printed. 7-Cmte on Indian Affairs: asked to be discharged from the consideration of the memorial of Lewis Ralston, & that it be referred to the Cmte of Claims: agreed to.

On Fri last Danl C Emery was arrested at Boston who is said to be one of the most expert forgers in the country since the death of Monroe Edwards. He was committed to jail.

House of Reps: 1-Letter from Capt Thos A Dornin, U S Navy, & documents referred to therein, respecting a claim of Chas L Denman, U S Consul at Acapulco, for relief afforded to two American citizens by paying their passage from Acapulco to San Francisco. There being no relief for American citizens other than seamen, & no appropriation under the control of the dept from which Mr Denman's claim can be paid, it is submitted to the adjudication of Congress: referred to the Cmte on Foreign Affairs.

Stock of jewelry, perfumery, & fancy articles: on Mar 1, at the store of Mr D Hirsch, 34 Louisiana ave, between 7th & 8th sts. -Jas C McGuire, auct

The Limantour claim to the land upon which nearly one-third of San Francisco is located has been confirmed by the U S com'rs. This claim is assessed at $5,000,000, & is considered too great a fortune for one man, now in Calif. Jose Y Limantour, in whom this vast estate will rest if the decision is sustained, is a Frenchman by birth, but now a citizen of Mexico. The land he claims was granted in 1843 by the then Govn'r of Calif in accordance with the laws of Mexico. It was 9 years afterwards before he made known his title in San Francisco, after his barren hills had been transformed into a well-built city.

Arrest of Mail-robbers. Geo Newell, alias Geo Anneville, & Lloyd Dawden were arrested at Cumberland, Md, on Feb 26, by a special agent, on the charge of committing depredations on the mails passing through the Cumberland post ofc. They were committed to jail to undergo further examination. Anothet-Oscar S Swift, postmaster at China Wyoming Co, N Y, was arrested on Feb 23, charged with abstracting money from leters passing through his ofc. He was committed for trial.

Mrd: on Feb 19, by Rev D T C Davis, at the residence of Raleigh Colston, of Albemarle, Chas M Blackford, of Lynchburg, to Susan Leigh, daughter of the late Thos M Colston, of Loudoun.

Died: on Feb 28, in Wash City, after a protracted illness, Jas M McKnight. His funeral is from his late residence on I st, near 10th, this afternoon at 3½ o'clock. [Mar 8 newspaper: a funeral discourse, occasioned by the death of the late Jas M McKnight, will be preached in the Fourth Presbyterian Church, 9th st, tomorrow at 3½ o'clock, to which services his friends & acquaintances are particularly invited.]

Died: on Feb 28, in Wash City, Mr Elema Beall, in his 62nd year, a native of Montg Co, Md, but for the last 3 years a resident of Wash City, & a soldier of the war of 1812. His funeral will be this afternoon at 3 o'clock, from his late residence, 7th st west, between L & M sts.

St Andrew's Society, Wash, D C: meeting Mar 3 at 7½ o'clock. -Jas MacWilliam, sec

The undersigned will apply to the Pension ofc for a renewal of Warrant No 24,369, for 120 acres, issued in the name of Danl Ryan on Oct 23, 1855, & has never come to hand. -P Williams, atty

SAT MAR 1, 1856
Destructive fire in St Martinsville, La, on Feb 19, took the life of 12 persons, 3 of them white: Richard, Parcel, & a gardener. Their deaths were occasioned by the explosion of barrels of gunpowder in Mr A Tertrou's store, under the ruins of which they were buried.

Mrd: on Feb 28, in Wash City, by Rev Mr French, Mr Wm H Newton, of St Paul, Minnesota, to Miss Sarah O Johnson, daughter of Philip C Johnson, of Wash.

Mrd: on Feb 27, in St Thomas' Church, Hancock, Md, by Rev Geo L Machenheimer, John W Baden, of Wash, to Nannie C, eldest daughter of Rev Geo L Machenheimer.

Died: on Feb 28, Mrs Lucy Brooke, aged 84 years. Her funeral is this day, from the residence of her son-in-law, Wm S Darrell, on L st, near 10th.

Died: yesterday, Elder David M Wilson, in the full triumph of the faith which he has so long exemplified among us. His funeral is at 2:30 o'clock, this day, at the Western Presbyterian Church, corner of H & 19th sts. [Mar 8th newspaper: the funeral sermon will be preached by Rev Mr Haskell, his pastor, at 11 A M next Sabbath, in the Western Presbyterian Church, new bldg, corner of H & 19th sts.]

Died: on Feb 28, in Wash City, Evelyn, in her 2nd year, daughter of John F & Jane E Tucker. Her funeral will tke place from her father's residence, on C st east, today at 3 o'clock P M.

Rev S H Worceser, of Balt, will preach in the New Jerusalem Church, on North Capitol st, near the railroad depot, at 11 o'clock this morning.

I have this day associated with me C Stribling, under the name of Howell & Stribling, for the transaction of the wholesale Grocery, Flour, & Genr'l Commission Business. -S H Howell, Gtwn, D C

H O Hood, 418 Pa ave, between 4½ & 6th st, Wash, has on hand a very good stock of superior gold & silver Watches; & an extensive assortment of very rich gold Jewelry.

For sale: the house & lot known as ***Clarens***, near the Theological Seminary, about 3 miles from Alexandria. The house is large & convenient & well built. Apply to J D Corse, or to the subscriber, in Alexandria. -Geo A Smith

Valuable hotel property for sale: commodious & well established ***Warren Green Hotel***, in Warrenton, Va, now in full operation; the house contains 45 chambers. -Inman H Payne or Jno S Moody, Warrenton, Va.

MON MAR 3, 1856
Senate: 1-Bill for the relief of the estates of Benj Bullitt, Danl M Heard, & John H Mahler, deceased, & of Wm Long: referred. 2-Bill for the relief of Amos Armstrong, of Ohio: referred.

Property in Gtwn for sale: the subscriber wishes to dispose of 2 or 3 houses in Gtwn, D C. One on Dumbarton st, nearly finished, in one of the best locations in the District: lot 120 by 120. One on Potomac st, an excellent, well-built house, two stories, brick, near St John's Church. One on Bridge st, in which my family now reside, 3 story brick. Prices reasonable & terms liberal. -R Cruikshank

Extensive sale of steam-engine, machinery, belting, lumber, doors, sash, window frames, & blinds: on Mar 12, by deed of trust, duly recorded: public auction at the superior Machinery & Fixtures of Mr T B Entwistle's factory, corner of 10th & La ave. -Saml Redfern, trustee -Jas C McGuire, auct

Mr Chas S Lounsbury, editor & proprietor of the Chronicle, published at Kosciusko, Miss, was murdered there on Feb 20 by a young man named Richd W Payne, who escaped the ofcrs of justice. He is thus described: 5 feet 5 & 6 inches high, 23 years of age, square built, & weighs 130 to 135 pounds, hair is dark yellow, eyes grayish blue, his front teeth rather wider than common & slightly separated from one another. About 18 months since Payne undertood to belittle & run over Lounsbury, & for that purpose sought a quarrel with him, in which he nearly lost his life, Lounsbury stabbed him with a dirk-knife over his left eye, for which he was indicted, stood his trial, & came clear, in the Circuit Court of this county. Payne then had a keen thirst for revenge.

Rev Danl Waldo, the venerable Chaplain of the House of Reps, has arrived in Wash City, & will commence his duties today. Mr Waldo is a native of Conn, & was born on Sep 10, 1762. [The year 1762 was double-checked & copied as written, as this is a Mar 1856 newspaper.]

The Mormons at Home, descriptive of a Tour through Kansas & Utah, & of a residence at the Great Salt Lake City, by Mrs B G Ferris, wife of the late U S Sec for Utah. One volume, 12 mo. Price .75. -Dix & Edwards, 321 Broadway, N Y

Richmond, Va, papers contain an account of a decision in the Circuit Court of Powhatan, refusing probate to the will of Dr Thos J Goode. In Aug, 1834, Dr Goode, a respectable citizen of Powhatan, murdered his infirm old father, aged about 85 years. A few weeks later, while in jail charged with the crime, he made his will. Some time subsequently he was pronounced by the court & jury to be insane, & taken to the lunatic asylum in Wmbsburg, where he remained until his death, a little more than 12 months ago. Judge Nash decided he was insane when he wrote the will. An effort will be made to carry the case to the Court of Appeals.

"Our Slave States," a new work, by F L Olmsted, author of "Walks & Talks of an American Farmer" in England, entitled "A Journey in the Seaboard Slave States." 1 vol, 12 mo, cloth, 725 pp. Wood cuts. Price $1.25. Mrs H B Stowe's opinion: the most complete & thorough work of this kind, expose of the economical view of the subject which has ever appeared.

TUE MAR 4, 1856
Senate: 1-Ptn from Dr Saml A Storrow, asking the establishment of a medical hospital in Wash City: referred. 2-Memorial from Jos A Seawell, late a passed midshipman dropped from the navy, asking redress in the premises: referred. 3-Memorial from John S Chauncey, late cmder in the navy, dropped by the recommendation of the late Naval Board, asking to be restored to his former position: referred. 4-Ptn from Wm Peck & Jas B Smith, asking the enrolment & registry of the schnr **Zadoc Pratt**, the keel of which was laid in Canada & the vessel finished in the U S: referred. 5-Memorial from Saml S Wood, for himself & Alex M C Wood, asking indemnity for property destroyed at the bombardment of Greytown by the U S sloop-of-war Cyane: referred. 6-Ptn from Chas A Price, asking to be allowed the right of pre-emption to a tract of land within a military reservation in Florida upon which he had settled: referred. 7-Cmte on Pensions: adverse reports on the following ptns: of Enoch S Moore; of Miles Devine; of John Brown; of Danl Brown; & of citizens of Ill, asking an increase of the pension of Valentine G Wehrheim: ordered to be printed. Same cmte: asked to be discharged from the consideration of the ptn of Simeon Summers, & that it be referred to the Cmte on Revolutionary Claims.

House of Reps: 1-Ptn signed by Henry Dawes. J Davis, T W Simpson, & others, asking for the construction of a railroad to the Pacific. 2-Memorial signed by Saml Hammantree & others, asking Congress to amend the pension laws. 3- Mr Perry, of Maine, presented the memorial of Jas A Milliken, claiming a seat in the House of Reps in place of Hon T J D Fuller, as Rep for the 6th Congressional district of that State: referred to the Cmte of Elections.

Local News: A cigar shop & dwlg, belonging to Mr J G Hall, & a tin shop & dwlg, belonging to Mr Grinnell, at F & 7th sts, Island, were destroyed by fire at an early hour yesterday morning. The proprietor of each is said to have been partially insured.

Criminal Court [Wash] commenced its Mar term yesterday. The juries were sworn in as follows: Grand Jury: Wm B Magruder, Jonathan Prout, Jos Bryan, Marshall Brown, V Harbaugh, Geo McNeir, John Purdy, Wm H Winter, Dr W Jones, Francis Mohun, Alex Ray, Isaac Clark, Joshua Pierce, A H Pickrell, Michl Shanks, G C Grammer, Wm M Morrison, John L Kidwell, Wm Orme, D B Johnson, Geo Mattingly, Richd Jones, Geo A Bohrer, Wm Noyes. Petit Jury: John Brady, Jas Barnes, E F Brown, A T Harrington, M R Coombs, Jos Lyons, R A Griffin, Walter Stewart, J T Devlin, Jackson Pumphrey, Jacob Vielmeyer, Wm D Aiken, G W Uttermahle, R Butt, W J Donohoo, John B Newton, Walter Warder, John Tolson, A Boscom, Z Williams, W R Spaulding, W V Waters, B Hackney, J H Durham, Leo Bowen, J D Evans, R W Dove, Geo D Spencer, D A Cardwell, D E Kealy.

Mrd: on Feb 28, by Rev R L Dashiells, Mr Danl L Morrison, formerly of Md, to Mrs Hettie A Stone, of Wash City.

Died: on Mar 3, in Wash City, of pulmonary consumption, Mrs Stella Jane Smith, wife of Chauncy Smith, formerly of Vermont, in her 49th year. Her funeral will be this afternoon at 3 o'clock, from Mr King's, 393 C st.

Died: on Mar 3, in Wash City, at the home of her parents, after a long & painful sickness, which she bore with Christian fortitude, Mrs May Jane Lightell, aged 28 years, wife of Mr John Lightell. She leaves a husband & 4 small children to mourn her loss. Her funeral is today at 2 o'clock P M, from the residence of Mr Jacob Luskey, I & 9th Navy Yard Hill.

N W Lakeman, mate of the ship **Ariel**, on trial at Charleston for the murder of Capt W H Eayres, has been acquitted. The murder was committed when the ship was a 1,000 miles from land, the captain being found in his berth in the morning with his head barbarously mangled.

The family of Mr Matthew Putnam, in North Danvers, was poisoned on Fri last by drinking tea made from the leaves of stremonium, alias henbane, alias apple of Peru, which had been mistaken for black tea. Mrs Putnam, aged 70 years, died of the poison on Sat. Mr Putnam & Mrs Curtis, who also partook, had medical treatment, & are now doing well. The apple of Peru was kept by the old lady, who fell a victim to it poisonous properties for smoking, to relieve her from fits of asthma to which she was subject. -Boston Herald

Valuable property for sale: 4 small frame houses, containing 2 rooms & kitchen, & 4 frame houses containing 8 rooms each; also bldg lot on 4th & L sts. Apply to the subscriber, at his residence, 191 14th st. -Josiah C Truman

Portland, Me, Mar 3. 1-The barque **David Nickels**, from Cardenas, sunk in our harbor yesterday from injuries caused by floating ice. Capt Sweet was drowned. 2-A fire on Sat destroyed 4 stores in Middle st, occupied respectively by Darius White, O H Perry, W S Richards, & Wm Russell.

For sale: 20,000 acres of land in Central Ohio, mostly in the vicinity of Columbus, improved & unimproved. I am anxious to sell. -M L Sullivant, Columbus, Ohio

WED MAR 5, 1856

Providence Post: two boys were drowned at Fall River, while skating, on Fri last. They were Chas Marvel, aged 16, & Wm Church, aged 13.

Trustee's sale of valuable property on 7th st: by deed of trust from Jas A Wise, dated Dec 30, 1852, recorded in Liber J A S No 50, folios 339 thru 341, of the land records for Wash Co: public auction on Mar 25, of all that parcel of lot of ground numbered 9, in square 453, in Wash City. -J N Callan, trustee -J C McGuire, auct

Senate: 1-Ptn from John H Swanton & Jas M Hunt, asking compensation for a vessel which was lost due to injuries received while engaged in the rescue of the passengers & crew of the steamship **Southerner**, wrecked on the Northwest coast. 2-Additional papers presented in relation to the claim of the heirs of Chas Lewis. 3-Ptn from Morris Powers, asking a pension for a wound received in the late war with Mexico. 4-Addition papers presented in relation to the claim of Enoch S More. 5-Ptn from Wm McKenney, chaplain in the U S Navy, of Norfolk, Va, father of Geo L McKenney, who was lost in the U S schnr **Grampus**, asking that the act of Jun, 1844, may be so amended as to embrace his case. This youth was captain's clerk on board the **Grampus** at the time she was wrecked off the coast of South Carolina in 1843, & as the act of 1844 embraced only the widows & orphans of seamen & marines, the father asks that the act my be so amended in consonance with the acts of Aug, 1848, & Feb, 1853, providing for the surviving relatives; & as in duty bound he will ever pray for the peace, prosperity, & perpetuity of the Gov't of the U S. 6-Ptn from Joshua Webb, asking to be allowed a pension for disability incurred in the service of the U S in the war of 1812. 7-Ptn from shipmasters, pilots, & others of N Y, asking that Cmder Gedney may be allowed leave of absence pay instead of furlough pay. 8-Cmte on Revolutionary Claims: memorial of Eliz A R Linn, with a bill for the relief of the distributes of Col Wm Linn, of the Revolution: passed. 9-Cmte of Claims: claim of John Y Laub, a clerk in the ofc of the First Comptroller of the Treasury: to be printed. Same cmte: asked to be discharged from the consideration of the ptn of Jas Harrington, a laborer at the Smithsonian Institute, asking additional compensation: referred to the Cmte to Audit & Control the Contingent Expenses of the Senate. Same cmte: papers relating to the claim of John Metcalf submitted: ordered to be printed. Same cmte: bill for the relief of Isaac Cook & others: ordered to be printed.

Genuine Garden Seeds for sale, supply direct from England & the Continent. Catalogues can be had on application. -John Saul, Seed Warehouse, 396 7th st, corner of H st.

For sale: a Brick Yard, with 5 or 6 acres of clay, Kilns, Machinery, Tools, & Shedding. 500,000 brick on hand for sale. Apply to Wm H Edes or Esau Pickrell, Water st, Gtwn.

Died: on Tue, in Wash City, after a protracted illness, Capt Leonard Adams, a native of Sandisfield, Mass, but for many years past a citizen of this District, aged 83 years. The veterans of the war of 1812 & the friends of the family are invited to attend his funeral this morning, at 11 o'clock, from the new Masonic Hall, corner of 9th & D sts. His remains will be taken to Alexandria, Va, for interment.

Died: on Monday last, Mary Jane, infant daughter of M W & Mary Jane Galt.

Foreign News: Grand Duke Nicholas, a brother of the Czar, has been married to Alex'r Petrona, the Princess of Oldenburg. [No date given-current item.]

Orphans Court of Wash Co, D C. In the case of Benj O Tayloe, Wm H Tayloe, & Edw T Tayloe, excs of John Tayloe, deceased: the execs & Court have appointed Mar 29 for the final settlement & distribution of the personal estate of said deceased, of the assets in hand. -Ed N Roach, Reg/o wills

Orphans Court of Wash Co, D C. In the case of Jas C McGuire, adm of John D Brown, deceased, the adm & Court have appointed Mar 25 for the settlement & distribution of the personal estate of said deceased, of the assets in hand.
-Ed N Roach, Reg/o wills

THU MAR 6, 1856
Senate: 1-Ptn from Isabella Budlong, widow of a Revolutionary soldier, asking to be allowed bounty land. 2-Cmte on Foreign Relations: bill for the relief of Geo P Marsh. 3-Cmte on Public Lands: adverse reports on the following memorials: of Edw D Tippett; of Wm Anderson; of John A Ragan; of Jas H Gale; & of McKinley Ward, guardian of Julia F Peebles. Same cmte: asked to be discharged from the consideration of the memorial of Wm G Mosely, & that it be referred to the Cmte of Claims: agreed to. Same cmte: asked to be discharged from the consideration of the memorial of John Dick, & that it be referred to the Cmte on Private Land Claims. 4-Cmte on Patents & the Patent Ofc: bill for the relief of Edwin A Stevens: ordered to be printed. 5-Cmte of Claims: ptn & papers of S Wood to be transmitted to the Senate.

Trustee's sale of lot D, in subdivision of square 500, with improvements, at auction: by deed of trust from Chas L Phillips & wife & John P Lashhorn, dated Mar 3, 1854, recorded in Liber J A S No 80, folios 299 thru 302, of the land records of Wash Co, D C: all of said lot D with improvements. The property is on the Island. -Hugh B Sweeny, trustee -A Green, auct

Mrd: on Mar 4, at the Church of the Epiphany, by Rev Mr French, Rev Dr John McCarty, U S Army, to Miss L W Stetson, of Charlestown, Mass.

Mrd: on Mar 4, in Wash City, at the residence of Maj Arnold Harris, by Rev Dr Gurley, Aristides Welsh, of Pa, to Miss Henrietta R Armstrong, daughter of the late Gen Robt Armstrong.

Mrd: on Tue, by Rev John C Smith, Mr Robt McAuley to Miss Catharine Wright, all of Wash City.

Died: on Mar 5, John Palmer, formerly of Loudoun Co, Va, but for many years past a citizen of Wash City & District, in his 46th year.

Died: on Mar 3, Anne Elizabeth, aged 7 years & 6 months, eldest daughter of Emily R & Chas C Hill.

Died: on Mar 5, after a long & severe illness, Mary J, daughter of John & Ellen Dougherty, in her 19th year. Her funeral will be from her late residence on G, between 1st & 2nd sts. [No time given.]

Died: on Mar 5, on 13th st, after a protracted & painful illness, which she bore with the greatest Christian fortitude & resignation, Miss Eliza A Miller, daughter of the late Maj Thos R Miller, of Port Royal, Va. Her funeral will take place at St Patrick's Church, F st, on Mar 7, at 10 o'clock A M.

Died: on Fri last, at **Collingwood**, his residence, in Fairfax Co, H Allen Taylor, son of the late Robt I Taylor, in his 36th year. He leaves to his family, relatives, & friends, the remembrance of his many virtues. -Alexandria Gaz

Obits: 1-John Braham, the vocalist, is dead, at the age of 78. The deceased Duke was at one time the head of the Roman Catholic interest in England, but on the celebrated Papal aggressions, a few years since, he joined the Anglican Church. He was the first Roman Catholic who took the oaths & his seat in the House of Commons after the passing of the Roman Catholic emancipation act in 1829. He is succeeded in the Dukedom & ancient family honors by his son, Henry Granville, Earl of Arundel & Surrey, born Nov 7, 1815, & married on Jun 19, 1838, to Augusta Mary, daughter of Admiral Sir Edmund Lyond, G C B, cmder-in-chief of the Mediterranean fleet.

2-John *Sadlier, M P, committed suicide. His body was found on Hampstead Heath, near Jackstraw Castle Hotel. A bottle containing essential oil of bitter almonds & a silver cream ewer containing the same poison were found beside him. He formerly possessed a large fortune, which he lost by recent speculations in mines & railways. [No death date given-current item.] [Mar 10th newspaper: It is said that the amount of frauds of which Mr *Saddlier, [who recently committed suicide,] was guilty was not much short of L1,000,000 worth of railway shares & mortgages. He had also committed crimes of the most diabolical description.] [Mar 17th newspaper: Letter from Mr J P Sadlier, M P, to Mr Robt Keating, just previous to his suicide: To what infamy have I come. Step by step, heaping crime upon crime. No one has been privy to my crimes; Stevens & Norris are both innocent. Oh, that I had never quitted Ireland! If I had had less talents of a worthless kind I might have remained as I once was, honest & truthful, & I would have lived to see my dear father & mother in their old age.] [Apr 1st newspaper: The coroner's inquest on the late Mr John *Sadleir, M P, has resulted in a unanimous verdict of felo de se-that he died by his own hand whilst in a perfectly sane state. The history of John & Jas Sadlier is curious enough when contrasted with their performances. Their father is at present living, a small tenant farmer, in the south of Ireland.] *Note the three spellings of Sadlier/Saddlier/Sadleir.

Avalanche recently at Cape Breton, about 30 miles from Sydney, destroyed the house of Mr Campbell, & buried Mr Campbell, his wife, mother, 3 children, & 2 young girls. Mrs Campbell, her 3 children, & 1 of the girls perished, but the others were rescued alive. A barn was overwhelmed & 18 head of cattle were killed.

FRI MAR 7, 1856
Senate: 1-Ptn from Wm J Sears, asking an increase of pension. 2-Ptn from Lt John C McFerran, assistant commissary in the army, asking to be allowed a credit in the settlement of his accounts for a sum of money of which he was defrauded by an assistant commissary of the army. 3-Cmte on Finance: asked to be discharged from the consideration of the ptn of the widow of John Scott, & that it be referred to the Cmte of Claims: agreed to. 4-Cmte on Military Affairs: joint resolution for the presentation of a sword to Col Benj S Roberts, submitted an adverse report on the same: which was ordered to be printed.

Geo W Owens died at his residence in this city, Mar 2, in his 70th year. For many years he was a prominent member of the Georgia Bar, & under a general ticket system represented this State in the representative branch of Congress from 1835 to 1839. After his retirement from Congress he took very little if any part in public affairs. Having accumulated a large estate, he sought that otium cum dignitate so agreeable to one so far advanced in life. -Savannah Republican

N Y, Mar 5. Chas G Hunter, late a lt in the U S navy, & familiarly known as Alvarado Hunter, died in this city yesterday, after a protracted sickness.

House of Reps: 1-Bill for the relief of the distributes of Col Wm Linn was referred to the Cmte on Revolutionary Claims. 2-Cmte on Private Lands Claims: bill to grant to L Jane Horner & children a section of land in Oregon: committed. 3-Ptn of the reps of Col Fred'k Weissenfels, of the Revolutionary army: referred.

This way, Ladies, if you please. Spring straw millinery just received; fancy goods, hosiery, & gloves; Bonnets bleached & pressed. -Wm P Shedd, 11th st, above Pa ave.

We are pained to learn that our highly-esteemed young friend & late fellow-townsman, Geo C Brooke, came to his death near Louisburg, Conway Co, Ark, on Feb 15, by the accidental discharge of a gun in his own hands. He expired in a few seconds after the fatal accident. He was in his 23rd year, & had entered upon the theatre of life with bright prospects of a brilliant future. He was a noble-hearted, chivalrous man, & a very devoted friend. Endowed with a strong & vigorous mind, which had been well cultivated, he gave promise to attain a high rank in the profession he had chosen. He was a son of the late John B Brooke, Marlboro Gaz

Died: on Feb 23, at his residence, in Carmichael, Green Co, Pa, Aaron Gregg, of congestion of the lungs, aged 65 years.

U S Patent Ofc, Wash, Mar 6, 1856. Ptn of Richd M Hoe, of N Y, praying for the extension of a patent granted to him May 30, 1842, for an improvement in a machine for grinding & pulverizing metallic plates, for 7 years from the expiration of said patent, which takes place on May 30, 1856. -Chas Mason, Com'r of Patents

U S Patent Ofc, Wash, Mar 6, 1856. Ptn of Marmaduke Osborne, of N Y, praying for the extension of a patent granted to him May 28, 1842, for an improvement in feltings for coats, for 7 years from the expiration of said patent, which takes place on May 28, 1856. -Chas Mason, Com'r of Patents

Orphans Court of Wash Co, D C. In the case of John W Patterson, adm of Saml S Whiting, deceased, the administrator & Court have appointed Apr 1 next, for the final distribution of the personal estate of the deceased, with the assets in hand.
-Ed N Roach, Reg/o wills

Orphans Court of Wash Co, D C. In the case of Wm G Gorsuch, adm of Jas Douglass, deceased, the administrator & Court have appointed Mar 29 next, for the final distribution of the personal estate of the deceased, with the assets in hand.
-Ed N Roach, Reg/o wills

SAT MAR 8, 1856
Trustee's sale of very valuable vacant lot on 7th st, one square north of the Northern Market-House: on Mar 20, by deed of trust from Geo W Mitchell & wife, dated Jul 28, 1855, recorded in Liber J A S No 102, folios 152 thru 155, of the land records of Wash Co, D C: sale of part of lot 11 in square 426, fronting on 7th st. -R J Powell, trustee -A Green, auct

First class farm for sale in Fauquier Co, Va, known as **Rock Hill**, late the property of Jas H Fitzgerald, containing by estimation 1,287 acres; mansion house is commodious, with all necessary out-bldgs attached thereto. Apply to the undersigned at Warrenton, Fauquier Co, Va. -Jas V Brooke

By virtue of a writ of fieri facias, issued by E H Bate, a Justice of the Peace for Wash Co, D C, at the suit of R W Carter, against the goods & chattels of Wm Groves. I have taken in execution furniture & fixtures of said Groves. I will offer them for sale on Mar 15 next, in front of the Centre Market-House, Wash City.
-H R Maryman, constable

Pay of Army Ofcrs: Senior Col $3,312 per annum, maximum
Jr major $1,860 per annum, minimum.
Company Ofcrs: Senior captain $1,914 per annum, maximum.
Jr lt $822 per annum, minimun

Mrd: on Mar 6, in Wash City, by Rev Andrew G Carothers, Mr John Ennis to Miss Eliza Poster, both of Wash City.

Mrd: on Jan 15, in Honolulu, Wm Cooper Parke, jr, Marshal of the Hawaiian Islands, formerly of Boston, to Miss Anna, daughter of the late Hon Luther Severance, of Augusta, Maine.

In Chancery. Rolf vs Jones As to Thos Evans, formerly of Hoxton, London, eldest son of John & Mary Evans, of that place, who, is is supposed, sailed from London for Boston, Mass, U S, about 23 years ago. Pursuant to a decree of his Honor, the Master of Rolls, an inquiry is being prosecuted as to who are the next of kin of Rachel Morgan, late of Panty Goytre, in Monmouth Co, England, Spinster, deceased, who died on Sep 2, 1854, & it is alleged that the children of the said John & Mary Evans are some of such next of kin: Notice is given that if the said Thos Evans was alive on & after Sep 2, 1854, he or his personal reps should forthwith give notice of his claim to Messrs J V & J T Harting, of 24 Lincoln's Inn Fields, London, G B, the Solicitor to the plntf in said cause. And any person who will furnish the Messrs Hartings with satisfactory evidence as to the said Thos Evans' present residence or death will receive a reward of 500 pounds sterling. Dated Nov 29, 1855. -J V & J T Harting, 24 Lincoln's Inn Fields, London, Plntsf' Solicitor

In Chancery. In the Circuit Court of Fairfax Co, Va, Feb Term, 1854. Orlando W Huntt, adm of John Chappel, deceased, cmplnt, against John Chappell & others, dfndnts. It is ordered that Thos Moore, one of the com'rs in chancery of this court, ascertain & report the number of heirs of John Chappell, deceased, entitled to distribution of the fund arising from the sale of the tract of land of which the said John Chappell died seized & possessed, & that he give notice for that purpose in the Nat'l Intell weekly for one month. -T D Richardson, clerk

+

The parties interested in the foregoing decree are to attend at the clerk's ofc of Fairfax Co Court on Apr 12, 1856, to execute the same, when & where they are required to attend with their evidence. -Thos Moore, com'r

In Chancery. In the Circuit Court for Worcester Co, Md, Feb 11, 1856. Saml Purnell vs Wm Whittington, Emeline C Smith, John W Smith, & Thos A S Smith. The object of this suit is to procure a decree for a sale of certain real estate in Worcester Co, of which Robt H Whittington, deceased, died seized, for the payment of his debts. The bill states that the said Robt was indebted to the cmplnt in the sum of $77.50, upon a bill obligatory, dated Oct 26, 1852, payable on demand, with interest from date; that, being so indebted, the said Robt died intestate in 1854, leaving no personal estate, but large real estate, which was liable for his debts; that the dfndnts are his heirs at law; & that the said Wm Whittington resides out of the State of Md. Absent dfndnt to appear in this Court, in person or by solicitor, on or before the 3rd Tue of Aug next. -Edw D Martin, clerk

In the Circuit Court for Worcester Co, Md, in Equity, Feb 13, 1856. Geo S Richardson & Brother vs Edwin & Geo S Bowen & others. The object of this suit is to procure a decree for the sale of the real estate of Zachariah Bowen, deceased, for the payment of his debts. The bill states that Zachariah died intestate in Jan, 1856, indebted to the said Geo S Richardson & Brother on account & to divers other persons in large sums of money; that said Zachariah hath left a widow & the following children, his heirs-at-law, to wit: Edwin, Geo S, Albert, Emma, & Irving M Bowen, of whom Edwin & Geo are of full age & non-residents of this State, & that Albert, Emma, & Irving are minors under the age of 21 years & reside in Worcester Co; that administration of the personal estate of said Zachariah hath been committed to Geo E Bowen, of said county, & that the personal estate is insufficient for the payment of the debts of said Zachariah, & pray a decree for the sale of his real estate. Absent dfndnts are to appear in this Court, in person or by solicitor, on or before the 3rd Tue in Aug next. -Edw D Martin, clerk

Died: on Mar 7, in Wash City, Robt B Leckie, eldest son of Martha & the late Jas Leckie, in his 21st year. His funeral will take place tomorrow at 2 o'clock, from the residence of Mr Lemuel Denham, on Pa ave, between 12th & 13th sts.

Died: on Mar 7, at the residence of his parents, Saml Southard Force, son of Peter & Hannah Force, in his 20th year. His funeral will be on Sunday at half past 2 o'clock, from the First Baptist Church, 10th st.

Died: Feb 29, at Phil, Wm P C Barton, M D, senior surgeon U S Navy, in his 70th year.

In Chancery, No 969. Circuit Court of Wash Co, D C. Selby B Scaggs & others vs Susan Brady & others. Henry Naylor, trustee in the above cause, reported the sales made by him on Sep 17, 1855: parts of lots 11 & 12 in square 823, in Wash City, to Selby B Scaggs, for $394.05½]; that he sold all of lot 13 & parts of lots 11 & 12 in same square, to said Selby B Scaggs, for $285.03; that on Sep 19, 1855, he sold part of lot 4 in square 535, with improvements, to said Selby B Scaggs, for $666; on Sep 17, 1855, he sold parts of lots 2 & 3 in square 825, to John L Fowler, for $89.04; that on the same day he sold the south part of lot 3 in square north of square 853, with improvements, to said John L Fowler, for $236; that on the same day he sold part of lot 1 in square south of square 825 to Richd Barry, for $348; on Sep 18, 1855, he sold lot 3 in square 834, & lot 4 in same square, to Jos Fugitt, who afterwards assigned the same to Francis H Hill, for $172.17½; & the purchasers have complied with the terms of the sales. -John A Smith, clerk

House of Reps: 1-Cmte on Naval Affairs: asked to be discharged from the consideration of the memorial of Cmder John De Camp, of the U S Navy, & that it be laid on the table. 2-Bill authorizing a settlement of the accounts of Chas P Babcock, late Indian agent at Detroit, Mich: referred. 3-Bill for the relief of the reps & sureties of Robt King, deceased: referred.

The Gold Medal of Honor has been awarded by the Paris Exhibition to Lt Maury for his Wind & Current Charts. Letter written Paris, Jan 26, 1856, by M Vattemare, ofcr of the Exhibition.

From New Mexico. Horace L Dickinson, auditor of Public Accounts for the Territory, died on Jan 2.

We chronicle this [Tue] morning the death of Roger Sherman, in his 88th year, probably the oldest male resident in our city. He was a son of Hon Roger Sherman, one of the signers of the Declaration of Independence, & one of the leading men in framing the Constitution of the U S, & one of the soundest statesmen that our country ever possessed.
-New Haven Journal

On Fri last negro Saul, convicted of the murder of Mr Porter, was hung at Centreville, Md, in the presence of some 4,000 persons.

MON MAR 10, 1856
Jas T McIntosh & Co, Drapers & Tailors, Pa ave, near 4½ st, American Hotel.

Drs Hunter & Williams, Physicians for diseases of the lungs, ofc 52 North Chas st, Balt, Md. Dr Hunter announces that Dr John B Williams will be associated with him in the Balt practice. Dr Williams has enjoyed in London & Paris long & great experience in the diagnosis & treatment of pulmonary diseases, & for some years has been connected with Dr Hunter's ofc in N Y. Ofc 260 Pa ave, over Mrs Voss' jewelry store.

Died: on Mar 9, in Wash City, Miss Margaretta Hill, aged 40. Her funeral will be from the residence of her mother, 366 21st st, between G & H sts, tomorrow at 2 o'clock.

Criminal Court-Wash. The jury in the case of Edwards charged with shooting & killing Avery in Wash City several months ago, on Sat, rendered a sealed verdict, & that manslaughter is the crime of which they pronounce him guilty. [Mar 17th newspaper: Wm B Edwards was on Fri last sentenced to confinement in the penitentiary at hard labor for 7 years. Edwards rented out one or more tenements near which he lived to evil persons, & he took upon himself the ofc of protector of his tenants, & ordered a young man Avery & others to leave the premises, &, to enforce his order, fired upon them, killing Avery & severely wounding another of the party.]

City Ordinance-Wash: 1-Act for the relief of Wm Van Riswick: that $5 be paid to him, that amount being overpaid by him for a license. 2-Act authorizing John P Pepper to pave the alley along the line of his property in square 491, to be done at his own expense.

For sale or rent: lot 1 in square 353, corner of E st south & 10th st west, recently occupied by Mr John W Martin for blacksmith & wheelwright shops. Also for rent, the whole of square 562, between 2nd & 3rd sts west & H & I sts north, containing 2½ acres, at present occupied by Mr H N Lansdale, on which for several years past was his carpenter's shop. Inquire of Jos Ingle

For rent: 3 story brick dwlg house on the corner of K & 25th st, No 63, with a large garden. Apply to Geo Lowry, 77, corner of 24th & K sts.

TUE MAR 11, 1856
Miss Martha Beach is prepared to give full & accurate courses of instruction on the Piano Forte to those who may desire her services. Pupils attended at their residences or her own. She refers, by permission, to Prof Foertsch, Miss Mary Murray, Mr J L Clubb, & Col Wm P Young. Apply at the residence of her parents, 310 North 9th st.

House of Reps: 1-Remonstrance of Lemuel Woodruff & 41 others, citizens of Beaver Co, Pa, against the extension of Woodworth's patent for planing. 2-Seven petitions, numerously signed by citizens of Pa, asking for the impeachment of John K Kane, Judge of the U S Court for the Eastern District of Pa. 3-Memorial of Absalom Boyd, of Muskingum Co, Ohio, asking the passage of an act to legalize & confirm the assignment of certain land warrants, which assignments were decided by the Com'r of the General land Ofc to be informal

The Hong Kong Register of Dec 15 confirms the report of the death of Cmdor Joel Abbott, of the U S Navy, Cmder-in-Chief of the U S Navy in these seas.. The event took place on Dec 14. He was 62 years of age, & died a christian's death. He was much esteemed by the ofcrs & men serving under his command. The remains of Cmdor Abbott will be conveyed from the residence of Robt P de Silver, U S Naval Storekeeper, on board the ship **Macedonian** this afternoon, to be conveyed to the U S for interment.

Senate: 1-Ptn from Sherlock Tillman & other citizens of Clarence, N Y, asking to be allowed bounty land for service in the war of 1812. 2-Ptn from Wm B Carrico & others, watchmen at the Navy Yard, asking to be allowed certain arrearages of pay. 3-Ptn from Michl Muse, asking indemnity for losses & injuries sustained by him in consequence of illegal & arbitrary imprisonment by the Mexican authorities. 4-Ptn from Chas A Suffield, asking increase of pension. 5-Ptn from Nathan B Marsh, asking a cmte to examine his invention for ascertaining the nature of bottoms in deep sea-soundings. 6-Ptn from Jos Dodds & Amos Irwin, soldiers of the war of 1812, asking an amendment to the bounty-land law. 7-Ptn from Henry Henry, late a captain in the navy, asking to be restored to his former position. 8-Ptn from Capt Conner, asking to be placed on the active instead of reserved list. 9-Memorial from Paul Zantzinger, late a captain in the navy, asking to be restored to his former position in the navy, complaining of having been treated with harshness & injustice, & asking redress at the hands of Congress. 10-Ptn from Smith Mowrey, jr, asking confirmation of his title to a certain island on the coast of Florida. 11-Cmte of Claims: bill for the relief of the legal reps of Zadock Thompson, of Vt, with a report.

Died: on Mar 10, in Gtwn, of consumption, Mrs Martha Ellen Hutchins, youngest daughter of Thos Payne, aged 23 years, 2 months & 14 days. Her funeral will be tomorrow morning at 10 A M, from the residence of her father, on Washington st, Gtwn.

Died: on Mar 9, in Balt, Wm Holliday, in his 49th year, a well known & highly esteemed citizen of that city, & for the last 17 years foreman of the Balt Clipper ofc.

WED MAR 12, 1856
Senate: 1-Ptn from Col Gardiner & other ofcrs of the army, asking an increase of army ration to forty cents. 2-Ptn from Mary Bennett, widow of a captain in the revenue service, asking to be allowed a pension.

An excellent lighographic portrait of Rev M D Conway has just been published by Mr C H Brainard, of Boston. It is for sale in Wash City by Taylor & Maury. The likeness is all that can be desired.

The body of Capt Palmer, of the schnr **Eudora Imogene**, the vessel scuttled & sunk near City Island, N Y, last fall, on her passage from Wmsburg to New Haven, & whose fate has since remained a mystery, was discovered on Sat near the foot of North Second st, Wmsburg. The body was sewed up in a course coal sack, & was recognized by Mr Kingsland, who was well acquainted with Capt Palmer. An incised wound was found on the side of the neck, exposing the carotid artery, & a cut from a sharp weapon was on the forehead, proving that he had been murdered. The negro charged with the murder is still under arrest. [Mar 31st newspaper: Geo Wilson, the man arrested & committed to jail at White Plains, Westchester Co, N Y, some time since, on suspicion of having murdered the captain, mate, & a boy belonging to the schnr **Eudora Imogene**, has been set at liberty; there not being sufficient proof to charge him with the murderers.] [Apr 3rd newspaper: Geo Wilson finds himself in jail again, at the instance of the U S Marshal, on the modified charge of having created a revolt on board the said schnr.]

Notice. The office of the **Oak Hill Cemetery** Company has been removed to room No 1, second floor, Cissel's bldg, on the northeast corner of Bridge & Congress sts, Gtwn. -Henry King

Fire broke out yesterday in the basement of the elegant house of Mrs Taggart on 21st st, near F. The fire caught from the furnace, & before it was discovered had made rapid progress. The house was wholly consumed, together with the one adjoining, which was unoccupied. Both houses belonged to Mrs Taggart, & were erected last summer. They were 3 stories high, of brick, & contained all the modern improvements. They were both fully insured, but there was not insurance on the furniture. We regret to state that Mr John G Anderson, who lived in **Bride's row**, on G st, was killed by the falling of the wall of the back bldg. The wall struck him on the head, & cut the top of it completely off, killing him instantly. He leaves a wife & 4 or 5 children in a destitute condition. He was a member of the Western Hose Co, & was engaged at the time in removing Mrs Taggart's furniture from the house. Mr Dorr, a sadler by trade, was also badly injured. The cords of his wrist were severed by his falling through a window sash. He bled profusely, & was carried to Dr Magruder's house, where his wounds were dressed.

Capt Benj H Arthur, of the 1st regt of infty, U S Army, died at **Fort Chadbourne**, Texas, Feb 11, 1856, of pneumonia.

Died: on Feb 14, near Belleville, Ill, Sarah Ann, beloved wife of Risdon Moore, & daughter of the late Wm & Sarah Duncan, of Wash. She leaves 2 small children to mourn her irreparable loss. May she rest in peace!

Died: on Feb 22, at Columbia, Texas, in his 50th year, Dr Mason L Weems, sr, 2nd son of the late Rev Mason L Weems, of Dumfries, Va. Dr Weems was favorably known to many in this city as a practitioner of medicine. He emigrated to Texas about 1838.

Phil, Mar 11. The steam-turning establishment in Master st was destroyed this morning by the explosion of the boiler. The establishment belonged to Mr Erhard Beck. Mr Eckart & his son Herman, age 14 years, who both worked on the first floor, were killed.

The arrival of the barque **Amelia** at St Thomas in distress has been announced. They finally arrived there after having been buffeted about on the ocean for 62 days, the vessel leaking to an alarming extent the entire time. Her cmder, Lt Reed Werden, has reached N Y in the ship **Black Warrior**, & Lt Erben, in whose charge the crew was placed, arrived at Balt in the barque **Amazon** a few days since. The sufferings experienced by these two ofcs of our navy & their crew were certainly very severe, & their escape from a watery grave almost a miracle. -Balt Patriot

THU MAR 13, 1856
Trustees of Berlin Female Seminary will receive proposals for a Principal, [male or female,] until May 1 next, to take charge of the Seminary for the scholastic year commencing in Sep next. The trustees will ensure to the Principal a salary of $600, with all excess which may accrue on school bills, out of which sum the Principal will pay a Female Assistant $200 & board, the Assistant to be furnished or approved by the trustees. The house can be occupied by the Principal after May 1, & it is possible an arrangement may be made for an interest in the school for the balance of this scholastic year. -F A Williams, Chairman of Cmte, Berlin, Md.

Fresh venison from Hampshire Co, Va. Just received, Jas H Shekell, 279 F st & 13th.

I offer for sale the Occoquan Cotton Factory, in the village of Occoquan, Prince Wm Co, Va, 22 miles from Wash City. The village has about 300 inhabitants. The original cost of the factory was $40,000. I will sell it for $16,000; one-fourth cash, the balance on terms to suit the purchaser. I will also sell my store & dwlg in the center of this village. I will sell the wharf attached to the property, for $4,000 in connexion with the factory. -Francis Hanna, Wash, D C

Selling out to change business, having determined to discontinue the perfumery, stationery, & fancy goods business, & keep solely a first-class Piano, Music, & Musical Instrument Store. -John F Ellis, 306, near 10th st.

Letter to the editor: Col Lewis Nicola was born in Ireland. According to the records of the Pa Society of the Cincinnati, of which he was a member, the writer has been unable to ascertain either the date of his birth or death. On Jul 6, 1775, we find him in Phil addressing the Cmte of Safety for a plan for the defence of this city. The writer has in possession a Genr'l Register of the Ofcrs in the American Army for 1779, entirely in the handwriting of Col Nicola, prepared with great care. On Jun 20th he was elected colonel. Ofcrs of the Corps of Invalids for 1779: Col Lewis Nicola, Capts David Woelpper, Will Williams, Robt Campbell, [killed Oct 4, 1779,] Moses McFarland, Will McElhalton, & Thos Arnold; Lts Osgood Carleton, Ephraim Minot, Will Honeyman, Abrah Wood, Jonath Pugh, Will Lamont, & Will Maynard. -H C B- Phil, Feb 28, 1856

Senate: 1-Ptn from Mary Haulbert, daughter of a soldier of the war of 1812, asking to be allowed bounty land. 2-Cmte on Military Affairs: bill for the relief of Dempsy Pittman. Same cmte: bill for the relief of Jas Harrington. Same cmte: adverse report on the memorial of John C McFerran: ordered to be printed.

Explosion in the steam saw-mill owned by Mr Wm Sears, near Henderson, Knox Co, Ill, on Feb 25. Mr Sears was severely though not dangerously hurt, & his eldest son, Francis, terribly bruised.

Dr Wm P Richardson, of New Kent Co, Va, charges the vaccine agent of the State of Va with having furnished "genuine" vaccine matter to him, in consequence of which 80 persons who had been vaccinated in that county with it are now sick with the small pox, & some of the cases very critical.

House of Reps: 1-Bill for the relief of Jacob Dodson was referred to the Cmte on Military Affairs.

Mrs Gassaway, D st, between 7th & 8th sts, has 2 rooms for rent, with or without board.

Brickyard for sale. The undersigned will dispose of their upper or eastern Brickyard, at N & South Capitol sts, [*Twenty-bldg Hill,*] with an abundance of the best quality clay. Apply to Richd Wallach or John Van Riswick. -Saml Byington & Co

Furniture varnishing & repairing; chairs & sofas recovered; mattresses restuffed. Shop: 446 north side E st, near 7th. -R J Walmsley

Died: on Mar 12, in Wash City, Mr Chas Pettit, in his 60th year, a native of Buck's Co, Pa, but for the last 39 years a resident of Wash City, & for 26 years past engaged in the ofc of the Sec of the Treasury. His funeral will take place from his late residence 484 E st, between 5th & 6th sts, on Friday at 3½ o'clock.

Circuit Court for Montg Co, as a Court of Equity. Mar Term, 1856. Henry Harding, adm of Thos F W Vinson, vs Jas N Allnutt, adm of Robt Lyles, Juliet [Lyles] Lyles, widow of Robt Lyles, & Robt J Lyles. The object of this suit is to procure a decree for a sale of certain mortgaged premises in said county which were, on Jul 4, 1835, mortgaged by one Robt Lyles, since deceased, to one Thos F W Vinson, since deceased, of whom the cmplnt is the administrator. The bill states that on Jul 4, 1835, the said Robt Lyles conveyed certain real estate, which is described in the bill & its accompanying exhibit, unto the said Thos F W Vinson in his lifetime, by way of mortgage, to secure the payment of the sum of $400, with interest, from Nov 1, 1830, which was then due & owing from the said Robt Lyles to the said Thos F W Vinson; that the said Thos F W Vinson has since departed this life & letters of administration on his personal estate been granted by the Orphans' Court of Montg Co to the cmplnt; that the said Robt Lyles has since departed this life, leaving a widow, Juliet Lyles, & Robt J Lyles, his heir-at-law, who reside in the State of Tenn; that letters of the administration upon his personal estate have been granted by the Orphans' Court of said county to the said Jas N Allnutt; that no part of the aforesaid sum of money or interest thereon has been paid, but that the whole of said debt, with interest, is still due & owing to the cmplnt as administrator as aforesaid. The bill prays that the said mortgaged premises, or so much thereof as may be necessary, be sold for the payment of the said claim of the cmplnt, as administrator as aforesaid, with interest as aforesaid. Absent dfndnts to appear in this court, in person or by solicitor, on or before the 4th Tue of Jul next. -Nich's Brewer, Circuit Judge -Jas G Hening, clerk

The trial of a man named Corrigan, about 70 years old, in Westmoreland Co, Pa, for the murder of his wife, has excited great interest. He was convicted of murder in the first degree & sentenced to be hung. The evidence was wholly circumstantial. The woman disappeared in Sept, & Corrigan said she had gone to Phil. Marks of blood were found about the house, & fragments of what seemed to be human bones were dug from a heap of ashes where Corrigan had been burning a brush-heap on his farm. These circumstances, & the fact they were known to have quarreled, procured his conviction.

Mrd: on Mar 9, in Wash City, by Rev Mr Holmead, Mr Jas B Pumphrey to Miss Agnes J Cline, formerly of Balt.

Mrd: on Mar 11, in Wash City, by Rev Mr Holmead, Tobias M Martin to Miss Mary E Henning.

Mrd: on Mar 11, in Ryland Chapel, by Rev J Morris Pease, of N Y C, Rev Wm C Steel, of Balt Conference M E Church, to Miss Pamela A, only daughter of the late Rev Lewis Pease, of the N Y Conference.

Died: on Mar 9, in Wash City, Wm C Poole, son of Lewis H & the late Eliz A Poole, aged 3 years & 1 month.

Died: on Feb 26 last, in Pensacola, Fla, in his 77th year, Robt Mitchell, a native of Fayetteville, N C, but for the last 34 years a resident of that place.

FRI MAR 14, 1856

The U S sloop-of-war **Portsmouth** is now preparing at the Norfolk [Va] navy yard, to join the East India squadron. Ofcrs who have been ordered to join her: Cmder, A H Foote; Lts, Wm H Macomb, H K Davenport, Edw Simpson, P G Watmough; Master, Fras E Shepperd; Surgeon, Andrew A Henderson; Assist Surgeon, John Vansant; Acting Boatswain, Paul Atkinson; Gunner, Jas A Gates; Carpenter, Jos G Myers, Sailmaker, Geo C Boerum.

Senate: 1-Ptn from the administrator of John Shorb, deceased, asking indemnity for French spoliations prior to 1800. 2-Ptn from the heirs of Chas Chapin, asking that they may be allowed a pension for services in the war of the Revolution. 3-Ptn from Geo M Weston, Com'r of the State of Maine, asking the settlement of the claims of that State against the U S growing out of the fourth article of the treaty of Wash. 4-Ptn from Jos Webb, asking an increase of pension. 5-Ptn from Lt L C Sartori, asking to be restored to his former position on the active service list. 6-Ptn from the widow of Cmdor Jesse D Elliott, asking the reimbursement of the expenses incurred by him when in command of the Mediterranean squadron in 1835. 7-Ptn from John S Vandyke, asking to be allowed back pay, pension, & bounty land as an ofcr in the military service of the U S. 8-Ptn from Eliz Speiden, asking a pension. 9-Memorial from Van Rensselaer Morgan, a lt, asking redress from the action of the late Naval Board. 10-Cmte on the Post Ofc & Post Roads: memorial of John H Scranton & Jas M Hunt, asking payment for carrying the mail to Puget's Sound, submitted a report, with a bill for their relief. 11-Cmte on D C, to which was referred the memorial of the Merchants' Exchange of D C, asking an increase of the banking & insurance capital of Wash: bill to incorporate an insurance company in Wash City. [This bill constitutes Silas H Hill, Wm B Todd, Saml Bacon, Wm Wall, Benj Beall, Chas Miller, Jos Bryan, M W Galt, Augustus E Perry, J C McGuire, Wm F Bayly, Walter Harper, Walter Lenox, & Wm T Dove, & their associates & successors, a body politic & corporate, by the name of Wash Ins Co.] 12-Cmte on Public Lands: adverse report on each of the following memorials, viz: of Mary Haulbert, asking to be allowed bounty land; & of Jonas P Levy, asking bounty land for services rendered in the war with Mexico.

The Army. 1-Capt Chas F Wooster, 4th artl, died at *Fort Brown*, Texas, Feb 14, 1856. 2-The resignations of Capt Thos R McConnell, 4th infty, & 2nd Lt Edwin F Townsend, 3rd artl, have been accepted by the Pres, to take effect Mar 11, 1856.

Fall of a warehouse, at Phil, on Thu: Messrs Buzby & Co, 365 Market st. It was erected in 1854. Mark Donohue, the measurer of the warehouse, aged 28 years; Jos Miller, agent for the Mechanicsburg line of cars; Jos Crawley, laborer; & Timothy Murphy, a porter, were crushed to death beneath the ruins.

House of Reps: 1-Bill for the relief of the heirs of Jane Irvine, deceased. 2-Bill to indemnify Mrs Lizzie R Smith for property lost in the destruction of the U S steamer **San Francisco**.

U S Patent Ofc, Wash, Mar 13, 1856. Ptn of Geo S Wright, of West Springfield, Mass, praying for the extension of a patent granted to him on May 28, 1842, for an improvement in machine for ruling letter paper, for 7 years from the expiration of said patent, which takes place on May 28, 1856. -Chas Mason, Com'r of Patents

J G Anderson, who perished at the fire on Tue, was buried yesterday, a large number of the firemen of the city & others uniting in the funeral procession.

Mrd: on Wed, in Wash City, by Rev John C Smith, Mr Wm Jones to Miss Mgt Parsons, all of Wash City.

Mrd: on Mar 12, in Wash City, by Rev J G Butler, John F Acker to Mary Brockenbrough Roane, daughter of Hon John J Roane, all of Wash City.

Mrd: on Mar 4, at *Fairfield*, the residence of her father, by Rev C M Callaway, Mr Jas E Marshall to Miss Mary M, eldest daughter of Henry M Marshall, of Fauquier Co, Va.

Mrd: in Wash City, by Rev Jas B Donelan, John Q Adams to Louisa Ragon, daughter of the late Chas Hartman, all of Wash City. [No marriage date given-current item.]

Died: on Mar 12, at his residence, near Wash City, Mr Wm Holmead, in his 40th year. His funeral will take place today at 3 o'clock.

Died: on Feb 28, in Boone Co, Mo, in her 68th year, Mrs Ann F Hamilton, widow of Robt Hamilton, deceased, of Prince Wm Co, Va, which place she with her family left in the fall of 1846, & where she left many relatives & friends. The deceased was for half a century a consistent member of the Methodist Episcopal Church.

Died: on Mar 13, at the residence of Mr Robt Brown, Capitol Hill, Mr Geo E Abbott, of Hampden, Maine. His funeral will take place this afternoon at 2 o'clock.

New Orleans, Mar 12. Recruits for Walker. 200 recruits for Walker left in the steamship **Daniel Webster** yesterday for Nicaragua. Among them was Col Parker H French.

Police ofcrs of the Wash Corp: John Davis, Chief of Police:

Washington Hurley	R R Burr	John A Willett
Jos B Peerce	Wm Martin	Isaac Stoddard
W H Barnaclo	A R Allen	U B Mitchel
Wm A Boss	John H Wise	J M Busher
E G Handy	J Simond	
J Gettings	Josias Adams	

Orphans Court of Wash Co, D C. In the case of Eliza A Brereton & John Hoover, adms of John Brereton, deceased, the administrators aforesaid & the Court have appointed Apr 5 next, for the distribution of the personal estate of said deceased, of the assets in hand. -Ed N Roach, Reg/o wills

SAT MAR 15, 1856
Senate: 1-Memorial from Augustus McLaughlin, late a master in the U S navy dropped by the action of the Naval Board, asking to be restored to his former position. 2-Ptn from R H Weightman, asking compensation for certain services rendered during the 32nd Congress as agent of the people of New Mexico. 3-Cmte of Claims: bill for the relief of Josiah S Little. 4-Bill for the relief of Richd Albritton: referred to the Cmte on Private Land Claims.

Obit-died: Isaac G Burnet, one of the oldest & most respected citizens of Cincinnati, died yesterday, in his 72nd year. He emigrated from N J to this city in 1804; entered the ofc of his brother, the late Judge Jacob Burnet, & completed his legal studies; removed to Dayton & began the practice of law in 1807; commenced the publication of a a newspaper, Dayton Dutchman, until after the war; in 1815 returned to this city & entered into partnership with Nicholas Longworth in the practice of law; about 1817 he became one of the proprietors of the Cincinnati Gaz & its editor; in 1819 he was elected Mayor, holding the ofc until 1831, when he declined to be a candidate again & returned to the bar. In 1833 he was elected clerk of the Supreme Court for this county. He was one of the earliest members of the second Presbyterian Church, & held the ofc of elder for many years. He resigned this when he removed out of the city. He was elected elder in the church at Walnut Hills, & remained so till his death. He left a large family of children, some of whom are among our most prominent citizens; one of them is a distinguished divine & another a lawyer of high standing. [From the Cincinnati Gaz of Mar 12.]

House of Reps: 1-Resolved, that the Cmte on Military Affairs inquire into granting a pension to Mrs Childs, widow of Brvt Brig Gen Childs, late of the U S army, & that they report by bill or otherwise.

Wm Gifford & Wm B McElroy, who stole $23,000 from the custom-house in Franklin, Texas, on Nov 8, didn't have very good luck. They took Cooke's route to Calif; 5 Apaches followed them, & on Florida mountain, shot Gifford dead & killed McElroy with lances.

The subscriber has 6 good farms for sale, within 9 to 10 miles of Wash, which he will sell low for cash or city property. Call on the subscriber at Geo F Kidwell & Co's Wood & Coal Yard, 14th st, opposite the Franklin Engine-house. -Henry N Lansdale

Trustee's sale: all persons holding claims against Messrs Huggins & Goldsby, of Selma, Ala, will present them to the undersigned by Jun 1 next. Assignment duly recorded in the Probate Court ofc of Dallas Co, Ala. -Wm M Byrd, trustee, Selma, Ala

Death of the oldest inhabitant. From the Loisville [Ky] Courier of Mar 10. Louisville has lost by death, yesterday, Old Ben Duke, as he has been styled from time immemorial at the age of 110 years, 8 months & 3 days. He was a man of color & a native of Md, from which State he emigrated when Ky was a complete wilderness & our city a frontier. He was many years a resident of Va, & at age 30 entered the service of Washington, of whom he retained the liveliest recollections. His death was without a pang of sickness. He was a member of the Baptist church, & a devout Christian. Yesterday morning there was prayer meeting at his residence, & after the service he walked to the door & became suddenly faint. His son ran to his aid, & assisted him upstairs to bed. He lay quietly for a few moments, & then peacefully expired. Ben Duke was originally a slave, but the entire race of his owners has become extinct, & he has been a free man for a long time. His beard & hair were long & white.

On the Island, yesterday, Clement Brooks, a free man of color, was shot in the right breast with a pistol by Danl Benett, another free man of color, jealousy being the motive. The wound is serious & may prove fatal. Bennett was arrested & committed to jail.

Mrd: on Mar 13, in Wash City, by Rev G D Cummins, Pierson B Reading, of Calif, to Fannie W Washington, daughter of the late Dr B Washington, U S Navy.

Died: on Mar 14, Julia, infant daughter of John D & Eliza B Thomson, aged 3 months & 3 days. Her funeral will be on Sunday afternoon at 3 o'clock, from 479 10th st, between D & E.

Orphans Court of Wash Co, D C. Letters of administration on the personal estate of Geo H Law, late of Great Britain & Ireland, deceased. -Edmund Law Rogers, adm

MON MAR 17, 1856

Mr Chas Maurice Smith, of the Washington Sentinel, has ceased his connexion with the editorial dept of that journal. Mr Beverly Tucker, its proprietor, announces his loss, & laments that he is now all alone. Three months ago the death of Mr Overton broke one of the bonds of friendship & political sympathy by which the three were closely united.

Col Fred'k B McNeill, of the U S Marine Corps, died on Mar 10, aged 49. He was a native of Mass, but removed to the South, & was appointed from Alabama in 1834.

Trustee's sale of valuable improved property: by deed of trust from Jos Davis & Geo W Garrett, dated May 5, 1854, recorded in Liber J A S No 83, folios 403 thru 405, of the land records of Wash Co: public auction on Mar 31, of lot 5 in square 381, with a 3 story brick bldg, occupied at present as a printing ofc. -Wm H Ward, J Y Davis, trustees -Jas C McGuire, auct

A tablet has been placed inside King's Chapel in honor of the memory of the late Saml Appleton, a Boston merchant, who died Jul 12, 1853, aged 87 years.

Two story frame house for sale: fronts 50 feet on the east side of High st, & runs back about 120 feet. Apply to M Adler, Gtwn

John W Forney, Clerk of the House of Reps during the 32nd & 33rd Congresses, was on Fri last complimented by the clerks who had served under him during those terms by the presentation of a silver pitcher & goblets of Messrs Galt's most beautiful manufacture. Mr John C Bowyer presented the gift.

Phil, Mar 15. This evening the ferryboat **New Jersey**, of the Phil & Camden Ferry Co, in crossing the Delaware to Camden, took fire in the middle of the stream. Three bodies only have been recovered, viz: those of John Little, Abraham Jannie, & Francis Fitzpatrick. Among the missing are Sallie Carman, Edw Meschamp, formerly conductor on the Amboy Road, an infant daughter of Saml Giverson, John Fidell, Matthew Miller, jr, broker, Mr Howard, clerk, Mrs Shade & child, & a large number of colored persons. [Apr 8th newspaper: The jury found the in-efficiency of Richd Letters, who inspected the boiler; the general unfitness of the boat for the transportation of passengers, & the omission of the company to properly man & equip the boat, & provide means of escape in case of fire, explosion, or collision, attributed to the disaster. The company was censured in the strongest manner.]

Died: on Mar 15, in Gtwn, Mrs Middleton Smith, wife of Anthony Smith, in her 79th year. Her funeral will be on Mar 17 at 3½ o'clock P M.

Obit-died: on Fri, from a severe illness, Dr Thos E Bond, sr, formerly of Balt, & for several years the principal editor of the N Y Christian Advocate & Journal, the leading paper of the Methodist Episcopal Church. Dr Bond was a Marylander by birth-a native, we believe of Harford Co, & came to Balt to reside about 1812. He was a local preacher & a member of the Methodist Episcopal Church. He lived to enter his 76th year. -Balt Patriot

TUE MAR 18, 1856
To the next of kin & the distributes of Edw Herndon, late of Campbell Co, Va. Said Edw Herndon died in 1845, without issue, & by his will, after certain specific bequests, he directed that the balance of his estate should be equally divided between his sisters, Sarah Samuels, Eliz Baker, Catharine Durham, Mary Herndon, & his brother Reuben Herndon. This will was duly probated in Campbell Co Court, & Y W Robertson qualified as executor. A suit has been instituted in the Circuit Court of Campbell Co by John T Irving & wife against the executor & legatees of said Edw Herndon for a settlement & division of said estate. And it appearing from the Com'rs report in that cause that all of the residuary legatees died in the lifetime of the testator, it is contended that said residuary legacy has lapsed, & is to be divided equally among the distributes of said Edw Herndon. Said residuary estate is worth $4,000 to $5,000. The following were the brothers & sisters of said Edw Herndon, viz: Lewis Herndon, Benj Herndon, Jas Herndon, John Herndon, Reuben Herndon, Mary Herndon, Sarah Samuels, Eliz Baker, & Catharine Durham. The parties interested will please state under which brother or sister of the testator they claim; the names & residences of all the children of said brother or sister, & in the case of the death of any child, the name of the widow or husband, as they case may be, & the children of the same; and, as far as practicable, will furnish the evidence of their relationship to said decendent. -Chas R Slaughter, Lynchburg, Va

Senate: 1-Ptn from Polly Fish, widow of a soldier of the war of 1812, asking to be allowed bounty land. 2-Ptn from Wm R Greble, claiming to be the original inventor of the apparatus for taking deep-sea soundings, & asking compensation for the use of same. 3-Ptn from John S Pendleton, asking compensation for services as special minister of the U S to the Gov't of the Argentine Confederation, the Republic of Paraguay, & the Oriental of Uraguay. 4-Ptn from Jas Morrow, asking compensation for services as agriculturist to the Japan Expedition. 5-Ptn from the legal reps of John Morrison & Chas Ginn, asking the confirmation of their title to certain lands in the Bastrop grant. 6-Bill introduced for the relief of Saml A Morse & others. 7-Ptn from Jas Junkins, asking to be allowed a pension.

Rev Mr Bailey, formerly pastor of Valley st Methodist Church, in Richmond, was drowned last week, with his wife, in the James river, in one of the lower counties. He was an active minister & truly pious man. [Mar 22nd newspaper: A letter from Chas City Co states that the reported drowning of Rev John Bailey, formerly of Richmond, & his wife, was incorrect. Both of them are alive & in good health. It is not very long since the same minister was reported to be frozen to death. -Richmond Dispatch]

Charlestown, Mass. While making an excavation at Bunker Hill, on Thu, a gang of laborers were suddenly buried by the earth caving in upon them. Michl Morrisey was taken out dead; Peter Gaffney dangerously injured; Danl Murphy & Timothy Kerwin with legs or arms broken; Wm Carroll was badly injured.

Hon Wm Parmalee, Mayor of the city of Albany, died at that place on Saturday.

The fine old ship **William Fane**, which nearly a 100 years ago bore Gen Wolfe to the conquest of Quebec, is now lying in the dry docks at Newport, England, to undergo a few slight repairs.

We are glad to learn that our young townsman, Wm D Washington, has returned to us for a time from Dusseldorf, but regret that his visit has been occasioned by the illness of two members of his family.

Sunnyside for sale: desiring to move South, I offer this beautiful improved farm, in Alexandria Co, Va; contains 200 acres; with a good dwlg house & necessary out-bldgs. Apply to Burke & Herbert, Alexandria, Va, or to the subscriber on the premises. -Edw B Powell

WED MAR 19, 1856
Jas McCoomb, convicted of murder at the court in Columbia, S C, on Wed was sentenced to be confined in jail until Apr 25 next, when he shall be conveyed thence & be hung.

Rev Jas S Belton, recently a missionary of the Methodist Episcopal Church South, died in N Y on Monday. He was a member of the Alabama Conference, & was sent as a missionary to China some two years since. He arrived in that country with his wife with every prospect of success, but the climate proved too severe for his condition. By the advice of his physicians & his colleagues he consented to return home, in the hope that in his native land the progress of his disease would be arrested.

Prize Beef! At my Stalls 29 & 31, West Market, on Friday, & Stall 66, Centre Market, on Sat, four of the finest cattle ever brought to market. They were raised by Mr Geo Roseberger, of Rockingham Co, Va. -Wm Linkins

Senate: 1-That Lt J M Gilliss, by his successful discharge of various public duties of a scientific nature, expecially his valuable astronomical observations in the late expedition to Chili, is entitled to the high consideration usually accorded to those who successfully devote themselves to such pursuits. 2-That the researches of Lt M F Maury on the subject of atmospheric & oceanic currents & other kindred phenomena, being of great value to the mercantile as well as the naval marine of the world, entitle him to the respect & gratitude of all who honor science & appreciate its application to practical results. 3-Ptn from Sophia Mason, heirs of an ofcr of the Revolution, asking to be allowed the commutation pay to which her ancestor was entitled. 4-Ptn from the surviving children of Ebenezer Murch, an ofcr of the Revolutionary army, asking compensation for the services & losses of their father. 5-Ptn from Effie Van Ness, widow of an ofcr of the Revolution, asking to be allowed a pension. 6-Ptn from Prudence Couch, asking a pension fort he services of her father in the Revolution. 7-Ptn from Wm Patterson, asking a pension as an invalid, occasioned by services in the war of 1812. 8-Ptn from Reuben Clough, asking to be allowed arrears of pension. 9-Ptn from D E Twiggs & other ofcrs of the army, asking an increase of the commutation ration. 10-Cmte on Pensions: asked to be discharged from the consideration of the ptn of Jno McDonald & others, & that it be referred to the Cmte on Public Lands: agreed to.

Virginia: **Mount Vernon**. The bill to incorporate the **Mount Vernon Ladies' Association** of the Union, & to authorize the purchase of a part of *Mount Vernon*, was passed by the House of Delegates on Monday by a vote of 106 to 2. The Senate concurred without a single negative.

Mr P T Barnum is just now under a rigid examination in N Y, at the instance of his creditors, in the Supreme Court. He testifies that though he had considered himself worth at least half a million last June, he has now but two suits of clothes in his possession, & not more than $25 in money; that at present his only means of support is the keeping of boarders in a furnished house now occupied by him in 8th st, except that his son-in-law in Conn furnished him with meat, & that he has some friends left who will not see him starve, some having already offered him money; that he owns no property in Alabama, though he has a mortgage on some slaves in Tenn; that he had $6,000 worth of stock in the Waterville Cuttlery Co [worthless] & $20,000 in the Jerome Clock Co, [also worthless,] besides $5,000 or $6,000 in the French Hat Body Manufacturing Co, a bankrupt concern; that his furniture at *Iranistan* has been sold for $2,000, including all his gold plate, valued at $500; that he had a gold watch which cost him $250 & a diamond pin & ring which cost $300, which he is ready to deliver up if so ordered; that his 5 horses at *Iranistan* brought less than $500, all he could get for them. The examination is to be continued this week. -Newark Daily Advertiser

Wash Corp: 1-Ptn from F A Hager for the remission of a fine: referred to the Cmte of Claims. 2-Memorial from V Harbaugh & others, cmte on behalf of the apothecaries' association, asking the privilege of holding their meetings in the chamber of this Board: referred to the Cmte on Police. 3-Ptn from Eliza M Hampton & others, asking that the curbstones may be set & the footway paved on the east side of square 352: referred to the Cmte on Improvements.

Orphans Court of Wash Co, D C. In the case of Jos W Webb, adm of Robt Mills, deceased, the administrator & Court have appointed Apr 12 next, for the final distribution of the personal estate of said deceased, with the assets in hand. -Ed N Roach, Reg/o wills

Mrd: on Mar 18, in Wash City, by Rev P D Gurley, D D, John F Clements, of Chicago, Ill, to Marion J McClery, daughter of Jas McClery, of Wash City.

For rent: 2 story brick dwlg on east Capitol st, between 1st & 2nd sts. Apply to Jas Lynch, Capitol Hill.

Orphans Court of Wash Co, D C. Letters of administration on the personal estate of Alfred G Ridgely, late of Wash Co, deceased. -David Ridgely, adm

THU MAR 20, 1856
The claim of the gallant Capt Reid's heirs for the loss of the brig **General Armstrong**, has been decided by the Court of Claims in favor of the claimants. It is a pity that some proper tribunal had not long ago been established by which claims against the Gov't could have been thoroughly examined & decided, &, when good, allowed before the claimants were in their graves. [Mar 21st newspaper: The venerable Capt Reid, of the privateer brig **General Armstrong**, so prominent in the history of the late war, is still alive, & in his 74th year, an active master in the navy. It was his venerable wife who died in the course of last year, & his son, Saml C Reid, being so long known as prosecuting the claim, led to the impression of the death of the father.]

Notice: to Jos Jenkins or his heirs. In pursuance of a decree of the Circuit Court of Jefferson Co, Va, information is required whether Jos Jenkins, who was a brother of Wm K Jenkins, deceased, is alive, & where to be found; or, if he be dead, whethere he left any children, & where they may be found. The said Jos Jenkins, if in life, or his children or ganrdchildren, if any, are entitled to a portion of the estate of said Wm K Jenkins, deceased, & will therefore find it to their advantage to furnish the information asked for to the undersigned, Com'r of said Court, Charlestown, Jefferson Co, Va. -Saml Stone, Com'r

Books: 1-Life of Govn'r Wise: a biographical sketch of Henry A Wise, with a History of the Political Camapign in Va in 1855, by Jas P Hambleton, M D, $2.50. 2-The Va Convention of 1776, a Discourse delivered before the Va Alpha of the Phi Beta Kappa Society by Hugh Blair Grigsby, $1.50. -Taylor & Maury's Bookstore, near 9th st.

Tough soldier. A private of the 11th regt of Huzzars, John Dryden, who received 31 wounds in one day at the storming of Sebastopol, is all recovered & again doing duty.

Died: Mar 19, in Wash City, of consumption, Mrs Eliz Robinson, aged 27 years, beloved wife of Sgt Maj John Robinson, U S Marine Corps. Her funeral will take place on Mar 21 at 2 o'clock, from her late residence, 8th st, opposite Odd Fellows' Hall, Navy Yard.

Health Report: ofc of the Com'r of Health, Mar 19, 1856. Interments in Wash City for Feb, 1856: 73. -A McD Davis, Com'r of Health

FRI MAR 21, 1856
Trustee's sale of lots of ground & improvements at auction: by deed of trust from John N Trook & wife, dated Oct 16, 1851: sale on Apr 21, in front of the premises, the following: lots 28 thru 33 in square 411, with improvements: fronts on 8th st west, between D & E sts south. -Saml Fowler, trustee -A Green, auct

Senate: 1-Papers in support of the claim of the heirs of Thos Jordan, a paymaster in the Revolutionary army for arrears of pension: referred. 2-Ptn from Brvt Col John L Gardner, U S Army, asking an amendment of the law of Apr, 1816, in respect to the allowance for forage. 3-Ptn from Benj Lanflant, asking compensation for property destroyed by the enemy during the last war with Great Britain. 4-Ptn from Oscar Piter, asking compensation for property destroyed in the bombardment of Greytown by the U S sloop-of-war **Cyane**. 5-Resolved, that the legal reps of Rhoda Lewis, widow of Seth Lewis, of Connecticut, be permitted to withdraw from the files of the Senate the original certificate of membership in the Cincinnati Society granted to Seth Lewis, & now with Rhoda Lewis' petition on the files of the Senate: provided that a certified copy be placed with the petition & papers aforesaid.

France: The Pope has consented to be god-father to the Imperial infant. The accouchment of the Empress is looked for almost immediately.

Runaways were committed to the jail of Wash Co on Mar 17, 1856, three negroes, viz: John Frasier, aged about 27 years; Charlotte Frasier, about 39; Lucy Frasier, a mulatto woman, aged 18 years. These slaves say they belong to Horace Luckett, of Loudoun Co, Va. Owner is to come forward, prove property, pay charges, & take them away, or else they will be discharged according to law. -B A Garlinger, Sheriff

House of Reps: 1-Ptn from Chas H Pointer, of Rockbridge Co, Va, for an increase of pension. 2-Memorial of Ashton S Tourison, late a lt of the 2nd regt Pa volunteers during the war with Mexico, praying for an increase of pension for wounds received during the said war. 3-Ptn of Shephard & Caldwell, for relief as to certain mail contracts, was withdrawn from the files. 4-Memorial of Junius J Balsley, Geo Cassady, Stephen Cooper, B S Howell, Wm T Young, & 24 others, citizens of Hamilton Co, Ohio, praying Congress to make provision for the construction of a Pacific railroad. 5-Memorial of Jas W Silby, S C Parkhurst, Wm B Casselly, C W West, R S Semple, & 109 others, citizens of the city of Cincinnati, praying Congress to aid in the construction of a canal around the falls of the Ohio on the Indiana side.

Fatal accident on the Phil Railroad on Tue at Aberdeen, when 2 trains collided in the snow storm. Geo Godwin, conductor, & Wm Todd, brakesman, were killed.

The remains of the late Capt H E Stevens, clerk of the steamer **Ohio Belle**, arrived here yesterday from Cairo, in charge of Mr Fee, an ofcr of the boat. Capt Stevens was shot by a man named Smith, after Stevens refused a note he had, saying it was counterfeit. Smith began using improper language in front of the Ladies, & when Stevens told him he would have to leave the boat, Smith pulled out a pistol & shot Stevens, producing almost immediate death. After the foul deed, Smith told Mr Riley, 2nd clerk, that his name was J B Jones, & that he resided in Mississippi. He said he was drunk, & that this was not the first man he had killed. -Cincinnati Commercial of Monday

Obit: the N Y papers announce the death, on Tue last, of Dr Thos Boyd, at the advanced age of 84 years. He had practiced medicine in this city for upward of 50 years. In every relation of life, as father, husband, physician, & above all as a Christian professor, the same unvarying rectitude governed his conduct.

The late Legislature of the State of Texas has passed a law giving to Mrs Eliz Crockett a league of land. She is the widow of the respected & lamented <u>David Crockett</u>, who, after serving his country honestly & faithfully in Congress, & other places of trust, was butchered at the Alamo, nobly fighting for the freedom of Texas. -Columbus Enquirer

Mrd: on Thu, in Wash City, by Rev John C Smith, Mr Andrew Jackson Lynn to Miss Nancy Ann Goodwin, both of Va.

Appointments made by the Conference of the Methodist Protestant Church for this vicinity: Wash, [9th st] Peter Light Wilson; East Wash Mission, [Navy Yard,] J R Nichols; Gtwn, Dr J J Murray; Alexandria, J T Murray; West Balt, S B Sutherland; East Balt, Washington Roby; Charleston, S C, D Evans Reese.

SAT MAR 22, 1856
Cmdor David Conner died at Phil on Mar 20. He was a native of Pa, & entered the Navy in Jan, 1809. Lt Wm A Nimmo, 4th artl, a native of N Y, died recently in Tennessee, of consumption.

Mrs Polly Beeman, of Birmingham, Conn, is in her 92nd year. Her husband, Tracy Beeman, died a short time since; he was 2 years the senior of his wife. They had lived in the same farm-house 69 years. They had a family of 9 children, the eldest of whon is now 73, & was married when she was 14. Of the grandchildren there are now 49, the oldest of whom is 56 years. There are 156 great grandchildren & 18 great great grandchildren. This venerable woman can call 230 of her lineal pedigree around her thanksgiving table. Their united ages now amount to 7,724 years. Our Connecticut old lady intends to take a long journey next week behind the iron horse. She ought to have a free ticket. -Hartford Courant

The Methodist Episcopal appointments: Potomac District, John Lanahan, P E Alexandria-L F Morgan, J N Coombs, A Griffith, Sup; Princess st, J S Gardiner. City of Wash-Foundry, S Regester; Wesley Chapel, W Krebs; Capitol Hill, R R S Hough; McKendree & Fletcher Chapel, Geo Hildt, M A Turner, Supt, T H Busey, Sup; Ebenezer, F H Richey; Ryland Chapel, J S Deale; Gorsuch Chapel, J H Ryland, S Rogers, W O Lumsdon, Sup, W R White, Sup. Gtwn-B M Brown, J M Hanson, Sup; West Gtwn & Tennellytown, T D Gotwalt, J W Hoover, Sup. Fairfax-D Thomas, R R Murphy, Sup. Stafford-W C Steele, R S McWilliams. Fredericksburg-E G Busey. St Mary's-J W Lambreth, F A Mercer, N Schlosser, Sup, J Bunting, Sup. Bladensburg-C G Linthicum, J H Wolf, Sup. Woodville-H C Westwood, Chas M L Hawley, J H Knotts. Rockville-W G Eggleston, Adam B Dolly, B Barry, Sup. Asbury & Mount Zion-Thos McGee. Jesse T Peck editor of Tracts & Corr Sec of the Tract Society of the Methodist Episcopal Church, Member of the Foundry Quarterly Conference. Elisha P Phelps Agent for Dickinson College.

Orphans Court of Wash Co, D C. Letters of administration on the personal estate of Robt Keyworth, late of Wash Co, deceased. -Mary Keyworth, admx

Died: on Mar 21, in Wash City, in his 60th year, John Devlin, clerk in the ofc of the Fifth Auditor of the Treasury. His funeral will move from his residence, in 12th st, at 9 o'clock on Monday morning; the services of requiem will commence at 10 o'clock in St Matthew's Church. No eulogium is deemed necessary to the memory of John Devlin. His high moral worth & deep impressions of religion have been long before his fellow-citizens. In intellectual attainments he displayed rare excellence.

Died: on Mar 18, in Wash City, at the residence of her niece, C L Brooke, Miss Catharine Shee, in her 85th year, daughter of the late Gen John Shee.

Died: on Mar 20, in Wash City, after a long illness, Mrs Sophia Jones, wife of Thos W Jones, & 2nd daughter of the late Geo Bean, in her 35th year, leaving a husband & 6 children. Her funeral is this afternoon at 3 o'clock, from the residence of her husband, on B st south, Capitol Hill.

Died: on Mar 20, in Wash City, Warrington, eldest son of Chas St J & Eliza C Chubb, aged 2 years & 5 months. His funeral is this afternoon at 1 o'clock, from the residence of the parents, 307 I st.

Funeral Notice: Capt W H Owen, son of Edw Owen, of Wash City, who died in New Orleans on Mar 8, will be buried from the residence of his brother, S W Owen, corner of K & 12th sts, on Mar 23, at 3 o'clock. The friends of the family & of the deceased, & his Calif friends in particular, are invited.

Wash City Ordinance: 1-Act for the relief of John Agnew: the sum of $231.50 be paid to him for repairing the Northern Liberty Company's Fire Engine.

Wm T Smithson: Dealer in land Warrants & Exchanges. Ofc next door, north, to the Bank of Wash.

MON MAR 24, 1856

The **Mount Vernon Ladies' Association** of the Union. Referring to the act lately passed by the Legislature of Va incorporating the "Mount Vernon Ladies' Association of the Union," for the purchase, by individual subscription of 200 acres of *Mount Vernon* place, including the mansion & tomb of Washington, with the intent that the same shall be ceded to the State of Va, & held sacred forever as the home & last resting place of the Father of his Country, the N Y Commerical advertiser remarks: "The sum asked by the present proprietor, Mr John A Washington, for the 200 acres, is $200,000, which is of course beyond its value as land. On that point, however, there is no need to say anything. The people of the U S, North & South, too deeply revere the memory of Washington to stand disputing about the price of the ground where his mortal remains rest. The sum can easily be raised, too, by the united efforts of the ladies in both sections of the country. We notice that the act in question invests the association with the title of the Mount Vernon Ladies' Association of the Union. We like that from Virginia-from the heart of the Old Dominion. It has the right cheering ring of former glorious days, & will, we doubt not, be promptly echoed from N Y & other Northern States in proffers of liberal co-operation with the Ladies of Virginia to raise the required sum for the purchase of the precious earth that hold the mouldering bones of the man who was, is now, & ever shall be, 'first in the hearts of his countrymen.' "

Mrd: on Feb 7, in Wash City, by Rev Francis E Boyle, Henry L Johnson to Miss Emily E Fitzgerald, both of Wash City.

The copartnership existing under the name of Worthington & Key has this day been dissolved by mutual consent. -Thos H Worthington, C M Keys. The Wood, Coal, & Sand business will be continued at the old stand, 14th & C sts, by Thos H Worthington. The Wood & Coal business will be conducted by C M Keys, corner of 12th & C sts. -C M Keys

It is our painful duty to record the death of the only son of Dr Geo Lynn. He was hunting with a young companion, & to cross his horse to the opposite side of the canal, he placed the guns in the ferryboard. As he went to move them an explosion occurred. One barrel entered his abdomen & he expired a few moments afterwards. He was a youth of much promise, the pride of his school-fellows & the joy & hope of devoted parents. -Cumberland Journal [No death date given-current item.]

The Detroit Tribune states that the wife of Horace Wilson, of Quincy, Branch Co, Mich, died last Sunday from the effects of chloroform, administered to her by Dr Berry for the purpose of extracting a tooth.

Died: on Mar 21, at his town residence, in Balt, Edw Gray, in his 80th year. He was a native of Ireland, but removed to the U S in his boyhood, & spent the greater part of his long life in Md, chiefly at Ellicott's Mills, where he was during many years extensively & successfully engaged in manufacturing pursuits.

Died: on Mar 22, in Wash City, Capt Benedict J L Railey, formerly of St Mary's Co, Md, but for the last 13 years a resident of Wash City. His funeral is on Monday at 2 o'clock, from his residence on Va ave, near 3rd st, Island.

Real Estate & Conveyance Ofc: French S Evans has opened at ofc, at his residence 520 north M st, to attend to claims of every description. He will also attend to the purchase & sale of Bounty Land Warrants.

For sale or rent, that valuable property known as Neale's Wharf, at the foot of South Capitol st, on which there is a dwlg & store-room. Apply at the counting-room of Stanislaus Murray, 57 Louisiana ave. -John E Neale

We offer our Drug Store for sale on reasonable terms. -R C Dyson & Co. Apply to W H Gilman, corner 4½ st & Pa ave, or as above.

Orphans Court of Wash Co, D C. Letters of administration on the personal estate of Wm P Ford, late of Buenos Ayres, South America, deceased. -P R Fendall, adm

TUE MAR 25, 1856
Superior Holland Gin at auction: on Mar 24, at the risk & expense of a defaulting purchaser, at the store formerly occupied by J T Neale, on 7th st. -C W Boteler, auct

Senate: 1-Memorial from Cmders Cadwalader Ringgold & Geo Adams, of the navy, complaining of the action of the Naval Board. 2-Ptn from Jos L Smith, asking that public documents printed by order of Congress may be furnished to each of the common schools & school districts throughout the U S. 3-Ptn from Dorcas Cary, asking to be allowed a pension. 4-Memorial of Jonas P Levy: to be referred to the Court of Claims. 5-Cmte for D C: bill for the relief of Michl Nash, of D C: to be printed. 6-Cmte on Indian Affairs: asked to be discharged from the consideration of the memorial of Lewis Campau. Same cmte: asked to be discharged from the consideration of the memorial of Dent, Vantine & Co, & that leave be granted to withdraw their papers: agreed to. 7-Cmte on Pensions: asked to be discharged from the consideration of the ptns of Jas Davidson & Martha Morris, & that the former be referred to the Cmte of Claims & the latter to the Cmte on Public Lands: agreed to. Same cmte: asked to be discharged from the consideration of the ptn of J L Elliott: agreed to. Same cmte: bill for the relief of Rebecca Halsey, widow of Zephaniah Halsey, an ofcr in the Revolution, with a report, ordered to be printed. 8-Cmte on Military Affairs: bill for the relief of John Tucker: passed. 9-Cmte on Naval Affairs: bill for the relief of Saml Forrest. Same cmte: adverse reports on the ptns of: Susannah Coddington; of John Woodworth; of Reuben Clough; & of Joshua Webb.

Valuable lots in square 375, in Wash City, for lease. The subscriber, duly authorized by the Orphans Court of Wash Co, D C, invites proposals for leasing for a term of 10 years the said lots belonging to the estate of the late Arthur Middleton: fronting on G & H sts, between 9th & 10th sts. -Rd Smith

Orphans Court of Wash Co, D C. In the case of Eliz Connolly, admx of Owen Connolly, deceased, the administratrix & Court have appointed Apr 15 next for the distribution of the personal estate of the said deceased, of the assets in hand.
-Ed N Roach, Reg/o wills

Mr Wm J Hatch, of Camden, N J, came to his death near that place on Sunday by violence. He pursued 3 German men who were trespassing on his father's farm, shooting birds. When he got close to them, one of the men shot him through the left temple, killing him instantly. They were Adolphe Delso, Jos Erben, & Jacob Linhart. His father had been fired at by a man who was shooting on his premises without leave, several years ago, & rendered a cripple for life. The Jersey farmers suffer greatly in their crops & fences from depredations committed by gunners from Phil. [Mar 27th newspaper: Wm J Hatch came to his death from a gun discharged in the hands of Jacob Lenairs; August Arnable Courcier was accessory & Adolphe Delascule a witness. The names of the parties were not correctly given on Tue.]

House of Reps: 1-Bill introduced for the relief of the heirs of the late Capt Geo Jacksen. 2-Cmte on Revolutionary Claims: bill for the relief of the distributees of Col Wm Linn, with amendments.

The Gallatin Argus states that on Friday last, at the store of Mr Allman, he was smoking in the store-room, & passed over a keg of powder, dropping fire into it, & it exploded. The house was leveled to the ground. Mr Allman was killed immediately & Mrs Allman was rescued from the ruins, hurt, but not dangerously.
-Natchez Courier, 18th

Mrd: on Mar 23, in Wash City, by Rev S A H Marks, Wm Moulder to Miss Mary C Crosby.

Mrd: on Mar 4, in Smithfield, Isle of Wight Co, Va, Mr Rowland D Buford, of Bedford Co, to Miss Josephine Victoria, daughter of Willis Wilson, of the former place.

Mrd: on Mar 19, at Spring Grove, by Rev Mr Stewart, Mr Saml Lockwood, of Niagara Co, N Y, to Miss Louisa J, daughter of Edw Bates, of Fairfax Co, Va.

Died: on Mar 23, in Wash City, Sister Mary Angela, known as Henrietta Martina Dyer, 2nd daughter of the late Edw Dyer, in her 20th year. Her funeral will take place at the residence of John F Boone, 447 8th st, between E & F sts, on Wed at 9 o'clock.

Died: on Mar 23, Edw G Handy, son of Edw G & Isabel Y P Handy, aged 11 years & 1 month. His funeral is today at 2 o'clock.

Died: on Mar 24, Jessie Bright, aged 1 year & 7 months, eldest child of Robt S & Mary Frances Sproule. His funeral will be this evening at 4 o'clock, from 355 F st.

Died: on Mar 20, in Fredericksburg, Va, Evalyn Wallace, infant daughter of Joshua T & Maria L Taylor, of Wash City, aged 1 month & 15 days.

WED MAR 26, 1856
On Mar 15, while the steamboat **Alabama** was on her upward trip from New Orleans to Minden, her boiler blew up some 5 miles about Grand Ecore, killing T S Bell, first clerk; S Parker, watchman; H M Prothro, passenger; Jos Ogden, assist engineer; C Butler, deck hand; Patrick Kelly, Tim Flaherty, Stephen McDonough, & John Laughlin, firemen.

Household & kitchen furniture at auction on: Mar 31, at the residence of Mrs Ladd, corner of north B & 1st st east. -Jas C McGuire, auct

Desirable property on the Heights at public auction: on Apr 1, the property lately occupied by Mrs Dr Gunnell, on 7th st, with a new & modern built dwlg, with back-bldg, & a pump of water. -Edw S Wright, auct

Premptory sale of valuable real estate in Gtwn, D C: by decree of the Circuit Court of Wash Co, D C, the subscriber will offer at public auction, on Apr 24, lot 16, in the original plan of Gtwn, part of the estate of Wm Nelson, late of Fairfax Co, deceased. This lot lies between Bridge & Prospect sts, & fronts 65 feet on each street, having a depth through from street to street of 240 feet. There is on it a large 3 story brick house, built for a tavern. -John Marbury, trustee -Edw S Wright, auct

Senate: 1-Memorial from Horatio Stone, sculptor, proposing to execute & erect within the Capitol a statue to represent "The Republic." 2-Ptn from Archangel Le Croix, asking compensation for property destroyed by the enemy during the last war with Great Britain. 3-Ptn from Henry L Rogers, asking the establishment of a uniform code of marine signals. 4-Memorial of the heirs of Saml Hammond was withdrawn & referred to the Cmte on Revolutionary Claims. 5-The reps of Moses Shepherd had leave to withdraw their petition & papers. 6-Cmte on Finance: asked to be discharged from the consideration of the memorial of Jas Morrow, & that it be referred to the Cmte on Foreign Relations: agreed to. 7-Cmte on Private Land Claims: to which was referred the resolutions of the Legislature of Michigan in relation to claims to lands of Jos Sansfacon & others, reported a bill appointing com'rs to ascertain facts relative to private land claims in the State of Michigan. Same cmte: bill for the relief of Cezarie Wallace, of the parish of Bossier, La. 8-Cmte on Naval affairs: adverse report upon the memorial of Wm Merrill: ordered to be printed.

A Lady in charge of a U S Fort. Lt Montgomery, of the U S Army, not long since lost his life in the service in Oregon. His death left his widow, formerly Miss Northrop, of Akron, & one child, in comparative penury, as is generally the case with those who devote their lives to their country's service. She returned, & Gen Jesup, with the kindness of heart of chivalry, immediately gave to her the trust of **Fort Gratiot**, now occupied by a garrison-a duty which she can fulfil, & the pay of which is very fair.

House of Reps: 1-Bill for the relief of Antoine Robedeau: referred. 2-Cmte on the Judiciary: asked that the bill for the relief of the reps & sureties of Robt King, deceased, be put upon its passage. 3-Ptn of Ezekiel Bowman, Jas C Conkling, B S Edwards, Jas Peters, & 20 other citizens of Springfield, Ill, asking the aid of Congress in construction of a Pacific railway: referred.

U S Patent Ofc, Wash, Mar 25, 1856. Ptn of J N & S W Lesh & Z Beeson & D Bowman, administrators of Jacob Deardorff, deceased, of Wayne Co, Indiana, praying for the extendion of a patent granted to them on Jun 27, 1842, for an improvement in the steam generator for 7 years from the expiration of said patent, which takes place on Jun 27, 1856. -Chas Mason, Com'r of Patents

Orphans Court of Wash Co, D C. In the case of Martha Wailes, admx of Isaac H Wailes, deceased, the administratrix & Court have appointed Apr 19 next, for the settlement of the personal estate of the deceased, with the assets in hand.
-Ed N Roach, Reg/o wills

The packet-ship **Germania**, Capt Wood, arrived at N Y on Sunday from Havre. On Feb 28 a ship's boat was seen ahead of the **Germania**. Inside the boat were found one living man & 4 dead bodies, one of the latter being that of a female. The survivor, Thos W Nye, of New Bedford, sat amid the dead, frozen in his hands & feet, & himself nearly dead from starvation. They were all that remained above the waters out of 13 who 9 days before had left the wreck of the ship **John Rutledge**, Capt Kelly, of N Y. On Feb 19th the **John Rutledge** encountered an iceberg, which stove a hole in her bow & she was a complete wreck. They had sailed from Liverpool on Jan 16. The mate, Mr Atkinson, went down with the wreck & Mrs Atkinson perished. The owners of the **John Rutledge** are Messrs Howland & Ridgeway, of N Y. The ship was built in Balt some 4 or 5 years ago, & is insured here for $70,000, while her cargo, consisting of 800 tons of merchandise, was insured in Europe.

Desperate affray on Sunday, in which Robt Childrey was killed & Geo S Butt & Thaddeus Butt were wounded. A strong feeling of animosity had for some time existed between Childrey & the young Butts, his step-sons, because of alleged maltreatment of their mother, the wife of Childrey. Childrey received a knife would which proved fatal. The Butts were stabbed but they should recover.
-Eliz City [N C] Democrat

Orphans Court of Wash Co, D C. Letters of administration on the personal estate of Patrick Magee, late of Wash Co, deceased. -Mary Magee, admx

Farm for sale in Alexandria Co, Va, 4 miles from the Long Bridge, 85 acres of improved land, with a good dwlg house & all other necessary out-bldgs. Inquire of Albert Gardiner, on the premises, near Ball's Cross Roads, or of the subscriber, 496 11th st, Wash. Title indisputable. -F A Tschiffely

THU MAR 27, 1856
The Marlboro Gazette states that Geo P Tiffany, has purchased the site of the old factory destroyed by fire a few months since at Laurel, & has contracted for the immediate construction of a new bldg of the same description: 4 story stone bldg, with a front of 50 feet & a depth of 300 feet, with all the modern improvements.

Handsome private residence at public auction: on Apr 2, 9th & E sts, recently occupied by W C Zantzinger, being lot 10 in square 407, fronting 50 feet on E st by 75 feet on 9th st, with a well finished 3 story brick dwlg house & a brick stable.
-Jas C McGuire, auct

Senate: 1-Memorial from Francis A Cunningham, paymaster in the army, asking to be released from responsibility for a sum of public money of which he was robbed while stationed at Santa Fe, New Mexico. 2-Memorial from Isaac H Sturgeon, assist treasurer of the U S at St Louis, Mo, asking the reimbursement of money paid by him for clerk hire, & to be allowed an additional clerk in his ofc. 3-Memorial from Anthony G Robinson, heir-at-law of Dr Jno Hamilton Robinson, asking the appointment of a new commission for the re-examination of his & other claims against the Mexican Gov't rejected by the late Board, & the provision may be made for the payment of such claims as may be found to be legally due. 4-Ptn from Eliza E Ogden, widow of a deceased paymaster in the army, asking to be allowed a pension. 5-Ptn from Wm Bell, asking to be allowed a pension for the time he received his wound. 6-Papers withdrawn from the files: those of R L Blair; of Jno Erick; & of the widow of Geo Wood. 7-Cmte on Private Land Claims: bill for the relief of Jos Smith; & bill to confirm Jos Wandestrand in his title to certain lands. 8-Cmte on Indian Affairs: bill for the relief of Wm B Trotter, asking additional compensation for subsisting emigrating Choctaw Indians. Same cmte: bill for the relief of Randall D Livingston. Same cmte: bill for the relief of Cephise Piseros, widow of Louis Labranche, of the parish of St Charles, in the State of Louisiana. Same cmte: bill for the relief of Richd Albritton: recommended its passage.

Miss Martha Burwell, of Bottetourt Co, Va, recently deceased, emancipated 13 slaves, & made provision for their removal to Liberia.

The Circuit Court on Thu took up the case of Eliz Campbell vs A LaGrange for breach of promise & seduction. The parties reside in New Scotland, N Y. The plntf is a fine looking woman about 20 years of age. The dfndnt is a bachelor, said to be worth $30,000. He not only denied the paternity of Miss Campbell's child, but sought to fasten it on an innocent person, a gentleman with whom she formerly resided. The jury returned a verdict of $9,000 for the plntf, one of the heaviest ever given in this State. -Albany Knickerbocker

<u>Oysters for Families.</u> Turtle, mock turtle, beef & all other soups at the usual prices. -J Wm Coke & Co, Proprietors, corner 6th & Pa ave.

$100 reward for runaway negro man Jim Johnson. -Eliz Walker, living in PG Co, Md.

Commencement ceremonies on Mar 25, of the Medical Dept of Gtwn College. The graduating class consisted of Messrs J H Jordan, of Va; F S Barbarin, of D C; J H Malone, of Ireland; C J P Girard, of France; & C M Hammett, of Md. Prof Flodoardo Howard, Dean, read the commission authorizing Gtwn College to confer the degrees of Medicine Doctor, which were then conferred by Rev Bernard A Maguire, Pres of that College.

Mrd: on Mar 25, in Wash City, by Rev Mr Hildt, Mr Peter Miller, of Anne Arundel Co, Md, to Miss Mary Dukehart, of Balt.

Mrd: on Mar 25, in Wash City, at the Western Presbyterian Church, by Rev T N Haskell, T W Johnson to Miss Frances L Earle, both of Wash.

Died: on Mar 25, in Wash City, Wm F Hamill, in his 76th year, a native of Limerick Co, Ireland, & a resident of Balt for 25 years, but for the last 4 years a resident of Wash City. His funeral is this afternoon at 3 o'clock, from his late residence, 519 I st north, between 6th & 7th sts.

Died: on Mar 25, in Wash City, Mrs Ellen Lucas, aged 73. Her funeral will take place at 2 o'clock today, from 10th & Pa ave.

Died: on Mar 23, at Jacksonville, Fla, whither he had gone for the benefit of his health, Isaac Munroe Chubb, of Wash City, aged 32 years. He was a native of Richmond, Va, & came to this city as a clerk in the house of Corcoran & Riggs 15 years ago, & has resided here ever since, for several years as the head of the house of Chubb Brothers. His death is lamented by a large circle of attached friends.

Died: on Mar 4, at Vincennes, Indiana, Jno R Jones, late register of the Land Ofc, aged 37 years.

Died: on Mar 22, in Balt, Miss Juliana M A Calvert, of Mount Airy, PG Co, Md.

FRI MAR 28, 1856
Senate: 1-Memorial from Wm B Todd, Geo Parker, P R Fendall, & other citizens of Wash, representing that the appropriations made by Congress for the completion of Indiana ave were insufficient for that purpose & the necessity of an early additional appropriation for finishing the bridge across the Tiber river & completing said avenue to the intersection of C st. 2-Ptn from Jane Stanbraugh, widow of a Revolutionary soldier, asking a pension. 3-Ptn from Mary F Henderson, only surviving child of Joseph Henderson, asking to be allowed bounty land in consideration of the services of her father during the war of 1812. 4-Ptn from Catharine E McKnight, asking a pension in consequence of her husband having been killed by an accident while in discharge of his duty as an artificer. 5-Cmte on Milirary Affairs: bill for the relief of Mrs Agatha O'Brien, widow of Brvt Major J P J O'Brien, late of the U S army. 6-Cmte on Public Lands: bill granting bounty land to Rebecca Freeman. 7-Cmte on Pensions: bill granting a pension to Nathl Mothershead. 8-Cmte on the Judiciary: bill for the relief of Adam D Steuart. 8-Cmte on Military Affairs: bill to authorize the Sec of War to cause to be paid to Capt Geo E McClelland, & the ofcrs & men composing his company of mounted volunteers, full pay for services rendered & subsistence & forage purchased in East Florida in 1840.

House of Reps: 1-Cmte on Indian Affairs: bill authorizing a settlement of the accounts of Chas P Babcock, late Indiana agent at Detroit, Mich: committed.

This is to certify that the original Land Warant, No 1,816, issued to Archibald Rose on account of his services as a sergeant of the Va State Line by the State of Va in the war of the Revolution, is lost, & that at the expiration of 3 months, application will be made to the U S Pension Ofc for the issue of scrip, pursuant to an act of Congress of Aug 31, 1852, on a duplicate of said warrant. -Jas Parker, Notary Public & Atty for the heirs.

Mr Thorington, of Iowa, has been suddenly called away from his seat in the House of Reps, & will be absent a couple of weeks. He has paired off with Mr Miles Taylor, of Louisiana. On Tue last Mr Thorington received the news from his brother, John H Thorington, that his nephew, E H Bradley, was in the last stage of consumption, & could not live but a few days. The second was from his brother-in-law, J M Parker, of the banking-house of Cook, Sargent & Parker, of Rock Island, that Mr John H Thorington, referred to above, had on that day been knocked down in their banking house [for whom he was a clerk] choked until he was insensible, & the house itself robbed of $3,000. Mr Thorington left in the cars on Wed for Rock Island, the scene of this double affliction.

Died: yesterday, in Wash City, Maj Chauncey R Johnson, a veteran of the war of 1812. He served on the Northern frontier during the war of 1812-15 as a non-commissioned ofcr, & was at the battle of Plattsburgh in Sep, 1814, as sgt-major of the 31st U S Infty. He was a brave man, a good citizen, & an exemplary Christian. He will be buried from the Assembly's Presbyterian Churcy [Rev Mr Carother's,] corner of I & 5th st, this afternoon, at 2 o'clock. Members of the Associated Soldiers of the War of 1812 of D C are to attend the funeral of Maj Johnson, a member of the association, at his late residence, on the west side of 11th st west, between H & I, at 1 o'clock this afternoon.

Died: on Jan 3, in Yadkinville, N C, Cynthia S, wife of Robt Williams, & daughter of the late Col John Williams, of Tenn, in her 32nd year. She has left a heart-stricken husband & 3 children, with a wide circle of relatives & friends, to mourn their separation from her.

Valuable farm in Alexandria Co for sale: by deed of trust from Peter Davis & wife, dated Jul 2, 1855: public auction on Apr 15 next, a tract of land containing 142 acres in said county, on the Columbia Turnpike road. Improvements consist of a good dwlg house & stable. Mr Peter Davis, who resides there, will show the land.
-Law B Taylor, trustee

At the late term of the U S District Court for the district of Missouri, Judge Wells presiding, the following were convicted for mail robberies: Chas J Gilbert, for stealing U S Mail, sentenced to 5 years in the penitentiary; Jos Clark, for like offence, 2 years; John Baker, for receiving letters & packages stolen from the mail, 2 years; John Johnson, for receiving U S mail as the driver of a mail stage & deserting the mail, was fined $50.

Dissolution of the firm of Johnson, Guy & Co, by mutual consent. -R C Johnson, B F Guy, W J Sibley. The business will hereafter be conducted by Wm J Sibley & B F Guy.

SAT MAR 29, 1856

The will of the late Mr Thos Cubitt is one of the longest on record, & extends to 386 Chancery folios, covering 30 skins of parchment. The personal estate exceeds L1,000,000; the scale of probate duty stamp being L15,000; the widow has an immediate bequest of L20,000, & an annuity of L8,000.

Chancery sale of valuable real estate on E st, between 14th & 15th sts, by decree of the Circuit Court of Wash Co, D C, made in the cause wherein Thos R Bird is cmplnt & Jas C McGuire, adm, & Rebeecca C Brown & Jos Brown, widow & heir at law of John D Brown & Alice C Brown, deceased, are dfndnts: public sale on Apr 22, on the premises, lots 3 & 4 in square 226, fronting on E st, with a small frame dwlg house, frame workshop, & lumber shed. -Chas S Wallach, trustee -J C McGuire, auct

The Phil papers state that Mr Buchanan, the American Minister, has sent home from London an original portrait of John Hampden, the celebrated English patriot, who was one of the first to resist the encroachments of the Stuarts, & to assail the prerogatives of the Crown in the great struggle for the popular rights which led to the establishment of the English Commonwealth. This portrait belonged to Mr John Macgregor, member of Parliament for Glasgow, & is presented by him, through Mr Buchanan, to the U S Congress. It is said to be one of the only two original portraits of Hampden now in existence.

The Lexington Observer & Reporter of Mar 16 advertises a public sale to be held at the residence of Cassius M Clay, in Madison Co, Ky, consisting of land, cattle furniture; also, about 22 slave, men, women, & children-which will be sold during said Clay's life.

Died: on Mar 27, in Wash City, after a few hours' illness, Ida M, infant daughter of Benj & S A Beall. Her funeral will take place from her father's residence, La ave, today at 3:30 P M.

The man named Russell, who was arrested a few weeks since on the charge of assaulting, with intent to kill, a storekeeper named Tubman, at Leonardtown, in Md, & robbing him, was brought before the court of that county on Fri last. He pleaded not guilty, but the proof being positive, withdrew his plea & entered another of guilty. He was sentenced to the penitentiary for 10 years. The stolen money was recovered. -Balt Clipper

Trustee's sale: by decree of the Circuit Court of Montg Co, Md, in a cause in said court pending, in which Robt Y Brent & others are cmplnts & Harriet Brent & others are dfndnts: public sale on Apr 23 next, on the premises, all the right, title, claim, & interest of Robt Y Brent, late of said county, deceased, in & to the farm known as the *Highlands*, it being the late residence of said deceased, & composed of a part of a tract of land called *Joseph's Park*, containing 400 acres. The dwlg house is 2 stories high, with kitchen, servants' quarters, smoke-house & ice-house. Apply to Mr W C Brent, on the premises. -John Brewer, Geo Peter, trustees

MON MAR 31, 1856
The station at Big Bend, having been abandoned several weeks previous, the Indians made a sudden attack on Feb 23, upon the farms, where some 10 or 12 men of Capt Poland's company of volunteers were encamped. The farmers were all killed. It is supposed there are now about 300 hostile Indians in the field, including those from Grave & Galaise creek & the Big Meadows, led by a Canada Indian named Enos, who was formerly a favorite guide for Col Fremont in his expeditions. Killed were: Capt Ben Wright, H Braun, E W Howe, Mr Wagnor, Barney Castle, Geo McClusky, Mr Lara, W R Tullus, Capt John Poland, Mr Smith, Mr Seaman, Mr Warner, Jno Geisell & 3 children, P McCullough, S Heiderick, Jos Seroc & 2 sons. Mrs Geisell & daughter are prisoners in the hands of the Micano band of Indians. Dr M C White escaped by jumping into a creek & hiding until the Indians gave up the search.

Superior cabinet furniture, French plate mirrors, silver-plated ware, choice old wines & liquors, table & mantel ornaments, & furniture for sale on Apr 18 next, at the residence of the late Russian Minister, A de Bodisco, Second st, Gtwn. The house will be open for visitors on the day previous to the sale. -Jas C McGuire, auct

Rev N S Prime, D D, died suddenly on Thu, in his 71st year. He was distinguished as an able preacher & earnest writer, & was well known as author of a History of Long Island, of which he was a native, having been born at Huntington in 1785. -N Y Com Adv

Died: on Mar 30, in Wash City, aged 13 months & 13 days, William Edwin, infant son of Wm E & Sarah Nott. He will be buried this evening, at 4 o'clock, from his father's residence on 9th st, between I & N Y ave.

Two persons of wealth & position, F B Morton & R T Morton, of Whateley, Mass, were tried last week in the Court of Common Pleas of Franklin Co, Mass, for abducting Isaac T Sheldon, a nephew of the former & grandson of the latter, & conveying him to Wisconsin, beyond the custody of his legal guardian, Harvey Kirkland, of Northampton, Mass. Young Sheldon is but 10 years old, perfectly blind, without father or mother, brother or sister, & the heir of property left by his parents to the amount of $50,000 on the death of his father in 1852. Mr Kirkland was appointed guardian of the children by consent of all parties. In 1855 the mother placed the boy in Dr Howe's Asylum for the Blind, South Boston, & a few months afterwards she & her little daughter died, leaving the boy without an immediate relative. When he attended his mother's funeral, he was conveyed to Wisconsin by his uncle, to get him out of the custody of Mr Kirkland. There the uncle was appointed guardian by one of the Wisconsin courts. The indictment was quashed. He still remains under the guardianship of Mr Kirkland.

Died: on Mar 23, at Jacksonville, Fla, Isaac Munroe Chubb, in his 32nd year. His funeral will be today at 2 P M, from his late residence, 139 F st.

Died: Mar 28, in Wash City, Jas Albert Burch, in his 23rd year. His funeral will be from the residence of his father, Fielder Burch, 14th st, between E & F sts. [No date given for the funeral.]

Circuit Court of Wash Co, D C-in Equity. Thos Sewell et al vs John Brereton's adms & heirs at law. An account to be taken of the personal estate of John Brereton deceased; account of the debts owing; & what real estate he left in this country: order to be executed at my ofc on Apr 9, City Hall. -Walter S Cox, Special auditor

Circuit Court of Wash Co, D C-in Equity. C H E Richardson vs Nicholas Gassaway, Lavinia Peter, Geo Peter, Alex'r Darnes, Mary Darnes, John H Gassaway, Jane H Gassaway, Wm A & Laura Gassaway. The bill states that one Robt J Allen, at Oct term, 1849, obtained a judgment for $149.19 against Hanson Gassaway, deceased, which was subsequently entered to the use of cmplnt, & which is unsatisfied; that Gassaway, having purchased several lots of ground, had them conveyed by an absolute deed to E M Linthicum, to secure a debt due to E M Linthicum & Co; that the property is more than sufficient to pay said debt, & there is a valuable equity of redemption in the property liable to said Gassaway's debts; that he died intestate, leaving no personal property, & said real estate descended to his heirs at law, who are the above dfndnts, excepting said Geo Peter & A Darnes; that the said real estate consists of lots 7 & 9 in Davidson's subdivision of square 367, lot I & K, in Wilson's & Callan's subdivision of part of same, & lot 6 & part of 2, in square 2, in Washington. It prays a sale of said real estate for the payment of cmplnt's claim & others. Absent dfndnts to appear in this Court on or before Aug 15 next.
-Jno A Smith, clerk

Died: on Mar 20, at the residence of her mother, Mrs Rebecca Pinkney, in the city of Balt, Eleanor Davidson.

TUE APR 1, 1856
Trustee's sale: by decree of the Circuit Court of Wash Co, D C, passed in a cause, wherein Geo McCallion & others are cmplnts, & Jos Peck, John Walker, & others are dfndnts: auction on Apr 24 next of two undivided third parts of lots 7, 22 thru 25, & 27, in square 106, in Wash City, upon which are several good dwlg houses.
-W Redin, Chas S Wallach, trustees -A Green, auct

Senate: 1-Ptn from Gotleib Kruman, asking to be allowed the right of pre-emption to a tract of land upon which he had settled. 2-Cmte on Naval Affairs: memorial of John Guest, asking compensation for surveying the coast between Apalachicola & the Mississippi, submitted a report, with a bill making a reappropriation from the surplus fund for the relief of John Guest & others. 3-Cmte of Claims: bill for the relief of Peter Grover. 4-Cmte on Military Affairs: bill for the relief of Mary McKnight, widow of Francis M McKnight, an artificer accidentally killed. 5-Cmte on Pensions: bills for the relief of Levi C Harris; of Betsy Whipple; increasing pension of Albert Hart; restoring Joshua Mercer to the roll of invalid pensions; increase the pension of Alpheus T Palmer, late a lt in the 9th regt of U S Infty; & a pension to Saml B Porter, a soldier in the late war with Great Britain. 6-Cmte on Pensions: adverse reports on the following petitions: of Jesse Barker; of Thos Coward, a lt on board the privateer **Chasseur**; of John Lamothe; of Lyman Treat; of Gitty Powers, of N J; & that of Lucy Bingham. Same cmte: asked to be discharged from the consideration of the ptn of Enoch S Moore: agreed to. 7-Cmte on Pensions: bill to increase the pension of Amaziah Goodwin. Same cmte: adverse report on the ptn of Abel Jackson, heir of Stephen Jackson. Same cmte: adverse reports on the following ptns: of Martha Stanton; of Nathan Cook; of Leslie Combs; of Mrs Mgt C Hanson; of Zachariah Corbin; of Robt Morton; of Wm J Sears; & of John Allen, asking a pension or tract of land for extraordinary bravery displayed in a conflict with the enemy during the war of 1812.

Household & kitchen furniture at auction on: Apr 15, at the residence of the late Lewis Smith, deceased, at High & West sts. -Barnard & Buckey, aucts

House of Reps: 1-Cmte of Claims: bill for the relief of West Drinkwater & others: committed. Same cmte: bill for the relief of the heirs & legal reps of Col Chas Simms, late Collector of the port of Alexandria; & a bill for the relief of Peyton G King, late receiver of public money at Monroe, La: committed. 2-Cmte on Commerce: bill for the relief of Wm Humphreys, jr, owner of the fishing schnr **Good Exchange**: committed. Same cmte: adverse reports on the ptns of John H Russell; & of the crew & owners of the schnr **Lapwing**.

The steamboat **Metropolis**, which left Pittsburgh on Tue last for New Orleans, burst one of her boilers at West Columbia on Thu. Out of 11 persons injured 9 had died, among whom were Capt E Z Hazlett, cmder of the boat, Mr Jas Roberts, a jeweler of Pittsburgh, & Mr Bryan, son of Rev A M Bryan, who, with his family, was moving to Memphis, Tenn. Mr Metz & Mr North, residence not given, are also among the dead. The **Metropolis** was a new boat, out on her first trip. It is said that her boilers were defective.

Mrd: on Mar 31, in Wash City, by Rev Dr O'Toole, S R Sylvester to Margaret, 3rd daughter of Mr Jas , all of Wash City.

Died: on Mar 30, after a long & painful illness, Rachael W, 3rd daughter of Robt & Sophia A Cohen, in her 24th year, leaving 2 small children to mourn their irreparable loss. Her funeral is this afternoon at 3½ o'clock, from the residence of her father, 418 6th st, between F & G sts.

Died: on Mar 31, of consumption, Marion W Hinton, in her 17th year, only child of the late Robt W & Emeline Hinton. Her funeral is this afternoon at 3½ o'clock, from the residence of her uncle, G W Hinton, 246 G st, between 17th & 18th sts.

Circuit Court of Wash Co, D C-in Equity. The Farmers' & Mechanics' Bank of Gtwn, D C, against Edw Dawes & Richd Smith. The dfndnt, Edw Dawes, being indebted to the Bank of the U S in the sum of $7,200, & to the cmplnts in the sum of $1,740, no divers notes drawn by said Dawes in order to secure the payment of the said debts or any debt due to the cmplnts not exceeding $2,000, by his deed dated Feb 23, 1831, conveyed divers tracts of land to the dfndnt, Richd Smith, & his heirs, in trust to sell the same, & apply the proceeds of such sales, pro rata, to the payment of the said debts; that the said Dawes enlarged his debt to the cmplnts to the sum of $2,000, as was contemplated & agreed by the parties at the date of said deed; that the said Smith has from time to time made sale of the property in the said deed mentioned for the objects contemplated thereby, & has received the purchase money; that there is in fact owing in arrears & unpaid to the cmplnts the full sum of $1,610, principal money, part of the said original debt, the payment of which is secured to them by said deed, with a large arrearage of interest thereon; that the cmplnts have from time to time applied to the said Dawes & to the said Smith, his trustee, to account for the proceeds of the said trust estate, & to be paid their pro rata portion thereof; that the said Smith has not rendered such account, or paid to the cmplnts any part of the proceeds of said sales, alleging that the said Dawes denies that the debt due the cmplnts & claimed by them is part of the debt secured by said deed; the cmplnts allege that the debt now owing to them by the said Dawes, & claimed by them of said Smith, is in fact part of the original debt, & the payment thereof is secured by the said deed. The object of the said bill is to have the cmplnts said debt established by a decree of the said Court; to have an account of the proceedings of the said Richd Smith, in the

execution of the trust confided to him by the said deed; to ascertain the portion of the trust found in his hands to which the cmplnts are entitled, & to have a decree against said Richd Smith that he pay the same to the cmplnts. Edw Dawes is not a resident of D C & cannot be served with the process of this Court. He is to appear in person or by solicitor on the first Monday of Sep next in the clerk's ofc of this Court.
-Jno A Smith, clerk

For sale, or exchange for Wash City property, about 100 acres of land in Fairfax Co, Va, in the vicinity of the grist & saw mills of Messrs Barcroft & Cloud. This place borders on Home's Run, which empties into the Potomac. Apply at 496 H st, corner of 8th, of the subscriber. -J Terrett

I have this day, Apr 1, brought out all the interest of Geo W Garrett in his stock & fixtures of his carpenter business, as carried on by him in his shop, between 3rd & 4½ sts. I shall continue the carpenters' business in all its branches at the same place.
-Henry A Garrett

Orphans Court of Wash Co, D C. Letters testamentary on the personal estate of Chas Morris, late of Wash Co, deceased. -Robt H Ives, exc

Obit: died on Mar 23, at Jacksonville, Fla, Isaac Munroe Chubb, in his 32nd year. As a son or father, husband or brother, his true affection was displayed. Mr Chubb has grown up among the people of Wash, known to all from earliest boyhood. He was in the warmer climate for his health, but in vain. The sorrowing mother, his only companion, returned with the body of her son to the bosom of his heart-broken family.

WED APR 2, 1856
Extensive sale of young trees, on Apr 5, in front of the Auction rooms. They were raised by Jas Maher, public gardener, at his private nursery. -Jas C McGuire, auct

Senate: 1-Ptn from Michl R Clark, of Mississippi, asking an increase of pension on account of wounds received in the late war with Mexico. 2-Ptn from Emma A Wood, asking compensation for the services of her deceased husband as a surgeon in the military service of the U S. 3-Ptn from A L Mason, guardian of J Duncan Mason, asking to be allowed a pension on account of the military services of his father. 4-Bill for the relief of Timothy Cavan: introduced.

House of Reps: 1-Cmte on Public Lands: adverse report on the ptns of J A Ragan & Absalom Boyd. 2-Cmte on the Post Ofc & Post Roads: act for the relief of Jas M Goggin: committed.

Another Revolutionary soldier gone. On Mar 23 Capt Josiah Parris, father of Hon Virgil D Parris, died in Buckfield, Maine, aged 95 years & 7 months. When but about 16 years old he enlisted in the army of the Revolution, & served through 6 campaigns. He was with Gens Greene & Sullivan in the battle at Rhode Island, Aug 27, 1778, & was supposed to be the last survivor of that hard-fought contest.

Tragedy in Scotland. At Dingwall, Rosshire, Scotland, last month, 3 men were poisoned at a private dinner party, given by John McIver, Provost of Dingwall. The maid servant went to the garden for some radish for the roast beef, & through a mistake, took monkshood root to the cook. The party consisted of Lewis M Mackenzie, of Findon; the Rev Messrs Mackenzie, of Eskdale, & Gordon, of Beauty, Roman Catholic priests; & John Macdonald of Torridon. Shortly after dinner the party fell sick. Before medical assistance could be brought the Rev Mr Mackenzie & the Rev Mr Gordon & Mr Mackenzie, of Findon, had expired.

Select School will open on Apr 7, at the house of the subscriber on L st between 9th & 10th sts. He feels that 12 years' experience as a teacher in the State of Maine qualifies him for the discharge of his duties. -Wm J Purington

Mr T F Gaszynski, Prof of Dancing, will instruct at Mr Carusi's Saloon. Mrs Gaszynski will assist him. Please address him through the post ofc.

Lost Land Warrant: No 38, 89_, for 120 acres, paid to Iver D Patterson, Mar 3, 1855, deposited in the post ofc in Wash Feb 20, 1856, addressed to the Hon Thos A Hendricks, Com'r of the Gen Land Ofc. A caveat has been filed against the issuing of a patent for said warrant, & an application will be made for a duplicate.
-J M Clarke & Co

I will sell the Farm on which I live at private sale: contains about 150 acres, on the Gtwn & Rockville turnpike, about 4 miles from Gtwn; dwlg house & out-houses upon the farm are commodious & in good order. The dwlg is new & spacious.
-Geo R H Marshall, near Tenallytown, D C.

Died: on Mar 31, in Wash City, Jos Howard, formerly of Ohio, & a member of the Senate of that State, but for several years past a resident of Wash, in his 58th year. His funeral will take place this morning, at 10 o'clock, from his late residence, 553 13th st, Island.

Norfolk, Va, Apr 1. Cmdor Isaac McKeever died this morning. He entered the service Feb 1, 1809, & received his commission of captain Dec 8, 1838.

THU APR 3, 1856
Senate: 1-Court of Claims report: adverse to the claims of Cyrus H McCormick & Wm W Cox, & in favor of the claim of Asbury Dickins & Jas H Lindsay, accompanied by a bill for their relief. 2-Ptn from the citizens of Hawkins Co, Tenn, asking that Jas Francisco may be allowed arrears of pension. 3-Cmte on Commerce: bill for the relief of Saml A Morse & others, reported it back with amendments. 4-Cmte on Foreign Relations: joint resolution allowing Dr E K Kane, & the ofcrs associated with him in their late expedition to the Arctic seas in search of Sir John Franklin, to accept such token of acknowledgment therefore from the Gov't of Great Britain as it may please to present. Mr Mason cited the case of Lt Maury, to whom a gold medal had been presented by the King of Sweden, & that ofcr had the permission of Congress to receive it, in 1854. To be considered.

Thos McDonald has been committed to jail at Indianapolis on a charge of robbing the mail at Michigan city. McDonald was the watchman at the ofc of the railroad where the mails were left when the trains failed to connect. This happened on Wed. The ofcrs had counted the mail & placed it where it could be seen if it was disturbed. They had hardly concealed themselves before they heard a window raised, & McDonald was caught. They searched his house & found a mail bag full of opened letters. His wife showed the ofcrs a trunk in which the plunder was concealed. McDonald was shipped for Indianapolis next morning, & committed to jail in default of $5,000 bail.

Hon Thos H Bayly reached Petersburg with his family from Charleston on Friday last. He is sojourning at the residence of his father-in-law, Judge May, where he will remain for some weeks. His health though still very feeble, is improved.
-Petersburg Dem

Suicide. Mr Jos Knox, who had stopped at the Judson House, Fla, hired a horse & buggy on Mar 19, & drove into the woods & shot himself. His brother keeps the Nat'l Hotel in Boston. During the day he gave Mr Salisbury, the superintendent of the Judson House, $1,000, & told him he thought he should not live but a short time, & said he had a mother in Boston, & that he wished him to send the money to her.

Mrd: on Apr 2, in Wash City, in the new Baptist Church, by Rev Dr Teasdale, Mr Palin Harris Sims to Miss Frances Rebecca Padgett, all of Wash City.

Died: on Apr 1, in Wash City, Mrs Ann Eliz Morgan, in her 64th year. Her funeral is this morning at 10 o'clock, from her late residence, on 11th st east.

Died: on Apr 1, in Gtwn, Otho M Linthicum, in his 61st year. His funeral is today at 4 o'clock, from his late residence, Third st.

Died: on Apr 2, in Wash City, of croup, Virginia, infant daughter of Richd M & Edmonia Heath, aged 14 months.

Wash City Ordinance: 1-Act for the relief of John N Lovejoy: the sum of $100 be paid to him as indemnity for excess of benefits assessed against him for opening & paving the alley in square 285.

Tudor for rent: this well known & beautiful residence is offered for Rent for a term of years. The house is one of the most spacious in this District, is on the Heights of Gtwn, & within the corporate limits. The premises contain between 7 or 8 acres of ground. And for sale a tract of land containing about 40 acres in Wash Co, a few hundred yards from Boundary st, & all of lot 303 in Wash City. Also, a handome bldg lot on the Heights of Gtwn, on the north end of ***Tudor Place*** square, containing a fraction less than 2 acres. -N Callan, Notary Public, 213 F st.

FRI APR 4, 1856
Senate: 1-Ptn from the widow of Chas Newbold, asking a grant of land as a remuneraion for the valuable services rendered & sacrifices of her late husband in discovering & bringing into use the cast-iron plough. 2-Ptn from Wm L Davidson, asking compensation for the distinguished military services of Gen Wm Davidson during the Revolution. 3-Ptn from Katy Vass, of Tenn, asking that the pension of her deceased husband may be increased, & the same continued to her. 4-Ptn from Jos L McDonald, asking compensation for his services as consular agent at the port of Powis, Prince Edward Island, in the Gulf of St Lawrence. 5-Cmte of Claims: bill for the relief of Saml V Niles. Same cmte: bill for the relief of Abraham Kintzing. 6-Cmte on Revolutionary Claims: bill for the relief of Hannah F Niles, with a report. 7-Memorial from Tench Tilghman, asking reimbursement of expenses incurred for outfit as U S Consul to Mayaguez, in the Island of Porto Rico, which consulship was abolished while he was on his way to take charge of his ofc. 8-Memorial from Gabriel Bradford, asking to be allowed a pension on account of a disease contracted while in discharge of his duty as a soldier. 9-Cmte on Private Lands Claims: bill for the relief of Wm Marvin, of Fla. Same cmte: asked to be discharged from the consideration of the memorial of the heirs of Lt Saml White, of the war of 1812, asking to be allowed bounty land to which their father was entitled, but died before receiving, & that it be referred to the Cmte on Public Lands: agreed to.

Great event of the day was the birth of an heir to the French throne. The Empress Eugenia gave birth to a son on Mar 16, 1856; health of her Majesty & the condition of the infant Prince are perfectly satisfactory. The name bestowed on the infant, Napoleon Eugene Louis Jean Joseph, fils de France, was entered in the parish register & signed by the Emperor.

House of Reps: 1-Bill granting lands to Jonathan Lambert, of Darke Co, Ohio: introduced. 2-Cmte on the Judiciary: bill for the relief of Christian Hax, of the State of Md. Mr Hax was a foreigner, naturalized in 1838 in the District Court of the U S at Balt. The clerk had recorded his name erroneously, & such time had elapsed that the judge did not think he had the right to change the record; the bill was to authorize the correction to be made: passed. 3-Bill directing payment of arrearages of pensions due Simon Smith, deceased, late a pensioner of the U S, to his heirs at law: referred. 4-Cmte on Revolutionary Claims: adverse report on the ptn of W D C Heard. Same cmte: bill for the relief of John Crawford: committed. Bill authorizing the legal reps of Manuel Gonzales Moro to enter certain lands in Missouri: referred. Bill for the relief of Jos Richards, of Berks Co, Pa: referred. Bill to authorize the legal reps of Pascal Le Cerre to enter certain lands in the State of Missouri. 5-Ptn of Stephen H Weems, of Md, late U S Consul at Guatemala, Central America, praying Congress to grant him compensation for services of a diplomatic character rendered by him & not covered by his consular appointment. 6-Memorial in behalf of Wm F Lynch, cmdr in the U S Navy, praying that Congress may allow to him the same compensation for the exploration of the Dead Sea which was allowed Lts Herndon & Gibbons for the exploration of the Amazon.

Died: on Mar 30, at Frankfort, Ky, in full assurance of a blissful immortality, John Nourse, formerly a clerk of the Treasury Dept.

Circuit Court of Wash Co, D C-in Equity. Edw Lockett, Henry D Johnson, & Jas G Berrett, vs John Pemberton, Liquidator of the Merchants' Ins Co. John Pemberton, in his capacity of liquidator of the said insurance company, established in the city of New Orleans on Dec 23, 1851, was the owner of a certain claim against the British Gov't for the value of certain slaves freed from the American brig **Creole** at Nassau, in the island of New Providence, in Nov, 1841, which slaves were liberated by acts of British functionaries, & the value of which slaves was afterwards paid for to the owners of the same by said insurance company; that the British Govn't having refused to allow said claim, the said John Pemberton, as liquidator, on Dec 23, 1851, executed & delivered an agreement in writing to said Lockett, Johnson, & Berrett promised, in consideration of services rendered & to be rendered by them in the prosecution of said claim, to allow them one half of any or all sums of money, principal or interest, which might be recorded on account of said claim. Convention was made on Feb 8, 1853, between the U S & Great Britain for the adjustment of claims. On Jan 9, 1855, the com'rs being unable to agree to said claim, the umpire selected by them awarded to said John Pemberton, liquidator, upon the claim, the sum of $28,460; & that the same has been placed in the hands of Hon Wm L Marcy, of Wash, for payment to the parties entitled to the same; & it states that without the exertions used by said cmplnts said award would not have been made, & that the cmplnts have received no compensation for their services & expenses in this behalf. The bill prays that a writ of injunction may be granted enjoining & commanding the said Pemberton & his attys not to demand & receive one-half of said award, & enjoining Hon Wm L Marcy from paying one-half of said award to other persons than the cmplnts, & prays that the Court will decree that one-half of said award, subject to the deductions prescribed by said convention be paid to said cmplnts, & that damages be paid to said cmplnts by said Pemberton; & it states that said Pemberton resides out of D C. Absent dfndnt to appear in this Court, in person or by solicitor, on or before the third Monday of Oct next. -Jno A Smith, clerk

SAT APR 5, 1856
Trustee's sale of valuable farm, on the turnpike road leading from Wash to Bladensburg, at auction: on May 7, on the premises, by deed of trust from Geo W Bowie & wife to the subscribers, dated Feb 24, 1854, recorded in Liber J A S No 74, folios 484 thru 489, of the land records of Wash Co, D C: part of a tract called ***Haddock's Hills***, part on Wm Hickey's line, formerly Wm Brent's line; containing 68 acres & 25 poles, more or less, except a small portion of said land which was conveyed to Wm Hickey, by Edw & Henrietta, by deed dated Sep 24, 1844, recorded in the land records of Wash Co, D C, in Liber W B, No 113, folios 30 to 32. Also, all that part of a cleared lot of land, number 5, in a division of a part of ***Haddock's Hills*** & enclosure, according to a survey, plat, & division of the same, heretofore made for & by the heirs of Richd Queen, deceased. -Benj Beall, Jos C G Kennedy, trustees -A Green, auct [Jul 17th newspaper: ***Haddock's Hills*** is advertised for sale again. The former purchaser having failed to comply with the terms of sale, we shall proceed to resell at his risk & cost, on Aug 4, 1856.] [Oct 17th newspaper: Trustee's sale of valuable farm, on the Turnpike road leading from Wash to Bladensburg, at auction. The former purchaser failed to comply with the terms of the sale; we shall proceed to resell, at his risk & cost, on Oct 27, 1856, on the premises.
-Benj Beall, Jos C G Kennedy, trustees -A Green auct]

On Sat Ephraim Whitehead, a boy 8 years old, son of R Whitehead, a poor man living on land of & in the vicinity of the residence of T Bolton, near Euclid road, was sent by his parents into a wood lot adjoining the premises of Wm Rogers to pick up chips. At noon he had not returned, & search being made he was found lying upon his face, almost lifeless, his clothes torn off & bites all over his body. Asked if dogs had done this, all he could reply was yes, & he died in a few minutes. -Cleveland Herald

House of Reps: 1-Bill for the relief of Mary Harris, widow of Newsom Harris, deceased, for services in the Revolutionary war: referred. 2-Bill for the relief of the heirs at law of Henry McGuire, deceased, for services in the Revolutionary war. 3-Cmte on Naval Affairs: bill granting a pension to Ansel Wilkinson: committed. 4-Cmte on Military Affairs: bill for the relief of Geo K McGunnegle, surviving partner of the firm of Hill & McGunnegle, of St Louis, Mo: committed. Same cmte: adverse report in the case of Levi Forbes.

Princess Royal of England, now in the 16th year of her age, is betrothed to Prince Frederick of Prussia, a young gentleman some 9 years her senior, & that they will be married probably in the course of the current year. Prince Fred'k Wm Nicholas Charles of Prussia was born on Oct 1, 1831, & is in his 25th year. He is the eldest son & heir of Fred'k Wm, Prince of Prussia, brother of the King, & heir to the throne. It is projected if the marriage takes place, that some time in the not far distance, the throne of Prussia will be occupied by a Princess of England. The young lady, Her Royal Highness Victoria Adelaide Maria Louisa, Princess Royal of England, was born at Buckingham Palace on Nov 21, 1840, & baptized on Feb 16 following. She was to be confirmed at Windsor Castle on Thu, the 20th ult. -N Y Post

Senate: 1-Ptn from the regt of drafted militia under the command of Lt Col John S Eddy, requesting to be placed on the same footing as other State troops during the war of 1812. 2-Ptn from Dr Moses Carter, who was captured by the enemy while serving as a surgeon on board a private-armed vessel during the war of 1812, asking a pension in consequence of infirmities growing out of his captivity. 3-Ptn from Mrs Augusta Ladd, asking indemnity for damages done to her property in Wash City due to a change of the grade of the streets on which it fronts by a surveyor acting under the authority of the U S. 4-Cmte on Public Lands: memorial of certain citizens of Ohio asking that a grant of land might be made to Jos McCunne for services of his father during the war of 1812: made an adverse report on the same.

For sale: a desirable country residence near Wash, between Piney Branch road & Rock Creek, near Maj Blagden's, formerly Mr Bodisco's place, containing 30 acres, more or less; having 2 new frame cottages, outbldgs, & other improvements. Title indisputable. -Saml D Finckel

Tribute of Respect: Princeton, N J, Mar 24, 1856. At a meeting of Whig Hall, on Mar 21, regarding: God in his wisdom has removed from earth Saml S Force, a graduate of the American Whig Society. Copy of the resolutions to be sent to his family & to be published in the Nat'l Intell. -John M Parker

Mrd: on Apr 3, in Wash City, by Rev Mr Boyle, Chas G Mauro, of St Louis, Mo, to Miss Charlotte E, daughter of Geo M Davis, of Wash City.

Mrd: on Apr 3, in Wash City, by Rev Mr Cummins, Richd Wallach to Rosa, daughter of Marshall Brown, all of Wash City.

Mrd: on Mar 27, at Terre Haute, Indiana, by Rev Mr Leach, Thos Dowling to Miss Sallie J Sibley, all of that place.

Mrd: on Apr 3, in Wash City, by Rev W Krebbs, Wm Trueman to Martha Ann Elliott, all of Wash City.

Died: on Apr 3, in Wash City, Mr Richd Purdy, in his 38th year. His funeral will be on Apr 6, at 3 o'clock, on 3rd st, between F & G Sts.

Died: on Apr 3, aged 55 years, John Keys, a native of Wexford Co, Ireland, but for the past 6 years a resident of Wash City. His funeral will be on Sat at 3 o'clock, from his late residence, corner of 27th & K sts.

MON APR 7, 1856
Household & kitchen furniture at auction on: Apr 14, at the residence of Thos Ewbank, on the east side of 6th st, between E & F sts. -Jas C McGuire, auct

Sale by order of the Orphans Court of Wash Co, D C: on Apr 15, of the stock of jewelry, silver ware, glass cases, fixtures, & tools of the late Robt Keyworth, in his late establishment on Pa ave, near 9th st. -Jas C McGuire, auct

Mrd: on Apr 3, in Wash City, by Rev G W Samson, Mr John Caperton, of Calif, to Mrs Mary E Coke, daughter of Hon Jas Guthrie, Sec of the Treasury.

Mrd: on Apr 3, at N Y, by Rev E Neville, D D, Lt Wm Lewis Maury, U S Navy, to Anne F, 2nd daughter of the late Wm Maury, of Liverpool.

Mrd: on Apr 3, at Upper Marlboro, Md, by Rev B J Maguire, Pres of Gtwn College, Mr P H Hooe, of Wash, to Miss Mary Augusta, daughter of C C Magruder.

Mrd: on Mar 26, in Macoupin Co, Ill, by Rev Mr Carroll, of Alton, Plutarch Dorsey, of that State, to Miss Olivia Williams, of Wash City.

Died: on Apr 6, Catherine, wife of Geo Vonderlehu, in her 60th year. Her funeral will be this morning at 9 o'clock, from her late residence 319 5th st, between I & K sts.

Died: on Apr 5, Ann C, beloved wife of Parker H Sweet, of the Gen Land Ofc. Her funeral is this afternoon at 3 o'clock, from the McKendree Chapel, on Mass ave, between 9th & 10th sts.

N Y, Apr 6. Gov Clark yesterday pardoned Dr Graham, of New Orleans, sentenced to be imprisoned for 7 years for killing Col Loring at the St Nicholas Hotel, in this city, some time ago.

TUE APR 8, 1856
By decree of the Circuit Court of Wash Co, D C, in the case of W S Nicholls against Jas B Frere's heirs, auction on Apr 26, of lot 14 in square 86, in Wash City, D C: fronting on north side of K st, 47 feet. -Jno Marbury, trustee -Jas C McGuire, auct

Chancery sale: by decree of the Circuit Court of Wash Co, D C, made on Dec 4, 1855, wherein Chrisopher S O'Hare & al are cmplnts, & Mary M Prather, admx, & al, heirs at law of Overton J Prather, deceased, are dfndnts: public auction on May 1 next, of lot 60 in square 448, & part of lot 12 in square 447, with improvements thereon. Lot 12 fronts on 7th st, between N & O sts, & lot 60 fronts on 6th st, between M & N sts. -A Austin Smith, trustee -A Green, auct

Senate: 1-Memorial from Lt E Lloyd Winder, of the navy, asking to be allowed the difference between full pay & leave of absence pay during the time he was detached from the ship in consequence of the accidental breaking of his arm. 2-Ptn from Don Piatt, asking compensation for services as Sec of Legation & as Charge d'Affaires at Paris during the sickness & absence of the Minister. 3-Ptn from Edw Ballard, asking to be allowed depreciation on the commutation pay of his grandfather, of the Revolutionary army. 4-Cmte on Military Affairs: bill for the relief of A S Bender. 5-Cmte on Pensions: adverse report on the ptn of Maria Price, asking a pension on account of the services of her husband in the war of 1812.

House of Reps: 1-Bill for the relief of Fred'k Stephens for services rendered in the late war with Great Britain: referred. 2-Bill for the relief of Hyacinth Riopell & others, heirs & assigns of Ambroise Riopell, deceased: referred. 3-Bill for the relief of the heirs of Jas Witherell: referred. 4-Joint resolution giving the consent of Congress to the acceptance by Lt Maury of certain medals presented by the King of the Netherlands & others. 5-Cmte on Patents: discharged from the consideration of the ptn of John A & Hiram A Pitts, & it was laid on the table.

Jefferson Co, Va, Apr 2,1 856. Davy Hall, aged 8 years & 9 months, only son of David C Hall, was accidentally shot & killed by a playmate, who did not know the gun he had picked up in the corner of the room was loaded. He now rests beside his mother, leaving a bereaved father.

Trustee's sale of handsome cottage & ground corner of 26th sts & Pa ave. Public auction on May 13 next, on the premises, by deed of trust executed by Chas Van Patten to me, recorded in liber J A S No 85, folios 167 & 168. Also, lots 6, 7, & 9 in square 14, with a cottage residence & out-bldgs. -G W Phillips, trustee -J C McGuire, auct

Died: on Apr 6, in Wash City, Mrs Mary H Fowler, wife of Henderson Fowler, & daughter of the late Henry Teachem, in her 42nd year. Her funeral is this afternoon at 2 o'clock, from her late residence, 717 3rd st, between L & M sts.

Died: on Apr 7, in Wash City, Francis Byrne Callan, youngest son of Nicholas & Christina V N Callan. His funeral will be today at 4½ o'clock, from the residence of Mr Callan, 213 north F st.

An old Calif family. Important case, involving land titles, was commenced yesterday in the Supreme Court. Don Jose Dario Arguello went to Calif in 1775, a lt in the Spanish army, & one of the pioneer chiefs chosen by Viceroy of Mexico for the purpose of reducing the Indian territory to the Spanish Crown, & protecting the missionary establishments to be founded there for the conversion & civilization of the Indians. The port of San Francisco was his destination. He established it as its commandant, the first military post, & hence the first settlement of white people that was founded on the waters of that bay. He served 40 years in this capacity. In 1815 he was transferred to Lower Calif, as general commandant & governor of that province, in which he continued till his death, about 1828. His son, Don Luis Antonio Arguello, succeeded in the command of the Presidio of San Francisco. He entered the army as a cadet in 1799; in 1805 was promoted to a lieutenancy, & afterward to a captaincy. He served as cmder at San Francisco till 1822, when a delegate from the new Empire of Mexico arrived in Calif to demand the formal transfer of the allegiance of the inhabitants. Arguello had early declared in favor of the revolution, & through his influence the Govn'r, Don Pablo de Sola, had also done so. The allegiance of the whole province was consequently declared transferred from Spain to the Mexican empire; Sola was elected a delegate to the Congress which was called to meet in Mexico; & Arguello was made governor & cmder of the province in his stead. In 1825 Don Luis had a distinction which has not happened, either before or since, to an ofcr commanding on the Calif coast, namely, to receive the capitualation of vessels of war. On Apr 27, 1825, the Spanish line-of-battle ship **Asia**, of 74 guns, & the brig **Constante** were driven into Monterey by stress of weather, & there capitulated to Govn'r Arguello-an event which concluded the Spanish war on that coast. Don Luis died at San Francisco in 1830, leaving his widow, Dona Soledad Arguello, & an infant family, who are the cmplnts in the present case. The property in question is alleged to have come into the family in the time of the founder, Don Jose Dario Arguello.

Mr Geo Punhard has retired from all business & editorial responsibility in the Boston Traveller, leaving the paper with an ample list of subscribers & advertisers.

We learn from the Ouachita Register that Mr T B Carrington, editor of the El Dorado Union, was shot & instantly killed in Camden, Ark, on Mar 17. He had called on Mr Jones & demanded of him satisfaction for alleged calumnies reflecting upon his character through the medium of the latter's paper. Jones refused to listen to Carrington. A fight ensued on the street, with Carrington firing 3 shots at Jones, which did not take effect, & Jones returned the fire, killing him instantly. Mr Carrington was a brother-in-law of Hon Albert Ruse, member of Congress from Ark, & leaves a young wife to mourn his death.

For rent, the house in *Gadsby's Row*, recently occupied by Capt Magruder, U S Navy. Apply at the corner of Lafayette Square & H st.

Eugene Pierce, aged about 8 years, an adopted child of Mr Leonard Prather, living on I st, was yesterday severely injured by a dog, a bull-terrier, belonging to Mr Prather. The child was running away from some one of the family who was in pursuit & ran near where the dog was chained. The dog sprang upon him & seized & held him by the thigh. Mr Hood, a neighbor, compelled the animal to desist by thrusting his arm down its throat. Dr Johnston was summoned to the aid the child, whose sufferings are very severe.

WED APR 9, 1856

Thos Allen Tidball, for nearly 30 years the popular & efficient Clerk of Fred'k Co, Va, died at his residence in Winchester on Apr 5.

Mr Wm M Ellis, formerly for many years the able & respected chief of the steam-engine shops in the Wash navy yard, has for some time past carried on the same business on his own account in Wash City, in connexion with his worthy brother, Jonas B Ellis, who was also, during 18 years, an engine builder & machinist in the navy yard. This firm has, in addition to other work, turned out no less than 12 steam engines of different sizes the last year, one of which, now nearly ready, is to stand in the large grist mill of Messrs Duncanson & Coltman, on Ohio ave, near 12th st. It is of 80 horse power.

John Fitzgerald, who deliberately murdered his own father, his mother, & his brother, some months ago, was hung at Auburn, N Y, on Saturday last.

Senate: 1-Memorial from Maj W W Morris & 20 other ofcrs of the U S Army, complaining of the insufficiency of the present army ration, & asking its increase to forty cents. 2-Memorial from the firms of F W Browne & Sons, Jno S Williams & Brother, Jas Hooper & Sons, & other merchants & shipowners of the city of Balt, urging the establishment of a marine hospital at that place. 3-Ptn from Geo G Henry, asking the passage of a law authorizing the Com'r of Patents to grant him a patent for 50 years for a valuable discovery. [He is solely in possession of a design, which from its nature he cannot here describe, that will be of great value to the human family.] 4-Memorial from Jos E Holmes, asking an appropriation to enable him to institute full & throrough investigation into the causes of the explosion of steam-boilers. 5-Cmte on Revolutionary Claims: bill for the relief of the heirs of Maj Saml Scott. 6-Cmte on Military Affairs: bill for the relief of F A Cunningham, Paymaster U S army. 7-Cmte on Revolutionary Claims: reports on the following petitions: of Thos A T Reiley; of Bracket Leavett; of Wm Allen, grandson of Jonathan Allen, deceased; & of the executor of Carter Page, asking to be discharged from the further considerationof the same, & that the petitioners have leave to withdraw their papers. Same cmte: adverse reports on the following petitions: of Mrs A E Donoho, on behalf of her mother, Sophia Turner; of Lucy Tate, & of Peter Van Buskirk: ordered to be printed.

The Columbus [Geo] Enquirer notes the arrival in that city, on Apr 3, of Mr Jefferson Buford, from Alabama, with a company of 70 men for Kansas. He was joined by 30 more from S C under Mr Bell, of that State. The party of about 130 departed from Columbus on Apr 4 by railroad, the company having given them a free passage.

House of Reps: 1-Memorial of Francis M Hodge, E C Beckwith, & others, in favor of the construction of a railroad to the Pacific. 2-Ptn of Wm E Lukins, J Wallace, Geo C Eaton, & 20 other citizens of Putnam, Muckingum Co, Ohio, asking the impeachment of Judge J K Kane, of Pa. 3-Ptn of Isaac Scaggs & other citizens of PG Co & Montg Counties, Md, praying Congress to make free that portion of the Balt & Wash turnpike road which lies within the limits of D C by purchasing the same.

Skilly & Sawny Procter, the Cherokee Indians tried & convicted of the murder of Milford Sumner at the last term of our Circuit Court, were executed on Mar 14, according to the sentence of the law. The prisoners acknowledged from the stand their guilt, & pronounced the sentence just & merited. -Van Buren [Ark] Intel, 22nd.

The Austrailia Times of Dec 3, printed at Ballarat: burned on Dec 1 in the fire of the U S Hotel in that town, & other bldgs, was Albion H Nichols, landlord of the U S Hotel. He was rescued from the burning bldg badly injured & died the same day. Mr Nichols went from Boston, & has a widowed mother, a sister, & brothers, who reside in Temple st. -Boston Courier

Mrd: on Apr 7, in Montg Co, Md, by Rev W L Childs, Henry L Bird, of Pa, to Eliz J Eld, of Montg Co.

Died: on Apr 7, in Wash City, Robt E Birnie, in his 22nd year. His funeral will take place today at 3 o'clock, from his father's residence, 55 Pa ave.

Died: on Apr 9, in Wash City, in her 27th year, Mrs Fanny Perkins, wife of John R Mitchell, & daughter of Dr John W Gantt, of Albemarle Co, Va. Her funeral is today at 5 o'clock, from her late residence on G st, between 8th & 9th sts.

THU APR 10, 1856
Household & kitchen furniture at auction on Apr 11, at the residence of the late John Devlin, on 12th st, between H & N Y ave. -Jas C McGuire, auct

Trustee's sale of valuale real estate: by two deeds of trust from Jas A Wise & Harriet Ann Wise, his wife, dated Apr 7 & Sep 8, 1855, duly recorded: public sale on May 13, on the premises, of part of lot 12 in square 429, on 7th st, with 3 story brick dwlg house. -Chas S Wallach, Jno C C Hamilton, trustees -Jas C McGuire, auct

Senate: 1-Ptn from Thos R Carman, a soldier of the war of 1812, asking a pension. 2-Additional papers in relation to the claim of the heirs of Jas Bell, deceased: submitted. 3-Cmte on Revolutionary Claims: bill for the relief of Eliz V Lomax, surviving child of Capt Wm Lindsay, of the Revolution. 4-Cmte on Pensions: bill for the relief of Lewis Wooster; & for relief of Danl Doland. Same cmte: adverse reports on the following petitions: of Catharine Jacobs, widow of Francis Jacobs, a waiter in the military household of Gen Washington; of Dorcas Carey, widow of of a soldier of the war of 1812; of citizens of DeKalb Co, Ala, in favor of a pension to Sarah Benge, & of Philemon Bacon. Same cmte: ordered to be printed: petition of Jas Francisco; of John Burkhalter; of Mrs Alison Logan; of Ebenezer Hitchcock; of Mrs Mary Bennett; of Michl R Clark; of Lucinda Peters; of Wm Patterson; & of Chas A Seefeld. 5-Bill for the relief of Christian Hax, of Md: referred to the Cmte on the Judiciary. 6-Cmte of Claims: for payment of Saml P Todd, John Shaw, of Wisc, & Isidore D Beaugrand. The Cmte of Claims amemded the bill so as to allow Saml P Todd interest from Dec 31, 1839.

On Tue, Geo W Hayden, a young man, a native of England, aged 21 years, employed in the clock dept of Ball, Black & Co, Broadway & Murray st, decamped with about $40,000 or $50,000 worth of his employer's diamonds & jewelry. He had been engaged with the firm for over 2 years to repair & put up clocks. He was arrested on the street & sent to the Tombs & committed for trial. -N Y Courier

Mrd: on Apr 8, in Wash City, at the Second Baptist Church, by Rev Mr Greer, J Frank Brown, of Balt, to Frances M, daughter of Dr Chas W Davis, of Wash City.

Mrd: on Apr 7, in Wash City, by Rev Dr Gurley, Mr Geo W Duval, of Wash City, to Miss Martha A, daughter of Asher D Bennett, of Montg Co, Md.

Iron fronts for store. Jacob Baily, Manufacturer of Iron Store Fronts, Columns, Girders, Window Heads & Sills: Foundry, Broad st, Phil.

FRI APR 11, 1856
For sale: that valuable square of ground, in the 4th Ward, Wash City, known as *Middleton Square*, numbered 624. The owner, being about to leave the country, now offers the property at a very low price. Inquire at the Ofc of the Gas Light Co, Pa ave & 8th st.

Capt Walter M Gibson, so generally known for his imprisonment in Netherlands India, & his escape therefrom, delivered a lecture in Balt on Tue last, to a large audience, on the geography, history, & pecularities of the Indian Archipelago. -Patriot

Wm F Morrill, depot & ticket master at Augusta, Maine, [says the Eastern Argus,] was arrested on Sat last in that city, on complaint of Hon Virgil D Parris, U S Post Ofc Agent, for robbing the mail of a package containing 4 land warrants, worth about $700. He was brought to Portland on Monday & taken before John Rand, U S Com'r. He waived an examination, & gave sureties in $2,000 for his appearance on Apr 23 before the U S District Court in Portland.

Senate: 1-Ptn from Harrison Sargent, a volunteer in the war with Mexico, asking to be allowed a pension. 2-Cmte on Public Lands: adverse report on the memorial of the heirs of Saml White. Same cmte: asked to be discharged from the consideration of the memorial of Wm Carey Jones, asking compensation for services as confidential agent of the U S to investigate titles to land in Calif: be referred to the Cmte of Claims: agreed to.

A friend of Mr Saml Bronbert, our late Consul at the free city of Hamburg, placed in our hands copies of the letters [Hamburg, Feb 24, 1853] soliciting the re-appointment of Mr Bromberg, as Consul for this port. Hamburg, Mar 1, 1856. Letter to Saml Bromberg, late U S Consul at Hamburg, from Wm Gossler: I am indeed very sorry having missed the opportunity of bidding you good-bye before you left our city.

U S Patent Ofc, Wash, Apr 9, 1856. Ptn of Stephen K Baldwin, of Gilford, N H, praying for the extension of a patent granted to him Jul 16, 1842, for an improvement in machine for cutting shoe pegs, for 7 years from the expiration of said patent, which takes place on Jul 16, 1856. -Chas Mason, Com'r of Patents

SAT APR 12, 1856

The Naval Medical Board convened at Phil on Mar 1st last, & reported the following Assist Surgeons in the navy for promotion:

Wm F Carrington	Saml F Coues	Jenks Harris Otis
Jas Suddards	Chas F Fahs	Fred'k Horner, jr
Jas F Heustis	Jacob S Dungan	
Arthur Lynah	Geo Peck	

The following, arranged in the order of their relative merit, were found qualified for the ofc of Assist Surgeons of the navy:

1-H A F Washington, of Wash.	5-Albert C Gorgas, of Pa
2-Richd C Dean, of Pa.	6-Alex'r M Vedder, of N Y.
3-H Lawrence Sheldon, of Conn.	7-Delavan Bloodygood, of N Y.
4-Philip S Whales, of Md	

A little girl, the daughter of Alonzo Clemens, some time during the day, on Mar 30th, took a mixture of cobalt, used for the purpose of poisoning flies, mistaking it for syrup. She died in a few hours. -Whitehall [N Y] Chronicle

We learn from the Rochester American that Dr F V Hayden, of that city, has just returned from a scientific exploration of the region of country surrounding the headwaters of the Missouri river, which has never before been visited for scientific purposes. He was absent for 2 years, & reports the country quite sterile, but very fruitful in objects of natural history. He spent 2 months among the Crow Indians picking up shells & Saurian remains. -Boston Journal

Elan P Littlefield, the Surveyor at Block Island, died Tue night, & within 24 hours afterwards 3 boat loads of sturdy Islanders arrived here to try for the ofc. It is thought that the island will be depopulated unless the vacancy is filled within 48 hours. -Newport News

Miss Cloyes was very serverely, if not fatally, injured Tue last, at Framington Centre, attempting to step from one car to another at the moment the train started. She fell between them & her right hand was completely torn off & one leg badly broken. She is 18 years of age, & was a daily passenger in the train, & for some time past has attended the school of design in this city. -Boston Transcript

On last Sat a son of David Huckelbury, of Craig Township, Switzerland Co, Indiana, in crossing a field, was attacked by a vicious horse, who with his teeth tore him & with his feet stamped him until life was extinct. His mother saw the transaction, & was so much excited that she swooned, & was carried into the house in a helpless condition. She died in a few hours. -Louisville Democrat, Apr 4

Senate: 1-Memorial from Henry Addison, Judson Mitchell, & Robt Ould, a cmte of the Corp of Gtwn, setting forth that the commerce of said town has been much injured in consequence of the accumulation of mud & other deposites in its harbor & channel, & very respectfully urging an appropriation of $5,000 for the removal of the same. 2-Ptn from Olivia W Cannon, widow of an ofcr of the U S navy, asking to be allowed a pension 3-Ptn from Geo W Gordon, asking the passage of a law to authorize the assignments made to him of certain warrants for land, he not being able to perfect his title to the same owing to the negligence of the Com'r of Pensions. 4-Cmte on the District of Columbia: memorial of John M Gilbert & others, asking that the direction of Delaware ave as laid down in the plat of Wash may be changed; & the memorial of Dr Storrow, asking the establishment of a hospital in D C: adverse report on the same. 5-Cmte on Private Land Claims: adverse report on the memorial of Susan Marlow. 6-Bill for the relief of the legal reps of John Morrison & Chas Ginn. 7-Bill to confirm the title of Henry Volcher to a certain tract of land in the Territory of New Mexico. 8-Bills passed-relief of: Capt Langdon C Easton, assist quartermaster U S Army; relief of Levi Robinson; pension to Benj Berry, a soldier of the Revolution; relief of Hall Neilson; relief of the heirs or legal reps of John Metcalf; relief of Isaac Cook & others; relief of John Y Laub, a clerk in the ofc of the First Comptroller of the Treasury; relief of Amos B Eaton, a commissary of subsistence in the U S Army; relief of the owners & sharesmen of the fishing schnr **Wanderer**, schnr **Mary**, schnr **Olive Branch**, schnr **Two Brothers**, & schnr **Brothers**. Relief of the owners of the fishing schnr **Brandywine**, schnr **Forrester**, schnr **Grampus**, schnr **Ursula**, schnr **Stephen C Phillips**, & the schnr **Union**. Also, relief of Dempsey Pittman; of Jas Harrington; of Joshua Shaw, of Bordentown, N J; of John H Scranton & Jas M Hunt; of Josiah S Little; of Rebecca Halsey, widow of Zephaniah Halsey, an ofcr of the Revolution; of Saml Forrest; of Michl Nash, of D C; of Cezaire Wallace, of the parish of Rossier & State of Louisiana; of Richd Albritton; of Jos Smith; of Wm B Trotter; of Randall D Livingston; of Cephise Piseros, widow of Louis Labranche, of the parish of St Chas & State of Louisiana; of Adam D Steuart; of Nathanl Mothershead, of Mo. Also a bill to confirm Jos Wandestrand in his title to certain lands. Also a bill to authorize the Sec of War to cause to be paid to Capt Geo E McClellan, his ofcrs & men, composing his company of mounted volunteers, full pay for services rendered & subsistence & forage furnished in East Fla in 1840. 9-Bills passed: relief of Mrs Agatha O'Brien, widow of Brvt Maj J P J O'Brien, late of the U S army; granting bounty land to Rebecca Freeman; relief of Peter Grover; pension to Albert Hart; relief of Levi C Harris; relief of Betsey Whipple; bill restoring Joshua Mercer to the roll of invalid pensions; & to increase the pension of Alpheus D Palmer, late a lt in the 9th regt U S infty. Bill making a re-appropriation from the surplus find for the relief of Lt John Guest, U S navy, & others; bill to increase the pension of Amaziah Goodwin, of the State of Maine; relief of Mrs M E McKnight, widow of Francis M McKnight; & granting a pension to Saml B Porter, a soldier in the last war with Great Britain. 10-Bill for the relief of Saml Morse & others [providing payment for capturing a British armed vessel during the war of 1812] gave rise to some discussion: pending.

A McScarlett, of Noble Co, Indiana, living near Wolf Lake, last week, accidentally shot & killed himself last week.

Charlotte Spineberg, aged 20 years, died at Balt on Thu by the discharge of a pistol in the hands of a boy named Wm Kuhlman. She arrived in this country from Germany a short time since, & some 7 months ago went to live in the family of Mr Yeakle, a butcher. The boy Kuhlman, an adopted son of Yeakle, while playing with a pistol, the cap discharged & the contents penetrated the right temple of Miss Spineberg. She lived but a few hours. -Clipper

On Sunday last the barn & stable of Mrs M F Weems, near Hunting Creek, Calvert Co, Md, with their contents, were destroyed by fire. Loss upwards of $3,000. No insurance.

Mrd: on Apr 10, in St John's Church, Gtwn, D C, by Rev T G Dashiell, of Westmoreland Co, Va, D F S Barbarin to Rebecca M, eldest daughter of Anthony Hyde, all of Gtwn.

Yesterday watchmen Mockabee & Elliott perceived a light in the shoe store of Mr Thos J Forrest, on Pa ave, near 12th st. Washington Naylor, a well-known blacksmith of Wash City, was found lying concealed upon the floor. His confederates had fled. Naylor was taken to the watch-house, & discharged in the morning by Capt Birch upon giving a bond, conjointly with John Mammack, his brother-in-law, in the sum of $500. His confederates were John Ray & Henry Croggan, who were found to have a quantity of stolen goods, & were committed to prison. Washington Naylor in the mean time disappeared. Mr Bushrod M Reed has identified some of the articles as being a portion of property stolen from him on Dec 23 to the amount of $250. The property of T G Forrest; of Mich Hoffer, jeweler; of G W Hinton; of M E Eckloff; of Nicholas Singer; of W T Bedinger; & of Jos Anker, was also identified in the stolen property. John W Demaine, who slept upon the premises of Mr Forrest as a guardian of his property, was arrested yesterday & committed to prison-stolen property was found on his person. The parents of this young man are worthy & respectable people. John E Baily, a few months ago appointed a constable for this county, was committed to jail. Stolen articles were found on his premises & person. [Apr 14th newspaper: Call Armstrong, a blacksmith in the First Ward, was on Sat arrested on suspicion of being a participant in the late acts of burglary in Wash City.]

Died: on Apr 11, in Wash City, of brain fever, Addie S Skirving, aged 3 years & 27 days, daughter of John & Fannie E Skirving. Her funeral is tomorrow afternoon at 3 o'clock.

Died: on Apr 11, in Wash City, William Ewing Harris, son of Rev Wm A Harris, in his 7th year. His funeral is today at 2 o'clock.

Mrd: on Apr 10, in Wash City, in his 32nd year, Arthur Lunt. His funeral is tomorrow at 2 o'clock P M, from the residence of Mrs Randall, on D, between 9th & 10th sts.

MON APR 14, 1856
Jos Roach, a stage driver, was taken to St Louis on Apr 7 charged with robbing the mail in Saline Co, Mo. He confessed his guilt & was committed to jail.

For several months the steamer **Columbia** has been hauled up in the ship-yard of Messrs Flannigan & Beacham, where extensive improvements have been made. The entire hull has been lengthened 25 feet, power overhauled & improved, & the decks painted & decorated. The joiner's work was done by Mr Geo Morris; painting by Mr Jos B Jenkins; carpeting of Gable, McDowell & Co; upholstering by Walter Crook, jr; plumbing by Mr Danl McCann. Mr Jas Harper, the excellent captain, continues in command of the boat, & the obliging & esteemed Mr P Kavanaugh clerk.
-Balt Patriot

Capt Wm Eaton, of Wells, Maine, met with a shocking death on Monday. He was sawing logs in his mill, when he fell across the carriage which supports logs, & was completely sawed in two. He was a highly respected citizen, & was aged 66 years.

Monument executed & erected by Mr Thos Hargrave, of Phil, in *Congress Cemetery*, to the memory of John W Maury. Inscription:
HE WAS BORN
IN CAROLINE COUNTY, VIRGINIA,
ON THE 15TH DAY OF MAY, A D 1809,
AND DIED IN THE CITY OF WASHINGTON
ON THE 2D DAY OF FEBRUARY, A D 1855.
HIS CHARACTER WAS BLENDED WITH ALL
THAT CAN ELEVATE OR ADORN; AND HIS LIFE
WAS A BRIGHT EXAMPLE OF THE NOBILITY
AND POWER OF VIRTUE
-Wash News

Veteran of the Revolution. A Brief Memoir of Col Fred'k Baron de Weissenfels; compiled from authentic papers left by his daughter & only heir, the late Mrs Harriet de la Palm Baker, deceased. Baron de Weissenfels was a native of Elbing, in the Kingdom of Prussia. A town in Germany bears the name of his family. He was trained to arms under Fred'k the Great; sought employment in the British service, in North America, in 1756; ascended the Heights of Abraham with brave Wolfe, & saw him expire in the arms of victory; was an ofcr in the Royal American Regt at the attack on *Fort Ticonderoga*, & participated in the descent upon & capture of Havana in 1762. When peace was concluded with France in 1763 Weissenfels settled in N Y. He served in the same regt with St Clair. He received from the American Congress in Mar, 1776, a commission of lt colonel, commandant of the Third N Y btln. He was at the battles of White Plains; at Trenton; & at Burgoyne. For his faithful services in the royal army before the Revolution he was entitled, by a proclamation of the King, to a large tract of land; this, together with his half-pay of lt, he lost by entering into the service of the United Colonies. He ever disdained to ask for remuneration for these losses, though he greatly needed it. Col Weissenfels is dead! & his daughter & only heir, the inheritor of his poverty as well as his exalted virtues, also is dead. Her children survive her, also needy, but trusting that the country which has become great & rich & powerful through the wisdom & the valor of the patriots of the Revolution, of whom their grandfather was distinguished one, will accord to them that justice when, had he demanded it himself, could hardly have been denied, & the claim to which has descended to them.

Mrd: on Apr 10, in Richmond, Va, at St Paul's Church, by Rev Geo Woodbridge, Edw L Handy, Cmder U S Navy, to Mary Gallego, youngest daughter of the late Peter J Chevallie.

Died: on Apr 12, in Wash City, Edw Godey, in his 34th year. His funeral will be this evening, at 2 o'clock, from his residence on I, between 4th & 5th sts.

Foreign news: 1-Sir Hyde Parker, cmder of the English naval forces in the East Indies, died at Devenport on Mar 21. 2-Sir Henry Pottinger died at Malta on the 18th.

TUE APR 15, 1856

Household & kitchen furniture, stock, farming utensils, & 1 negro servant man-a valuable servant, & 2 servant girls, between 8 & 12 years old, & 1 servant boy, 2 horses & 1 cow, & a large lot of chickens, a family carriage & a gun, & a 1 horse cart: at auction on May 7 next, at the late residence of Geo W Bowie, deceased, on the Turnpike Road leading from Wash to Bladensburg, in D C. -B L Jackson, adm -A Green, auct

Bailiff's sale of very handsome household furniture, Piano Forte & stool, at auction, by order of distrain for house rent due to Saml Stott by Theodore Kane, I will expose at public sale, on Apr 17 next, at the residence of said Kane, on G st, between 18th & 19th sts, in Wash City, the above goods. -S C Davison, bailiff -A Green, auct

Trustee's sale of improved real estate: on Apr 22, at public auction, lot 12 in square 904, with 2 neat frame dwlgs, fronting on 7th st, formerly the property of D Klinehause.
-A Lloyd, Jos H Bradley, jr, trustees -Jas C McGuire, auct

Senate: 1-Memorial of Jas H Lane was presented. Mr Harlan addressed the Senate at great length, giving a history of the services of Col Lane in the Mexican war & to the Democratic party.

Narrow escape from death was made at the country residence of Capt Ezra Nye, near Irvington, N J, on Wed. The family had just returned for the summer, & fires were kindled in the furnace for the first time, but an obstruction in the chimney diverted the noxious gases to the apartment in which his 2 daughters had retired. Mrs Nye fortunately rose unusually early in the morning, & in attempting to arouse them she became so alarmed at their silence that she procured the door to be forced open, & found them both insensible. Medical aid was sent for, & Capt Nye promptly applied restoratives, by which the patients were brought back to consciousness, & are now nearly restored to health.

Mrd: on Apr 14, by Rev Mr Alig, Mr Michl Conner, of Balt, to Miss Margaret Conner, of Wash City.

Died: on Apr 13, in Wash City, in his 40th year, Jas F Harvey. His funeral is this day at 2 o'clock, from his late residence, 410 7th st west, between G & H sts.

Died: on Apr 11, in Montg Co, Md, after a brief illness, Hon Otho Magruder, in his 63rd year. He was one of the Judges of the Orphans' Court, & for 36 years past has been a ruling elder in the Presbyterian [Rev Mr Eva's] Church. He attended a meeting of the Presbytery of the District, in Alexandria, on Apr 4, & was appointed Alternate Com'r to the General Assembly. "He was a good man, & full of the Holy Ghost & of faith."

Died: on Apr 14, Anne Roberta, daughter of Jas & Henrietta Keleher, aged 3 years. Her funeral is today at 4 o'clock, from the residence of her parents, 17 Missouri ave.

Died: on Apr 8, in Balt, of scarlet fever, Clementina Eliz Grierson, aged 5 years; & of the same disease, on Apr 9, Fred'k Latimer, aged 6 years, daughter & son of F P & Ann E Schleicker, of that city.

Died: Apr 14, of consumption, Mr Jas Ingliss Martin, in his 45th year, formerly of Balt, but for the last 16 years a resident of Wash City. Requiescat in pace! His funeral will be Apr 16 at 3 P M, at his brother-in-law's, Mr Scott, 473 14th st, so Pa ave.

Phil, Apr 14. Col Hughes, special agent of the Post Ofc, this morning arrested Geo W Townsend, who broke jail at Newcastle while waiting sentence for stealing a letter from the Wilmington post ofc. He had 3 revolvers on his person, & every barrel charged. When he escaped from prison he liberated 7 other prisoners. He is about 20 years of age.

Public sale: by deed of trust recorded in Liber J A S No 95, folios 239 thru 241, of the land records of Wash Co, D C: public auction on Mar 3, of one undivided ninth part of that part of square 186 which was conveyed by W W Corcoran to Thos Ritchie. -Jos H Bradley, trustee -C W Boteler, auctioneer

WED APR 16, 1856
Senate: 1-Mr Weller presented resolutions of the Legislature of Calif complaining of the action of the Naval Board, &, in consideration of the irreproachable character of Fabius Stanley & Thos H Stevens, of that State, & of their well known good conduct & efficiency in their country's service, instructing their Senators & their Reps to use all proper efforts to remedy the injustice committed by the said Board: ordered to be printed. 2-Memorial from Jas T Barclay, of Wash City: he has discovered a certain process by means of which a portion of the precious metals may be abstracted from gold or silver at the cost of a fraction of a cent for every dollar's worth thus withdrawn. 3-Ptn from Ethan H Allen, Mary A Weir, & Ethan Allen Hitchcock, grandchildren of Gen Ethan Allen, asking to be recompensed on accout of the extraordinary & very meritorious services of their ancestor during the war of the Revolution. [Resolution in 1778, stating what was due at the time of Gen Allen's

death, has never yet been paid.] 4-Ptn from Obed Hussey, asking an extension of his patent for a reaping machine. 5-Ptn from Isaac S Sterrett, a cmder in the navy, asking to be restored to his former position. 6-Ptn from Nancy Mann, asking to be allowed bounty land for the services of her husband in the Revolutionary war. 7-Ptn from Cyrus McCormick, asking an extension of his patent for a reaping machine. 8-Ptn from Isaac Seymour, asking arrears of pension. 9-Ptn from Jessee Wyatt, a volunteer in the war of 1812, asking a pension. 10-Ptn from Tacitus Clay, heir of Thos Clay, deceased, asking indemnity against loss on a military land warrant issued to his ancestor for Revolutionary services. 11-Ptn from J M Gould & others, of Rock Island city, Ill, asking permission to establish a military institute on the military reservation on that island. 12-Cmte on Finance: bill for the relief of Franck Taylor. 13-Cmte on Pensions: bill for the relief of Moses Powers; & bill granting a pension to Olivia W Cannon, widow of Jos L Cannon, late a midshipman in the U S Navy. Same cmte: adverse reports on the following petitions: of Dr Moses Carter; of Jacob W Morse; of Eliz Dowdale; & on the claim of Jos Colby, son of Ebenezer Colby, deceased. Same cmte: bill for the relief of Timothy Cavan, with a recommendation that it do not pass.

House of Reps: 1-Cmte on Invalid Pensions: to inquire into the claims of Geo Bond & Claiborne Vaughn to be placed upon the pension roll, & that the said cmte have leave to report by bill or otherwise. 2-Cmte on Revolutionary Pensions: to inquire into the claim of Rebecca Smith, widow of David Smith, a Revolutionary soldier, & that the said cmte have leave to report by bill or otherwise. 3-Cmte on Indian Affairs: adverse reports on the petition of Robt A Jones & on that of Albert Jackson & others. Same cmte: resolution authorizing the Sec of the Interior to settle the accounts of Oliver M Wozencraft. 4-Cmte on Military Affairs: bill for the relief of Jacob Dodson, a colored man who, when labor was very scarce in Calif & commanded high rates, entered the service of the U S & received an honorable discharge. This bill was necessary to enable him to receive compensation of his services, as the laws of the U S did not provide for the mustering of colored men into the service of the country: passed. Same cmte: bill for the relief of J P Hatch, of the U S Army; & a bill for the relief of the heirs of the late Col John Hardin: both committed. Same cmte: bill for the relief of Jacob Price: committed. Same cmte: bill for the relief of the legal reps of Capt Jos H Whipple, deceased: committed. Same cmte: adverse reports on the petitions of Daniel de Moisille, & of Thos Smithers. Same cmte: bill for the relief of the sureties of the late Lt Chas E Jarvis, of the U S Army: committed. 5-Memorial of Geo A Fairfield, Com'r of the State of Maine, praying indemnity for lands conveyed by said State to enable the Gov't of the U S to fulfil the stipulations in the treaty of Wash. 6-Memorial of Geo Dana, jr, Capt E Benedict, & others in favor of the construction, at the earliest day practical, of a railroad to the Pacific. 7-Remonstrance of 54 citizens of Erie, Pa, against the extension of Woodworth's patent for a planning machine.

An old Calif family: Don Jose de la Guerra y Noriega, a native of the province of Santander, in Spain, arrived in Upper Calif in 1801, as first ensign of the Presidial company of Monterey; in 1806 promoted to a lieutenancy in the company of the Presidio of Santa Barbara, till Aug, 1810; was appointed Commissary General of the troops of both Californias, & embarked for the capitol of Mexico-or rather of New Spain, as it then was; returned to Calif in 1812, the war of independence was raging in Mexico; in 1817 was appointed captain of the company of Santa Barbara till 1819; in 1822 the then Govn'r of the Province,was Don Pablo Vicente de Sola, the Deputy to the new Congress of Mexico. In 1824 the Indians of various missions revolted; they were defeated through the activity of Capt de la Guerra; in 1827 he was elected Deputy to the Nat'l Congress at Mexico till 1829; then he resided permanently in Santa Barbara as a retired captain, & in the repose of private life. In 1801 he married Dona Maria Antonia Carrillo, daughter of Don Raymundo Carrillo, likewise one of the founders of the country, & now in a hale old age of 78 years upwards of 80 descendants, all native of the country which he so long served. The sons & grandsons of this venerable gentleman area among the most respectable citizens of Calif. Don Pablo de la Guerra, & others of the family have filled important trusts, civil & military, under Mexico & the present State Gov't. Wash, Mar 14, 1856.

Business Directory-Balt, Md.
Agricultural Warehouses: Rice & Norris; E Whitman & Co.
Attys at Law:
Sprague & Root   R Stockett Matthews
Alfred H Byrd   Jas J Robbins
Jesse H Magruder   Francis D Tormey
Auction Stores: F W Bennett & Co; Cannon & Matthews.
Bakeries: Jas D Mason & Co
Banks & Bankers:
Jno S Gittings & Co   McKim & Co
Johnston Brothers & Co   Appleton & Co
Bell & Brass Foundries: Baker, Holmes & Brown; Clampitt & Regester
Boarding Houses: Mrs Williams
Bookstores:
J W Bond & Co   Cushings & Bailey
W S & J Crowley   Whitney, Cushing & Comstock
Boot & Shoe Stores:
Alfred D Evans   Watkins, Dungan & Waesche
Benj Russell   E Williams
Breweries: W Clagett & Co; Francis Dandelet
Carriage Factories:
Burr, Haight & O'Connell   John Curlett
Wm McCann   G W Mason
Chair Factory: A Mathiot

China, Glass, & Queen's Ware:
Robt T Banks   Geo W Herring & Co
E Brooks & Co   D Preston Parr
Jos S Hastings, jr
Cigar Store: Albert Nicolassen
Clothing Stores: Noah Walker & Co; Asbury Jarrett
Centre Market Place: Asbury Jarrett
Cloth Store: J W Richardson & Co
Commercial School: Chamberlin's Commercial College
Commission Merchants:
Coover, Tysinger & Stow   Ball, Clarke & Co
Neale, Harris & Co   Haslup & Co
Lyman, Reed & Co
Confectionary: L G Curlett
Copper Smith: Jno M Bruce
Cotton Factories: Mount Vernon Co, R H Humphrey's, sec; John H Haskell
Daguerrean Gallery: D R Stiltz
Dentists: Dr E Davidsohn; Dr M A Hopkinson; Snowden
Drug Stores: Popplein & Thompson; Seth S Hance; Andrews & Thompson
Dry Goods:
Sowman Brothers   R W Dryden
Thos R Rich   Perkins & Co
Merrefield & Stinchcomb Wroth & McCreery
Hamilton, Easter & Co   A Hecht
J Edw Bird & Bro   M Myers
Stephen L Bird & Co
Engine Works: A & W Dunmead & Sons
Flour Stores:
Duer & Johns   Walter & Co
C D Hinks & Co   Willis & Co
Forwarding & Shipping Merchants: Foley & Merceret; Magraw; Koons
Foundry: Poole & Hunt
Fruit Stores: Butt & Ricketts; Higgins & Pontier
Furnishing Store: Wm P Towles

Furniture Stores:
E Mount   S S Stevens & Sons
Sears & Phillips   J R Ward & Coo
Meachan & Haywood   John T Watkins
Gas Fixtures: D Leeds Smith & Co; Dukehart & Kaflinski
Gas Machines: Md Portable Gas Co of Balt, E R Sprague, treasurer.
Genr'l Agent: John M Walker
Glass Factory: Baker & Brother

Grocers, wholesale:
Butt & Ricketts
Duvall & Iglehart
Ellicott & Hewes
Harding & Carroll
G A Martin & Bro
T T Martin & Bro
Thos R Matthews & Son
Scwartz & Dix
D Whiteford & Co

Guano Depots:
P Malcolm & Co
Wm Robinson
Stirling & Ahrens
Robt Turner

Guns & Pistols: A McComas; D B Frimble
Hair Dye Factory: John A Jones
Hardware:
Baker, Holmes & Brown
Dugan & Jenkins
Hiss & Cole
R B Porter & Co
Schaeffer & Loney

Hat & Cap Stores:
Thos L Hughes & Co
J L McPhail & Brother
S Hindes & Son
Towson & Brenton

Hose Factory: Wm Dukehart
Hosiery: Amos Lovejoy
Hotels:
Barnum's City Hotel
Gilmor House
Eutaw House
Fountain Hotel
Maltby House
Nat'l Hotel
U S Hotel

House-furnishing Stores: Coryland & Co; Alfred H Reip; Samson Carriss & Co
Insurance Offices:
Nat'l Fire Ins Co of Balt: J B Seidenstrikcer, Pres
J R Magruder, Sec
Balt Fire Ins Co: J I Cohen, jr, Pres, Fred Woodworth, sec
Fireman's Ins Co: John Reese, Pres, Henry P Duhurst, sec
Associated Firemen's Ins Co: John R Moore, Pres, John Dukehart, sec
The Merchants' Mut Ins Co of Balt, Marine: Geo Wm Graham, Pres, B Coale, sec
The Ocean Mut Ins Co of Balt: Wm Buckler, Pres, Wm Krebs,sec
Balt Life Ins Co: John I Donaldson, Pres, H F Thompson, sec
The Mut Benefit Life Ins Co: M Lewis, Agent
Iron Railing Factories: Jas Bates; Newsham & Co
Iron Store: J Hopkinson Smith
Jewelry Stores:
Canfield, Brother & Co
J Alexander
Gould, Stowell & Ward
J Thompson Laws

Justices of the Peace: Wm H Hayward; Malcom W Mearis; Sam M Lawder
Leather Stores: E Larabee; Grupy & Stansbury

Livery Stables:
Nat'l Livery Stables: J H Colston   Paca Street Stables: Jos H McGee
Northwestern Stables: L Hartzell   Jno R Hynson's Livery Stables
Lock Factories:
Gibson & Kirk   John A Stewart & Son
Sanders & Smith
Looking Glasses & Picture Frames:
Barrett & Debeet   Thos Seagers
C H Leonard & Co
Lottery Ofcs: Saml Winchester; R M Beam & Co; Jas Fletcher;
Consolidated Lotteries of Md: R France & Co
Lumber Merchants: Burns & Sloan
Marble Works:
Md Stone Dressing Co: Jno W   Sisson & Baird
Maxwell   Andrew H Lyeth
Balt Steam Marble Works: Levi Taylor
Merchant Tailors:
Johnston & Marsden   Byers & Crise
M Tracy & Sons   J A Griffith
Millinery:
Armstrong, Cator & Co   Elias Bonney
Benj Crane & Co   T W Webster
Carroll & Reed
Mill Stones: B F Starr & Co; Wm Hogg & Son; Morris & Trimble
Music Stores: Miller & Beacham; C H Eisenbrandt
Oculists & Aurists: Dr E P Morong; Dr Von Meschziker
Oil & Paint Stores: G R Dodge & Co; W & H Spilcker
Oyster Packers: Price & Littig
Painters: Weaver & Brother
Paints, Chemicals, Varnishes: Wm Davison & Co
Paper Hangings:
J C Golder & Bro   Jno W Myers
Howell & Brothers   Michael & Brother
B T Hynson
Paper Stores: A L Knight; Wheelwright & Mudge; Jas S Robinson; Hunckel & Son
Pawnbrokers: S & J Benjamin
Physician: Dr J W Perkinson
Piano Forte Warerooms:
Wm Knaube & Co   J Fetri & Co
Neill, Duross & Co   F D Benteen
Wm Gaehle & Co   Kuhn & Ridgeway
Newman, Bro & Sons   Chas M Stieff
Planing Mill: Hugh D Gelston

Plate Glass: R Edwards, jr & Co
Pork Packers: Smith & Nicodemus
Powder Works: Geo J Beatty; Elder & Webb
Printing Ink: B F Fellows
Produce & Provision Stores:
Cornell & Dorsey   J G Harvey & Coo
S & J Klinefelter   Philip P Pendleton
Coulter & Co
Queensware Factory: E & W Bennett
Real Estate Agents: Jas Boyd; B Franklin Cole
Restaurants:
Reilly's Saloon   F Lagroue, [French]
Wm H Rose
Roofing:
Balt Stucco Works: Jacob F Grove,   C M Warren & Co
agent
Sadlery, Harness & Trunks:
J D Hammond   John R Yeatman
Robt Lawson   E W Briding
Safes:
S J Sharp & Co   Tilton & McFarland
Thompson & Oudesluys
Sash & Door Factory: Rouse & Bennett
Scale Factories:
Richd Murdock   J A Weston & Co
Jesse Marden
Seed Stores: Saml Ault & Son
Shirt Factories: Constable, Walker & Co; Carman & Baden
Shoe Findings, & Tools: John A Solze; Christian Barth
Show-case Factory: Woodroffe & Wyberd
Sign Painting Establishment: Roach & Cline
Silver Plating: Jesse Seger
Spice Mills: W H Crawford; Geo W Wait & Son
Stationery Store: Saml E Turner
Steamship Agent: A C Hall
Storage: Ellicott & Hughes; Thos Poultney, jr
Stoves, & Tin Ware:
Ward & France   Collins & Co
Andrews & Stran   J Weatherby & Co
H L McAvoy & Co   John W Bechtel
Sugar Refiners: Md Steam Sugar Refining Co, F W Brune & Sons, Agents
Surgical Instruments:
Chas C Reinhardt, Manufacturer   G W S Nicholson, Surgical, Dental

Tea Stores: Geo Sanders & Co
Tin & Sheet Iron Ware: Robinson & Kremer; Keen & Hagerty
Tin Plate, Sheet Iron, Wire: E L Parker & Co
Tobacco & Cigar Stores:
Courtney & Cushing   Wm A Boyd & Co
Jacob Heald & Co   Chas D De Ford & Co
J E Montell & Bro   Warwick & Armistead
R W Gray   Wm H Ereck
Trimming Store-Ladies Fancy: Jas M Haig & Bro
Trunk Stores: John McGee; Silas Phelps; J V D Van Nostwick
Turning & Sawing Works: Jas S Suter
Type Foundry: Ryan & Rickets
Variety & Notion Stores: E R Horner & Bro; Isaac Wechsler
Window Shades: Baker & Cushman
Wine & Liquor Stores:
F L Brauns   Thos Robinson
Graff & Co   Chas H Ross & Co
Jas Haxlitt & Co   Sloan & Calwell
Heim, Micodemus & Co   Spence & Reid
John Higinbothom   C Morton Stewart
McCoy, Bro & Co   Laurence Thomsen
Wm McGowan   P Tiernan & Son
Mehens & Schumacker   W F Walters & Co
Chas H Myers & Bro
Wire Works: H Balderston & Son
Wood Carvers: Hays & Morse

Orphans Court of Wash Co, D C. Letters of administration on the personal estate of Otho M Linthicum, late of Wash Co, deceased. -Jno Marbury, adm

Orphans Court of Wash Co, D C. Letters of administration on the personal estate of Geo W Bowie, late of Wash Co, deceased. -B T Jackson, adm

Orphans Court of Wash Co, D C. Letters of administration on the personal estate of Abraham Hines, late of Wash Co, deceased. -C M Hines, adm

THU APR 17, 1856
Senate: 1-Ptn from Sallie C Northup, asking that her title under certain land warrants may be confirmed. 2-Bill for the relief of John S Pendleton: referred to the Cmte on Foreign Relations.

Bishop O'Reilly, of Hartford, Conn, who was supposed to have been on board the missing steamer **Pacific**, is safe, & came passenger in the steamer **Cambria**.

A beautiful Gold Medal has been received from Holland at the State Dept, struck by order of his Majesty the King of the Netherlands in honor of Lt Maury. On its face is the image of the King, Wm III; on the reverse, an inscription in the Dutch language, of which the following is a translation:
"To M F Maury,
The Investigator of Nature, the Guide of the Ocean, and
The Benefactor of Seamen.
The King-1855.

Fatal accident on Sat when a carboy of nitric acid was accidentally spilled on the floor of Carlton's lamp factory, 12 Beach st, Boston. Sawdust was thrown upon the liquid & the workmen continued their work. Deleterious vapor arose. Jacob Geer, about 50, & Jos Kraus, 26 died Sunday. Albert Yuhl, residing in Ruggles st, Roxbury, & John Lang, residing in Plymouth st, are both suffering severely, but not considered in a dangerous condition. Jos Herms was not much affected, & will probably recover.
-Boston Atlas

House of Reps: 1-Cmte on Naval Affairs: bill for the relief of Capt Thos Ap Catesby Jones: committed. Same cmte: adverse report on the ptn of Wm Black. 2-Cmte on Invalid Pensions: bill for the relief of Mrs A W Angus, widow of the late Capt Saml Angus, U S navy: committed. Same cmte: bill for the relief of Mary E Tillman: read twice. Mr Books, of S C, urged the immediate passage of the bill. When a requistion was made upon South Carolina for service in the Mexican war this lady gave to her country every member of her family at the time capable of bearing arms, a husband & 3 sons. All went, but not one returned to dry a mother's tears with the gallantry of her soldier boys. The bones of one of this family now lie at Saltillo, another fell at Jalapa, another lies buried by the castle walls of Perote, & the last found the close of his earthly career & youthful ambition at the capital of Mexico. By a strange fatality, the only remaining son, a boy too young to discharge the duty of supporting the family in the absence of his elder brothers, by an accidental fall from his horse injured his spine, & is now a paralytic for life. This lady is left, in the decline of life, with a helpless child & a little daughter entirely dependent on her exertions for their & her own support. One of her sons enlisted in the Alabama regt; the father & the remaining sons mustered in the service of the U S under my command. Mr Mace, of Indiana, examined the bill & it simply proposed to pay this widow $8 per month. He moved that the $8 per month be stricken out & $50 inserted. At the instance of many gentlemen, he would modify his motion so as to make it $20 a month. Bill was passed. 3-Cmte on Invalid Pensions: bill for the relief of Mrs L Browning: passed. Same cmte: bills committed: relief of Betsy Nash; of Edmund Mitchell; & of Evelina Porter, widow of the late Cmdor David Porter, U S navy.

Orphans Court of Wash Co, D C. Letters of administration on the personal estate of Danl Roemle, late of Wash Co, deceased. -Chas Walter, adm

J Connelly, Undertaker, 423 7th st, west side, between G & H sts, informs he is prepared to attend to all orders at the shortest notice & on most liberal terms.

FRI APR 18, 1856

Reminiscence: Delegates representing the various sections of the District of Columbia, & who commenced their sessions on Nov 19, 1804, in Stelle's Hotel, Wash City:
Corp of Washington: Saml H Smith, Nicholas King
Corp of Gtwn: Benj Stoddert, Henry Foxall, John Mason
Levy Court of Wash Co: Thos Corcoran
Inhabitants of Gtwn: Danl Reintzell
Inhabitants of Wash: Cornelius Coningham, Benj Moore
Alexandria & County: Francis Peyton, Robt Alexander, Presly Gunnell, Walter Jones, Abraham Fow, Lewis Summers, Henry Rose
Various subjects were taken into considertion & voted on by yeas & nays, memorials drawn up for presentation to Congress for various alterations & amendments to the laws of Md & Va unsuitable to the District.

The ship **Peruvian**, which arrived here yesterday, brought out the entire family of the late Mr Glass, commonly called Govn'r Glass, of the Island of Tristan d'Acunha. There were upwards of 20 in the whole, women & children. We believe the Glasses have concluded to abandon the island altogether & take up their permanent residence in the U S, probably in this State. Tristan d'Cunha may therefore be considered as annexed to Connecticut. -New London Chronicle, Apr 8

Mr Sibbern, Ex-Minister from Sweden at Wash, & his lady, were amongst the passenger who sailed from N Y on Wed in the steamship **Asia** for Liverpool.

Household & kitchen furniture at auction on: Apr 22, at the residence of Theodore Kane, on north G st, between 18th & 19th sts. -A Green, auct

Senate: 1-Cmte of Claims: which was referred the decision of the Court of Claims adverse to the claim of Cyrus McCormick, asked to be discharged from the consideration of the same, & that it be referred to the Cmte on Patents & Patent Ofc: agreed to.

The fine mansion of Edmund J Lee, near Shepherdstown, Va, with its furniture, was destroyed by fire on Apr 12. The loss is stated at $2,000 above the insurance.

Large sale of Marble Statuary, the importation of Signor Vito Viti & Sons, will continue this evening at 4 o'clock. The lovers of art will do well to attend the sale.

Late news from Central America-Mar, 1856. Cmder-in-Chief of the Republic of Costa Rica, Headquarters, Liberia, Mar 21, 1856. To the Minister of War: The assault of the hacienda of *Santa Ross*, a splendid military position, elevated & surrounded by walls of stone in all its extent has been glorious for our army. The attack was rapid & instantaneous. The field is strewed with the dead. The honorable, valiant & loyal Capt Jose Maria Guliarrez, Capt Manuel Quiros, & Lts Justo Castro & Manuel Rojos met a glorious death, as well as 12 soldiers whose names are not yet knowns. May God preserve you! -Rafael Mora [A battle had taken place between a detachment of Walker's troops, 400 strong, under Col Schlesinger, & a body of Costa Ricans, 500 in number, under Gen Mora, near the hacienda of *Santa Rosa*.]

Obit-died: on Apr 5, at his residence in Winchester, Thos Allen Tidball, for more than 30 years the popular & efficient clerk of Fred'k Co, Va. A large concourse of citizens attended his remains to their resting place in *Mount Hebron Cemetery*. An eloquent sermon was preached by Rev Dr Boyd. Mr Tidball was born in Phil, Jan 14, 1756. His father, who had been a merchant in that city, removed to Winchester when his son Thos was about 4 years of age. He entered the duties of clerk in 1804. He was nominally a deputy in the ofc from 1804 to 1824, though really the whole responsibility of the ofc rested upon him, Mr Jas Keith, the actual occupant, having his residence in Alexandria. After the death of Mr Keith, in 1824, Mr Tidball was appointed his successor. He held this ofc until his death. As a husband & father he was everything that could be desired.

House of Reps: 1-Bill for the relief of F W Armstrong: referred. 2-Bill for the relief of Isaac T Washburne: referred. 3-Bill for the relief of John W Cox: referred. 4-Cmte on the Judiciary: adverse report on the memorial of R L Hendricks & others, praying the abolition of the ofc of chaplain.

Chicago Democrat of Tue: distressing accident on the Calumet, some 10 or 12 miles from Chicago, a day or two before, by which a son of John Whitney, of that city, lost his life. Young Whitney & a lad named Vincent Bell were out shooting, when Bell accidentally shot Whitney, when his thumb slipped down on the hammer. Whitney died soon after. .

$500 reward for the apprehension & conviction of Washington Nailor, who was arrested for burlglary & admitted to bail, & who has since absconded. He is about 36 years of age, about 5 feet 8 inches, dark complexion, weight about 140 pounds; when spoken to has a downward look, & is very talkative & speaks quick. He had a full suit of hair when he left, & was unaccustomed to shave any portion of his beard, which was very long when he left. -Jno T Towers, Mayor, Wash City, Apr 17, 1856.

Large sale of Marble Statuary, the importation of Signor Vito Viti & Sons, will continue this evening at 4 o'clock. The lovers of art will do well to attend the sale.

The Boston Atlas states the Capt Chas Kerman, who, in the summer of 1854, was sentenced in that city to imprisonment in the county jail for 3 years & to pay a fine of $1,000, for being concerned in the fitting out of the schnr **Glamorgan** for the slave trade, has received an unconditional pardon from the Pres of the U S.

Mrd: on Apr 17, in Wash City, by Rev G W Samson, Mr Jas W Sarten to Miss Mary Ellen Kane, both of Alexandria.

Died: on Apr 18, in Wash City, Jura Esther, infant child of B S & Jane A Howard.

C Buckingham has this day associated with himself Jas H Mead, to conduct the business of Black & Whitesmithing in general, under the firm of Buckingham & Mead. New firm, at my old stand, on C st, between 10th & 11th sts.

For sale or rent the well-known residence of the late Maj A A Nicholson, near *Duddington*. Apply to John C Brent, Atty at Law, 30 La ave, or to Buckner Bayliss, Missouri ave, between 4½ & 6th sts. The key of the house will be found at *Duddington*.

SAT APR 19, 1856

The whaling barque **Maria** is said, by the New Bedford Mercury, to be the oldest vessel in the U S. She has just returned to that port from the Pacific. She was the first ship that hoisted the American flag in the river Thames at the conclusion of the war of the American Revolution.

Senate: 1-Ptn Mrs A P Derrick, widow of of the late chief clerk of the Dept of State, asking to be allowed compensation for the services of her husband while acting as Sec of State. 2-Ptn from Andrew A H Knox, asking the confirmation of his title to certain lands in the Bastrop grant, in the State of Louisiana. 3-Additional papers presented relating to the claim of Maj Jas Belger, of the U S Army, to be released from liability for public money of which he was defrauded by his confidential clerk. 4-Cmte of Claims: bill for the relief of the legal reps of Rinaldo Johnson & Ann E Johnson. 5-Bill to continue half-pay to Mrs Lewright Browning for a further term of 5 years: referred. [Mr Seward hoped the Senate would pass the bill at once; Mr Toombs objected.] 6-Bill for the relief of Mary Tillman: passed. 7-Following bills were passed-relief of: Saml V Niles; of Abraham Kintzing; of Wm Marvin, of Fla; of Saml Scott; of F A Cunningham, paymaster in the U S Army; of the legal reps of Jas Bell, deceased; of Eliz V Lomax, only surviving child of Capt Wm Lindsay, of the Revolution; of Lemuel Worster; of Danl Doland; of the legal reps of John Morrison & Chas Ginn; & of Franck Taylor. Also, granting a pension to Mrs Olivia W Cannon, widow of Jos L Cannon, late a midshipman in the U S Navy, now deceased; & to confirm the title of Henry Volcker to a certain tract of land in the Territory of New Mexico. 8-The bill for the relief of Timothy Cavan was rejected.

The Carlisle [Ill] Democrat notices the death in that place, on Thu week, of Sgt John L Hays, an old resident of Carlisle & a soldier of the war of 1812. Sgt Hays was born on the day of the battle of Lexington, & was 85 years old. He was the son of the celebrated Milly Pitcher, who distinguished herself at the battle of Monmouth, & of whom the Life of Washington gives the following account: "It was during this part of the battle, when Lee was struggling nobly against the overwhelming numbers that pressed on him, that an Irishman, while serving at his gun, was shot down. His wife, Molly, but 22 years old, employed herself, while he loaded & fired his piece, in bringing water from a spring near by. While returning with a supply she saw him fall, & heard the commanding ofcr order the gun to be taken to the rear. She immediately ran forward, seized the rammer, declaring she would avenge his death. She fought her piece like a hero to the last. The next morning Gen Greene, who had been struck with her bravery, presented her to Gen Washington, who immediately promoted her to be a sgt, & afterwards put her name upon the half pay list for life. Previous to this she fired the last gun when the Americans were driven from **Fort Montgomery**." At the close of the Revolution Molly took up her residence in Carlisle, where she was known as Molly McCauley. She lived to an advanced age, much respected by all, & was buried with military honors.

Dr F N Ripley, in company with Mr McLelland, in the latter part of Feb, left Glenco, about 55 miles s w of this place, for Forrestville, a new town located in the early part of the past winter. They lost their way & wandered until Mar 1, when they reached Round lake, 5 miles away, when the doctor laid down, completely exhausted. Mr McLelland used all means to arouse him, but in vain. He proceeded alone. On Mar 20th a surveying party heard the sad story, & returned with him to Shakopee, former residence of Dr Ripley, for whose frozen remains they made fruitless search. Mr McLelland is now under the care of physicians, his feet badly frozen, as to render amputation necessary just above the ankle. Possible he may recover. -Minneapolis [Minn] Democrat of Mar 29.

Rev Geo B Jewett, late a professor in Amherst College, but for the last year pastor of a church at Nashua, N H, was visited with a sad affliction on Tue last. Whilst, in a carriage with his wife & only child, a boy 8 years old, he was crossing the Concord railroad track in Nashua, his horse became frightened & backed upon an approaching freight train, by which the horse was killed, the carriage crushed, & its inmates terribly mangled. The child lost an arm & leg, & died that evening. Mr Jewett had his right ankle crushed so as to require the amputation of his leg, & it was feared he will not recover. Mrs Jewett had her left hand crushed, a portion of which has been amputated; her other bodily injuries are not severe. Mr Jewett is a brother of John P Jewett, of Boston, & of Chas C Jewett, late of this city.

Mrd: on Apr 17, in Wash City, at St John's Church, by Rev Dr Pyne, John W Jones, of Delaware, Ohio, to Kate Jessie, daughter of the late Wm A Williams, of Wash Ctiy.

Obit-died: Francis Gibson, the eldest son of Col Geo Gibson, who fell at St Clair's defeat, & the brother of the late Chief Justice Gibson, of Pa, died recently at the old family homestead in Sherman's Valley, Perrty Co, aged about 88 years. He made for himself an excellent violin & taught himself to play on it very well; made a capital rifle, & became a first-rate marksman with it; & he worked in wood & iron better than many who made trades of such work. He was a member of the Carlisle Infty & marched to Pittsburgh to assist in putting down the Whiskey Insurrection. He was appointed a lieutenant in the corps of the U S artl in 1798, & held his commission for several years. He volunteered for the war of 1812, & performed the double capacity of sgt & fifer. There are persons living at Harrisburg who distinctly remember his gigantic figure & his quaint appearance. For many years he has lived a simple quiet life in Sherman's Valley, devoting himself to the care of his farm, his mill, & a very large family, several generations of which had grown up around him. He retained his vigorous intellect to extreme old age. The last surviving member of the family of the late Col Gibson is now Gen Geo Gibson, of Wash, who has been for many years Commissary Genr'l of Subsistence in the U S Army. -Phil Bulletin

Died: Apr 18, in Wash City, Mrs Eliza Henley, widow of the late Com John D Henley, U S Navy. Her funeral is tomorrow at 3 P M, from her residence, 338 H st.

Died: on Apr 12, at her residence in Vansville district, PG Co, Md, Mrs Mary Scaggs, at the advanced age of 86 years. Mrs Scaggs was the relict of the late Jas Scaggs, & a native of Fred'k Co, Va. She left numerous relatives in Va & some of the Western States. She was a devoted mother, a kind & sincere neighbor, & died deeply regretted by all who knew her.

Attractive bldg site for sale: n e corner of 10th & O sts; 233 feet on 10th & 100 on O; the highest point in the city. -Estwick Evans, 467 , near s e corner of 9th & L sts.

MON APR 21, 1856
Auction sale: by 2 deeds of trust from Otho M Linthicum, deceased, to the subscriber, one dated Oct 23, 1849, the other Nov 29, 1855: sale on May 20th next of a perpetual leasehold estate in part of lot 47, in the original plan of Gtwn, being the s w corner, formed by the intersection of Bridge & High sts, fronting 30 feet on High st & 43 on Bridge st with the 3 story brick store & warehouse thereon, subject to an annual ground rent of $49. The bldg on this lot has been occupied as a drug & medicine store from a period beyond the memory of the oldest inhabitant to the present day. Also, a lot of ground that fronts 22 feet 3 inches on Cherry st; a brick carriage house, with the use of the ground between it & said house to pass to & from Beatty st. Also, parts of lots 152 & 153 in Beatty & Hawkins' addition to Gtwn, on the south side of Third st, fronting 25 feet on the same, with frame tenement. All previous liens & charges shall be paid out of the proceeds of the sale. -John Marbury, trustee -Barnard & Buckey, aucts

Meeting of the Whigs of Lexington, Ky, Apr 12, 1856.
Present:

Joshua F Bell, of Boyle Co	J B Temple, of Franklin
Thos J Helm, of Glasgow	John S McFarland, of Daviess
P Dudley, of Frankfort	L M Flournoy, of McCracken
Adam Beatty, of Mason	Wm G Talbot, of Bourbon
Richd Collins, of Mason	N S Ray, of Marion
Thos B Stevenson, of Mason	R Apperson, of Montg
Beverly D Williams, of Boyle	John D Taylor, of Mason
Lewis E Harvie, of Franklin	Marshall Key, of Mason
Jas B Clay, of Fayette	

Hon Richd Hawes, of Bourbon, chosen Pres; Thos B Stevenson, of Maysville, Sec. Address & platform unanimously adopted, the same subscribed by the following:

R Hawes, of Bourbon	J B Temple, of Franklin
Thos B Stevenson, of Mason	Lewis E Harvie, of Franklin
P Dudley, of Franklin	Beverly D Williams, of Boyle
Squire Turner, of Madison	Philip Speed, of Jefferson
Archie Dixon, of Henderson	D L Price, of Woodford
Joshua F Bell, of Boyle	J C Lemon, of Scott
Jas B Clay, of Fayette	A S McGroarty, of Boyle
John M Clay, of Fayette	Thos P Jacob, of Louisville
Wm R Thompson, of Bullitt	G H Cochran, of Louisville
John A Holton, of Franklin	W K Taylor, of Frankfort
W N Haldeman, of Louisville	Asbury Evans, of Covington
John Onan, of Woodford	John Todd, of Covington
R Blain, of Lincoln	

The schnr **Searsville**, which arrived at N Y on Sat from Trinidad, was loaded principally with old iron guns & an anchor from the remains of the Spanish men-of-war that were burnt in the Gulf of Paria, near the port of Spain, in 1797, at the time they were blocked by the British fleet. The American schnr **Silver Ray**, Capt Clark, which belongs to the Submarine Diving Co, of Boston, visited the Gulf of Paria, & obtained permission from Govn'r Elliott, of Trinidad, to operate in that vicinity. In Chayuaramas Bay, about 10 miles to the west of the port of Spain, he found, in about 6 fathoms of water, the remains of the Spanish fleet, commanded by Apodaca at the time the English expedition, under Harvey & Abercrombie, sailed from Martinique for the subjugation of the island of Trinidad in 1797. The principal part of the present cargo of the **Searsville** is taken from the wreck of the 5 Spanish vessels, & consists of about 90 guns. They are of Spanish manufacture, having been cast in Seville, & are marked Aug 5, 1776 & Apr 14, 1777.

Household & kitchen furniture at auction on: May 30, at the residence of P de Ausoategui, 117 West st, Gtwn. -Green & Scott, aucts

New Orleans Bee of Apr 11. The steamship **Charles Morgan**, which sailed yesterday for San Juan del Norte, took out 208 men who intend to join Gen Walker as soon as they arrive in Nicaragua, & whose services will doubtless at this critical time be of great value to him. Among the passengers were Gen C C Hornsby, Capt Moncasis, Chas Callahan, of the Picayune, Henry E Walker, of Tenn, [a brother of Gen Walker,] & L P Ellis, a member of the bar of this city.

I O O F: annual session of the Grand Lodge of Va, was held at Richmond last week. The following are the ofcrs elected for the ensuing year:

Nicholas K Trout, Grand Master
John R Jackson, Deputy G M
Thos J Evans, Grand Warden
Michl Seagers, Grand Sec
Geo W Toler, Grand Treas
W H Cook, Rep to Grand Lodge of the U S
Rev Wm L Hyland, Grand Chaplain
Wm H Peters, Grand Consuctor
Alex Grant, Grand Guardian
J W Poindexter, Grand Marshal
John W Childress, Grand Herald

Mr B H Clark, formerly of Troupe Co, Ga, writes us from Alexandria, La, Apr 5, that a fracas on board the steamboat **Bellfair**, between the Irish boat hands & the deck passengers, resulted in the loss of deck passengers, either in the flames or by drowning. The following from this State are: J B Taylor, of Macon Co; N G Rise, of Pike Co; John C Mathews, of Randolph Co; John G Hoges, of Upson Co; & B M Jones, of Pike Co, Ala. -Columbus [Ga] Enquirer

The *Congress Cemetery*. The *Congressional Cemetery* at Washington does not compare favorably with the cemeteries of note in various parts of the country. It contains about 10 acres & dates back to 1807. The first objects that attract the eye are the small plain cenotaphs erected in memory of those members of Congress who have died at Washington. These are arranged in double rows, & number 128 in all. In some instances the graves beneath them are tenantless, as in the cases of Henry Clay, John Quincy Adams, & others, but most of them have not been disturbed since the remains of the great men of our nation were deposited there. Most interesting & striking monuments: the remains of Henry Stephen Fox, nephew of the celebrated Chas Jas Fox, for many years British Minister to this Gov't, are enclosed in a plain massive marble sarcophagus, near the Congressional cenotaphs. The monument erected to the memory of Maj Gen Alex'r Macomb consists of a beautiful marble shaft, with appropriate military emblems, surmounted by a helmet with the visor down. The epitaph runs as follows: "It were but a small tribute to his memory to say that in youth and manhood he served his country in the profession in which he died, during a period of more than forty years, without stain or blemish upon his escutcheon." Maj Gen Jacob Brown, who died in 1828, lies under a massive broken marble column, erected by order of Congress. One of the finest, perhaps the most attractive, monument here is the one erected to Wm Wirt. Cmdor Chas W Chauncey, who died in Mexico in 1847, has a light & graceful marble shaft, with appropriate emblems & inscriptions. One of the handsomest is a tall spire of white marble, like Cleopatra's needle, rising over the grave of the late John W Maury, of this District, who died only about a year ago. The inscription is: "His character was blended with all that can elevate or adorn, and his life was a bright example of the nobility and power of virtue." One of the prettiest designs is an inverted cannon, in marble, standing on 3 cannon balls, erected to the memory of Lt John T McLaughlin, late of the U S Navy; another to the memory of Lt Geo Mifflin Bache, of the coast survey, & the ofcrs & crew who perished with him in the brig **Washington**, which was lost in the Gulf Stream in 1846. Capt Geo W Taylor, the inventor of the submarine armor, reposes under a little plain marble slab, 3 feet by 18 inches. The most eleborate monument is that of the family of Jacob Gideon, beneath which are deposited the remains of his deceased wife. On the upper part of the shaft are the simple words, "To my wife,", & below is a large daguerreotype set in the marble. The effect is very pretty. Elbridge Gerry, formerly Vic Pres, who died in 1814, at age 70, while on his way to the Capitol to take his seat as Pres of the Senate, has a richly ornamented monument, in the old style, which was erected by order of Congress. He realized his own memorable words, which constitute the epitaph on his tomb: "It is the duty of every citizen, though he may have but one day to live, to devote that day to the good of his country." Near by is another erected to the memory of Geo Clinton, also once Vice President. Push-ma-ta ha, a Choctaw chief, who died at Washington in 1824, has a plain granite cenotaph, erected by his brother chiefs. The celebrated eccentric Lorenzo Dow is said to have been buried here, but I was unable to find any clue to his resting place. -Connecticut

Mrd: on Apr 17, in Gtwn, D C, at St John's Church, by Rev N P Tillinghast, Rev Thos G Addison to Marie E, daughter of Thos B Addison, of Gtwn.

Died: on Apr 18, at his residence, Cmder Geo Adams, of the U S Navy.

Died: on Apr 18, at Balt, after a short but painful illness, in her 37th year, Honora S, wife of Geo Guest, & daughter of Gen Jas Bankhead, of the U S Army.

Wash City Ordinances: 1-Act for the relief of Jesse Williams: the sum of $75 be paid to him to indemnify him for injury to his horse by breaking through the flooring of the bridge across the canal at 4½ st, on Mar 20, 1856. 2-Act for the relief of Robt P W Balmain: the sum of $11.85 payable to him to correct an error in certificate 422 of the Wash Corp stock, which occurred in transferring the interest account of the quarter ending Mar 31, 1840.

Notice: Thos J Galt & Wm M Galt has this day entered into copartnerhsip, under the firm of T F & W M Galt, for the purpose of conducting the Wood & Coal business. Ofc n w corner of 12th & C sts.

Orphans Court of Wash Co, D C. Letters testamentary on the personal estate of Jas F Harvey, late of Wash Co, deceased. -Maria E Harvey, excx

U S Patent Ofc, Wash, Apr 18, 1856. Ptn of Jos Whitworth, of Manchester, England, praying for the extension of a patent granted to him on Aug 2, 1842, for an improvement in machine for sweeping & cleaning streets, for 7 years from the expiration of said patent, which takes place on Aug 2, 1856. -Chas Mason, Com'r of Patents

TUE APR 22, 1856
Rare chance to obtain a small country seat near Wash City: private sale of that beautiful tract of land called *St Elizabeth*, generally known as *Poplar Point*, on the Eastern branch of the Potomac, opposite the Navy Yard. It will be sold in lots of from 5 to 25 acres. Apply to Jno C C Hamilton, Atty at Law, La ave, or to T M Hanson, 512 7th st. A plat will be exhibited on the day of sale, with division of the land. -C W Boteler, auct

The fate of Bishop O'Reilly, of Connecticut, who was reported to have arrived from Europe in the steamer **Cambria**, is at last settled. A letter from his brother at Belfast, Ireland, dated Mar 27, says he certainly took passage on the ill-fated steamer **Pacific**. Rev Mr O'Reilly who arrived on the **Cambria** was not the Bishop.

Hon W G D Worthington, for many years one of the Associate Judges of Balt City Court, died suddenly on Sunday night of apoplexy, at his lodgings in Balt. Judge Worthington was formerly Govn'r of the Territory of Florida, & its first delegate in Congress. He had reached his 74th year, & was remarkable for his unvarying good humor, his ready wit, & for the benevolence & kindness of his disposition.
-Balt Patriot

A tornado on Apr 12, 1856, was felt with much severity at Elkton, Md. The house of Mr John Knight, a new frame, about 4 miles south of that place, was blown down, & an old lady, Mrs Wollenham, & a young man, Cyrus Walker, were killed. Four children of Mr Knight escaped without serious injury.

Ex-Pres Tyler is about to deliver a Lecture at Petersburg on the dead of his Cabinet- Webster, Calhoun, Upshur, Gilmer, & Legard.

The barn & stables of Mr John P Martin, of Westmoreland, Va, were destroyed by fire on Sat last. Loss estimated at $2,500 to $3,000.

The Culpeper [Va] Observer learn that the barn of Smith H Rixey, near Griffinsburg, in that county, was destroyed by fire one day last week, with his entire crop of grain.

On Sat the dwlg occupied by Mr Jas W Hope, near Carter's run, Fauquier Co, Va, was totally consumed by fire, with its contents.

Decision of the Supreme Court of Louisiana on Apr 14 was that of Jas Costello, under sentence of death for the murder of policeman John Dunn. The Court affirmed the judgment of the District Court, & Costello is to expiate his crime upon the gallows. Judge Lea, who pronounced the opinion of the Supreme Court, held that the simple empanelling of a jury, no other steps having been taken towards a trial, could not be held as placing the prisoner in jeopardy any more than he was before such empanelling. -New Orleans Bulletin

Trustee's sale: by a decree of the Circuit Court of Wash Co, D C, passed in a cause wherein Francis Wheatley & others are cmplnts & Chas H Winder & Wm H Winder are dfndnts: sale at auction, on May 16, lots 1 thru 5 in square 170, in Wash City, according to Davidson's subdivision of original lots 9 & 10 in said square.
-W Redin, trustee -A Green, auct

$200 reward for runaway mulatto slave Phil Barker, age about 23 years. Phil was purchased of Thos Green, of Washington. He ran off without cause. Address the subscriber, Warrenton, Va. -Wm H Gaines

Senate: 1-Memorial from Edw D Tippett, urging the appointment of a cmte to examine his navigating balloon & his new theory of generating steam without boilers. 2-Ptn from Jas Ladd & others, heirs of ofcrs & soldiers of the Revolution, asking to be allowed bounty land. 3-Cmte on Pensions: bill for the relief of Nancy Bowen & Sarah Larrabee. 4-Cmte on Naval Affairs: bill for the relief of Oscar F Johnson, a passed midshipman in the U S navy.

John Hancock as he appeared in 1782. One who saw him in June, 1782, relates that he had the appearance of advanced age. He had been repeatedly & severely afflicted with gout, probably owing in part to the custom of drinking punch-a common practice in high circles in those days. He was nearly 6 feet high & a thin person, stooping a little, apparently enfeebled by disease. His face was very handsome. He wore a blue damask gown lined with silk, a white stock, a white satin embroidered waistcoat, black satin small clothes, white silk stockings, & red morocco slippers. Gentlemen wore wigs when abroad, & commonly caps when at home. His equipage was splendid, with such as is not customary at this day. He rode, especially upon public occasions, six beautiful bay horses, attended by servants in livery. He wore a scarlet coat, with ruffles on his sleeve, which soon became the prevailing fashion.

Died: on Apr 20, in N Y, in her 22nd year, Mrs Mary Virginia, wife of J Wilson Kemp, & daughter of the late Robt Fenwick, of Wash City. Her funeral will take place this afternoon at 3 o'clock, from the residence of Mrs Milburn, corner of 7th st & Va ave.

On the train of cars which left Phil for Pittsburgh on Wed last one of the passengers, Jas P Williams, of New Brunswick, N J, came to his death in a very strange manner. His wife was sleeping beside him, & his son, a small boy, on the seat in front of him. When about 2 hours out from Phil, it was observed that his head hung down outside of one of the windows of the car in which he was seated, &, on being pulled inside, he was found insensible, apparently dying, the blood flowing profusely from a severe contusion or wound on the head. At the next station he was taken off the car & soon expired. The supposition is that the wound was inflicted on passing a water tank or some cars standing on the other track. -Pittsburgh Post

Died: on Apr 20, in Wash City, after a short illness, Jas Mead, a much respected citizen of this place, in his 74th year, formerly of PG Co, Md, but for 25 years a resident of Wash City. He was a soldier of the war of 1812. His funeral will take place today at 2 P M, from the residence of his son, Jas H Mead, 6th st, near Pa ave.

WED APR 23, 1856
Senate: 1-Ptn from John Mitchell, asking to be allowed arrears of pensions: referred. 2-Bill for the relief of Wm Allen, of Maine, asking an increase of pension & arrearages of pension. 3-Ptn from Lewis W Ludlow, a contractor for carrying the mail, asking an increase of compensation or to be released from his contract: referred. 4-Additional papers presented in relation to the claim of McKinley Ward.

House of Reps: 1-Cmte of Claims: bill for the relief of Emma Bidamon: committed. Same cmte: adverse report on the ptn of Edw Van Ness. 2-Bill for the relief of Joshua Knowles: committed. 3-Bill for the relief of Levi Robinson: committed.

Died: on Apr 21, at Annapolis, in her 14th year, Mary Alice, eldest daughter of Professor Jos E Nourse. Her funeral will take place from the residence of her Grandfather, Col M Nourse, on Wed at 11 o'clock.

Died: on Apr 21, in Wash City, Capt Geo T Hills, of Boston. His funeral will take place today at 11:30, at his late boarding-house, [Fitzgerald's] between 3rd & 4½ sts, Pa ave.

Died: on Apr 21, in Wash City, Mrs Hannah E, wife of Benj A Thorn, in her 48th year. Her funeral will take place today at 2 P M, from her late residence on 8th st, near L.

Obit-died: on Apr 19, at his residence in *Hoboken*, in his 68th year, Robt L Stevens. Mr Stevens was one of the wealthiest citizens of N Y, & with his brothers was the possessor of a large part of the land upon which *Hoboken* now stands, & which formed the principal portion of their patrimonieal estate. As he was never married, his property will, we suppose, fall to his surviving brothers. His disease was inflammatory gout, terminating in paralysis.

New Orleans, Apr 19. W C Labatt, late city atty, is reported to be a defaulter to the city to the amount of a quarter of a million of dollars.

Having bought out the entire interest of J W Shiles in the late firm, I shall in future carry on the business at the old stand, [Md ave & the Canal,] where I will keep a general assortment of all kinds of Lumber. -Saml Norment

THU APR 24, 1856
Hon Thos J Rusk, one of the Senators from Texas, has been summoned home by the extreme illness of his wife. Hon Geo S Houston, a Rep from Alabana, is occasioned by the death of his wife, which took place in this city on Sunday last. The remains of Mrs Houston are now on their way to Alabama for interment.

Senate: 1-Memorial from Sarah B Webber, widow of a late military storekeeper at Watertown, Mass, asking compensation for an improvement in the construction of gun-carriages invented by her husband. 2-Cmte on Foreign Relations: bill for the relief of Wm K Jennings. Same cmte: bill for the relief of John Randolph Clay, asking compensation for certain diplomatic services. Same cmte: adverse report on the memorial of Wm Foster, asking compensation for his services & expenses in obtaining the opening of the port of Manzanillo, Mexico. 3-Cmte on Commerce: bill for the relief of Saml A Morse & others-recommitted. 4-Cmte on Public Lands: bill granting bounty land to Jarel L Elliott.

On Sat morning Francis Nesby, a somnambulist, while asleep, jumped out of the 3rd story of the house corner of 10th ave & 18th st. He was conveyed to the N Y hospital, where he died on Sunday morning. -N Y Commercial advertiser

Mrd: on Apr 22, by Rev Mr Rolph, Lt Thos R Young, U S Navy, to Maria R Hodges, eldest daughter of John Hodges, of PG Co, Md.

Died: Wed, Luke Richardson, aged 72 years, a native of Lincolnshire, England, but for the last 40 years a resident of Wash City. His funeral will take place today at 3 o'clock P M, from the residence of his son-in-law, Jas Goddard, L st, between 13th & 14th sts.

Died: on Apr 16, at Harrisburg, Pa, Mrs Priscilla Louisa King, wife of Wm King, late of the Navy Dept, & daughter of Robt G Harper, of Gettysburg, Pa, in her 28th year.

Died: on Apr 23, in Wash City, in her 46th year, Mrs Catherine Emily Wilson, wife of John Wilson & daughter of the late Fred'k D Tschiffely. Her funeral will be tomorrow at 4 o'clock, from the residence of her husband, on 17th, between H & I.

Died: on Apr 17, at Lafayette, Indiana, Mrs Marietta Bartlett Ellsworth, wife of Hon Henry L Ellsworth, formerly Com'r of Patents, Washington.

New Orleans, Apr 22. The reported defeat of Schlessinger is confirmed. Fifty of his men were killed. The cause of the defeat is alleged to have been negligence on the part of Schlessinger. The remnant of his party had arrived at Rivas. They loudly cursed their cowardly colonel. Capt Thorpe faced him with pistols on the field of battle & threatened to shoot the coward. All was useless, however; his cowardice had created a panic. Capt Thorpe came passenger in the ship **Charles Morgan**. [Apr 25th newspaper: New Orleans, Apr 24: Parker H French has fallen out with Gen Walker & left San Juan for Aspinwall. Walker, at the head of 7,000 men, was marching against the Costa Ricans, who were expected to invade Nicaragua.]

FRI APR 25, 1856
Senate: 1-Ptn from David W Rogers, asking to be allowed bounty land & remuneration for losses sustained in consequence of rendering assistance to American prisoners in Montreal during the war of 1812. 2-Ptn from Jeremiah Pendergrast, asking to be allowed an increase of pension. 3-Ptn from John McKesson, setting forth that he holds certain "promises to pay" which were issued for the services of his ancestors in the Revolutionary war, & asking that the same may be duly redeemed. 4-Ptn from Geo J Knight, asking compensation for a vessel impressed into the service of the U S in 1814. 5-Cmte on Military Affairs; bill for the relief of John Davidson, of Ky. 6-Cmte on Foreign Relations: bill for the relief of John S Pendleton: recommended its passage.

Cmdor David Conner departed this life, at Phil, on Mar 20, 1856. He was of Irish descent, his family, emigrating to this country about the middle of the last century, settled in the valley of Wyoming, in the State of Pa. Escaping narrowly from the massacre by which that beautiful region was desolated, the parents of Conner took refuge at Harrisburg, where, many years after, he was born, in 1792. After the death of his father, he came to Phil in 1806, being then in his 15th year. On Jan 16, 1809, he was made a midshipman, & performed his first cruise in the frig **President**. Through a long & active career he maintained a character that was never clouded by even a breath of detraction. He passed the remainder of his life in Phil. He was interred with military honors in Christ churchyard. He was married in 1818 to a daughter of the celebrated Dr Physick, of Phil; this lady & 2 sons survive him.

Mrd: on Apr 24, in Wash City, by Rev R L Dashiell, G T Woodward, of Chicago, Ill, to Rebecca, daughter of Richd W Polkinhorn, of Wash, D C. [Apr 28th newspaper: Mrd: on Apr 24, in Wash City, by Rev Mr Dashiell, Geo Thos Woodward, of Chicago, Ill, to Miss Rebecca Polkinhorn, of Wash City.]

Jas R Lofland vs Chas B Jones & others. The object of this petition is to obtain an order directing the trustee for the sale of Wm Jones' real estate to pay out of the proceeds of such sale to this petitioner the sum of $1,758.82. The ptn states that Wm B Jones in his lifetime executed his single bill for the said sum of money to Jos Brown or order, payable on demand; that said Wm Jones died; that Chas B Jones was appointed trustee to sell the real state of said Jones, that said trustee sold said real estate according to the term; of said decree. The ptn further states that said Jos Brown, on Aug 10, 1853, assigned the said single bill to the petitioner, Jas R Lofland. The ptn further states that Jas D Jones, Jos Jones, & Wm Jones, three of the heirs-at-law of said Wm Jones, reside out of the State of Md. Absent dfnts are to appear in this Court, in person or by solicitor, on or before Jul 10 next. -J B Hopper -Thos F Garey, Clerk of the Circuit Court for Caroline Co, Md.

Mrd: on Apr 24, in Wash City, by Rev Wm Krebs, Saml H Young to C Jennie, eldest daughter of J C McKelden, all of Wash City.

Mrd: on Apr 24, in Gtwn, at the Methodist Episcopal Church, by Rev R D Gotwalt, Mr Nathl M Marden, of PG Co, Md, to Miss Martha D Lutz, of Gtwn.

SAT APR 26, 1856
Senate: 1-Ptn from Thos C Rollins & 91 others, citizens of Gloucester Co, Va, asking that Jos A Seawell, late a midshipman in the U S navy, may be restored to his former rank in the service. 2-Ptn from Harrison H Cocke, a furloughed captain in the U S navy, protesting against the action of the late Naval Board, & asking to be restored to his former position in the active service list. 3-Ptn from the widow of Ellet Turner, asking to be allowed a pension. 4-Ptn from Jos Graham, asking compensation for diplomatic services performed at Buenos Ayres, South America. 5-Ptn from Wm G Gildersleeve, of Wilkesbarre,Pa, setting forth that within the last 5 years a doubt has taken strong hold on the public whether there ever has been any legal slavery in the U S, & whether there can be now any slavery consistent with the Constitution. He asks Congress to inquire into the subject. 6-Cmte on Foreign Relations: memorial of Eugene Relliend, claiming compensation for losses sustained due to the bombardment of Greytown by order of Gov't, asked to be discharged from the consideration of the same, & that it be referred to the Court of Claims: which was agreed to.

Mrd: on Apr 24, in Wash City, at St Paul's Church, by Rev J G Butler, Ogden I Edwards, of Springfield, Ohio, to Louisa A Lloyd, of Wash City.

Died: on Apr 24, in Gtwn, D C, Mary Stuart, daughter of John G & Cecilia A Hedgman, aged 3 years & 6 months.

Anthony Buchly, Undertaker, Shop & Residence 303 Pa ave, south side, between 9th & 10th sts. N B: Residing on the premises, orders will be promptly attended to at all hours, day or night.

The Greenbrier Era states that Mr Jackson Huddleson was hunting in Fayette Co a few days ago & fired at a deer, but failed to kill it. He pursued it for some time, & seeing a little boy at a distance took him to be the deer & shot him. The little fellow survived a few hours & died.

MON APR 28, 1856
Skirmish with the Indians in Florida: whilst scouting in the Big Cypress, with the available force of his command, composed of Capt Dawson, 2nd Lts Langdon & Gardner, Assist Surgeon Moore, & 108 enlisted men, Maj Arnold was attacked on Apr 8 by Indians, estimated from 80 to 100. The fight & pursuit occupied about 6 hours. The loss was: Private John Simms, Co L, 2nd artl, mortally wounded, [survived about 15 minutes;] Cpl Jos Carson; privates John Muller, John Strobell, Co C, 2nd artl; & Thos Newton, Co L, 1st Artl, severely wounded, & privates Silas M Watkins & Wm Abbott, Co C, 2nd artl, slightly wounded.

Geo Wilds, a young man, while shooting muskrats above the Passaic Falls, at Paterson, on Wed last, accidentally killed himself. He was aged about 18 years.

$100 reward for runaway negro man Joe Campbell, about 32 years old. He has a brother living in Wash, D C. -John Hamilton, living near Port Tobacco, Chas Co, Md.

Orphans Court of Wash Co, D C. In the case of Hopkins Lightner, exc of Stephen Pleasanton, deceased, the executor & Court have appointed May 20 next, for the final settlement of the personal estate of said deceased, of the assets in hand.
-Ed N Roach, Reg/o wills

Mrd: on Apr 23, in Portland, Maine, by Rev Alex Burgess, Capt Albert Tracy, U S Army, to Miss Sarah Whitman, daughter of Hon Albion K Parris.

TUE APR 29, 1856
Chancery Sale: by decree of the Circuit Court of Wash Co, D C, dated Apr 23, 1856, passed in a cause wherein Halsey & others are cmplnts & Gorman's heirs are dfndnts: sale on May 22 next, of lot 12 in square 580, with 2 small frame tenements.
-John F Ennis, trustee -A Green, auctioneer

Household & kitchen furniture at auction on: May 1, at the residence of Mr T Fitch, on North G, between 13th & 14th sts: an excellent assortment of furniture.
-A Green, auct

Valuable & beautiful farm or country seat, about 3 miles from the Capital, at auction: on May 22, the residence of the late John Agg, known as the *Vineyard*, on the Heights, north of Washington, adjoining the farm attached to the Military Asylum. The farm contains 75 acres, water near the dwlg, & good roads leading to it. Apply to E J Middleton, at the City Hall, H N Gilbert, 548 Pa ave, between 1st & 2nd sts, or to A Green, auctioneer.

Senate: 1-Ptn from Capt Hiram Paulding, of the U S navy, asking to be reimbursed for expenses incurred by him in receiving & entertaining on board the U S frig **St Lawrence** the heads of certain foreign Gov'ts. 2-Ptn from Sally G Mathews, widow of Wm P Mathews, asking compensation for the services of her late husband as a clerk in the Treasury Dept. 3-Ptn from Wm S Bliss, asking compensation for services in raising & subsisting volunteers for the Mexican war. 4-Ptn from Mathew Hines, asking payment for a lot of ground in Franklin square, in Wash City, which said square was purchased by the Gov't. 5-Ptn from Laurent Millandon, of Louisiana, asking the confirmation of his title to certain lands purchased on the eastern side of Mobile bay, in the State of Alabama. 6-Resolved, That the Court of Claims be requested to return to the Senate the ptn & papers relating to the claim of Eliz Montgomery, heir of Capt Hugh Montgomery, an ofcr in the Revolutionary war, referred to that Court by the Senate on Feb 19, 1856.

Letter published in the Austin Times of Apr 12th says: Capt Callahan & Wm S Johnson are both killed & E Clement Hinds dangerously wounded. Woodson Blasengame, his son Calvin, & his wife have been taken into custody for the perpetration of these horrible crimes. The painful tragedy took place at Pittsburg, on Martin's Fork of the Blanco. Blasengame is an old man about 60 years of age.

U S Patent Ofc, Wash, Apr 26, 1856. Ptn of Reuben Rich, of Oswego Co, N Y, praying for the extension of a patent granted to him on Jul 8, 1842, for the improvement in water wheels, for 7 years from the expiration of said patent, which takes place on Jul 8, 1856. -Chas Mason, Com'r of Patents

Died: on Apr 28, after a lingering illness, Wm T Truton, aged 83 years. His funeral will be tomorrow at 4 o'clock, from the residence of his brother, John B Turton, on H st, between 21st & 22nd sts.

Died: on Apr 6, at Shallotte, Pitt Co, N C, of paralysis, John H Burney, aged 52 years.

Died: on Apr 12, at his residence, on *Good Hope Hill*, Mr Thos Perkins, in his 58th year, leaving a wife & 5 children to mourn his irreparable loss.

Mrd: on Apr 29, in Wash City, by Rev Dr Pyne, Geo B Warren, jr, of Troy, N Y, to E Phebe W, daughter of B Ogle Tayloe, of Wash City.

WED APR 30, 1856
Extensive sale of saddles, harness, trunks, & saddler's hardware at auction: Mr Danl Campbell intending to change his business. Sale on May 8, at his Saddlers' Establishment, 396 Pa ave, between 4½ & 6th sts. -A Green, auct

Jas McCombs, duly convicted of murder, was hung on Fri last at Columbia, S C. The scene was the more painful from the breaking of the rope when the culprit was first swung off, which rendered necessary his second suspension. The sufferer had been intemperate, & in a moment of excitement shot a police ofcr who, in discharge of duty, was endeavoring to preserve the peace.

On the day of the funeral of Thos R Borden, a respectable citizen of Greene Co, Ala, who was shot dead in his bed, it was found that his son had decamped with his father's horse & $4,000. He was pursued & arrested on suspicion of being the murderer.

Wash Corp: 1-Ptn of Henrietta Shryock, praying for the remission of a fine: referred to the Cmte of Claims. 2-Ptn from Leonora S Butler, asking to be relieved from the payment of certain expenses incurred at a tax sale: referred to the Cmte of Claims. 3-Cmte of Ways & Means: bill for the relief of F B Poston: passed. 4-Cmte on Improvements: bill for the relief of Chas Stewart: passed. Same cmte: bill for the relief of W Doroty & B K Gladmon: rejected.

Mrd: on Apr 29, in Wash City, at the E st Baptist Church, by Rev Dr Binney, J W Helmer to Miss Ellen A Petrie, both of Little Falls, N Y.

Desperate affray at Panama on Apr 15 between the American transit passengers & the natives, in which the former had 30 killed & 40 wounded. Among the killed were Michl Bettern, of Vt; R W Marks, of Pa; M Dubois, of Louisiana; & Mr Stokes, an ofcr of Walker's army. Among the wounded are Wm H Hunter, Theodore De Sabila, Sec of the American Consul at Panama, & Mr Palmer, an employe of the railroad company, all residents on the Isthmus; also Geo O Fields, of N Y, & Rev John Selwood, late of Grahamville, S C. The riot originated with a drunken man who refused to pay a native a dime for a piece of watermelon.

$100 reward for runaway negro boy Daniel, about 16 years of age. -Wm J Berry, living near Upper Marlboro, PG Co, Md.

THU MAY 1, 1856
Mrd: on Apr 29, in Wash City, by Rev Andrew G Carothers, Mr John Humphrey to Miss Ann Sophia Hoover, both of Wash City.

From Central America. War between Costa Rica & Nicaragua. Persons taken prisoner at *Santa Rosa* & shot on Mar 25:

Jas Salomon, Ireland	Philip Johmit, Germany
John Perkin, Italy	Peter Connan, Ireland
Andrew Constantine, Samos	Jas Hollin, Ireland
Manuel Grege, Corfu	Antoine Pornu, France
Theodore Lidecker, American	David Koch, Germany
Henry Dunn, Ireland	Wm West, Prussia
Isaac A Rose, American	Francis Narvaez, Panama
Henry Johsierder, Germany	Theodore Heining, Prussia
Peter Pyne, Ireland	

Senate: 1-Ptn from L M Joslin, asking an act of incorporation for a Granite Manufacturing Company in Wash City, for the manufacture of a new material known as Foster's improved bldg block: referred. 2-Additional documents presented from Philo C Shelton & his associates in relation to their wishes. 3-Ptn from John P Andrews, asking the adoption of measures for the suppression of the Coolie slave trade in American vessels. 4-Memorial from Henry P Schell, in relation to the slave question; submits a bill which he recommends as curative of the evil.

Died: on Apr 30, Mr Saml Dunwell, in his 55th year, a native of Balt, but for the last 25 years a resident of Wash City. His funeral will take place this evening at 5 o'clock, from the residence of his brother-in-law, Geo Savage, 9th st, near Pa ave..

Equity-No 969: Selby B Scaggs & wife, Francis O Brady, & Eliz Ogden, against Nathl B Fugitt & Susan Brady. Parties named & Henry Naylor, trustee, are to attend at my ofc, in City Hall, Wash, on May 7, where I shall state the trustee's account & the shares of the parties in the trust fund. -W Redin, auditor

U S Patent Ofc, Wash, Apr 29, 1856. Ptn of Alfred Hall, of Perth Amboy, N J, praying for the extension of a patent granted to him Sep 3, 1842, for an improvement in brick presses, for 7 years from the expiration of said patent which takes place on Sep 3, 1856. -Chas Mason, Com'r of Patents

FRI MAY 2, 1856
Senate: 1-Cmte of Claims: bill for the relief of Norwood McClelland, master of the steamboat **New World**. 2-Cmte on Commerce: memorial of Henry J Rogers, submitted a report, with a bill to provide for the general introduction of a uniform national code of marine signals.

The State Convention of the Democracy of Md assembled in the Hall of the Md Institute at Balt on Wed last, & was organized by the choice of the following ofcrs: Pres, Hon John C Legrand. Vice Presidents: Richd C Holliday, Richd Waters, A Willison, Col Wm Slater, & Wm J Byrd. Secs: Col Geo Gale, Dr L Macklin, Wm H Hiss, Jas H Grove, & A P Sorden. On the motion of Hon Wm T Hamilton, of Wash Co, a cmte of one from each county & the city of Balt was appointed. The Convention appointed Presidential Electors for the State, as follows: First district, Henry Goldsborough, of Talbot; second, Richd W Ringgold, of Kent; third, Levi K Bowen, of Balt; fourth, Francis Gallagher, of Balt City; fifth, Josiah H Gordon, of Allegany; sixth, Geo W Hughes, of Anne Arundel. John M Robinson, of Queen Anne's, [Eastern Shore,] & Walter R Mitchell, of Charles, [Western Shore,] for the State at large.

Brvt Capt Edmund L F Hardcastle, Corps of Topographical Engineers, & 2nd Lt Wm A B Jones, first cavalry, have resigned their commissions in the Army.

J F Caldwell, Dentist, is not connected with Dr Baily, but has removed to the house first above Pa ave, on 11th st, adjoining Farnham's bookstore, where he is ready to operate on teeth. He will be glad to receive visits from recent patrons, as well as those whom he has professionally served 20 years since.

Mrd: on Apr 15, by Rev Calvin A Frazer, Rev David Kerr, D D, Rector of the Church of the Epiphany, Opelousas, La, to Miss Maria Louisa, daughter of the late Thos B Fitch, of Louisville, Ky.

Mrd: on May 1, by Rev S H Mirick, Mr G L Sheriff to Miss Susie, 4th daughter of A Rothwell, all of Wash City.

Mrd: on Apr 30, by Rev Wm Krebs, Jos S Boss to Susan A Banks, all of Wash City.

Wash City Ordinance: 1-Act for the relief of Benj K Morsell: the sum of $359.10 be paid to Morsell, police magistrate for the 4th district, for extra services officially rendered by him. -Approved, Apr 25, 1856.

Land for sale in Buckingham Co, Va. The undersigned wishes to close his farming operations in said county, & offers for sale upon reasonable terms, or in exchange for city property, 2 tracts of land lying within 6 miles of Buckingham Court-house. The *Owen's Mills* tract contains 230 acres; with a small dwlg house & necessary out-houses; steam saw & grist mill. The other tract contains 216 acres & lies within 1/4th mile of the first mentioned. Consult Mr S W Owen, 212 Pa ave, or the subscriber, at present on the premises. -Edw Owen

N Y, May 1. Hon Ogden Hoffman, recently Atty Gen of this State, died this afternoon after a short illness.

SAT MAY 3, 1856
Senate: 1-Ptn from Putnam W Taft & others, of Worcester, Mass, against the renewal of the patent for a planing machine. 2-Additional papers in support of the claim of Anne Rice, legal rep of John Jones, deceased: presented. 3-Cmte of Claims: asked to be discharged from the consideration of the memorial of Francis C Elliot, widow of Cmdor Jesse D Elliot, & that it be referred to the Cmte on Naval Affairs: which was agreed to. Same cmte: bill for the relief of Wm G Ridgely; & a bill for the relief of the heirs & reps of the late Robt Sewall.

House of Reps: 1-Bills & resolutions to which no objection was made: to grant L Jane Horner & children a section of land in Oregon. Relief of: Anson Dart; of the reps & sureties of Robt King, deceased; of the heirs of Col Chas Simms, late collector of the port of Alexandria; & to settle the accounts of Chas P Babcock, late Indian agent at Detroit, Michigan. Relief of Wm Humphrey, jr, owner of fishing schnr **Good Exchange**, lost at sea. Relief of Jas M Goddin; of John Crawford; of Capt J P Hatch, of the U S Army; of Jacob Price, of Jefferson Co, Va; of the legal reps of Capt Jos H Whipple, deceased; of Emma Bidamon; & of the heirs of the late Col John Hardin. Settle the accounts of Oliver M Wozencraft. Joint resolution for the relief of Dr Wm P A Hall, late of the Tenn volunteers in the Mexican war.

Trustee's sale of a dwlg house: decree of the Circuit Court of Wash Co, D C, passed in a cause in which E M Linthicum & others are cmplnts & Ephraim Wheeler & others are dfndnts: sale on May 26 next of: lot B, in Wm B Todd's subdivision of part of square 352, & part of lot C, in the same subdivision, with improvements thereon. Also the residue of said lot C. The house occupies lot B & part of lot C.
-John Marbury, trustee -A Green, auct

Mrd: on Thu, at St Luke's Church, Balt, by Rev Chas W Rankin, Hon Geo Vail, M C, of N J, to Miss Mary Lewis Lightfoot, of Port Royal, Va.

Obit-died: on Apr 24, at **Waverley**, [the residence of her beloved daughter, Mrs Etheldra Harris, of Chas Co, Md,] Mrs Eliz Parker Chapman, the venerable mother of Hon John G Chapman, in her 78th year. She was nurtured & educated from her earliest youth in the faith of the Protestant Episcopal Church.

MON MAY 5, 1856
Two youths, sons of Messrs Wm C Burton & Geo Burks, of this city, while bathing in Black Water Creek, yesterday evening, drowned. -Lynchburg Virginian

Trustee's sale of valuable bldg lot on 10th st west, on May 26, 1856, by deed of trust from Estwick Evans & wife to the subscriber, dated Oct 10, 1855: recorded in Liber J A S 101, folios 399 thru 402, of the land records for Wash Co, D C: sale of lots 7 thru 9 in square 339, in Wash City. The lots front on 10th st west between N & O sts north. -Hugh B Sweeny, trustee -A Green auct

Hon Robt B Gilchrist, Judge of the U S District Court of S C, died at his residence in Charleston on Thu last. The condition of his health has for some time prepared his friends to a degree for this melancholy issue.

Mrs Washington French, of Atala Co, Miss, recently presented, at a single birth, to the astonished Mr Washington French, two boys & two girls. The parties had been married only one year.

Hon Ogden Hoffman died at his residence in this city on Thu. The disease was congestion of the lungs, being the sudden determination of a slight sickness, which had been but of a few days' duration. He was born in N Y C, & at the time of his death was in his 63rd year. He was the son of Josiah Ogden Hoffman, who in his day was one of the most eminent lawyers of this city, & at one time Atty Gen of this State. Mr Hoffman graduated at Columbia College in 1812; just after the declaration of war against Great Britian; he received a midshipman's warrant, & was attached to the command of Cmdor Decatur. During the period while the U S frig **President**, commanded by Cmdor Decatur, was blockaded in the harbor of N Y, Mr Hoffman remained on board, & when finally, in Jan, 1815, she put out to sea, he was on her decks ready to encounter all the risks of battle. A bloody running fight, through long hours, followed. The President was captured & he became a prisoner of war, was taken to Bermuda, & remained there for some months, until an exchange of prisoners of war effected his release. He was admitted to the Bar & practiced in Goshen, Orange Co, N Y, & in 1828 represented it in the Legislature of the State. In Nov 1853 he was elected Atty Gen of the State of N Y. Mr Hoffman was twice married. His first wife was the daughter of Jonathan Burrall, cashier of the first U S Bank. His second wife, who survives him, is the daughter of the late Saml L Southard, formerly Sec of the Navy. His funeral took place at the Church of the Annunciation on Sat. -N Y Courier

Madame Chegary's Boarding & Day School for Young Ladies. A report that she is about to give up her school, Mme Chegary informs she will continue; her niece, Mme Prevost, [formerly Mlle Louise Berault,] will reside with her & take an active part in the school. Her country residence is in N J, & she will receive students during the summer.

Orphans Court of Wash Co, D C. Letters of administration on the personal estate of Seth M Levensworth, late of Indiana, deceased. -Isaac Beers, adm

Mrs Emily P Lesdernier was greeted by a delighted audience at Carusi's Saloon on Sat. She will this evening appear in the costume of an Indian girl & read Longfellow's celebrated poem of Hiawatha.

Horse-shoe Robinson, a drama founded upon the celebrated novel by Hon J P Kennedy, will be produced at the Nat'l Theatre this evening.

Mrd: on Apr 15, at the residence of Mrs M A Glover, Marengo Co, Ala, by Rev Mr Blanche, Danl F Prout, of Mobile, to Miss Laura D Glover.

Died: on May 3, Wm Steele McNair, aged 25 years & 10 days, only son of Col D R McNair. His funeral will take place at the residence of his father, 461 E st, on May at 10½ o'clock.

Died: on May 3, Mrs Mary E, wife of John W England, of N Y C, & eldest daughter of Judson & Deborah Mitchell, of Gtwn. Her funeral will take place today, at 4 o'clock, from the residence of her father, 23 First st.

Died: on May 3, in Wash City, Dr Geo W Cherry, a native of N Y, aged about 55 years. For many years he was a practicing dentist; but during the latter period of his life devoted himself almost exclusively to a series of mechanical inventions, in which he gave evidence of much genius, though it was not permitted him to live to realize their practical benefits.

Columbia, S C, May 4. Ex-Gov Troup, of Ga, died in Laurene Co, S C, on Apr 26.

Geo C Thomas, of Wash, being in Europe attending to important Patent business, hereby informs his clients that he expects soon to return & resume his practice of his profession. -London, England, Apr 7, 1856.

For rent, the valuable farm the ***Highlands***, the residence of the late R Y Brent. It is 9 miles out on the 7th st Plank Road, & contains 400 acres. Inquire of B L Jackson & Bro, Wash.

TUE MAY 6, 1856
Casualties. 1-Mr Smith mistook Mr Atkins for a wild turkey in the woods of Alabama, & shot him dead-both plantation overseers. 2-A M Cobb of Hickman, Ky, was instantly killed a few days since, by the falling of a heavy stick of timber from the frame of a new church. 3-A little son of Mr Bower was drowned in Memphis, Tenn, by falling into the immersion pool of the Baptist Church. 4-Sarah B Bates, aged 14, fell from a boat in Cumberland, Me, one day last week, & was drowned.

Senate: 1-Ptn from Jas A Girardin, asking payment of a balance due for the services of his ancestor as a volunteer in the war of 1812. 2-Ptn from F C Treadwell, asking that all volunteers engaged in the defence of Salem & its vicinity in the last war with Great Britian may be placed on the same footing as other volunteers who served in that war. 3-Additional papers submitted relating to the claim of Capt S D Sturgess, of the U S Army. 4-Cmte on the Judiciary: bill for the relief of Christian Hax, of Md, reported it back, & asked for its immediate consideration: which was agreed to. 5-Cmte on Pensions: bill for the relief of the heirs-at-law of Sarah Crandall, deceased. Same cmte: bill granting 5 years' half-pay to Mrs Ann Turner, widow of Ellert Turner. Same cmte: bill granting pension to Nancy M Gunsolly, widow of Lyman M Richmond. 6-Cmte on Private Land Claims: adverse report on the memorial of Smith Mowry. 7-Cmte on Naval Affairs: adverse report on the memorial of E L Winder, & asked that the memorialist have leave to withdraw his papers: which was granted. 8-House bills referred-relief of: the legal reps of Capt John H Whipple; of the heirs of the late Col John Hardin; of Capt J P Hatch, of the U S Army; of Dr Wm P A Hail, late of the Tenn volunteers in the Mexican war; of Jacob Price, of Jefferson Co, Va; of John Crawford; of the heirs of Col Chas Simms, late Collector of the Port of Alexandria; & of Emma Bidamon. Also, granting a pension to Ansel Wilkinson; & to continue the pension of Mrs Nancy Weatherford. Also to construe the act entitled "An Act for the relief of Jas M Goggin, approved Jul 27, 1834." 9-Act to grant to L Jane Horner & children a section of land in Oregon: referred.

Household & kitchen furniture at auction on: May 13, at the residence of Louis Janin, 15th & H sts. -Jas C McGuire, auct

The entire set of Pews in St Peter's Church, Capitol Hill, will be disposed of at private sale. They are of the best materials & workmanship, & in excellent condition. They maybe seen at any hour of the day, & full information as to price & terms will be given upon application to the pastor on the premises, or to J C Fitzpatrick, 294 south B st.

Henry N Lansdale & Jonathan Kirkwood have entered into partnership, under the firm of Lansdale & Kirkwood, for the purchase & sale of all kinds of city property; also, farms & land. Ofc 514 7th st, opposite the Nat'l Intelligencer.

Melle Manvers, Parisienne, has removed to 451 10th st, between E & F sts, & will continue to give lessons in the French & Spanish languages & Piano & Singing lessons, at her own residence or that of the scholars. Melle Manvers speaks English.

Mrd: on May 4, in Wash City, at St Paul's Church, by Rev J G Butler, Isaac Angney to Matidla Clark, all of Wash City.

Died: on May 4, in Wash City, Mrs Harriet H, wife of Hiram Richey, in her 35th year. Her funeral is this evening at 4 o'clock, from St Patrick's Church, F st, between 9th & 10th sts.

Died: on May 5, in Wash City, after a lingering illness of several months, Wm Clare, aged 48 years. His funeral is this evening at half-past 4 o'clock, at his late residence, over the Bank of Washington.

Died: yesterday, at Mount Holly, N J, Jas Eakin, who was nearly 50 years a faithful ofcr in the Treasury Dept, the greater part of the time, & until 1848, the assiduous & able chief clerk in the ofc of the 2nd Auditor. Mr Eakin united the manners & habits of a gentleman, & was respected in this community, where he spent nearly all his life.

Orphans Court of Wash Co, D C. Letters of administration on the personal estate of John Poor, late of Wash Co, deceased. -Sarah Poor, admx

Orphans Court of Wash Co, D C. Letters of administration on the personal estate of Thos H Busey, late of Wash Co, deceased. -Sarah N Busey, admx

Orphans Court of Wash Co, D C. In the case of Wm R Woodward, adm of Eliz McGarvey, deceased, the administrator & Court appointed May 27 for the final settlement of the personal estate of said deceased, of the assets in hand.
-Ed N Roach, Reg/o wills

WED MAY 7, 1856
Household furniture at auction on: May 16, at the House Furnishing store of Wm Dowling, on High st, Gtwn, a few doors north of Bridge st: all his furniture & housekeeping articles. -Jas C McGuire, auct

The venerable & distinguished Dr John C Warren, [nephew of the celebrated patriot, Gen Warren, who gloriously fell at Bunker Hill,] died at Boston on Sunday last, universally respected & regretted.

One day last week a dog in the family of the late Mr Isaac Pearson died from actual grief for the loss of his master. The dog was 10 years old, & Mr Pearson had always taken the utmost care of him. The dog refused to eat or drink, & it appeared he pined away & died without any appearance of disease. Do dogs reason? -Newburyport Herald

House of Reps: 1-Remonstrance of Geo W Thompson, J S Sharp, & others against the extension of the Woodworth patent. 2-Remonstrance of Albert Arnold, Thos Hancock, & others, for the same object. 3-Ptn of Ann H Allen, asking a further allowance as the legal rep of Saml Allen, an invalid pensioner.

The Indian war in Florida; hostile Indians are variously estimated at from 200 to 500. The U S troops in the State consist of 3 companies & 2 detachments, in addition to which there are 4 companies in the State service, the whole under the command of Col Munroe, 2nd artl. List of the ofcrs & their posts:

Fort Brooke, Tampa
Brvt Col J Munroe, 2nd Artl, commanding 2nd Regt Artl & troops in Peninsula of Fla.
Maj H Leonard, Pay Dept
Capt J C Casey, Indian Agent
Brvt Maj J McKinstry, Assist Quartermaster
Capt C S Kilburn, Commissary Substance
1st Lt T J Haines, Adj 2nd Artl
1st Lt T M Vincent, 2nd Artl, acting assist Adj Gen.

Fort Myers:
Brvt Col H Brown, 2nd Artl, commanding on the Caloosa-Hatchee
Capt W S Hancock, Assist Quartermaster
Assist Surgeon W F Edgar, Medical Dept
Assist Surgeon J Moore, Medical Dept, on duty in the Big Cypress Swamp.
Capt H C Pratt, 2nd Artl, in command of expedition to Cho-ka-lis-ka
Capt A Elsey, 2nd Artl, on duty at Cho-ka-lis-ka
Capt H A Allen, 2nd Artl
1st Lt J M Robertson, 2nd Artl, A A C S
1st Lt H Benson, on duty at Cho-ka-lis-ka
1st Lt T K Walker, 4th Artl, assist Indian Agent, on duty at Cho-ka-lis-ka
1st Lt C L Hartsuff, 2nd Artl
2nd Lt J T Greble, 2nd Artl
2nd Lt M P Small, 2nd Artl

Fort Reynaud:
Brvt Maj L G Arnold, 2nd Artl, commanding expedition in the Big Cypress Swamp
Assist Surgeon R L Brodie, Medical Dept
Capt A A Gibson, 2nd Artl, on duty at Tampa, **Fort Brooke**, Fla
1st Lt F H Larned, 2nd Artl, A A C S & A A Q M
1st Lt A J S Mohnard, 2nd Artl
2nd Lt G G Garner, 2nd Artl, on duty in Big Cypress Swamp
2nd Lt Thos Grey, 2nd Artl, on duty in Big Cypress Swamp
2nd Lt A S Webb, 2nd Artl, on duty at **Fort Centre**

Died: yesterday, in Wash City, Mrs Eliz R Larned, consort of Col Benj F Larned. Her funeral is this afternoon at 4 o'clock, from her late residence on 13th st.

Died: on May 5, in Wash City, Albert O'Neal Wall, son of C O & A E Wall, aged 5 months & 13 days. His funeral is this afternoon at 3 o'clock, from their residence on 6th st, between E & F sts.

The stable belonging to Mr Shreve, at 7th & I sts, was destroyed by fire yesterday-loss from ten to fifteen hundred dollars. It was believed to be the work of an incendiary. Mr Benj C Greenup, aged about 24 or 25, lost his life while aiding in conducting the engine to the fire down Capitol Hill, whether by a violent fall or by being run over by the carriage, appears uncertain. He was a marble-cutter by trade, extensively known in the city as a good vocalist, & was highly esteemed.
+
Died: on May 5, in Wash City, Benj C Greenup, in his 25th year. His funeral is this afternoon at 2 o'clock, from the Columbia Engine house, Capitol Hill.

Mrd: on Apr 8, at **Fort Fillmore**, New Mexico, by Rev Mr Tallhirst, 1st Lt L W O'Bannon, Regimental Quartermaster 3rd U S Infty, to Miss May Chase, daughter of Col D S Miles, U S Army.

Mrd: on May 6, in Wash City, at the Methodist Protestant Parsonage, by Rev P Light Wilson, Mr Richd Bell to Miss Christina Vermillion.

Mrd: on May 6, in Wash City, at the Methodist Protestant Parsonage, by Rev P Light Wilson, Mr John R Shinn to Miss Martha E Barkman.

Columbia, S C, May 5. The State Convention to elected delegates to the Democratic Nat'l Convention met this evening, Hon Francis W Pickens chosen permanent Pres. On May 6 Hon Jas L Orr delivered an address. The following were selected as delegates:

At Large:
F W Pickens	W D Porter	J L Orr
J L Manning	C McBeth	Jas Farrow
A McGrath	J D Allen	F J Moses
Gen Gadberry	B H Brown	E J Palmer
B H Wilson	P S Brooks	
C W Dudley	C P Sullivan	

THU MAY 8, 1856
Trustee's sale of bldg lot in square 559 at auction: on May 28, by deed of trust from Jos S Boss, to the subscriber, dated Jun 1, 1855, recorded in Liber J A S No 107, folios 118 thru 120, of the land records for Wash Co, D C: west half of lot 8 in square 559, fronting on L st north 30 feet, between 1st st west & N J ave.
-John Mills, trustee -A Green, auct

Died: on May 6, in Wash City, after a short illness, David Hoover, in his 59th year.

Died: on Feb 23 last, at his residence, **Hanson's Green**, near Port Tobacco, Chas Co, Md, Jos Young, a universally esteemed & valued citizen.

The Telegraph brought yesterday the sad intelligence of the sudden death of Hon Wm C Dawson, of Georgia. He had been successively Representative & Senator in Congress. He died at his residence in Greensborough, of neuralgia of the heart. [May 19th newspaper: Meeting of the Wash Encampment, No 1, Knights Templars, held in Wash City, May 14, 1856: in memory of Hon Wm C Dawson. Copy of resolutions of respect to be sent to the widow & afflicted family of Hon Dawson. -Wm J Rhees, recorder]

Ex-Govn'r Geo M Troup died at his residence in Laurens Co, Ga, on May 3, in his 76th year. He was a native of Georgia, & filled in succession all the highest official honors his State could bestow on him, & he deserved them all. He was Rep & Senator in Congress & Govn'r of the State. He possessed Roman virtue & inflexibility.

Telegraphic dispatch from Marion, S C, about a fatal duel on Sat last, near Fair Bluff, between Dr Wm C Willkings & Jos H Flanner, both young men & citizens of this place. On the third fire the former received a ball through the lungs, & in a few minutes expired. The difficulty grew out of a speech made by Mr Willkings on Wed last at the Democratic meeting at the court-house. They fought with pistols, at 10 paces, Mr Willking being the challenger. -Wilmington [N C] Herald

Before the Circuit Court of King & Queen Co, Va, now in session, [Judge Lomax presiding,] Philip Eustis, a citizen of the county, was found guilty of drunken & disorderly conduct at the "Old Church," by which the exercises of a Methodist meeting were seriously interrupted. The offender was sentenced to pay a fine of $50 & to be imprisoned 6 months in the county jail. -Alex Gaz

Trustee's sale of house & lot on the Island: by deed of trust from Henry Thomas & wife, dated Mar 26, 1855, recorded in Liber J A S No 94, folios 460: public sale on May 30th next, of lot 7 in square 389, fronting 12 feet 7 inches on G st south, between 9th & 10th sts, with a well-built frame dwlg-house. -Chas S Wallach, trustee -Jas C McGuire, auct

Senate: 1-Ptn from Geo Watt, asking an extension of his patent for an improvement in ploughs. 2-Ptn from H R Rooker, for herself & other children of Jabez B Rooker, asking compensation for the services of their father as clerk to the Com'r of Public Bldgs. 3-Ptn from Franklin Peale, of Phil, setting forth his claims to certain improvements made by him in the machinery & processes for refining & coining the precious metals while engaged in the service of the mint, of which the U S has received the benefit, & asking to be recompensed therefor. 4-Cmte on Revolutionary Claims: adverse reports on the memorials of Stephen Tuthill, & of Robt H Coggeshall.

Dr Jas G Percival, one of our American poets of extensive popularity, died on Friday last in Wisconsin, having for some time held the ofc of Geologist of that State. He was the son of a physician, & was born Sep 15, 1795, in Berlin, near Hartford, Conn. He received his collegiate education at Yale, & entered the Medical School of the same institution, receiving the degree of Dr of Medicine in 1820. His first volume of poems was published in 1821, & it was well received. For a short time he held a commission as assist surgeon in the U S army, but resigned soon & removed to Boston. Of late years he had led a quiet bachelor life in New Haven, until recently, when he undertook the ofc of geologist of Wisconsin, in the performance of whose duties he has just died, at the age of 61. -Phil Bulletin

Circuit Court of Wash Co, D C-in Equity. Re. Petition of Jno Cox, trustee, & al. The ptn of Gideon Pearce represents that in pursuance of a decree in this cause, dated Jan 16, 1844, the trustee, John Cox, sold to the petitioner lots 22, 32 thru 34, in Peter, Beatty, Threlkeld, & Deakins' addition to Gtwn, for $2,000; that said purchase money has been since fully paid; that the trustee, John Cox, is dead, & petitioner is entitled & asks to have a trustee appointed in place of said deceased trustee to convey the premises to him. The peititioner further asks that the___ que trusts interested in said property may be made parties & required to answer the petition, & states that of said parties Eliz Underwood, wife of Jos R Underwood, John T Cox, & Robt M Cox are non-residents. Said non-residents are to appear in this Court, in person or by solicitor, on or before Sep 15 next. -Jno A Smith, clerk

Yesterday the large brick livery stable of Mr Jas Shreve, jr, [adjoining that of Mr Jas Shreve, sen, which was destroyed on Tue,] was discovered on fire, & was totally destroyed, the horses & vehicles only being saved. The adjoining stable, belonging to Mr Paulus Thyson & occupied by Mr Allen Dorsey, was also nearly destroyed. Among the persons who entered Mr Shreve's stable for the purpose of rescuing his horses was Mr Ebenezer Lord, grocer, whose store is at 9th & N Y ave, & while he was there the rear wall fell upon him. He was extricated & removed as soon as possible, when it was found that his right thigh was broken, his left arm bruised & burnt, & his left hand burnt, & his forehead cut. At 10 o'clock last night Mr Lord was regarded as doing well. He is a son of Mr Francis B Lord, an old & respected citizen of Wash, & a young man of fine character & amiable deportment. Two or three negroes were arrested on suspicion of firing the stable yesterday & confessed that & other recent acts of incendiarism, & they were going to fire other bldgs last night. [May 8th newspaper: Mr Lord is doing well & in a fair way to recovery.]

Wash City Ordinances: 1-Act for the relief of L Godfrey: the sum of $250 be paid to him for the purpose of indemnifying him for damages sustained by him in the change of the grade on 14th st west. 2-Act for the relief of John W Stevens: to pay him $7.50, a refund for 2 licenses taken out by him for carrying on certain business which he was forcibly compelled to relinquish. 3-Act for the relief of F A Hager: the fine imposed on him for an alleged violation of the law relating to huckstering is remitted: provided Hager pay the costs of prosecution. -Approved, May 1, 1856

Mrd: on May 6, in Wash City, by Rev S A H Marks, Mr Robt Sauvan to Miss Margaret Ann Pickford.

FRI MAY 9, 1856
Senate: 1-Bill for the relief of the legal reps of Jabez B Rooker. [This bill was passed at the last session & lost in the House of Reps from want of time, & had been again reported unanimously by the Cmte of Claims.] 2-Cmte on the Post Ofc & Post Roads: bill for the relief of the legal reps of Geo Mayo. 3-Inquiry to be made to inquire into the propriety of paying to F B Gilbert, late a page in the Senate, the same extra compensation as was allowed other pages of 2nd session of the 30th Congress.

Desirable Market-house property at auction: by power of the atty from the executors & trustees of Chas Marquand, late of the State of Ohio, deceased: sale on May 24, of 2 lots of ground, each fronting 20 feet on the east side of Market Space, in Gtwn, & running back 127 feet 9 inches to Warehouse alley. One has a 2 story brick house, & the other a 3 story brick house, both excellent business stands. Title believed to be good. -John Mountz, atty of Peter Marquand & Chas E Marquand. -E S Wright, auctioneer

Household & kitchen furniture at auction on: May 12, at the residence of Mrs Raymond, 367 C st, between 4½ & 6th sts. -A Green, auctioneer

Trustee's sale of valuable Farm in PG Co, Md, at public auction, by deed of trust from Robt W Burrows to the subscriber, dated Apr 10, 1854, recorded in Liber O N No 1, folios 643 thru 645, one of the land records for PG Co, Md. Auction on Jun 9 next, of the Farm, which contains 175 acres, more or less, in said county, about 3 miles west of Beltsville, adjoining the **White House, Buck Lodge**, & Capt Eversfield's Farms. The improvements consist of a good dwlg house, barn, & all necessary out bldgs. -Chas McNamee, trustee -A Green, auctioneer

Trustee's sale of valuable real estate in Gtwn, D C: by deed of trust dated Dec 15, 1855, & lodged for record in the ofc of the Clerk of the Circuit Court of said District on Apr 25, 1856, the subscriber will offer for sale the eastern most of the two three story brick dwlg houses on the north side of Bridge st, & opposite Mrs Lang's Tavern, lying between the west gable-wall of the warehouse built by Thos Cramphin & the dividing-wall between the house now offered for sale, & the westernmost of the said 2 dwlg houses, now owned & occupied by R Cruikshank. -Lloyd W Williams, trustee -Edw S Wright, auct

Chancery sale: by decree of the Circuit Court of Wash Co, D C, dated Nov 2, 1855, passed in a cause wherein Jos Bryan & others are cmplnts, Wyatt S Berry & others dfndnts, I shall sell, on May 30, lot 21 in square 457, between D & E sts north, with 2 small brick houses & 1 frame house. -Chas Edmonston, trustee -A Green, auct

U S Troops taken to Lawrence, Kansas, by Col Sumner, consist of 4 companies of cavalry, numbering 300 men, composed of Co B, Capt D B Sackett & Lt A V Colburn; Co C, Capt T J Wood, 1st Lt A Iverson, & 2nd Lt J R Church; Co G, Capt W S Walker; & Co H, 1st Lt E A Carr, 1st Lt A Ranson, jr, Adj & 1st Lt J E B Stewart, A Q M. -Union

Local Items. Thos Keating, a waiter at Willard's Hotel in Wash City, was yesterday morning killed by a pistol shot fired by Hon Philemon T Herbert, a Rep in Congress from Calif. Public curiosity would no doubt require of us a minute account of this melancholy occurrence; but we believe the public justice forbids this gratification at present. Let it suffice to say that at the breakfast table, a little after 11 o'clock, an altercation occurred between Mr Herbert & the deceased; that other persons interfered in the melee; & that it terminated with the catastrophe we have recorded. Mr Herbert passed out of a side door, took a hack, & fled from the scene, but soon after surrended himself to the legal authorities, & was held in the custody of the Marshal until 4 o'clock in the afternoon, when an examination was commenced before Justices Smith & Birch, & continued until half-past nine o'clock last night, when it was postponed until this afternoon. The deceased was an Irishman, above 30 years of age, having a wife & 2 children & that he sustained a good name alike among his fellow-servants & with the proprietors & guests of the hotel. [Jul 26th newspaper: Criminal Court-Wash: the trial of Mr Herbert was brought to a close last evening. The jury returned a verdict of acquittal.]

Mr Brady, a young men whose arm was amputated at the Infirmary several days ago, in consequence of an accident which occurred to him at the Capitol, is doing well, & in a fair way to recovery of his usual health & strength.

Mrd: on May 8, in Wash City, by Rev Geo D Cummins, Edw Baldwin to Lizzie T, only daughter of W W Birth, all of Wash City.

Dr W B Magruder & D R Hagner have entered into partnership for the practice of the various branches of their profession. Ofc 209 H st, between 18th & 19th sts. Dr Margruder's residence is on Pa ave, near 21st st; Dr Hagner's next door to the office.

Professional Notice. Conway Robinson, of Va, will practice in the Supreme Court of the U S as well as in the Court of Appeals of Va & the Federal Courts at Richmond. He may be communicated with by letters directed to Richmond, Va.

SAT MAY 10, 1856

The examination of Hon Philemon T Herbert, of Calif, charged with shooting & killing Thos Keating, a waiter at Willard's Hotel, was commenced on Thu, before Justices Smith & Birch. The District Atty, Mr Key, appeared for the U S, & Senator Weller, Mr Phillips, of Alabama, & Messrs Bradley & Ratcliffe, of Wash City, appeared for the prisoner. The evidence of some of the waiters who were examined was that Mr Herbert came into the dining room, with a friend, at half-past eleven o'clock, & called for breakfast; but, it being past the usual hour, he was informed by the servant that he could not have his meal without an order from the office. Mr Herbert directed several servants who spoke to him on the subject to retire, & called them harsh names. The deceased, made a reply, when Herbert struck him with his fist or napkin. The deceased picked up a plate or tray, making a movement as if to throw it, when Herbert threw his chair at the deceased, the latter returning the assault with the plate. During the melee, Patrick, a brother of the deceased, entered, having heard of the proceedings, when Herbert seized him, & the 2 brothers closed on Herbert. The struggle now became intensely exciting, & as it proceeded crockery & chairs were broken profusely by the parties to the contest. Col McKay testified that he saw, when he entered the dining-room, 6 or 7 persons in a scuffle, & thought it was a general fight among the servants of the hotel. He beheld one of the servants knock down Mr Gardiner with a chair, & he saw 3 servants striking Mr Herbert & holding him by the wrists. One of them struck him with a chair, when witness seized a chair to defend Herbert, who was sinking under the weight of those upon him. Gardiner was beating them promiscuously. After Herbert fired his pistol the other two servants still clinched him. Mr Smith rushed forward with a cane, saying, "If you don't' release him I'll kill you." Mr Herbert was injured, & the witness placed a patch on his nose. Herbert's pistol was a single barrel. Capt J Smith confirmed Mr McKay's statement, saying a crowd of servants had Mr Herbert in their power, striking him on the head with plates. Mr Bishop, a member of Congress, testified he was positively certain that the pistol was discharged while the struggling was going on. Capt Blanding corroborated the statement that several servants were pressing a man down [Mr Herbert] previous to & at the time of the firing of the pistol. Capt Dupont's testimony was confirmatory of the above. Messrs Arnold Harris, John E Reynolds, Wm A Gardiner, & Maj Graham were examined for the defence. From the testimony it appeared that Mr Herbert did not retreat from the hotel by a side door, but through the main entrance, & that he repaired to the magistrate's office to surrender himself as soon as possible after hastily adjusting his dress at his room, on the opposite side of the avenue. [Jul 3rd newspaper: The Grand Jury made presentment against Mr P T Herbert for the murder of Thos Keating on May 8 last. He was yesterday arrested by the Deputy Marshal & committed to jail for trial at the current term of the Circuit Court of Wash Co, D C.] [Jul 16th newspaper: The jury declared themselves unable to agree & were dismissed by the Judge. 7 for acquittal & 5 for manslaughter.] [Jul 26th newspaper: Criminal Court-Wash: the trial of Mr Herbert was brought to a close last evening. The jury returned a verdict of acquittal.]

The U S steamer **Waterwitch**, Cmder Thos J Page, has returned to Wash City from the survey & exploration of the River La Plata & its tributaries. List of her ofcrs: Cmder, Thos J Page; Lts, W N Jeffers, Wm L Powell, Wm H Murdaugh, & E W Henry; Assist Surgeon, Robt Carter; Engineers, 2nd Assist, R C Potts, Wm J Lamden, 3rd Assists, T B C Stump, & P H Taylor, Captain's Clerk, E R Bushell.

Tragedy in Memphis, Tenn: on Apr 30, at the house of Mrs Dallman, Main & Jefferson sts, in that city, Benj Conner, a daguerreotypist, was seen emerging from the door with a pistol & parrot. He had mortally wounded Williams, who was demanding possession of the bird. Mr W C Mathais fired at Conner, & he returned the fire, shooting Mathais in the heart, & he expired in a few minutes. A brother of Mr Mathais wished to avenge his relative's death on the spot, but the city Marshal prevailed, & Conner was locked in the calaboose. Mr Williams died in the evening. It appears that he had given the parrot to a young lady in the city, who had returned it to him, but wishing afterwards to repossess it she had sent Conner to get it.

Senate: 1-Bill for the relief of Mary A Jones. 2-Cmte of Claims: bill for the relief of Mrs A P Derrick, widow of W S Derrick. Same cmte: bill for the relief of Emma Bidamon, & recommended its passage. Same cmte: bill for the relief of Sallie T Matthews; also a bill for the relief of Jas T V Thompson. Same cmte: bill for the relief of John M McIntosh. 3-Bill for the relief of Norwood McClelland, master the steamship **New World**: passed. 4-Bill for the relief of John Hastings, collector of the port of Pittsburg, Pa: postponed.

The many friends of Senator Rusk in Wash City will deeply regret to learn that news has been received here of the death of that gentleman's wife.

Obit-died: Rev T E Gill, PP, of Oranmore & Ballinscourty, in the county of Galway. For several years he discharged the duties of his sacred office of pastor of those parishes with a pious & exemplary zeal. He was possessed of literary abilites of a high & sterling order. -Irish paper, Apr 11, 1856 [No death date given-current item.]

Handsome & valuable square of ground, being square 739, with improvements, at auction: on May 28, being the former residence of Mr Thos Blagden, & recently vacated by Theodore Mosher, on N Y ave, south of the Capitol. The improvements are of the first order. The house contains 20 good & conveniently arranged rooms, with wide passages; carriage house, garden, & a large vinery of delicious grapes. This square has a front of 244 feet on N J ave. Mr White, who has charge of the premises, will show the property. For particulars apply to Theodore Mosher, at his lumber-yard, Blagden's Wharf, or to the subscriber. -A Green, auctioneer

Mr Chas Boughter, whose trial on a charge of embezzling the funds of the Lancaster Savings Institution, was going on at Lancaster, Pa, last week, has been acquitted.

Mrd: on Thu, in Wash City, in the Fourth Presbyterian Church, by Rev John C Smith, John H Smoot to Miss Charlotte Q Campbell, all of Wash City.

Died: on May 9, in her 14th year, Lavinia S, only child of Edw & Virginia Auld. Her funeral is at 2 o'clock tomorrow, from her late residence, C st, between 1st & 2nd sts.

Hotel in Washington for rent. The proprietor of that well known established Hotel, near the Wash & Balt Railroad Depot, having urgent & important business in Europe, wishes to rent or lease out his establishment, & sell his stock & furniture. The proprietor has had the establishment built for himself & under his own direct superintendence. Address the Proprietor, J Casparis, Wash City.

Orphans Court of Wash Co, D C. Letters of administration on the personal estate of Thos W Perkins, late of Wash Co, deceased. -Mary A Perkins, admx

MON MAY 12, 1856
Two thousand volumes of rare & valuable books at public auction: on May 20 & 21, a portion of the library of Thos Ewbank, formerly Com'r of Patents. Terms cash. Persons at a distance will be furnished with catalogues upon application. -Jas C McGuire, auct

Excellent household & kitchen furniture at auction on: May 16, at the residence of Maj St C Denny, on H st, between 17th & 18th sts. -Jas C McGuire, auct

U S ship **Jamestown**, Porto Praya, Mar 28, 1856. You will greatly oblige the Ofcrs of this ship by publishing the following list of ofcrs & reporting all well: Thos Crabbe, Cmdor; Jas F Armstrong, Lt Commanding; Thos H Patterson, 1st Lt; Julian Myers, 2nd Lt; Jos M Bradford, 3rd Lt; John E Hart, 4th Lt; E P Williams, 5th Lt; Geo Clymer, Fleet Surgeon; T Marston Taylor, Purser; Chas W Thomas, Chaplain; Danl R Swann, Assist Surgeon; Wm L Shuttleworth, Capt Marines; John McKinleey, Acting Boatswain; Wm Cope, Gunner; Jos R Smith, Carpenter; Wm A Maull, Sailmaker; H B Johnson, Capt's Clerk.

Highly valuable real estate at public sale: on May 15, 3 bldg lots on the east side of Union st, between King & Prince sts, in Alexandria city, Va, belonging to John S Miller & the devisees of John C Vowell, deceased. Sale positive.

Excellent household & kitchen furniture at auction on: on May 19, at the residence of Mrs Foy, at the corner of N J & D st, near the Railroad Depot. -A Green, auct

On Friday evening Miss Jones, daughter of Mrs Melinda Jones, made her debut as Parthenia in the play of Ingomar at Cincinnati. Miss Jones is a native of Washington.

Edw F Randolph writes to the Intelligencer from Iowa that a grand-daughter of Gen Nathl Greene is now an inmate of the house of Dr Geo M Hinkle, of Decatur Co, in that State. Her father, John Neville Greene, left 5 children, who are orphans & destitute. The grand-children of the man who was second only to Washington in the services rendered to his country in the Revolution are dependent upon the charity of strangers for their daily bread. -Boston Post
+
It is stronge how such unfounded stories obtain circulation & belief. Gen Greene left no son John Neville, & of course his orphan children are not destitue & dependent upon charity for their bread. The General left 2 sons. The oldest, Geo Washington, was taken to France by Lafayette in 1785, [the year of his father's death,] when about 9 years of age, & was cared for & educated by that distinguished patriot. After the execution of Louis XVI his mother, fearing for his safety, sent for him, & he arrived home in 1794, & was soon after unfortunately drowned in the Savannah river, then only 18 years of age, & left no posterity. His youngest son, Nathl Ray, is now living in this State, in independent circumstances. Gen Green left 3 daughters, Martha Washington, Cornelia Lott, & Louisa Catharine. They all married Southern gentlemen-two of them twice-& they & their posterity have always occupied highly respectable positions in society. The second of them, Mrs Littlefield, in now living at the South, & is 79 years of age. She is an intelligent & accomplished lady, & last summer published an interesting letter written by her respecting a portrait of Washington by Stuart. There are now living in this State many of the family & the blood of Gen Greene. -Providence Journal

Trustee's sale of valuable bldg lot on Delaware ave at auction: on Jun 11, by deed of trust from John Riggles to the subscriber, dated Aug 12, 1854, recorded in Liber J A S No 85, folios 4 thru 7, of the land records of Wash Co, D C: being part of lot 4 in square 684, in Wash City, D C, containing 4,600 square feet, more or less.
-P J Steer, trustee -A Green, auct.

Peremptory sale: on May 16, of a certain lot of ground, with 2 small brick tenements thereon, at 17th st west & G st north, being the same property conveyed to me by Louisa Lincoln Lear, recorded among the land records of Wash Co, D C.
-C St J Chubb -C W Boteler, auct

Mrd: on May 8, in Wash City, at Trinity Church, by Rev Mr Cummins, Dr Wm E Walker, of Louisiana, to Miss Lucy E Hilliard, of North Carolina.

Mrd: on May 8, in Wash City, by Rev Wm Krebs, Jos H Allen to Mary A Blades.

Dissolution of partnership under the name of B W Ferguson & Co, by mutual consent. John T Downs, the remaining partner, is authorized to use the name of the late firm in settling their business. -B W Ferguson, John T Downs

The Examining Magistrates, Messrs Smith & Birch, having concluded not to take bail in the case of the killing of Thos Keating at Willard's Hotel on Thu last, but to refer a matter of so much gravity to the Criminal Court as the proper tribunal, the counsel for the accused forthwith procured a writ of habeas corpus & on Saturday brought the party before Judge Crawford. Wm A Gardiner sworn: he was with Herbert; they were too late for breakfast; Herbert wanted breakfast and he called the waiter, the deceased man, a damned rascal & told him to go away & get him some breakfast. The waiter said to Herbert, you are a damned son of a bitch. At this time the waiters were getting around pretty thick & Herbert threw a chair, the waiter threw a plate. Herbert took out his pistol & walked towards the deceased & shot him with a single-barrelled Deringer pistol. [May 3rd newspaper: Decision in the case of Philemon T Herbert yesterday: The order of the Court is, that the prisoner enter into a recognizance with one or more good surety or sureties in the sum of $10,000, conditioned for his appearance at the next term of the Criminal Court of the Dist of Columbia, to be holden on the 3rd Monday of June next, to answer to the charge of manslaughter of Thos Keating, & not to depart the jurisdiction of the Court without the leave thereof; and, on his failure to do so, that he be remanded to the jail of Wash Co, D C. -Thos H Crawford]

Died: on May 10, in Gtwn, Mr Everett Krouse, in his 57th year. His funeral is today at 3 o'clock, from the residence of his son, Mr John Krouse, on Water st, Gtwn.

For sale: a pleasant family Horse, 9 years old, kind in harness, & without fault; also, a new Rockaway, built by one of our best city workmen. Inquire at the stable of Mr Cowling, G, near 13th st.

TUE MAY 13, 1856
Members of the Board of Visiters to the Military Academy for 1856.
Wm H Duncan, N H
Thos P Shepard, R I
Hon John Wheeler, Vt
Hon L Kirkpatrick, N J
Rev John B Spotswood, Dela
Col F H Smith, Va
Hon R F Simpson, S C
Wm B Read, Ky
E G Eastman, Tenn
Maj John Hendricks, Ind
Dr W W Roman, Ill
Hon Epaphroditus Ransom, Mich
Dr John J Lowry, Mo
[Appointment not yet made,] Ark
Franklin B Sinton, Texas
Judge Wm T Barbour, Calif

Household & kitchen furniture at auction on: May 19, at the residence of Capt Thom, U S A, on 17th st, between H & I sts. -J C McGuire, auct

Norfolk Herald: Capt Thos A Donin has been appointed to the command of the Gosport navy year, & has entered upon his official duties.

Appointment of Cadets appointed by the Pres at large & from D C for 1856.
Edmund Kirby, son of Col Kirby, deceased, late of the U S Army.
Guy V Henry, son of Capt Henry, deceased.
Justin Dimick, son of Maj Dimick.
Franklin Harwood, son of Capt Harwood, U S Navy.
Campbell Emory, son of Maj Emory, U S Army.
Lewellyn Hoxton, son of Dr Hoxton, deceased, formerly of the U S Army.
Robt L Eastman, daughter of Capt Eastman, U S Army.
Jefferson D Bradford, son of David Bradford, deceased, served in the war of 1812.
Henry A Dupont, Delaware.
Frank A Davis, Pa, orphan; family rendered much service in the war of 1812 & subsequent wars.
Wright Rives, Dist of Columbia

Mrd: on Apr 11, by Rev R R S Hough, Jos Bounds to Eliz A Laker, both of Savage, PG Co, Md.

Died: on May 10, at his residence, near Tenallytown, D C, Mr Giles Dyer, for many years a clerk in the ofc of the Auditor for the Post Ofc Dept. His funeral is on Wed morning, at 7½ o'clock, at Trinity Church, Gtwn.

Died: on May 8, of a brief illness, at the residence of Mr Geo Mattingly, in Wash City, Miss Maria Costigan, daughter of Mr Jos Costigan, of Somerset, Ohio, in her 20th year. The death of this young lady, far from home & kindred, though among kind friends, is the more distressing as she was but the day before in fine health & spirits, in the full discharge of her duties as teacher of a flourishing school, & in the daily expectation of a visit from her father.

Died: on May 3, in Wash City, James William, infant son of John B & Mary Ann Davidson, & grandson of the late Richd Rock, of Alexandria, Va, aged 1 month & 21 days.

Senate: 1-Memorial from Isaac N Cary, Andrew Foot, & other agents of the Columbian Harmony Society, asking that the restriction in the deed of conveyance on the power to sell a square of ground purchased of the Com'r of Public Bldgs for a burial ground by that society may be removed. 2-Cmte on Patents & the Patent Ofc: bill for the relief of Cyrus H McCormick.

Orphans Court of Wash Co, D C. Letters of administration on the personal estate of Luke Richardson, late of Wash Co, deceased. -Kezia Richardson, admx

The subscriber offers for sale the well arranged Boarding House at Mossy Creek Academy, Augusta Co, Va; with dormitories & stable; with house & lot. Apply to the Postmaster, Mossy Creek, Va, free. -Jed Hotchkiss, Mossy Creek

Middle Circuit of Florida, Wakuita Circuit Court. Jos Mitchel & Basil T Elder & Josephine his wife, cmplnts, vs Angelique Mitchel & Matilda Mitchel, dfndnts. A bill of cmplnt having been filed in this suit, the object of which is to procure partition of the premises therein mentioned, in which premises the above-named cmplnts & dfndnts are alleged to be respectively interested; & it appearing to the Court, by the affidavit annexed to the said bill, that the said dfndnts are non-residents of this State, it is ordered that the said dfndnts appear & answer the said bill within 9 months from this date, else that the same be taken as professed. The premises for the partition of which the said bill is filed are 4 certain tracts, pieces, or parcels of land, in Wakulla Co, Fla, known as Forbes' Purchase, numbered respectively 2 thru 5 on the Wakulla Book or Survey, the said tract number two containing 519 acres, or thereabouts; tract 3 containing 40 acres, or thereabouts; tract 4 containing 464 acres, or thereabouts; & tract 5 containing 316 acres, or thereabouts. Done at Chambers, Apr 18, 1856.
-J Wayles Baker, Judge

WED MAY 14, 1856
Senate: 1-Ptn from Mrs E E Ogden, widow of Capt E A Ogden, late of the U S army, asking to be allowed commissions on certain disbursements of public money of her late husband. 2-Ptn from Ruth Phillips, asking to be allowed a pension. 3-Ptn from Wm Reynolds, late naval storekeeper & acting purser at Valparaiso, asking to be released from responsibility for certain naval stores stolen while under his charge. 4-Ptn from E F Hassler, asking the establishment of a marine hospital at Cape Vincent, N Y. 5-Cmte of Claims: bill for the relief of Mrs Jane McCrabbe, widow of the late Capt John W McCrabbe, assist quartermaster U S Army. Same cmte: asked to be discharged from the consideration of the memorial of Sarah B Webber, & that it be referred to the Court of Claims: agreed to. 6-Cmte on Patents & the Patent Ofc: bills for the relief of Hiram Moore & John Hascall or their legal reps; & for the relief of Obed Hussey. 7-Cmte on Naval Affairs: bill for the relief of Richd W Meade. 8-Bill for the relief of the widow of of Adj Gen Roger Jones: introduced.

Sale by order of the Orphans Court of Wash Co, D C of the personal effects of Thos W Perkins, deceased, at his late residence, 1½ miles from the Anacostia or Navy Yard bridge, on the Marlborough road, adjoining Good Hope, on May 21, all the stock, farming utensils, wagons, carts & furniture of the deceased. -Mary A Perkins, admx -A Green, auct

An original portrait of Danl Webster is on exhibition at Mr Wagner's store, south side of Pa ave, near 12th st. It was executed by Willard, of Boston, at a late period of Mr Webster's life. It is a strong & clear resemblance of the great statesman.

The only son of Mr Thos Thornley, Warden of the Penitentiary, a child between 4 & 5 years of age, was accidentally drowned yesterday. So distressing a bereavement cannot but command general sympathy.
+
Drowned, yesterday, May 13, off the Penitentiary wharf in Wash City, Thos James Thornley, only son of Thos & Martha Thornley, aged 4 years, 3 months & 15 days. His funeral will take place from the Warden's apartments of the Penitentiary on May 15 at 2 o'clock P M.

The powder mill at Gorham explosed yesterday killing Mr Alfred Allen, who leaves a family. The mill was owned in Massachusetts. -Portland Argus, Wed.

Mrd: on May 12, in Wash City, by Rev P Light Wilson, Mr John W Stern, of Wash Co, Md, to Miss Laura Virginia Smoot, eldest daughter of Wm Smoot, of Prince Wm Co, Va.

Circuit Court of Wash Co, D C-in Equity. Geo McCallion & others against Jos Peck, John Walker, Lewis Walker, Mgt Peck, Louisa Ballard, & Jas Walker. Wm Redin & Chas S Wallach, trustees reported that on Apr 24, 1856, they made the following sales: Two undivided 3rd parts of lot 7 in square 106, in Wash, with improvements, to Geo Parker, for $3,333.33. Two-thirds of lots 24 & 25 in square 106, with improvements, to Geo Parker, for $2,333.34; two-thirds of lot 27 in square 106, with improvements, to Robt M Sutton, for $750; two-thirds of the west part of lot 22 in square 106, fronting 20 feet on K st, to Jas Pool, for $354, who, after the sale, assigned his purchase to Chas S Schneider; two-thirds of the east part of lot 22, with the same front, to Chas A Schneider, for $310.52; & two-thirds of lot 23 in square 106, with improvements, to Wm T Williams, for $570.28. The purchasers have complied with the terms of the sale. -Jno A Smith, clerk

Died: on May 8, in Montpelier, N Y, Sarah, wife of the late U S Senator Wm Upham, aged 60 years, a most estimable lady.

Phil, May 13. Robt Hancock, a farmer belonging in the vicinity of Coote's Mills, N J, was killed this afternoon near Bordentown by a train of cars on the Camden & Amboy railroad. He was in a wagon with his wife & attempted to cross the track in advance of the train. His horse was killed & his wife severely injured.

THU MAY 15, 1856
Accident on the Little Schuylkill Railroad on Wed when engine No 6 blew up at Ringgold, a station between Tamaqua & Port Clinton. Killed instantly were: the brakeman, L Carey; fireman, E Hildredth; & baggage master, Andrew Fleming.

The steamer **Persia** sailed from N Y yesterday for Liverpool. Among her passengers is Hon John P Kennedy, who is accompanied by Mrs Kennedy, Miss Gray, & Miss Pennington, all of Balt. They purpose making a tour of Europe, & returning in Oct next. Mr Kennedy goes for the benefit of his health, which is somewhat impaired, & on business connected with the Northern Central Railroad.

Public sale: by deed of trust executed to me, recorded in Liber J A S No 100, folios 388 thru 392, of the land records of Wash Co, D C: sale on Jun 5, all the piece of land in Wash City, D C, known as part of lot 3 in square 512, containing or estimated to contain 3,330 square feet of ground being the same piece or parcel conveyed to Fred'k Aueroches by David A Hall & wife, on Oct 30, 1853, by deed recorded in Liber J A S No 67, folios 476 thru 479, of the land records of Wash Co, D C. Terms cash. Property to be resold at the risk & expense of the purchaser unless terms are complied with within 3 days from day of sale. -Edw C Carrington, trustee
-A Green, auctioneer

Senate: 1-Ptn from Thos Osbourn, late lt in the revenue service, asking that he may be allowed the pay of a lt of the navy while he served in the navy. 2-By Mr Bright: Asking that John L Metsereau have leave to withdraw his memorial & papers. 3-Cmte on Claims: bill for the relief of John H Scranton & Jas M Hunt, owners of the steamer **Major Hopkins**. Same cmte: bill for the relief of the heirs of Col Chas Simms, late Collector of the Port of Alexandria: recommended its passage. Same cmte: asked to be discharged from the consideration of the ptn of memorials of Manuel A T Barboza, of Alexander Joze da Cruz, Luis Vidal Cezar, & of Beuto des Santos, & that they be referred, with the papers pertaining thereto, to the Court of Claims: agreed to. 4-Cmte on Military Affairs, referred the following House bills: recommended their passage: relief of Capt J P Hatch, of the U S Army; relief of the legal reps of Capt Jos W Whipple, deceased; relief of Dr Wm A Hail, late of the Tenn volunteers in the Mexican war; & relief of the widow of Adj Gen Roger Jones. Same cmte: adverse report on the memorial of David Butler, late military storekeeper in the service of the U S, asking additional compensation for services while acting in that capacity. Same cmte: asked to be discharged from the consideration of the memorial of David W Rogers, & that it be referred to the Cmte on Public Lands: agreed to. 5-Cmte on Foreign Relations: bill for the relief of Horatio J Perry. Same cmte: bill for the relief of Chas E Anderson. 6-Cmte on Military Affairs: referred the memorial of John B Walbach; & reported a bill for the relief of Brvt Brig Gen John B Walbach, of the U S Army.

Summer Millinery: E E McDonald, No 70 Bridge st, Gtwn, informs the ladies that she will on May 15, open a beautiful assortment of Millinery.

Mrd: on May 13, by Rev Mr Marks, Mr Wm Garner to Miss Sarah White.

Wash City Ordinance: 1-Act for the relief of Chas Stewart: to pay him $28.51 being the balance due for taking up & relaying the pavement on the west front of square 398, as per bill certified by W W Demaine, Assist Surveyor. Approved, May 9, 1856

Notice. The public are cautioned not to purchase of Saml Strong part of lot 1 in square 756, on C st north, & now in my possession, as it belongs to me, my uncle, Saml Scott, having conveyed it to me in fee for the consideration of $600, & the deed having since been lost or mislaid by Walter Davidge, which whom I deposited it to be recorded. The said Strong claims title to said property by reason of a deed from the said Scott to him dated Apr 7, 1856; but the same was executed under a false representation made by him to said Strong, that I had authorized the said Scott to convey the property to him, & I hereby pronounce the instrument in virtue of which the conveyance was made a forgery. -Wm H Swain

For sale: 620 acres of land, within 1½ miles of Staunton, Va. The heirs of J B Breckinridge, deceased, will on Jul 16 next, offer at public sale, the farm near Staunton, known as the **Red Bud**, containing about 620 acres; with all the necessary farm bldgs, new & well arranged. It can be divided into 2 farms. Possession will be given on Aug 1 next. -A N Breckinridge, Staunton, Va

For sale or rent: elegant House on 4½ st, between Pa ave & C sts. Apply to P W Browning, under U S Hotel.

Orphans Court of Wash Co, D C. Letters testamentary on the personal estate of Eliz R Larned, late of Wash Co, deceased. -Benj F Larned, exec

FRI MAY 16, 1856
Senate: 1-Ptn from the widow of Curtis Hine, late a lt in the U S revenue service, asking to be allowed a pension. 2-Memorial from John Nugent, setting forth that, while in discharge of his duty on board the U S sloop-of-war **Germantown**, in firing a salute in honor of the Queen of Spain, he had both arms so shattered as to require them to be amputated, & that therefore he is compelled to look to the bounty of his country for subsistence. 3-Ptn from Jas Dunlop, of the Pa bar, asking for a subscription by Congress to his digest of the Laws of the U S. 4-Ptn from John Hughes, a seaman in the navy during the war of 1812, asking to be allowed a pension in consequence of a wound received in battle. 5-Motion of Mr Bell, of Tenn, the papers relating to the case of Gen Nathan Towson, in relation to the capture of the British ship **Caledonia**, were taken from the files & referred to the Cmte on Naval Affairs; & the papers in the case of Robt P Carrin were referred to the Court of Claims. 6-Cmte on Public Lands: bill to vest the title to certain warrants for land in Geo M Gordon. 7-Cmte on Military Affairs: bill for the relief of Adam D Stewart & of Alex'r Randall, exc of Danl Randall. 8-Bill for the relief of the widow of Adj Gen Roger Jones: passed.

Household & kitchen furniture & superior Rosewood Piano Forte at auction on: May 22, at residence of Col W F Wilson, 441 I st, between 9th & 10th sts. -A Green, auct

Household & kitchen furniture at auction, Jun 2, at residence of Prof Rual Keith, on Beall st, near Christ Church, his entire household furniture. -Barnard & Buckey, aucts

The population at the Navy Yard yesterday was thrown into a state of high excitement due to the meeting between 2 young men, Danl W Jarboe, aged 22, & John Rufus Nally, aged 20, resulting in the shooting of Jarboe by Nally. It appears that Jarboe & his sister Sarah Jane, aged 17, walked in company into the house of an acquaintance on 9th st south, where they remained a short time. As they were coming out 2 young men, Jno R Nally & his brother, Wm, were passing on the sidewalk to their work in one of the shops in the Navy Yard, when Jarboe stepped forward & asked Nally what he intended to do in reference to his [Jarboe's] sister, to whom it seems Nally had formerly paid attention in the capacity of a lover, but had criminally deceived her. Nally's reply was that he would see what he would do, when Jarboe, pushing his sister aside, advanced & discharged the contents of one barrel of a revolver into Nally's left side, & then exclaimed, "I will shoot the other damned rascal [meaning Wm] too. As soon as shot, Nally commenced running rapidly towards his home, some 100 yards away, when he fell & almost instantly expired. Jarboe was arrested & duly committed to jail for trial at the Criminal Court. On his way to jail Jarboe was informed of Nally's death, when he shed tears & said he was sorry, but acknowledged having done the deed.

Mrd: on May 15, in Wash City, by Rev Byron Sunderland, D D, Wm B Donaldson to Arabella A, daughter of the late John H Wade.

For **Mount Vernon & Fort Washington**: fare, round trip, $1. From Alexandria, 75 cents. The boat **Thomas Collyer** will make 2 trips a week, Tue & Fri. -Saml Gedney, Captain

SAT MAY 17, 1856
Fatal railroad accident on Wed on the Boston & Worcester railroad, near Newton Corner, which resulted in the serious injury of Mr McFarland, a baker, residing in West Newton, who was driving to Newton Corner in a covered carryall, in which were also seated his wife & her sister, Miss Heutis, a beautiful young lady 21 years of age. He had just reached the railroad crossing when the train from Albany approached. He whipped his horse & drove across the track, but the locomotive struck the rear part of the wagon. The two women were found to be dead & shockingly mangled. The usual alarm was sounded, which it is thought Mr McFarland must have heard, but, being unable to stop his horse, made a bold push to drive across in time to avoid the train.

Senate: 1-Memorial from Lt J C Carter, asking compensation for carrying, in 1852, the Brazilian Minister & family in the steamer **Massachusetts** from Valparaiso to Rio Janeiro at the request of the American Minister & of the cmder of the American squadron. 2-Cmte on Private Land Claims: bill granting to L Jane Horner & children a section of land in Oregon, reported it back without amendment & recommended its passage. Same cmte: bill for the relief of John Crawford: recommended its passage. 3-Cmte of Claims: bill for the relief of Wm H Chase, reported it back without amendment & recommended its passage. Same cmte: bills for the relief of Asbury Dickins; for the relief of Michl Nourse; & for relief of John Robb: reported them back in each case, with substitutes for the original bills. 4-Cmte on Public Lands: adverse reports on the several memorials of Sarah Baker, John L Williams, Jas Ladd, & others, on the ground that they came within such class of cases as Congress had refused to provide for under any general provision. 5-Bill for the relief of Jas Davidson, of Ky: passed.

House of Reps: 1-Bill for the relief of West Drinkwater was taken up. 2-Bill for the relief of W M F Magraw: passed.

Explosion of a steam boiler at Albany, N Y, which was 3 days previously placed into the distillery of Cyrus Edson, on South Broadway, demolished the bldg & killed Mr Cyrus Edson, owner of the establishment; Geo Henderson, engineer; & Jas Donavan, laborer.

We announce the unexpected death of Mr Brunet, the editor of the Abington Democrat. We sympathize with his family in the sudden & distressing blow.
-Richmond Enquirer

Six cents reward for runaway, Andrew Curtain, an indented apprentice to the coachsmithing. All persons are hereby cautioned against harboring or employing said apprentice. -Michl McDermott, living in Washington.

U S Patent Ofc, Wash, May 14, 1856. Ptn of Matthias W Baldwin, of Phil, Pa, praying for the extension of a patent granted to him on Aug 25, 1842, for an improvement in the manner of constructing locomotive steam-engines, for 7 years from the expiration of said patent, which takes place on Aug 25, 1856.
-Chas Mason, Com'r of Patents

Mrd: on May 15, in Wash City, at Trinity Church, by Rev Geo D Cummins, Chas A James to Julia Hobbie.

Died: on May 12, in Phil, in her 69th year, Martha Mitchell, consort of Andrew Caldwell Mitchell, formerly of Wash City.

Died: on May 16, in Wash City, of consumption, Mrs Rachel B Barnard, consort of the late E F Barnard, of Wash City. Her funeral will be tomorrow at 2½ o'clock, from her late residence, 367 15th st.

Died: on May 15, at his residence, near Beltsville, PG Co, Md, Thos McKnew. This kind & noble-hearted man leaves an interesting family & a large number of friends to mourn his loss. None knew him but to love him. J P B

Trustees' sale of valuable real estate. Alex'r Keech & others vs Eleanor H Callis & Anthony Addison. In the Circuit court for PG Co, sitting as a Court of Equity. By decree of said court, passed Feb 19, 1856, in the above cause, the undersigned, as Trustees, will expose to public sale, on Jun 5 next, at **Barnaby Mansion House**, the residence of the late Henry A Callis, a portion of the real estate of which the late Henry A Callis died seized & possessed, containing 160 acres, more or less. This land has been divided into 3 lots: 36 1/5th acres; 64 5/6th acres; & 59 acres, more or less. The land adjoins the lands of Messrs Thos Berry, Col Maddux, Geo Walker, & others. Premises shown by Mr J E Thompson, residing at **Barnaby**. -J Contee Mullikin, C Smith Keech, trustees -G N Boteler, auct: Upper Marlboro, Md

MON MAY 19, 1856
Desirable dwlg house & lot near the Navy Yard at public sale: by order from the Orphans Court of Wash Co, D C: sale on Jun 12, of part of lot 8 in square 904, fronting on 7th st, with improvements, a neat well built frame dwlg house, containing 6 rooms. -Zebedee Kirwan, Guardian -Jas C McGuire, auct

Trustee's sale of improved property in the First Ward: by deed in trust from Nicholas Funk & wife, dated Jan 10, 1855, recorded in Liber J A S No 90, folios 288: sale on Jun 24, on the premises, east half of lot 24 in square 101, fronting 20 feet on north I st, near 20th st, with a 2 story brick dwlg-house. -Owen Murray, trustee -Jas C McGuire, auct

Household & kitchen furniture & superior Rosewood Chickering Piano-forte, at auction on: May 22, at the residence of the late Peter Brady, on N Y ave, between 11th 12th sts. -Jas C McGuire, auct

Conviction of forgers of land warrants: Diogenes Wetmore & T K Wetmore, of St Louis, Mo, indicted for presenting fraudulent claims at the Pension Ofc, have been convicted, after a trial of 12 days, & sentenced to the penitentiary, the former for 10 & the latter for 8 years.

St Louis, May 16. Hon John G Miller, member of Congress from the 5th district of Missouri, died at his residence on Sunday last.

$200 reward for runaway negro man Sandy Green, about 22 years of age.
-Wm J Berry, living near Upper Marlborough, PG Co, Md.

Hon John G Miller, a Rep in Congress from the 5th district of Missouri, died on May 11. [Despatch from St Louis, dated May 16th.] [May 23rd newspaper: Senate-Mr Miller was born in Mercer Co, Ky, & at the time of his death was under 45 years of age. He acquired the rudiments of a classical education at Centre College, in Ky, & prepared himself for the practice of the legal profession by his studies at Transylvania Univ. In 1835 he emigrated to Booneville, Mo, & engaged with great success in the practice of the law. He married the daughter of Hon Thos L Williams, of Tenn. He was a kind, devoted husband, a fond, indulgent father. Time alone can soothe the sorrows of the widow & his orphan children.]

Haul of counterfeiters: arrested in this city yesterday, John Stewart, Wm Hall, & Augustus Stisser, all residents of Detroit; also Malcom Burham, who resides opposite Newport, C W. They are now in jail for passing & having in possession counterfeit bank bills & coins. -Detroit Daily Advertiser, of May 18.

Trustee's sale: by deed of trust from Andrew Rothwell & wife, dated Nov 3, 1853: sale on Jun 20th, of lot 3 in square north of square 4, in Wash City. Terms: $340 cash, & the residue upon such terms as Mr Rothwell may direct. -W Redin, trustee -A Green, auct

Died: on May 2, at Pike, Wyoming Co, N Y, Mrs Eliz Besancon, aged 77 years.

Died: on May 16, of a lingering disorder, in Phil, Eliz Upshur, wife of J Murray Rush, & daughter of the late Lyttleton Upshur Dennis, of the Eastern Shore of Md, in her 29th year.

St Louis, May 16. Hon John G Miller, member of Congress from the 5th district of Missouri, died at his residence on Sunday last.

$200 reward for runaway negro man Sandy Green, about 22 years of age.
-Wm J Berry, living near Upper Marlborough, PG Co, Md.

TUE MAY 20, 1856
Trustees' sale of a valuable Farm: by deed of trust from John Saul to us, dated May 22, 1854: sale on Jun 3, of the Farm containing 80 acres on the Wash & Rockville turnpike, about 2 miles from Wash City, & now occupied by Mr John Saul.
-Walter S Cox, Chas S Wallach, trustees -Jas C McGuire, auct

Mrd: on May 15, in Wash City, at Trinity Church, by Rev Geo D Cummins, Chas A James to Julia, daughter of the late Hon S R Hobbie, all of Wash City.

Died: on May 18, in Wash City, Mrs Ann Duvall, wife of Washington Duvall, in her 66th year, & for the last 50 years a resident of Wash City. Her funeral will take place today at 11 o'clock, from her late residence, on 11th st east, near the Navy Yard.

Wash City Ordinances: 1-Act for the relief of F B Posten: the sum of $92.26 be paid to him for the construction of an ofc & fish-stands for the Western Market. 2-Act for the relief of Jos Hill: that the bed of the alley between lot 13 & lots 14 thru 17 in square 528, be moved 2 feet & 7 inches north of its present location; & that Jos Hill be & he is hereby allowed to occupy, & the Mayor is hereby authorized to convey to said Jos Hill, whenever the Corp may possess the power, the southern portion of said alley fronting on lot 13, equal in the extent to the parcel of ground purchased by said Jos Hill & set apart as a portion of said alley. Approved, May 14, 1856.

Senate: 1-Memorial from the executors of Gen John Armstrong, late of N Y, claiming pay for the services of said Armstrong as com'r extraordinary & plenipotentiary for the purpose of negotiating with Spain under a commission dated Mar 7, 1806, & for other services. 2-Ptn from Hannah Walker widow of a soldier of the Revolution, asking to be allowed a pension under the act of 1853 & arrears of pension due her late husband. 3-Memorial of Aaron Haight Palmer, on the files of the Senate, was referred to the Cmte on Foreign Relations. 4-Cmte of Claims: bill for the relief of the heirs of Maj Gen Arthur St Clair. 5-Cmte on Indian Affairs: message of the Pres of the U S in relation to the claim of Richd W Thompson, agent of the Menominee Indians: asked to be discharged from the consideration of the same, on the ground that no further legislation was necessary. 6-Cmte on Private Land Claims: bill for the relief of Martin Fenwick. Same cmte: bill giving to Joshua Kirby & the widow of John McNarey the right to enter land covered by the life reserve of John McNarey under the Cherokee treaties of 1817 & 1819, submitted a report, concluding with the recommendation that the bill do not pass.

Church Directory.
Presbyterian Churches:
First Presbyterian Church, 4½ st, between C st & La ave. Rev B Sunderland, pastor.
Second Presbyterian Church, N Y ave, near I st. Rev J R Eckard, pastor.
F st Presbyterian Church, F st, between 14th & 15th sts. Rev Dr Gurley, pastor: residence west side of 12th, between G & H sts.
Fourth Presbyterian Church, 9th st, between G & H sts. Rev J C Smith, pastor.
Assembly's Church, I & 5th st, Rev A G Carothers, pastor..
Sixth Presbyterian Church, 6th & Md ave. Rev Mr Moore, pastor.
Seventh Presbyterian Church, 7th st, between D & E, Island. Rev E B Cleghorn, pastor.
Western Presbyterian Church, G st, between 19th & 20th sts. Rev T H Haskell, pastor.

Episcopal Churches:
Christ Church, Navy Yard, G st, between 6th & 7th sts. Rev Mr Morsell, rector; parsonage adjoining the church.
Trinity Church, 3rd st west & C st north. Rev G D Cummins, rector; dwlg 6th st, between D & E sts.
Church of the Ascension, H st, between 9th & 10th sts. Rev Mr Stanley, pastor.
Church of the Epiphany, G st, between 13th & 14th sts. Rev Mr French, rector.
St John's Church, opposite the Executive Mansion, at H st north & 16th st west. Rev Dr Pyne, rector.
Grace Church, D st, between 8th & 9th sts, Island. Rev Alfred Holmead, rector; dwlg on B st, south of Smithsonian Institution.

Baptist Churches:
First Church, 10th st, between E & F sts. Rev S P Hill, pastor; residence on H, between 15th & 16th sts.
Navy Yard Church, Va ave, & 7th st. Rev Mr Greer, pastor; residence on Va ave, between 7th & 8th sts.
E st Church, E st, between 6th & 7th sts. G W Samson, pastor; residence on 6th st, between D & E sts.
Fourth Church, 13th st, between G & H. Rev T C Teasdale, pastor; residence on 13th st, between G & H sts.

Methodist Episcopal Churches:
McKendree Chapel, Mass Ave, between 9th & 10th sts. Rev Geo Hildt, pastor; residence 9th st, between L & M sts.
Foundry Church, 14th & G sts. Rev Saml Regester, pastor; parsonage adjoining church, on G st.
Union Chapel, 20th st, between Pa ave & H st. Rev Wm S Rogers, pastor.
Ryland Chapel, Md ave & 10th st. Rev John S Deale, pastor; parsonage 10th st, adjoining Ryland Chapel.
Gorsuch Chapel, 4½ st, between L & M sts. Rev J H Ryland, pastor; residence, parsonage above.
Wesley Chapel, F & 5th sts. Rev Wm Krebs, pastor; residence F, between 6th & 7th sts.
Capitol Hill Church, corner A & 2nd sts. Rev R R S Hough, pastor.
Ebenezer Church, 4th st east, between E & G sts south, Navy Yard. Rev Francis H Richey, pastor; residence 7th st, between G & I sts.
Fletcher Chapel, N Y ave & 4th st. In charge of the McKendree Chapel station.
Providence Chapel, I st & Delaware ave. In charge of the Capitol Hill station.
Methodist Episcopal Church South, 8th st, between H & I sts. Rev Dr Doggett, pastor. This church edifice undergoing repairs, the congregation worship, for the present, in the old Trinity Church, on 5th st, opposite the City Hall.

Methodist Protestant Churches:
Methodist Protestant Church, 9th st, between E & F. Rev P L Wilson, pastor; dwlg, parsonage adjoining church.

Methodist Protestant Mission Church, Va ave & 5th st, near the Navy Yard. Rev John R Nichols, pastor.

Catholic Churches:
St Patrick's Church, F st west, between 9th & 10th sts. Rev T J O'Toole, pastor; F E Boyle, assistant. Parsonage adjoining the church.
St Matthew's, corner 15th st west & H st north. Rev Jas B Donelan, pastor; Jno B Byrne, assistant. Parsonage adjoining the church.
St Mary's [German] 5th st west, between G & H north. Rev Matthias Alig, pastor. Parsonage adjoins the church.
St Peter's [Capitol Hill,] 2nd st east. Rev Edw A Knight, pastor; Rev R J Lawrence, assistant. Parsonal adjoins the church.
St Dominick's [Island,] F st, between 6th & 7th sts. Rev J A G Wilson, pastor; J N Clarkson, assistant. Parsonage opposite the church.

Lutheran Churches:
German Evangelical Church, 20th & G sts. Rev P Finkle, pastor; dwlg near the church.
English Lutheran Church, H & 11th sts. Rev J G Butler, pastor; dwlg 12th st, between K & L sts.
German Lutheran Church of the Unaltered Augsburg Confession north side of E, between 3rd & 4th sts. Rev Wm Nordman, pastor; dwlg next door.

Jews' Synagugue: Tenth st, between E & F sts.

New Jerusalem Church: On North Capitol st, between B & C sts. Minister temporary.

Friends Meeting House: I st, between 19th & 20th sts.

African Churches:
Colored Presbyterian Church, 15th st, between I & K. This church is temporarily supplied by Dr Jas Wilson.
First Colored Baptist Church, 19th st, corner of I st Sampson White, pastor.
Second Colored Church, Missouri ave, between 6th & 7th sts. Gustavus Brown, pastor.
Asbury Methodist Episcopal Church, 11th & K sts. Rev Thos McGee, pastor; residence 8th, between I & K sts.
Little Ebenezer Methodist Episcopal Church, C st, between 4th & 5th sts. Rev F S Evans, pastor.
Israel Bethel African Methodist Episcopal Church, south Capitol st, near Capitol Hill. Rev Saml Watts, pastor.
Union Bethel African Methodist Episcopal Church, 15th & M sts. Rev W H Waters. Pastor.
John Wesley Chapel, between 17th & 18th sts. Rev T J Clinton, pastor.
Zion Wesley Chapel, on D, between 2nd & 3rd sts, [Island.] Rev Mr Jones, pastor

White Sulphur & Chalybeate Springs, at Doubling Gap are in Cumberland Co, Pa; the house & grounds have all been improved. Boarding $1.25 per day; $8 per week. Scott Coyle, Proprietor, Newville post ofc,

Fauquier White Sulphur Springs, Va: will be opened for visitors on Jun 1, under the joint management of the subscribers, having been leased by one of them for a term of years. -Thos B P Ingram, Alex'r Baker

Teacher wanted: the Trustees of Wash Academy, at Princess Anne, Somerset Co, Md, wish to employ a Principal Teacher to take charge of said institution on the first Mon in Oct next: salary of $800 per annum, payable semi-annually.
-Edw Long, Isaac D Jones, Wm J Byrd, Cmte

Orphans Court of Wash Co, D C. In the case of Jane H Dement, adms of Richd Dement, deceased: the admx & Court have appointed Jun 10 next, for the final settlement & distribution of the personal estate of said deceased, of the assets in hand.
-Ed N Roach, Reg/o Wills

WED MAY 21, 1856
During the recent trip of the steamer **Empire City** from Havana to New Orleans, on the same day the steamer left Havana, Apr 11, it was reported to Capt Windle that one of the cabin passengers, Mr Jos Waterman, formerly of Galveston, Texas, had died at 3 o'clock of consumption, & in accordance with the customary usages observed at sea, the remains were placed in a hammock & laid upon the quarter-deck in order to be buried at sunset. The deceased was a Royal Arch Mason, formerly attached to a Lodge & Chapter of the Fraternity in the city of Galveston; &, as there were several of the mustic tie on board, it was resolved that he should be interred with the Masonic honors peculiar to the order. As the sun was about sinking beneath the wave the remains were placed in charge of such of the Fraternity. The remains were covered by the U S flag, & laid upon a plank at the stern, & as the ship's bell began to toll the intervals the brethren formed a circle around the corpse, & the Masonic burial service was delivered by Past Master J E Elliott, of N Y, who presided as Master upon this occasion. The Wordshipful Brother pronounced the words, "We therefore commit the body of our departed brother to the great deep; his memory shall remain engraven upon the tablets of our hearts, while his spirit shall return unto God who gave it," a single plunge was heard. -New Orleans Picayune

Senate: 1-Papers in relation to the claim of Jacob Kerr, of N Y: referred to the Court of Claims. 2-Memorial & papers of Jean Baptiste Farribault to be taken from the files & referred to the Cmte on Military Affairs. 3-Cmte on Foreign Relations: bill for the relief of Peter Parker. Same cmte: bill for the relief of J E Martin. 4-The Senate proceeded to consider the bill for the relief of the legal reps of Rinaldo Johnson & of Anne E Johnson, deceased.

House of Reps: 1-Cmte on Patents: bill for the relief of Isaac Adams: committed.

Wash Corp: 1-Ptn from Mary J Martin, asking permission to erect a brick wall in front of her house: referred to the Cmte on Improvements. 2-Act for the relief of Thos McNaney. 3-Ptn of Hugh Latham, praying the remission of a fine: referred to the Cmte of Claims. 4-Cmte of Claims: bill for the relief of John P Hilton: passed.

Splendid farm for sale of 320 acres in Fairfax Co, Va, about 6 miles from Wash, Alexandria, & Gtwn. Apply, with stamp enclosed, to Prof Chas G Page, Wash, D C.

Beautiful country residence for sale: the subscriber, intending to move nearer to his place of business, offers at private sale the place at which he now resides: on north Boundary st, between 2nd & 4th sts, outside the city limits. The house is large, 17 rooms, with high & lofty ceilings; is heated by furnace; hot & cold water in the bath room & kitchen; with a never failing pump of excellent water at the door. Apply to Z D Gilman, New Drug store, 350 Pa ave. City property will be taken in part payment if desired.

Further examination of the case of Danl W Jarboe, charged with shooting John R Nally, took place yesterday at the jail. The witnesses examined were Susanna Erwin, Henrietta Cook, Wm W Nally, John A Willett, Dr McKim, Dr Dove, Thos Erwin, Ann Armistead, Js Buckley, & John T Johnson. The prisoner was remanded for trial for murder at the next term of the Criminal Court.

Headquarters Volunteer Regt, Wash, May 16, 1856. Regular annual parade of the Regt for inspection, review, & exercise will take place May 26, on the parade ground in front of the City Hall precisely at 4 o'clock P M. By order of Col Hickey. Henry A Ober, Adj

Died: yesterday, in Wash City, suddenly, Isaac Goddard, in his 43rd year. His funeral will be this evening at 4 o'clock, from his late residence, corner of 12th & G sts.

THU MAY 22, 1856
Trustee's sale of improved property at auction: on Jun 4 next, by deed of trust from Judson Milstead to the subscriber, dated Feb 4, 1839, recorded in liber W B No 73, folios 20 thru 23, of the land records for Wash Co, D C: sale of part of square 742, with improvements, a 2 story brick house: fronts on N J ave between L & M sts south. Also, part of lot 5 in square south of square 744, with a 2 story frame house- this property is near Mr Lambel's brick yard. -Zadock Williams, trustee -A Green, auct

Died: on May 20, George Shedden, eldest son of George W Riggs, aged 6 years & 5 months. His funeral is this afternoon at 4 o'clock.

House of Reps: 1-Cmte of Claims: reported without amendment Senate bills for the relief of Eliz V Lomax, only surviving child of Capt Wm Lindsay; & for the relief of the heirs of Saml Scott: which were committed.

Senate: 1-Cmte on the Judiciary: bill for the relief of Chas Stearns. 2-Cmte on Military Affairs: bill for the relief of John Nugent, & asked its immediate consideration. [Nugent, an intelligent & worthy seamen, had both arms so shattered in firing a salute in honor of the Queen of Spain as to require them to be amputated. This bill allowed about $30 a month for his support. He was unable even to feed himself without the aid of an assistant, & had been compelled to appeal to the bounty of the Gov't. There was a precedent for this in a like unfortunate case, where a seaman had likewise lost both arms in firing a salute of some foreign potentate at Gibraltar in 1850.] The bill was then read a third time & passed.

Wash Corp: 1-Ptn from John H Munroe, asking compensation for the loss of a longboat in the Eastern Branch: referred to the Cmte of Claims. 2-Bill for the relief of John P Hilton: passed.

For rent, during the warm season, my residence, ready furnished, 2½ miles n w of Gtwn, with garden planted & orchard. Also, several small farms for sale, within 3 miles of Gtwn. -H Loughborough, **Grassland**

FRI MAY 23, 1856
Senate: 1-Ptn from Thos Howard, asking to be allowed a pension on account of an injury sustained while he was employed as a laborer in the navy yard at Phil. 2-Ptn from Wm D Young, asking an incease of pension on account of disability incurred while in discharge of his duty as an assistant engineer. 3-Ptn from the heirs of Isaac Bowman, of the Revolutionary army, asking to be allowed the bounty land or scrip to which he was entitled. 4-Ptn from Chas Holmes, asking that a register may be issued for the foreign-built vessel **Mary St John**. 5-Ptn from Henry Fried, asking the redemption of certain continental money issued to his father for services as a volunteer in the Revolutionary war. 6-It was ordered the J W Nye have leave to withdraw his memorials & papers. 7-Cmte on Pensions: bill granting a pension to Mary A Jones.

Painful occurrence at the Capitol yesterday. Mr Senator Sumner having in his speech of Tue last, made some offensive personal reflections on Senator Butler, of S C, [who is now absent at home,] his nephew, Hon Mr Brooks, of the House of Reps, sought Mr Sumner yesterday in the Senate chamber, & made an attack on him with a cane. Several Senators & others interposed, when Mr Brooks withdrew. Mr Sumner was a good deal hurt & bleeding, & was conveyed to his lodgings.

Household & kitchen furniture at auction on: May 27, at the residence of the late Mrs Barnard, 367 15th sts, between L & M sts. -J C McGuire, auct

The Spirit of Jefferson learns that while 3 small children of Mr Vault, toll-keeper on the bridge at Harper's Ferry, were playing in an old bldg, on Fri last, adjoining his residence, the bldg was by a gale of wind blown over, instantly killing 2 of the children, & the 3rd was so seriously injured that it was not expected to survive.

Obit-died: this morning, at his residence in this town, Col John Sloan, an aged & distinguished man. He had been unwell for several days, but was not ill enough to excite any special alarm among his friends. However, he was taken suddenly down, & expired almost instantly. He had filled many posts of honor in his life. In 1818 he was elected Congressman from this district, which position he held for 6 years. He had attained the ripe old age of 78 years. -Wayne Co [Ohio] Democrat

The Providence Journal of this morning reports the death of Judge Thos Burgess, of that City. Judge Burgess leaves a widow & 6 children. Two of his sons are Hon Thos M Burgess, late Mayor of this city, & Rt Rev Geo Burgess, Bishop of the Protestant Episcopal Church in the diocese of Maine.

The Hotel & Restaurant near the Railroad Depot, formerly kept by the late Mr John Foy, has been leased by Mr Jas T Lloyd, who will open the house for business Jun 1st.

Wash City Ordinance: 1-Act for the relief of Thos McNaney: the sum of $185.63 to be paid to him for grading & gravelling K st north, at the West Market-house.

New Orleans, May 22. Messrs R W Estlin & M Cuddy, merchants of this city, fought a duel at Pass Christian yesterday morning. Mr Cuddy was killed & Estlin was slightly wounded.

SAT MAY 24, 1856
One Lennairs, of Phil, convicted of the homicide of Mr Hatch, of N J, during an altercation which arose between them on account of the former's trespassing & gunning over Hatch's farm on a Sunday, has been sentenced to 20 years' imprisonment with hard labor.

Peter Mattocks was executed yesterday in Phil for the murder of Eliz Gilbert, by shooting her with a pistol. Though denying his guilt of the particular charge, he acknowledged having previously been implicated in numerous crimes of a heinous stamp, including 2 murders. He was about 47 years of age.

Household & kitchen furniture at auction on: Jun 3, at the residence of Capt Sawyer 57 Pa ave, near the Circle. -A Green auct

Senate: 1-Cmte on Private Land Claims: bill for the relief of the heirs & legal reps of Pierre Cazelar, deceased. Same cmte: bill for the relief of Chas Lucas or his legal reps, & for other purposes. 2-Cmte on the Post Ofc & Post Roads: bill for the relief of Wm M F McGaw: reported it back with an amendment. 3-Bills taken up & passed-relief of: A S Bender; of the legal reps of Rinaldo Johnson & Ann E Johnson, deceased; of Oscar F Johnston, a passed midshipman in the U S Navy; of Wm K Jennings & others; of J Randolph Clay; & of Hannibal Faulk & Eliza S Collier, [formerly widow Scriber,] & the heirs & legal reps of Benj Scriber, deceased. 4-Bill for the relief of John Hastings, collector of the port of Pittsburgh. 5-Bills passed-relief of Wm G Ridgely; of the heirs & reps of Robt Sewall; of Anthony Rankin, of Tenn; of the heirs-at-law of Sarah Crandall, deceased; of the legal reps of Geo Mayo, deceased; of Sally T Matthews; of Jas T B Thompson; of John M McIntosh; of Mrs Jane McCrabb, widow of the late Capt John W McCrabb, assist quartermaster U S Army; & of John J Pendleton. Bill granting a Revolutionary pension to Sarah Blunt. Bill granting 5 years' half-pay to Mrs Ann Turner, widow of Elbert Turner, deceased. Bill granting a pension to Mrs Sally M Gunsally, formerly widow of Lyman M Richmond, deceased. 6-Bill for the relief of Cyrus H McCormick: rejected. 7-Bill for the relief of Obed Hussey, was passed, & the vote passing it reconsidered. 8-Bill for the relief of Hiram Moore & John Hascall, or their legal reps: was also reconsidered. 9-Received & referred: ptn from Jas Connelly, a soldier in the late war with Great Britain, asking arrears of pension. Also, ptn from John R Tucker, asking a pension & bounty land for the services of his father, who was killed in battle during the war of the Revolution. 10-Cmte of Claims: bill for the relief of Franklin Peale. Same cmte: bill for the relief of John Bronson. 11-Cmte on Foreign Relations: bill for the relief of Jos Graham.

Trustee's sale of valuable improved property at auction: on Jun 17, on the premises, by deed of trust from Fred'k Hagar to the subscriber, dated Sep 30, 1847, recorded in Liber W B No 136, folios 466 to 470, of the land records for Wash Co, D C: sale of lots 6 & 7 in square 32, fronting 125 feet on F st, with a good frame dwlg house, containing 12 rooms, with wide passage, kitchen & cellar. Also, a fine stone ice house; brick & frame slaughter & store house, 2 stables, & carriage-house, smoke & lumber houses. -Henry Naylor, trustee -A Green auct

MON MAY 26, 1856
Trustee's sale of valuable & improved & unimproved property belonging to the estate of Jas Douglass, deceased, at auction: on Jun 2 next, by authority from all the heirs, the following property, belonging to the estate of the late Jas Douglas, viz: all of lot 3 in square 567, with improvements: fronts 23 feet 11 inches on north F st, running back 120 feet. Also, lots 6, 7, 13, 14, in square south of square 562, with improvements: fronts on north H st & Mass ave, between 2nd & 3rd sts. Also, lot 11 in square 493: fronting on C st, between 4 ½ & 6th sts: unimproved. -Wm G Gorsuch, trustee. -A Green auct

Sale of groceries & liquors, on May 28, at Mr L R Holmead's store, Md ave & 7th st west, [Island.] -Jas C McGuire, auct

For rent: the house lately occupied by Capt Magruder, U S N, & the one adjoining in Gadsby's Row. Apply corner of H st & Lafayette Square.

Fire broke out yesterday in a frame bldg not long since erected in the rear of the residence of Mrs Col Brent, on Capitol Hill, & used partly as a workshop by Mr Brumidi, the fresco-painter, & partly as a foundry for bronze, silver, & ornamental castings by Mr Vencinti, both in the employ of the Gov't. A good many valuable designs & artists' materials were lost by Mr Brumidi. The frame bldg was quite destroyed, as well as the kitchen of Mr Brent's establishment, immediately adjoining. The main residence was saved.
+
Mrs E Brent desires to make her acknowledgments to the firemen for their prompt & efficient services in arresting the fire which threatened yesterday morning to destroy her entire property, & to return to them & to all who proffered their aid her grateful thanks.

U S Patent Ofc, Wash, May 23, 1856. Ptn of Wm Baker, of Utica, N Y, praying for the extension of a patent granted to him for an improvement in window blinds, hinges, & fastenings, for 7 years from the expiration of said patent, which takes place on Sep 17, 1856. -Chas Mason, Com'r of Patents

TUE MAY 27, 1856
Mr Redfield, of N Y, is now printing & will soon have ready for publication a <u>History of Immigration</u> to the U S from Sep 30, 1819, to Dec 31, 1855, compiled entirely from official data. This work is by Mr Wm J Bromwell, a clerk in the Statistical Ofc of the State Dept, & is so prepared as to exhibit not only the extent of each year's immigration, but also the character of that immigration. The tabular statements contained in it for each year comprise: 1-The number & sex of the passengers arriving at the several ports; 2-the age; 3-the occupation; 4-the country where born.

House of Reps: 1-Provision was made for payment to the widow of Hon John G Miller of the pay & mileage due to him to the day of his death. 2-Cmte on Foreign Affairs: bill for the relief of Don Piatt: committed. 3-Cmte in Invalid Pensions: bill for the relief of S Knapp: committed.

The most profound metaphysician of the age, Sir Wm Hamilton, died in Edinburgh on May 6. He had been in delicate health for many years. -Boston Post

Mrd: on May 20, by Rev Mr Hildt, Jos J Colclaser to Miss Hester L Powders, both of Wash City.

John F Staples, inspector of lumber at the Gosport navy yeard, committed suicide on Fri. He was discovered suspended by a rope in one of the timber sheds in the navy yard. For several months his health had been impaired, which was produced by water on the brain. The deceased for many years had been a most exemplary member of the Presbyterian Church. He leaves a devoted wife & a family of interesting children.

Died: on May 24, in Wash City, Sidney Danforth Bassett, aged 30 years.

Died: on Apr 27, at her residence, in the city of Richmond, Mrs Charlotte Wooldridge, in her 58th year. She was an earnest, steadfast Christian. Blessed with an abundance of wordly goods, she dispensed it with a generous heart & liberal hand to the needy.

Died: **at Rock Hill**, in Alexandria Co, Va, near Gtwn, D C, of fever of the brain, Mr Wm Thos Miles, in his 31st year, leaving a disconsolate wife & 2 children. Mr Miles was formerly of Chas Co, Md. [No death date given-current item.]

Died: May 26, in Wash City, Sarah Fannie, infant daughter of Mr Jno C & Susan C Wilson, aged 17 months. Her funeral will take place today at 4 o'clock, at their residence, 417 Pa ave.

Senate: 1-Ptn from John Ottinger, asking to be allowed a pension for services in the Revolutionary war. 2-Bill for the relief of Mrs Ann E Derrick, widow of Wm S Derrick, was passed, so as to read for the relief of the widow & children of Wm S Derrick.

New Orleans, May 25. The trial of the case of the U S vs ex-Postmaster W G Kendall, founded on the Marshal Hanson letters, was concluded last night. The jury rendered a verdict of not guilty.

WED MAY 28, 1856
Senate: 1-Memorial & papers of Wm Carey Jones, in relation to services rendered as confidential agent of the Gov't, returned from the Court of Claims, referred to the Cmte on Public Lands. 2-Ptn from Ed Patton, asking indemnity for property destroyed & damage sustained by the bombardment of Greytown. 3-Ptn from Otway H Berryman, of the navy, asking to be allowed an amount equal to the balance found against him on the settlement of his accounts as acting purser while in command of the U S schnr **Onkahye**, & which amount he had been obliged to pay over to the U S.

On Sat week, at Timberville, Rockingham Co, Va, Rachel Topper, aged 13, & Eliz Zigler, aged 14, daughters of John Topper & Saml Zigler, fell into the Shenandoah river while attempting to cross & were drowned.

Ofc removed. Dr Van Patten, Dentist, will be happy to serve his patrons at his residence, *Cedar Hill*, on Pa ave, near Gtwn.

$50 reward for the return of a horse stolen from my stable on May 26. -Parke G Howle, 14th st, Island.

Mrd: on May 22, at Portsmouth, Va, by Rev Chas A Davis, E Brison Tucker, of Wash City, to Sue W Davis, daughter of the officiating minister.

Died: on May 25, at the residence of her father, L Lance, near Wilmington, N C, Mrs Augusta Hardin, wife of L B Hardin, of the Navy Dept. Her funeral will take place from St Paul's Church, Alexandria, this morning at 9 o'clock.

Died: lately, in Phil, Redwood Fisher, of that city, at an advanced age. He was the founder & for a year or two the able editor of the Nat'l Magazine & Industrial Record, a valuable statistical & economic work, published in N Y, devoted to the cause of American industry. Possessed of a philanthropic heart & generous impulses, he was a warm friend, & in the domestic & gentle affections his character was unsurpassed.

Died: on May 10, at his residence, near Gtwn, D C, Giles Dyer, in his 49th year, after a protracted illness & extreme sufferings. A thousand recollections will crowd upon the memories of an innocent boyhood, a blameless youth, a useful & edifying manhood.

On Sunday last two young men, De Garris, of Alabama, & Wheeler, of Ga, who lately arrived here & boarded at the Exchange Hotel, were arrested on a charge of having robbed Mr Denton Porter, a fellow boarder, of between three & four hundred dollars. For want of bail they were put in jail for safe keeping. A young white woman, a servant in the house, who had received money from them, was also committed.

New President of the Gaslight Co. At a meeting of the Board of Directors on May 24, Geo W Riggs, of the firm of Riggs & Co, bankers, was chosen Pres of the Wash Gas Light Co, in the place of Silas H Hill, resigned.

Meeting of the Union Association on May 28, at Coomb's rooms, Pa ave, near 10th st. By order, Z K Offutt, sec

THU MAY 29, 1856
Elegant household & kitchen furniture at auction on: Jun 3, at the residence of Col B F Larned, 13th st, between E & G sts north. -Jas C McGuire, auct

Senate: 1-Additional papers submitted in relation to the claim of Lucy Tate. 2-Ptn from the heirs of Cornelius Russell, deceased, lt in the Continental line, asking to be allowed the benefit of the resolution of Congress of Oct 21, 1780. 3-Two memorials from A S Taylor, an ofcr in the marine corps, asking to be allowed additional pay for the performance of certain staff duties, & remuneration for certain losses sustained by the burning of the U S steamer **Missouri** in the harbor of Gibralter. 4-Cmte on Foreign Relatins: bill for the relef of Horatio J Perry: passed, with amendments. 5-Bill for the relief of John Crawford: passed. 6-Bill for the relief of Wm M F Magraw: passed.

House of Reps: 1-Bill for the relief of Mrs Charlotte Turner, of Louisiana: referred. 2-Joint resolution for the relief of the persons who composed the Darien exploring expedition under Lt J G Strain, U S Navy. 3-Cmte on Foreign Affairs: bill for the relief of Dr Jas Morrow: committed. 4-Cmte on Commerce: bill for the relief of Fred'k Stevens, with a recommendation that it do not pass: laid on the table. 5-Cmte on the Post Ofc & Post Roads: bill for the relief of John H Scranton & Jas M Hunt: committed. Same cmte: adverse reports on the ptns of J W Post & of Nathan Cook. 6-Cmte on Naval Affairs: bill for the relief of Cmder John L Saunders: committed. Same cmte: adverse report on the ptn of Wm P S Sanger. 7-Cmte on Indian Affairs: bill for the relief of the heirs of Mary Jemison, deceased: committed.

For sale: on the Heights of Gtwn, **Mont Alto**, containing about 16 acres. This celebrated spot is so well known as to need but little description. For particulars address Dr Bohrer, Gtwn, D C.

Mrd: on May 27, in Wash City, by Rev Geo D Cummins, Albert H McRea to Mary M, daughter of the late Capt Jas Ricketts, of the British Navy.

FRI MAY 30, 1856
Administrator's sale of Millinery Goods: on Jun 3, by order of the Orphans Court of Wash Co, D C, a small stock of goods belonging to the late Anne E Marselus. &- Anthony Buckley, adm -Jas C McGuire, auct

Senate: 1-Ptn from Mrs Susan Decatur, widow of Cmdor Stephen Decatur, asking to be allowed an increase of pension. 2-Ptn from Jas Smith, asking to be allowed right of pre-emption to certain lands in Alabama upon the performance of certain duties. 3-Ptn from Henry Cartner, a soldier in Wayne's army, asking to be allowed a pension. 4-Ptn from Emarine Young, widow of a soldier in the late war with Mexico, asking to be allowed a pension.

Mrd: on May 27, at **White Cottage**, Fairfax Co, Va, by Rev Wm B Lipscomb, Mr Wm Quail, of Wash, Pa, to Miss Phebe Degge, youngest daughter of the officiating minister.

Sir Wm Hamilton, the Scotch philospher, died on May 6, at his residence in Great King st, Edinburgh, Scotland, after 10 days' illness. By the death of this illustrious man the Univ of Edinburgh has lost its most distinguished ornament & the world its greatest philosopher. He was born at Glasgow, Scotland, in 1788.

House of Reps: 1-Cmte on the Judiciary: bill for the relief of Wm Burdell, Saml Medary & others, sureties of John T Arthur, assist quartermaster U S army: committed. 2-Bill for the relief of Wm Humphrey, jr, owner of fishing schnr **Good Exchange**, lost at sea: passed. 3-Bill authorizing a settlement of the accounts of Chas P Babcock, late Indian agent at Detroit, Mich: referred. 4-Bill to authorize the legal reps of Pascal L Cerre to enter certain lands in the State of Missouri: passed. 5-Bill for the relief of Chas J Ingersoll was considered. 6-Joint resolution authorizing the Sec of the Interior to settle the accounts of Oliver M Woozencraft: referred. 7-Ptn of John H Monroe, of Lincoln Co, Mo, asking to be placed on the pension roll & to be allowed arrears of pension. 8-Memorial of Benj D Tubman, Russel K Compton, & 37 other citizens of Chas & PG Counties, Md, praying the establishment of a mail route from Piscataway, PG Co, to Pomonkey, in Chas Co.

SAT MAY 31, 1856
Excellent household & kitchen furniture at auction on: Jun 6, at the residence of the late Dr O M Linthicum, deceased, on 3rd st, near Market, all his furniture, horse carriage, & piano. -Jno Marbury, trustee -Barnard & Buckey, aucts

From Oregon. The Oregonian of Apr 19 published a report from Col T R Cornelius, commanding the first regt of Oregon mounted volunteers, dated Apr 13, at the Dalles of the Columbia. On Apr 10 Capt Hembree & an exploring company of 4 were suddenly surrounded by about 70 hostile Indians, under chief Kamoikin, who fired upon them, killing Capt Hembree. This was the signal for a general Indian attack upon the camp, for which at all points the Indians commenced marching, but the attack was prevented by the activity of the troops. A band of 300 Indian warriors was subsequently dislodged from a fortified position up the creek. No other white man was killed.

Mr Brochieri, the inventor of the celebrated hemorrhagic water which bears his name, has just died in France. He has just willed to his widow a fortune of a million of francs & his secret to the Faculty of Medicine. -Courier des Etats Unis

Died: on Fri, in Wash City, after a lingering illness, Mrs Eliz Nailor, aged 38 years, wife of Washington Nailor. Her funeral will be this afternoon at 3 o'clock, from her late residence on D st, between 13½ & 14th sts.

Died: on May 29, at **Oak Hill**, Montg Co, Md, Edmund H, son of Edmund H & Emily Brooke, aged 7 years & 10 months. His funeral will be this afternoon at 5 o'clock, at the residence of his father.

Died: on May 23, at New Orleans, in his 58th year, Gen Wm De Buys. He was a native of New Orleans; & represented it in the House of Reps of the State, over which he presided as Speaker. He was the prdecessor of Gen Lewis, as Maj Gen of the First Division of Louisiana Militia, & was a veteran of the war of 1812-'14. As a father, husband, & friend, he was exemplary in the faithful discharge of his duties.
-Picayune

Mount Zephyr, originally a part of the **Mount Vernon** Estate, is for sale: contains 648½ acres; & the **Laurel Spring Farm**, 237 acres; & the **Union Farm**, 715½ acres, formerly a part of the estate of Gen Geo Washington, bounded 3 miles on the east by Mount Vernon, near the farm of David Walton: all for sale. In 1785 Gen Washington built a spacious brick barn & shed upon it, the largest in America, since destroyed, but enough of the remains of his work in farming is yet visible to distinguish the master mind in peace as in war. There is a large & commodious dwlg house, with a deep & dry cellar. Three old tenements remain on the **Laurel & Union Farms**. For terms apply to Messrs Geo & Thos Parker & Co, Wash, Messrs Smith & Beach, Alexandria, or to the undersigned, care of Messrs J Macy's Sons, N Y.
-Aaron Leggett

Isthmus of Panama. List of the killed by an accident on the Panama railroad. Killed at the time of the accident: males: Danl Stuyvesant, Norman J Baker, *Thos Crowley & son Thos; +Dennis Crowley, +Moses Walton, John Morton, John Nichter, Thos Holloway, N Eide, *C Harve, *S Hoffman, *A Pether, *M Read, *J F Krauter, Robt Chesborough, *Geo Zindell. Females: Julia Cronan, +Mrs Thos Crowley, +Mrs Dennis Crowley, +Mrs J Bulger, + Mrs Murphy. Passengers from Cornwall, England: John Blight, +John James Gale, +Ryan Johns, +John Richd Johns, +Thos James, +Benj Archer, + Thos Ford. Residents of Aspinwall: Henry Alvarenga, 30 years of age, a native of Kingston, Jamaica; J Ross Dalhosie, aged about 33, a native of Kingston, Jamaica. A list is also given of 50 persons wounded, who remained in the hospital. Some 8 or 10 went on to Panama to take the steamer for San Francisco. Died since the accident: Jas Martin, died May _, Antonio Domingo, died May 7; Mr King, Ohio; Wm Thraves, American, aged 19 years, from Ohio. His brother gives the information. El Panameno states that some arrests of persons engaged in the Panama riot of Apr 15 had been made, & a portion of the property stolen recovered. The disturbances in the interior had been quelled. The Panama Star & Herald states that a treaty has been concluded between Ecuador & the U S.
*:Recognized by steerage tickets or other papers found on them
+: Identified by their friends.

From Central America: the Aspinwall Courier of May 13 gives particulars of Gen Walker's successful attack upon the Costa Ricans at Rivas. Battle commenced on Apr 11. Walker lost 80 killed & disabled, including almost all his official staff. Lts Gillis & Winter were among the killed. Capt Casey lost an arm & had his other hand badly wounded. The Costa Ricans lost over 200 killed & 400 wounded.

Orphans Court of Wash Co, D C. Letters of administration on the personal estate of Benedict J L Railey, late of Wash Co, deceased. -Christiana Railey, admx

Circuit Court of Wash Co, D C-in Equity. Stephen Whitney et al vs A Dey et al. Duncan P Campbell, Dudley L Gregory, Luke Hemenway, & Saml Swartwout having each filed his petition in said cause, praying to be allowed & paid the dividend on their respective shares as stockholders in the Galveston Bay & Texas & Co, that is to say, 5 shares to said Campbell, 8 to Gregory, 4 to Hemenway, & 1 share to Swartwout, & it appearing by said petitions that the certificates of the said petitioners have been lost or mislaid. Same to be published in in Wash, & N Y C, once a week for 3 weeks prior to Jul 1 next. -Jno A Smith, clerk

MON JUN 2, 1856
Trustee's sale: by deed of trust from Jas Crutchett to the subscriber, recorded in Liber J A S No 48, at folio 478, of the land records of D C: public sale on Jun 16 of lots 1 thru 22, in square 720, Wash City. -Hugh Caperton, trustee -E S Wright, salesman

Hugh Miller, the distinguished Scotch geologist, the author of Old Red Sandstone, is about to visit American on a lecturing tour. He will be received every where with cordiality & attention.

E F Page, a 1st class clerk, has been promoted to the 2nd class, [$1,400,] vice Wm F Sherrod, resigned. Lewis Jourdan, jr, of Indiana, has been appointed to a 1st class [$1,200,] clerkship, vice Page, promoted.

The celebrated Englishwoman Fanny Kemble, whose talents & character are an honor to her sex, arrived in N Y in the ship **Africa**. She will have a warm welcome from her friends, & the hills, streams, & waving vegetation of Berkshire with gladness will acknowledge her presence. -Boston Post

Trustee's sale of valuable bldg lot on 10th st west, between north N & O sts: at public auction, on Jun 23, by deed of trust from Estwick Evans & wife, dated Oct 10, 1855, recorded in Liber J A S No 101, folios 399 thru 402, of the land records of Wash Co, D C: sale of lot 7 thru 9 in square 339, in Wash City. Terms cash. -Hugh B Sweeny, trustee -A Green auct

Household & kitchen furniture at auction on: Jun 4, at the residence of Mr Jas R Roache, 407 13th st, between G & H sts. -A Green auct

From the Santa Fe Gazette for Apr: Gov't surveyors under Mr Garretson had again commenced. Col Chandler returned to **Fort Craig** from the expedition to the Gila Apache country on Apr 2. He had been in pursuit of a body of Indians who had been stealing stock. Thirty men under Lt Moore & Bendal completely routed the band composed of 40 to 50 warriors. The Indians had 2 killed & 1 wounded. Col Chandler's casualties were 2 wounded, Pvt Allen of Co I, & Pvt Fox, of Co D 1st Dragoons.

Florida Indian outrage: the Tampa Peninsula of the 12th ult says that on the 14th a number of Indians fired upon the house of Capt Bradley, in Hernando Co, & killed 2 of his children. On the 16th the same band of savages attacked men guarding the train carrying provisions to the State troops from Tampa to Ichepuckarana, a boy named Stallings & his boy, & a man named Roach were killed. Hinson & Hatfield, guards, escaped.

Piqua [Ohio] Register of Apr 17: two daughters & a little son of Mr M Withers, of that city, were out fishing in the canal. The little boy slipped in, & the eldest sister, about 18, sprang to his resuce. Both sank & drowned. The youngest sister leaped in to assist them, & would have drowned too but for the presence of mind of a little boy, a son of Mr Wolsey, who reached the end of his fishing rod to her, & saved her.

Mrd: on May 28, at Trinity Church, N Y, Mr Geo W Fellows to Miss Sarah M, youngest daughter of Christopher Walton, of Fordham, Westchester Co, N Y.

Died: on May 30, at N Y, aged 40 years, John M McEneany. He was a printer who has been employed as compositor for some years past in N Y, where he enjoyed the confidence & esteem of all who knew him. He was also favorably known in Wash City, where he resided for a time for a few years back.

Masonic: regular communication of B B French Lodge, No 15, will be held on May 2. -C L Lombard, sec

The employes in the different Jewelry stores having requested their employers to close their stores at 7 o'clock P M from Jun 2 until Sep 28, & their request having been granted by all but a single exception, they give notice that hereafter the store of the following parties will be closed as stated above: M R Galt & Bro; Saml Lewis; Augustus Lang; H Semken; C E Heydon.

TUE JUN 3, 1856
Hon John M Niles, formerly Postmaster Gen & Senator from Conn, died at his residence in Hartford on Sat last.

Election for Pres & Board of Directors of the Chesapeake & Ohio Canal Co took place yesterday: Wm P Maulsby, of Fred'k city, Pres. Board of Directors: Thos Devecmon & Jas Fitzpatrick, Alleghany Co, Md. Jas Cowdy & Jacob H Grove, Wash Co, Md. John Brewer, Montg Co, Md. Robt P Dodge, Gtwn, D C.

Notice of copartnership under the name of Stanislaus Murray & Co: counting room, 57 La ave, up stairs. -Stanislaus Murray, T F Sweeny, Jun 3. [We are prepared to order Teas, Wines, & Liquors of every grade for dealers.]

Terrible affray at Helena, Ark: on Sat last, had it s origin in an article in the State Rights Democrat which reflected on Mr Rice. A duel had been talked of between Mr Rice & Mr Hindman, one of the editors of the Democrat. On Sat Hindman & his partner, Claiborne, while in the street encountered Mr Rice & his brother-in-law, Dr Merritt. Pistols were drawn & fired. Dr Merritt & Mr Claiborne were mortally wounded. Hindman's condition was considered favorable, but still precarious.

Fresh strawberries: from the Washington Nursery, 5th st, corner of K & N Y ave. -M Griffiths

H O Hood has removed his stock of fine Gold watches, rich Gold Jewelry, Silverware, & Plated Goods from his old stand to the newly fitted up store formerly occupied by Mr Keyworth, 3 doors above 9th st.

WED JUN 4, 1856
Fraud upon the Pension Ofc: the agent, armed with the proper legal processes, assisted by the marshal & deputy marshal of Augusta, proceeded to Columbia Co, & there arrested Richd W Jones & Dr Henry A Ramsay, the latter appearing to have been the originator & chief actor in the villainous plot against the Treasury. They were arraigned before the U S Com'r, Chas S Henry, for preliminary examination, Ramsay giving bond of $5,000, with his father as security, for his appearance from time to time, while Jones was committed to jail for lack of a sponsor. Ramsay has since fled, & a reward of $500 is offered for his apprehension. Jones is still in jail. -Savannah Republican

Last week, at Baskinridge, N J, Miss Charlotte Janes, the eldest daughter of Rev Bishop Janes, was so severely burnt by the explosion of a camphene lamp that her life is despaired of. She is about 18 years of age.

On Friday, a young woman, Mary Ann Young, was badly burnt at her residence in Wash st, Phil, by the explosion of a fluid lamp, by the light of which she was sewing. She is only 18 years of age, & was engaged in making her wedding garment at the time.

Fatal rencontre: Mr Marks, editor of the Ledger, at Bayou Sayra, La, killed Mr Robertson, editor of the Chronicle, in that place, on May 26, in a street rencontre.

Henry Hopkins, the lawyer & postmaster who robbed the mail at Island Point, Vt, has been found guilty & sentenced to 10 years' imprisonment.

The mill belonging to Lawrence Washington, near Pope's Creek, in Westmoreland Co, Va, was destroyed by fire on Fri last. Supposed to be the work of an incendiary.

Yesterday afternoon 3 young men, somewhat flushed with drink, of whom John Essex, a powerfully built stalwart stone cutter, was one, were walking along Pa ave when they passed a single person, Owen Quigley, who cried "Hurrah for Magruder." Essex dropped back & overtook Quigley & gave him a blow, felling him to the ground. Mr Chas Wood, a respectable citizen of Wash, & Dr Jas Finks, of Warrenton, Va, were both passing by at the time, & witnessed the assault. Quigley was removed from the scene & Essex was arrested by ofcr Duvall. Quigley died about 10 minutes after the blow. Essex has since escaped and fled Wash City.

Died: on Jun 3, in Wash City, on 5th st, between F & G sts, Mr Richd Elmore, late of Richmond Co, Va, in his 29th year. His funeral is this morning at 10 o'clock.

Fresh Milk, from R Nicols Snowden's farm of Fairland, for sale by O V Durfee, 485 10th st, Wash.

THU JUN 5, 1856
Sale on the Heights of Gtwn of elegant furniture, rich china, fine cut glass, horses & carriages, on Jun 12, at the residence of his Excellency J F Crampton, British Minister, on Road st, between Congress & Wash sts. -Barnard & Buckey, aucts

Sale of fine stock of Fresh Family Groceries & Liquors at auction: on Jun 9, at the Grocery Store recently occupied by Bernard Devine, deceased, at the corner of south B st & N J ave, Capitol Hill. -A Green auct

Brooke Hall Female Academy, Media, Delaware Co, Pa: Miss Maria L Eastman, Principal. This Seminary will be open on Sep 10, 1856.

News from Nicaragua by the Orizaba: Judge J Caleb Smith, well known in Calif & Va, died at Granada on Apr 25, after a short attack of fever. He was the son of Ex-Govn'r Smith, of Va, & was on his way, we believe, to Calif at the time of his death. -Alexandria Sentinel

Reward of $500: Ofc U S Marshal D C, Wash, Jun 4, 1856. For John Essex, who is charged with the murder of Owen Quigley, in Wash City, on Jun 3. -Jonah D Hoover, Marshal for D C. [Jun 6 newspaper: A charge of complicity in the escape of John Essex was yesterday laid before Justice John D Clarke, on the oath of Constable Wilson, against Justice Hollingshead. A hearing of the case will take place this afternoon.] [Jun 7th newspaper: the accused presented himself, but the principal witness did not, & so nothing was done, & the whole affair assumed a very absurd & ridiculous aspect.]

$25 reward for the apprehension, or any information which will lead to the apprehension of, Chas Harris, who, for some time prior to Mar 5, 1856, resided in this place in the capacity as bar keeper. Harris is an Englishman by birth, about 25 years of age, of small stature, with black hair & eyes, & lame in his right leg. He possessed himself of money & merchandise upon false pretence of carrying on the business of pedlar. He is probably making his way to the West. -Vass & Brother, Warrenton, Fauquier Co, Va

Sheriff's Ofc, Jun 2, 1856. Notice: to the heirs & legal reps of Patrick Murphy, late of Carnarvon township, Lancaster Co, Pa, deceased. By order of the Orphans' Court of said county, I will hold an inquest to divide, part, or value the real estate of the said deceased, on Sep 6, at the public house of Mrs Albright, in the village of churchtown, in said township, when & where you may attend if you think proper.
-Geo Martin, Sheriff

Mrd: on Tue, in Wash City, by Rev John C Smith, John Wood to Miss Maria Louisa, daughter of John T Fales, of Burlington, Iowa.

Mrd: on Jun 3, in Wash City, by Rev J W French, Mr Henry C Fillebrown to Miss Margaret H Paine.

FRI JUN 6, 1856
Judge Slaughter, of Hamptonburg, N Y, was picking up a measure of sale in the pasture among his horses, & received a violent kick from one of his colts, above the eyes, crushing in the frontal bones, & entirely depriving him of sight. He now lies in a dangerous situation.

Died: on Jun 4, after a lingering illness, Mary F, wife of John R Murray, in her 37th year. Her funeral is this morning at 10 o'clock, from 26 4½ st.

Mrd: on Jun 5, in Wash City, by Rev Dr Sunderland, Mr Sheppard Homans, Actuary of the Mutual Life Ins Co of N Y, to Miss Sallie L Houston, daughter of John W Houston, of Wash City.

Mrd: on Jun 5, in Balt, at the Central Presbyterian Church, by Rev Stuart Robinson, Jos Shillington, of Wash City, to Lizzie Cummings, of the former place.

Obit-died: on May 23, in Chillicothe, Ohio, Mrs Margaret Vanmeter, wife of Jos H Vanmeter, in her 26th year. She was the daughter of Col Franklin Fullerton, of Newark, Ohio, where her life was mostly spent, & where she was the charm of the social circle. Less than a year ago she was married & removed to Chillicothe, & although she resided there but a few months she had endeared herself to all who knew her.

Wash City Ordinances: 1-Act granting permission to Mary J Martin to erect a brick wall in front of her premises, at the corner of C st north & 1st st east & that said wall may be placed 4 feet outside of the bldg line: Provided that said wall shall be removed at the pleasure of the Corp. 2-Act for the relief of John P Hilton: the sum of $6.93 be refunded to him, he having erroneously deposited that amount to the credit of the surplus fund.

Laws of the U S passed at the 1st Session of the 34th Congress of the U S A: Act to incorporate St Thomas' Literary Society, in the District of Columbia: that Nicholas D Young, Geo J A Wilson, & Sidney A Clarkson, & their successors, are hereby made a body politic & corporate forever, by the said name, for purposes of charity & education.

Public sale of young negroes of both sexes: on Jun 14, at the Court-house door in Upper Marlborough, Md: one young negro man, one boy about 11 years old, one young woman with a child 12 months old, & one young woman. The women are house servants, the one a first-rate cook & the other a first rate house servant & nurse. They are sold for no fault whatever, the undersigned expecting to leave the State. Terms cash. -Robt J Young

Sam Chilton & Geo M Williams have associated as partners in the practice of the law. Ofc 49 La ave, Wash.

St Louis, Jun 5. Govn'r Price, of Missouri, has ordered an election on the first Monday of Aug next to fill the vacancy occasioned by the death of Hon John Miller.

Kinderhook, Jun 5. Ex-Pres Van Buren was thrown from his horse this morning, receiving a severe wound upon his head, but not considered dangerous.

SAT JUN 7, 1856
Rev Alex'r McCain died in this city on Sunday last, in his 84th year. He had been engaged in preaching the Gospel for 49 years. He moved from Alabama to this city last winter in order that he might be enabled to spend the remainder of his days with his only & beloved daughter, Mrs Jas Brett. -Augusta [Geo] Sentinel

Dr of Med-ladies. On Monday Mr Newkirk, Vice Pres of the Penn Medical Univ of Phil, conferred the degree of Dr of Medicine upon the following ladies: Esther C Williams, of Ohio; Sarah H Young, of Mass; Ellen J Miller, of Phil; Mary M Halloway, of Indiana; & Eliz Calvin, of Pa.

Charleston Courier of Monday mentions the following casualties: 1-Capt Howard, of the brig **Victor of the Wave**, was drowned on Sat, near Robert Island, by the capsizing of his boat. 2-Louis Warkman & John Maent, Germans, were drowned on the same day & during the same squall while on a fishing excursion. 3-Wm Madden, a native of Ireland, was killed on Sunday. The deceased was on the city guard, & was about relieving Cummins, who was stationed in charge of the jail yard in consequence of repairs there going on, when he received the fatal wound. It is said the parties were on friendly terms, which gives probability to the accounts which refer the said affair to some strange mistake.

Died: on Fri, of a lingering disease, which she bore with Christian fortitude, Mrs Mary Whitelock, relict of John Whitelock, of Balt, aged 86 years. Her funeral will take place from the Smithsonian Institution tomorrow, Sabbath, at 4 o'clock P M, to which her friends & the friends & acquaintances of Mr Wm McPeak are invited.

Circuit Court of Wash Co, D C-in Equity, No 1,050. Cadwallader Wallace vs Elijah S Maddox, Felix Richards, & Jas B White. The bill filed in this cause states in substance that on May 30, 1840, land ofc military land warrant 8,809, for 1,233 1/3 acres of land, was issued from the land ofc of Va to Elijah S Maddox, one of the heirs of Joshua Johnson, deceased; that prior to the issue of said warrant, viz on Apr 8, 1840, the said Elijah S Maddox executed a power of atty to Felix Richards, by which he appointed the said Richards his atty to prosecute his claims for land or money due him from the State of Va, & also to sell & assign any land warrants or warrant that he might under said power obtain in his name; that, but virtue of said power, the said Richards did prosecute the claims of the said Maddox, & did obtain the issue of the aforesaid land warrant No 8,809, & did further under & by virtue of said power, transfer & assign the same to one John F Webb for a valuable consideration, & did deliver the same to the said Webb; that the said Webb made the purchase aforesaid from the said Richards as the agent of & for the benefit of the cmplnt, Cadwallader Wallace, & filed the same in the Genr'l Land Ofc at Wash City in his, the said cmplnt's, name; that the said Felix Richards did further execute a power of atty to the cmplnt, in which, under & by virtue of the power of atty aforesaid from the said

Maddox to him, he did appoint & substitute the said cmplnt in his place, to receive & transfer the aforesaid warrant, 8,809; that afterwards, viz on Jan 24, 1854, the said Maddox did file in the Genr'l Land Ofc aforesaid an affidavit, setting forth that he had never received from the said Richads any satisfaction for said warrant, & on Jan 28 aforesaid did execute an assignment of said warrant to Jas B White, one of the dfndnts, & a new power of atty, by which he did empower the said White to receive, assign, & transfer all scrip that might be issued upon said warrant No 8,809, & did revoke & annul all former powers; that the said White has filed a caveat in the said Genr'l Land Ofc against the issue of scrip upon said warrant to the cmplnt, & asks that the same may be issued to him. The bill prays for an injunction & a decree that the first power of atty may be recognized as having full force & vigor, notwithstanding the power to White; that the cmplnt may be decreed to be the assignee of said Maddox & the present proprietor of said warrant, & that the Com'rs of the Genr'l Land Ofc may be ordered to issue the scrip due upon said warrant to the cmplnt, or that, failing this, a decree may be had against the said Felix Richards, ordering him to assign to the cmplnt an amount of scrip equivalent to that due upon said warrant, or to pay a sum of money to said cmplnt equal to the value of said scrip. It appearing to the Court that Elijah S Maddox is not a resident of D C, & is warned to appear in Court, in person or by solicitor, on or before Oct 3 next.
-Jno A Smith, clerk

$50 reward for servant man Jas Anderson, who got permission on May 31 to go to Dr S Cook's, in PG Co, Md, to see his children, & has not been there. -W G W White, corner 8th st & Market Space, Wash.

MON JUN 9, 1856
Household & kitchen furniture at auction on: Jun 16, by order of the Orphans Court of Wash Co, D C: at the residence of the late Oliver Whittlesey, on La ave, between 3rd & 4th sts, near the City Hall. -A Green auct

Trustee's sale of valuable private residence at auction: on Jun 19, by order of the trustee, that valuable property in Gtwn, being the late residence of Dr O M Linthicum, deceased, on 3rd st & extending through to 4th st. This property is improved by a large 3 story brick dwlg with back bldgs. -John Marlang, trustee -Barnard & Buckey, aucts

Mr Henry Davis, jr, of Bulloch Co, Geo, was bitten by a large rattlesnake while walking a few hundred yards from his house one day last week & died from its effects. After he was bitten he corded his leg with his suspenders, & then killed the reptile. He proceeded towards his house, but finding he could go no further, hung his hat upon a bush & lay down, where he was found. He was much respected, & has left a wife & some 5 or 6 children & numerous friends to mourn his loss. -Georgian

Worcester, Mass, May 7. Lawrence M Cleary was instantly killed today by premature discharge of a cannon being fired in honor of Mr Buchanan's nomination.

Trustee's sale of valuable real estate. Alex'r Keech & others vs Eleanor H Callis & Anthony Addison. In the Circuit Court for PG Co, sitting as a Court of Equity. Be decree of the said court, passed on Feb 19, 1856, in the above cause, the undersigned, as trustee, will expose to public sale, on Jul 3 next, on the premises, a portion of the real estate of which the late Henry A Callis died seized & possessed, containing, by a survey made under this decree, 160 acres, more or less. This land has been divided by the surveyor, as will appear by a plat which will be exhibited on the day of sale, into 3 lots: 34 1/5 acres, 64 4/5 acres, & 59 acres, more or less. The land adjoins the lands of Messrs Thos Berry, Col Maddux, Geo Walker, & others. Those desiring to purchase will be shown the premises by Mr J E Thompson, residing at Barnaby. -J Contee Mullikin, C Smith, Keech, trustees -F N Boteler, auct, Upper Marlboro, May 14.

I hereby certify that John Lighter, of Wash Co, D C, brought before me, as a stray trespassing on his enclosures, a sorrel gelding, about 12 years old. -B K Morsell, J P [Owner of the above horse is to come forward, prove property, pay charges, & take him away. -John Lighter]

Mrd: on Apr 19, in Fred'k City, Md, by Rev B Villiger, Walter Hay, M D, of Fla, to Rebecca B, youngest daughter of the late Gen Saml Ringgold, of Wash Co, Md.

Died: on Jun 6, Mrs Mary Dunn, in her 72nd year. Her funeral is today at 4 P M from the residence of her daughter, Mrs E Cudlipp, 427 Pa ave, between 3rd & 4½ sts.

TUE JUN 10, 1856
Trustee's sale of bldg lots in square 545, on Jun 21, at public auction, by deed of trust from Peter Emrich to the subscriber, dated Feb 4, 1854, recorded in Liber J A S No 73, folios 459 thru 461,of the land records of Wash Co, D C: all of lots 42 & 32 in Joel W Jones' subdivision of square 545, in said city, with improvements. The property fronts on 3rd st west, between N & M sts, & contains 4,390 square feet of ground. -E M Hamilton, trustee -A Green, auct

Trustee's sale of 24 acres 3 roods & 7 perches of valuable land in PG Co, Md, at auction: on Jun 27, by deed of trust from Wallace Kirkwood to the subscriber, dated Sep 1, 1848, recorded in Liber J B B, No 5, folios 391 thru 394, one of the land records of said county: all that piece or parcel of land, being part of a tract known as parts of **Lonehead & Chillum Castle**, in said county, fronting on the Bladensburg & Rockville road, & near the farm of Mrs Diggs. -David A Gardner, trustee -A Green auct

Valuable foundry property in the 1st Ward at auction: on Jun 25, we will sell lots 9 thru 11 in square 15, known as ***Rock Creek Foundry***, on corner of Pa ave & 26th st, with the foundry, blacksmith shop, ofc, & other bldgs thereon. The view of the Potomac, Gtwn, & Va shore from there unsurpassed. -Wall, Barnard & Co, aucts

Died: on Jun 9, in Wash City, of pneumonia, Mr John Fleming Butler, printer, in his 49th year. He was a nephew of the late Dr Robt Butler, Treasurer of the State of Va, & well known in this community as a high-minded & honorable man. His funeral will be this afternoon at 4 o'clock, from the residence of Josiah Melvin, 411 10th st.

For sale: horse, wagon & harness. The describer has no further use of them. Wagon was built by Mr J W Martin, of Wash City. Apply to Julius De Saules, 389 9th st.

Orphans Court of Wash Co, D C. Letters testamentary on personal estate of Isaac M Chubb, late of Wash Co, deceased. -Caroline A Chubb, excx -Wm H Dougal, exc

Mr Geo P Buell, of Wash City, who was stabbed in an affray at Cincinnati, is recovering from the wound. His brother left Wash for Cincinnati on Sat. [Jun 11th newspaper: he has been removed from Cincinnati to Lawrenceburg, Indiana.]

WED JUN 11, 1856
Senate: 1-Ptn from Elias Hall, asking compensation for his services as superintendent of the repair of small arms during the war of 1812 on the Northern frontier.
2-Ptn from Jason Harrison, Clerk of the District Court of the U S for the district of Missoui, asking to be reimbursed expenses incurred by him for rent of ofc.

Beautiful residence & valuable farm in Orange Co, Va, for sale: the farm upon which I now reside, known as ***Linden***, containing 848½ acres: with a very comfortable dwlg house, overseer's house, & all necessary out-bldgs, in good repair. -Henry Massie

The wife of Edw Cooper, of Sutton Mills, Mass, was drowned on Wed night in Hodge's mill-pond. It is supposed she fell in while attempting to dip water. Mr Cooper was aroused by the crying of an infant, when he found her gone.
-Andover paper

Our citizens were shocked on Thu by the news of the massacre of the family of Jacob Friend, a worthy citizen living about 3 miles south of this city. Seven distinct smouldering skeletons were traced in the ruins of the yet burning house. These comprised Mr Friend, his wife, & 5 children. The coroner's jury found they had come to their death by assassination. Suspicion has rested upon certain parties living near the scene, who are now undergoing examination. -St Joseph [Mo] Gaz of May 30.

David Martin, one of the editors of the Democratic paper, the Baton Rouge Advocate, died in that city on Sunday. He has long been connected with the press of Louisiana. -New Orleans Bulletin

Castle Garden, at N Y, was crowded on Monday. Passengers from 6 ships, nearly 2,000 in number, landed there, &, coming from almost as many different quarters of Europe, the variety of costume & the confusion of tongues was bewildering. The ship **James R Keeler**, from Liverpool, with 350 passengers. The ship **Emerald Isle**, from Liverpool, with 782 passengers. The barque **Meridian**, from Leghorn, with 34 passengers. The barque **Mississippi**, from Bremen, 228; the ship **Johanna Elisa**, Hamburg, 216;& the barque **Gerhard**, Hamburg, 149. Among these immigrants were a number from Hesse Cassel. N Y Courier

Mrd: yesterday, in Wash City, at St John's Church, by Rector, Rev Dr Pyne, Thos H Holt, of Calif, to Adelaide L, daughter of Hon Thos L Smith, Auditor of the Treasury.

Died: on Jun 7, at the residence of Capt Z F Johnson, Rockville, Md, in her 67th year, Mrs Matilda Holland, relict of the late Solomon Holland, of Montg Co, Md.

Died: on Jun 2, in Alexandria, Falkland Lary, aged 16 years, eldest son of the late Archibald Lary, of Cumberland, Md.

Died: on Jun 10, in Wash City, suddenly, Joanna, wife of Mr Sylvester Mudd, & daughter of Charlotte & the late Thos Peake, aged 20 years & 3 months.

Died: on Jun 10, Mary Jane Downey, aged 11 years, daughter of the late Michl & Mary Downey. Her funeral is today at 3 o'clock, from the residence of her mother, *Spring Tavern*, Bladensburg road.

Died: on Jun 10, in Wash City, John Proud, only child of Thos M & Mary P Hanson, aged 1 year & 10 months. His funeral is today at 5 o'clock P M, from his father's residence, 22 East Capitol st.

THU JUN 12, 1856
Kansas Matter. Letter to Col Anderson, Capts Shelby, Trigg, Walton, Sawyer, & E Windsor. Westport, Jun 2, 1856. Gentlemen: A messenger has just arrivd from Capt Pate, of the Lawrence Sharpshooters, stating that he is in great danger & surrounded. He has several prisoners. John Donaldson has been killed. Foreman & 4 others are taken prisoners by the Abolitionists, & before this they are probably murdered. Whitfield starts tonight for Hickery Point, the place of the last Massacre, to aid our men or die. -C E Kearney, Henry F Hereford, A S Johnson, J Buford

Household & kitchen furniture at auction on: Jun 17, at the residence of Mrs Blunt, corner of 8th & E sts. -Jas C McGuire, auct

On Thu, says the Shelbyvile [Ky] Banner, while Mr J C Bushy, his little 6 year old son, & Mr A J Odel were planting corn near Fairland, in that county, they discovered a root which they took for spikenard, & about 10 minutes after they had eaten of it the boy was seen to fall. He died in two hours after suffering terrible agony.

Senate: 1-Ptn from Lemuel Wooster, asking to be allowed bounty land on account of his services as a waiter to an ofcr during the war of 1812. 2-Chamber of Commerce of N Y, in favor of an appropriation for the purchase by the U S of Lt Sands' invention for taking deep-sea soundings. 3-Ptn from the heirs of Dr John Lore, asking to be allowed the commutation pay & pension to which the widow of said Lore was entitled after his decease. 4-Ptn from Jos Clarke, a man of color, asking to be allowed a pension in consequence of a wound received in the war of 1836 with the Creek Indians.

Mrd: on Jun 10, in Wash City, in the Methodist Protestant Church, 9th st, by Rev P Light Wilson, Mr John P Lashhorn to Miss Marion H Proctor, all of Wash City.

Died: on Jun 6, at his residence in St Lawrence Co, N Y, Wm F Gurley, elder & only brother of Rev P D Gurley, of Wash City.

FRI JUN 13, 1856
Confectionary, household & kitchen furniture at auction on: Jun 18, at the Confectionary Establishment of Mr Eckhardt, at 9th & F sts. -A Green auct

Very handsome farm near Beltsville, PG Co, Md, at auction: on Jul 10, the residence of Lt Thos T Hunter, containing between 200 & 300 acres, near the Beltsville depot. The improvements are a substantial dwlg house, nearly new, with 13 rooms, & necessary back bldgs. A pump in the yard of excellent water. -A Green, auct

Senate: 1-Ptn from the heirs of Jos Packwood, asking remuneration for the extraordinary & meritorious services of their ancestor, & indemnity for losses & sacrifices in the Revolutionary struggle. 2-Ptn from Alex'r Jones, asking to be allowed bounty land. 3-Ptn from Geo S Setton, asking that he may be allowed to enter a quantity of land equal to that of which he has been deprived by errors in the survey of a tract claimed under a Spanish concession, & confirmed to him by a decree of the Spanish Court. 4-Ptn from Mary E Heard & other heirs of Gen Danl Morgan, an ofcr in the army of the Revolution, asking to be allowed depreciation on his commutation pay. 5-Ptn from A C Harper, asking to be allowed bounty land for the services of his father in the war of 1812.

Our worthy fellow-citizen & old friend, Nathl Carusi, so well known in our community, leaves us soon to make a new home in the flourishing & refined metropolis of Virginia, Richmond, where he opens a large music establishment, & is to be the sole agent for Chickering's pianos in that city.

Mrd: on Jun 5, in Christ Church, Middletown, Conn, by Rt Rev Thos C Brownell, Bishop of the Diocese, Col Saml Colt, of Hartford, to Miss Eliz Hart Jarvis, eldest daughter of Rev Wm Jarvis.

$150 reward for runaways, brothers, Ben & Jas: both of a light brown complexion. James is about 18 or 20 years old. They were last seen in Westmoreland, Va, on their way to the Potomac, which they intended to cross, & make their escape through Md for Pa. I think they were intimated by a free negro named Fortune alias Ware. Dandridge Sale, Loretto, Essex Co, Va.

New Orleans, Jun 11. In San Francisco a man named Jas P Casey shot Jas King, of Wm, editor of the Bulletin, in the street, on May 14. Casey was arrested & committed to jail. Mr King died on Jun 16, & on the 18th, 3,000 citizens, completely organized into divisions & companies, armed with muskets, marched to the jail & took possession of it. They took Casey & the gambler Cora, & carried them to the cmte room. It was supposed they would be hung. The whole city was draped in mourning for the death of Mr King, who was highly esteemed. He was a native of Gtwn, D C. [Jun 14th newspaper: Calif news. All business closed on the afternoon of Jun 20th, in respect to Mr King. Casey, the murderer, was a member of the Board of Supervisors, & editor of the Sunday Times. The prisoners, Casey & Cora, were both executed on the day following the funeral of Mr King.] [Jun 16th newspaper: Casey published a communication reflecting upon the character of Mr King, & Mr King sought the name of the author, which Casey refused to give, saying that he would assume the responsibility himself. An article appeared in the Bulletin exposing the character of Casey, & stating among other things, that he had been an inmate of Sing Sing prison in N Y. Casey went to the ofc of the Bulletin & demanded an explanation, which was decidedly refused by Mr King, who showed Casey the door. This is the same day that Casey met Mr King in Montg st, & without warning drew a revolver, which he pointed at Mr King's breast & fired.] [Jun 30th newspaper: The funeral of Mr King took place at the Unitarian Church at San Francisco, where services were conducted by Rev Messrs Cutler, Taylor, & Lacy. The remains were conveyed to their last resting place in the **Lone Mountain Cemetery**.]

SAT JUN 14, 1856
Excellent household & kitchen furniture at auction on: Jun 25, at the residence of Maj Deas, U S A, 231 I st, between 18th & 19th sts. -Jas C McGuire, auct

At Salem, Tue, we learn that from the Traveller, Mr Jacob K Christian, of Salem, while getting on board a train of cars, made a mis-step & got between them, & was so badly injured that he died during the night. He leaves wife & child.

Senate: 1-Ptn from Eliza B McNeill, widow of an ofcr of the revenue service who died of disease contracted in the discharge of his duty, asking a pension. 2-Papers of Santiago E Arguello were taken from the files & referred to the Cmte of Claims. 3-Bill for the relief of the heirs of Col Chas Semmes, late collector of Alexandria: passed.

The late Jabez Barber, of Chicago, Ill, who, with his wife & daughter, was on board the steamer **Pacific**, has been opened for probate. His estate is valued at $250,000, & his will bequeaths $1,000 to the American & Foreign Missionary Society, $1,000 to the American Home Missionary Society, $1,000 to the American Bible Society, & $3,000 to the Third Presbyterian Church, Chicago. A little orphan girl is sole heir to the estate.

Baton Rouge [La] Advocate of May 30. Wilson, a soldier of the U S army, stationed at that place, suffered the penalty of death by hanging, for the murder of a fellow-soldier. He met his fate calmly, but did not deny the murder.

Public sale of valuable farm in Jefferson Co, Va: by decree of the Circuit Court of said county, pronounced on Jun 3, 1856, in the case of S Howell Brown, guardian of the infant children of John M Macfarland, vs Fanny D Macfarland & others. The undersigned com'rs appointed will offer at public sale, on Jul 24, a valuable farm in said county, being the property bought by Jno M Macfarland, deceased, of Dr Philip R Hoffman, know as *Woodbury*, formerly the residence of Judge Henry St Geo Tucker, situated on the Smithfield & Shepherdstown Turnpike: containing about 356 acres, more or less: with a very large & fine stone dwlg house, built at a cost of some $13,000, containing 16 large rooms, with all the necessary out-houses.
-Thos G Green, Edmund I Lee, Com'rs

Mrd: on Jun 4, in Allamance Co, N C, by Rev Dr Mason, Upton Bruce Gwynn, of Raleigh, to Miss Sally R, youngest daughter of Hon Thos Ruffin.

MON JUN 16, 1856
Trustee's sale of bldg lot on 6th st, between P & Q sts, at auction: on Jul 16 next, by deed of trust from Wm R Woodward & wife to the subscriber, dated Apr 14, 1855, recorded in Liber J A S No 96, folios 34 thru 37, of the land records for Wash Co, D C: all of that piece or parcel of ground in Wash City known as the north part of lot 5 in square 478, having a front of 44 feet 6 inches on 6th st, running back the same width 93 feet 4½ inches. -Geo F Kidwell, trustee -A Green auct

Chancery sale: by decree of the Circuit Court of Wash Co, D C, made in the cause of Henry P Van Bibber vs Fred'k & Mary Ann Van Bibber, dated Jun 14, 1856: public auction, on Jul 8 next, of lots 17 & 18 in square 172, in Wash City. -Walter S Cox, trustee -J C McGuire, auct

Executor's sale of valuable brick houses on 7th & 9th sts & the whole of square 152: public auction on Jun 24 next: lot 7 fronts on 9th st west, between D & E sts, with three 3 story brick dwlg houses. Lot No ___ [blank as copied] in square 424, fronting on 7th st, between M & N sts, with three new 3 story brick dwlg houses. Two are occupied, as dry goods stores & the other as a grocery store. Square 152 has a 2 story brick dwlg on it. Title indisputable & sale positive. -Chas Uttermuhle, Augustus Uttermuhle, Geo W Uttermuhle, excs. -Jas C McGuire, auct

New Port [Florida] Wakulla Times of Jun 4. We are pained to record the destruction by fire on Fri last, of the oil works & turpentine still of Mr E C Holbrook, of this place, & with the loss of the life of Mr Patrick Collins, formerly of Brooklyn, N Y, but for the last 6 months an industrious & valuable citizen of our town. Mr Collins, who was superintendent of the works was making varnish, & while mixing naptha with hot rosin the gas ignited, causing a report similar to the escape of steam from the safety valve of a steam boiler. The flames spread instantly to every part of the bldg, which was entirely destroyed. Mr Collins, covered with flames, ran for the river, some 200 feet distant, & plunged in. He was taken from the water in excruciating pain & lingered about 30 hours before he died.

Jas McFittrick was brought before Com'r Newhall yesterday, charged with robbing the mail at our post ofc. It appears that Dr Vattier, the postmaster, had for some time been doubtful of McFittrick's honesty. $60 was found missing from a letter, & he confessed the theft. He also endeavored to conceal $100 among some old papers. He was held to bail in $1,000 to appear for examination.
-Cincinnati Columbian of 13th.

U S Patent Ofc, Wash, Jun 14, 1856. Ptn of Cullen Whipple, of Providence R I, praying for the extension of a patent granted to him Aug 18, 1842, for an improvement in machine for cutting the threads of wood screws, for 7 years from the expiration of said patent, which takes place on Aug 18, 1856.
-Chas Mason, Com'r of Patents

Notice: All persons are warned against purchasing lot 7 in square 163, in Wash City, a deed or conveyance of which lot was obtained Oct 4, 1853, fraudulently & by false pretences, by one Wm B Smith of John C Roemelley & Fanny Smith, recorded on said city records, folio No 65, page 484, as a bill will immediately be filed in the Court of Chancery of the said city to set aside said illegal transaction. -Fanny Smith

Obit-died: on Jun 9, at his residence, PG Co, Md, in his 61st year, Geo W Duvall. The deceased was long & favorably known throughout his native county & State; & for several years he was elected to serve in the legislative councils of the State. No man exhibited more solicitude for the welfare of his family & the peace of the community. Throughout his life he gave liberally to the support of the gospel, & when health permitted, was always an attendant on the public worship of the sanctuary. -N

Mrd: on Jun 12, in N Y C, by Rev Francis L Hawks, D D, Robt D Tweedy, of Wash City, to Lizzie, daughter of Wm E Bird, of the former place.

Circuit Court of Wash Co, D C-in Equity, No 1,114. Halsey & others, Gorman's heirs. John F Ennis, trustee, reported on May 22, 1856, that he sold lot 12 in square 580, in Wash City, to Edw H Pendleton for $1,000, & the purchaser has complied with the terms of the sale. -John A Smith, clerk

Circuit Court of D C. U S A against Selden, Withers & Co, & others. Upon the motion of Andrew Wylie he is admitted a dfndnt in this cause, & thereupon he filed his answer, & this cause having been set for hearing as to the dfndnts who have answered by consent of parties by counsel, & the plntf having proceeded by publication against the dfndnts, John Withers, Lawrence P Bayne, Geo W Carlyle Whiting, & Robt W Latham, who are non-residents of this District, in conformity with the order of publication made by the Court on Jan 28 last, & the said non-resident dfndnts not having appeared & answered as by said publication they were warned to do, the said bill is taken pro confesso as to them. Thereupon this cause came on to be heard upon the bill. Answer of the dfndnts, John A English, Wm Bayne, Wm Selden, Andrew Wylie, A G Allen, A B Little, J T Shugert, Danl J Browne, Chas E Mix, [acting Com'r of Indian Affairs,] the exhibit, was argued by counsel. On consideration whereof, the Court, not now deciding any question arising in this suit, does this Jun 13, 1856, order & decree that it be referred to the Auditor of this Court to inquire from the firm of Selden, Withers & Co, to the plntfs upon the claim alleged in the bill, also who are the creditors of said firm & what amounts due them respectively & in the aggregate; what the amount of the assets of said firm transferred to the dfndnts, English & Bayne, their trustees, & to dfndnt, Andrew Wylie, & the character & description thereof; what sum of money has been realized & probably will be realized by said trustees & said Wylie from said assets; whether the same will be sufficient to satisfy all the liablilites of said firm, & if insufficient what the pecuniary ability of the members of said firm individually to make up the deficiency; & said Auditor will report his proceedings to the Court, with any matter specially stated he may deem pertinent, or any party interested may require to be so stated. -Jno A Smith, clerk [Statement of accounts on Jul 29 next, at my ofc in City Hall, Wash, at 11 o'clock. -W Redin, auditor]

TUE JUN 17, 1856

Senate: 1-Memorial from Jas H Byson, one of the legal reps of the N C Cherokee Indians, asking that the provisions of the fourth section of the act of 1848 & the 3rd section of the act of 1855 may be extended to all who were embraced in the census rolls of John C Mulloy. 2-Memorial from John L Hayes, in behalf of many citizens of the U S & British North American provinces, asking that the principle of reciprocity may be applied to the patent laws of the U S & Great Britain, so as to secure the benefits of their inventions to the people of both countries. 3-Additional papers submitted in relation to the claim of Sallie C Northrop.

The Pension Bureau has received information that John H Steil & Marcus A Wolff, of St Louis, Missouri, indicted for presenting fraudulent papers at that ofc to obtain bounty land warrants, have been found guilty & sentenced-Steil to the county jail for 1 year & $2,000 fine; Wolff to 5 years in the penitentiary.

$200 reward. I will pay the above reward for the apprehension of John H Ray, Henry Crogan, John E Bailey, & David Y Moore, or $50 each if taken in this District. -J D Hoover, U S Marshal for D C. [They broke confinement on Sunday from the jail. The first 3 named were part of the Naylor gang; the last was inprisoned for trial on a charge of perjury at the polls at the late municipal election.

Criminal Court-Wash-June term opened yesterday. Grand Jury called:

Geo W Riggs, foreman	Jeremiah Orme	Benj Beall
Geo McCeney	Wm B Scott	A W Miller
Jno P Ingle	Saml Pumphrey	Z W McKnew
Steph P Franklin	Selby Scaggs	Robt S Patterson
Jos C G Kennedy	Henry Haw	Wm F Bayly
Gregory Ennis	Wm Selden	Robt White
Wm A Bradley	P M Pearson	Jno R Queen
Geo S Gideon	Jenkin Thomas	B J Simms

Fratricide in Alexandria County: on Sat last, on the road leading past the residences of Messrs Reach & Frazier, by Saml Howard on his brother Wm. They were residents of the country part of the county, of bad character, & both were drunk at the time. An altercation occurred between them. Saml used his knife upon Wm, inflicting 5 or 6 terrible & fatal wounds. Saml was arrested yesterday.

Died: on May 6, at San Francisco, Calif, Lewis Walker, a native of Wash, D C, leaving a wife, 7 children, & a large circle of connexions to mourn his loss. His last moments were cheered by the kind & affectionate attentions of sincerely sorrowing friends. -San Francisco Bulletin

Mrd: on Jun 15, in Wash City, by Rev Mr Samson, Mr John H Wallis to Miss Mary Sloan, both of Wash City.

WED JUN 18, 1856
New Book. Memoir of Rev Jas Chisholm, A M, late Rector of St John's Church, Portsmouth, Va, with Memoranda of the Pestilence which raged in that city during the summer & autumn of 1855. By David Holmes Conrad, N Y, 1856, 12mo. Pgs 193.

Hon Jas G Hardy, Lt Govn'r of Ky, died at his residence in Barren Co, Ky, on Jun 12, after a serious & protracted illness. He was a native of Va, but long a resident of Ky; about 60 years of age; a warm hearted man; a prominent member of the Baptist Church.

The ship **Thornton**, Capt Collins, which arrived at N Y on Sat from Liverpool, brought 758 Mormons, bound to Utah.

There was an Otter captured on the farm of Jno D Rogers by Wm Feagens on Sat last, which measured 3 feet long & weighed 15 pounds. "Quite a stranger," in this neighborhood. -Middleburg, Va, Mon, Jun 16, 1856.

Abingdon [Mass] Standard: Mr David Humble 2nd, a workman in the shoe manufactory of J L Nash & Co, died suddenly in that town, from eating a large quantity of skimmed milk cheese.

Victor Hugo is about to take up his permanent residence in the island of Guernsey. He has already purchased a large house, surrounded by fine grounds & beautifully situated near the seashore, & is about to occupy it with his family.

Glenwood Cemetery, Ofc 292 Pa ave, corner of 10th st, over the Savings Bank. This Cemetery is laid out on the plan of the celebrated Greenwood, of N Y, situated on the high ground distant one fourth mile north of the capitol, North Capitol st leading directly to the gateway. This Company received a charter from Congress, appropriating their ground forever to burial purposes, making a fee title to the purchaser, & prohibiting all encroachments from legislation or otherwise, which is of vast importance to those who wish their dead to repose where they have placed them, for it has become a custom in all cities, when the burial ground has become valuable for other purposes, to sell it & throw the dead promiscuously into one large pit, & legal measures cannot prevent it, as no titles are given to the ground. N B. Office open from 10 to 12 o'clock A M, where pamphlets, with a map, the charter & bye-laws, & all other information, can be obtained at the office; also, all orders for interments left with Mr Jas Harvey, 410 7th st, or any other undertaker, will be promptly attended to.

Baron Sina, the Vienna banker, who recently died in that city, left a fortune of ninety million florins, of which sixty millions were in real estate. His oldest son, Baron Simon Sina, was constitiuted his universal legatee, & succeeds him in business.

A monument is to be erected in Paris to Louis XVI & Maria Antoinette.
-Evening Post

The city of Saragossa, Spain, is to build a palace for the Duke de la Vittoria, as a mark of their gratitude for his exertions in introducing railroads into Spain.

THU JUN 19, 1856
Trustee's sale of valuable improved property at auction: on Jul 14, by deed of trust from Fred'k Hagar to the subscriber, dated Sep 30, 1847, recorded in Liber W B No 136, folios 466 to 470, of the land records for Wash Co, D C: sale of lots 6 & 7 in square 32, having a front north F st of 125 feet, & on 25th st 51 feet, with a good frame dwlg house, containing 12 rooms, wide passage, kitchen & cellar under the whole. -Henry Naylor, trustee -A Green auct

Chas F M Garnett, of Richmond, Va, now chief engineer of the Va & Tenn railroad, has received the appointment of chief engineer of Don Pedro railroad, Rio de Janeiro, Brazil, with a salary of $15,000.

Soldiers of the war of 1812 had their first anniversary celebration of the Association of Soldiers of D C of the War of 1812 yesterday at the City Hall, on Jun 18, in that year, having been the day on which war was declared against Great Britain. Ofcrs for the ensuing year: Pres, Col Wm W Seaton; 1st V Pres, Col John S Williams; 2nd V Pres, Gen Skinner; Sec, Maj Richd Burgess; Surgeon, Dr Wm Jones; Treas, Jas McCleary; marshal, Col Wm P Young.

Died: on Jun 18, in Gtwn, Mr Jane Heath, relict of the late Maj Jas P Heath, formerly of Balt. Her funeral is on Fri at 5 o'clock P M, from the residence of her son-in-law, Robt P Dodge, Montgomery st.

Died: on Jun 18, Richd Gibson, the artist. His funeral will be on Fri morning at 10 o'clock, from his late residence, corner of D & 12th sts, to St Matthew's Church.

FRI JUN 20, 1856
Naval: the frig **Constellation**, Capt Bell, was at Marselles May 27; crew in good health. The U S steamer **Saranac** left Gibralter on May 1 for Phil, where she was to refit. She has been now out 43 days, & there are some apprehensions that she has met with an accident to her machinery.

West Point Military Academy. The annual examination closed on Wed; names of the graduates, all of whom are now entitled to the commission of brvt-lt in the army:

1-Geo W Snyder, N Y
2-David C Houston, N Y
3-Miles D McAlister, Mich
4-Chas C Lee, N C
5-Henry V DeHart, at large
6-Orlando M Poe, Ohio
7-John Tipton, Iowa
8-Herbert A Hascall, N Y
9-A Parker Porter, Penn
10-Francis L Vinton, at large
11-Geo D Bayard, at large
12-Thos C Sullivan, Ohio
13-John W Barriger, Ky
14-Lorenzo Lorain, Pa
15-John Bennett, Ohio
16-Wesley Owens, Ohio
17-Guilford D Bailey, N Y
18-John D Shinn, Ohio
19-Hylan B Lyon, Ky
20-Ed C Bainbridge, at large
21-Lunsford L Lomax, at large
22-Richd Loder, N J
23-Jas P Major, Missouri
24-Jeremiah H Gilman, Maine
25-Thos E Miller, Ky
26-Chas H Stivers, Ky
27-Wm Gaston, at large
28-Jas W Forsyth, Ohio
29-Thos W Walker, Iowa
30-Geo Jackson, Va
31-Jos H Taylor, at large
32-John F Ritter, Penn
33-John K Mizner, Mich
34-Frank S Armistead, at large
35-Herman Biggs, N Y
36-Wm T Gentry, N Y
37-J B S Alexander, Va
38-Wm H Jackson, Tenn
39-Owen K McLemore, Ala
40-Richd S C Lord, Ohio
41-Wm P Sanders, Miss
42-Jas McMillan, N Y
43-Wm B Hughes, Tenn
44-Saml S Carroll, D C
45-Fitzhugh Lee, at large
46-J McLean Hildt, at large
47-Brayton C Ives, N Y
48-Herbert M Enos, N Y

Hon Lot M Morrill, of Augusta, Pres of the last Senate of Maine, has renounced his connexion with the democratic party, having written to the State Cmte, of which he is a member, his repudiation of the platform adopted at Cincinnati.

Receding Gtwn. Senate: Resolved, that the cmte for the District of Columbia inquire into the expediency of receding to the State of Md Gtwn & all that part of the District of Columbia which lies west of Rock Creek, upon such terms & conditions as will secure to Gtwn an amount of money equal to that which was appropriated for the benefit of Alexandria while it was a part of the territory of the District of Columbia; & that said cmte have leave to report by bill or otherwise.

Marceron's estate: such of the creditors of said Marceron as proved their debts in the chancery cause can receive their dividends on application to me. -W Redin

From Southern Florida. Cpl Manning, of the U S army, was shot by a sentinel at **Fort Myers** a few days ago. He was attempting to pass the sentinel on his hands & knees, &, failing to answer the challenge, was shot dead.

Wm Hughes, the Calif pedestrian, has just completed in Boston the feat of walking 100 consecutive hours without intermission. He undertook to walk on hour extra, but fell exhausted after 25 minutes.

Mr Thos Applebee, a grocer in Chicago, was brutally murdered in his store on the night of Jun 12th. A reward of $1,500 has been offered for the apprehension of the murderer.

Mrd: on Jun 17, in Wash City, at Trinity Church, by Rev Dr Cummins, Wm N Barker to Miss Rebecca Delaney, daughter of Saml Hanson, all of Wash City.

Died: on Jun 19, in Wash City, suddenly, Jas Barry, aged 40 years. His funeral will be this afternoon at 4 o'clock, from the residence of his brother, Richd Barry, Mo ave.

SAT JUN 21, 1856
The English papers bring us new of the conviction for willful murder of Wm Palmer, the poisoner, & of his having been condemned to expiate his guilt upon the scaffold. Palmer was a surgeon in some practice in Rugeley, a small town in Staffordshire, England, & had for some years been engaged in betting transactions connected with horse-racing. He became acquainted with Mr Wm Parsons Cook, a well know sporting character, an owner of race horses, whose murder he has just been declared guilty. Palmer was in desperate condition & administered strychnine in repeated doses to Cook until he was dead. In 1854 Palmer murdered his wife, in the following year he murdered his brother, Walter Palmer, & 2 months later he murdered his friend, Wm Cook. -Journal of Commerce

John Stadley, who plead guilty some time since in the U S District Court to an indictment for embezzling money from the post ofc in this city, in which he was employed, was yesterday sentenced, by Judge Wilkins, to 12 years' imprisonment in the penitentiary. -Detroit Press, Jun 17

Escape of prisoners. John A Cullen, of Va, & E J Wilson, of Ky, 2 of the passengers of the barque **Archibald Gracie**, seized some 6 months ago at La Paz, Mexico, as a filibuster, have arrived at New Orleans. All on board the barque were thrown into prison, & have ever since been confined. Recently six of them made their escape, & the two referred to allege that, after traveling a dreary journey on foot of some 1,500 miles through Mexico, they reached Vera cruz, & there embarked for New Orleans.

Household & kitchen furniture at auction on: Jun 26, at the residence of Mr John Hands, 469 I st, next to 9th st. -A Green auct

Valuable farm & pleasant residence in Fairfax Co, Va, at private sale: by a decree of the Circuit Court of said county: sale of **Collingwood**, the residence of the late H Allen Taylor, about 5½ miles below Alexandria, & contains about 244 ¼th acres. The improvements consist of a new & commodious frame dwlg, kitchen, & other out houses built of the best materials, & in the best style. -W Arthur Taylor, John A Washington, Com'rs of sale.

A German family of 7 persons was murdered & their bodies burnt in their dwlg near St Joseph, Mo, some 2 weeks since. Five men have been arrested as concerned in the crime, John Patterson, Geo W Lincoln, Warner Hoops, Davis, & Myers. Patterson & Myers have confessed & implicated the rest. All are in jail, held for their trial. -Chicago Press

A young German, Gottfried Frick, was shot through the body on Monday evening by Geo Helfrich, in Henrico Co. The murderer escaped & has not since been apprehended.

Local: last evening a fatal accident occurred at the corner of F & 5th sts, whereby a worthy man, Danl Smallwood, was instantly killed, & Chas Medford severely injured. The two, carpenters, engaged with others, were pulling down the bldg known as the Wesley Chapel, preparatory to the erection of a new & larger church edifice in its place, when a whole section of the brick wall fell on them, killing Smallwood instantly. Medford tried to pull him away, but failed. Smallwood was removed to his residence on the Island. He was about 35 years of age, & leaves a widow & one child,

Mrd: on Jun 19, in Wash City, by Rev John C Smith, Mr Emor K Reynolds, of Phil, to Miss Kate Pleasants, youngest daughter of Geo Cochran, of Wash City.

Mrd: on Jun 18, by Rev B N Brown, Mr Joshua W Offutt to Miss Rose A Jackson, all of Farifax Co, Va.

MON JUN 23, 1856
Splendid launch of the steam-frig **Colorado** on Thu. About 200 persons were on board at the time of the launching, & the ceremony of christening was performed by Miss Annie Dornin, daughter of the Commandant of the yard. We believe she is the last of the six new steam-frigs ordered by Govn't. -Norfolk Herald

Sad occurrence at Westminster, Md. Conrad Schellings, aged 25, was killed by the accidental discharge of his gun on Sat last, in Westminster, Carroll Co, where he had resided for some time. The gun had been loaded with beans, & he accidentally struck the cock against a window-sill, & it exploded, producing death in a few hours.

House of Reps: 1-Cmte on Patents: bill for the relief of Nathl Haywood: committed. 2-Bill for the relief of the estate & sureties of Andrew H Kincannon, late marshal of the northern district of Mississippi: referred to the Cmte on the Judiciary.

Murders at New Orleans: 1-Michl Higgins, a clerk in a cotton house, came home Sat intoxicated & shot his wife with a double-barrelled shot gun. She died the next morning. They were both born in Ireland. She was only 21 years old & they had been married several years & had several children, the youngest about 14 months old, survive. Higgins was arrested & is now in prison. 2-On Sat Edw Wisely & Capt Jos Gibson had some ill feelings between them. Wisely stabbed Gibson with a bowie-knife-Mrs Gibson sprang between her husband & Wisely, & received a stab to the abdomen. Capt Gibson drew a dirk & stabbed Wisely to the heart, & he fell a corpse. Mrs Gibson was pronounced past recovery, & she is in all probability before this dead. -Bulletin

U S Patent Ofc, Wash, Jun 21, 1856. Ptn of Jeptha A Wilkinson, of Suffolk Co, N Y, praying for the extension of a patent granted to him on Jan 4, 1853, for an improvement in printing presses, for 7 years from the expiration of said patent, which takes place on Jan 4, 1857. -Chas Mason, Com'r of Patents

Valuable farm for sale cheap: in Montg Co, Md, with a new frame dwlg house, kitchen, stable, & out houses; on the road leading from the Great Falls to Rockville, Md. Inquire of Dr J D Stewart, Md ave & 7th st, or to the subscriber, on the premises. -E D Whitcomb

Mrd: on Jun 17, in Balt, by Rev John W Hedges, Capt John E Wyett to Miss Georgiana E Shields, only daughter of Thos A Shields, deceased, of Wash.

Died: on Jun 21, in Wash City, Sarah E Morris, aged 21 years, wife of Thos Morris, & only daughter of Washington Lewis, of Wash City. Her funeral will take place this morning at 10 o'clock, from the residence of her father, on I st, between 4th & 5th sts.

Died: on Jun 20, at his residence, near Phil, Dr Fred'k S Eckard, only brother of Rev J R Eckard, of Wash City.

Died: on Jun 19, in Balt, in his 26th year, Nathan Smith, M D, 2nd son of Prof Nathan R Smith.

Died: on Jun 20, in Wash City, Catharine Wysong, beloved & only daughter of Wm W & Anna E Young, aged 2 years, 10 months & 20 days.

TUE JUN 24, 1856
Senate: 1-Memorial from Nathan M Loundsbury, of Rutland Co, Vt, a soldier in the war of the Revolution, asking to be allowed arrears of pension. Mr Foot gave a description of the memorialist, who is upwards of 100 years of age, & yet so full of the vis vita as to be enabled to walk several miles to receive his pension & then back to his home on the same day. This old patriot had made application under the act of 1818 for his pension, but was unable to obtain it until 1826. The whole amount allowed him was $100 a year, out of which he had to support a wife. This memorialist was the youngest son, & is the only survivor of a family of 8 persons who devoted themselves to the service of the country in the Revolutionary war, [a father, & 7 sons.] One of the brothers fell at the battle of Bunker's Hill, another died a prisoner of war with the enemy, & a 3rd died at Newburg, N Y, from the effect of wounds received at the siege of Yorktown, while standing by the side of the memorialist. When the gallant but unfortunate Maj Andrew was brought in a prisoner he [the memorialist] was the first to stand guard over him. 2-Ptn from Harriet C Read, sister & excx of the late Lt Col A C W Fanning, asking to be allowed his commission for disbursing of public moneys. 3-Memorial from Lt W B Whiting, complaining that great injustice had been done him by the late Naval Board in placing him on the reserved list, & asking such relief in the premises as Congress may deem proper. 4-Ptn from the executor of Francis Hutinack, asking that the arrears of pension to which the said Hutinack was entitled may be paid to his surviving children. 5-Additional papers submitted relating to the claim of Geo W New, a soldier in the war of the Revolution & in that of 1812, asking that his pension may be increased. 6-Ptn from Sallie Keys, widow of a soldier of the Revolution, asking to be allowed a pension. 7-Cmte on Naval Affairs: bill for the relief of Dr Chas D Maxwell, a surgeon in the U S navy. 8-Cmte on Military Affairs: bill for the relief of Jean B & Pelage Farribault, of Minnesota Territory. 9-Bill for the relief of Jas Earl or his legal reps: introduced.

Extensive assortment of furniture at auction on Jun 23, at the **Washington House**, formerly **Gadsby's Hotel**, on the corner of Pa ave & 3rd st: all the furniture, kitchen furniture & cooking requisites; linens, china, & silver plate. -Benedict Milburn, trustee -C W Boteler, auct

The recent advices from England announce the death of the eminent London banker, Saml Gurney. He was at the head of the firm of Overend, Gurney & Co. Mr Gurney was a member of the Society of Friends & brother of Mrs Eliz Fry, whose acts of beneficence, so far as they involved money expenditure, were at the expense of this her brother, whose fortune was colossal.

Assassination at Beaver Island. Before this time, in all probability, Jas J Strang, the leader of the Mormon settlement on Beaver Island, is among the dead. On Monday, Capt McBride, of the U S iron steamer **Michigan**, [which was lying at the pier there,] sent his pilot, Alex'r St Aubin, with a request for Strang to come on board upon some business. Strang returned with St Aubin, but when on the dock 2 men fired a revolver at him, striking him about nose level, the ball passing into his head. The men, Alex'r Westworth & Thos Bedford, made no attempt to escape, but surrendered themselves up to Capt McBride. Bedford had been whipped 40 lashes on the bare back, upon a charge of neglecting to disclose facts concerning a robbery. This was done by Strang's orders. Both Bedford & Wentworth had been Mormons, but had seceded & joined with the McCulloch faction. Both had families, & Capt McBride brought them with their families, & 5 other families to Mackinaw. Strang was the heart & soul as well as the intellect of the Mormon gang, & it is hoped that his death will break them up & scatter them abroad. There remains no man among them capable of wielding Strang's influence or of supplying his place. -Detroit Adv 20th.

Affray at Kanawha House, Charleston, Va, on Jun 14, in which Mr Edw Kenna lost his life, having been shot through the head with a pistol. Another of the belligerents, a Mr Watt, was slightly wounded. It is not known who fired the fatal shot.

The **Mount of Olives**, near Jerusalem, has been purchased by a Madame Polack, a widow of a wealthy banker of the Hebrew persuasion at Konigsberg, in Prussia. She intends to beautify the place & improve the whole neighborhood at her sole expense. The first thing she did was to plant the whole area with a grove of olive trees, & thus to restore it to the original state from which it derives its name.

One of the escaped prisoners from the Washington jail, David Y Moore, has been arrested, & is now restored to safe-keeping.

Criminal Court-Wash. Two boys, aged 10 & 12, Wm Harrod & Oscar Wilson, were on trial for larceny, having, on Apr 22, entered the Centre Market & forced the lock of the box in which Mr Homiller stored his butcher knives & with one of them pried open the box of Mr Clisk, & took articles valued at about $30. They then stole 5 bacon hams & wrapping paper. They were found guilty. This was not the first time they had been arrested.

On Sat, Mr J Knox Walker, of Memphis, Tenn, a guest at the Dexter House, on 7th st, was robbed a jewelry & property of value of $500. Police are on the track of a party they suspect to have had connexion with the deed.

Mrd: on Jun 12, in Gtwn, by Rev B F Brooke, Thos McElderry Mullikin, of Balt, to R Eliz, daughter of Saml S Rind, of the former place.

Mrd: on Jun 12, at Stateburg, S C, by Rev J J Roberts, Lt F L Childs, U S Army, to Mary Hooper, only daughter of Dr W W Anderson.

Mrd: on Jun 19, in Boston, Mass, by Rev Fred'k D Huntington, Saml B Parris, of Wash City, to Annie Kinsman, daughter of the late Geo Willis.

Mrd: on Jun 22, in Wash City, by Rev Andrew G Carothers, Mr Henry J Keller to Miss Margaret Miller, both of Wash City.

Handsome farm on the Colesville & near the Wash Plank Road at auction: on Jul 7 next, on the premises, the farm, about 6½ miles from Washington Market, on Colesville road, Montg Co, Md, adjoining the farm of R Burche: contains 57 acres, & a house with 5 rooms, & all necessary out-bldgs, well fenced, & a more healthy location not to be found in Christendom. -A Green auct

Orphans Court of Wash Co, D C. Letters of administration with the will annexed, on the personal estate of Philip Mohun, late of Wash Co, deceased. -Catherine Mohun, admx, with the will annexed

WED JUN 25, 1856
City residence, with fine grounds, at public auction, on Jun 30, the desirable residence at the corner of F & 21st sts, now occupied by Capt A W Whipple. The lot fronts 67 feet on F st, with a depth of 136 feet 6 inches on 21st st. There are 16 rooms in the house, completely fitted with gas, & heated by a furnace. -Jas C McGuire, auct
+
Excellent household & kitchen furniture at auction on: Jun 30, at the residence of Capt A W Whipple, corner of F & 21st sts. -Jas C McGuire, auct

Senate: 1-Memorial from Fred'k Koones, for himself & other clerks & messengers in the ofc of the Navy Agent at Wash, asking to be allowed the 20% on their pay that was allowed to other employes of the Gov't of Washington. 2-Wm A Richardson was allowed to withdraw his papers from the files of the Senate. 3-Cmte on Indian Affairs: asked to be discharged from the consideration of the memorial of Ziba T Peters, delegate of the Stockburdge & Munsee tribes of Indians: which was agreed to.

Drowned on Sat: a man about 21, Thos Haley, employed by A Bronson, who went out in a skiff in search of the bodies of 2 boys who had drowned. He was the same man who jumped into the mill race a few nights since & rescued Mrs Chumascero who accidentally fell through the Court st bridge. -Rochester Union of Sat.
[The names of the boys were not given.]

Mrd: in Wash City, at Ryland Chapel Parsonage, by Rev John S Deale, Jas McCausland, of Phil, to Miss Mary Eliz, daughter of Jos Davis, of Wash City. [No date given-current item.]

Sale of U S land near Richmond, Va. Ordnance Ofc, Wash, Jun 28, 1856. Proposals will be received at this ofc for the purchase for cash of a parcel of land, with the bldg thereon, on the James river, Chesterfield Co, known as **Bellona Arsenal**. This land was purchased by the U S from Wm Trabue & wife & Mary Ready, by deed dated Sep 21, 1815. -Henry K Craig, Colonel of Ordnance.

Storm in N Y Sunday. A boat belonging to Red Hook, containing Mgt Crane, Mgt Sullivan, Robt Hanin, & 2 others, a brother & sister of Miss Sullivan, capsized. The 2 latter saved themselves by clinging to the boat, but the 3 named were drowned. Another boat capsized & it is feared that Hugh McNichols, Thos Hays, & Wm Monaghan, who are missing, have not been heard of since last evening, may have perished. Lightning struck the house of Mr York, in Atlantic st, Brooklyn, instanting killing his wife Catharine. She leaves 6 children. Mr York was unhurt. In Jersey City the 14 year old son of John Maxwell was instantly killed when he sought refuge in an unfinished bldg, which was blown down. Mr Jas Brann, a young man who is studying for the Catholic ministry, was so badly injured that his life is supposed to be in danger. Others were slightly hurt. -N Y Commercial Advertiser

Denmark. Frederic VII, the present King of Denmark, is 47 years of age, & succeeded his father, Christian VIII, Jan 20, 1848. At the age of 20 years he married the daughter of King Frederick VI, but was divorced from her at the age of 29. Four years afterwards he married a princess of Mecklenburg, & was divorced again in 1846. After his second divorce he became enamored of a milliner of Copenhagen of the name of Rasmussen, whom he has since raised to the nobility, with the title of Countess Danner. The King & his favorite have been united in what is called a morganatic marriage, by which she & her children are excluded from the rank of her husband. The aristocracy of Copenhagen are much scandalized at the conduct of the King in introducing a plebeian queen among them, & seem to make no secret of their displeasure. The King has turned his back upon them, & lives in the retirement of private life with his wife, whom, it is said, he intends to raise to the rank of Duchess next New Year. He is far inferior to his father, who was a man of fine taste & elegant manners. The present King has no children & no brothers or sisters. He has an uncle who will succeed to the throne in case he outlives his nephew. The uncle is already 63 years of age & childless. On the death of the King & his uncle the direct of line of decent in the royal house will be extinguished. According to the Danish law of succession, the crown would then descend to the aunt of the King & her heirs.

Tragedy in Charleston, Va, on Jun 14. Edw Kenna, a member of the Charleston bar was killed by the discharge of a pistol or pistols, during a scuffle with Mr C Smith, in the Kanawha House. A coroner's inquest rendered a verdict that Mr Kenna's death was caused by wounds inflicted by Jas V & Andrew D Lewis, his brothers-in-law. All the parties are of high social position.

Criminal Court-Wash. 1-Lynes Sanford, charged with robbing a watch from Diedrich Rankin on Capitol Hill, in Apr last, during a scuffle, was found not guilty. 2-Thos Ferguson, free colored, was found guilty of stealing a ham from the store of Mrs Horstkamp, on 7th st, & sentenced to 6 months' imprisonment in the county jail. 3-John Foreman, free colored boy, accomplice of Harrod & Wilson in their larcenies in the market house, was sentenced to 2 years in the penitentiary. Harrod & Wilson to be sentenced.

THU JUN 26, 1856
Trustee's sale: by decree of the Circuit Court of Wash Co, D C, passed on Mar 27 last, in a cause wherein Henry Toland, Thos Biddle, Henry J Williams, Benj Gerhard, & Geo P Meade are cmplnts, & Geo Stewardson, Alfred Ingraham & Eliz M his wife, Richd W Meade, Wm Patterson & Salvadora his wife, Hartman Bache & Maria C Wise, Thos B Huger & Mariamme his wife, Alex'r J Dallas, Jas D Graham, & Salvadora, Wm M, Richd W M, & Jas D Graham, the younger, are dfndnts, being No 905 on the equity docket of the said court, the subscriber will, on Jul 28 next, sell at auction, in front of the premises, the part of square 143, in Wash City, with the excellent dwlg house & other bldgs on said part, now occupied by the said Richd W Meade. -W Redin, trustee -A Green auct [Nov 8th newspaper: W Redin, trustee, reported that he sold the above parcel, part of square 143, fronting on F st, with dwlg house & other bldgs on said moiety as then occupied by said Richd W Meade, to Jas M Waterbury, for the price of $8,025, & that he hath complied with the terms of the sale. -Jno A Smith, clerk]

Trustee's sale: by deed of trust from the late Geo Cover, recorded in Liber W B No 95, folio 264, & at the request of the party secured thereby, on Jul 29 next: sale of one undivided moiety or half part of lots 8 & 9 in square 287, in Wash City, with the bldgs thereon, where the tanning business has been carried on; & also the south half of lot 7 in square 323, in said city. —Geo Parker, B B Curran, trustees -A Green auct

The Annual Columbia College Commencement took place yesterday in the E st Baptist Church, Wash. Address by Mr Thos M Scott, candidate for the degree of bachelorship of philosophy. Addresses by Mr Jas G Board, of Va, Mr J Boulware Kidd, Mr Mahlon A Hensley, of Va, & Mr Chas H Uttermehle, of Wash, candidates for B A followed. The oration of Mr Geo F Bagby, of Va, candidate for degree of Master of Arts followed.

Circuit Court: Anthony Preston died intestate, leaving a large real estate in Wash City. His widow & heirs applied to the Court for the appointment of com'rs to make partition of it, which application was granted. The com'rs reported the lands could not be equally divided. The Court thereupon, at the request of the petitioners, directed the lands to be sold & the shares duly paid over, except that of Mrs McKnight, who was a daughter of Preston. Her husband was insolvent & largely indebted to sundry judgment creditors, who sued out attachments thereon against him, & levied them upon Mrs McKnight's share, while in the hands of the com'rs. The creditors contended that the sale & confirmation thereof by the Court converted her share into personal property, & that as such it belonged to her husband & became liable to be attached for his debt. In behalf of Mrs McKnight it was insisted that her share of the proceeds of her real estate continued hers until it came into the actual possession of her husband or until he had exercised a legal control over it. A motion was made in her behalf to quash the attachments. During the pendencey of this motion Mr McKnight died, his wife & 2 children surviving him. The Court held that the attaching creditors acquired no right to Mrs McKnight's share in the proceeds of said sale. She will now come into possession of a respectable property sought to be taken from her by creditors of her late husband. Counsel for attaching creditors, Messrs Bradley, Davidge, & Chilton; for Mrs McKnight, R H Gillet & J M Carlisle. -Union [No dates given: entitled-Interesting Case.]

Savannah Republican of Jun 21. The ship **Elvira Owen**, Capt Alexander, arrived at Tybee 2 days ago from Balt, via Hampton Roads, to receive a number of colored emigrants who were waiting here to take passage to Liberia. Mr Wm Duncan, of this city, provided the following interesting particulars: of the emigrants: 5 from Va liberated by will of Mr Noel; 43 from Va, liberated by will of Mr Kelly, & by him furnished $15,000; 12 from Halifax, N C, liberated by will of Mr Simmons; 29 from Ky, liberated by will of Mr Graves, & by him furnished $14,800; 7 from Missouri, liberated by Mr Fullerson; 7 from Gallatin, Tenn, liberated by Mr Barr; 2 from Tuscaloosa, Ala, liberated by Lincoln Clark; 24 from Columbus, Miss, liberated by Mr Holderness; 2 from Augusta, Ga, liberated by Mrs Bryson; 3 from Augusta, Ga, liberated by Mrs Marks; 19 from Rocky Plains, Ga, liberated by David Floyd; 1 from Columbia, Tenn, liberated by Judge Kennedy; & 41 from Gwinnett Co, Ga, liberated by will of Geo M Watters.

Naval: the U S ship **Macedonia**, Capt John Pope, had left for Boston, Mass, after having been full 3 years upon the East India station. She brings home the remains of the late Cmdor Joel Abbott, who died at Hong King in Dec last.

Orphans Court of Wash Co, D C. Letters of administration with the will annexed on the personal estate of Kitty Bowie, late of Wash Co, deceased. -Thos Baltimore, adm with the will annexed.

Senate: 1-Claim from Saml A Belden & partners, urging upon Congress compensation for property confiscated by the Mexican Gov't. 2-Ptn from John Etheridge, foreign corresponding clerk in the Navy Dept, asking compensation for his services as superintendent of the s w Executive bldg. 3-Ptn from Nancy Fisher, asking arrears of pension due to the widow of John Chisom at the time of her death. 4-Ptn from Eliz Moast, widow of a Revolutionary soldier, asking a pension. 5-Ptn from John A Brunner & Brothers, asking compensation for supplies furnished the Oregon volunteers during the Rogue River war. 6-Mary B Dusenbery: granted leave to withdraw her papers from the files.

Hon Thos Henry Bayly, late member of Congress from Va, died of consumption on Jun 23, at his late residence, **Mount Custis**, Accomac Co, in his 47th year, after a long & painful illness. In private life he was a most affectionate father & husband. -American Democrat [Jun 28th newspaper: Senate: Gen Bayly was born on the eastern shore of Va, in Accomac Co, on Dec 11, 1810, & departed this life at his home, in the county of his birth, on Jun 22, at the age of 45 years & 6 months. He was re-elected to the present Congress, &, though emaciated & feeble, took his seat at the commencement of the session. He came to the bar in 1830, a graduate in law, in the collegiate schools of the Univ of Va.]

Mrd: on Jun 24, by Rev Stephen P Hill, Jas M Miller, of Louisiana, to Isabel C Laurie, daughter of Cranstoun Laurie, & grand-daughter of the late Rev Dr Laurie, of Wash City.

Mrd: on Jun 25, by Rev A G Carothers, Mr Geo Eslin to Miss Anne Douglas, both of Wash City.

Died: on Jun 25, in Gtwn, John Mitchell, only child of John W & the late Mary E England, aged 2 months & 7 days. His funeral will take place this afternoon at 5 o'clock, from the residence of his grandfather, Judson Mitchell.

Died: on Jun 24, Mr Wm H Clarke, son-in-law of C P Sengstack, in his 40th year, leaving a wife & 4 children to lament his loss. The deceased was a man of correct moral habits & honorable in all his relations of life. His funeral will take place from his late residence on 12th st, this afternoon, at 2 o'clock.

Died: on Jun 24, in Gtwn, Margaret Parks, infant daughter of John P & Ellen M McEldery.

For sale: tract of land, containing about 45 acres, on the Heights of Gtwn, being a part of the **Valley View Farm**, the residence of the late John H King, deceased. Also, a large frame dwlg house & lot on corner of 5th & H sts west, Wash. Apply at **Valley View Farm**, or to Dr H King, 80 Prospect st, Gtwn, D C. -E J King

FRI JUN 27, 1856
Mr Rufus Cogswell, a Revolutionary pensioner, died in Essex, Mass, on Jun 17, aged 100 years. He was a soldier of the Revolutionary war, & was in the American army under Gates at the capture of Burgoyne. He had been blind for the last 15 years.
-Salem Gaz

Senate: 1-Memorial from the citizens of Gtwn, D C, asking the retrocession of that city to the State of Md. 2-Ptn from Saml P Todd & John De Bree, pursers in the navy, asking to be released from the liability as sureties of John N Todd, deceased, late a purser in the navy. 3-Ptn from Wm R West, a soldier in the war of 1812, asking to be allowed a pension. 4-Cmte on Indian Affairs: asked to be discharged from the consideration of the memorial of the firm of J A Brunner & Brothers, & that it be referred to the Cmte on Military Affairs: which was agreed to. 4-Cmte on pensions: bill to continue the pension of Mrs Nancy Wetherford, reported it without amendment, & recommended its passage. 5-Joint resolution introduced for the benefit of Susan Decatur, widow of Stephen Decatur, late of the U S Navy: referred to the Cmte on Naval Affairs.

House of Reps: 1-Cmte on Revolutionary Pensions to inquire into placing Jas Saxton, of Catooza Co, Ga, on the Revolutionary pension rolls. 2-Cmte on Invalid Pensions: to inquire into the propriety of placing John Graddy on the rolls as an invalid pensioner. 3-Mr Bowie, of Md: Ptn of Mary B Dusenbery, widow of Maj Saml B Dusenbery, who died while in the military service of the U S, praying to be allowed a pension. 4-Ptn of S W Eldridge, of Lawrence, Kansas, asking the U S to compensate him for the destruction of his property by a body of men headed by S J Jones.
Affray at Bayou Sara on Jun 17 between S H Lurty, the sheriff of the parish, & Mr John Turnbull, planter. Both pistols & bowie knives were used. Mr Turnbull was mortally wounded & died soon afterwards. Mr Lurty had his leg broken by a shot, & he was also wounded in the neck with a bowie knife, but he is not considered in any danger.

Criminal Court-Wash. 1-Yesterday a young man, Dunigan, about 20 years of age, was found guilty of assault & battery, with intent to kill ofcr E L Keese. He was sentenced to 3 years' hard labor in the penitentiary. 2-John *Brant, Jas Eddington, & Geo Eddington, tried for stealing gillnets, the property of Mr Ellis, valued at $30. The former was found guilty, the 2 latter were acquitted under suggestion of the District Atty. [Jun 28th newspaper: John Brand, convicted on Thu of stealing gillnets, was yesterday sentenced, on 2 indictments, one year on the one & 18 months on the other, to imprisonment in the penitentiary.] *Two spellings-Brant/Brand.

On Sat a truckman, Winslow Eddy, residing in Boston, Mass, instigated by jealousy, stabbed his wife with a dirk knife, causing her death in a few hours. He surrendered himself to the police.

Mrd: on Jun 18, at **Mount Sharon**, Orange Co, Va, the residence of Mrs Louisa C Taliaferro, by Rev Jos Ernest, Cassius Carter, M D, of Fairfax Co, Va, to Miss Jane A Taliaferro, daughter of the late Rev Chas Taliaferro.

Died: on Jun 26, at Hopeton, near Washington, at 7 o'clock A M, Willie Dunham, aged 16 months, & at 12 o'clock Florence Ella, aged 4 years & 6 months, children of Jos C & Mary K Lewis. Their funeral is this evening at 5 o'clock.

Died: on Jun 25, in Wash City, William Bakewell, infant son of Allan & Susan E Pollock, aged 1 year & 20 days. His funeral will be from their residence, 349 K st, opposite **Franklin Row**, this afternoon at 4 o'clock.

St Louis, Jun 26. Advices from Kansas received in this city state that Wm Guy, agent for the Shawnees & Wyandots, was murdered by the Indians. It is rumored that Mr Brown, editor of the Herald of Freedon, has been killed; also, that Col Sumner has had a fight with a party of Missourians & lost 2 men, but drove the Missourians out, the latter having several killed.

SAT JUN 28, 1856
Senate: 1-Court of Claims: favorable opinions of the Court on: claim of Jos White; of Moses Noble; of Geo A Magruder; & of Thos H Baird. There were adverse decisions on the claims of Cassius M Clay & of Susan Decatur, widow of Cmdor Decatur. All of which were referred to the Cmte of Claims & ordered to be printed. 2-Memorial from Lewis J Williams, a passed assistant surgeon in the navy, asking to be allowed the pay of surgeon for the time he performed the duties of that grade. 3-Ptn from Jas Reed, asking to be allowed bounty land for service rendered by him as bearer of dispatches during the late war with Mexico. 4-Ptn from Eliz Emmons & Brothers for leave to apply to the Com'r of Patents for the renewal of the patent of Uriah Emmons for improvement in planing machines. 5-Cmte on Revolutionary Claims: asked to be discharged from the consideration of the ptn of Eliz Moast & Nancy Fisher, & that they be referred to the Cmte on Pensions: which was agreed to.

Died: on Jun 26, in Wash City, in her 12th year, Mary Virginia, daughter of Christopher S & Ann E O'Hare.

Obit-died: on Jun 23, Mrs Maria Campbell, the wife of our esteemed fellow-townsman, Mr Alex Campbell. She was the 2nd daughter of the late Alex Jas Dallas, & the sister of the present American Minister in Great Britain. She had been most remarkable for intellect & genius. Coming into social life when her father was a member of the Administration of Pres Madison, she adorned the circles of Washington with charms of a most lively wit. She added a constant attention to her duties as a wife & mother. -Pennsylvanian

The two remaining escaped prisoners, Croggan & Bailey, were captured at the house of Mr Cross, on 15th st. In company of the fugitives was a young man named Lloyd Cross, late of the Auxiliary Guard, & whose father keeps a tavern on 15th st, to which they repaired on the night of their escape. But one more, Ray, remains to be captured.

Trustee's sale of bldg lots at 10th & O sts north, at auction, on Jul 18 next, by deed of trust from Estwick Evans & wife to the subscriber, dated Sep 4, 1854, recorded in Liber J A S No 83, folios 286 thru 289, of the land records of Wash Co, D C: sale of lots 7 thru 9 in square 339, which fronts on 10th st west 233 feet 4 inches, & on north O st 99 feet 10½ inches. Terms cash. -Hugh B Sweeny, trustee -A Green auct

Died: on Jun 26, in Wash City, Linnie R Young, 2nd daughter of A H & M A Young, aged 20 years. Her funeral will take place from the Foundry M E Church tomorrow at 3 o'clock.

MON JUN 30, 1856

House of Reps: 1-Cmte on Pensions: to inquire into granting to Jas H Huey, a Revolutionary soldier, a pension under the act of 1832; also to inquire into paying to Francis & Judy Welchel the arrearages due them under the act of Mar 4, 1846. 2-Cmte of Claims: adverse report on the bill for the relief of Almanston Huston, originating in the Court of Claims: it was committed.

The jurors convened at the coroner's ofc on May 22, 1856, & determined that Chas Cora & Jas P Casey died on May 22, 1856, by hanging by the neck, which hanging was done by a body of men styling themselves a Vigilant Cmte of San Francisco. [See Jun 13th newspaper: death of Jas King of Wm.]

From California: 1-Jas, alias Yankee Sullivan, committed suicide in his cell at the cmte rooms, where he was confined. He has made a free & unreserved confession of all his crimes & rowdyisms, & expressed a determination to reform if he should be liberated. 2-On Jun 1 Chas Duane & John Cooney were arrested by order of the cmte. Others in custody were Billy Mulligan, Martin Gallagher, Wm Carr, Edw Culgers, & Wooley Kearney. Reports were current that the opponents of the cmte were supplying themselves with arms, & a conflict was expected between the two.

Farmers' & Mechanics' Bank, Gtwn, Jun 26, 1856, declared a dividend of 3% out of the profits for the 6 months ending Jun 30, payable Jul 1 next. -W Laird, jr, cashier

Total depravity. Two men, Henry Eggers & Carl Sleder, have been detected placing obstructions on the Michigan Central railroad. Their hostility to the road was caused by the loss of a dog, which had been killed by a passing train. They never asked remuneration for the loss, but commenced the fiendish system of obstructions.

Lost military bounty land warrants: No 29,616, for 80 acres, issued to Segus Rutherford, widow of Peter Rutherford; No 29,563, for 80 acres, issued to Nicholas Tyrce; No 27,852 for 80 acres, issued to Nancy Hargrove, widow of Beverly Hargrove; No 43,639 for 120 acres, issued to Jas Labban. I shall apply at the Pension Ofc for duplicate thereof. -W M Cabell

We are pained to record the accidental drowning on Sat of John A T Wade, aged 12 years, son of Mr John Wade, living near the corner of H & 6th sts. John had been in the habit of bathing in the Tiber, but on Sat, with other boys of his own age & size, & for the first time & without his parents' knowledge, went to the river, at the Point, near the **Washington Monument**. John, like Patrick Mills who was drowned in Rock Creek on Fri, was unable to swim, & ventured beyond his depth.

Criminal Court-Wash. 1-Bridget Curtis was convicted & sentenced to one year's imprisonment for stealing articles worth $14. 2-Richd Thomas was convicted of setting fire to the house of Mr Philip Mackay. Two other cases against Thomas being yet to be tried, the Court deferred sentence. 3-The case of Hon Preston S Brooks for the assault on Senator Sumner will be put on trial. 13 witnesses have been subpoenaed.

A subscription for the relief of the widow & children of the late Thos Keating was put in circulation soon after the death of Keating, & the amount subscribed & paid is $632. The money collected has been disposed of as follows: for the purchase of a 2 story house, near the corner of E & 20th sts, which has been conveyed to the widow & 2 children as joint tenents: $600. Paid for recording the deed: $1.25. Paid to Mrs Keating: $30.75. The foregoing amount was contributed by 75 individuals, in sums from $1 to $50.

Mrd: on May 29 last, at Whittaker's Chapel, N C, by Rev L H B Whittaker, Thos C Hunter, of Halifax, N C, to Mrs Annie H Wheat, formerly of Wash City.

Died: Jun 29, in Wash City, George Benedict, youngest son of Geo T & Ann E Raub, aged 5 months & 6 days. His funeral will take place this afternoon at 4 o'clock, from 15th & C sts.

Must be sold: our entire stock of fancy & plain bonnets. Call at Mrs R G Etchison's. [No address given. Appears local.]

TUE JUL 1, 1856
Copartnership notice. The undersigned has this day, Jul 1, associated with him in business Mr Edw F Simpson, under the firm of Fitzhugh Coyle & Co.
-Fitzhugh Coyle

Sale of **Haddock's Hill Farm** by trustees, in Chancery: by decree of the Circuit Court of Wash Co, D C, made in a cause, No 1,066, wherein Agnes M Easby is cmplnt, & Horatio N Easby, John W Easby, Wm R Smith & Wilhelmina M his wife, Henry King & Marian E his wife, & Cecilia J Hyde are dfndnts: sale at auction, on Jul 30, all that suburban residence known as part of **Haddock's Hills**: lies on the turnpike road from Wash City to Bladensburg, containing 46 acres 1 rood & 7½ perches.
-W P Webb, Richd H Clarke, Jos H Bradley, jr, trustees -J C McGuire, auct
+
Sale by trustees in Chancery of very valuable improved & unimproved real estate, by a decree of the Circuit Court of Wash Co, D C, made in a cause, No 1,066, wherein Agnes M Easby is cmplnt & Horatio N Easby, John W Easby, Wm R Smith & Wilhelmina M his wife, Henry King & Marian E his wife, & Cecilia J Hyde are dfndnts, the undersigned, trustees, will sell at auction the following:
Jul 31: lots 5 & 6 in square 1, corner of Va ave & 28th st.
Lot 2 in square 16, fronting on I st.
Parrt of lot 2 in square 11.
Lot 9 in square 12, fronting on E st, between 26th & 27th sts.
Lot 21 in square 37, fronting on 23rd st, between L & M sts.
Lot 18 in subdivision of square 38.
Lot 3 in square 40, fronting on 24th st, between H & I sts.
Lot 6 in square 41, fronting on 24th st, between H & I sts.
Lot 4 in square 42, corner of G & 24th sts.
Lots 2 & 3 in square 44, fronting on E st north, between 23rd & 24th sts.
Lot 3 in square 32, fronting on F st north, between 24th & 25th sts.
Lot 14 in square 32, fronting on Va ave & G st, between 24th & 25th sts.
On Aug 1:
Lot 7 in square 61, fronting on 23rd st west, between D st & N Y ave.
Lot 3 in square 88, fronting on Water st, between 21st & 22nd sts.
Lot 3 in square 89, fronting on Water st, running to the channel of the river.
Lots 1, 5, & 6 in square 57, on F & G sts north, between 22nd & 23rd sts.
Lot 6 in square 104, fronting on 21st st, between E & F st north.
Lot 8 in square 104, corner of E st north & 20th st west, fronting on E st.
Lots 5 & 6 in square 143, each fronting on 19th st west, between E & F sts north.
Lot 13 in square 100, fronting on 21st st west, between L & M sts north.
On Aug 2:
Lot 1 in square 574, B st & 1st st west, with 2 frame houses.
Lot 8 in square 631, fronting on N J ave, between C & D sts north.
Parts of lots 1 & 10 in square 559, fronting on K st, between N J ave & 1st st.
Part of lot 7 & all of lot 8 in square 728, fronting on North Capitol st, with a 3 story brick house with back bldg.
Part of lot 4 in square 730, fronting on 2nd st east, corner of south A st.
Lot 20 in square 702, fronting on ½ st east, between N & O sts.

Lot 9 in square 708, fronting 30 feet on an alley back of South Capitol st, between Q & R sts south.
Lot 20 in square 740.
Lot 1 in square 705, fronting on Ga ave, at 1st st east & south P st.
On Aug 4:
Lots 1 thru 8 & lot 12 in square 925.
Lots 6 & 13 in square 1028.
Lots 7 in square 1031.
Lot 5 in square 1034.
Lot 11 in square 1070.
Lot 10 in square 1111.
Lots 5 & 6 in square 1121.
Lot 8 in square 1122.
-W B Webb, Richd H Clarke, Jos H Bradley, trustees -Jas C McGuire, auct

Trustees' sale, pursuant to the provisions of a deed of trust executed by Wm H Clarke & wife, dated Dec 9, 1853, recorded in Liber J A S 75, folios 87 thru 91 of the land records of Wash Co, D C: sale on Jul 31, of the north half of lot 19 square 293, containing 2,233 square feet, fronting 294 feet 4 inches on 12th st west, running back 100 feet to an alley between C & D sts north, improved by a 2 story brick dwlg.
-J B H Smith, Silas H Hill, trustees -A Green auct

Senate: 1-Memorial from Wm R Talbot, in behalf of himself & other pursers in the navy, asking increase of compensation. 2-Additional papers submitted in the case of Lewis W Ludlow. 3-Ptn from Jacob Hatt, asking additional compensation for carrying the mail on account of Indian disturbances on the road from Missouri to Oregon. 4-Ptn from Thos O Selby, of Calif, asking compensation for injuries sustained by him in 1852 by a company of U S dragoons occupying a part of his premises. 5-Ptn from Thos J Churchill, asking to be relieved from liability for public property on account of lost vouchers during the battle of Buena Vista, in the Mexican war. 6-Cmte on the District of Columbia: memorial of E M Joslin, of Wash City, asking for an act of incorporation for a granite manufacturing company in said city: adverse report on the same. Same cmte: to which was referred the memorial of the city of Gtwn, asking an amendment of their charter so as to extend the right of suffrage, reported a bill to amend the charter of Gtwn, D C. [This bill give the right of suffrage to every free white male citizen who has attained the age of 21 years, who may have resided within the corporate limits of said town one year preceding the day of election, & who may have been returned on the books of the Corporation as subject to a school tax, except vagrants, paupers, persons non compos mentis, or convicted of any infamous crimes.] 7-Cmte of Claims: bill for the relief of Santiago E Arguello. Same cmte: bill for the relief of John P Baldwin, owner of the Spanish brig **Gil Blas**. 8-Bill for the relief of Richd W Meade: passed. 9-Bill for the relief of John H Scranton & Jas H Hunt, owners of the steamer **Major Tompkins**: passed.

Died: on Jun 30, at **Hopeton**, near Wash City, Herbert Denny, son of Jos C & Mary K Lewis, aged 9 years & 6 months, being the 3rd child within one week. His funeral will be this afternoon at 5 o'clock.

Died: on May 26, in Wash City, after a short illness, much lamented by a large circle of friends, Major J J P Kingsbury, formerly of the 6th Regt U S Infty, aged 57 years.

Sudden death. Yesterday, Mr Wm Palmer, the well-known professor of singing & the flute, walked into Liberty Hall, on Pa ave, between 14th & 15th sts, & attempted to seat himself on a chair; but failing to do this he fell to the ground. On being lifted up he said "it is all right,' & was then seated in a refreshment box close adjoining. The keeper of the establishment soon perceived Mr Palmer was sick, & removed him to the air in the house passage. Mr Palmer was then seized with a fit, which was removed by frictions of brandy. In about 5 minutes death convulsions came on & the patient died. His attending physician pronounced the death was caused by heart disease, which Mr Palmer has had for a considerable time.
+
Died: yesterday, suddenly, of conjestion of the brain, aged 42 years, Mr Wm Palmer. His funeral will take place from the house of his nephew, 266 F st, at 13th, at 3 P M.

Trustees' sale of very valuable property at auction: by decree of the Circuit Court of Wash Co, D C, sitting in Chancery, passed on Jun 14, 1856, in the case of Hezekiah Clagett & others vs John Walker & others: public auction on Aug 2 of the following: Lots 1 & 2, & 5 thru 19, in square 555, & all the east half of square 554 as laid down on the plat of Wash City. -Jno A Linton, Thos Brady, trustees -C W Boteler, auct

Orphans Court of Wash Co, D C. Letters of administration on the personal estate of Wm Holmead, late of Wash Co, deceased. -Mary A Holmead, admx

WED JUL 2, 1856
Last evening, while J W Paramore was replenishing a lighted lamp with camphene, it caught fire & exploded. He & his niece, Miss E J Rowland, were enveloped in flames. Mr Paramore was slightly burnt. Miss Rowland had her clothes entirely burnt off. Drs Dodge, Wheeler, & Beckwith were soon on hand. Her state is critical, but not without hope. -Cleveland Herald, 28th.

Mrd: on Jul 1, in Wash City, by Rev Wm Krebs, Henry C Windsor to Hattie R, eldest daughter of the late Albert J Baker, all of Wash City.

Died: on Tue, in Wash City, Mary Sophia, youngest child of T W & the late Sophia Jones, aged 6 months & 4 days. Her funeral will be this afternoon at 4 o'clock, from north B, between 1st st east & N J ave.

Senate: 1-Memorial from Christian Hansen, showing the importance of establishing a regular line of mail steamers from N Y to the north of Europe. 2-Ptn from Wm F Harrington, asking to be allowed the pay of a passed assist surgeon in the navy during the time he acted in this capacity previous to his promotion. 3-Communication from Cmder Thos J Page, addressed to the Cmte on Naval Affaris, in relation to the propriety of allowing additional pay to the ofcrs of the navy recently engaged in an exploration & survey of the La Platte river & its tributaries. 4-Cmte on Military Affairs: asked to be discharged from the consideration of the memorial of Mrs Harriet O Read: which was agreed to. 5-Cmte on Naval Affairs: joint resolution for the benefit of Susan Decatur, widow of Cmdor Decatur, late of the U S Navy, recommended its passage. Same cmte: bill for the relief of Fred'k Chatard, of the U S Navy. 6-Cmte on Post Ofcs & Post Roads: bill for the relief of J R Powell, for compensation for extra services as mail contractor in Alabama, allowing reasonable compensation for additional expenses incurred.

Jos F Brown resigned his 4th class clerkship [$1,800] in the Adj Genrl's Ofc, War Dept.

Missing. The St Louis Republican asks the aid of the eastern papers in an effort to discover the whereabouts of Mr Jas H Stewart, of Jefferson Co, in that State, who left his home on May 16, with the intention of going to Phil, by the way of the Balt & Ohio Railroad & Washington, & has not been heard of since. His object in visiting Phil was to receive certain moneys due him in the partition of an estate & of making a deed for the same. Mr Stewart is about 6 feet high, rather broad, of robust appearance, & florid complexion, hair dark & inclined to curl, eyes grey, & features regular. His habits are steady & manners reserved towards strangers.

THU JUL 3, 1856
House of Reps: 1-Bill for the relief of Jas P Fleming, of Augusta, Ga: committed. 2-Bill to test the usefulness of J S Richardson's atmospheric telegraph: committed.

Senate: 1-Memorial from John Taylor, heir of a Cherokee reservee, asking that the heirs or assignees of Cherokee reservees may be paid the full value of their reservations: referred. 2-Memorial of Hezekiah Miller, on the files of the Senate: referred to the Cmte on Territories. 3-Cmte on Military Affairs: bill for the relief of Thos J Churchill, late a lt in the 1st Ky regt of volunteers.

Advices from Beaver Island assure us that King Strang was alive on Tue, & there was a fair prospect of his recovery. His lower limbs are entirely paralyzed by the shot in the back. -Detroit Free Press

Gtwn College. The exercises appointed for this evening consist of a public defence of Theses in Intellectual Philosophy by the following students: Messrs Wm Cleary; Jos King; John F Callan, of D C; & John Rieckelmann, of Ohio.

The public are cautioned not to receive 2 notes of $1,500 each, dated Mar 1, 1855, one payable on Dec 1, 1856, & the other on Dec 1, 1857, which I executed payable to Warren Somers, as I shall dispute the same; they being given for the purchase money of certain land & premises sold to me by him to which he had not a legal title. These notes were intended to be secured by a mortgage on the said land executed by me. Mr Somers & wife gave me a deed for the said land, but their title was defective. -Marcus Bickford.
[Jul 26th newspaper: It is entirely false that he ever gave me a mortgage on said land for the payment of the noted referred to in said notice; & it is equally false that my title to said premises at the time of the deed by myself & wife to said Bickford was in any manner defective. -Warren Somers]

The Alumni Association of Princeton had a meeting at the college chapel: Hon W C Alexander was elected Pres; Rev R K Rogers, Sec; speeches by J P Jackson, sr, B B Vaughn, & Prof Duffield. On its catalogue for this year we find the names of 253 students & 18 instructors. -Newark Daily Adv, Jun 30, 1856

Mrd: on Apr 17, at *Oak Lawn*, St Paul's Parish, S C, by Rev C C Pinckney, Ambrosia Jose Gonzalez, formerly of Cuba, to Harriett Rutledge, youngest daughter of Hon Wm Elliott.

Died: on Jun 26, in St Louis, Mo, Dr Robt S Holmes, formerly of the Army, aged 39 years, & a native of Pittsburg, Pa.

Teacher wanted: a single gentleman to fill the situation as Principal of the Clasical Dept in my school. -Caleb S Hallowell, Alexandria High School, Va.

FRI JUL 4, 1856
Chancery sale of valuable improved real estate: by decree of the Circuit Court of Wash Co, D C, passed on Jun 17, 1856, in a cause wherein Nicholas W Goertuer & wife are cmplnts, & Wm Mechlin & others are dfndnts: the subscriber will, on Jul 29, 1856, sell at public auction, the following property in Wash City: lot 7 in square 118, & that part of lot 8 in the same square, adjoining lot 7, fronting on I st, with the 3 story brick dwlg house & other improvements on the same. The property is situated at the corner of 20th & I sts. -Thos P Morgan, trustee -Jas C McGuire, auct

Household & kitchen furniture at auction on: Jul 9, at the late residence of Mr Worcester, on 14th st, between H & I sts. -A Green auct

Chillon Castle Manor Farm at auction: executor's sale, by the last will & testament of the late Wm Easby. Public auction on Aug 8, on the premises, that valuable farm, lying partially in Wash & PG Co, Md, containing in all 62 acres of land, more or less. Improvements consist of a small frame dwlg-house & a large well built new barn.
-H N Easy, J W Easby, Agnes M Easby, excs of Wm Easby, deceased.
-J C McGuire, auct

Sale of valuable real estate near Wash City under a decree in Chancery, by a decree of the Circuit Court for PG Co, Md, in equity, & passed in a cause wherein Marion M Taylor & Sarah V Taylor, his wife, John W Van Hook, & John Fox, are cmplnts, & Mgt A Scott & Rachel P Scott are dfndnts, dated Jun 20, 1856. Public sale on Jul 20, that portion of the county commonly known as ***Spaulding's District***, adjoining the lands of Messrs Jessie Ridgway, Nathan Masters, Jas Addison, & others; the New Cut road from Good Hope running through the land, containing in all about 350 acres of land, being the tract of land of which Geo B Scott died seized & possessed, & made up of portions of several tracts of land known as ***Gum Spring***, ***Gum Spring Enlarged***, ***Three Brothers***, & ***Silver Hills***. For particulars inquire of the trustee or of Messrs Fox & Van Hook, 490 7th st, Wash. The title believed to be indisputable.
-S S Williams, trustee -A Green auct

Executor's sale of valuable quarry & other lands lying on the Potomac river, between the ***Aqueduct & Little Falls Bridge***: on Aug 7, the subscribers, as executors of the last will & testament of the last Wm Easby, will sell a body of valuable quarry lots, numbered from 1 thru 43, all lying on the Potomac river. Title indisputable. -H N Easby, J W Easby, Agnes M Easby, excs of Wm Easby, deceased.
-J C McGuire, auct

Accident on Monday at the sugar-house of Harris Evans & Co, 28 Leonard st, N Y, cost the life of Jas Covens, a laborer, & caused fearful injuries to Jos Nazeraw & Jas Malony, also laborers. Only one man at a time should ride on the frame used for hoisting sugar, but the 3 men got upon it at the same time, & when they reached the 6th floor, one of the ropes gave way, & they fell headlong with the freight to the 1st floor.

Died: on Jul 3, in Gtwn, Mrs Eliza Pearce, aged 61 years, wife of Gideon Pearce, of Gtwn, D C. Her funeral will take place on Jul 5 at 4½ o'clock, from her late residence on Prospect st.

I offer for sale the farm on which I reside, containing 700 acres; in Culpeper Co, Va. My depot & post ofc is Brandy Station, Culpeper Co, Va. -Jos Morton

MON JUL 7, 1856

The U S practice ship **Plymouth** arrived off Old Point on Jun 30 from Annapolis. In addition to the regular ofcrs there are 50 acting midshipmen on board. List of her ofcrs: Cmder, Jos F Green; Lts, Robt H Wyman, Wm H Wilcox, J Van Ness Philip, J Taylor Wood, Wilson McGunnegle; Purser, B Frank Gallaher; Passed Assist Surgeon, John Ward; Carpenter, Henry P Leslie; Gunner, John Webber; Sail Maker, Wm B Fugitt; Boatswain, Philip J Miller.

Gen Memucan Hunt, of Texas, died in Haywood Co, Tenn, on Jun 26. His health had been failing for some months previously. His name is identified with the early struggles of Texan independence & interwoven with her political history as a separate republic & as a State of this Union from that day to this. He was a brave & true man; in public life patriotic, & loyal; in the social relations all that endears man to his fellows. -Memphis Bulletin

The honorary degree of Dr of Laws has been conferred by the Delaware College on Lt Jas M Gilliss, U S Navy, & Dr of Divinity on Rev Chas H Read, of Richmond, Va.

Mrd: on Jun 29, in Wash City, by Rev Mr Brown, of Gtwn, John Hoover to Mrs Sarah Franklin, both of Wash City.

Died: on Jun 29, in Richmond, Mrs Margaret Topham, [formerly Margaret King, of Wash City,] in her 48th year.

Died: on Jul 6, in Wash City, Hannah P Munday, daughter of the late Capt Wm Munday, of the Army of the Revolution. Her friends & those of J P Keller are invited to attend her funeral, this afternoon, at 5 o'clock, from the residence of the latter, 469 13th st.

Chancery sale of valuable real estate near Gtwn, D C: by decree of the Circuit Court of Wash Co, D C, passed on Jun 7, 1856, in a cause wherein Guinilda Spencer is cmplnt & Jos Spencer & others are dfndnts: sale on Jul 31, at auction, on the premise, all that piece of land in Wash Co, D C, being parts of the tracts called ***Pretty Prospect & Resurvey on Lucky Discovery***, as is described in a deed from Jos Spencer & Jas A McKenney to Guinilda Spencer, dated Apr 20, 1847, recorded in Liber W B 134, folios 5 thru 7, one of the land records for said county, containing 31 acres 3 roods & 26 perches, saving & excepting there from the part known as ***Mount Alban***, on which stands the church of St Alban's. This property is about 1½ miles north of Gtwn, adjoining the land of Jas Causten. -John Carroll Brent, A Austin Smith, trustees -J C McGuire, auct

Mexico. Salvator Iturbide, the most talented & worthy son of the Emperor, drowned near Tepic while bathing.

N Y: 1-Hannah Wiadean, residing at 122 Broome st, was killed by the discharge of a pistol in the hand of a woman residing next door named Amelia Stewart. It appears the pistol had been handed to her by A Beirnheim, who dared her to fire it. The woman had no intention to injure the deceased. Beirnheim was found guilty of culpable carelessness. 2-Mrs Louisa Segelboum, of 8th ave, stood in her doorway & discharged a pistol, not knowing it contained shot, & severely wounded Mgt Skoote, a little girl, 4 years old. She was arrested & held to bail.

Murder on Fri last at Beckert's, near the Park, on 7th st, when a party of 5 intoxicated & disorderly persons wanted to enter the premises, a portion of which the Germans had engaged for their own sole use. The gate-keeper, Chas W Bell, [whose right name was Casper Kohman, changed because under that designation he had been suspected of being in the African slave trade,] the murdered man, refused admission, & a fight commenced. Wm Sullivan confessed to having stabbed Bell; Conrad Jost was a witness. Verdict of the jury: Bell came to his death by a blow inflicted either by John Eggleston or Wm Sullivan during a riot, in which Danl & Isaiah Stewart were also involved. Bell or Kohman left a wife & child about 5 years of age. He bore the character of a quiet & inoffensive man.

Wm Lewis Dayton, candidate for the Vice Presidency, is a native of Somerset Co. His ancestors for many generations were also native Jerseymen. His great grandfather, Jonathan Dayton, who was of English descent, settled at Elizabethtown, Essex Co, as early as 1725, & about the same time his mother's grandfather removed to Baskenridge, Somerset Co, where he erected the first frame dwlg in that section of the country. His ancestry on both the fathers' & mother's side took an honorable part in the Revolutionary struggle. Elias Dayton, the brother of the grandfather, became a Brig Gen, & his son, Jonathan Dayton became eminent as the Speaker of the House of the 4th Congress. His maternal grandfather, Edw Lewis, was a commissary in the Revolutionary army, & served as such during the entire war. The mother of the late Saml L Southard [who died while presiding ofcr of the Senate] was the sister of this grandfather. Robt Dayton, the grandfather of the candidate, removed his family shortly after the Revolutionary war from Elizabethtown to a farm near Baskenridge, & here he afterwards continued to reside. Here his son Joel resided, & here Wm L Dayton was born, on Feb 17, 1807. He was the eldest of the family, & was placed, while in his 12th year, under the care of the celebrated Dr Brownlee, afterwards of N Y. Dr B prepared him for the college of N J at Princeton, from which institution he graduated in 1825. His health suffered severely in college. He then read law with Gov Vroom & was admitted to the bar in 1830. He settled in Monmouth Co, opening an ofc in Freehold, where he continued to reside for about 7 years. He entered political life at age 30. Hon Saml L Southard died in Jun, 1842, & Mr Dayton took his seat on Jul 6, 1842. He was the youngest man in the body, having barely attained the age of 35.

Mr John Kissel, residing near Fairview, Cumberland Co, Pa, was found on Monday last with a gun-shot wound on his forehead. He was a bachelor & lived alone, doing all the housework duties himself, & generally disliked the presence of visitors. It was known that he had a large sum of money which he always carried with him, & the fact that his pockets were cut open proves that this caused his assassination.

Rowland B Perry, of Grand Blanc, in this county, was gored to death by a favorite bull on Monday last. Mr Seymour Perry, nephew of the deceased, who, with Mr Bates, was working nearby, ran to the spot. Mr Perry was then insensible. On being carried to the house he revived, but sunk rapidly & died within the hour. Mr Perry had raised the bull since it was 6 months old & had been constantly in the habit of handling it.
-Flint [Mich] Citizen

The Union Railroad Company have provided a <u>funeral car</u> to run upon the horse railroad from Boston to Mount Auburn, which was used for the first time yesterday. The price charged is $6. The car can convey the remains & 20 persons. $4 is charged for a carriage to Mount Auburn. Every facility will be afforded by Mr Styles, superintendent.

Mr W T Balestine, of N Y, arrived in Wash City by the Southern boat on Sat morning, & was conveyed in a weak & dying condition to the Kirkwood House. Dr Berry & Dr Miller attended him until his death, which took place this afternoon. The Masonic fraternity, of which the deceased was a member, have taken the body in charge, & are making suitable arrangements for the funeral.

TUE JUL 8, 1856
The royal baptism of the infant Prince took place on Sat, Jun 14, in France. The 13th century cathedral was decorated with crimson & gold drapery. The Empress was robed in blue, veiled with white lace; her brow was ornamented with a superb ornament of diamonds & pearls. The hair being drawn back a la Imperatrice. Their Majesties took their seats before the altar as the guardian of the <u>Imperial child</u> advanced. The baptismal register, first witnessed by the envoy of the Pope, was signed by Prince Oscar of Sweden, Prince Napoleon, the Duchess of Hamilton, the ofcrs of State, & others. The shouts of the multitude outside the bldg proclaimed the close of an event which has baptized the heir of Napoleon III to the hereditary rights of Emperor of the French. The godfather of the child, the Pope, was represented by the Legate, while the Duchess of Baden represented the godmother, the Queen of Sweden.

Wanted: a Teacher well qualified to act as an assistant in an English, Classical, & Mathematical Academy. -P A Bowen

Mr Geo Guy, living at Ocean View, near Norfolk, set fire to his house on Monday night, & it was consumed, with one of his children. He had been on a spree for some time previous to the tragedy, & for the past few days had shown evident signs of a return of insanity with which he was afflicted.

Senate: 1-Ptn from the widow of Geo Davis, a sailing master who died of disease contracted in the service, asking to be allowed a pension. 2-Ptn from John P Eldredge, asking that the ofcrs of the company of the Clinton Guards, of the Michigan militia, called into the service of the U S by the Govn'r of Michigan in 1838, may be allowed compensation for their services. 3-Ptn from Henry J Benson, a lt in the revenue cutter service, asking to be allowed bounty land for his services in the Mexican war. 4-Ptn from Capt Israel Warner, of the 2nd regt of Ohio militia during the war of 1812, asking payment for money adanced for subsistence of his company. 5-Ptn from Moses Olmstead, asking to be allowed a pension. 6-Ptn from Geo J Knight, asking indemnity on account of a vessel impressed in the service of the U S & subsequently destroyed in 1814. 7-Papers relating to the claim of Chas West were withdrawn from the files & referred to the Cmte on Pensions. 8-Cmte on Public Lands: memorial of Wm Carey Jones, asking compensation for services as special agent to examine land titles in Calif: claim to be settled. 9-Cmte on Naval Affairs: memorial of John B Montgomery, asking to be relieved from liability for public money entrusted for security purposes, which was lost due to the failure of the bank in which he deposited it: asked to be discharged from its further consideration of the memorial & it was referred to the Cmte on Finance. Same cmte: asked to be discharged from the consideration of the memorial of John Etheridge, of the Navy Dept, asking compensation for services as superintendent of the s w Executive bldg: referred to the Cmte of Claims. 10-Cmte on Naval Affairs: memorial of Gen Nathan Towson in behalf of himself & other captors of the British ship **Caledonia**, submitted a report, with a bill for the benefit of the captors of the **Caledonia**. [The bill appropriates $25,000 to be paid to the legal reps of the late Capt Jesse D Elliot, of Gen Nathan Towson, & ofcrs & men engaged in the capture.] 11-Mr Cass asked the Senate to indulge him in taking up the bill for the relief of Brvt Brig Gen Wallach, giving as a reason that the gallant old soldier was now 92 years of age, & there could be no more appropriate time than immediately after Jul 4th to pay such a tribute to such a man: bill was passed. 12-Bill granting a pension to Mary A M Jones, widow of Gen Roger Jones, was passed.

Public sale of valuable real & personal estate in Alexandria Co, Va: on Jul 15 next, on the premises, that tract of land & county seat in said county called **Hampton**. The entire farm contains 354 acres, from which 3 lots, two of 20 acres & one of 50 acres, have been laid off. The dwlg is commodious, with all necessary out-houses. Also, a number of horses, mules, milch cows, wagons, carts, threshing machine, & farming implements will be sold. -Saml J McCormick, auct, Alexandria, Va.

Both John Eggleston & Wm Sullivan, the parties implicated in the murder of Chas W Bell, alias Kohman, have been captured. Eggleston had been staying at the house of his brother-in-law at the west end of Wash City, but the brother-in-law advised him to surrender, which he did on Sunday. Sullivan was found in his house in an out-of-the-way closet, where he had secreted himself. He, too, was placed in jail.

Died: on Jul 7, in Wash City, Ann Eliza, wife of Danl Quinn, aged 35 years, a native of Norfolk, Va, & for the last 15 years a resident of Wash City. Her funeral will take place from her late residence, 13th & G sts, this afternoon at 5 o'clock.

Died: on Jul 3, in Wash City, of inflammation on the brain, William Henry, infant son of John T & Sarah E Stanley, aged 9 months & 16 days.

Died: on Jul 7, in Wash City, Grayson H Edwards, aged 3 months & 2 days, infant son of John S & Susan W Edwards.

Balt, Jul 7. Accident this evening on the Balt & Ohio Railroad, near the Relay House. The switch was broken & half opened, & the train which left Wash at 4½ P M was thrown from the track. Engineer Jas Gough & Henry Nagle, newsman, were killed. Mr Hedges, mail agent, Mr Worthington, lawyer, of Annapolis, Wm Bridges, confectioner, & Mr Russell, fireman, were badly injured. [Jul 9th newspaper: Mr Jas Gough was thrown from the locomotive directly under the wheels, which passed over his breast & neck, killing him instantly. Mr Gough resided in Wash City, & leaves a wife & 3 children. Mr Henry Nagle, a newspaper carrier, who attended the trains to sell papers, was instantly killed when thrown from the platform & run over by the wheels of the smoking car. John Russell, fireman, had one arm broken & his face badly scalded & bruised. Wm Bridges, confectioner, of Balt, received a fracture of one arm, besides sustaining great internal injury. Brice Worthington, of Annapolis, sustained 2 severe fractures of one of his ankles & thighs. He was taken in a carriage by Hon Reverdy Johnson & conveyed to a neighboring farm-house. A gentleman named Cumminsky was badly bruised about the head & face. The verdict was that the train was thrown off the track by the displacement of the switch by some persons unknown. The Railroad Co has offered a reward of $2,000 for the arrest of the guilty party.]

For rent: the desirable store No 558 7th st, opposite Centre Market, fitted up with shelving, counters, gas fixtures, & awning. Possession given immediately.
-Robt C Brooke

WED JUL 9, 1856
Died: on Jun 10, at **Fort Pierre**, Nebraska Territory, Jas M Mason, aged 20 years, 4th son of Gen John Mason, of Wash City.

Serious accident at Gloucester, N J, on Friday, while a party of inexperienced men were engaged in firing a salute. The piece was not swabbed out, &, the vent not being properly attended to, the gun was discharged prematurely, & Geo Huntsman, Edw Noble, Saml English, & Jesse Daisey were seriously injured. Huntsman had one hand blown off.

Senate: 1-Memorial from Wm Lorell, of the U S navy, asking that the same extra pay may be allowed to the ofcrs & seamen who accompanied Dr Kane's expedition as was allowed to those under Lt De Haven. 2-Memorial from Capt David Geisinger, of the navy, placed on the reserved list, asking such redress as Congress may deem just. 3-Ptn from Alfred Bassett & other members of a company of Connecticut militia in the war of 1812, asking to be allowed bounty land. 4-Cmte on Revolutionary Claims: bill for the relief of Catharine V R Cochran, sole surviving child of the late Gen Philip Rutledge. 5-Cmte on the Post Ofc & Post Roads: bill for the relief of John Scott, Hill W Houre, & Saml O Houre. 6-Cmte on Pensions: asked to be discharged from the consideration of the memorial of Thos Howard, of Pa, asking for a pension for injuries sustained while in the naval service & that it be referred to the Cmte on Naval Affairs: which was agreed to. 7-Cmte on Revolutionary Claims: adverse report on the ptn of Lucy Tate, widow of an ofcr of the Revolution. 8-Cmte on Naval Affairs: adverse report on the memorial of Thos Ewbank for an appropriation to test certain improvements in the mode of constructing the paddles of steamers; the cmte saw nothing to justify the appropriation. Same cmte: adverse report on the memorial of Jas Shackleford & other temporary watchmen guarding the steamer **Minnesota** for extra compensation. 9-Cmte on Pensions: adverse report on the ptn of the widow of Michl Custner; & on the ptn of Saml Warner.

Valley View, a new private boarding house, to be open about Jul 10 for the reception of some 15 or 20 boarders. It is situated upon the Manassas Gap Railroad, which runs through the farm, within full view of the mansion, & but 5 hours' ride from Wash. The house will be superintended by a lady from Alexandria, of superior qualifications. Address Mrs Maria Hambleton, Markham Station, Va.

My brother, Jeremiah Conolly, who came to this country about 16 years ago & settled in some part of Pa, & as I am informed lived with a farmer about 3 years in that State, will gratify his brother, Jeremiah Conolly, who now resides in Gtwn, D C, if he will write to him, & hopes this notice will reach him or some person who knows him. He lived in the parish of Cuharra, Ireland. -Jeremiah Conolly.

Female teachers needed at the Pennsylania Female College. Address the President, J Warrenne Sunderland, Perkiomen Bridge P O, Pa.

Orphans Court of Wash Co, D C. Letters of administration on the personal estate of Hugh McMillen, late of the U S Marine Corps, deceased. -John Robinson, adm

THU JUL 10, 1856
Executor's sale of stock: at the auction rooms of Jas C McGuire, the undersigned, excs of the late Wm Easby, will sell 84 shares, of $100 each, Chesapeake & Ohio Canal Stock. 10 shares, of $10 each, Temperance Hall Stock. -H N Easby, J W Easby, Agnes M Easby, excs. -Jas C McGuire, auct

Trustee's sale of bldg lots, by deed of trust from Richd B Lloyd to the subscriber, dated Dec 24, 1855, filed for record Jun 23, 1856, in the Clerk's ofc for Wash Co, D C: auction of lots 8 & 9 in square 653; lot 19 in square 36; lot 21 in square 51; & lot 2 in square 6. -Hamilton G Fant, trustee -A Green auct

Desirable farm for sale: the undersigned offers his farm in Orange Co, Va, known as **Prospect Hill**: contains about 500 acres, & is situated on the Rapidan river, 3 miles below the Raccoon Ford mills. The undersigned, intending to return to the State of Missouri, [where he was raised,] will dispose of his farm on favorable terms. Apply to Benj Farish, of Culpeper; & to Hon G Porter or H G Fant, Wash, for information. -Jas W Farish

The copartnership existing under the firm of Boyne & Brock is this day, Jul 10, dissolved by mutual consent. Thos J Boyne will continue the business at the old stand, 522 Pa ave. -Thos J Boyne, Wm G Brock

Jul 4th accidents. 1-Wm Dinge, aged 15, was killed at Wolcotville, Ct, by the bursting of a small cannon while firing a salute. 2-Arthur, aged 12 years, son of Capt H S Soule, was injured at New Haven, Ct, on Thur while playing with fireworks, & died on Sat. 3-At East Berlin, Ct, Jas Beckwith, a bystander, had his head blown off by the bursting of a cannon with which a party were firing a salute. 4-At Walpole, Mass, Mr Robt Smith was probably fatally wounded. He was marking a target for two of his companions who were firing with rifles; & although he was standing 30 feet from the target, one of his friends accidentally shot him through the body just below the heart.

Accidents on Jul 4th in Phil from careless use of firearms. Injured were Thos McElmoth, aged 14; Chas Smith, aged 54; Patrick Farley, aged 8; Jas Quinn, aged 24; Geo Dubois, aged 15, & Jas Smith, aged 18. John Welsh, aged 16, fell from a pile of lumber. Abner Winslow, a sailor, was burnt by the explosion of some powder in a bottle. -Ledger

Wanted, a situation at the South, Sep 1, by a Lady capable of giving instruction on the Piano; who would like home in some family in the country, where she might instruct children in the rudiments of an English education. Good Washington references. Address Miss Clara E Bradley, Wash.

Teacher wanted to take charge of a school of boys, not exceeding 15 in number, for the ensuing year. He must be qualified to teach & devote his time to the advancement of his pupils. Address either of the undersigned, at Middleburg, Loudoun Co, Va. -H B Powell, Dr F W Powell, or Dr Wm B Cochran

$50 reward for runaway negro man Jim Boon, 22 years old. -M P Morton, living near Benedict, Chas Co, Md.

FRI JUL 11, 1856
Trial of Hon P T Herbert. Jury consists of Edw M Edelin, Peter F Bacon, John Scribner, John T Bradley, John Sessford, jr, Robt Cohen, Enoch Moreland, Geo W Cochran, Nimrod Garrettson, Henry Wilson, John F Bridgett, & Henry D Gunnell. Witnesses for the U S: Patrick Keating, [brother of the deceased,] Thos Broderick, John Enwright, Chas Quinn, Jas Quinn, Jeremiah Reardon, Henry H Willard, Fred'k Warren, [resides in Boston,] Dr Thos Miller, Gabriel De Venois, [chief cook,] Michl Carrol Francis Maynard, & John Riley. With the District Atty is associated, at the request of the deceased's relatives, John M Brewer, formerly of the Western Md bar, but now of Wash. Witness for the defence: Messrs A J Smith, Jas Bishop, W R J McKay, Arnold Harris, John C Reynolds, W A Gardiner, Danl Smith, Mr Graham, Mr Colt, & Capt Birch.

Sad accident in Claremont, N H, on Jul 4. Wm Griffin broke his back & died when the Massoma Fire Co at Lebanon were passing over a suspension bridge of the Claremont Manufacturing Company when it broke, & they were precipitated into the water.

Fatal affray in St Peter's Parish, S C, on Jul 3, Hon Edmund Martin in the chair. Mr Jesse Peeples, a member of the House of Reps of S C, asked Mr Martin why he had not placed him on the cmte. On Mr Martin stating that he had not thought of him Mr Peeples knocked him down. A general fight ensued, in which Dr E H Martin, of Savannah, son of Hon Edmund Martin, was severely cut, & Mr Peeples was killed.

Recent English papers report that 2 wealthy ladies, Misses Ann & Eliz Sherwood, of Sheffield, have just been liberated, by the intervention of their friends, after 14 years' imprisonment for contempt of the Court of Chancery. They continued in prison rather than produce an unimportant document in their possession. -Transcript

Information reached this city that a party of Sioux recently came in the night to Platte Lake, & killed Francis Brunett & his whole family, of 5 persons. He was a well-known half-breed, & had been a Chippewa trader for 30 years. The Sioux payment was stopped because they refused to deliver up a party of murderers. -St Paul Democrat of Jul 1.

Senate: 1-Ptn from Stephen Hoyt, asking an amendment of bounty land law of Mar, 1855. 2-Memorial from Jonas P Levy & other citizens of Wash, D C, asking an incorporation of the Wash Gas Light Co. 3-Ptn from Danl Fowler, a soldier in the war of 1812, asking to be allowed a quarter section of land in lieu of his bounty land sold by the State of Ill without his knowledge or consent. 4-Ptn from the surviving children of Richd Furbee, an ofcr of the Revolution, asking to be allowed the amount of pension to which their father was entitled. 5-Ptn from Clement C West & other employes of the Gov't at Wash, asking to be allowed an increase of 20% on their salaries. 6-Ptn from E Lloyd Winder, of the U S Navy, asking to be allowed the difference of pay between passed midshipmen & masters during the time he acted in the latter capacity. 7-Ptn from Chas Kinkead, in behalf of Livingston Kinkead & Co, asking indemnity for depredations committed by the Sioux Indians. 8-Ptn from Wm J Appleby, clerk of the Supreme Court & First District Court of the U S in the Territory of Utah, asking an increase of compensation. 9-Ptn from Wm Heine, asking compensation for his services as an artist in the Japan expedition. 10-Ptn from Ambrose Lanfear, asking confirmation of his title to certain lands in Louisiana. 11-Ptn from N T West, dropped as passed midshipman in the navy, asking to be restored to the service. 12-Cmte on Private Land Claims: adverse reports on the memorial of Silas Stockwell & on that of Sallie C Northup: which was agreed to. 13-Cmte on Pensions: adverse report on the memorial of John G Watmough, for increase of pension: which was agreed to. 14-Cmte on Private Land Claims: bill for the relief Laurent Millandon. 15-Bill for the relief of John Rogers: referred to the Cmte on Indian Affairs. 16-Bill for the relief of Wm J Appleby, Clerk: referred to the Cmte on the Judiciary. 17-Bill for the benefit of Susan Decatur, widow of Cmdor Stephen Decatur, late of the U S Navy: postponed.

South Florida: Capt F M Durrance, in command of one of the mounted volunteer companies stationed at **Fort Frazier** gives an account of an attack by a party of Indians on the house of Willoughby Tillis at sunrise on Jun 14. Lt Carlton, who happened to be at **Fort Meade** on a visit to his family, heard the report of guns, & with 6 others went to the aid of Tillis & his family. The Indians fled to a thicket nearby. Lt Carlton & his men charged them. Lt Carlton & Lott Whidden, of my company, were killed, & Danl Carlton wounded. Wm Parker, of Capt Hooker's company, was killed, & J H Hollingswroth wounded. Jun 16: Nineteen men were in the swamp in search of the enemy. A charge was ordered, & a well-contested battle fought. Robt F Prine & Geo Howell were killed, & Jas Whidden, Wm D Brooker, & John L Skipper wounded.

Mrd: on Jul 2, at Urbana, Ohio, by Rev J P Stuart, Miss Gertrude Vanuxem James, daughter of John H James, to Mr Henry Thayer Niles, Greek Professor in Urbana University.

Died: on Jul 10, in Wash City, Ella, aged 6 months, youngest child of Martha E & Thos W Howard. Her funeral will take place today at 4 o'clock P M.

SAT JUL 12, 1856
Senate: 1-Ptn from Nathl Hayward, asking for an extension of time on his patent for an improvement in the manufacture of India rubber goods. 2-Additional papers presented relating to the claim of Eliz Moast, widow of John Moast. 3-Additional papers presented in the case of D A Hays for arrears of pension. 4-The memorial & papers of Edw Hart were referred to the Cmte on Patents & the Patent Ofc. 5-The papers of Hezekiah Miller were conferred to the Cmte of Claims. 6-Cmte of Claims: bill for the relief of Jos White; of Geo A Magruder; of Moses Noble; of Jas M Lindsay: ordered to be printed with the bills. 7-Cmte on Pensions: bill for the relief of Eliza B McNeill. Same cmte: bill for the relief of Nathan M Lownsbury: recommended its passage. Same cmte: bill for the relief of Jacob Price, of Jefferson Co, Va: passed. Same cmte: asked to be discharged from the consideration of the ptn of John Hughes, & that it be referred to the Cmte on Naval Affairs: which was agreed to. Same cmte: asked to be discharged from the consideration of the ptn of Ruth Philips: which was agreed to. 8-Cmte on Revolutionary Claims: adverse report on the claim of the surviving children of Lt Ebenezer March, of the Revolution, for compensation for the services & losses of their father. 9-Cmte on Pensions: adverse reports on the ptns of Jas Connelly; of John R Tucker; of Alex'r Wilson; of Sallie Keyer; & of Hannah Walker: all of which were severally ageed to. 10-Bill for the relief of Susan Decatur, widow of the late Cmdor Stephen Decatur: agreed to Mrs Decatur to receive a pension for 5 years at the rate of $50 per month. 11-Bills passed- relief: of Capt J P Hatch, U S Army; of the legal reps of Capt Jos H Whipple, deceased; of Dr Wm P A Hail, late of he Tenn volunteers in the Mexican war; of Chas E Anderson; of Adam D Steuart & of Alex Randall, exc of Danl Randall; of Asbury Dickins; of Michl Nourse; of John Robb; of Wm H Chase; of the heirs of Maj Arthur St Clair; of Martin Fenwick; & of Peter Parker. 12-Bill to vest the title to certain warrants for land in Geo M Gordon: passed. 13-Act to grant to L Jane Horner & children a section of land in Oregon: passed.

House of Reps: 1-Bill introduced & referred-relief: of Simon Myers. 2-Cmte of Claims: bill for the relief of Jos White: committed. Same cmte-committed-relief: of John Tucker; of Josiah S Little; of Anthony Rankin, of Tenn; of Jabez B Rooker; of John M McIntosh; of Peter Grover; & of Isaac Cook & others. Same cmte: bill for the relief of Sally T Matthews: committed. Same cmte: bill for the relief of Moses Noble: committed. Same cmte: bill for the relief of Jos C G Kennedy; of Abraham Kintzing; & of the sureties of Danl Wilson: committed. 3-Cmte on Naval Affairs: bill for the relief of Thos B Steele, passed assistant surgeon in the U S Navy: committed.

In Providence, on Sunday, a little girl about 2 years of age, Anna Bergman, was so severely burnt by the upsetting of a fluid lamp that she died the next day.

Mrd: on Jul 10, in Wash City, by Rev G W Samson, John H Tretler to Miss Fannie Dougherty, both of Wash City.

Mrd: on Jul 10, in Wash City, at St Paul's Lutheran Church, by Rev J G Butler, J Alexander Gregory, of Md, to Maria L Starbuck, of Wash.

Died: on Jul 9, in Gtwn, aged 9 months, Eva Kate, infant daughter of Gustavus & Kate M Harrison.

Died: on Jul 9, in Wash City, infant daughter of Geo W & Josephine Hodges. [No name given.]

Trustee's sale of valuable property: on Jul 16, on the premises, lately occupied by Mr Danl Shryer as a Morocco Factory & Sumac concern, 2 large Sumac Mills complete; kettles, dye boxes, oil casks; large tubs; etc. At the same time & place, will be offered the lot, with the bldg thereon, located about 140 feet on Princess st, adjoining the Beverley property, & extending from Princess st to Oronoko st. -Thos Davy, trustee N.B. The title is believed to be indisputable, but I convey only such title as is vested in me as Trustee. [Gtwn Advocate]

MON JUL 14, 1856

Valuable market farm [belonging to & occupied for the past 14 years by the late Ninian Beall] for sale, lying in Wash & Montg Counties, about 3 miles from Gtwn: farm contains about 54 acres; the improvements are a good & nearly new 2 story framed dwlg-house, with back bldg, a cottage for overseer or gardener, barn, stable, corn-house, spring house, chicken houses, & cowpen & stable. Apply to the subscriber, 120 Bridge st, Gtwn, D C. -Geo W Beall, for the heirs -Barnard & Buckey, aucts

Great excitement at Brighton, Mass, on Thu, by an attempt made to blow up the house of Thos Wethern, a butcher. A keg of powder was placed in the cellar & exploded causing great destruction to the house & kitchen. The family was sleeping in the chambers, & escaped injury. No clue is found to the perpetrators of the diabolical outrage.

Trustee's sale of house & lot at auction: on Aug 13 next, by deed of trust from Robt Clark & wife to the subscriber, dated Apr 30, 1849, recorded in Liber J A S No 4, folios 199 to 203, of the land records of Wash Co, D C: sale of the west part of lot 1 & part of the east part of said lot, in square 928, with a good brick house, situated on south K, between 8th & 9th sts, Wash City, D C. -Walter Lenox, Henry Naylor, trustees -A Green auct

The Cincinnati "Columbian" announces the death on Jul 10, in his 65th year, of Prof John Locke, long & favorably known for his unremitting & profound researches in the cause of science. He was a graduate of Yale College at an early age; he invented the famous magnetic clock, still in use in the Observatory at Wash; he came West in 1826, & at first established a female academy in Lexington, Ky, where Henry Clay's daughters were among his pupils. He moved to Cincinnati & opened a similar institution. He became Prof of Chemistry & Pharmacy with the Ohio Medical College in 1836. In 1853, broken in health, he retired to a quiet life.

On Sunday morning, Jul 6, Miss Eleanor & Jane Comstock, daughters of Mr Levi Comstock, of Grenadier Island, near Chippeway Bay, were upset in a skiff while proceeding from the island to the bay, & were drowned. They were 18 & 22 years of age respectively. -Ogdensburgh Republican

Academy of the Visitation, B V M, Gtwn, D C: Annual Distribution of Premiums was held on Jul 9, the premiums were distributed by Rt Rev Richd P Wheelan, assisted by Rt Rev John McGill & Rev B A Maguire, S J, Pres of Gtwn College. Premiums were distributed to the following students:

Caroline Davis, N Y
Susan Savage, Wash, D C
Frances Beckham, Warrenton, Va
Rosa Cole, of Balt Md
Anna Evans, San Antonio, Texas
Gale Evans, Marshall, Texas
Alice Murray, Gtwn, D C
Martha Smith, Middleburg, Va
Priscilla Neale, Chas Co, Md
Amelia Lancaster, Wash, D C
Laura Ridgely, Balt, Md
Anna Horne, Milledgeville, Ga
Lolula Johnson, Milledgeville, Ga
Hannah Mabee, Ohio
Elviana Moore, Louisiana
Mary Hinton, Petersburg, Va
Lavinia Clements, Gtwn, D C
Mary Pizzini, Richmond, Va
Ada Semmes, Gtwn, D C
Mary Duncan, Montg, Ala
Anna Le Compte, Norfolk, Va
Martha Bisselle, Wash, D C
Adelaide Frederick, Augusta, Ga
Kate Potter, Binghamton, N Y
Mary Dooley, Richmond, Va
Jane Poe, Gtwn, D C
Kate Smith, Reading, Pa
Maria Briscoe, Wash, D C
Lucy Rainey, Gtwn, D C
Amanda Payne, Gtwn, D C
Alice Edelin, St Mary's Co, Md
Alecia Evans, Marshall, Texas
Cleorah Palmer, Montg Co, Md
Bena Gilliam, Dinwiddie Co, V
Florence Poe, Gtwn, D C
Agnes Hays, Opelousas, La
Caroline Hickey, Wash, D C
Kate D Miller, Raleigh, N C
Cecilia Coad, St Mary's Co, Md
Leila Bonner, of Columbus, Ga
Nora Bonner, of Columbus, Ga
Vandalia Lancaster, Wash, D C
Susan Plowden, St Mary's Co, Md
Louisa Jamieson, Martinsburg, Va
Fannie Evans, San Antonio, Texas
Louisa Keigan, New Orleans, La
Maria Bradley, Wash, D C
Marion Harrison, Wash, D C
Pauline Seymour, Gtwn, D C
Jeannie Springer, Cincinnati

Mary Bowie, PG Co, Md
Helena Ward, Balt, Md
Lizzie Price, Wash, D C
Josephine Hurdle, Gtwn, D C
Mary Sis, Gtwn, D C
Georgiana Gray, Gtwn, D C
Catharine Ghearity, Gtwn, D C
Emma Malbon, Gtwn, D C
Kate Suit, Gtwn, D C
Ellen Potter, Binghamton, N Y
Mary Callan, Gtwn, D C
Mary Fowler, Gtwn, D C
Mary Moxley, Gtwn, D C
Lilla Barbarin, Gtwn, D C
Mgt Kengla, Gtwn, D C
Virginia Payne, Gtwn, D C
Mary Kelly, Albemarle Co, Va
Mary Waring, Montg Co, Md
Alice Knight, Gtwn, D C
Josephine Herron, Gtwn, D C
Teresa Favier, Wash, D C
Ellen Potter, Bingham, N Y
Anna Pickrell, Gtwn, D C
Sarah Thorington, Iowa
Cecilia O'Donnoghue, Gtwn, D C
Charity Southern, Gtwn, D C
Laura Laub, Gtwn, D C
Emily Long, Northampton, N C
Lucinda Clements, Chas Co, Md
Ellen Kelly, Albemarle Co, Va

Clementina McWilliams, Cobb Neck, Md
Helen Clements, Gtwn, D C
Mary Jane Cannon, Wash, D C
Alice Knowles, Gtwn, D C
Mary Ellen Smith, PG Co, Md
Naomi Thorington, Iowa
Mary Rainey, Gtwn, D C
Mary Hinton, Petersburg, Va
Mary Delaigle, Augusta, Ga
Thersa Keigan, New Orleans, La
Fanny Marquis, Phil
Rose O'Connell, Balt, Md
Celestia Semmes, PG Co, Md
Victoria Moreno, Pensacola, Fla
Ella Bibb, Gtwn, D C
Pauline Seymour, Gtwn, D C
Jennie Springer, Gtwn, D C
Clara Crouse, Lynchburg, Va
Kate Tierney, Gtwn, D C
Virginia Cooledge, Gtwn, D C
Emma Lubert, Phil
Anita Lubert, Phil
Mgt Edelin, Wash, D C
M Dorsey, Gtwn, D C
Octavia Prudhomme
Elviana Moore, Louisiana
Rosa Cole, Phil, Penn

Mrd: on Jul 9, in Richmond, Va, by Rev J Peterkin, Mr F Plummer Hobson to Annie J, daughter of Hon Henry A Wise, Govn'r of Va.

Died: on Jul 12, in Wash City, Mary Pauline, infant daughter of S B & Maria Louisa Boarman, aged 8 months & 14 days.

Died: on Jul 4, at Urbana, Fred'k Co, Md, Henry Becket, aged 7 months, son of Purser T P McBlair, U S Navy.

Died: on Jul 13, in Gtwn, Mary Frances, eldest daughter of Capt C K & Helen M Stribling, in her 30th year. Her funeral will be from the residence of her brother, Mr C Stribling, Gay & Green sts, Gtwn, D C, tomorrow at 6 o'clock P M.

I O O F: regular meeting of the R W Grand Lodge of D C, this evening at 7½ o'clock. -J Thos Bangs, Grand Sec

TUE JUL 15, 1856
Sale by order of the Orphans Court of Wash Co, D C, of fishing tackle, seines, & boats, at auction on Jul 23: belonging to the estate of Thos W Perkins, deceased: at the residence of Mr Henry Perkins, at **Blue Plains**, known as the **Head of Frazier**. -Mary A Perkins, admx -A Green auct

Trustee's sale of house & lot at auction: on Aug 14, by deed of trust from Thos D Allen & wife to the subscribers, dated Dec 4, 1849, recorded in Liber J A S No 9, folios 267 thru 273, in the land records in Wash Co, D C: sale of lot 8 in square 436, together with a good house thereon: property at 8th & F st. -Walter Lenox, Henry Naylor, trustees -A Green auct

Senate: 1-Ptn from Geo E Hand, U S Atty for the district of Michigan, asking compensation for his services in prosecuting trespassers on the public lands in that State. 2-Ptn from Passed Assist Surgeon Jas Sudders, asking to be allowed the difference between the amount of pay of assist surgeon & passed assist surgeon from May 17, 1851, to Apr 9, 1856. 3-Ptn from the citizens of Michigan, asking that the pension granted to Hon Henry Fitzgerald, wounded at the battle of Lundy's Lane, in the war of 1812, may be extended to his children. 4-Cmte on Military Affairs: bill for the relief of the heirs of the late Col John Hardin: recommended that it do not pass. Same cmte: asked to be discharged from the consideration of the memorial of Thos O Seeley, & that it be referred to the Court of Claims: agreed to. Same cmte: adverse report on the memorial of Maj Jas Belger. Same cmte: asked to be discharged from the consideration of the ptn of Brvt Col John L Gardner: which was agreed to. 5-Cmte on Pensions: bill for the relief of Jos Hill. 6-Cmte on Private Land Claims: bill for the relief of Ambrose Lanfear, of Louisiana, & asked its immediate consideration: bill was passed. 7-Bill for the relief of Jas R Powell: passed. 8-Bill for the relief of Eliza P McNiel: passed.

Died: on Jul 11, at Lexington, Va, Mrs Matilda Ratcliff, of Wash City, aged 45 years.

Died: on Jul 14, in Wash City, Harriet Farrel, infant daughter of Otis W & Harriet E Marsh, aged 10 months & 12 days. Her funeral is this morning at 9 o'clock, from the residence of her parents at 391 N Y ave, between 12th & 13th sts.

From Calif, Jul 14. The following have been arrested & were awaiting trial: Thos B Cunningham, the murderer of Col Weymouth, of New Orleans; Thos Mullory, highwayman; Bill Lewis, ballot-box stuffer; Robt Lipsey & Philander Bruce, murderers. The Vigilance Cmte number some 1,000 men armed with revolvers.

Fireboard prints & paperhanging of every description executed with skill & punctuality, in city or country. -John Markriter, 500 7th st.

Public sale, by decree of the Circuit Court of St Mary's Co, Md, in Equity: sale on Aug 19, at the court-house door in Leonardtown, St Mary's Co, Md: that beautiful farm in said county, called **Smithwood**, the late residence of Elwiley Smith, deceased, containing about 400 acres, more or less. -Fred'k Stone, trustee

WED JUL 16, 1856
The Buffalo Commercial of Fri mentions the drowning of 3 persons: Wm Ray, aged 22, drowned in one of the slips; McConner, an Irishman, drowned in the canal slip; & a girl named Kelly drowned in Buffalo creek.

Senate: 1-Memorial from Wm Ramsay, late a captain in the U S Navy, dropped by the action of the late Naval Board. The memorialist sets forth a service of 43 years, having entered the service shortly after the declaration of war. 2-Memorial of J Horsford Smith, late U S Consul at Beirout, Syria, asking an increase of compensation for his services as counsul & for incidental services. 3-Ptn from Lt J W A Nicholson, of the navy, asking compensation for services performed as master on board the U S ship **Princeton** in 1844 & 1856. 4-Ptn from J W Sullivan, of Calif, asking to be compensated for losses sustained by him in consequence of repeated failures of the great Southern mail. He deposes he has lost $12,351 from Oct 9, 1854, to Mar 19, 1856. 5-Ptn from Wm Russell, asking compensation for property destroyed while occupied as a military post by the U S in Florida. 6-Cmte of Claims: bill for the relief of Salvador Accardi: to be printed. 7-Cmte on the Post Ofc & Post Roads: act for the relief of Jas M Goggin: recommended its passage.

Calif Chronicle: on Jul 5 Wm Mulligan, C P Duane, Billy Carr, John Bulger, Woolley Kearny, & Martin Gallagher, who were proved to have stuffed votes in the ballot boxs, & dangerous characters, were sent out of the country by the Vigilance Cmte, partly by the steamer **Golden Age**. On Jul 6 John Crowe, Jas Hennessey, Jno Lawler, Jas Cusick, J W Bagley, Wm Hamilton, Wm alias Jack McGuire, & Terrence Kelly, looked upon as suspicious characters, have also received orders to leave Calif. On Jul 9, Gen Sherman resigned his commission as Major General of militia.

House of Reps: 1-Memorial of Martha Elliott, widow of Saml Elliott, praying a pension for wounds received by her husband in the war of 1812.

Mrd: on Jul 14, in Balt, Md, by Rev Thos Foley, Martin P King to Alice Virginia, daughter of the late Alexius Simms, all of Wash City.

Died: on Jul 13, at the Infirmary, in Wash City, Miss Ann Hobbs, aged between 60 & 70 years.

Died: yesterday, in Wash City, after a long & painful illness, Mrs Mgt Ann Thompson, wife of Wm H Thompson, & daughter of Mgt Delaney. Her funeral will be from the residence of her mother, on C st, between 13th & 13½ sts, this afternoon at 3 o'clock.

Toronto, Jul 15. Richd Metcalf House, alias Richd Stanford Graves, was brought before the Chief Justice of the Court of Common Pleas under the Ashburton extradition treaty, charged with being a defaulter to the State of Mississippi to the amount of nearly $200,000. He was formerly treasurer of that State, but has been a resident here for 15 years. After full examination he was discharged, the judge holding that the treaty does not provide for embezzlement. House has been a magistrate here for 10 years, & owns considerable property.

For sale: the real estate of the late I Jos Jones, in PG Co, on the Balt & Wash Railroad, within a quarter of a mile of the Beltsville depot: tract contains between 400 & 500 acres. Apply to Luther D Jones, or to Geo & Thos Parker, of Wash.

THU JUL 17, 1856
Unreserved sale of an extensive assortment of foreign & domestic dry goods: on Jul 22, at the store of Jas L White, 8th & Market space, all his stock in trade.
-Jas C McGuire, auct

Naval Promotions: The Senate's Executive session yesterday confirmed the promotions of Cmder G J Pendergrast & Cmder W C Nicholson, to be captains.

A San Francisco paper gives the following as the results of the labors of the Cmte of Vigilance of San Francisco up to Jun 20. Jas P Casey, & Chas Cora: executed. Yankee Sullivan, committed suicide. C P Duane, Wm Mulligan, & Woolley Kearny: shipped on the ship **Golden Age**. Bill Car, Martin Gallagher, & Edw Bulger: sent to the Sandwich Islands. Jim Burke, alias Activity, ran away. Peter Wightman, Ned McGowan, & Jim White: ran away. John Crowe, left on the ship **Sonora**. Bill Lewis, Terrance Kelley, John Lawler, T B Cunningham, Alex Purple, Jas Hennessey, Tom Mulloy, Frank Murray, Jas McGuire, Wm Hamilton, & Philander Brace, shipped on the ship **Sierra Nevada**. Jas Busick, ordered to leave, but refused to go. J W Bagley-no information.

Senate: 1-Ptn from Thos Quantrell, an ofcr in the war of 1812, asking to be allowed arrears of pension. 2-Ptn from Christine Barnard, widow of an army ofcr, asking for a renewal of her pension. 3-Ptn from Rachel Posey, widow of a Revolutionary soldier, asking a pension. 4-Ptn from Wm J Hubard, asking to be allowed to place in the Capitol at Washington a facsimile of Hudon's statue of Washington, now at Richmond, Va.

After the publication of this notice for 6 weeks, application will be made to the Com'r of Pensions for the issue of a duplicate of Warrant No 48,908, for 120 acres, act of Mar 3, 1855, issued to Nancy Norwood, widow of Croxton Norwood; the same having been lost, & a caveat against its location entered in the Gen Land Ofc.
-J T Stevens, atty, Wash, D C

Notice. R B Donaldson, Dentist, will be absent from Wash City until Aug 18.

Sunday afternoon a very sad accident occurred at Cohoe, N Y. Two little girls named Harvey, while playing on the bridge which crosses the canal in that village, fell from it into the water & were drowned. One was 9 & the other 4 years of age.

Died: on Jul 15, in Wash City, Eben Sage Stevens, son of the late Com Stevens, U S navy, in his 23rd year. His funeral will be this afternoon at 5 o'clock, from the residence of Mrs G S Oldfield, 151 F st, between 19th & 20th sts.

Died: on Jul 16, in Wash City, Robt I, eldest son of the late H Allen Taylor. His funeral will take place this evening at 4:45 o'clock from the residence of his grandmother, Mrs Robt I Taylor, in Alexandria.

Died: on Jul 13, in Wash City, Mrs Sarah S Baden, in her 46th year.

Orphans Court of Wash Co, D C. Letters testamentary on the personal estate of Richd Gibson, late of Wash Co, deceased. -Sarah Gibson, excx

FRI JUL 18, 1856
New book: "A New Chapter in the Life of Washington," by Col John Pickell, of Md. The author is a Director of the Chesapeake & Ohio Canal Company, having a joint control with his associates over the original papers of the old Potomac Company. This company was chartered to execute an internal improvement project which should facilitate communication between the East & West. The object of that company was warmly favored by Washington, as a means of strengthening the bonds of unions between the 2 sections of the country divided by the Alleghany Mountains; & he acted as its President from 1784, when it was organized, during a period of 4 years.
-Journal of Commerce

We learn from Vera Cruz that Lt A J Gwin, of the U S revenue service, has been missing from his hotel since Jul 13, & fears are entertained by his friends that he is no more. Lt Gwin is a nephew of Dr Gwin, late member of the U S Senate from Calif.
-Boston Post

Mrd: on Jul 16, in Wash City, in the Western Presbyterian Church, by Rev T N Haskell, Mr Ephraim K Wilson to Miss Kate B Steiger, all of Wash City.

Senate: 1-Memorial from Geo Washington Greene, asking that Congress may take a certain number of copies of the correspondence of Maj Gen Greene, commencing at the camp before Boston in 1775 & coming down to the close of the war. The memorialist says the undertaking will involve an expense far beyond his means, & for that reason he asks the assistance of Congress for what he considers may be justly styled a work of great national interest. 2-Ptn from Geo Colvin, asking to be allowed a pension on account of injuries sustained while in the military service of the U S. 3-Ptn from John H Piatt, one of the reps of Lewis Piatt, asking to be allowed a pension on account of the services of his father during the Revolution. 4-Ptn from Robt M Stratton & others, asking that they may be authorized to contract with the Gov't for conveying the U S Mails between N Y, St Thos, Barbadoes, Demarara, & Para, in first class steamers. 5-Additional paper in the case of J Horsford Smith: presented. 6-Resolved, that the finding of the late Naval Board, approved & executed by the Pres of the U S, in the case of Lt Washington Bartlett, violated the constitutional rights of the accused, & is therefore null, void, & of no effect.

Wm J Clark informs his numerous friends & patrons in this District & elsewhere that he has relinquished all connexion with the Gtwn Female Seminary, over which he has presided during the last 4 years, & has assumed charge of St Anne's Episcopal Institute for young ladies in Wash City.

Mrd: on Jul 16, in Wash City, in the Western Presbyterian Church, by Rev T N Haskell, Mr Ephraim K Wilson to Miss Kate B Steiger, all of Wash City.

Died: on Jul 14, at the residence of her cousin, Judge Allen, in Botetourt Co, Va, Miss Mary E Cutts, of Wash City, daughter of the late Richd Cutts. [Jul 24th newspaper: includes a poem entitled, "On the death of Miss Mary E Cutts," by Sheelah.]

Terrible disastrous railroad collision. Phil, Jul 17. As an excursion train of the children of St Michael's Roman Catholic Church, in Kensington, was proceeding on the North Penn railroad this morning, it came in collision with the down train. Six cars were entirely demolished. Among the killed are Rev Danl Sheridan, chorister of the church, Hugh Campbell, Mary Lelly, Jas McIntire, John Dogan, Edw Hall, John Rivers, Jas Hickey, Wm Barnard, Henry Haines, Mary McDelain, Catherine McGurk, Ellen Clark, Sarah McGrugan, Catherine McGrugan,] Kate McGirr, John Brady, Mgt Meany, John McGuire, Jas Carney, & Henry Harrison, engineer of the up train. Wm Vaustavern, the conductor of the down-train, has committed suicide by swallowing arsenic. Wm Lee, the engineer, of the same train, has been arrested & committed for examination. [Jul 19th newspaper: Mr Wm Swaim was at Chestnut Hill, about 3 miles distant, when the disaster occurred. He immediately hastened to the spot. At least 53 were killed on the spot, & the wounded exceeded 100.]

Died: on Jul 16, in Wash City, Jos Dudley Ward, formerly of Onslow Co, N C, but for the last 25 years a resident of Wash. He had been a very popular & efficient member of the Legislature of his native State, & filled various posts under the Gov't here. His brethren of the Masonic fraternity took charge of his remains & accompanied them to the last resting place of man. May he rest in peace!

SAT JUL 19, 1856

Harvard Univ Annual Commencement was held on Jul 16. Among the graduates are Mr Robt G Thrift, of Md, & Mr Richd Archer, of Va, upon whom the degree of L L B was conferred. The honorary degree of Dr of Laws was conferred upon Hon John Jas Gilchrist, Judge of the Court of Claims in Wash City.

Oliver Nash, an intelligent & respectable citizen of South Amherst, fell from a load of hay on Wed last, & almost instantly expired. He was about 70 years of age.

Senate: 1-Ptn from the widow of John D Prescott, a soldier of the war of 1812, asking to be allowed a pension. 2-Cmte of Claims is to appoint an agent to receive proof as to the claims of individuals described in the memorials of Geo M Weston, Com'r of Maine, to be reported to Congress at its next session. 3-Cmte on Private Land Claims: bill for the relief of John Dick, of Fla; & for the legal reps of Manuel Gonzales Moro. Also, bill for the relief of Andrew A H Knox & Jos C Campbell, of the State of Louisiana. Same cmte: bill for the relief of John Temple, of Louisiana. Also, bill giving to Joshua Kirby & the widow of John McNary the right to enter the land covered by the life reserve of John McNary, under the Cherokee treaties of 1817 & 1819, with an amendment.

Died: on Jul 18, in Wash City, W W Curran. His funeral is this evening at 5 o'clock, from his late residence, Capitol Hill, north side.

Died: on Jul 15, in Wash City, of consumption, Alex'r Moran, formerly of Chas Co, Md.

Died: on Jul 13, in Randolph, Vt, of paralysis, Chauncey H Hayden, aged 85 years.

Died: on Jul 17, near Balt, Mrs Sarah A Connolly, wife of John F Connolly, aged about 42 years.

Died: Jul 18, in Wash City, Harriet, aged 14 months & 13 days, daughter of W H West, of the Treasury Dept.

Kingston, [C W] Jul 18. The propeller **Tinto** was burnt to the water's edge yesterday off Windmill Point. 12 lives were lost, including Capt Campbell & Mrs Harrison.

Wash City Ordinances: 1-Act for the relief of Maurice Holloran: to pay him $15, for cleaning a sewer, said sewer having been ordered to be cleaned by Geo W Harkness, former Com'r of the 2nd Ward. 2-Act for the relief of Chas Steedman: to pay him $9.37, taxes he erroneously paid.

MON JUL 21, 1856

The steamer **Northern Indiana**, which left Buffalo for Toledo on Wed, took fire on Thu, when off Point au Pelee. The steamer **Mississippi** & propeller **Republic** were near at hand & the former took off most of the passengers & crew & carried them to Detroit. Passengers known to be lost: Sewell Turner & Danl Gray, of Rome, Maine; Michl Burke & Thos Farre, firemen, of Buffalo; Mrs Eliza Blanchard, of Augusta, Me; Henry Nims & child, of Tully, N Y; Augustine Fulvalle, of Buffalo; Geo Dawson, of Brookport, N Y; Mrs Mary Ledyard, of England; Mrs Mary Ackroyds, her father, mother, husband, & 2 children, of England; G Smith, of Buffalo; Eugene Cary & child, of Greenbush, Wis; Miss Jenning, of Waverley, Ill; Hezekiah Thomas, of Buffalo; Nichlas Commerford, of Rochester; a lady & child of Louisville.

Richmond [Va] Despatch: on Fri week, Mr Wm M Kelley, of Caroline Co, was suddenly roused from his sleep, &, under the impression his house was being broken into, as he thought, entering the door; but, to his horror, he found he had shot his wife, who was fastening it. Two physicians were called but she was beyond hope. She died on Sat, leaving an almost distracted husband, an infant son 11 months old, & a large number of relatives & connexions to mourn her loss.

House of Reps: 1-Cmte of Claims: adverse report on the ptn of Edw L Norfolk, of Mass. 2-Cmte on Commerce: bill for the relief of Solomon Hopkins: committed. 3-Cmte on Public Lands: bill granting bounty land to Jared L Elliott: committed. Same cmte: bill for the relief of Francis Wlodecki: committed. Same cmte: bill granting bounty land to Jonathan Lambert, of Duke Co, Ohio, with a recommendation that it do not pass. Same cmte: bill for the relief of Mark & Richd H Bean, of Ark: committed. 4-Cmte on Revolutionary Claims: bill for the relief of Nancy D B Holker: committed. Adverse reports on the ptns of the heirs of Col Ethan Allen & of Jane W Ballard, widow of John Osgood Ballard. Same cmte: bill for the relief of the heirs of Alex'r Stephenson, a soldier of the Revolutionary war: committed. Joint resolution in favor of J W Nye: committed. Same cmte: joint resolution for J W Nye, assignee of Peter Bargy, jr, & Hugh Stewart: committed. 5-Cmte on Private Land Claims: bill to confirm the title of Ethan Ray Clark & Saml Ward Clark to certain lands claimed under a grant from the Spanish Gov't, & a bill for the relief of Roswell Minard: committed. 6-Ptn of Thos L Disharoon, reported adversely on, was re-referred to the Cmte on Private Land Claims, additional evidence having been presented in the case. 7-Cmte on Military Affairs: bills committed: relief of John C McConnell; & of Jos McClure, a paymaster in the war of 1812. Same cmte: bill for the relief of A S Bender & for the relief of Jas Davison, of Ky: committed. Also, bill for the relief of

John A Sims, adm of L Sims & Brother: committed. Same cmte: bill for the relief of F A Cunningham, paymaster in the U S Army; relief of Jesse Morrison, of Ill; relief of Anne E Bronaugh, widow of the late John W Bronaugh; relief of Antoine Robidoux; & relief of Wm Kendall: committed. 8-Cmte on Naval Affairs: adverse reports on the ptns of Moses Davis, of Portland, Maine, & Isaac Cobb, of Cape Elizabeth, Maine. Bills for the relief of Geo P Marsh & of J Randolph Clay: committed. 9-Cmte on Territories: bill for the relief of Richd H Weightman: committed. 10-Cmte on Revolutionary Pensions: bill providing an increase of pension to Danl Waldo, of Onondaiga Co, N Y; pension to Benj Berry, a soldier of the Revolution; relief of Hannah F Nile; granting a Revolutionary pension to Sarah Blount; bill for the relief of Rebecca Horsey, widow of Zephaniah Horsey, an ofcr of the Revolution; relief of Maria Burgher, widow of Jeremiah Burgher, deceased, a Revolutionary soldier; bill for the relief of Letty Griggs, widow of Simeon Griggs, a Revolutionary soldier; & relief of the surviving children of John Gibert, a Revolutionary soldier: all committed. 11-Cmte on Invalid Pensions: bill for the relief of Lewis Hembert. It proposed to increase from $8 to $16 per month the pension of Hembert, who lost both legs in the Mexican war: passed. Same cmte-relief: of Richd Philips; of Mary Kirby Smith; of Sarah Hildreth; of Jas M French, of N Y C; of Isaac P Washburne; of Nehemiah Ward; of Anthony W Bayard; of Wm Craig; of Geo W Whitten; of Jas A Glanding; of Edw Rumery; of Geo Cassady; of Cornelius H Latham; of Robt H Stevens; & of Nancy Bowen & Sarah Larrabee. Bill granting a pension to Thos Allcock, of Rochester, N Y. Bill for the relief of the heirs-at-law of Sarah Crandall, deceased: committed. Bill granting a pension to Nancy M Gunsally, formerly widow of Lyman M Richmond, deceased: committed. Bill granting 5 years' half-pay to Mrs Ann Turner, widow of Elbert Turner, deceased: committed. Same cmte: bill for the relief of Henry Stewart; & relief of Danl Doland: committed. Same cmte: adverse reports on the ptns of Lanson Jones, Wm Baird, & F B F Martin. Same cmte: bills for the relief of Isaac Langley & of Jonathan Cilley: committed. Same cmte: bill directing the payment of arrearages of pension due Simeon Smith, deceased, late a pensioner of the U S, to his heirs at law: committed. Bill for the relief of Roxana Kimball; of Mrs Rachel McMillan; of Wm Kingsbury; & relief of Lemuel Worster: committed. 12-Cmte on Commerce: bill to indemnify Henry Leef & John McKee for illegal seizure of a certain barque: committed. 13-Cmte on Patents: bill for the relief of Edwin Stevens; & relief of Jos Nock: committed. 14-Cmte on Indian Affairs: bill for the relief of Geo D Dousman, one of the securities for Wm H Bruce, late sub-Indian agent at Green Bay, Wisc: committed. 15-Cmte of Elections: bill for the relief of Abelard Guthrie: committed. 16-Bill for the relief of the heirs & legal reps of Danl Renner & Nathl H Heath was considered & discussed. 17-Mr Jones, of Tenn, rose & remarked that it was known to most of the members that Mr Curran, jr, some years the head of the Globe reporters of the House, died yesterday, & that his funeral would take place this evening. His friends were desirous of attending the funeral & the House adjourned.

Though we cannot name the first Spanish discoverer of ***Chesapeake Bay***, still there is no doubt that it was known to the Spaniards already in the first half of the 16th century, under the name of Bahia de Sta Maria, [St Mary's bay.] The most remarkable Spanish exploration of this bay is that of Pedro Menendez Marquez, a nephew of Pedro Menendez de Aviles, who surveyed in the year 1573 the whole Atlantic coast from Cape Florida to St Mary's Bay, who made a pretty good report on this bay. The new name was spelled & changed in many different ways. Milineux, an English geographer of the time of Queen Elizabeth, on his Globe, 1592, writes Chesepiook; Purchas writes Chesepioc; & calls the bay also sometime "The Bay of Chesapian." Whtflieth, a Dutch geographer, has on his map, 1597, Chesipook Sinus, [Chesipook Bay.] If not the whole large bay, the entrance was sometimes called the "The Barre of Virginia." Capt John Smith, the father of the new Virginian colony, spelled it Chesapeack, afterwards changed to Chesapeake. The old Spanish name Sta Maria was, however, re-introduced to the bay by the son of Sir Geo Calvert, Lord of Balt, in 1633, when he planted at the northern half of the bay his colony of Terra Sancta Maria, the land of the Holy Mary. It is true that the Calverts chose this name, as they officially stated, in honor of the Queen Henreitta Maria, the wife of Charles. -T G Kohl

Chancery sale: by decree of the Circuit Court of Wash Co, D C, made on Dec 4, 1855, in a cause wherein Christopher S O'Hare & al are cmplnts, & Mary M Prather, admx & al, heirs at law of Overton J Prather, deceased, are dfndnts: public auction on Aug 14 next, in Wash City, lot 60 in square 448; & lot 12 in square 447. Lot 12 fronts on 7th st, between N & O sts, & lot 60 fronts on 6th st, between M & N sts. -A Austin Smith, trustee -A Green auct

Died: on Jul 15, in Columbia, S C, Ruth, the loved & only daughter of Benj F & Emma J Wilkins, in her 5th year.

TUE JUL 22, 1856
Senate: 1-Cmte on Patents & the Patent Ofc: memorial of Eliz Emmons & brothers for leave to apply to the Cmte of Patents for the renewal of the patent of Uriah Emmons, deceased, for an improvement in planing machine, submitted an adverse report on the same. Same cmte: memorial of Nathan Scholfield, asking a renewal of his patent for a machine to regulate the motion of water wheels, submitted a report, accompanied by a bill for his relief. 2-Cmte on Private Land Claims: bill to authorize the legal reps of Pascal L Cerre to enter certain lands in the State of Missouri, reported back the same with an amendment.

Landon Academy & Military Institute will commence on the first Monday in Sept & close on Jul 4th following. References: Col B P Smith, City Hall: Gen R C Weightman, Wash; C W Pairo, Wash; Rev Alfred Holmead, Wash. -J R Jones, Principal, Urbana, Fred'k Co, Md.

U S Patent Ofc, Wash, Jul 21, 1856. Ptn of G W & E B Robinson, of Boston, Mass, praying for the extension of a patent granted to them on Sep 30, 1842, for an improvement in steering apparatus for vessels, for 7 years from the expiration of said patent, which takes placed on Sep 30, 1856. -Chas Mason, Com'r of Patents

Mrd: on Jul 20, in Wash City, at the Assembly's Church, by Rev Andrew G Carothers, Mr Robt Slatford to Miss Mary Jane Lynch, both of Wash City.

Died: on Jul 18, in Wash City, Ann Eliz, only child of Prof Wm E & Harriett L Jillson, aged 1 month & 10 days.

Died: on Jul 19, in Wash City, Margaret, wife of Alex'r Gau, of the Prussian Legation, & daughter of the late Jas Campbell, of N Y.

Cincinnati, Jul 21. Wm Arrison was today convicted of manslaughter on the third trial, for causing the death of Mr Allison by the explosion of an infernal machine about 2 years since. Great dissatisfaction is expressed with the verdict. The sentence will be deferred, & he will be put on trial for the murder of Mrs Allison, & application will be made for a change of venue.

Yellow Sulphur Springs, Montgomery Co, Va, is open for the reception of visiters. -Fowks, Edmundson & Gardner

Valuable coal lands for sale, by decree of the Circuit Court of Kanawha Co, entered by consent in the cause therein pending, in which the administrator of the estate of Jas E Couch & others are cmplnts, & Geo H Warth & others are dfndnts: sale on Aug 22, in front of the house of Ruffner, Hale & Co, in the **Kanawha Salines**, the following: one equal third part of the Salt & Coal property of Warth & English, estimated about 400 acres, on which Job English now resides, which third of said tract of 400 acres lies on the lower side of the river, & adjoining the salt property of Jas H Fry. And a tract back of the salt property containing about 1,400 acres. The interest of Warth & English in a tract of land containing 19 acress, near the town of Malden. Also, their interest in a tract of 266 acres, being the Geo Alderson survey, adjoining said tract of 19 acres. Also, the interst of Geo H Warth & Co, in the lot of land called the **Beam Lot**, in what is known as the Buzzard Roos' property, in the **Kanawha Salines**.
-Jas M Laidley, N Fitzhugh, C Hedrick

WED JUL 23, 1856
Household & kitchen furniture at auction on: Jul 25, at the residence of the late Mrs Washbourne, on 12th st, between G & H sts. -Jas C McGuire, auct

Orphans Court of Wash Co, D C. Letters of administration on the personal estate of Matilda Radcliff, late of Wash Co, deceased. -Wm F Speake, adm

Senate: 1-Ptn from John W Salyer, a solder of the war of 1812, asking to be allowed a pension for injuries received while in service. 2-Cmte on Naval Affairs: referred the memorial of Washington A Bartlett, submitted with a voluminous report. [This report recommends nothing but simply states the evidence in the case, & recommends that it be printed: which was ordered.]

National Theatre at auction: by deed of trust from Wm H Winder to the subscribers, dated Dec 7, 1850, recorded among the land records of Wash Co, in Liber J A S No 20, folios 220: sale of lots 3 & 4 in square 254, [excepting the part in lot 3 conveyed to Allison Nailor,] together with the bldgs thereon, known as the Nat'l Theatre. The above sale will be subject to a prior trust, given to secure a debt of $7,000, as stated in the deed above cited. -Anthony Hyde, Thos R Suter, trustees -A Green auct

Wash Corp: 1-Ptn from Richd Adams for the remission of a fine: referred to the Cmte of Claims. 2-Ptn from J C Offutt & others for changing an alley into a street: referred to the Cmte on Improvements. 3-Cmte of Claims: asked to be discharged from consideration of the ptn of John H Munroe, asking compensation for a long-boat lost in the Eastern Branch: cmte discharged accordingly.

From the Kingston [C W] News of Jul 19: on Jul 17, the propeller **Tinto**, from Montreal, bound to Lake Erie, passed Kingston harbor when fire was discovered in the firehold, where a quantity of wood was in a blaze, & the flames rapidly spread with great fury to the upper cabins. The only small boat attached to the vessel was immediately manned, & 4 women & 3 children, some of the crew & passengers embarked. The boat was then lowered from the davits, &, owing to the rapid motion of the vessel, on striking the water, immediately capsized, & all are doubtless drowned. The following are their names: Patrick Campbell, master; Alex'r Henderson, engineer; R Lemmon & G Marchand, wheelsmen; Louis ___, fireman; Frank Farmer, Thos Baylis, & Wm McMillen, deck hands; R Kincaid, steward; female cook, name unknown, female friend of the steward, named Sarah ___ supposed to have been betrothed to him; Mr Benton, her nurse & 3 children; a Fench Canadian passenger, named Jaques LeBois, & Nicholas Butler, lamp boy. Among the saved were Mr Benton, late of the Montreal & Champlain Railway, husband to Mrs Benton & father of one of the children, the two other being under his care; Mr W D Handyside, purser, saved by clinging to the rudder for about an hour or more, with 2 other men. The schnr **Mary Adelaide**, Capt Davis, & schnr **Flying Cloud**, Capt ___, hastened to the burning vessel & rescued those floating in the water.

Dr John Potter, one of the most skillful surgeons in the State of N Y, recently dressed a man's arm which had been mutilated in the cog-wheels of some machinery. He called his brother Hazard Potter to assist him. He cut himself accidently, & in a few days the poison from the cut had mingled in his system. He died on Friday. His brother, Hazard, had a slight scratch, & his life is despaired of. -Geneva [N Y] Gaz

Died: on Jul 22, at the residence of Mrs Clark, over the Bank of Wash, Robt Emmett Daily, late of Alabama, in his 19th year, of disease of the heart. The friends & acquaintances of the deceased, of his mother, Mrs E F Sprague, & of Mrs Clark & family, are invited to attend his funeral, from the residence of Mrs Clark, tomorrow at 4 o'clock.

Died: on Jul 20, in Balt, Alice Lee, daughter of the late Philip A L Contee, of Va, & grand-daughter of the late Gov Kent, of Md, aged 18 years.

Died: on Jul 21, in York, Pa, Henry Wise, infant child of Geo D & Laura Wise, aged 5 months & 12 days.

Died: on Jul 19, at Lewenville, Fairfax Co, Va, John Libbey, infant son of Rev B F & C Malvina Bittinger, in his 10th month.

Died: on Jul 21, at Bruington, King & Queen Co, Va, Miss Hannah Chapin, daughter of the late Stephen Chapin, D C.

Farm for sale & dwlg house for rent: farm continuing 167 acres of land; a log dwlg & convenient out bldgs, near Beltsville station. Also, a dwlg house on G st, near 5th sts. Apply for further particulars at 398 D st, near 7th st, second story. -W G Deale

THU JUL 24, 1856
Hon John F May died at his residence in Petersburg, Va, last Monday, in his 72nd year. He was formerly Judge of the Superior Court of the second judicial district. He was father-in-law to Hon Thos H Bayly, whose lamented decease we not long since had the duty of announcing. His bereaved wife has now to mourn the loss of a father as well as her husband.

Promotions in the Navy: confirmed by the Senate on Friday last:
Captains:

G J Pendergrast	Wm W McKean	Wm L Hudson
Wm C Nicholson	Franklin Buchanan	Geo A Magruder
Jos B Hull	Saml Mercer	John Pope
John Kelly	Chas Lowndes	Levin M Powell
Wm H Gardner	L M Goldsborough	Chas Wilkes
David G Farragut	Geo N Hollins	Thos O Selfridge
Stephen B Wilson	Duncan N Ingraham	Henry Eagle
T Aloysius Dornin	John Marston	G J Van Brunt
Rob B Cunningham	Henry A Adams	Wm M Glendy
Victor R Randolph	Wm S Walker	Geo S Blake
Fred'k Engle	Geo F Pearson	Saml Barron
John Rudd	Saml F Du Pont	Andrew A Harwood

Commanders:
Chas H McBlair
John W Livingston
A B Fairfax
Henry K Thatcher
Jas H Rowan
Wm McBlair
John S Misroon
Richd L Page
Fred'k Chatard
Benj J Totten
Arthur Sinclair
Robt B Hitchcock
C H A H Kennedy
Thos W Brent
Jos Lanman
John K Mitchell
Thos Turner
Chas H Poor
Jas F Schenck
Timothy A Hunt
Sylvanus Wm Godon
Wm Radford
Saml F Hazard
John M Berrien
Geo A Prentiss
Alfred Taylor

Lieutenants:
Edw Simpson
Wm G Temple
Geo P Welsh
Saml P Carter
Wm Nelson
Chas W Aby
Edw C Stout
Reuben Harris
Jas B McCauley
Thos S Phelps
Alex F Warley
Garrit V Denniston
Leonard Paulding
Francis S Conover
Edw Barrett

Saml Phillips Lee
John P Gillis
Saml Swartwout
Raphael Semmes
Jas P McKinstry
Oliver S Glisson
John A Dahlgren
Stephen C Rowan
Edw R Thompson
Guert Gansevoort
Chas Green
Edw L Handy
Melancthon Smith
Cicero Price
J R Goldsborough
Chas S Boggs
Theodore P Green
John R Tucker
Thos J Page
Geo Minor
Percival Drayton
Robt F Pinkney
Thos R Rootes
Edw M Yard
Wm S Young
Jos F Green

Colville Terrett
John W Bennett
Homer C Blake
Clark H Wells
S P Quackenbush
Earl English
Jos M Bradford
Reigart B Lowry
Jonathan H Carter
Wm H Parker
J Pembroke Jones
David A McDermot
Wm P Buckner
Richd L Law
Wm H Willcox

John De Camp
Chas W Pickering
Overton Carr
Luther Stoddard
Wm M Walker
John A Winslow
Benj More Dove
Thornton A Jenkins
John Rodgers
John B Marchand
Wm Rogers Taylor
Henr J Hartstene
Benj F Sands
Henry French
Saml Larkin
H S Stellwagen
Jas L Henderson
Danl B Ridgely
Wm T Muse
Chas Steedman
Wm Lewis Herndon
Jas Alden
Augustus L Case
Roger Perry

John T Barrand
Thos Roney
John H Upshur
John Van N Philip
Saml R Franklin
Wm D Whiting
Wm L Powell
S Ledyard Phelps
Edw Y McCauley
Theodore L Walker
Wm Mitchell
Francis A Roe
Jos B Smith
Wm H Murdaugh
John M Brooke

Wm Gibson	Leonard H Lane	L Howard Newman
Edw Renshaw	Milton Haxtum	Chas E Thorburn
Jos D Danels	Robt Selden	Richd T Bowen
John T Walker	Albert Allmand	Chas W Flusser
J C P De Krafft	Robt Stuart	Wm S Lovell
John Van McCollum	Theodoric Lee	John R Eggleston
John E Hart	Geo H Bier	Andrew B Cummings
Oscar C Badger	P G Watmough	Bayard E Hand
Thos C Harris	Geo W Young	Geo E Belknap
John Kell	John H Russell	Edw P Williams
John L Davis	Edw M Stone	Jared P K Mygatt
Alex A Semmes	Dawson Phenix	John D Rainey
John B Stewart	Robt F R Lewis	David B Harmony
M Patterson Jones	Chas P McGary	Wm Gwin
Watson Smith	Hunter Davidson	John J Cornwell
Alex M De Bree	Andrew W Johnson	Jas P Foster
Jos E De Haven	Stephen B Luce	Henry Wilson
Alex W Habersham	Dulany A Forrest	A E K Benham
Wm T Truxton	Robt W Scott	Robt T Chapman
Greenleaf Cilley	Walter W Queen	Wilson McGunnegle
Horace N Crabb	Robt R Carter	John Irwin
Saml Magaw	Edmund W Henry	Jos S Skerrett
Jas H Rochelle	Thos T Houston	Jas A Greer
Robt D Minor	Ralph Chandler	Chas H Green
Wm C West	John R Hamilton	Francis H Baker
N H Van Zandt	Jas Parker	Isaac W Hester
Franics G Dallas	Philip C Johnson	Edw T Spedden
Simeon S Bassett	John Watters	Elias K Owen
Robt C Duvall	K Randolph Breese	Wm T Glassell
David P McKorkle	Oscar F Johnston	Aaron W Weaver
Geo H Hare	Lewis A Kimberly	Austin Pendergrast
Wm Sharp	Beverly Kennon	Jos P Tyffe
Jas I Waddell	S Livingston Breese	Wm P McCann
Wm M Gamble	Geo U Morris	Jas Stillwell
Jonathan Young	Edwin F Gray	Julius G Heileman
Wm K Mayo	John G Sproston	Jos D Blake
Thos Gonng	Bancroft Gherardi	Jas H Gillis
Jas E Jouett	Danl L Braine	
Jos Fry	John Taylor Wood	

Chief Engineers:
*ElLridge Lawton; Robt Danby; Robt Long [*Copied as written.]
Prof of Math: Jos Winlock

Chief of the Bureau of Ordnance & Hydrography of the Navy Dept:
Capt Duncan N Ingraham

Mrs Henrietta Harden died in St Mary's Co, Md, on Jun 29, having attained, it is said the rarely precedented age of 118 years. The Leonardtown Beacon says she was the widow of a Revolutionary Soldier, & as such applied for a bounty land warrant under the act of Congress; but owing to the loss or destruction of marriage records of that early period, & the fact that there was no other person living in the county old enough to bear testimony to such a fact, the old lady was unsuccessful in her application to prove her marriage.

The Phil papers state the entire number of deaths thus far resulting on the North Penn railroad at 63. The following is the most complete list of the dead that has yet been published. Nine of the victims were buried without having been recognized:

Rev Danl Sheridan	Danl Marlow	Bridget McCain
Hugh Campbell	John McGuire	John McVey
Jas McIntire	Mary McErlain	Hugh Tracy
Barney Green	John Grebbens	Lewis Rivel
Sarah McGuigan	Henry Core	Catharine Cokely
John Dugan	Sally McGee	Rosanna Mulholland
John Riners	John McGraw	Patrick Flanigan
Jas Hickey	Sarah McGraw	Thos Kelly
John Brady	Jos Conlin	Michl O'Brian
Wm Barnard	John Devlin	___ Fleury
Henry Harris	Patrick Hickey	Eliz Gunn
John Dudson	John Sloan	Edmund P Gilian
Jas Rey	Francis Wells	Thos Kelly
Jas Hurley	Edw Flannigan	Jas Mulholland
Kate McGurk	Michl Burns	Michl Fras Haggerty
Jas Congdon	___ McAleer	Anna Lilly
Henry Harvey	Caroline M Korsner	
Edw Hall	Jas Gallagher	
Ellen Clark	Lawrence Dillon	

Died: on Jul 15, Edmonia Churchill, aged 5 months & 11 days, only daughter of C St George & Mary E Noland.

Bloomfield Academy, situated in Albemarle Co, Va, will commence on Sep 1 next & close during the last week in June. -P H Goodloe, Principal

Homicide in Gtwn on Wed: adverse partisan feelings have existed for some time between Bernard Magee & Jas Semmes, the latter being a "Know-Nothing," the former a "Democrat." It was the object of Semmes to cut down a Democratic pole reared near the "Twenty Bldgs," which, coming to the knowledge of Magee, he prepared for resisting the assault on the pole. Semmes & another, Hilleary Hutchins, came to cut down the pole, the former standing guard whilst the latter performed the work, & it was in this way that they were were employed when Semmes was shot by Magee, who was posted in his house at the time. The shooting was not fatal, for Semmes rushed to Magee's house & entered it, receiving a second shot, which yet did not kill him. Following Magee up stairs, the latter fired a third & fatal shot. Magee surrendered himself to justice & is now in jail. [Jul 26th newspaper: Political animosity does not appear to have been the cause. A jealousy about business affairs had for some time existed between Magee & Simms.]

Senate: 1-Court of Claims: opinions of said Court on the claims of Wm Neil & others & of H L Thistle, & also the decisions of the Court in favor of the claim of Thos M Newall & the claim of Gibbons & Kelley, accompanied by a bill for the relief of Thos M Newall, & a bill for the relief of Francis A Gibbons & Francis X Kelly; which, on motion of Mr Brodhead, was referred to the Cmte of Claims. 2-Ptn from Rebecca Adams, widow of a soldier, asking to be allowed bounty land. 3-Additional papers submitted in relation to the claim of Geo Colvin. 4-Ptn from Geo H Giddings, contractor for carrying the mail from Santa Fe, Mexico, to San Antonio, Texas, asking compensation for services performed under his contract, & that the compensation now allowed be increased or his contract cancelled. 5-Cmte on Military Affairs: memorial of Dr Chas McCormick, asking compensation for extra services performed by him in New Orleans in 1847 thru 1849, submitted a report, accompanied by a bill for his relief. 6-Cmte on Naval Affairs: resolved-that Surgeon Thos Williamson & Passed Assist Surgeon Jas F Harrison, of the U S Navy, be authorized to accept the gold medals recently awarded to them by the Emperor of France; that Lt M F Maury, of the U S Navy, be allowed to accept the gold medals recently presented to him by the Gov't of Prussia & Holland. 7-Cmte on Naval Affairs: referred the memorial of Lt Wm F Lovell, submitted a report, with a joint resolution authorizing the Sec of Navy to pay to the ofcrs & seamen of the expedition in search of Dr Kane the same rate of pay that was allowed to the ofcrs & seamen of the expedition under Lt De Haven. Same cmte: bill for the relief of Wm Heine. Same cmte: adverse report on the memorials of the chaplins of the navy to have a relative rank assigned them; & also an adverse report on the memorial of Wm Reynolds. 8-Cmte on Indian Affairs: memorial of the heirs of Robt McConnell, asking indemnity for a negro captured & taken away by the Creek Indians in 1813, submitted a report, with a bill for the relief of the heirs of Robt McConnell.

Yesterday a man named Umberfield, whose remaining term of confinement in jail is only about 3 months for an attempt at jail-breaking some time ago, escaped from the bldg by breaking through a bar in the window of the north passage.
[Jul 25th newspaper: Wm Umberfield was captured on the same night, at his own house on 6½ st south, on the Island. He was probably preparing for a start, but he was hopelessly surrounded by a posse, & delivered himself up & was returned to jail.]

Heirs wanted: from the Raleigh [N C] Register: some months ago an old woman, pretending to be an object of charity, came to this city & called upon most of our citizens soliciting alms. Her name was, so she said, Catharine Alberti, & she passed herself off upon the credulous as a fortune teller & a female doctress. On Monday last she died, & among her effects was found money, in gold, silver, & bills, amounting to some $2,000. Also found among her effects were certificates of 20 shares of stock in the New Albany Railroad, evidences of her owning a plantaion in Ky, & a small sign-board with her name painted thereon. If no heir is found her property escheats to the Univ of N C.

Valuable Elkridge farm for sale: by decree of the Circuit Court of Howard Co, passed in a cause in which Mary A Dorsey, et al, were cmplnts, & Alex M Mackey others were dfndnts, the subscribers, as trustees, will offer at public sale at the Exchange, in the city of Balt, on Aug 21 next, the Farm called *Waveland*, in said county, 6 miles of Ellicott's Mills: contains 260 acres; with a well built 2 story brick house 52 feet front, a commodious barn, corn house, dairy, & other out-houses. -Robt J Brent & Wm H G Dorsey, trustees

FRI JUL 25, 1856
Cmdor Robt F Stockton has written a letter withdrawing from the contest for the Presidency. His associate on the ticket, Kenneth Rayner, withdrew some time ago. Messrs Fillmore, Fremont, Buchanan, & Gerrit Smith are the only men now regularly before the people as candidates for the Presidency.

Senate: 1-Court of Claims: bill for the relief of Jos D Beers, of N Y: referred to the Cmte of Claims. 2-Cmte on Foreign Relations: memorial of R P Eldredge, reported a bill for the relief of the ofcrs & privates of the Clinton Guards, of Macomb Co, Mich. 3-Act for the relief of the reps of John Donelson, Stephen Heard, & others: referred to the Cmte on Public Lands.

The oldest Pastor in N Y is Rev Dr Spring, who has presided over Beekman st church for 46 years; Rev Dr Knox, of the Collegiate Church, [Dutch Reformed,] is next, having occupied his present position for 40 years; Rev Dr Seabury is third in respect to time; & Rev Dr Marsellus, of Bleecker st church, fourth.

Hugh Corrigan, convicted in Westmoreland Co, Pa, for the murder of his wife, for which he was under the sentence of death, committed suicide on Sat in his cell in the jail at Pittsburg.

The Ladies' School, Coombe Cottage, Fairfax Court-house, Fairfax Co, Va, under the superintendence of Mrs H M Baker, will re-open on Sep 1, 1856.

Died: on Jul 24, in Wash City, Mr Franklin Edmonston, printer, in his 63rd year. His funeral is this afternoon at 5 o'clock. His friends & acquaintances, the members of the Typographical Society, & printers generally, are respectfully invited.

SAT JUL 26, 1856
Household & kitchen furniture at auction on: Jul 31, at the residence of Rev Geo R Moore, 9th st south, in *Wallach's Row*, near Grace Church. -A Green auct

Senate: 1-Ptn from Edw Hillen & others, asking the passage of an act granting extra pay to the seamen who served in the Gulf squadron as was allowed to those who served in the Pacific squadron during the Mexican war. 2-Cmte of Claims: bill for the relief of Jos D Beers, of N Y C; & of Thos M Newell. Same cmte: to which were referred the decisions of the Court of Claims adverse to the cases of Hezekiah L Thistle, J P McEldery, & Wm W Cox, submitted a resolution confirming the decision of the Court aforesaid: agreed to. 3-Bill for the relief of Jos Hill, a poor mutilated invalid: passed. 4-Bill for the relief of Obed Hussey; of H More & John Hascall or their legal reps; of J E Martin; of Chas Stearns; of Franklin Peale; of John Bronson; & of Jos Graham: passed.

House of Reps: 1-Cmte of Ways & Means: bill for the relief of Franck Taylor: committed. 2-Cmte on the Judiciary: bill for the relief of Pollard Brown, a soldier of the Revolution: committed. Bill for the relief of John T Robertson: committed. Act to provide compensation for the services of Geo Morrill in adjusting titles to land in Michigan: committed. Adverse report on the ptn of A T Pratt. Bill for the relief of John G Camp: committed. Bill for the relief of Robt T Birchett: committed. 3-Cmte on Private Land Claims: bill for the relief of Geo F Baltzell, assignee of Jas Baltzell, & a bill for the relief of John L Vattier: committed. Bill for the relief of Jas L Disharoon, of St Louis, Mo: committed. Bill for the relief of Harriet Peet, child & only heir of John Peet, deceased: committed. Bill for the relief of the heirs of Jaques Godfroy & a bill for the relief of Wm Packwood, a citizen of Wash Territory: committed. 4-Cmte on Military Affairs: Bill for the relief of Saml P Haight: committed. Same cmte; bill granting a pension to Martha Elliott, widow of Saml Elliott, a soldier in the war of 1812; & a bill for the relief of Harriet S Fisher, admx of M W Fisher, deceased; & Richd M Bouton: committed. Same cmte: bill for the relief of Brvt Brig Gen John B Walbach, of the U S Army; & a bill for the relief of Danl Waldo: committed. 5-Cmte on Foreign Affairs: adverse report on the ptn of Robt M

Hamilton, U S Consul at Montevido. 6-Cmte on Invalid Pensions: bills for the relief of Terence Kirby, & of John Draub: committed. Same cmte: bill for the benefit of Wm L Oliver; & bill granting a pension to Franklin W Armstrong, of Hardin Co, Ky: committed. Same cmte: adverse report on the ptn of citizens of Hart Co, Ky, praying that a pension be granted Danl Robinson. Same cmte: bill for the relief of Mary F Swann; of Eliza B McNeil; of Nathan N Lounsbury; of the heirs of Solomon Van Rensselaer; of John Houser; & granting a pension to Mary A M Jones: committed. Same cmte: adverse report on the ptn of John Morrison. 7-Bill for the relief of Chas J Ingersoll: laid on the table. 8-Bill for the relief of Anson Dart: laid on the table. 9-Bill for the relief of Don Piatt: referred to the Cmte on Foreign Affairs. 10-Recommended that they pass: bill for the relief of Edmund Mitchell; of Levi Robinson; of the owners & sharesman of the fishing schnrs **Wanderer, Mary, Olive Branch, Two Brothers, & Brothers**. 11-Bill for the relief of the heirs of Saml Scott; of the legal reps of Zadock Thompson, of Vt; of John Y Laub, a clerk in the ofc of the 1st Comptroller of the Treasury. 12-Recommended that they pass: resolution to pay John Lee $390 in full compensation for 5 horses killed while in the service of the House of Reps: bill for the relief of John Poe, of Louisville, Ky; of John Otis; of Wm Jones; of Wm B Cozzens; of Henry L Robinson; of John Nash; of Robt Mitchell; of the heirs of Wadleigh Noyes, deceased: & settlement of the account of David Gordon. Also, bill to authorize the entry of certain lands in the State of Iowa by Mrs Caroline Newington. 13-Adverse reports from the Court of Claims, with the recommendation that the decision of the Court in each case be confirmed: adverse report in the case of Robt Roberts; of Saml M Pucket; of John P McElderry; of Louis G Thomas & others; of Shepherd Knapp; of Cyrus H McCormick; of Wm W Cox; of J D Holman, exc of Jesse B Holman, deceased; & of John C Hale. 14-Cmte of the Whole: bill for the relief of Calvin Hall, assignee of Wm Jones: passed.

Verdict on the late railroad disaster on the North Penn Railroad: the collision was caused by the criminal negligence of Alfred Hoppel, who, as conductor, was in charge of the excursion train running from Phil to **Fort Washington**, & who carelessly & negilently ran his train beyond the sideling at Edge Hill.

Thos Doughty, the landscape painter, died at N Y on Wed of a softening of the brain. He struggled with poverty through life, & his last days were embittered by want.
-N Y Post

Mrd: on Jul 23, in Wash City, at the Church of the Epiphany, by Rev Mr French, Mr John Tobias to Miss Susan H Keech, daughter of the late Jas Keech, of St Mary's Co, Md.

Died: on Thu, in Gtwn, Dr Peregrine Warfield, in his 77th year. His funeral is this afternoon at 6 o'clock, from his late residence, on Market st.

Teacher wanted: Trustees of the Allegany Co Academy, Cumberland, Md, desire to obtain the services of a Principal. -Thos J McKaig, Pres Board of Trustees

MON JUL 28, 1856

Orphans Court of Wash Co, D C. In the case of Chas S Wallach, adm of Chas W Stewart, deceased: the administrator & Court have appointed Aug 19 next, for the final distribution of the personal estate of said deceased, of the assets in hand. -Ed N Roach, Reg/o wills

Senate: 1-Bill for the relief of the heirs & legal reps of Danl Renner & Nathl H Heath: reported to the House with the recommendation that it do not pass: rejected. 2-Bill for the relief of Peyton G King, late receiver of public money at Monroe, La: recommended that it pass: passed.

Shirley Female Institute, Urbana, Fred'k Co, Md, will open on Sep 3. -Geo G Butler, A M, Principal.

Died: on Jul 26, in her 28th year, Eliz P, wife of Wm A Elliott. Her funeral is this afternoon, at 5 o'clock, from her late residence on 20th st, between G & H sts, First Ward.

Died: on Jul 26, at *Gisboro*, near Wash, Henrietta Brent, infant daughter of John Carroll & Sarah T Brent, aged 22 months & 18 days. Her funeral is this morning at 9 o'clock, at St Peter's Church, Capitol Hill.

Died: on Jul 26, Edmond Henry, infant son of Benj C & Mgt E Ridgate, aged 4 months & 26 days.

TUE JUL 29, 1856

A death in the cars which left Boston on Thu on the Lowell railroad: a male passenger appeared to be in a swoon, & in 5 minutes was dead. The name of John W Bradford, of Keene, N H, was found in his pocket-book.

The Negro, Geo Wilson, who murdered the captain & mate of the schnr **Eudora Imogene** near N Y C last winter, acknowledged his guilt, but subsequently denied it, & died protesting his innocence.

H Corson's Female Collegiate Institution, Wash. Hiram Corson, jr, Principal; Mme Caroline Rollin Corson, Vice Principal: this Institution will commence its 4th session on Sep 15, n w corner of Pa ave & 21st st.

Died: on Jul 24, in Wash City, William Henry, infant son of Richd H & Mary Jane Campbell, aged 28 days.

Information of Thos Ready, of Washington, [Savage, by the mother.] He left his father's house on Jun 23. He worked for some months in the Intelligencer ofc. He is a smart intelligent boy, 14 years old, from 4 feet 7 inches to 4 feet 8 inches high, dark hair & eyebrows, blue eyes, & pretty features. He is the oldest of 6 orphans. Anybody knowing his whereabouts would confer a favor on his disconsolate father by writing to Thos Ready, blacksmith, corner of 4th st & Wash alley, D C, stating all particulars respecting him.

French & English Female Seminary, for boarding pupils, by M A Tyson & Sisters. Seminary is at Alnwick, midway on the Balt & Wash Railroad & Turnpike. The Fall term will commence on Sep 1. For particulars circulars may be had at Dr Tyson's Drug store, corner of 10th & I sts, Wash.

Criminal Court-Wash. The trial of Danl W Jarboe for the shooting of Jas R Nally was resumed yesterday. Wm W Nally, the brother of the deceased, was the first sworn on the part of the prosecution. Deceased was engaged to Miss Jarboe, but broke off the engagement, alleging as the reason criminal inconstancy on her part. Witness, when informed of the state into which his brother's intimacy with Miss Jarboe had brought her, said that if it was true & his brother refused to marry her he was a "d__d rascal." Mrs Susanna Irwin testified to the coming of Jarboe & his sister to her house on May 15, just prior to the shooting. Jarboe looked like a crazy man, & she thought he had broken from the asylum. It was for this reason that she called to have her child taken from the street at the time. His eyes looked as large as her fist. The Court adjourned. [Jul 30th newspaper: Mr Benedict Jarboe, father of the prisoner, testified to the facts of his daughter's engagement with Rufus Nally; they were to have been married last Sept or Oct; time passed, he failed to come up to his promise; & discontinued his visits. His daughter is age 17 years. Mrs Jeffers testified full knowledge of the two young people's engagement. Rufus Nally, when out of work, visited Sarah Jane Jarboe morning, noon, & night. Ignatius Atchison deposed to seeing Rufus Nally on the day of the shooting try to return a pistol to his pocket, after he was shot. The Jury returned a verdict of acquittal. The young man Jarboe was then released & accompanied by his father home.]

Died: on Jul 27, at Weston, of disease of the heart, Mrs Eliza Causten, consort of Jas H Causten, in her 64th year. Her loss will be sincerely mourned not only by her immediate family, but by numerous friends & also by the poor, to whom her charity was freely dispenses. Her funeral will be at St John's Church, today, at 12 M.

Died: on Jul 26, at her residence, near Bladensburg, in her 34th year, Margaret M A, wife of Dionysius Sheriff, of that place, & daughter of the late Marmaduke Dove, of Wash City.

Senate: 1-Ptn from Jos Holman, asking to be allowed bounty land for military services during the Revolution. 2-Ptn from Jas Hall, asking that a contract may be entered into for carrying the mail between the U S & South America & other immediate ports. 3-Ptn from Henry Lucas, asking that certain public land in the State of Alabama may be disposed of at auction, & not by private entry. 4-Ptn from C Vanderbilt, proposing to run a line of steamships between N Y & Southampton, proposing to carry the mail there, & asking compensation for the same. 5-Cmte on Public Lands:asked to be discharged from the consideration of the memorial of Francis Treadwell: which was agreed to. 6-The following House bills were referred to the Cmte of Claims-relief of: Henry L Robinson; of Wm B Cozzens; of Calvin Hall, assignee of Wm Jones; of John Otis; of John Poe, of Louisville, Ky; & of Peyton G King, late receiver of public money at Monroe, La. 7-Act for the relief of Edmund Mitchell: referred to the Cmte on Pensions. 8-Act for the relief of West Drinkwater & others: referred to the Cmte on Finance. 9-Act for the relief of the heirs of Wadleigh Noyes, deceased: referred to the Cmte on Revolutionary Claims. 10-Act directing the settlement of the accounts of David Gordon: laid on the table.

From Calif: 1-Several suicides have taken place, among others that of G H Yates, a writer for the press. 2-Nearly half a dozen murders have happened during the last fortnight. Two murderers, Saml L Garrett & Wm S Kelly, were executed at Sacramento. Three more, Nathan Cottle, Beverly Wells, & John Williams, were convicted & sentenced to death, the first at Jackson, the second at Benicia, & the third in Calaveras Co. 3-Mining & other casualties have been about an average. Dr Dickerson & a young lady, his daughter, were drowned while crossing the Merced river. 4-On Jun 21 an assault with a bowie knife was made by David S Terry, Judge of the Supreme Court, upon Sterling A Hopkins, as the latter, a Vigilance Cmte man, was attempting to arrest one Reuben Maloney. Terry & Maloney fled, but were soon captured. 5-On Jun 22 Dan Aldrich, a notorious gambler & rowdy, was arrested by the Vigilance Cmte, & is now in confinement. 6-On Jun 23 Wm Ford, a law & order man, was found shot in First st, by a man named Wright. Ford is doing well, & the excitement upon the subject died away.

The public are informed that Julian Vannerson is no longer in my employ, & no longer authorized to do business for me. -J H Whitehurst, Daguerrean Gallery, Pa ave.

Book: The Life & Adventures of Jas P Beckwourth, Mountaineer, Scout, & Pioneer & Chief of the Crow Nation of Indians, with illustrations, written from his own dictation, by T D Bonner. Just received & for sale by R Farnham.

WED JUL 30, 1856
San Francisco: Order was issued for the arrest of Jas R Maloney, better known as Reuben Maloney. Terry & Maloney were captured, along with Dr Ashe, Ham, Bowie, & Martin Reese.

Texas: A large body of lawless characters, the Regulators, have killed some of the good citizens of Orange Co & compelled others to leave. They have already killed Dr Mages, Burwell, Alexander, Chas Sexton, John Fielden, & ___ Baxter. The sheriff of the county has been forced to leave, his deputy, Burwell Alexander, having been killed. They attempted to assassinate Mr Hugh Ochiltree, a quiet & most respectable citizen, living at Gree's Bluff, for refusing to join them. He saved himself by last accounts by barricading himself in his own premises. The Govn'r is expected to send a body of men to the scene to put an end to them.

Senate: 1-Ptn from Sarah Adams, asking to be allowed the half-pay & commutation due on account for the services of her father as an ofcr of the Revolution. 2-Ptn from John Ferguson, contractor for carrying the mail from San Francisco to Sacramento, asking to be released from certain liabilities incurred by him in the execution of his contract. 3-Ptn from Louis F Tasistro, asking compensation for services rendered in examing the materials for a new volume of the American archives, under & by direction of the Sec of State. The memorialist states that he had to devote 5 to 6 hours in the afternoons & mornings for several months in discharge of his laborious task, much to the detriment of his health & comfort. 4-Ptn from Algernon S Taylor, asking to be allowed the same difference of pay as an ofcr of the line doing duty in the staff as had been allowed to other ofcrs of marine corps under similar circumstances. 5-Ptn from Maurice K Simons, a soldier wounded in the Mexican war, asking an increase of his pension. 6-Cmte on Military Affairs: bill to continue a pension to the widow of the late Brvt Maj Moses J Barnard, of the U S Army. 7-Bill for the relief of John Nash. 8-Cmte on Patents: bill for the relief of Nathl Hayward. 9-Cmte on the Post Ofc & Post Roads: settlement of the accounts of Chas M Strader & Edw P Johnson, mail contractors: passed. 10-Cmte on Finance: asked to be discharged from the consideration of the bill for the relief of West Drinkwater & others, & from the memorial of Capt John P Montgomery, & that they be referred to the Cmte of Claims: agreed to. 11-Cmte on Naval Affairs: adverse reports on the memorials of Hans Nelson, alias Hans Kunston, & of J P Milton.

Jemmy Johnson, head chief & warrior of the Tonawandas, & who was successor of the celebrated orator, Red Jacket, has died. He had reached a very advanced age. We trust his successor Jabez Grounds, will prove an equally faithful & valuable counselor & friend to his people. -Batavia [N Y] Times, Jul 19

On Monday, Mr Graves on Graves' Station, Chesterfield, while out hunting with his son, by accident, the gun young Graves had on his shoulder fell, & as his father caught the muzzle, it went off, killing the father almost instantly. -Petersburg [Va] Express

Died: on Jul 28, in Wash City, Edward Perry, infant son of Harrison P & Eliz B Lewis, aged one year.

Wash Corp: 1-Ptn from B Wood for the remission of a fine: referred to the Cmte of Claims. 2-Ptn from F Glenroy for the introduction of vocal music into the public schools: referred to the Cmte on Public Schools. 3-Cmte of Claims: asked to be discharged from the consideration of the ptn of Henry Carl for the remission of a fine. 4-Cmte on Wharves: Act granting permission to Thos P Morgan & Wm T Dove to construct a wharf at the foot of G st north. 5-Ptn of Jas Curtin, praying for the remission of a fine; ptn of Mrs Visser, praying for the remission of a fine; & ptn of Jeremiah Carmady, praying for the remission of a fine: referred to the Cmte of Claims.

THU JUL 31, 1856

Senate: 1-Ptn from Jos E Holmes & his associates, asking that an act of incorporation may be passed for the Washington Paper Mill Co, in D C: referred. 2-Ptn from Noah Smith, a soldier in the war of 1812, asking to be allowed a pension: referred. 3-Ptn from Harry L Goodwin, complaining of certain regulations at the post ofc of San Francisco, respecting the delivery of letters, as being unlawful: referred. 4-Bill for the relief of Thos J Churchill, late a lt in the 1st Ky regt of volunteers: passed.

Sketch of the life of Gen Arthur St Clair: born in Thurso, Scotland, in 1736; was a descendant of the noble family of Roslin, &, being the second son, he received a professional education; procured for himself an ensign's commission in the British army. When the war of 1756, between Great Britian & France was declared, at age 20 years, he joined the 42nd regt of Highlanders & came to America under Gen Wolfe. After the death of Gen Wolfe he served under Gens Moncton & Murray til the close of the war, when he received an appointment from Gen Gage, the cmder of the British forces in America, to take command of the forts in Pa, & have the military stores contained in those forts removed to the headquarters of the army at N Y. As a reward for his meritorious services, he received a grant of 1,000 acres of land from the British Crown, which land he laid out, in the vicinity of **Fort Ligonier**, in an octangular form. He had several appointments from Govn'r Penn, as Prothonotary, Register & Recorder of Bedford Co, & appointed the same offices in Westmoreland Co, when Hannahstown was the seat of justice. His first connexion with the U S was in 1775. He had a colonel's commission tendered him by the United Colonies, without any application on his part. He was, to use his own expression rich to his utmost wish, & had a dearly loved family, a wife & 5 children. He served on the northern frontier during the summer of 1776, in the fall, ordered to join Gen Washington in his retreat through N J. In the spring of 1776 he was made major general & sent to take command of Ticonderoga under Gen Schuyler. Knowing the weakness of the fort, not wishing to surrender his troops prisoners of war, abandoned the works in the night time, & conducted the retreat so skillfully that not one man was lost. This was not discovered by Gen Gates until the next morning. He was suspended from his command, but did not leave the army. He remained under Washington during nearly the whole war, at Valley Forge, at Monmouth, & at Brandywine, where he had his horse shot fron under him. He was soon reinstated in his former office, when Arnold deserted the American cause he was appointed to take his place at West Point. Upon his advance towards Williamsburgh, the enemy retired & he therefore proceed immediately South. He joined Green on Jan 3, 1782, & remained under his command during his brilliant campaign in the Carolinas. Here ended St Clair's services as a soldier of the Revolution. At the close of the war he was made auctioneer of the city of Phil, & held that post until 1786, when he was elected to Congress & chosen President of that body. He received his first commission as Govn'r of the N W Territory, which ofc he held for 15 years. It was the continuance of this office that St Clair made his well-known & unfortunate expedition against the Indians. He received his commission for this purpose on Mar 4, 1791, & set out in Sept. On Nov 3 encamped on the banks of the Wabach, he was sturck by the Indians & suffered a total defeat. He died at his home on the Chestnut Ridge on Aug 1, 1818. The citizens of Greensburgh desired that his remains should be buried in the St Clair cemetery at that town; & his fellow Masons erected a neat little sandstone monument over his last resting place.

The Western papers tell of the death of Mr Done, the valuable railroad ofcr, who made a false step & was thrown under the wheels of the train, 7 miles out of Chicago. He was found on the track bleeding profusely. He lost too much blood to be saved.

Dr Vick, of Sussex, Va, while conducting a post morten examination a few days since upon a dead body, accidentally cut his hand. A portion of the virus from the body entered the wound causing his death in a short time.

San Francisco: result of the labors of the Vigilance Cmte to date, so far as expulsion of notorious persons is concerned: Jas P Casey, executed; Chas Cora, do; Yankee Sullivan, commtted suicide; C P Duane shipped on the ship **Golden Age**; Wm Mulligan, do; Wooley Kearney, do; Bill Car, sent to the Sandwich Islands; Martin Gallagher, do; Edw Bulger, do; Jim Burk, alias Ativit, ran away; Pete Wightman, do; Ned McGowan, do; Jim White, do; John Crowe, left on the ship **Sonora**; Bill Lewis, shipped on the ship **Sierra Nevada**; Terrence Kelley, do; John Lawler, do; T B Cunningham, do; Alex Purple, do; Jas Hennessey, do; Tom Mulloy, do; Frank Murray, do; Jack McGuire, do; Wm Hamilton, do; Philander Brace, do; Jas Cusick, ordered to leave, but refused to go; J W Bagley, do.

Criminal Court-Wash, yesterday. 1-Wm Lyons found guilty & sentenced to 4 years in the penitentiary for entering & robbing the house of Hon J B Ricaud. 2-Richd Burns, colored, for misdemeanor, convicted & sentenced to 9 months' imprisonment in jail. 3-Geo Smith, colored, for an assault & battery on a colored woman: convicted & sentenced to 1 year in the penitentiary.

Died: on Jul 30, in Wash City. Anna E Leeke, only daughter of Henry & Julia A Leeke, in her 26th year. Her funeral will be this afternoon at 5 o'clock, from her father's residence, on 6th st, near H st.

Died: on Jul 23, in Toledo, Ohio, in her 28th year, Harriet M, wife of John E Hunt, jr, & grand-daughter of Elisha Whittlesey.

Died: on Jul 30, in Wash City, in his 10th year, James Laurie Colegate, son of James & Eliz Colegate. His funeral is today at 5 o'clock, from the residence of his father, 441 E st.

FRI AUG 1, 1856
Trustee's sale of 2 small frame house & lots: on Aug 9, on the premises, by deed of trust from Geo Barker & wife, dated Mar 12, 1853, recorded in Liber J A S No 52, folios 316 thru 318, of the land records of Wash Co, D C: part of lot 6 in square 214, fronting on 15th st west, between north L & M sts, improved by 2 comfortable frame dwlg-houses suitable for a small family. -N Callan, trustee -Jas C McGuire, auct

The small steamboat **John Jay**, on her way from Ticonderoga to Caldwell on Thu took fire near Garfield's & burned to the water's edge. The bodies of five persons have been recovered: Mrs Belknap, wife of Edw Belknap, of N Y C; Miss Renshaw, of New Orleans; Mr Metcalf, of Cherry Valley, N Y; Mrs S C Thwing, of Boston; Miss C A Fleet, of Brooklyn. Five persons jumped overboard & were drowned.

Cincinnati papers give account of a violent storm which passed over the city on Monday. The rains fell on a small house occupied by a man named Gammell, with his wife & child; Mrs Gammell was killed instantly & her little daughter had her thigh broken.

Senate: 1-Ptn from Ann C T Partridge, widow of Capt Allen Partridge, formerly superintendent of the military academy at West Point, asking to be allowed compensation for services of her late husband; for extra services of great importance to the country & calling for severe labor & sacrifices her husband had received no compensation whatever. 2-Ptn from V G Audubon, asking that Congress may pass a bill authorizing the Sec of State to purchase 100 or more copies of his work on the Birds of America & the Quadrupeds of North America, for the purpose of sending copies thereof to foreign Governments that have made presents of valuable works to the U S. 3-Cmte on Military Affairs: adverse report on the memorial of Jas Girardin, asking to be allowed the amount due him for rations while in military service in the war of 1812. 4-Cmte on Public Lands: asked to be discharged from the consideration of the memorial of Chas A Price, & that it be referred to the Cmte on Military Affairs: which was agreed to. 5-Bill for the relief of Danl Gordon: passed.

Nebraska as it is: Jun, 1856. The present Govn'r is Mark W Izard, a Kentuckian by birth, but appointed from Arkansas, where he has resided for many years. The Judiciary is in the hands of Chief Justice Ferguson, of N Y, [appointed from Mich,] Bradley, of Pa, [appointed from Indiana,] & Hardin, of Ga-all men of great ability.
-J A P, of Va

Chestnut St Female Seminary, 525 Chestnut st, Phil, Pa. Principals: Mary L Bonney & Harrietta A Dillaye.

Mrd: on Jul 9, in Gtwn, by Rev B N Brown, Mr Wm H Palmer, of Balt, Md, to Miss Jane P Furse, of Wash City.

I have this day, Aug 1, associated with me in the Wholesale & Retail Grocery Business Norvall W Burchell, & it will be hereafter named King & Burchell.
-Z M P King

One cent reward & no thanks for his return. I will pay the above reward for the return to me of Christopher Reiny, an apprentice who ran away from me on Jul 8, 1856. All persons are warned from harboring him, as the law will be strictly enforced.
-J Aigler

SAT AUG 2, 1856

Senate: 1-Opinion in the case of Wm R Glover & Thos W Mather & their associates: laid on the table & ordered to be printed. 2-Court of Claims: adverse decision in the case of Mrs Letitia Humphrey. Favorable opinion on the claim of Mrs Mary Reeside, excx of Jas Reeside: referred to the Cmte of Claims. 3-Ptn from John Brannan & other laborers in the Dept of State, asking that the compensation now allowed may be continued to them. 4-Cmte of Claims-recommended their passage-act for the relief: of Peyton G King, late receiver of public moneys at Monroe, La; of John Poe, of Louisville, Ky; of Calvin Hall, assignee of Wm Jones; of Henry L Robinson; & of Wm R Cozens. 5-Cmte on Pensons: memorial of the citizens of Michigan, asking that the children of Thos Fitzgerald have the pension to which he was entitled continued to them: bill for the relief of the children of Thos Fitzgerald. 6-Cmte of Claims: recommended the passage of the bill from the House for the relief of West Drinkwater & others. 7-Cmte on the Judiciary: bill for the relief of the reps & sureties of Robt King deceased. 8-Cmte of Claims: bill for the relief of Anthony S Robinson, heir & legal rep of Hamilton Robinson, deceased. 9-Cmte on Pensions: asked to be discharged from the consideration of the claim of C Vass, & that the parties have leave to withdraw their papers: which was agreed to. 10-Bill introduced for the relief of Catharine M Hamer, widow of the late Gen Thos Hamer: referred to the Cmte on Pensions. 11-Mr Wade moved to reconsider the bill passed yesterday for the relief of David Gordon: which was done.

Household & kitchen furniture at auction on: Aug 4, at the residence of Mr R C Wetenhall, on Bridge st, between High & Congress sts, all his furniture. -Barnard & Buckey, aucts

Elijah Fillmore, an uncle of the ex-President, died at his residence in Bennington, Vt, a few days since. He was very highly respected by his neighbors & townsmen, & was one of the oldest living native residents in Bennington. The ex-President's father was born in Bennington. Millard himself was born at Summer Hill, Cayuga Co, N Y, to which place his father had removed from Bennington.

House of Reps: 1-Bills to which no objection was made-relief: of the heirs of Sarah Ann Dye; of the heirs & legal reps of Mrs Magdalena Broutin, widow of de la Ronde; of the heirs & legal reps of Ignacio Delino; of the heirs & legal reps of Lewis Reggio; of the heirs & legal reps of Bernard Hemkin; of Richd Albritton; of Randall D Livingston; of Cephise Piseros, widow of Louis Labranche, of the parish of St Charles, & State of La; of Benj La Fonte, Wm Altenburg & others; of Talbot C Dousman; of Napoleon B Gill, of Perry Co, Mo; of Bridget Maher; & of Mrs M E McKnight, widow of Francis M McKnight. Bill to confirm the title of Ruhama Whitaker & Rebecca Whitaker to certain lands in the State of Louisiana. To confirm Jos Wandestrand in his title to certain lands.

Governess wanted for 4 or 5 children, competent to instruct in all the branches of an English education, & proficient in Music & the French language, with at least the knowledge of Latin. Salary $500. Address Philip St Geo Cocke, Jefferson P O, Powhatan Co, Va.

Dreadful accident yesterday at the planing mill of Messrs Ager & McLain, 13th st & the canal. Whilst Saml Cunningham, about 8 years old, & son of the foreman of the establishment, was passing a board-planing machine, his shirt sleeve caught in the pulley & his arm was literally chopped to pieces as high as the shoulder. Both he & his father displayed great fortitude under their painful misfortune. It is feared that his life is in imminent danger.

Master Wm Robinson, son of Wm Robinson, of the Navy Dept, but resident on the heights of Gtwn, drowned in Rock Creek, on Thur. He was about 15 years of age. This is the second time Mr Robinson has been called to suffer in this severe way, having lost an elder son in the ill-fated brig **Arctic**.

Mrd: on Jul 31, at the Assembly's Church, by Rev Andrew G Carothers, Mr Chas Beall to Miss Rachel A Pumphrey, both of Wash City.

Virginia Female Institute, Staunton, Va: next session will commence on Sep 24. -Rev R H Pheillips, Hugh W Sheffey, Staunton, Va.

Criminal Court-Wash-Thu. 1-Geo Watson alias Wm H Taylor convicted of obtaining money under false pretence from Hon Jas H Woodworth: sentenced to 4 years in the penitentiary. 2-Wm Smith & Calbert Drury convicted for riot on Capitol Hill & fined $30 each. 3-Martin King, for an assault & battery with intent to kill: indictment quashed. 4-Ellen Dillon, convicted of assault & battery on a child, sentenced to pay $1. 5-John Baltzer found guilty in 2 cases of assault & battery. Not yet sentenced. 6-Yesterday Conrad Heissler was found guilty of assault & battery, but strongly recommended by the Jury to the mercy of the Court. Fined $1 & costs.

MON AUG 4, 1856
House of Reps: 1-Cmte of Claims: bill for the relief of Jos Hardy & Alton Long: committed. Same cmte: bill for the relief of the widow & children of W S Derrick: recommended that it do not pass. Same cmte: bill for the relief of the heirs of Maj Gen Arthur St Clair: committed. Same cmte: bill for the relief of John H Scranton & Jas M Hunt, owners of the steamer **Major Tompkins**: committed. 2-Cmte on the Post Ofc & Post Roads: bill for the relief of Jacob Hall, contractor on mail route 8,912, from Independence, Mo, to Santa Fe, New Mexico: committed. Same cmte: adverse reports on the ptns of John F Wills, & of Jos Hall, of Alabama. 3-Cmte for the District of Columbia: adverse report on the ptn of Matthew Hines. 4-Cmte on Revolutionary Claims: bill for the relief of the legal reps of Gen Henry Miller, deceased: committed. 5-Cme on Private Land Claims: bill for the relief of Ambrose Lanfear, of Louisiana, & Senate bill for the relief of Hannibal Faulk & Eliza S Collier, [formerly widow Scriber,] & the heirs & legal reps of Benj Scriber, deceased: committed. Same cmte: bill for the relief of Benj R Gantt: committed. Same cmte: adverse reports on the ptns of Jos Roy, sen, & of Louis A Latil. 6-Cmte on Indian Affairs: bill for the relief of Arthur Sizemore & John Semi, Simmance, or Semoice: committed. Same cmte: bill for the relief of Horatio Boultbee: committed. Same cmte: adverse report on the memorial of O H Woodworth. Same cmte: bill for the relief of Whitemarsh B Seabrook & others; of Chas Stearns; & of C B R Kennerly: committed. 7-Cmte on Naval Affairs: bill for the relief of Van Rensselaer Hall; & resolution for the benefit of Susan Decatur, widow of Cmdor Stephen Decatur, late of the U S navy: both committed. Same cmte: bill for the relief of Lt John Guest, U S navy: committed.
8-Cmte on Revolutionary Pensions: bill for the relief of the surviving children of Peter Hubert, a Revolutionary soldier, & a bill for the relief of the children of Jas Phelps, a Revolutionary soldier: committed. Same cmte: bill for the relief of the heirs of Mary Hocker; & bill directing the pension due Jas Huey, deceased, & Jane Huey, his widow, deceased, to be paid to their sole heir, Alex'r B Huey, of Ga: committed. 9-Cmte on Invalid Pensions: adverse report on the ptn of Richd Reynolds. Same cmte: joint resolution to pay the pension due Parmelia Slavin, late the wife of John Blue, deceased, to her administrtor: passed. Same cmte: bill for the relief of Wm Walton, a soldier of the war of 1812; a bill for the relief of Chas Parish, a soldier of the war of 1812; & a bill for the relief of Mary B Dusenbury: committed. 10-Cmte on

Foreign Affairs: report in the case of Capt Walter M Gibson. Mr Stanton, of Ohio, stated to the House that this was a memorial praying compensation for damages sustained by Capt Gibson by his imprisonment at Batavia, in the East India Islands. The cmte did not recommend the payment of any money, but a renewal of negotiations, with the view of securing to Capt Gibson compensation from the Gov't of the Netherlands, in India. There was embodied in the report a somewhat valuable memoir, containing information with regard to the geography, products, & population of the East Indian Archipelago, with a large original map. The report recommends that the Executive be instructed by Congress to urge Capt Gibson's claim for indemnity, amounting to $100,000; to provide for the more thorough protection of American citizens trading in the Eastern seas; & to send a special envoy to make treaties of amity & commerce with the Sultan of Jambee, whose independence is recognized, with other independent native princes of the East Indian Archipelago. The motion was referred to the Cmte on Printing. 11-Bill for the relief of Jos Hill: passed. 12-Cmte of the Whole: bill for the relief of the heirs & legal reps of Mrs Magdalena Broutin, widow of de la Ronde; for the relief of the heirs & legal reps of Ignacio Delino; & to confirm the title of Ruhama Whitaker & Rebecca Whitaker to certain lands in the State of Louisiana: passed. Also passed-relief: of the legal reps & heirs of Bernard Hemkin; of the heirs & legal reps of Lewis Reggio; of Richd Albriton; of Randall D Livingston; of Cephise Piseros, widow of Louis Labranche, of the parish of St Charles, La; of Talbot Dousman; of Benj La Fonte, Wm Altenburg, & others; of Napoleon B Gill, of Perry Co, Mo; of Bridget Maher; of Mrs M E McKnight, widow of Francis M McKnight; & of Sarah Ann Dye: passed. Bill to confirm Jos Wandestrand in his title to certain lands: passed.

House of Reps: 1-Ptn of Martin H Clapp, of Mass, praying for the expulsion of Hon Anson Burlingame from the House of Reps.

Gen Henry Stanton, one of the assist quartermaster generals in the U S army, died, on Aug 1, at **Fort Hamilton**, N Y. He entered the army in 1813 as a lt in the light artillery & resigned in 1817. In 1818 he was reappointed assist deputy quartermaster general, & received the brevet of Brig Gen in 1847 for meritorious services in Mexico. He was a native of Vermont.

Richd R Crawford, of Gtwn, D C, was on last Fri unanimously elected by the Corporate authorities of that place to fill the vacancy occasioned by the death of the late D W Edmondson in the Revisory Board, created by the late act of Congress, in reference to the codification of the laws of the District of Columbia.

Mrd: on Aug 4, in Wash City, by Rev Thos Duncan, Mr Milton T Fristoe to Miss Sarah E Stinson, both of Bentonville, Warren Co, Va.

Died: on Jul 31, Wm Robinson, aged 16 years, son of Col Wm & Frances H P Robinson, of Gtwn.

Died: yesterday, in Wash City, P Fitzpatrick, aged 35 years. His funeral is this afternoon at 5 o'clock, from the residence of his nephew, corner of 7th & N sts.

I offer for sale on a credit of one to seven years 1,000 acres of my land, on the York river, above, below, & around Yorktown, with or without some dwlg or storehouses, steam-saw & grist-mills, & other valuable improvements. I offer also for sale some houses & lots in the center of Williamsburg. -Robt Anderson, Yorktown, Va

Grand Excursion: the Franklin Fire Co announce an excursion & picnic to the White House Pavilion on Aug 6: tickets $1. The boat will leave Gtwn at 7 A M; Wash at 8:30; Navy Yard at 9:30; & Alexandria at 10 o'clock. Cmte of Arrangements:

Robt E Doyle	Wm H Fanning	Floor Managers:
John Coumbs	Geo R Crossfield	Wm L Jones
Milton Clarke	Chas Leaman	L R Thomas
Wm H Beardsley	John Medley	Wm M Payne
Conrad Finkman	P Newman	Wm Stansbury
Danl Driscoll	Henry Knight	

Genr'l Collection Agency, 384 5th st, north of G. st. -John W Wells

A number one **Albemarle Estate** for sale: I offer my farm upon which I reside, containing 1,038 acres, 8 miles of the Univ of Va. The bldgs are spacious. Stock included in the sale if required. -D G Smith, Morven, Charlottesville post ofc.

Teacher wanted. Subscriber wishes to employ a gentleman to take charge of a small school in his family. A few boys wanted as boarders. -Rob E Peyton, the Plains Post Ofc, Fauquier Co, Va.

Notice is given that Land Warrant No 7,643, for 160 acres, issued in favor of Henry Fagan, under act of Sep 28, 1850, has been lost; & we have filed a caveat against the location or patenting of the same, & will in due time make application for a duplicate issue thereof. -Birchett & Downing, Attys for Henry Fagan.

WED AUG 6, 1856
Bailiff's sale: by order of distrain issued by Mr Hall against the goods & chattels of D Hersh for rent due & in arrears: sale of fans, laces, pencils, pocket books, mits, gloves, shirts, satchels, sewing silks, spool cotton, needles, show cases, etc, on Aug 9 at the Auction Store of A Green, 7th & D sts. Terms cash. -B T Watson, bailiff -A Green auct

House of Reps: 1-Cmte on the District of Columbia: bill for the relief of Michl Nash, of D C: recommended that it do not pass: laid on the table.

Senate: 1-Ptn from John H Waggaman, asking that the decision of the Court of Claims for arrears of pay for his services as a clerk in the Genr'l Land Ofc may be reversed, or that his case may be referred for a rehearing to that court. 2-Ptn from Jas L Cathcart, asking an appropriation to test his invention of an improved method of attaching ships' propellers to the driving shaft. 3-Ptn from S P Todd, a purser in the navy, asking to be relieved from liability for certain public stores lost or stolen while in his custody. 4-Cmte on Naval Affairs: to which was referred the resolution in relation to the use by the Gov't of the copyright of the great circle protractor, invented by Prof Chauvenot, submitted a report favoring the same. 5-Cmte on the Post Ofc & Post Roads: bill for the relief of John Ferguson & others. 6-Cmte on Naval Affairs: House bill granting a pension to Ansel Wilkinson, reported it with an amendment, & asked its immediate consideration; but objection was made. 7-Cmte on Pensions: bill for the relief of Maurice K Simons; bill granting a pension to Mgt Davis, widow of Geo Davis, a sailingmaster in the U S navy; & bill for the relief of Katharine M Hamer, widow of the late Thos L Hamer: with reports in each case. 8-Cmte on Military Affairs: adverse reports on the memorials: of Saml W Owen, S D Sturgis, Ann E T Partridge, & of R H Chilton, in relation to extra pay to the troops at **Fort Kearney**: all of which were agreed to.

Executor's sale: on Aug 9, the subscriber, as executor of the last will & testament of the late Dr Geo W Cherry, will sell at public auction, for cash, all the personal effects of the said Dr Cherry, consisting mainly of a U S patent-right for the sole & exclusive use of a stone saw. -Wm K Masters, exc -J C McGuire, auct

Mr Enoch W Clark, of the firm of E W Clark & Co, of Phil, bankers & exchange brokers, died on Sunday, after a long & painful illness. He was 54 years of age. -Ledger

Hon Edw Curtis, formerly a Rep in Congress from N Y C, & afterwards Collector of the port of N Y, died in that city on Sunday last, aged about 54 years. He had been afflicted for some time previous to his death. [Aug 8th newspaper: Mr Curtis commenced the practice of the law with his brother Geo Curtis, about 1824. They afterwards formed a partnership with the late Judge Danl B Tallmadge. He leaves a wife, but no children.]

Hon Peter De Forrest, an aged minister of the Methodist denomination, & a citizen of Richmond, was found near the half-way house on Petersburg railroad last Thu in a dying condition. His death occurred in a short time afterward. The supposition is that he wandered from his home while laboring under aberration of mind.

Orphans Court of Wash Co, D C. Letters testamentary on the personal estate of Geo W Cherry, late of Wash Co, deceased. -Wm K Masters, exc, 37 N Wharves, Alexandria, Va

$5,000 reward to the children or grand-children of ofcrs of the Revolution who served to the end of the war in the Continental line. The undersigned, late an accountant on Revolutionary Claims in the ofc of the Third Auditor of the Treas Dept, having a list of the names of the ofcrs who served to the close of the Revolutionary war, will attend to the prosecution & collection of claims under the new act of Congress, just passed, granting half-pay from the time of the reduction of the army in 1783, during the life of the ofcr, to his children, or to his grand-children if none of his children are now living. -W T R Saffell, Wash, D C

Orphans Court of Wash Co, D C. Letters of administration on the personal estate of Patrick Fitzpatrick, late of Wash Co, deceased. -Jas Fitzpatrick, adm

Mrd: on Jul 29, in Hamilton, N Y, by Rev R W Cook, Mr R T Taylor, of Wash, Principal elect of the Newark Wesleyan Institute, to Miss Amelia E Spencer, of the former place.

Died: on Jul 28, at **Babina Plantation,** Parish of West Baton Rouge, La, of congestion of the brain, Lafayette, the eldest son of Col Lafayette & Fannie Constance Caldwell.

Died: on Jul 27, in Anna, Union Co, Ill, Henry Holland, son of Wm A & A P Hacker, & grandson of Isaac Holland, of Wash City; age 1 year, 2 months & 7 days.

THU AUG 7, 1856
Senate: 1-Ptn from Wm Y Hansell, & Wm H Underwood, reps of Saml Rockwell, asking compensation for services as atty & solicitor, for the Cherokee nation. 2-Ptn from Jas Worden, asking to be allowed back pay & an increase of his pension. 3-Ptn from M F Bailey, an ofcr in the late war with Mexico, asking an increase of pension. 4-Cmte on Commerce: asked to be discharged from the consideration of the memorial of Chas Holmes: which was agreed to. 5-Cmte on the Post Ofc & Post Roads: bill for the relief of Geo H Giddings, contractor for carrying the U S mail on route 12,900. 6-Cmte on Indian Affairs: bill for the relief of Bridget Maher: passed.

The subscriber offers for sale his farm, **Llangollen**, [formerly the residence of Hon Cuthbert Powell, deceased.] This estate contains 792 acres, in Loudoun Co, on the eastern slope & at the foot of the Blue Ridge Mountain, within 3 miles of the village of Upperville, Fauquier Co; with a stuccoed brick dwlg house, of modern style, & numerous out-bldgs. Apply to J G Gray, M D, through the Post Ofc at Upperville, Va.

John Griswold died on Monday at Hyde Park, Dutchess Co, N Y, aged 73 years. For many years he has been one of the most respectable & eminent shipping merchants of N Y C.

$50 reward for return of runaway mulatto woman Nelly West, aged 45 or 50 years. She ran away on Aug 2, from *Free Branch*, residence of R O Mullikin, PG Co, Md. Deliver to R O Mullikin, or to Frank S Shulze, 404 I st, Wash, D C.

Criminal Court-Wash-Wed. 1-Henry Croggin guilty of robbing the store of Mr Geo W Hinton. 2-John E Bailey guilty of larceny of Mr Geo W Hinton, having stolen 5 overcoats of the value of $140, vests, & other property. Stolen articles were found at his house. 3-John W Demain, about 18, found guilty of robbing the store or workshop of Michl Hoffa, a silversmith & watch-maker tools, worth in all about $150. The tools were found in prisoner's bedroom at his father's house. He was also arraigned for a robber of the dry goods store of Mr John E Latham, at 19th & Pa ave.

Died: on Aug 5, in Wash City, in his 60th year, after a long & painful illness, Phillip O'Reilly, a native of Granard, County Longford, Ireland. His funeral is this afternoon at 4 o'clock, from the residence of his brother, East Capitol st.

Died: on Aug 5, at Norfolk, Va, after a protracted illness, H F Loudon, of the firm of H F Loudoun & Co, of that city.

Died: on Aug 1, at his residence in Pittsburgh, Pa, T J Fox Alden, a member of the Pittsburgh bar. He was born in N H in 1802, & graduated at Allegany College, of which his father, Rev Timothy Alden, was the founder, & at that time President. He studied law under Hon Patrick Farelly, & entered upon his practice at Meadville, Pa, where he resided until about 12 years since, & then at Pittsurgh, in which place he published several volumes. -P

Portland, Me, Aug 4-the Corning & Glazing Mills connected with the powder works at Gorham blew up, killing Peter Ritchie, of Canada, Messrs Gerry, of Portland, & White, of Acton, Mass.

Sale of valuable real estate: by decree of the Circuit Court of Hampshire Co, Va: public sale on Aug 23 next, before the door of the Nat'l Hotel, in Cumberland, all the lands of the late Lucy Perry in Hampshire Co, Va, conveyed to the said Lucy Perry by deed of partition from John Hoye & wife & John Rogers & wife, duly recorded in said county. This land is known as the *Perry Farm*, & a portion of the *Middle Farm*, about 1 mile above Cumberland, with an excellent double house, barn stabling, & other out-bldgs. In the whole tract there are 193 acres of bottom land. Part of this land is known as the *Race-course*. -Roger Perry, Special Com'r

Mrd: on Jul 17, in Winchester, Va, by Rev C Walker, J Peyton Clark to Cornelia Lee, daughter of Dr Robt T Baldwin, all of that place.

Green Hill Female Institute, 385 Girard ave, near Girard College, Phil, will re-open Sep 1st. -Enoch H Supplee, Principal

FRI AUG 8, 1856
Desperate affray at Oakland House, Lousiville, Ky, on Monday between Edmund Shipp & Hercules & Wm Walker, in which Shipp was killed & the two Walkers were dangerously wounded. Mr Shipp received one shot & 6 stabs in the heart. Hercules Walker will probably died. His lower limbs were paralyzed from a pistol shot in the small of the back. The difficulty arose from some misunderstanding relative to a horse-race. Mr Shipp was universally liked for his generous qualities. -Lou Jou

Doctress Lydia Sayer, lecturer on the Wrongs of Women, was last week married at Warwick, Orange Co, N Y, to Mr J W Hasbrouch, editor of the Whig Press, at Middletown. The ceremony was performed by the parties themselves, without the assistance of a minister, at the house of the bride's father.

Criminal Court-Wash. 1-Wm D Bell, convicted of an aggravated assault on Dr Henry Haw, was sentenced to 2 months in the county jail & fined $30. Edmund J Ellis, implicated in the same matter, failed to present himself in Court. 2-Biddy Macnamara was fined $10 for an assault on another woman.

Senate: 1-Ptn from Chas Waterman, asking to be confirmed in his title to certain lots in Milwaukee, Wisc. 2-Ptn from Jos Menard, asking to be allowed to locate certain warrants for land granted to the late Marquis de Lafayette, of which he is the assignee. 3-Ptn from Gustave A Lundberg, asking that his pension may be increased. 4-Ptn from Geo V Vandivir, a private in the military service, employed to remove the Cherokee Indians, asking to be allowed a pension in consequence of a chronic disease incurred while in that service. 5-Cmte on Public Lands: bill for the relief of Robt Mitchell: passed. 6-Cmte on Private Land Claims: recommended the passage of: relief of the heirs & legal reps of Mrs Magdalene Broutin, widow of De la Ronde; relief of the heirs & legal reps of Ignacio Delino; relief of the heirs & legal reps of Louis Reggio; relief of the heirs & reps of Bernard Hemkin; & to confirm the title of Ruthama Whittaker to certain lands in the State of Louisiana. 7-Cmte on Military Affairs: bill for the relief of Susanna T Lea, widow & admx of Jas Maglennen, late of the city of Balt. 8-Cmte on Indian Affairs: adverse on the memorial of Wm Leonard, asking indemnity for depredations committed by the Pawnee Indians on cattle driven from the Atlantic States to Calif.

On Fri last 2 negroes named Henry & Smith, convicted of the murder of Mr Thos Terry, were executed at Goochland court-house, Va, in presence of an immense crowd.

Mrd: on Aug 6, at Christ Church, Gtwn, by Rev Dr Norwood, C N Thom, of St Paul's, Minn, to Kate, eldest daughter of the late Col Thos Corcoran, of Wash City.

Died: on Aug 3, at Yellow Sulphur Springs, Montg Co, Md, Mrs Mary E Bennett, wife of Mr Alex'r Bennett, aged 38 years.

Died: on Aug 7, Martha Anna, daughter of Robt & Mary Kearon, aged 2 years & 27 days. Her funeral is today at 4 P M, from the residence of her parents, 314 8th st.

On Sunday last, during the prevalence of a storm in Anne Arundel Co, Md, Mr Wm T Wilburn's wife & his sister-in-law, formerly of this county, living near Davidsonville, were instantly killed by a flash of lightning, &, strange to tell, Mr Wilburn & the house in which they lived were not harmed in the least. -Marlborough Adv

Orphans Court of Wash Co, D C. Letters testamentary on the personal estate of Giles Dyer, late of Wash Co, deceased. -Jane C Dyer, excx

SAT AUG 9, 1856
Senate: 1-Memorial of J B Williams, asking the payment of $800, with interest from 1778, to the heirs of Jos Biggs, that being the amount paid by him for nursing & medical attendance in consequence of a wound received at the Kirkwood blockhouse, opposite the present city of Wheeling. 2-Cmte of Claims: bill for the relief of Thos H Baird: passed. Same cmte: bill for the relief of Ephraim Hunt: passed. 3-Cmte of Claims: bill for the relief of Ernest Hedler; & of Sturgis Bennett & Co, of N Y: passed. 4-Cmte on Private Land Claims: bill for the relief of Benj La Fonte, Wm Altebury, & others: passed. 5-Cmte on Public Lands: adverse report on the memorial of the widow of Alfred J Adams for bounty land for military service in the Florida war.

Select School for Girls, Friends' Meeting House, I st, between 18th & 19th sts, will be resumed on the first Mon in Sept. -E E Janney

Cottage & furniture on Gtwn Heights for rent: the house & grounds known as ***Duffey's Cottage***, recently occupied by M Boileau, of the French Legation: immediate possession. Apply to the subscriber, 122 Wash st, Gtwn, or through the Wash P O. -A Hyde

House of Reps: 1-Cmte on Revolutionary Pensions: bills committed-relief of the surviving children of Sarah Van Pelt, widow of John Van Pelt, a Revolutionary soldier; relief of the legal reps & heirs of Jos Bindon, a Revolutionary ofcr; & relief of the heirs of Peter Charlant, a Revolutionary soldier. Same cmte: adverse report on the ptn of Enoch Fisher. 2-Cmte on Patents: bill for the relief of Edwin M Chaffee: committed. 3-Cmte on the Post Ofc & Post Roads: bill for the relief of J R Powell: passed. Adverse on the ptn of Alonzo Weir, of N Y. 4-Cmte of Claims: bill for the relief of Mary Reeside: committed; & bill for the relief of Cyrus Buckland: committed. 5-Cmte on Foreign Affairs: adverse reports upon the ptns of John M Barker & Francis A McCauley. Same cmte: bill for the relief of Francis Dainese: committed. Same cmte: bill for the relief of Horatio J Perry, stating it was a case of peculiar hardship: committed. 6-Cmte on Invalid Pension: bill for the relief of Randolph Kussmaul; of Elijah Close, of Tenn; of Amos Armstrong, of Ohio; & of Eliz Riker: committed. 7-Cmte of Claims: adverse report on the ptn of Josiah Ray. 8-Cmte on Naval Affairs: adverse report on the ptns of Lewis Warrington & Thos Hurst.

The U S sloop-of-war **Macedonian**, arrived at Boston on Wed from the East Indies, absent from the U S nearly 3 years & 4 months, cruising in the India, China, & Japan seas. She was one of the squadron under Cmdor Perry which effected the treaty with the exclusive Japanese, & was afterwards flag-ship of the East India squadron under Cmdor Joel Abbott, who died at Hong Kong on Dec 14 last, & whose remains have been brought home in the ship. During her absence she had been nearly 2 years & 3 months in port, principally the treaty ports of China, the disturbances there rendering her presence necessary for the protection of American residents. This detention in port has had an injurious effect upon the health of her ofcrs & crew, & she brings back to their native shores scarcely one-half of the gallant crew with which she set out on her noble errand. -Boston Journal

Circuit Court, for Dorchester Co, Md-in Equity. Mary Jones for herself & as next of friend of Jos P Skinner & Thos Skinner, vs Thos Jones, Henry Jones, Matilda Jones, & Wm Jones, her husband, & others. The object of this writ is to procure a decree for a sale of certain land lying on **Peter's Neck**, Dorchester Co, containing some 76 acres of land, for division. The bill states that a certain Wm Jones, of said county, deceased, by his last will devised said land to the cmplnt, Mary Jones, for life, & at her death equally to the dfndnts in this cause; that only about 4 acres of said land is cleared, & it is unproductive & not under rent, & by reason of the taxes & expenses is a loss to those entitled to the same; that it will be for the benefit & advantage as well of the cmplnts as the dfndnts that the same be sold & the proceeds divided to those entitled, in the proportions to which they are entitiled; that the said Jos P Skinner & Thos Skinner are minors & reside out of the State of Md. Absent dfndnts are to appear on or before Jan 15th next, in person or by guardian. -Thos A Spence -Francis J Henry, clerk -Griswold & Jefferson, solicitors

The New Orleans papers announce the death of Andrew Hodge, formerly of Phil, but for many years a highly respected & prominent citizen of the former place. He was a brother of our fellow-townsman, Wm L Hodge.

Brvt Maj D Fraser, of the U S Army, in command of *Fort Taylor*, Florida, died on Jul 27th.

On Monday last Mr Andrew Shealy was shot dead & a son of his dangerously wounded whilst they were riding in the vicinity of their residence in Macon Co, Ga. The assassin is not known. Mr Shealy was 60 years old.

Criminal Court-Wash-Fri. 1-John Crown, of Gtwn, not guilty of keeping a disorderly house. 2-Henry Croggin pleaded guilty of robbing the store of Michl Hoffa, & others. 3-John E Bailey pleaded guilty to robbing the store of Mr John E Latham on Mar 24 last. 4-Sentencing: Croggin was sentenced to 3 years' imprisonment & hard labor in the penitentiary of D C, & a similar term in a second case, to commence at the expiration of the first. John E Bailey was sentenced to exactly the same punishment. John W Demaine sentenced to 2 years in the penitentiary on each of 3 charges, to commence, at the special instance of his father, 3 days hence, on Monday next. 5-Amon Duvall, a police ofcr, was put on trial for adding & abetting the escape of John Essex, charged with the murder of Owen Quigley on Jun 3 last. Duvall was acquitted. 6-Henry T L Wilson's case for the same offence, returned a verdict of guilty.

Died: on Aug 6, in Wash City, Robt S Hamill, in his 39th year. His funeral is tomorrow at 4 o'clock, from the residence of his brother-in-law, Moses Hogg, N Y ave & 1st st.

Obit-died: on Jul 13, of apoplexy, at Windsor Forest, near New Madrid, Mo, Judge Edw Broughton, aged 71 years & 38 days. He was a native of the Eastern Shore of Md, whence he removed to Balt about 1812. He was elected an ofcr in one of the companies for the defence of *Fort McHenry*. In 1815 he crossed the mountains & settled in Tidalia, La. As a parent, husband, & a friend he was ever devoted & kind. He has left an aged widow & 8 children to mourn his death.

Died: recently, in Orange Co, Va, in his 31st year, Dr Cassius Carter, of Prince Wm. The deceased had been united in marriage but a few hours to an accomplished young lady when, amid the innocent festivities common to such occasions, he was arrested by the hand of death. The mysterious dispensation filled many hearts with the sincerest grief. He had quite recently settled as a practitioner of medicine at Brentsville, Prince Wm, where he commanded an extensive practice. He was an ornament to society & a most useful member of the Methodist Episcopal Church. Our loss will be his gain.

Mrd: on Aug 7, at Green Valley, Va, by Rev Dr Packard, M Ross, of Lake Providence, La, to Mary E, 2nd daughter of Anth R Fraser.

Died: on Aug 4, in Salisbury, Conn, aged 85 years, Mrs Polly Averill, wife of Nathl P Averill, & only sister of Elisha Whittlesey.

Died: on Aug 8, in Wash City, Hollis Lavinia, 2nd daughter of Jno W & Rebecca E Shipley, aged 2 years, 5 months & 8 days.

Alexandria Boarding School: 33rd annual session will commence on Oct 1: number of students is limited to about 50. Circulars can be obtained by addressing Benj Hallowell & Sons, Alexandria, Va. -Benj Hallowell, Henry C Hallowell, & Francis Miller

MON AUG 11, 1856
Closing out sale of Dry Goods: on Aug 12, at the store of Mr Jas L White, 8th & La ave. -Jas C McGuire, auct

Senate: 1-Ptn from the legal reps of Carlile Pollock, asking to be released from liability as sureties of Wm McQueen, deputy postmaster at New Orleans. 2-Ptn from Edwin M Chaffee, asking an extension of his patent for an improvement in the process of manufacturing India rubber goods.

Mrs Julia Sayles, wife of John Sayles, of Blackstone, died on Jul 14 of dropsy, from which she has suffered for 5 years. During that time she has been tapped upward of 149 times, & more than 3,000 pounds of water were extracted. -Woonsocket [R I] Patriot

Mrd: on Jul 15, in Brunswick, Va, by Rev Dr Pryor, of Petersburg, Jas A Cunningham, of the same place, to Miss Ann F Tally, daughter of Wm W Tally, of Brunswick.

Mrd: on Aug 5, in Wash City, by Rev Mr Clarkston, Chas H Anderson, of N Y, to Josephine Beardsley, daughter of the late Mrs Catharine Purdon.

Died: on Aug 10, in Wash City, after a brief but severe illness, Benj Shaw, of Frankfort, Maine. His funeral is this afternoon at 5 o'clock, from the Fourth Presbyterian Church, 9th st, near the Patent Ofc.

Died: on Jul 21, in Brunswick, Va, after a protracted illness, Mrs S Harris, consort of Maj John S Harris, merchant & postmaster at White Plains.

Died: on Jul 22, in Brunswick, Va, at the residence of her father, D J Claiborne, jr, Mrs Cornelia A Turnbull, wife of Wm Turnbull, near Petersburg, in her 25th year.

Died: on Jul 31, in Brunswick, Va, Miss Sally Orgain, youngest daughter of Dr John Orgain.

Died: on Aug 8, in Wash City, Dora, daughter of Chas B & Jane E Young, aged 13 years.

Died: on Aug 10, Francis, infant son of Jas & Martha Riordan, aged 9 months & 17 days.

House of Reps: 1-Cmte of the Whole: bill for the relief of Abner Dickson: passed. 2-Cmte of the Whole: discharged from the consideration of the bill to increase the pension of Danl Waldo, the chaplain of the House, from $26.60 per annum to $8 per month, commencing on Mar 4, 1831. Mr Waldo entered the service of the U S in Apr, 1779, & was a private in the Connecticut line; at the close of that year he was taken prisoner by the British & confined in the old stone Sugar House, in N Y C, where he remained for 2 months. His extreme sufferings in that loathsome & horrid prison, where 400 American prisoners were crowded into a bldg not 60 feet square, amid starvation, pestilence, & death, well-nigh cost him his life & made him an invalid for nearly a year. By a firm constitition, temperate habits, & a vigorous mind he recovered & obtained a liberal education. Making divinity his profession, he entered the ministry of the Congregational Church in early life. The bill was passed. 3-Cmte of the Whole: bill for the relief of John Connoly, late a private in Co A, 6th Infty, U S Army: passed.

A tasteful monumental stone to the memory of the late Andrew J Downing has just been placed in the Smithsonian grounds by the friends of that valuable & lamented citizen. The Gov't & public of Wash are indebted to the taste & judgment of Mr Downing for the beautiful arrangement of the parks & public squares of Wash City.

On Monday last Bradley S Osborn, a young man employed in the express ofc of Wells, Fargo & Co, at N Y, clandestinely left that establishment. He was soon missed, & it was discovered that 2 bags of gold, containing each $1,000, had disappeared. Capt Wm Stokely, of the Independent Police immediately started in pursuit of the fugitive, whom he arrested at Phil, with gold & bank bills in his possession. He was taken back to N Y.

Criminal Court-Wash: 1-Wm McFarland, charged with assaulting Chas C Edelin at the Navy Yard, was fined $5 & costs. 2-Henry Liesburger found guilty for receiving stolen goods: found not guilty.

A graduate of Rutger's College desires a situation as Tutor in a private family or school. He is competent to teach Latin, Greek, Mathematics, & French. Please address, with full particulars, C H Suydam, New Brunswick, N J.

TUE AUG 12, 1856
Painful coincidence. John J Speed, who studied law with the late Danl Kellogg, of Skaneateles, & who became a celebrated lawyer in Md, was lost on the steamboat **Henry Clay**, burnt on the Hudson 3 or 4 years ago. Edw Stanford, of N Y, from the same ofc, was lost on the brig **Arctic**; & John C Beach, of N Y, from the same ofc, was killed by the explosion of the steamer **Empire State** on Sat last.
-Seneca [N Y] Courier

Senate: 1-Ptn from Tobias Martin, a settler upon lands in Florida under the armed occupation act, asking to be indemnified for the loss of his land, in consequence of its being embraced in a military reservation. 2-Ptn from Wilson Nason & others, heirs & legal reps of John Lord, asking compensation for his services as a seaman in the navy during the Revolutionary war. 3-Cmte on th Post Ofc & Post Roads: bill for the relief of Garman, Wigle, & Beuford. 4-Cmte on Patents & the Patent Ofc: bill for the relief of Edw Haste, asking compensation for services performed under direction of the Com'r of Patents. 5-Cmte on Private Land Claims: bill for the relief of Talbot C Dousman, recommending its passage.

Clarke Co Land for sale, on Sep 1 next, the premises, **Benlomond**, the farm adjoining the one on which I reside, containing about 240 acres. Also, **Rockland Meadow**, contiguous to the above, containing about 125 acres. The two together will make a beautiful farm, with all the necessary bldgs. -Robt C Randolph, M D, Milwood, Clarke Co, Va.

Obit-died: Mr John Griswold, at Hyde Park, N Y, resided over 40 years in this city, & was well known as one of our most prominent shipping merchants. He was born at Lyme, Conn, removed early in life to this city, became the founder of the London line of packets, its agent & principal owner, & having acquired a large fortune retired to Hyde Park, where he closed his life at the age of 74 years. -N Y Courier
+
The death of Chas Sedgwick, at Lenox, Mass, on Sunday last, is also announced. He was the youngest son of the late Judge Sedgwick, of the Supreme Court of Mass, & was brother of Theodore & Henry & Robt Sedgwick, all of whom had preceded him to the grave. He was educated for the bar, but early in his professional life he was appointed to the ofc of Clerk of the Supreme Court of the State, which obliged him to remove from the family seat at Stockbridge to Lenox, the county town, where he resided, still holding the same ofc, until his death at the age of 64 years. -N Y Courier

Criminal Court-Wash: 1-Michl Macnamara found guilty for larceny & sentenced to 8 months in the county jail & to pay a fine of $1. 2-David Y Moore, indicted for illegal voting at the last municipal election, was fined $50 & costs & 2 months in the county jail. 3-Henry Michelette, indicted for larceny, was acquitted.

Died: on Aug 2, in Wash City, William Clifford, only son of Ebenezer & Mary E Piggott, aged 1 month & 19 days.

Notice: Bounty Land Warrant, No 61,504, for 120 acres, issued Mar 14, 1856, to Wm C Megee, act of 1855, for services in Capt Dobbins' company of Illinois Mounted Volunteers, & sent to "John Underwood, Present," has not been received by me. A caveat has this day been filed in the Gen Land Ofc, & application made to the Com'r of Pensions for a duplicate of said warrant. -John Underwood

WED AUG 13, 1856
Senate: 1-Cmte on Commerce: bill for relief of J Hosford Smith. 2-Cmte on Foreign Relations: bill for relief of Dr Jas Morrow. 3-Cmte on Indian Affairs: bill for relief of Mrs Mary Gay. 4-Bill for relief of the heirs of Col John Hardin, of Ky: to reconsider the vote rejecting the bill. Mr Crittenden advocated the justice of the claim, spoke of the patriotic services of that gallant son of Ky, Col Hardin. Consideration of the bill was postponed. 5-Bill for relief of Nathl Hayward, to extend the patent for 10 years; Mr Hayward sold his patent for improvement in making India rubber goods many years ago, & other persons had grown rich on the efforts of this genius, while the inventor had become poor. Mr Jones, of Tenn, thought it extremely strange for an inventor who had sold his patent should come to ask its renewal. Mr Hunter would be compelled to vote against the extension of the patent.

House of Reps: 1-Bills to which no objection was made: authorizing the legal reps of Manuel Gonzales Moro to enter certain land in Missouri; bill for the relief of the Geo K McGunnegle, surviving partner of the late firm of Hill & McGunnegle, of St Louis, Mo. Relief of the legal reps of Thos Gordon, deceased; of the sureties of the late Lt Chas E Jarvis, U S Army; of Capt Thos Ap Catesby Jones; of Jas M Lindsay; of Betsey Nash; of Salvador Accardi; of Wm H Chase; of Collins Boomer; of Ransdell Pegg; of Cezaire Wallace, of the parish of Bossier & State of Louisiana; of Jos Smith; of Dempsey Pittman; of J W Todd, a lt of ordnance in the U S Army; of Geo Schellenger; of Amos B Eaton, a commissary of subsistence in the U S Army; of Saml Forrest; of Mrs Agatha O'Brien, widow of Brvt Maj J P J O'Brien, late of the U S Army; of Chas S Denman; of Rebecca Smith; of Mary B Winship, widow of Oscar F Winship; of Ursula E Cobb, widow of Chas Cobb; of Albro Tripp; of Dolly Empson; of Lyman N Cook; of Betsey Whipple; of Claiborn Vaughn; of Geo Bond; of Richd J Murray; of Levi C Harris; of Robinson Gammon; & of John Campbell. Resolution to pay Wm Cooper $400 for his services as laborer at the Capitol during the 31st & 32nd Congresses. Bill to increase the pension of Geo W Torrence; & to increase the pension of Alpheus T Palmer, late a quartermaster in the 9th regt U S Infty. Bill granting a pension to Mrs Olivia W Cannon, widow of Jos S Cannon, late a midshipman in the U S Navy, now deceased. Bill for the benefit of Robt S Wimberly. Bill restoring Joshua Mercer to the roll of invalid pensioners. Bill granting a pension to Nathl Mothershead, of Missouri; & a pension to Morris Powers.

Household & kitchen furniture at auction on: on Aug 20, at the residence of Mrs Redwood, 365 C st, near 4½ st. -Jas C McGuire, auct

Wash Corp: 1-Ptn from A N Clements; from Thos Kenney; & from Ann Dunlop, for the remission of a fine: referred to the Cmte of Claims. 2-Ptn of Geo H Miller, asking compensation for the loss of a cow: referred to the Cmte of Claims. 3-Cmte of Claims: asked to be discharged from the consideration of the ptns for the remission of a fine from: Bazell Bell; Mgt Ring; M Ryan; Mrs Visser; Jeremiah Carmady; Jas Curtin; & Hugh Latham. Also, from Thos M Fugitt, asking compensation for certain services as Com'r of the eastern section of the claim. 4-Cmte of Claims: bill for the relief of Peter Little; of Z M P King; & of Robt Downing: passed. 5-Ptn of Thos Welsh, praying compensation for injuries sustained by his horse in crossing 14th st bridge: referred to the Cmte of Claims. 6-Ptn of Maurice Halloren, asking compension for work done by him on 13th st: referred to the Cmte of Claims.

Died: on Aug 11, Mary Lizzy, youngest child of M J & E A Callan, aged 11 months. Her funeral is this evening at 4 o'clock, from 474 H st, between 9th & 10th sts.

John O Lawler, aged 28 years, recently became a soldier on Bedlow's Island, N Y, & a few days ago wrote to the Chief of Police that he had in 1852, while a schoolmaster in the work-house of Rathdrum, Wicklow County, Ireland, became enamored with a girl named Mary Dunn. He made proposals to her, which she rejected. H committed an assault on her, which he feared she would complain of, & consign him to prison for many years. He watched his opportunity & threw her into the stream. She was drowned, but her murderer was never known until this confession. He is held for examination, & will probably be sent to Ireland under the Ashburton treaty. -Courier

Orphans Court of Wash Co, D C. In the case of Lemuel Etchison, executor of Ruth A Peaco, deceased, the exec & Court have appointed Sep 2 next, for the final settlement of the personal estate of said deceased, of the assets collected. -Ed N Roach, Reg/o wills

THU AUG 14, 1856
Teacher wanted: the trustees of Wash Academy, Princess Ann, Somerset Co, Md, wish to employ an Assist Tutor at said institution. -Edw Long, Isaac D Jones, Wm J Bird, Cmte

Senate: 1-Cmte on the Library: memorial of Harriet L B Ruth, reported a resolution directing the Sec of the Senate to pay Harriet L B Ruth, mother of J S Ruth, deceased, $2,500 in full for his services in preparing for publication the observations on terrestrial magnetism, made at the observatory of Girard College, & published under the order of the Senate on Feb 12, 1845. 2-Resolved, that in the proceedings before the Senate in the matter of the memorial of Washington Allen Bartlett, late a lt in the U S Navy, complaining of the action had under the act of Congress entitled "An act to promote the efficiency of the navy," approved Feb 28, 1855, nothing appears which impeaches his promptness & efficiency as an ofcr of the navy or his character as a gentleman.

Wm & Mary College, Wmsburg, Va, will begin its next session on Oct 15.
Faculty: [The necessary expenses for the session do not exceed $240.]
Benj S Ewell, Pres & Prof of Mathematics & Natural Sciences.
Morgan J Smead, Ph D, Prof of Languages.
Rev Silas Totten, D D, prof of Moral & Intellectual Philosophy, Belles Lettres, & Logic.
Henry A Washington, Prof of History & Constitutional Law.
Lucian Minor, Prof of International & Municipal Law.
Thos T L Snead, Adj Prof of Mathematics.

Tract of land for sale, containing 120 acres; improvements consist of 2 log-houses, one of which is very comfortable. The land is within 3 miles of the Navy Yard Bridge, adjoining the lands of Messrs Young, Wankowiectz, & Capt Gibson, a little east of the Piscataway road leading from said bridge. A plat of the land can be seen in the hands of H Naylor, at the City Hall. -John H Surratt

Court of Chancery at Nashville, Tenn. August Rules, 1856. Wm E Watkins & Oliver P McRoberts, excs of the last will & testament of Montgomery Bell, deceased, against Jas L Bell & others, legatees & devisees of Montgomery Bell. Montgomery Bell died in Tenn on Apr 1, 1855; by his last will he devised the residue & the remainder of the proceeds of his real & personal estate to his nephews & nieces & grand nephews & grand nieces, children & grandchildren of his 8 brothers & sisters, in the proportion to which each brother & sister would have been entitled, the distribution to be made as expressed in the will. Many of his legatees are unknown, & the object of the bill is to have a distribution, & for all the legatees to come in & prove their relationship on the 1st Monday in Nov next at the Chancery Court at Nashville. -C D O'Brien, C & M

Rev John Donelly, a missionary Catholic priest, was accidentally killed by a train of cars at Rochester on Sat. At the time of the accident he was awaiting a train to proceed eastward, & whilst standing upon the river bridge was crushed by an incoming train.

Criminal Court-Wash-yesterday: 1-H T L Wilson, the county ofcr convicted for aiding the escape of John Essex: sentenced to 2 years' imprisonment & a fine of $20. 2-West Adams, convicted of a libel on Jas Mockabee, in asserting on oath that he was a man of color, was sentenced to 3 months' imprisonment & fined $50. 3-The trial of Bernard Magee for the shootng of Jas Simms in Gtwn was taken up. Dr Cragen & Dr Snyder, both of Gtwn, a daughter of the deceased, & other witnesses were exaimined.

Local: annual election of Public School teachers-meeting took place yesterday.

First District:
Mr S John Thomson:	Principal 1st District School
Miss Mary P Middleton:	Assist Principal, Female Dept
Mrs M E Rodier:	Principal Male Primary
Miss Geraldine Wells:	Principal Primary No 1
Miss Adeline H Lowe:	Principal Primary No 2
Miss A V Bates:	Assist Principal No 2
Miss Jane N Thompson:	Principal Primary No 3
Miss M Richie:	Assist Primary No 3
Miss L E Moore:	Principal Primary No 4

Second District:
Mr Thos M Wilson:	Principal 2nd District School
Mrs Susan P Randolph	Assist Principal Female Dept
Mrs Emily Myers	Assist Principal Male Dept
Mrs Rebecca M Ogden	Principal Male Primary
Miss Eliz Parsons	Principal Primary No 1
Miss Emily V Billing	Principal Primary No 2
Miss Ellen Hawkins	Assist Primary No 2
Miss Frances L Henshaw	Principal Primary No 3
Miss Lucy H Randolph	Principal Primary No 4
Miss Kate McCarthy	Assist Primary No 4
Miss Eliza Titus Ward	Principal Primary No 5

Third District:
Mr John Fill	Principal 3rd District School
Mr Wm W McCathran	Assist Principal Male Dept
Miss Mary A Myrick	Assist Principal Female Dept
Mr H Henshaw	Principal Male Primary
Miss Frances Elvans	Principal Primary No 1
Miss Isabella F Acton	Assist Principal No 1
Miss Laura Hilton	Principal Primary No 2
Miss Rebecca St John	Assist Primary No 2
Mrs Eliza W Clarke	Principal Primary No 3
Miss Jane G Moss	Principal Primary No 4
Miss Harriet N Henshaw	Principal Primary No 5
Miss M Freeman	Principal Primary No 6

Fourth District:
Mr John E Thompson	Principal 4th District School
Miss Mgt A Milburn	Assist Principal Female Dept
Mr Augustus Edson	Principal Male Dept
Miss Annie M Adams	Principal Primary No 1
Miss Mary A Lee	Principal Primary No 2
Miss E E Ashdown	Principal Primary No 3

The resignation of the present secretary, Mr G J Abbot, was accepted, & a vote of thanks for his valuable services was expressed by the Board. Dr S A H McKim was elected his successor.

The youth, Thos J Padgett, who was arrested in Balt on suspicion of being concerned in an outrage on a female in this city about 3 weeks ago, was discharged from custody on Tue, there being no evidence against him.

Mrd: on Aug 12, in Wash City, by Rev Mr Hildt, Capt John F Haynie, of Balt, to Miss Kate, daughter of Mr Francis Walker, of Balt.

Died: on Aug 12, in Wash City, Mr Wm Archer, a native of Scotland, & an old & highly respected citizen of this place. His funeral is this evening at 4 o'clock, at the residence of his son-in-law, Dr Purrington, on G st, near 15th sts.

Died: on Aug 2, at **Blakely Grove**, Calvert Co, Md, [the residence of his brother, Jos Blake,] Dr Richd Blake, of Terre Haute, Indiana.

Obit-drowned: on Jul 20th last, in the Red Lake river, Minnesota Territory, Madison Rush, of Phil, late Lt in the U S Navy, in his 35th year. After a long career of active service in the navy, he resigned his commission a few months ago in consequence of broken health, brought on in tropical latitudes, while in squadron on the coast of Africa. In company with a valued naval friend he recently left Phil on an excursion to the far West, in the hope of benefiting his health. While bathing in the water of the above river, which are deep & rapid, his strength failed & he drowned. [Aug 26th newspaper: He was the 3rd son of Hon Richd Rush, & a mother of wide spread social accomplishments. He was named after Pres Madison, of whose Cabinet his father was a member. He received his midshipman's warrant from the hand of Pres Jackson in 1836. Wash. Aug 23, 1856]

Yarmouth, Me, Aug 13. A sail-boat was sunk by a whirlwind in this harbor yesterday. Mr Winslow & 2 children, Mrs John Brown & 2 children, & a daughter of Adam Baker were drowned.

FRI AUG 15, 1856

Mrd: on Aug 11, at the residence of the bride's father, in Wash City, by Rev J W Cummins, Mr Theobald B Tiers, of Phil, with Donna Maria Da Gloria, only daughter of his Excellency the Cmder de Figantiere e Moras, Envoy Extraordinary & Minister Plenipotentiary of his Most Faithful Majesty near the Govn't of the U S.

Died: on Aug 11, at Andalusia, Bucks Co, Pa, Mrs Jane M Biddle, widow of the late Nicholas Biddle, in her 64th year.

Senate: 1-Ptn from Mary Gay, widow of Wm Gay, late Indian Agent in the Territory of Kansas, asking that provision may be made for her support in consequence of her husband having been murdered by armed men while in the discharge of the duties of his ofc. 2-Ptn from Lindsay Muse, assist messenger in the Navy Dept, asking an increase of his compensation. 3-Ptn from Wm McKenney, chaplain in the navy, asking that the act of Jul 1854, for the relief of the widow & orphans of the ofcrs & seamen of the U S schnr **Grampus**, lost at sea, may be so construed as to extend relief to him. 4-Ptn from L A Latile, asking a pension on account of disability incurred while master armorer at Baton Rouge. 5-Cmte on the Post Ofc & Post Roads: favorable report on the claim of Ramsay & Cannick. 6-Cmte on Patents: bill for the relief of Isaac Adams, asked its immediate consideraton. 7-Cmte on Indian Affairs: bill for the relief of John Rogers: recommended its passage. 8-Cmte on Revolutionary Claims: bill for the relief of the legal reps of Thos Gordon, deceased: recommended its passage. 9-Cmte on Pensions recommended the passage of the act for the relief: of Lewis Hembert; of Abner Dickson, a soldier in the war of 1812; of John Connolly, late a private in Co A, 6th Infty, U S Army; of Ursula E Cobb, widow of Chas Cobb; of Antoine Robedeau; & of Edmund Mitchell. Also, an act providing an increase of pension to Danl Waldo, of Onondaga Co, N Y. 9-Cmte on Military Affairs: bill for the relief of Mrs Agatha O'Brien, widow of Brvt Maj J P J O'Brien, late of the U S Army, recommended that the Senate concur in said amendment: which was agreed to. 10-Cmte on Private Land Claims: bill authorizing the legal reps of Manuel Gonzales Moro to enter certain lands in Missouri: recommended its passage. 11-Bill introduced to confirm the title of Benj C Edwards to a certain tract of land in the Territory of New Mexico: referred to the Cmte on Private Land Claims.

SAT AUG 16, 1856

Valuable real estate for sale: by a decree of the Circuit Court for Chas Co, as Court of Equity, public sale, at the Court-house door in Port Tobacco, in said county, on Sep 16 next, that large & desirable estate of which John Beale Fergusson, late of said county, died possessed, called **Wellington**, containing a 1,000 acres of land, more or less. The estate lies upon the Potomac river, just below Md Point. There is a small but new & comfortable dwlg house, with other out-bldgs. -John W Mitchell, trustee

By order for distress, I shall expose to public sale, for cash, on Aug 22, at the house of Wm Feeney, on Pa ave, between 2nd & 3rd sts west, Wash City: household furniture. -R R Burr, Bailiff -A Green auct

Being anxious of changing my location & pursuits, I will sell my 3 fine estates, adjoining each other, all lying upon a portion of Port Tobacco Valley: first, **Linden**, my present residence; second, **Friendly Hall**; & third, **Hanson Hill**, containing in the whole about 1,500 acres. There are on these farms 3 dwlgs & all necessary outhouses. -Walter Mitchell, Linden, near Port Tobacco, Md

Mrs Rodman, of New Bedford, Mass, who had reached the advanced age of 99 years, quietly passed off the stage a few days ago. She belonged to the Society of Friends; a native of England, she passed most of her life in the U S; endowed with a large fortune, she was distinguished equally for her public spirit & her charities. Her mental faculties continued nearly unabated to the last. She continued the supervision of her affairs, though she was, by infirmity, confined to her bed [Aug 19th newspaper-correction: Mrs Rodman was born in our island of Nantucket, on Dec 9, 1757, & I am pretty sure she never was in England. Her parents & ancestors for several generations were natives of Massachusetts. Her grandfather, Jos Rotch, may be said to have been the founder of New Bedford, & of the whale fishery in that place, then a small village, he having previously commenced the business in Nantucket, & was the first person to ship from this country whale oil to England. Her father, soon after the war of the Revolution, was invited by the French Gov't, with especial privileges, to carry on the whale fishery, which he prosecuted extensively & with great success from Dunkirk, as his descendants have since done in New Bedford. I am unwilling that our country, & the State of Massachussets especially, should be deprived of the honor due to the birthplace of so excellent a woman. -P, Balt, Md, Aug 16, 1856]

Died: on Aug 15, in Wash City, Clarence, youngest son of A D & M Melcher, in his 5th year. His funeral is this afternoon at half-past 5 o'clock, from the residence of his parents, N Y ave, near 4th st.

Senate: 1-Cmte on Finance: bill for the relief of Geo L Bowne & Wm Curry: passed. 2-Cmte of Claims: bill for the relief of Thos Rhodes & Jeremiah Austell: asked its immediate consideration: which was objected to. 3-Cmte of Claims: recommended the immediate passage of the bill for the relief: of Salvador Accardi; of Jas M Lindsay; of Wm H Chase; of the sureties of the late lt Chas E Jarvis, U S Army; of Capt Thos Ap Catesby Jones; & of John Otis. 4-Cmte on Military Affairs: bill for the relief of J W Todd, a lt of ordnance in the U S Army, reported it back without amendment.

Boston, Aug 15. A yacht was sunk in our harbor yesterday by a collision with a ferry-boat. Ten persons on board, 5 of whom drowned, viz: Mrs Saml Robinson, Mrs S Erving, Miss H Greenough, Miss Mary E Hamilton, & Miss Mary C Hamilton.

Trustee's sale of house & lot in Gtwn, on Sep 24, on the premises, by deed of trust from Henry B Walker, dated Aug 7, 1850, recorded in Liber J A S No 16, folios 416 thru 420, of the land records for Wash Co, D C: sale of part of lot 12, in Holmead's addition to Gtwn: improvements consist of a 2 story frame dwlg-house.
-Jno W McKim, Richd H Clarke, trustees -Jas C McGuire, auct

MON AUG 18, 1856
Died: on Aug 15, in Wash City, Thos W Mahorney, in his 39th year.

Senate: 1-Cmte on Revolutionary Claims: memorial of the heirs of Isaac Shelby, submitted a report, with a bill providing payment for the Revolutionary services of Col Isaac Shelby. 2-Ptn from Danl Ammen, asking to be allowed the pay of a master in the navy for services rendered in that grade previous to his promotion. 3-Cmte to Audit & Control the Contingent Expenses of the Senate, made unfavorable reports upon the memorial of Jas Harrington, to increase the pay of the superintendent of the document room & assistants, & the resolution of Mr Sebastian to increase the pay of the mail-boys of the Senate: which was agreed to. 3-Memorial of Harriet L B Ruth, mother of Jos S Ruth, deceased: referred to the Cmte to Audit & Control the Contingent Expenses of the Senate: which was agreed to. 4-Bills passed: relief of the reps & sureties of Robt King, deceased; of Talbot C Dousman; & of John Poe, of Louisville, Ky.

Yesterday a party left Mariner's House, North Square, for a sailing excursion. The sail-boat crossed the wake of the steamer, when the progress of the ferry boat was impeded by some mudscows, & the helmsman could not see the sail boat, & ran afoul of it & capsized her. One of the paddle wheels smashed the boat & struck the ladies, who sunk to rise no more. The men tried to save the ladies, but the wheel struck them & in an instant they were out of sight. Mr Hamilton, the landlord of the Mariner's House, lost his daughter, Mary C, aged 14, & his sister, Mary E, aged 22; Miss Henrietta Greenlaw, 20, Mrs Jane Erwin, 28, & Mrs Ellen Robinson, 20, were the other ladies drowned. The five men with them escaped with no injury.
-Boston Atlas, Aug 15

Trustee's sale of valuable property: by deed of trust from R W Latham & Catherine C, his wife, dated Oct 11, 1852, to secure $6,000: sale on Sep 19 of: parts of lots 1 & 2 in square 405, with excellent dwlg thereon. -Geo Thomas, trustee -A Green auct

Sale of stock of farming utensils & crop in the field: on Aug 27, at the farm of Capt Gibson, 3 miles from the Navy Yard bridge, near the road leading to Piscataway, adjoining the farms of Mrs Livingston & Weir. -A Green auct

Died: on Aug 16, in Wash City, Ella Rebecca D Wroe, only child of Everett & Mgt E Wroe, aged 5 months & 5 days.

House of Reps: 1-Bills to which no objection was made: bill for the relief of Amos B Corwine; of Geo H Giddings, contractor for carrying the U S mail on route No 12,900; & of John H Scranton & Jas M Hunt. 2-Cmte of Claims: bill for the relief of Francis A Gibbons & Francis X Kelly: committed. 3-Bills-recommended they pass: relief of-John Tucker; of Josiah S Little; of Anthony Rankin, of Tenn; of the heirs of Jabez B Rooker, deceased; of John M McIntosh; of Sally T Matthews; of Isaac Cook & others; of Abraham Kintzing; of Jas Davidson, of Ky; of F A Cunningham, paymaster U S army; of Rebecca Halsey, widow of Zephaniah Halsey, an ofcr of the Revolution; of Nancy Bowen & Sarah Larrabee; of Franck Taylor; of Brvt Brig Gen John B Walbach, U S Army; of Eliza B McNeill; of Nathan M Lounsbury; of Ambrose Lanfear, of Louisiana; of Hannibal Faulk & Elisa S Collier, [formerly widow Scriber,] & the heirs & legal reps of Benj Scriber, deceased; of John Scrantion & Jas M Hunt, owners of the steamer **Major Tompkins**; of Adam D Steuart & of Alex'r Randall, exc of Danl Randall; & of Francis A Gibbons & Francis X Kelly. Also: Pension to Benj Berry, a soldier of the Revolution; Revolutionary pension to Sarah Blount; pension to Nancy M Gunsally, formerly widow of Lyman M Richmond, deceased; & granting 5 years' half-pay to Mrs Ann Turner, widow of Elbert Turner, deceased. Resolution for the benefit of Susan Decatur, widow of Cmdor Stephen Decatur, late of the U S Navy. 4-Cmte on Military Affairs: bill for the relief of Jane McCrabb, widow of the late Capt Jno W McCrabb, assist quartermaster U S army: committed. 5-Settlement of the accounts of Chas M Strader & Edw P Johnson, mail contractors: passed. 6-Cmte of the Whole discharged from the consideration of the bill for the relief of Mary Reeside; & also the bill for the relief of Dr Jas Morrow: both read a third time & passed. 7-Ptn of Jos E Griffith, of Texas, for a grant of land: referred.

A young man named Smith, of Boston, grandson of Arthur McArthur, of Limington, Maine, accidentally shot himself through the lungs while out gunning on Sat at the latter place. It is supposed he cannot recover.

Legacy to Harvard College: Dr John G Treadwell, who died in Salem on Friday last, left the greater portion of his property, estimated at upwards of $100,000, [after the decease of his mother, now 80 years old,] to Harvard University, for the founding of a new medical professorship. He also donated to the institution, his valuable library. In case the College authorities do not accede to the conditions of the will, the whole amount goes to the Massachusetts Genr'l Hospital without condition. Dr Treadwell was a bachelor, & a graduate of Harvard in the class of 1825.

Henry Polkinhorn informs that he has removed his Printing Ofc to the new bldg on D st, between 6th & 7th sts, having added a steam-engine to his facilities for executing every description of Job Printing.

Disaster occurred at Yarmouth, Mass, on Tue last, when a party started in a sail-boat on an excursion among the island. A whirl wind struck the boat containing Mr John Brown, wife, & 2 children, & sister, Asa P C Winslow, wife, & 2 children, & a daughter of Adam Baker, drowned. The women and children went into the cuddy of the boat when the rain first came on. Every person in the cuddy was drowned. Those on deck were saved by getting upon the bow of the boat.

Private sale, a small farm, 5 miles from Wash, bounded on the south by the farm of Dr Gunton, of Wash, on the north by the farm of Mr Fox, of Union Town; contains about 35 acres. -Richd Bryan

Wash City Ordinance: 1-Act for the relief of Z M P King: to pay him $23.92 for the redemption of part of lot 2 in square 199, said lot having been erroneously sold by the Collector of Taxes on Jun 2, 1832. -Approved, Aug 15, 1856

Equity Docket, No 1,064. Circuit Court of Wash Co, D C, Mar Term, 1856. Hirst, wife, & others vs H S Nelson. The trustee reported he has sold part of lot 43, in the original plan of Gtwn, D C, part of the estate of Wm Nelson, deceased, to Jas Nelson, who is one of the heirs at law of said Wm Nelson, for $1,450; & the portion numbered 16, in the same plan, [the same having been divided into 3 lots of 22 feet each, fronting on Prospect st, running back 120 feet,] to Wm Kirkland, for the aggregate sum of $759; & a portion of the same lot, fronting on the north side of Bridge st 29 feet, running back 120 feet, on which stands a 3 story brick house, to Wm Dowling, for $675; that the said Wm Kirkland & Wm Dowling have complied with the terms of sale, & the said Jas Nelson hath proposed to pay interest on the purchase money of said part of lot 43, until the distribution among the heirs of the Wm Nelson of the proceeds of the sale made & to be made by the trustee.

Equity Docket, Circuit Court of Wash Co, D C, Mar Term, 1856. Edw M Linthicum & others vs Ephraim Wheeler. John Marbury, trustee, reports he sold lots B & C, in Wm B Todd's subdivision of part of square 852, in Wash City, on May 26 last, at public auction, to Edw M Linthicum, John Marbury, jr, & Chas A Buckery, the cmplnts, for $2,650. The court ordered that the said sale be ratified & confirmed.

Fire broke out on Sat in the large carpenter's shop on Conn ave, between H & I sts, belonging to W W Corcoran, which, with its contents, was entirely consumed. The fire was of incendiary origin. Mr John Wilson, carpenter, who resides in the neighborhood, came near sacrificing his life, when he attempted to save some tools & property within. Messrs Potts, father & son, went to the assistance of Wilson. He was found lying on his back on the ground, his face & hands much burnt. Dr Miller attended him throughout the night. The injury was very severe, but he is not considered in any serious danger. A few hours later a fire was discovered in a small tenement, owned by Mr Frush, jr, of Gtwn.

In Chancery, Circuit Court of Wash Co, D C, Mar Term, 1856. Wm S Nicholls vs the heirs at law of Jas B Frere. The trustee appointed reports the sale of lot in square 86, in Wash City, to Owen Murray, for $1,046.15, & the purchaser has complied with the terms of sale.

Public sale of farm & fishery: by decree of the Circuit Court for Chas Co, sitting as a Court of Equity: I will sell on Aug 26, in front of the Court-house door in Port Tobacco, Chas Co, Md: **Hopewell Landing Farm**, the residence of the late Wm F Pye, in Cornwallis Neck, Chas Co, immediately on the Potomac river, containing about 350 acres, more or less, with an island attached of about 13 acres.
-N Stonestreet, trustee

Died: on Jul 14, at Decatur, Ill, Wyatta, infant daughter of Mary Eliz & of the late Wyatt Staff Berry, formerly of Wash City.

TUE AUG 19, 1856
Senate: 1-Bills from the House passed-relief: of Rudolf Kussmane; of Thos Ap Catesby Jones; of Wm H Chase; of J W Todd, a lt of ordnance, U S Army; of Jas M Lindsay; of Salvador Accardi; of the sureties of the late Lt Chas E Jarvis, U S Army; of John Otis; of the legal reps of Thos Gordon; of Abner Dickson, a soldier in the war of 1812; of John Connolly, late a private in Co A, 6th Infty, U S Army; of Ursula E Cobb, widow of Chas Cobb; of Edmund Mitchell; of Antoine Robedeau; of the heirs & legal reps of Louis Reggio; of the heirs & legal reps of Bernard Hempkin; of the heirs & legal reps of Ignacio Delina; of the heirs & legal reps of Mrs Magdalene Brouten, widow of De La Ronde; of Wm B Cozens; of Henry L Robinson; of Peyton G King, late receiver of public money at Monroe, La; of John Nash; of Calvin Hall, assignee of Wm Jones; & of Wm Humphreys, jr, owner of fishing schnr **Good Exchange**, lost at sea. Also, an act to increase the pension of David Waldo, of Onondagua, N Y; act authorizing the legal reps of Manuel Gonzales Moro to enter certain lands in Missouri; & to confirm the title of Ruhama Whitaker & Rebecca Whitaker to certain lands in the State of Louisiana. 2-Act increasing the pension of Geo W Torrence: laid on the table. 3-Bill postponed: act for the relief of Louis Hembert. 4-Act for the relief of the heirs of the late Col John Hardin was rejected; but the motion was reconsidered, & the bill lies over until next session.

Valuable farm adjoining the town of Winchester, Va, at public sale: by authority of the will of Thos A Tidball, deceased: sale on Sep 25 next, the farm of the late Thos A Tidball, containing about 267 acres, with a fine large dwlg house; brick kitchen & servants' rooms attached to the main dwlg, & a store-room in the same wing; with the necessary out-houses. At the same time will be sold 2 young negro children, girls, 4 & 6 year; & a library, consisting principally of the theological collection of the late Rev Dr Hill, containing some rare & valuable works not easily procurable elsewhere.
-Jas Marshall, Province McCormick, excs

Household & kitchen furniture at auction on Aug 22, at the late residence of Doct P Warfield, deceased, Fayette & 1st sts, his entire personal effects, including his Library; pew No 52 in Christ's Church, eligibly situated; pair of dueling pistols, & surgical instruments. -Thos Sappington, adm -Barnard & Buckley, aucts

In consequence of the death of one of the partners of the firm of H F Loudon & Co, merchant tailors of Wash City, the business will be closed. The business will then be carried on under the former name at the old stand. -H F Loudon & Co, under Brown's Hotel.

Gen O'Donnell, the Prime Minister of Spain, is as his name indicates, of Irish descent. His family progenitors came to Spain about the middle of the last century. His father attained the rank of Count d'Abispol. Leopold was his 2nd son, & the Count obtained for him a place in the army as Sous-Lt. In the War of the Succession, in 1833, he was rapidly promoted, & finally attained the rank of Genr'l of Division. His family all took sides with Don Carlos, he alone choosing the cause of the young Queen Isabella. Two of his brothers lost their lives in that war. O'Donnell rendered the Regent Queen Christina invaluable service by his military skill, & always stood high in her good graces, but was forced to leave the country in 1840, when the reaction came. He came back to Spain with Narvaez & was made Capt-Genr'l of Cuba. On his return from Cuba he was chosen member of the Senate & made Genr'l-in-Chief of the Cavalry. Murillo's Cabinet put him out of favor & he joined the opposition. Now he is again in power, & neither friends nor foes seem to know what to expect from him.

Died: on Aug 16, at Salem, N J, Wm Morgan Thompson, aged 29 years, late member of Kunkel's opera troupe; was a printer by trade. His death will be regretted by his numerous friends.

Died: on Aug 18, after a long & painfull diarrhoea, Jas Knox Polk, in his 7th year, son of Hon Wm F & Mary F E Purcell. His funeral is this morning at 10 o'clock, from L st, between 9th & 10th sts west.

Died: on Aug 14, in Snow Hill, Md, in his 34th year, Edw D Martin, Clerk of the Circuit Court, & an estimable & popular citizen of Worcester Co.

Died: on Aug 13, in Wmsburg, Long Island, of bilious fever, Ann, wife of Robt O'Hara, aged 52 years.

Died: on Aug 18, in Wash City, James, youngest son of James & Josephine Stone. His funeral will take place from 233 5th st, this afternoon at 5 o'clock.

WED AUG 20, 1856

Mrd: on Aug 14, in Columbus, Ga, by Rev Dr Hawks, Lt Geo G Garner, U S Army, to Lizzie, daughter of Col Wm L Wynn, of Assumption Parish, La.

Mrd: on Aug 18, by Rev Geo W Samson, Lt Chas D Anderson, U S Army, to Miss Lucy A Hazard, of Wash City.

Mr Wm Macleod: instructions in Drawing & Painting, at his Class Rooms, s e corner of 13th & F sts, Wash.

Sashes, Doors, Blinds, & Mouldings: all work will be sold at factory prices.
-Job W Angus, 562 7th st, opposite the Market.

THU AUG 21, 1856

A patent has been recently granted to Mr Peter Hannay, of Wash City, for an improved method of producing blanks for bank-notes, bills, stock certificates, checks, & warrants, so as to prevent their successful imitation by any means now known to science or art.

Criminal Court-Wash-Wed: the case of Bernard Magee for the murder of Jas Simms in Gtwn was disposed of by the acquittal of the accused.

Yesterday the body of a man was observed floating on the surface of the water of the canal just east of the 7th st bridge. He was recognized as Mr McEwen, who formerly was a huckster in the Centre Market. During the storm of Tue evening cries for help were heard by a boatman, but he could not find him. Supposition is that in crossing 7th st bridge he mistook his way, & fell from the dangerous stone steps at the end of the bridge. He had been drinking, but was not intoxicated. He was about 55 years of age.

Mrd: on Aug 19, in Wash City, at St Matthew's Church, by Rev Mr Byrne, John W Nixon, of New Orleans, to Kate, daughter of Wm T & A M Maddox, of St Mary's Co, Md.

Died: on Aug 16, at the residence of Mrs C A Latimer, Prince Wm Co, Va, Harriet Cecilia, aged 1 year & 4 months, only child of Wm T & Rebecca M Weir.

U S Patent Ofc, Wash, Aug 19, 1856. Ptn of Jno P Sherwood, Wash Co, N Y, praying for the extension of a patent granted to him on Dec 17, 1842, for an improvement in door locks, for 7 years from the expiration of said patent, which takes place on Dec 17, 1856. -Chas Mason, Com'r of Patents

FRI AUG 22, 1856
New Orleans Picayune of Aug 15: reliable particulars of the disaster at Last Island, forwarded by the obliging Jona C White, of the Thibodaux, Minerva, & by Mr Brashear, of Brashear. News from Last Island on Aug 13 states that every house had been unroofed & thrown down save one; that those saved were on the hull of the steamboat **Star**, which occupies the site of the Muggah Billiard House; that 116 persons are missing; that many of those saved have broken limbs. Mrs Maskell & child, Mrs Rentrop, Wm Rochell & child, & Mrs Robt Royster are among the missing. One house only remaining, Mrs Bishel's. Drs McLeod & Scuddy have gone down in a sail-boat to render assistance to the wounded survivors. The following is a list of the victims with which we are furnished by our reporter:

Thos A Miller, wife, & 2 servants
Capt Schelatre, wife, & 7 children
Mrs Thos Maskell, 3 children & 1 servant
Mrs Telesphore Landry, 2 children, & 4 servants
Mrs Antoine Como, 5 children & 3 servants

Mrs Pruett, 2 children & 3 servants
Mrs Dorsine L Rentrop & daughter
Mr & Mrs Turner
Mr & Mrs Read & child
Mrs Flash & sister
Servant of Thos Ellis
John Muggah, wife & 2 children
A M Foley & wife
Mrs Cooziere & 3 servants
J C Beatty, wife, & 2 children
Mrs Bordis & servant
Henry Landry & 3 servants
Michl Landry
Jos Dugas
Ulysses Simonica
C A Berreditt
Infant child of W W Pugh
A Fidre, wife, child & servant
S Grevenburg
Wm Rochell

Capt Ratler
F Fitzpatrick
A Gennan, jr
Mr & Mrs Royster
Child of Ette
Child of Berard
Child & servant of Marsh
Mrs Gerard & child
Servant of Dr Hawkins
Mr Miller, wife, & child
Mrs Roumage
Mr Voisin & daughter
M Babbin, Mrs E Babbin
Jas Muggah & son
Mr Bell J Snyder
Servant of G A Bryant
2 children of Bouttbon
Pecam
Robbinett

[Aug 28th newspaper: Persons saved, some of whom passed not less than a day or two on the water: Mr A Read; a slave of Mr Muggah; a servant of Mr Read; Mr Michl Landry, of Assumption; Messrs Thos Mille; Capt Schlatre; a servant girl of Mr Telesphore Landry.]

Mrd: on Aug 21, in the old Trinity Church, by Rev W Krebs, Geo Burns to Sallie H Hammond, all of Wash City.

[Aug 30th newspaper: The New Orleans papers announce the recovery of several more bodies of the victims by the calamity at Last Island: Jean B Avet, Mrs Roumage, Mr Gimble, & Seymour A Stewart, son of Saml Stewart, of New Orleans. Mrs A M Dickinson, 2 children, & servant; Mrs M A Leftwich; Mr Wm Hart, wife, 2 children, & servant; & Mr Trosclair & wife, of Bayou Geula. They were rescued by the steamer **Blue Hammack**.] [Sep 4th newspaper: Mrs Toffier, of Bayous Goula, with her mother & brother, & infant child in her arms, passed the night on a piece of timber & were rescued in the morning. Messrs Mille & Schlatre got on a door & were carried into the Gulf, reaching the bay shore on the 15th. Capt Smith made one heroic effort to save Mr Turner, his wife, Col Fisher & daughter, but the sand half-blinded him & he no longer could find them. Henry Turero, son of Francis Turero, aged 16, saved his half sister Henrietta, daughter of Boudreau, 3 times; she kept separating from his arms. He is now lying very ill at the house of that honorable, though sorely afflicted husband & father, Antoine Como, one of the survivors on Last Island. A negro girl belonging to Antoine Como, aged 15, named Molly, saved a little girl aged 3, daughter of Mr Como, only child saved out of 6 he had on the island. The children were already orphans on the father's side, & made doubly so by the loss of their mother on the island.]

Vocal Instruction: Mr F Nicholls Crouch, Composer & Singing Master: proposes opening a Musical Vocal Academy on Sep 15 next. Apply at Mr Richd Davis' or at Geo Hilbus' music store, Pa ave, for necessary information.

St Louis, Aug 21. Leavenworth Journal of the 17th: 300 Freesoilers, headed by Brown, drove a colony of Georgians near Ossawattomie into Missouri, destroying their property. On Aug 15 the Treadwell settlement was attacked by 400 Freesoilers & sent to Gov Shannon for aid. Fight on Aug 14 near Ossawattomie between 200 Freesoilers & 12 pro-slavery men-the latter in a fort. 23 Freesoilers were killed & wounded. On Aug 16 Lecompton was attacked by 800 of Lane's men. The U S troops, having in charge Robinson, Brown, & others, surrendered without firing a gun. Col Titus was absent at the time. His house was burnt. Mr Clowes, editor of the Southern Advocate, & another person, were killed.

Died: on Aug 21, in Wash City, Mary Virlinda, only child of Richd B & Mgt Ann Norment, aged 2 years & 24 days. Her funeral will take place this afternoon at 4 o'clock, from the parent's residence, 611 H st.

Trustee's sale of improved property: by deed of trust from Nicholas Funk & wife, dated Jan 10, 1855, recorded in Liber J A S No 90, folios 288: sale on Sep 24, on the premises, the east half of lot 24 in square 101, fronting 20 feet on north I st, near 20th st, with a 2 story brick dwlg house. -Owen Murray, trustee -A Green auct

Household & kitchen furniture at auction on: Aug 28, at the residence of Mr Dart, on E st north, between 2nd & 3rd sts-very superior furniture. -A Green auct

SAT AUG 23, 1856
First-class residence in Gtwn, D C, for rent. The subscriber offers her late residence at the corner of Fayette & 4th sts, Gtwn, immediately opposite to the Convent of the Visitation. This is one of the largest & best finished houses in D C, having all the modern improvements. Attached is a large cistern in the yard & carriage-house & stables for several horses. A pump of the purest water is in the immediate vicinity. Possession given immediately. Inquire next door to the premises of Mrs Anne R O'Neale.

Senate: 1-Bills which failed to receive the signature of the Pres from want of time at the last session, have since been presented to the Executive under the joint resolution of the 2 houses adopted yesterday-act for the relief of: J W Todd, a lt in the U S Army; of the legal reps of Thos Gordon, deceased; of Calvin Hall, assignee of Wm Jones; of Jas M Lindsay; of Salvador Accardi; of John Otis; of Antoine Robedeau; of Abner Dickson, a soldier of the war of 1812; of John Connolly, late private in Co A, 6th Infty, U S Army; of Ursula E Cobb, widow of Chas Cobb; & of Rudolph Kussmaul. Also title of Ruhama Whittaker & Rebecca Whittaker to certain lands in Louisiana; increase pension of Danl Waldo, of Onondaga Co, N Y; & authorize the legal reps of Manuel Gonzales Moro to enter certain lands in Missouri.

Household & kitchen furniture, & excellent rosewood piano forte & stool, at auction on: Aug 29, at the residence of Wm Lewis Herndon, U S Navy, corner of H & 20th sts. -Jas C McGuire, auct

Died: on Aug 21, in Wash City, John Elliot, infant son of Chas E & Susannah Brown, aged 6 months.

Died: on Aug 18, in Wash City, Sylvester Kane, infant son of M A E & Jas J Kane.

Died: on Aug 22, in Wash City, Emma Amelia, infant daughter of Wm & Jane M Thomas. Her funeral is this afternoon at 4:30 P M from the family residence, corner of 11th st & Mass ave.

Died: on Aug 21, in Wash City, Oliver Fannin, infant son of Philip & Leonora Clayton, aged 18 months.

Fred'k Female Seminary will be resumed on the first Monday of Sept, 1856. Boarding & Tuition, including furnished rooms, lights, fuel, & washing: $200 per scholastic year, payable half-yearly in advance. Address H Winchester, President

Wanted, a teacher to take charge for the ensuing scholastic year of 3 youths, about 16 & 17 years of age. An Episcopalian & a Southerner preferred. Address Mrs Geo Carter, Upperville, Fauquier Co, Va.

MON AUG 25, 1856
Wash City Ordinance: 1-Act for the relief of Wm Bean: $5 to be paid him for arranging the premises for holding the annual general election in the 1st precinct of the 5th Ward.

Died: on Aug 23, in Gtwn, Mrs Mary Ann McKenney, wife of Saml McKenney. Her funeral will be this morning at 10:30 A M, from her late residence on Dumbarton st.

Hartford Times of Aug 21. The noble old **_Charter Oak_**, of Hartford, which stood on the grounds of Hon Isaac W Stuart, late the Wyllys' estate, in this city, so noted in song & history, fell with a tremendous crash during the great store this morning, Aug 21, 1856. About 3 years ago some boys built a fire in the hallow of the tree, which burnt out the punk. Fresh sprouts sprung out the next spring, & Mr Stuart took great pains to preserve this valued relic of the original forests of New England, but more especially interesting as the tree in which the old Brititsh Charter of Connecticut was secreted & preserved. The charter of King Charles the Second for the colony of Connecticut arrived in Hartford in 1662. On Oct 9 it was publicly read to the assembled freemen of Connecticut. It was the organic law of Conn till the present constitution took its place in 1818. In 1686 a new Gov't was instituted with Jos Dudley as President of the Com'rs. On Oct 31, 1687, Sir Edmund Andross, attended by members of his Council & a body guard of 60 soldiers, entered Hartford to take the charter by force. The Genr'l Assembly was in session. The charter was brought in & laid on the table, when suddenly the lights were all put out & total darkness followed. The candles were again lighted, & the charter was gone. Sir Edmund Andross declared the gov't of Conn to be in his own hands, & that the colony was annexed to Mass & other New England colonies, & proceeded to appoint ofcrs. Whilst he was doing this Capt Jeremiah Wadsworth, a patriot of those times, was concealing the charter in the hollow of Wyllys' oak, now known as the Charter Oak. In 1689 King James abdicated, & on May 9, 1689, Gov Treat & his associate ofcrs resumed the gov't of Conn under the charter preserved in the old hollow oak.
[Nov 20th newspaper: The Hartford Times states that the roots of this fallen oak still live, & that at a distance of 10 feet from the ground on the stump is a new shoot; but we fear this king of trees is laid low forever. -Union A citizen of Washington has now 6 young oaks growing, produced from acorns taken from the old charter oak. The acorns were sent to him at his request by the late venerable Judge Williams, of Conn. -Nat Intel.]

A farmer, Silas Gravel, died in Montg Co, Pa, a few days since in consequence of handling guano with his hands, when there were some slight sores upon them. This should warn others not to handle guano if they have even a scratch upon their hands.

Died: on Aug 23, in Wash City, David S Waters, sen, in his 66th year. His funeral is this evening at 4 o'clock, from his residence on N Y ave, between 6th & 7th sts.

Died: on Aug 24, in Wash City, Mrs Lucy A Burdine, wife of Mr Alfred Burdine, in her 22nd year.

Died: on Aug 20, at the residence of her cousin, Wm Watts, in St Mary's Co, Md, after a severe illness of bilious dysentery, which she bore with Christian fortitude, Miss Sue C Milburn, of Wash City, aged 21 years & 2 months.

Middlebury, Vt, Aug 23. Hon Jas Meacham, member of the U S House of Reps from the first district of this State, died at his residence in this town this morning, from congestion of the brain, at the age of 46 years. His illness had been brief. [Aug 26 newspaper: Mr Meacham was a native of Rutland, Vt, where he was born in 1810 of humble but respectable parentage. He was bereft of both parents in his early youth. He has left a wife & children to mourn his loss.]

TUE AUG 26, 1856
Leavenworth Journal of Aug 17. An express from Lecompton brings intelligence of the attack on Franklin by Lane's men. They attacked Judge Fain & shot him in the shoulder; attacked the post ofc & robbed it, treating the postmaster & his family in a most dastardly manner. Mr Crain's energy as a justice of the peace being the cause of the unheard of atrocities perpetrated upon him. More outrages. Col Titus murdered; the house of G W Clark, Indian Agent was also attacked. Andre Preston was wounded; Mr Sisterre & Mr Cweos, [editor of the Southern Advocate] were killed.

Appointment confirmed by the Senate: Mr Curry as Govn'r & Benj F Harding, Sec of the Territory of Oregon; John J Taylor, of N Y, & Geo P Bond, of Cambridge Univ, Chief Astronomer, to run the boundary line between Wash Territory & the British possessions; Franklin H Clark, U S Atty for the eastern district of Louisiana, vice McCay, resigned; Danl Ratcliff, Assist Solicitor of the court of Claims; A T Haven, of Mich, U S marshal for Utah, vice Howard, removed; Matthias R Andrew, Collector of Customs at St Augustine; John Thorne, of N Y, Consul at Singapore; John Laws, Com'r, & Jas G Mayes, Receiver of the Land Ofc at Vincennes, to examine & decide on land titles there.

Criminal Court-Wash-Monday. 1-Danl O'Keefe pronounced guilty of larceny & sentenced to 18 months' imprisonment.

Police Magistrates elected last evening by the City Council:
Saml Drury   Benj K Morsell   Jas H Birch
Paul Stevens   Thos J Williams
John S Hollingshead   Saml S Briggs

On Sunday John Tuell, son & only child of Mr L A Tuell, of the 6th Ward, was drowned in the Eastern Branch. He was in a boat with other youths crossing from the direction of Mrs Woodruff's farm, when he fell off backwards off the boat into the river. He was 14 years of age, intelligent, & the pride of his father's heart.

Died: on Aug 24, in Gtwn, Mrs Mary O Reiley, aged 63 years. Her funeral is this morning at 9½ o'clock, from her late residence on Congress st.

Died: on Aug 22, in Wash City, Mary Lizzie, infant daughter of Wm A & Catharine B Baird.

From Kansas: Aug 16, near Lecompton, 500 Freesoilers marched upon Col Titus' camp. & took all the inmates prisoners. Capt Chabere, of Indiana, was wounded & will die. Titus was badly wounded.

WED AUG 27, 1856
The valuable property advertised by Chas B Calvert, at private sale is not sold, & will be sold at public auction on Sep 2 next, in the grove adjoining the *Spa Spring* at Bladensburg, PG Co, Md. 1-Tract containing 216 acres. 2-Meadow land containing 25 acres, having several houses on ground rent. 3-Beautiful bldg lots in the village of Ellaville, each containing from 3 to 10 acres. -A Green auct

Wash City Corp: 1-Referred to the Cmte of Claims-act for the relief: of Henrietta Shryock; of Maurice Holloran; of J B Williamson; & of Jas H Boss. 2-Bills passed- relief: of Henrietta Shryock, Anne Dunlop, & Richd Adams. 3-Cmte of Claims: asked to be discharged from the consideration of the bill for the relief of Ann Sharkey; which was disagreed to, & the bill was passed.

$50 reward for runaway negro boy Jos Gallaway, about 15 years old, a bright mulatto, with straight hair. He has relations near the Alexandria [Va] Ferry. -J Alfred Osbourn, living near Upper Marlborough, Md.

Criminal Court-Wash-Tue. Jury:
Jno Scrivner   Josh Worthington   Amos Davis
Enoch Moreland   John T Bradley   John Ashford
Thos J Davis   Thos E Baden   Ephraim Wheeler
Henry G Murray   Patrick McKenna   David A Baird

Criminal Court-Tuesday. The U S vs Wm Sullivan, for the murder of Caspar Kohrman, alias Chas W Bell, on Jul 4 next. Kohrman was about 35 years of age. Sworn in: Ofcr Keese; Dr Johnson Eliot; Urban Geier; Conrad Jost; Mrs Padgett; & Simon Heisman, his evidence in German interpreted to the Jury. He & his wife were sitting on a bench at the time of the occurrence. [Aug 28th: Valentine Dingel, barkeeper at Mr Schussler's, testified. Mrs Eggleston, she being the wife of the other party indicted, was not permitted to testify. Mrs Schussler; Thos Dawson; Columbus Estlin; Jas Bowen, & Danl Stewart were examined.] [Aug 30th newspaper: Henry Hood; Chas Frankinberger; Allen Dorsey; Thos Dawson; Franklin Birckhead, a watchmen; Jas H Shreeve; & John Grimes: testified. Mr Donaldson, captain of the watch in Gtwn, & Sullivan's father-in-law, deposed that on the day following the murder his daughter, Sullivan's wife, came to him to consult about Sullivan's delivering himself up. Jas Ward, jailor of the Wash Co jail testified.]

Died: on Aug 26, in Wash City, Amela Ann Gallant, wife of Peter Gallant, & daughter of the late John Hoburg, in her 32nd year. Her funeral is this morning at 9 o'clock, from her late residence, on Mass ave, between 5th & 6th sts.

Died: on Aug 26, in Wash City, Kate, daughter of the late Jos & Mary A McEvoy, in her 22nd year. Her funeral is on Thu at 3 o'clock, from the residence of Mrs Murphy, on 9th st, between F & G sts.

Died: on Aug 19, at Berryville, Va, whither she had gone for the benefit of her health, Hannah J Washington, daughter of Perrin Washington, of Wash City.

Died: on Sunday, John Francis Tuell, aged 14 years, son of Mr L A Tuell, of Wash City. His funeral is this afternoon at 3 o'clock, from the residence of his father, 577 7th st east.

THU AUG 28, 1856
Orphans Court of Wash Co, D C. Letters of administration on the personal estate of Jane Birth, late of Wash Co, deceased. -Wm W Birth, adm

Orphans Court of Wash Co, D C. In the case of John Kelley, exc of Wm Donovan, deceased: the Court & executor had appointed Sep 16 next, for the final settlement of the personal estate of said deceased, of the assets in hand. -Ed N Roach, Reg/o wills

Died: on Aug 27, at the residence of his grandfather, in Wash City, Walter Smith Hill, youngest son of Wm B & Catharine B Hill, of PG Co, Md, aged 13 months.

From Calif: the Vigilance Cmte was still in power. They hung on Jul 29 Jos Herrington for murder, & Dr Sandall a few days previous; also, a man named Brace, for a murder committed a year ago. Judge Terry was still a prisoner.

FRI AUG 29, 1856
Mrd: on Aug 28, in Wash City, at the E st Baptist Church, by Rev G W Samson, Mr Geo W Stidham, of the delegation from the Creek Nation, to Miss Sarah C Thornberry, of Wash.

Died: on Aug 28, in Gtwn, Clara Eliz, daughter of Henry & M J King. Her funeral is this afternoon at 3 o'clock, from the residence of her father 48 Third st.

Household & kitchen furniture at auction on: Sep 4, at the residence of Mrs Gassaway, 59 First st, Gtwn, opposite *Cox's Row*. -Jas C McGuire, auct

Desirable property for sale on the Heights of Gtwn: the pleasant Cottage opposite the residence of Richd L Mackall. It is new & contains 7 or 8 rooms. Apply to M Adler.

Maj Cornelius A Ogden, Corps of Engineers, died at Brandon, Vt, on Aug 23, according to advices received at the War Dept.

Two young men named Girard Clifton & Jas Williams were detected on Monday in the act of picking ladies' pockets at the Jane st Methodist Church, N Y, when the funeral service of Mr Thos Braum was being performed. They were arrested & committed to prison.

Orphans Court of Wash Co, D C. Letters of administration with the will annexed on the personal estate of Mary Calna-, late of Wash Co, deceased. -P Gallant, adm with the will annexed. [Calna_: last letter missing.]

SAT AUG 30, 1856
Fr Schaffieiter, A Roman Catholic priest of the Redemptionist order, fell down within the rails of the altar while singing the Magnificat, in St Mary's Church during vespers on Sunday. He lived only about half an hour. The cause of his death was disease of the heart. He was a very learned & benevolent priest, & much beloved by his people. -Buffalo Commercial Advertiser

Dr Crawley Finney, a much respected resident of Nansemond Co, Va, died a few days ago from taking morphine by mistake for quinine. He was about 63 years of age.

Six persons drowned on Wed off Bellport, Long Island, when a pleasure boat was upset. They were all of N Y: Mrs Dr Kemf, Mrs J E D Funk & Jas Funk, wife & son of Capt Stansberry Funk, Linda Harriott, daughter of Carman Harriott, Eddie Northrup, wife of John Northrup, & a servant girl in the employ of Mr Harriott.

Mrs B E Gittings has just opened a choice lot of French Flowers, Straw Bonnets, Ribands, & Embroideries, at her store, 14 Pa ave, between 8th & 9th sts.

Mrd: on Aug 26, at Oak Hill, PG Co, Md, by Rev H C Westwood, Mr Geo W Scaggs, of Wash, to Miss Mary P Nailor.

Mrd: on Aug 20, by Rev Thos J Addison, at the residence of Col Dickinson, Caroline Co, Va, Maj Jas P Corbin to Miss Eliza Lewis Hoomes, of the same county. The bridal party celebrated the nuptials on the same evening at *Moss' Neck*, at the magnificent mansion of Maj Corbin, where the usual festivities were enjoyed by a large party of friends from Wash, Richmond, Balt, & the immediate vicinity, the ceremonies being greatly enlivened by the sprightly performances of the State Band from Richmond. -A Washington Friend

Coal for sale at H B Riehle's Wood & Coal Yard, N Y ave, between 11th & 14th sts.

Mutual Fire Ins Co of D C: Ulysses Ward, Pres: Chas Wilson, Sec; Mathew G Emery, Treas. Managers: Thos Blagden, Ulysses Ward, John Dickson, T J Magruder, John Van Riswick, Mathew G Emery, J C McKelden. Ofc: adjoining the Bank of Wash.

Boston, Aug 29. Amos A Lawrence has declined the nomination for Govn'r tendered him by the Fillmore Convention.

Aza Arnold, Patent Agent, 448 7th st, opposite the Patent Ofc.

Female teacher wanted to instruct in all the branches of an English education & music on the piano, to take charge of a school in my family of some 10 or 12 pupils: salary of $200 per annum & board. A lady belonging to the Episcopal church would be preferred. Address Wm Ferguson, Chas Co, Md.

MON SEP 1, 1856
Calif: Two more persons executed by the Vigilance Cmte: Jos Hetherington, for the murder of Dr Randall in a hotel on Jul 24, the other a young offender, Philander Brace. David S Terry, a Judge of the Calif Supreme Court, was arrested by this cmte for the crime of defending his own life in a quarrel forced upon him for the discharge of his duty as a conservator of the peace. There are over 1,500 unnaturalized aliens in armed opposition to the laws & constitution of this country, & one-third cannot speak English. Maj Lee, U S Army, who has served his country over 25 years, had a pistol pointed at his breast by one of these people for attempting to pass the street, & was told to stand back. Such is the libery in San Francisco. I will enumerate some of those who belong to this party & condemn the acts of the cmte. From their names & position you will be able to guess the true state of the case: Judge J H Thornton, formerly of Alabama, appointed a member of the Land Commission by Pres Fillmore. Judge Thompson, late of Va, & a member of the Land Commision. He is now with you. Jos G Baldwin, of Alabama; Henry P Irving, formerly of Va, a prominent Whig in the Buckingham district; Col Peter de La Torry, of S C, one of our best lawyers;

A P Crittenden, of Texas, a lawyer & nephew of Senator Crittenden; Jas E Calhoun, atty at law, a son of the late John C Calhoun; Calhoun Benham, U S district atty under Mr Fillmore; Col Edw Baker, ex-member of Congress from Ill; Hon Ogden Hoffman, Judge U S District Court; Hon M H McAllister, Judge of the U S Circuit Court; W B Dameron, U S naval ofcr; L Q Washington, deputy collector of customs, formerly of Wash, D C; Col John C Hays, formerly of Texas, U S Surveyor Genr'l; Chas Neller, U S Postmaster; R P Ashe, U S Navy Agent; Maj R B Lee, U S Army, late of Wash City. San Francisco, Aug 3, 1856. The last mail steamer carried away Reuben Maloney, one of the witnesses for the U S Gov't, in the case of the U S vs Durkee, charged with piracy. He was forced to leave by the Cmte of Vigilance. Judge Terry's property on the San Joaquin river, valued at $35,000, has been burnt down, the work of an incendiary.

Wash City Ordinances: 1-Act for relief of Ann Sharkey: fine imposed on her for selling liquor without a license is remitted, provided she pay the costs of suit. 2-Act to compensate Jos Radclif as clerk to examine the accounts of R J Roche, late Collector of Taxes: to be paid $357. 3-Act for relief of Richd Adams: fine for violating a city ordinance by keeping his bar open after 12 o'clock is remitted, provided he pay the costs of prosecution. 4-Act for relief of Peter Little: sum of $15.25 be paid him for cleaning the snow from the Eastern Market-House in Jan last.

Loss of the steamer **Nautilus**: details furnished by the Purser of the steamship **Perseverance** & Lt Stevens, of the U S engineers, who left Galveston on Aug 20, for Timballer Island, on the Govn't schnr **Essayons**. The largest part of the hull was on Caillou Island. Jim Frisbee, the steward of the **Nautilus**, was picked up on the 20th by the towboat **F M Streck**, near **Fort Livingston**, Barrataria bay, after floating on a drift log. Capt Thompson was washed off the ship. Mr Johnson, the first engineer, was with Frisbee 5 days, when he became delirious & jumped into the sea & drowned. A body of a man with black whiskers, having blue clothes on, was found, & thought to be Capt Thompson. List of passengers containing all whose names could be learned by our informants: R P Deaver, N C; Micajah Thomas & lady, Houston, Texas; H G Bullock, Fayette Co, Texas; W A Kirwin, Freestone Co, Texas; Rev Jerome Twichell, Houston Texas; Wm Dean, Brownsville, Texas; Adolphe Holff, Liberty, Texas; S A Ingraham, Lagrange, Texas; J D Ellis, Washington, Texas; Thos A Mallory, Galveston, Texas; Judge Jas Scott, Grimes Co, Texas; Dr R Graves, Wheelock, Texas; Miss H Gay, Wheelock, Texas, C H Short, New Orleans; Capt Wm Muir, New Orleans; Anderson Marsh, New Orleans; J Newman, Marshall, Ala; J M Adams, Marshall, Ala. It appears that the ship was suddenly overturned, & that the passengers were not anticipating their fate, but were in an instant launched into eternity. -New Orleans Bulletin of the 25th.

Jas E Heath, of Richmond, Va, formerly Com'r of Patents, had his thigh bone fractured by a fall on a hard pavement at Warrenton on Sat last.

Mrd: on Aug 28, in Gtwn, by Rev Dr Norwood, L Martin, of Va, to Anne M Harrison, of Gtwn.

Died: on Aug 29, in Exeter, N H, of consumption, Mrs Anne Richardson French, wife of Hon Henry F French, & sister of Mrs B B French, of Wash City. An angel-woman on earth, she has gone to add one to the angel choir in Heaven.

A son of Mr Wm Phipps, engraver, aged about 3 years, was so seriously burned last evening, by his clothes taking fire from a friction match, with which he was playing, that he is not expected to survive the injury.

TUE SEP 2, 1856
Sandwich Islands: we have before us the first number of a handsome new paper, printed in English, at Honolulu, Hawiian Islands, dated Jul 2, entitled the Pacific Commercial advertiser, & is published weekly, by Henry M Whitney.

John Fox, convicted of the murder of John Henry at New Brunswick, N J, was executed at that place on Wednesday.

Home School for Young Ladies: repairs to be made at Mrs Archer's, the school formerly kept in her house will be temporarily transferred to my residence, ½ mile, near the Piedmont Station, on the Manassas Gap Railroad, Fauquier Co, Va.
-John Thos Smith

To parents & guardians: the subscriber has engaged a young gentleman to tutor in his family, & desires to get some 6 or 8 boys as boarders. The school will be conducted upon the parental system. The situation is pleasant & within a mile of the Manassas Gap railroad. -Robt E Peyton, near the Plains P O, Fauqier Co, Va.

Mrd: on Aug 19, in Wash City, by Rev Thos Duncan, Mr Jas H Meacham to Miss Jennie F Lynch, both of Va.

Mrd: on Sep 1, in Wash City, by Rev Thos Duncan, Mr Wm B Shaw to Miss Belle Burke, all of Wash City.

Mrd: on Sep 1, in Wash City, in the Fourth Presbyterian Church, by Rev John C Smith, Chas A Shafer to Miss Mary, daughter of the late Anthony Preston.

Mrd: on Aug 28, at **Evergreen Park**, Manhasset, Long Island, N Y, by Rev Mr Demerest, Dr H Coust Simms, of Wash, D C, to Maria, 2nd daughter of Hon Judge H G Onderdonk, of the former place.

Died: on Sep 1, in Wash City, of congestion of the lungs, Peter Little, sen, in his 80th year. His funeral is this afternoon at 4:30 o'clock, from his late residence, on L st south, near the Navy Yard.

Died: on Jul 28, in Marysville, Calif, at the residence of his brother-in-law, Saml W Langton, Robt Grant Keefer, formerly of Thorold, Canada West, aged 26 years & 3 months. [Note: A difficult to read "word of codolence" was included under the death notice by a Downieville [Cal] Citizen]

WED SEP 3, 1856
Cmder Hoff, U S Navy, will proceed immediately to take command of the U S frig **Independence**, now in the Pacific.

Trustee's sale of drugs, medicines, soda apparatus, store fixtures, & gas fixtures, at auction, by deed of trust to the subscriber, dated Dec 11, 1855, recorded in Liber J A S No 102, folios 423 ro 426, in the land records of Wash Co, D C: in the apothecary store & house of Wm T Evans, north H & 7th sts; & all the furniture in the house. -John S Evans, trustee -A Green auct

Chas W Welch, Chief Clerk of the Dept, has been appointed by the Pres acting Sec of the Navy, in the temporary absence of Mr Sec Dobbin, who has gone to his home in N C for the benefit of his health.

While Dr Irving Webster, of Plymouth, his father, from Vt, his brother, from Kansas, & his little son, 4 years of age, were sailing on Billington Sea [a large pond by that name] yesterday afternoon the boat upset, & Dr Webster & his little son were drowned. His age was 35. -Boston Chronicle, Aug 29

H Fulkurt, pastermaster at Haskinsville, Ohio, for 10 years, has been arrested on the charge of robbing the mail.

Wash Corp: 1-Ptn from Emma C Berry & others for improving First st east, between B & C sts: referred to the Cmte on Improvements. 2-Ptn from John & Philip Bigler for the remission of a fine: referred to the Cmte of Claims. 3-Cmte of Claims: act for the relief of Jas H Boss: passed. Same cmte: act for the relief of Wm G Deale: read twice.

Two little sisters, Ann & Emily Clappsaddle, aged 6 & 10 years respectively, were found drowned in a mill pond, near Elmira, last Monday evening. It is supposed they were at play on some saw logs lying in the water, as their dinner baskets were found on the bank near by. -Syracuse Journal

Died: Sep 2, in Wash City, after a lingering illness, Miss Eliz Bellinger. Her funeral is this afternoon at 4 o'clock, from the residence of Mrs Tucker, on 9th st, near I st.

THU SEP 4, 1856
Stone & Marble Yard; prices moderate: E st, between 12th & 13th sts.
-Wm Rutherford

Mrd: on Aug 30, near N Y, by Rev Jos Quartier, Wm S Forrest, of Wash City, to Miss Eliz S, daughter of the late Dr Joel Martin, U S Army.

Died: on Sep 3, in Wash City, Walter M Clarke, in his 39th year. His funeral will be tomorrow morning, at 9 o'clock, at St Patrick's Church, F st.

C Woodward & Son have opened a New Stove, Grate, & House Furnishing Establishment, next door to C Woodward's old stand, 318 Pa ave, between 10th & 11th sts. They have the well known Morning Star Cooking Stove, which has a first rate bake oven.

$400 reward for runaway, my negro man Danl, 25 years of age, & my negro woman, Maria, 40 years of age, a bright mulatto. -Geo Parker, Wash, D C

FRI SEP 5, 1856
A happy colony of young people left N Y for the West, under the guardianship of Rev Mr Vanmeter. The number of little immigrants was about 50 of both sexes, & varied in ages from 6 years to 14 years. They were accompanied to the cars by Messrs Macy, Mead, & C C Tracy, of the Newsboys' Lodging House, & fitted out for the West by the Five Points Ladies' Mission, the Children's Aid Society, & the Home for the Friendless. -N Y Evening Post

Columbia Statesman dated Aug 29: Kansas exaggerations: Col Titus was not killed; the State prisoners, Robinson, Brown, & others, have not been rescued, but are all in safe custody; the U S troops have not been whipped; Capt Moore's company are all well mounted & equipped; Capt Bill Martin, an old Texas ranger, with his 600 Kickapoo Rangers, had also arrived at Lecompton. -St Louis Democrat

Gen P A Herran, Minister from New Grenada, & Don Rafael Pombo, Sec of Legation, are in Wash City.

The Navy Dept has selected Cmder Hartstene to command the ship **Resolute** on her voyage to be presented to the British Gov't, in pursuance of the recent act of Congress.

A young man, John Curtis, was shot dead a few nights ago, near Cincinnati, by a gentleman whose house he had entered to rob.

For rent: 299 & 305 of the row houses on I st, between 15th & 16th sts. Pew No 35 in Christ Church, Gtwn, [Dr Norwood's,] for sale. Apply at Riggs & Co's, to A Hyde.

Md Military Academy, Oxford, Talbot Co, Md. John H Allen [graduate of the U S Military Academy, West Point,] Superintendent. The 10 annual session of this Institution will commence on the 1st Monday of Oct next: tuition for 5 months, $100.

C W Schuermann, from the Conservatoire de Music of Leipzig, Germany, will continue to give instructions on the Piano & Vocal Music. Residence 512 L st, between 9th & 10th.

$100 reward for runaway negro man Ben Fletcher, about 26 or 27 years of age. The said boy has recently been hired on the farm of W G W White, near 7th st tollgate. -Henry Martin, near Rock Creek Church

Died: on Jul 31, at **Camp Cooper**, Texas, 2nd Lt Geo McGunnegle Dick, of the 1st Regt of Infty, & oldest son of Hon John Dick, member of Congress, of Pa. By the death of this meritorious young man the service has been deprived of one whose many excellent qualities as an ofcr presaged an honorable career in the profession he already adorned.

Died: on Sep 4, in Wash City, Julius A Peters, a native of Neufchatel, Switzerland, aged 48 years. His funeral will be on Sat at 10 o'clock A M, from his late residence on D st west, between 21st & 22nd sts.

Died: on Sep 4, in Wash City, Mr Jas Galligan, in his 74th year. His funeral is this afternoon from his late residence, corner 1st & C st, Capitol Hill, at 3 o'clock.

Orphans Court of Wash Co, D C. Letters of administration on the personal estate of Danl Ross, late of the U S Navy, deceased. -Lewis Clephane, adm

SAT SEP 6, 1856
Household & kitchen furniture at auction on: Sep 11, at the residence of R S Sproule, on F st, between 9th & 10th sts. -Jas C McGuire, auct

The subscription books for the "History of the Invasion & Capture of Washington," by J S Williams, Brig Maj & Inspector of the Columbian Brigade in the war of 1812, will be found at the bookstores of R Farnham & Taylor & Maury for the signatures of such as may desire to subscribe for this work.

Reminiscences. Yesterday, the 5th, was the anniversary of two small but well contested battles with the British fleet in the Potomac, at the White House, & on the Va side, under Cmdor Porter, & at Indian Head, on the Md side, under Cmdor Perry. Capt Gordon commanded the British squadron, which ascended the river as far as Alexandria, comprised of the frig **Seahorse** & the frig **Euryalus**, the bomb-ships **Devastation**, **Aetna**, **Meteor**, **Erebus**, & **Fairy**, & the dispatch-boat **Anna Maria**. On the Sunday evening previous Com Rodgers, with 4 barges, encountered the enemy with 7 barges, & repulsed them, destroying one barge & having only 2 or 3 men slightly hurt. The month of Sep, 1814, was an era distinguished for brilliant achievements on the Northern frontier & lakes & at Balt. One of the most distinguished ofcrs of the British navy, Sir Peter Parker, fell in an attack upon a detachment of Md Militia under Col Philip Reed, on Aug 30, near Belle Air, on the eastern Shore of Md, & Gen Ross, the cmder of the military forces who invaded Wash City, fell in a conflict with the militia at North Point, near Balt.

Jas H Weakley, of Florence, Ala, died suddenly of disease of the heart at Wilmington, N C, on Wed last. He had just arrived with his wife & niece, all of them being on their way to one of the Va springs.

Mademoiselle de Boye, Instructress in Vocal & Instrumental Music announces her purpose of remaining here another season. Her residence is at 466 13th st, between Pa ave & E st.

Public sale of valuable real estate: in pursuance of the last will of Elisha W Williams, deceased, & in obedience to an order of the Orphans' Court of Montg Co: sale in Poolesville, on Oct 11, the Farm, on the Potomac river, in said county, equidistant between the mouth of Seneca & Edwards' Ferry, containing 175 5/8th acres of land: adjoining the lands of the late Thos J Bowie on the west, & on the east by the lands of Mrs Jane Williams. Geo W Dawson, living in the vicinity, will show the land.
-Jane Williams, excx of Elisha W Williams, deceased.

Circuit Court of Wash Co, D C-in Equity, No 1,183. John Withers vs Chas S Wallach, Richd Wallach, Edwin Walker, John A Linton, & Wm Linton, adm of Enoch Glasscock. 1,017-Chas H Tavener vs Jos Peck, Robt W Latham, & Chas S Wallach. The above causes are referred to me to take & state an account of the fund in the hands of the dfndnt, Chas S Wallach, & of the grounds & particulars of the respective claims upon said fund, which are referred to in the answers of said Wallach to the bills filed in these causes. Above parties are to appear before me at the Auditor's room, City Hall, on Sep 13. -Walter S Cox, Special Auditor

Died: on Sep 5, in Wash City, at the residence of her nephew, Col Abert, Miss Sally Ming, in her 93rd year. Her funeral will take place today at 4 o'clock.

Died: on Sep 4, in Wash City, of congestion of the brain, Mrs Caroline Adams, mother of Mr Edwin Adams, of the Nat'l Theatre, in her 50th year.

MONDAY SEP 8, 1856
Last evening in Augusta, Geo, J W Blount, who had arrived the previous day at the U S Hotel, threw himself from the 3rd floor. His condition at a late hour last night was such as to hold out hopes of his final recovery. -Augusta [Geo] Sentinel

Union Gazette of Thu. Martin Stowell was brought before the U S Com'r Boyce yesterday charged with complicity in the recent extensive mail robbery at Oswego. The prisoner & his alleged confederate, Alex'r Powell, were seen in very suspicious circumstances, & the evidence against them is very strong.

Emma Jane, [age 8 years,] daughter of Danl Elliott, of Smithfield, R I, died on Sunday of hydrophobia, from a bite in the arm by a mad dog 5 weeks since.

On Sep 6, the Mount Vernon Hotel, at Cape Island, burnt to the ground, & Mr Cain & his family all perished in the flames, except young Philip, & he lies at the point of death. Mr Philip Cain, sr, with Col Frank T Foster, of this city, were the proprietors of the ill-fated hotel. Mr Cain resided at Vincenttown, N J, & went to Cape Island the present season for the purpose of opening the hotel. He was 65 years of age. Andrew Cain, his son, about 20 years of age; Martha was in her 17th year, & Sarah but 13. Mrs Albertson was 35 years of age. She was a widow & had gone to the island to act as house keeper at the hotel. The elder Mr Cain leaves a wife & several children at Vincenttown. Mrs Albertson also resided there. Young Philip Cain is about 18 years of age. The Mount Vernon was built at a cost of $125,000, upon which there is not one cent of insurance. The bldg was first occupied in 1853; Messrs Cain & Foster did not become the lessees until the past season. There were no guests in the house at the time, & Col Foster, the surviving proprietor, was in this city.

Abraham Miller, committed to the Carlisle, Pa, jail last week charged with the murder of John Kissell, hung himself in his cell on Sat. He left no confession, but was generally supposed to have been guilty.

Died: on Sep 6, at the residence of his nephew, Col Henry Naylor, near Wash City, Capt Thos Young, aged 91 years. His funeral is this morning at half past 10 o'clock.

Died: on Sep 1, in Wash City, Mrs Therza A Yerby, consort of Wm W Yerby, of Mississippi, in her 52nd year.

Died: on Sep 6, in Wash City, John, infant son of B F & H W Rittenhouse, aged 13 months & 10 days.

Died: on Aug 28, at Bladensburg, Md, after a painful illness, Miss Margaretta A Ross, in her 85th year. She lived to mingle with 3 generations, & for some years her intercourse was with the elite of New England's noblest sons & our own. She retained her faculties undimmed to the last. Bladensburg was the place of her nativity. She was on a visit to it, in the house her father built, where she was born, in sight of the spot where reposed the remains of her revered parents, when disease overtook her. -P

TUE SEP 9, 1856
Mrs Geo Fricks, residing close to by the Alleghany Valley railroad track, was run over & killed on Sep 2. She was deaf, & had just stepped on the track out of some bushes, when she was struck & killed by the locomotive.

Zeno Orso, of Citronelle, near Mobile, Ala, was dangerously shot on Aug 24 by Saml Jackson, a school teacher, with whom he had had a difficulty. Jackson has been arrested. Mr Orso was one of the oldest citizens of the county.

Wash City Ordinances: 1-Act for the relief of Maurice Holloran: the sum of $123.30 be paid to him for extra grading & gravelling on 13th st. 2-Act for the relief of Henrietta Shryock: to be paid $6.50 for taxes erroneously paid. 3-Act for the relief of John B Williamson: the sum of $20 be paid to him for putting up fences at polls in the 2nd Ward. 4-Act for the relief of Jas H Boss: to pay him $10 for the rent of room & fitting up of same for the first election precinct of the 4th Ward.

Land for sale: being desirous of locating my servants in Texas this fall, I will sell the Farm on which I reside, in Madison Co, on the Rapid Ann river, containing 607 acres. For particulars refer to Hon Jeremiah Morton, Culpeper Co; R B Somerville, Richmond; or to the subscriber on the premises, whose address is Somerset post-ofc, Orange Co, Va. -Geo A Smith

Mrd: on Aug 28, at Brooklyn, N Y, by Rev Dr Constantine Pise, Dr Henry Constantine Simms, of Wash City, to Miss Maria Onderdonk, daughter of Judge H G Onderdonk, of **Evergreen Park**, Long Island.

Died: on Sep 6, in Wash City, in her 26th year, Jennette, wife of Irvin S Barker, & daughter of Jas Tucker.

Died: on Sep 6, in Wash City, Israell Wayson, in his 41st year.

St Louis, Sep 6-from Kansas. Several Freesoilers were killed, & 7 taken prisoners. Two were afterwards shot. Brown & his son were killed. They also confirm the killing of Wm Phillips at Leavenworth by a party of Southerners under Capt Emery.

WED SEP 10, 1856
Three story brick house on Bridge st, Gtwn, D C, at public auction, by decree of the Circuit Court of, D C; sale on Oct 1 next, of the s e part of lot 16 in the original plan of said town, with the brick house & back bldg, part of the estate of Wm Nelson, late deceased. -Jno Marbury, trustee

Sale of U S land near Richmond, Va, known as **Bellona Arsenal**: Ordnance Ofc, Wash, Sep 9, 1856. The property to be sold consists of 27½ acres on the James river, some 14 miles above Richmond; part is covered with the arsenal bldgs, among which are a brick store house, 100 by 25 feet; brick barrack, a magazine of stone, 81 by 26 feet, with a slate roof, etc. Apply to Mr McArthur, on the premises.
-H K Craig, Col of Ordnance

On Aug 27, near Wesly, Tipton Co, Tenn, two brothers by the name of Collier, of respectable & wealthy parents, aged 20 & 21 years, disputed about a pony, when the younger brother stabbed the other & killed him. -Memphis Inq, Aug 29

Died: on Sep 6, in Gtwn, of water on the brain, Charlotte, infant daughter of Stephen T & Virginia Brown, aged 10 months.

Died: on Aug 23, at Brandon, Vt, Maj C A Ogden, of the U S Engineers, aged 56 years. Maj Ogden was a native of N J, & was an 1819 graduate of West Point; in 1820 was appointed to the command at Mobile Point, where he remained until 1834, superintending in the mean time the construction of **Fort Morgan**; in 1831 ordered to Cumberland road & stationed at Terre Haute, Indiana; returned to **Fort Morgan** in 1841; ordered to Balt in 1847 to superintend the construction of the fortifications at Soler's Point, now **Fort Carroll**; in 1848 appointed a member of the joint commission of naval & engineer ofcrs for the examination of the Pacific coast. He returned to Washington in 1850, where he continued as a member of the Board of Engineers of the Pacific coast until 1851, when he was ordered to Boston, where he was stationed at the time of his death. -Mobile Advertiser

Wilmington, Del, Sep 9. Geo M Townsend pleaded guilty this morning before the U S district court to the charge of robbing the post ofc in this city in Aug, 1855. He was sentenced to 2 years' hard labor in the State prison, the lowest term for the offence.

Sale of land: by authority vested in me, I will sell, in Alexandria Co, Va, at auction, on Sep 25, 48 acres of land; joining the farms of Mrs Hamilton, R Cruit, & Rev A Hays, about 1½ mile from Gtwn; with a comfortable log house thereon. Inquire of Robt Ball, sr, near Ball's cross Roads, or of the subscriber, 558 G st, near 3rd.
-Robt Ball, jr, exc for Wm Ball, deceased.

Quebec, Sep 9. Four days later from Europe. 1-Sir Wm Temple, Minister to Naples, & Lord Palmerston's only brother, is dead. 2-Napoleon is said to be suffering much from a diseased liver.

THU SEP 11, 1856
Mr Levi Hamilton, a resident o Alleghany Co, Md, whilst in the act of gaping dislocated his lower jaw, which caused him intense pain, & he was unable to close his mouth. Dr P A Healey arrived & set the disjointed member.

The entire family of Mr Peabody Atkinson, resident a few miles from Wheeling, are lying in a critical situation for the deleterious effects of corrosive sublimate, sold them by some druggist of that city, & mixed with their bread, instead of salaeratus.
-Richmond Whig

Alexandria Gaz: a son of Capt Rhett, U S A, about 4 years old, was accidentally drowned in a bath tub, one day last week, at Chestnut Hill, Loudoun Co, where the family was residing during the summer.

Rev Joshua Upson, of Dayton, Ohio, abstained from eating & actually died on Sunday week of starvation.

Died: yesterday, in Wash City, after a long & painful illness, of consumption, Miss Sarah Berry, aged 44 years. Her funeral is tomorrow at 4 o'clock, from the residence of A Sioussa, 417 11th st, between G & H sts.

Died: on Sep 9, in Wash City, of disease of the heart, Jacob Schmidt, in his 64th year. He leaves a wife & 8 children to mourn his loss.

Orphans Court of Wash Co, D C. Letters of administration on the personal estate of Peter Little, sen, late of Wash Co, deceased. -Franklin Little, adm

Orphans Court of Wash Co, D C. Letters of administration on the personal estate of Julius A Peters, late of Wash Co, deceased. -M A Peters, excx

FRI SEP 12, 1856
Richmond Enquirer: Dr Basil L Gildersleeve has been appointed by the Board of Visitors to the chair of the Greek Language & Literature of that institution. He is a native of S C, but has lived for many years at Richmond.

Orphans Court of Wash Co, D C-Sep 9, 1856. In the case of Edw A Gallaher, adm of Marcellus Gallaher, deceased, the administrator & Court have appointed Oct 4 next, for the final settlement of the personal estate, of the assets in hand.
-Ed N Roach, Reg/o wills

On Tue Louisa H Brown, wife of Geo W Brown, one of the free-State prisoners in Kansas, appeared before Justice Curtis, of the U S Supreme Court at Pittsfield, Mass, with a petition for a writ of habeas corpus in her husband's behalf. Cassius M Clay was named as a suitable person to execute the writ, & the petition was signed by the principal free-State men of Kansas. It was refused. Judge Curtis held, on the authority of Kane's case, [14 Howard, 193,] that he had no power to issue any process save the process of the circuit court for his own circuit, which could not avail, because, unlike the process of the Supreme Court, it can be served only within the district where it issues.

Orphans Court of Wash Co, D C. Letters testamentary on the personal estate of Eliz Chinn, late of Wash Co, deceased. -Richd H Clarke, exc

Died: on Sep 7, Walter Ann, youngest child of E W & Tracenia Latimer.

Died: on Sep 11, Josephine Lyles, daughter of A F & E A Offut. Her funeral will take place this morning at 10 o'clock, from the residence of her father, First st.

Died: on Sep 11, Miss Leah J Wilson, sister of the late David M Wilson, in her 57th year. Her funeral is this afternoon at 4 o'clock, from the residence of her brother-in-law, Saml Grubb, 599 M st, between 6th & 7th sts.

SAT SEP 13, 1856
Household & kitchen furniture at auction on: Sep 18, by authority of the last will & testament of Eliz Chinn, deceased, late of Wash Co, D C: public auction, on the premises, on 6th st west, between south I & K sts. Also, on the same day, I shall sell the house & lot, it being part of lot 13 in square 499, fronting on 6th st 27 feet, running east 100 feet, with a good frame house & enclosed fence. -Richd H Clark, exc -A Green auct [Nov 8th newspaper: the house & lot 13 in square 499 is advertised a second time.]

If Wm Rowley, who, in or about the year 1793, sailed from England with his brother John for India, but left the ship at Cape Good Hope & ultimately settled in the U S, &, as it is supposed, at Chartiers, in Wash Co, Penn; or, in the event of his death, his next of kin, will apply to John Wm Howard, of No 69 Fenchurch st, London, solicitor, they will hear of something considerably to their advantage. The said Wm Rowley was the son of a very respectable gentleman, who for some period of his life resided in Yorkshire. Any person who can give satisfactory information respecting the death of the said Wm Rowley will be rewarded on application as above.

N Y, Sep 11. The death of Seth Cheney, the well known artist in crayon, is recorded. He died yesterday at Manchester, Conn, of consumption. He was about 55 years of age.

Trustee's sale of valuable bldg lots in Wash City: by deed of trust dated Nov 29, 1854, from the late firm of Selden, Withers & Co, to the undersigned trustees, duly recorded in the land records of Wash Co, D C: sale of lots 22, 23, 24, 30, 31, & 32, in square 513: fronting 181 feet 6 inches on north N, between 4th & 5th sts. The whole property, including a portion of Ridge st, is inclosed by a substantial board fence. -J A English, Wm Bayne, trustees -A Green auct

Chancery sale of valuable improved real estate in Gtwn: beautiful suburban residence & extensive grounds. By decree of the Circuit Court of D C, made in the cause wherein Richd W Templeman & Annie W Templeman are cmplnts, & John Miller & Mary Templeman & others are dfndnts, No 860, in Chancery, the subscriber, trustee appointed by said decree, will sell at public sale on Oct 9 next, on the premises, lots 20, 21, 30, & 31, in Peter Beatty, Threlkeld, & Deakin's addition to Gtwn, the whole fronting 120 feet on Bridge st, 244 feet on Fayette st, & 120 feet on Prospect st, with the bldgs, which consist of a commodious & well built 2 story dwlg house, brick summer-house, brick meat-house, brick wash-house, & frame offices, & other necessary out bldgs. -Chas S Wallach, trustee -Jas C McGuire, auct

In Chancery: Circuit Court of Wash Co, D C. Austin Sherman, against John F Callan & Sarah A Callan, his wife, Michl P Callan, Nicholas Callan, Wm Robinson, Alice Octavia Robinson, Benj N Robinson, Needler R Jennings, John Brooks, Jas Jennings Brooks, Robinsonora Clarke, Amanda C Jennings, & others. The bill states that, on Apr 1, 1855, the cmplnt recorded, on the law side of this Court, against John F Callan, 6 several judgments, as follows: One for $2,000 damages, to be released on the payment of $1,300, with interest thereon from Apr 9, 1853, until paid, & $11.26 costs; another for $2,000 damages, to be released on the payment of $1,494, with interest thereon from Apr 13, 1853, until paid, & $11.26 costs; another for $1,260 damages, to be released on the payment of $875, with interest thereon from Mar 22, 1853, until paid, & $11.26 costs; another for $1,000 damages, to be released on payment of $755, with interest thereon from Apr 15, 1853, until paid, & $11.26 costs; another for $1,500 damages, to be released on the payment of $1,075, with interest thereon from Apr 19, 1853, until paid, & $11.26 costs; & another for $3,000 damages, to be released on the payment of $2,143, with interest thereon from May 18, 1853, until paid, & $11.26 costs. That, on Mar 31, 1825, Henry M Morfit sold & conveyed to Wm Robinson, since deceased, trustee for Alice C Jennings, also since deceased, lot 8 in square 456, in Wash City, D C, with the appurtenances, which conveyance was in trust for the said Alice C Jennings, her heirs & assignees; that said Wm Robinson & Alice C Jennings, by indenture dated Nov 2, 1840, leased said property to John F Callan for the term of the natural life of the said Alice C Jennings, in which lease, after a recital that said Callan had contracted to purchase the fee-simple in said property, after the death of the said Alice C Jennings, for $3,000, to be paid to said Robinson, his heirs, or assigns, it was covenanted by said Callan so to purchase, & by said Alice C Jennings that upon said payment said Robinson should

stand seized to said Callan's use in fee, & the said Robinson covenanted to convey in fee; that said Callan, at the time of the execution of said lease, occupied said property, & has since continued to occupy the same & has added valuable improvements thereto; that the said Alice C Jennings died in May, 1851, leaving a will, by which she devised said property to her four daughters, Robinsonora Clarke, Alice Octavia Robinson, [the wife of Wm Robinson, heir at law of said Wm Robinson, deceased] Amanda C Jennings, & Indiana H Jennings, to be divided amongst them share & share alike, & appointed Wm Robinson [her said trustee] & her son, Needler R Jennings, execs, the former of whom died intestate before the testatrix, & later qualified as executor; that Indiana H Jennings, in Oct, 1851, intermarried with John Brooks, & shortly afterwards died, leaving her husband & John Jennings Brooks, an infant child, surviving her; that before said intermarriage a marriage settlement was made between said Indiana H Jennings & said John Brooks, a copy of which is filed; that after the death of said Alice C Jennings the said Callan tendered the said sum of $3,000, & having complied with the conditions of said lease, was entitled to a conveyance in fee; that, in 1854, said property, with the improvements, was worth upwards of $15,000, & on Oct 16,1854, was conveyed, together with other property charged to be worth upwards of $3,000 to John F Callan, who was then insolvent, to Mich P Callan, for the pretended consideration of $4,900, which conveyance, it is alleged, was fraudulent & void, being designed to delay, hinder, & defraud the cmplnt in the collection of his said debts; & that said Wm Robinson & Benj N Robinson are heirs at law of Wm Robinson, trutstee of Alice C Jennings. The bill further states that John F Callan, being indebted unto Mary Ann Nalley in the sum of $4,700, conveyed to her absolutely certain real estate in Wash City, which conveyance he afterwards insisted was designed merely as security for the debt, &, having paid $5,000 or thereabouts, prevailed on said Mary Ann Nalley to execute a deed for the said property to Nicholas Callan, in trust for his [John F Callan's] wife & children, which deed was executed in Dec, 1853, & has never been recorded, & is alleged to be null & void, & to have been procured by John F Callan in order to delay, hinder, & defraud the cmplnt in the collection of his debts; that a part of the property conveyed to Mary Ann Nalley was subject to a deed of trust to Nicholas Callan, made to secure to Mich A Guista a debt of $2,200, which debt is charged to have been paid; & that the said Wm Robinson, Alice Octavia Robinson, Benj N Robinson, Needler R Jennings, John Brooks, Jas Jennings Brooks, Robinsonora Clarke, & Amanda C Jennings reside out of the District of Columbia. The object of the suit is to obtain a decree annulling the deed from John F Callan to Michl P Callan, & from Mary Ann Nalley to Nicholas Callan, respectively, & for the sale of the property conveyed by them, the proceeds of such sale, after the satisfaction of the $3,000 & interest agreed to be paid by John F Callan for the property leased, to be applied to the payment of the cmplnt's judgments. Absent dfndnts are to appear in this Court, in person or by solicitor, on or before the 3rd Monday of Jan next. -Jas S Morsell, assist Judge.
-Davidge & Ingle, Solicitors for cmplnt

The Pensacola Gaz announces the death, on Aug 29, at the U S naval hospital in Warrington, near Pensacola, after a long & protracted illness, of Surgeon Isaac Hulse, of the U S Navy. He was a native of N Y & entered the navy in 1823.

Dr Henry A Ramsey has just committed suicide in jail, at Sparta, Ala, to avoid punishment for a most extraordinary series of forgeries. The forgeries were all traced to & proven on him. His father arrived at Sparta from Atlanta, & told who he was. He then poisoned himself by drinking coffee containing the seed of the Jamestown weed, & died there-from. He was a graduate of the Medical College of Ga, & once had a large practice in Columbia Co, Ga.

U S Patent Ofc, Wash, Sep 12, 1856. Ptn of Saml Hewitt, of Rochester, Wisc, praying for the extension of a patent granted to him for an improvement in hay presses for 7 years from the expiration of said patent, which takes place on Dec 30, 1856. -Chas Mason, Com'r of Patents

Died: on Sep 6, of consumption, Richd Tilden Robbins, aged 18 years & 9 months, son of Z C Robbins, of Wash City.

MON SEP 15, 1856
Orphans Court of Wash Co, D C. In the case of Wm G Cranch, exc of Wm Cranch, deceased, the Court & executor have appointed Oct 7 next for the final settlement of the personal estate of the deceased, with the assets in hand. -Ed N Roach, Reg/o wills

Orphans Court of Wash Co, D C. In the case of Thos F Semmes, adm of Jos L C Hardy, deceased, the Court & administrator have appointed Oct 7 next for the final settlement of the personal estate of the deceased, with the assets in hand.
-Ed N Roach, Reg/o wills

An old man named Simeon Pfouts, residing near Lock Haven, Pa, was bitten in the wrist by a rattle snake, on Thu last week, & killed. He was in the habit of playing with them.

Fire yesterday in the brick grocery store at 20th & Pa ave, owned by Mr Saml Stott, but in the occupation of Mr J L Rider was burnt out. The adjoining property of Messrs Hines & O Funk were also burnt out.

Died: on Sep 14, in Wash City, Calvert, son of Chas K & E C King, in his 4th year. His funeral will be from his father's residence, 167 H st, between 20th & 21st sts, this afternoon, at 4 o'clock.

Died: on Jul 2 last, at Forbes' Town, Butler Co, Calif, Gen Thos H Bowen, formerly of Wash City.

Died: on Sep 12, at **Preston**, near Alexandria, in her 72nd year, Mrs Frances Swann, relict of the late Wm T Swann, formerly of Alexandria Co, Va. Her funeral will be this evening at 4 o'clock, from **Preston**, her late residence.

Calif: The Vigilance Cmte unconditionally released Judge Terry on the 7th.

For rent, a fine dwlg house & 2 stores or warehouses. The house is in **Franklin Row**, being 250 K, between 12th & 13th sts; well furnished, & will be rented with of without the furniture. The storehouses are on 6th st, between Pa & Missouri aves. Apply to Mrs S T Hugh, 444 6th st, between E & F sts.

TUE SEP 16, 1856
Household & kitchen furniture at auction on: Sep 25, at the residence of M Snyder, in Corcoran's Bldgs, on I st, between 15th & 16th sts. -Jas C McGuire, auct

Household & kitchen furniture at auction on: Sep 21, at the late residence of R W Latham, 8th & O sts. -A Green auct

Rev Jos Upson, a Universalist clergyman of Dayton, Ohio, died a few days since, after having existed some time in a remarkable state of monomania. He would abstain from nourishment for weeks in succession.

Died: on Sep 14, in Wash City, after a long & painful illness, Fred' W A, eldest son of Chas & Harriet C Mallard, aged 19 years & 9 months. His funeral is this afternoon at 3 o'clock, from his father's residence, 10th & C sts, Island.

Died: on Aug 10, in San Francisco, Calif, in her 21st year, Mrs Augusta Virginia, widow of Robt G Keefer, [who died at Marysville on Jul 28 last,] & daughter of Mrs Catherine Langton, formerly of Wash.

Foreign News: The marriage between the Infanta Amelia of Spain & Prince Aldabert was celebrated on Aug 25.

WED SEP 17, 1856
Trustee's sale of house & lot at auction: on Oct 17, by deed of trust from Edw Fuller to the subscriber, dated Sep 1, 1855, recorded in Liber J A S No 109, folios 177 thru 180, of the land records of Wash Co, D C: being part of lot 38 in square 500, with a good dwlg house, in said city. -John L Smith, trustee -A Green auct

Alfred L Rives has been selected to make the surveys for a permanent bridge over the Potomac, under authority vested in the Sec of the Interior.

Jas Aldrich, recently announced the associate editor of the Home Journal, has died. He was born in Suffolk Co, in 1810, & early in life came to this city. He leaves a family & a large circle of friends, who knew his worth & deeply feel his loss. [No death date given-current item.]

Land sale: within the past few weeks a number of sales of land have taken place in Fairfax Co, Va: Geo W Hunter, jr, has sold his residence near Fairfax courthouse, with 100 acres of land, to Thos R Love, for $60 per acre. Mr Francis Fish sold his farm on the Little River turnpike, containing 250 acres, for $36 per acre. Mr Thos Ayre sold his farm, on the same turnpike, containing 318 acres, to Mr Hamilton, of Loudoun, for $47 per acre.

Died: on Aug 24, at Panama, David Ochiltree, late U S N, aged 28 years, a native of Fayetteville, N C.

N Y, Sep 16. One death, that of Dr Crane, at New Utrecht, of fever. There were 2 new cases at the relief hospital at **Fort Hamilton**.

Orphans Court of Wash Co, D C. In the case of Wm Gunton, adm of Thos Gunton, deceased: the Court & administrator have appointed Oct 7 next, for the final settlement of the personal estate of said deceased, of the assets in hand.
-Ed N Roach, Reg/o wills

THU SEP 18, 1856
Mrd: on Sep 16, in Wash City, by Rev G W Samson, Mr John W Jones, to Miss Mary E Thompson, of Montg Co, Md.

Mrd: on Sep 15, in Balt, by Rev Jas A Ward, of Loyola College, Balt, Mr Wm H Brawner to Miss Emily B Orme, all of Wash City.

Died: on Sep 6, at Freeport, Pa, Frank G May, in his 35th year, a native of Md, but for the last 5 years a resident of N Y C.

Household & kitchen furniture at auction on: Oct 1, at the residence of W M Corcoran, 493 17th st: the entire household furniture. -Wall, Barnard & Co, aucts

Wash City: contractors for removing garbage in the several Wards of the city: John O Dea Geo Fosnaught; Hanson Brown; John Callihan; John Cusick; Mr White. Mr Wm Dixon elected assessor of the 6th Ward in place of Israel Wayson, deceased.

Hon W W Irwin, formerly Mayor of Pittsburg, Rep in Congress, & Charge d'Affaires to Denmark during Mr Tyler's administration, died at Pittsburg on Sep 15.

Beautiful farm *Huntington*, for sale: located in Montg Co, Md, on the road leading from Gtwn to Rockville, contains 302 acres of land. Persons desirous to purchase are to call soon, as the subscriber will be absent for some time after this month.
-Thos M Macubbin

On Tue a small child of Mr Richd Shields, of Balt, Md, got hold of some friction matches & ate the ends off. It was seized with spasms & died the next morning.

Orphans Court of Wash Co, D C. In the case of Geo W Riggs, exc of Hannah Blackford, deceased: the Court & exec have appointed Oct 7 next, for the final settlement of the personal estate of said deceased, of the assets in hand.
-Ed N Roach, Reg/o wills

FRI SEP 19, 1856
Criminal Court-Wash-Thu. John Eggleston, tried for the murder of Caspar Kohrman on Jul 4 last, was found not guilty.

Died: yesterday, in Gtwn, in her 60th year, Mrs Johann Lane, long a resident of that place. Her funeral will be today at 4 P M, from her late residence on Bridge st.

Died: on Sep 16, in Wash City, after a short but painful illness, William Jones, infant son of Jas B & Alexine Williamson, aged 1 year & 11 days.

Lost, on Wed last, on Pa ave, a certificate of the freedom of Eliz Boyd from the Clerk of PG Co, Court; also, her certificate of residence from the Corp of Wash. A reward of $3 will be paid for the return of the papers to the subscriber, immediately back of Mr Faulkners' Shirt Manufactory, Pa ave, between 3rd & 4½ sts. -Eliz Boyd

N Y, Sep 18. Wm T Coleman, Pres of the San Francisco Vigilance Cmte, was arrested today on complaint of Jas Maloney, on charge of his being instrumental in expelling the latter from San Francisco. Coleman was held to bail in $50,000.

SAT SEP 20, 1856
Nat'l Whig Convention assembled at Balt, Md, in the Hall of the Md Institute, on Sep 17. Wm Schley called the Convention to order, & nominate ex-Govn'r Washington Hunt, of N Y, as temporary chairman. [Cheers.] Hiram Ketchum, of N Y, read the most interesting portions of the Farewell Address of Geo Washington. The following cmte was appointed to report permanent ofcrs for the Convention:

Hon Jas D Green, of Mass	Hon Francis Granger, N Y
Rush Fuller, Conn	Dr Chas G McChesney, N J

David Paul Brown, Pa
John Jones, Dela
Hon John G Chapman, Md
Jas C Bruce, Va
John H Bryan, N C
Jas W Jones, Ga
L B Hansford, Ala
Thos Mount, Miss
M R Jennings, La

Wm Y Strong, Ohio
John S McFarland, Ky
Edw Cooper, Tenn
Hon Jas E Blythe, Ind
D A Brown, Ill
Thornton Grimsley, Mo
J P Sanderson, Fla
J M Graham, Ark

The cmte submitted the following report: for Pres: Hon Edw Bates, of Missouri

For Vice Presidents:
Jos Paxton, of Pa
Luther V Bell, of Mass
Dr Jas W Thomson, of Dela
Chas P Krevals, of Conn
Jas A Hamilton, of N Y
Gov Chas Stratton, of N J
Ezekiel F Chambers, of Md
Wyndhan Robertson, of Va
Gov Wm A Graham, of N C
Elbert A Holt, of Ala
A M Foute, of Miss

Dr Geo W Campbell, of La
Gov Allan Trimble, of Ohio
Henry T Duncan, of Ky
John Shanklin, of Ind
Walter Coleman, of Tenn
Jas H Matheny, of Ill
Gov Wm C Lane, of Mo
John Finney, of Fla
E A Holbrook, of Ark
G T Dortie, of Ga

For Secretaries:
Laz Anderson, of Ohio
Jas M Townsend, of Conn
Hon Thos Jones Yrok, of N J
E V Machette, of Pa

S H Kennedy, of La
Jas H Charless, of Mo
Col Huntingdon, of N Y

The nominations were unanimously confirmed.

The *Mariposa* claim is a tract of land 10 leagues in extent, lying upon a creek of the same name in the San Joaquin valley. It was purchased for me by Mr Larkin in the beginning of 1847, & during my absence with the battalion in the south, from D Juan B Alvarado, to whom it had been granted in consideration of his public services. Mr Larkin paid for it $3,000. The purchase was made before Calif was ceded to the U S & long before any gold had been discovered. I had always intended to make my home in the country if possible. On my return to the country in the present year I visited the place with Dr Corrie, Mr Reed, & other gentlemen, & for the first time saw the land. I have always supposed that at some future time the validity of the claim would be settled by the proper courts. I am satisfied to await the decision.

Lewis Clark, aged 16, went to Frostburg on Sep 8, obtained liquor, & became deeply intoxicated. He was carried home speechless & died on Wed. -Cumberland Civilian

MON SEP 22, 1856
In Equity. Eliz Braiden vs Richd Smith et al. The object of this suit is to procure a conveyance of the legal title to a part of lot 13 in square 319 in Wash City. On Nov 9, 1841, John P Van Ness leased to Sarah A Payne all that part of lot 13 of square 309, in Wash City, together with the bldgs & appurtenances there unto belonging, for & during the space & term of 7 years, commencing for the same on Oct 1, 1841, at the yearly rent of $50, payable semi-annually; & that there was incorporated in said lease, as one of its provisons, an agreement that said Sarah A Payne & her assigns might at any time during said term purchase the fee-simple in said premises for the consideration of $800; that afterwards, viz, on or about Jun 6, 1843, said Sarah A Payne agreed to purchase said premises for $800; &, having made part payment thereof subsequently, sold & assigned said lease to cmplnt, who, as such assignee, made payment on account of said purchase money to said Van Ness; that said Van Ness died in Mar, 1846, intestate, leaving Cornelius P Van Ness, Gertrude Hoffman, [intermarried with Martin H Hoffman,] Peter Van Ness Van Allen, Matilda E Van Ness, Chas W Van Ness, Edw Van Ness, & Eugene Van Ness, his heirs at law; that at the death of said John P Van Ness there was yet due of said puchase money the sum of $200, with interest from Oct 1, 1844; that after the death of said John P Van Ness, Cornelius P Van Ness took out letters of administration on his estate, & the cmplnt paid to him the amount due of said purchase money, with all interest due thereon; that at the death of said Cornelius P Van Ness thereafter letters of administration de bonis non on the estate of said John P Van Ness were granted by the proper authority to Eugene Van Ness; that said Cornelius P Van Ness, by his will duly made & executed, devised all his real estate in Wash City, to his daughter, Christina, giving his wife, Madalina Van Ness, also an interest therein; that all the heirs of John P Van Ness, except Peter Van Ness Van Allen, joined in a conveyance for the purpose of passing all their interest in the real estate of John P Van Ness to Richd Smith, upon certain trust as therein set forth, &, among others in trust, to fulfil such contracts or agreements, of any made & entered into by said John P Van Ness, for the sale & conveyance of any part & parcel of said property; that said Peter Van Ness Van Allen, by his deed duly executed & recorded, conveyed one-third of his interest in said estate to Cornelius P Van Ness, one-third to Catharine D Philip & Wm H *Phillip, & the remaining third to Matilda E Van Ness, Chas W Van Ness, Edw Van Ness, & Eugene Van Ness; that Wm H Philip & Catherine D Philip subsequently conveyed their interest in said real estate to said Richd Smith upon trust similar to those declared in the deed from the heirs of John P Van Ness to said Smith before mentioned. And it appearing to the satisfaction of the Court that Matilda E Van Ness, Chas W Van Ness, Edw Van Ness, Eugene Van Ness, Madalina Van Ness, Christina Van Ness, & Catharine D Philip are now residents of the District of Columbia; it is ordered that they appear at the ofc of Clerk of the Circuit Court of D C, on the first Monday of Feb, 1857. -Jas S Morsell, Assoc Judge -Jno A Smith, clerk -Stone for cmplnt. [*Copied as written.]

$100 reward for runaway negro man Heny Sly, about 37 years of age.
-Geo H Gardiner, farm near Beantown Post Ofc, Chas Co, Md.

Wash City Ordinance: 1-Act for the relief of Robt Downing: to pay him $21.42, erroneously paid for taxes.

Needler R Jennings, of New Orleans, whose name appeared in the proceedings of the Balt Convention as M R Jennings, was a delegate from the Whigs of La. He was upon the Cmte of Organization, but took no active part in the proceedings after. [Note: His name was spelled Jannings; since corrected.]

Mr E C Clarke, a merchant of Omaha City, Nebraska, writes to his father in this city, under date of Sep 10, stating that a Mormon train had been slaughtered by the Cheyenne Indians a short distance west of that city. All their horses were stolen. The Pawnees attacked the Cheyennes, killing a number of them & recovered the horses.

Don Vincente Hernandez de Ayala, pretended Minister Plenipotentiary & Envy-Extraordinary from the Republics of Venezuela & Granada, was arrested at Mobil charged with forgery & swindling. After his arrest he made an attempt to swallow forged drafts to the amount of $6,000 but was prevented. [Current item.]

The English papers announce the death of the celebrated Arctic navigator, Sir John Ross, Rear Admiral in the British Navy, at the age of 80 years. He entered the navy in 1786; in 1818 he accompanied Sir Edw Parry in his expedition to the Arctic seas; & he received the honor of knighthood from Wm IV, for his distinguished services. [No death date given-current item.]

TUE SEP 23, 1856
The death of Lorenzo B Shepard in his bath tub should be a renewed caution to abstain at night from the powerful stimulus of cold water upon an exhausted system. Mr Shepard had made an exhausting political speech in the evening in N J, reached him home about 1 o'clock in the morning, & went into a bath. He was found dead in it. -Albany Journal [No death date given-current item.]

Public sale: having rented my *Ashland Farm*, on Rock Creek, I will offer at public auction, on Sep 30, farming utensils, a crop of corn, & a quantity of provender. I will also on the same day offer *Beechwood*, lying directly south of *Ashland*, & a part of the original tract, containing about 120 acres of land, within 1½ miles of Rockville. This farm has been neglected & is out of order, but it offers a rare opportunity to a person of moderate means for a good location & safe investment. -A B Davis

Manchester Guardian: inquest held on the body of John Day, of Goulden st, who was struck by glass when a soda water bottle burst on Tue. He bled very much & died at the Royal Infirmary.

I offer my farm for sale near Beltsville, Md, containing about 200 acres; house nearly new, with all necessary out-houses. It will be sold a great bargain, as I am determined to sell it at once. Inquire on the premises of Fred Hunter, who is authorized to sell, & will take pleasure in showing it. -Thos T Hunter

Mrd: on Sep 20, in Wash City, by Very Rev Chas Henry Stonestreet, S J, of Gtwn College, Dr Alphonso T Semmes, of Canton, Miss, to Sabina, daughter of the late Raphael Semmes, of Gtwn.

The Copartnership existing between the undersigned in the Stove & Tin Ware Manufactory was dissolved on Aug 1, 1856, by mutual consent. -Berry & Naylor
The business will be carried on by W O Berry.

WED SEP 24, 1856

Indian massacre on the plains: account given in the Council Bluffs Eagle of the murder & robbery of B W Babbitt's train of Gov't property by the Cheyenne Indians. On Aug 25, the little train, with Alex'r Nichols, one of our citizens, as captain & conductor, & Mrs Wilson & infant, from St Louis, a young man, Orren Parrish, a man from Penn, & another, name unknown, were encamped upon Prairie creek, & were suddenly attacked by a band of Cheyennes. Some days later a detachment from the fort, 20 miles away, found the dead bodies of Mr Nichols, the man from Pa, & the child. The torn wardrobe of Mrs Wilson was found but her body was nowhere found. Parrish managed to escape. The Indians were pursued by Capt Stewart's company & a detachment under Lt Wheaton. On Aug 22 they came upon them in camp, charged & killed 10 of them.

Political riot a few days ago, at Bourbon, Indiana, between Hon Mr Colfax & Judge Stuart, resulted in Mr John Leffler being mortally wounded.

Geo Witman, Justice of the Peace, Com'r for States & Territories, & Conveyancer. Ofc on C st north, near 7th st.

Farm for rent containing upwards of 200 acres, lying in Montg Co, Md, on the road from Rockville to the Great Falls. Apply to the subscriber on the farm. -E Waterman

Died: on Sunday last, in Wmsport, Maury Co, Tenn, of pulmonary consumption, at the residence of Mrs Jane H Y Greenfield, Wm Brogden Dorsett, aged 20 years. He was on a visit to the relative at whose house he died. -C F C

Orphans Court of Wash Co, D C. In the case of Mary A Sprigg, admx of Thos B Sprigg, deceased, the administratrix & Court have appointed Oct 14 next for the distribution of the assets in hand. -Ed N Roach, Reg/o wills

THU SEP 25, 1856
Cmdor French Forrest arrived at Norfolk on Sunday. He will hoist his flag on board the frig **St Lawrence** & go out in her as cmder of the squadron on the Brazil station.

On Sat, Mr Josiah Montgomery, one of our city police, residing in Jay st, swallowed 4 grains of strychnine, mistaking it for a powder prepared for an opiate which had been prescribed. Mr M had some time since procured the strychnine for the purpose of killing dogs during the hot season. On discovering his mistake, he ran into Dr Swinburn's ofc, a few doors away, where he procured an emetic. Dr Bly was also sent for. Mr M went into spasms, which Dr Bly relieved by applying chloroform. He was in a comfortable state yesterday, with a clear mind & a good pulse.
-Rochester Democrat, Sep 15.

While the Light Artl were firing a Fillmore salute at Boston on Sat one of the gunners, whose duty it was to thumb the vent, removed his thumb while Mr Solomon W Cutting was in the act of ramming the cartridge. A premature explosion of the charge followed, & Mr Cutting's hands were so mangled that amputation will be necessary. His face & neck were also badly burnt.

Died: on Sep 24, in Gtwn, D C, Wm B Golding, aged 68 years. His funeral will take place tomorrow at 3 o'clock, from his late residence on Washington, between Bridge & Water sts.

Notice to the heirs & legal reps of Lewis Urban, late of Lancaster, Lancaster Co, Pa, deceased. Take notice that, by virtue of an order of the Orphans' Court of said county, I will hold an inquisition to divide, part, or value the real estate of said deceased, on the premises, in the city of Lancaster, on Oct 25, 1856, when & where you may attend, if you think proper. -Geo Martin, Sheriff of Lancaster Co

FRI SEP 26, 1856
Superior cabinet furniture, household effects, carpets, & kitchen furniture at auction on: Oct 2, at the residence of T Kilby Smith, in the center house of the Demenou Bldgs, on H st, between 13th & 14th sts. -Jas C McGuire, auct

Household & kitchen furniture at auction on: Sep 30, at the residence of Col Woodley, 297 F st, between 12th & 13th sts. -A Green auct

John Drinker, jr, died at N Y on Thu from burns received about a week ago since by the explosion of a camphene lamp.

N Y-Sep 24: A sudden death occurred here today in the family of Judge Roosevelt, of our Supreme Court. The eldest son of the Judge, a very promising law student about 20 years of age, fell back as he was dressing & almost instantly expired, the cause being disease of the heart. [The son's name was not given.]

Natchitoches [La] Chronicle. Matthew Bresente, convicted of the murder of John Rodrigo, was hung at that place on Sep 5, in accordance with the sentence of the law.

Died: at the **Caves**, in Balt Co, Md, after a painful & protracted illness, John Henry Carroll, in his 57th year, a gentleman of rare literary acquirements, a ripe scholar, & firm believer in the promises of the Gospel. Mr Carroll was a native of the city of Annapolis, descended from one of the oldest & most respectable families in the State of Md. After having attained his majority he removed to his estate in Balt Co, where he devoted himself to the pursuits of agriculture, & several times represented that county in the Legislature of the State with marked efficiency & ability. He leaves a wife & child, an aged & only brother, bowed down with grief, to mourn their loss. May "He who tempers the wind to the shorn lamb" soothe their sorrows & comfort them in affliction. -M

Milwaukee, Sep 25. The steamer **Niagara** was burnt last evening near **Fort Washington**, Lake Michigan. There were 100 lives lost. Hon John B Macy is supposed to be among the lost. Among the passengers saved were: Harvey Ainsworth, Henry Luce, J Locke & Henry Locke, of Vt, J B Curtis, of Steuben, N Y, & Dr S Allen, of Concord, N H. Hugh Kennedy lost his wife & daughter. The bodies of 3 women, names unknown, are now at **Fort Washington**. One has a ring marked Z D G. The **Niagara** was heavy with freight, which was all lost. [Sep 29th newspaper: Known to have been lost on the **Niagara**: Almond Atwood & wife, of Vt; M J Clark, [the steward,] of Buffalo; Hon John B Macy, of Wisc; & Harvey Ainsworth, of Royalton, Vt, lost his wife, 3 children, father, & sister-in-law.] [Oct 3rd newspaper: Hon John B Macy was a native of Nantucket, Mass, & after having resided for some years in N Y & in Michigan, he took up his residence at Fon du Lac, Wisc. His age was about 58 years. -Toledo Blade] [Oct 18th newspaper: The entire family of Mr Ainsworth, of Vt, was lost. He had gathered his wife, his aged father of 70 years, & 3 children about him & lowered them from the deck, away from the flames. This hardy son of Green Mountains, swam from one to another to assist them in holding on to some buoying object. He saw his youngest child of 3 years sink to its cold grave. Then came the death struggle of his aged parent, whom he saw disappear forever. His wife & daughter were buried by the waves. All were gone save his little boy of 8 years. He watched desperately as his son disappeared to the depths of Michigan. The only member of a happy family watches the beach at Ozaukee, in hopes that some friendly wave may send him up from the bosom of the lake his lost, forever lost, family, that he may lay them with his own hands in the ground. -Milwaukee American]

L J Brown, of Stockbridge, Vt, came to his death in Chicago from blowing out the gas in his chamber at the Massasoit House instead of shutting it off.

The copartnership of H F Loudon & Co, dissolved this day, Aug 5, 1856, is caused by the death of H F Loudon. The business will be settled at the old stand by Geo W Farant, surviving partner. G W Farant, F J Hieberger, & J H King, will continue the business under the title of J F Loudon & Co.

Application to be made to Com'r of the Gen Land Ofc of the U S for the issue of U S land scrip in lieu of the following Va Military Land Warrants issued by the Register of the Land Ofc for the state of Va for military services in the war of the Revolution, to wit: Warrant No 1,390 for 100 acres, issued to Henry Bohennon, private, on Jul 18, 1783. Warrant No 471 for 400 acres, issued to Wm Belvin, a sergeant, on Apr 19, 1783. Warrant No 676 for 100 acres, issued to Wm Tuaold, a private, May 29, 1783. Warrant No 4,452 for 200 acres, issued to Jas Lipscomb, a sergeant, on ___, 1785.

I certify that Geo Thomas, of Wash Co, D C, brought before me, as a stray, a dark bay Horse. -C H Wiltberger [Owner is to prove property, pay charges, & take him away from my place, on the road leading from Bladensburg to Rock Creek Church road, & north of the Military Asylum about quarter of a mile. -Geo Thomas]

The creditors of the late Richd Dement, deceased, are notified that a distribution of the assets of said estate will be made on Sep 30, at 12 o'clock, under the order of the Judge of the Orphans Court of Wash Co, D C, at the court room of said Court. -Jno Marbury, Atty & agent of the admx.

SAT SEP 27, 1856
Trustee's sale, by deed of trust from John A Throckmorton & wife, dated Mar 15, 1854, recorded in Liber J A S No 75, folios 100 thru 104, of the land records of Wash Co, D C: sale on Oct 27 next, the west 20 feet front of half of lot 14 in square 455, improved by a brick tenement, on G st, between 6th & 7th sts. -J B H Smith, Silas H Hill, trustees -A Green auct

Moscow, Sep 7. His Imperial Majesty the Emperor Alexander II was solemnly crowned today in the Uspenski Ssobor, & the act of coronation was performed by Archbishop Philaretes, the Metropolitan of Moscow. Count Orloff was created a Prince, Prince Woronzoff a field marshall, & Generals de Berg & Soumarokhoff counts.

Valuable property for sale: 4 small frame houses, containing 2 rooms & kitchen, & 4 small frame houses, containing 8 rooms each, on 4th st, running back to L st. Apply to the subscriber, at his residence, 191 4th st. -Josiah C Truman

Trustee's sale of gold mine stock at auction: by authority vested in us as trustees of the New Mexico Mining Co Assoc: public auction, on Nov 27, at the Auction Store of Jas C McGuire, Wash Co, D C: 321 shares upon the books as belonging to N M Miller; 83 shares belonging to Oscar W Turk; & 125 shares belonging to Wm M Moseley & John F Miller. -A Renihen, Lewis S Coryell, trustees -Jas C McGuire, auct

Beautiful unimproved tract of land on the Potomac, for sale: contains 166 2/3rd acres, about 3½ miles below Alexandria. Address W Arthur Taylor, Alexandria, Va.

John Spicer met with an accident in St Louis on Wed last, when his leg became entangled in the wheel of a buggy at great speed, & was completely wrenched off at the knee. He was sent to the hospital, but there are little hopes of his recovery.

Mrd: on Sep 25, in Wash City, by Rev G W Samson, Mr John A W Clarvoe to Miss Rosella Beyer, both of Wash City.

On Thu, Stratton Hood, about 14 years of age, son of Mr John Hood, of the Gen Land Ofc, lost his life. He had gone out to play with his usual companions in the street, & was engaged in the sport called short fox or leap frog, but, throwing himself with too much force, fell over upon his head & dislocated his neck. He died very soon after.
+
Died: on Sep 25, in Wash City, suddenly, Stratton, 3rd son of John & Rebecca R Hood, in his 15th year. His funeral will be this afternoon at 3 o'clock, from the residence of his parents, 358 9th st.

Died: on Sep 25, in Wash City, within the Navy Yard, Josephine, infant daughter of Jos & Ann Cornelia Lanman.

MON SEP 29, 1856
Trustee's sale of 5 1/16th acres of land with improvements, near Wash, at auction, on Oct 30, by deed of trust from Ann Brown, dated Apt 19, 1853, recorded in liber J A S No 54, folios 227 thru 230, of the land records of Wash Co: lot 3, of Geo Taylor's subdivision, being a part of the land whereof Anthony Holmead, sen, died seized, & part of the tract called **Pleasnt Plains**, lying on the east side of the Wash & Rockville turnpike road, near the lot sold to J C Lewis; being the land & premises which the said Ann Brown purchased from John F Sharretts, with a dwlg & necessary outhouses. -Hugh B Sweeny, trustee -A Green auct

Died: on Sep 27, in Wash City, after a brief illness, in his 40th year, Jas Henry Ellsworth, printer, a native of Wash City.

Died: on Sep 26, in Wash City, Capt Job G Williams, of the Marine Corps, while in command of the marine guard stationed at the navy yard.

Late from Calif: 1-The <u>Vigilance Cmte</u> of San Francisco disbanded. 2-Judge Terry took his seat on the bench of the Supreme Court on Aug 26. 3-John L Durkee & Chas Rand, who took the State arms from a vessel by order of the Cmte, were indicted for piracy in the U S Court & refused bail. 4-J D Musgrove, late member of Supervisors, & one of Casey's associates, has been ordered to leave the State. He is given until the 20th to arrange any business affairs. He fled into the interior several weeks ago.

Wm A Densmore, formerly of Dunham, Canada East, now of Montpelier, Vt, was arrested in the latter place on Sep 21 for having counterfeit coin in his possession.

The N Y papers bring the sad intelligence of the death of Geo Steers, the eminent shipbuilder. He was driving on the Long Island plank-road, when his horse took fright, throwing him to the ground. His injuries were so severe that he died on Thu, a few hours after the accident occurred. Mr Steers was a native of Washington, but had lived in N Y since his boyhood. He first earned distinction by the construction of the famous yacht **America**, which won the prize in the yacht race of all nations at Cowes in 1851. He died in the prime of life, being but 35 years of age; a mechanical genius.

TUE SEP 30, 1856
Trustee's sale, by 2 deed of trust to us, as trustees of the Union Bldg Assoc of Gtwn, [one from Wm T Collins, dated Feb 17, 1855, & the other from Danl A Smallwood, dated Nov 19, 1855,] public auction, on Oct 31 next, on the premises, the following lots in Wash: parts of original lots 21, 56 thru 58, in square 387. Part of lot 10 in square 297, improved by a 2 story frame dwlg. -Walter S Cox, Hugh Caperton, trustees -Jas C McGuire, auct

The coroner's jury, in the case of Kelly who was killed in a late prize fight, have returned a verdict implicating John Roach, Kt Burns, Barney Aaron, J Lafferty, Henry Gribben, John Montgomery, Michl Murphy, Jerry Reardon alias Billy Cotton, Philip Clare, & Patrick Cosgrove as aiders & abettors at the fight. Warrants have been issued for their arrest. [Place not given.]

Mrd: on Sep 24, in Wash City, by Rev Jas B Donelan, at St Matthew's Church, Mr Henry McConvey to Miss Ellen M, 2nd daughter of John L Burck, of Fairfax Co, Va.

Died: on Sep 26, in New Haven, Conn, at the residence of her son-on-law, J W King, Ann, the aged relict of Judge Josiah Masters, of Chayticoke, & sister of Col Wm Smith, one of the aids-de-camp of Gen Washington during the war of the Revolution.

Fiendish assassination: the New Orleans Delta has a letter dated at Marion, Texas, on Sep 4. On Aug 26 A E Moore, his wife, & a lovely orphan girl, 12 years old, who was, by adoption, one of the family, had just seated themselves at the supper table, when the assassin discharged a double barreled gun at them. Mr Moore fell first, followed by Mrs Moore and then the orphan girl. The Moores had taken in 3 homeless orphans, now but 2, a young lady of 16, & a boy 14, has been left her large estate.

Public sale of land, by deed of trust from Geo H Montsanet & wife to the subscriber, recorded among the land records of PG Co, in Liber O N No 1, folios 481 thru 483: sale on Oct 31, of all that tract of land in PG Co, Md, commonly called **Oakland**, containing 430 acres, more or less; located about 2 miles from Piscataway, with a dwlg & other necessary out-houses. By the trust deed sufficient cash will be required to take up a note of $1,400 due Jan 1 last, & to defray the expenses of the trust. -John W Mitchell, trustee

Mrd: on Sep 27, in Wash City, by Rev Mr Boyle, Doctor W A Williams to Miss Susanna J Williams.
+
Died: on Sep 29, in Wash City, Mrs Susanna J, wife of Doctor W A Williams, & youngest daughter of the late Alex'r Williams. Her funeral is this afternoon at half past 3 o'clock from the residence of her mother, Mrs Williams, on M st.

WED OCT 1, 1856
Wash Corp: 1-Cmte of Claims: bills for the relief of John B Lord; of Terrence Keenan; of Chas Wilson; of Saml Payne; of Alex'r Bradley; & of Franklin Little: each passed. Same cmte: adverse reports & asked to be discharged from the consideration of the ptns of: Isaiah Hitchcock; of John Fitzgerald; of Geo H Miller; & of Edgar H Bates. 2-Ptn of Chas Magee, asking the remission of a fine: referred to the Cmte of Claims.

Died: on Sep 30, in Wash City, Sallie Boyle, daughter of Jas & Sarah E Owens, aged 1 year & 11 months. Her funeral is this evening at 2 o'clock, from the residence of her parents, on A st north, between 5th & 6th sts.

Died: on Sep 26, at **Gisboro**, near Wash, in his 15th year, Ashton Stevens, son of Henry Stevens, formerly of Va.

The funeral of John H Ellsworth will take place this afternoon, at 4 o'clock, from the residence of his brother-in-law, Ferdinand Jefferson, on 11th st, between L & M sts.

Charleston, S C, Sep 29. Wm R Taber, one of the editors of the Mercury, was killed this afternoon in a duel by Edw Magrath. He fell mortally wounded at the third fire.

THU OCT 2, 1856
Andrew Joyner, aged 72 years, died a few days ago, at Halifax, N C, a highly valued citizen of that virtuous State. At the time of his death, he had been a continuous & punctually-paying subscriber to the Nat'l Intelligencer for 51 years.

Ann Murray, aged 40, has been arrested at N Y on a warrant charging her with causing the death of Patrick Glenn, a child 6 months old, by giving him laudanum. The child was left with Murray by the mother for a brief visit to a neighbor, when the child became fretful & laudanum was freely administered to quiet him. The prisoner was held for trial.

Supreme Court at Boston: on Sat a verdict against the city for $2,250 damages in favor of the heirs of Geo Palmer, who died from injuries caused by slipping on the ice on the pavements in 1853, was awarded.

Mrd: on Sep 26, in Paris, Maine, by Rev Nathl Butler, Hon Hannibal Hamlin to Miss Ellen V, daughter of Hon Stephen Emory.

FRI OCT 3, 1856
Mrd: on Sep 30, at Balt, Md, by Rev Mr Coskery, Geo W Hazzard, U S Army, to Mary E, eldest daughter of Francis W Elder.

Mrd: on Oct 2, at St John's Church, in Wash City, by Rev Smith Pyne, Dr Thos S Mercer, of West River, Md, to Violetta, daughter of Hon Thos Carroll, of Wash City. [See Oct 4th newspaper notice. Hon has been omitted]

Mrd: Sep 25, by Rev P L Wilson, Amos F Martin to Cornelia Redman, all of Wash City.

Died: yesterday, in Wash City, Mr Geo Walsh, aged about 86 years, from the county of Kilkenny, Ireland. His funeral will be this afternoon, which will proceed from the Infirmary at half-past 3 o'clock.

Orphans Court of Wash Co, D C. Letters of administration on the personal estate of Jas Fitzgerald, late of Wash Co, deceased. -Margaret Fitzgerald, admx

On Sep 25, the dwlg house of Mr Jackson Dawson, at West Union, Doddridge Co, Va, was entirely destroyed by fire, & in it all of his 5 children; also Miss Lavinia Myers, a girl that lived with him. Mr Dawson, in attempting to save his children, was so badly burnt that his recovery is doubtful. The fire is supposed to have originated in the kitchen.

Wm Arrison, convicted at Cincinnati of manslaughter upon an indictment charging him with murder in the first degree by killing Isaac Allison by means of an infernal machine or torpedo, was on Monday sentenced to the penitentiary for 10 years. He was first conviced of murder in the first degree & sentenced to be hung, but obtained a new trial.

Rev David Moore, D D, the eldest son of the late Bishop Moore, of Va, died on Tue, at the rectory of St Andrew's Church, Staten Island, N Y, in his 70th year of his age, & 48th year of his rectorship on Staten Island. -Com Adv

Rev J Morris Pease, agent of the N Y Colonization Society for exploring Western Africa, died at Auburn, N Y, on Sunday last. His loss will be severely felt.

SAT OCT 4, 1856
The Gtwn Advocate, for a number of years past issued by Ezekiel Hughes, has been purchased by Mr John C Parker, & will hereafter be conducted by him.

Trustee's sale: by deed of trust from Saml B Fowke & Ellen E T his wife, dated Apr 9, 1855: auction on Nov 6, in front of the premises: lots 1 & 2, & the southern part of lot 14, in square 439, with improvements thereon. -W Redin, trustee -A Green auct

Mrd: on Oct 2, at St John's Church, Wash City, by Rev Smith Pyne, Dr Thos S Mercer, of West River, Md, to Violetta, daughter of Wm Thos Carroll, of Wash City.

Mrd: on Oct 2, at the First Presbyterian Church, by Rev Dr Sunderland, Lovell L Lawrence, of Indiana, to Sue I, daughter of John Underwood, of Wash City.
+
Mrd: on Oct 2, at the First Presbyterian Church, by Rev Dr Sunderland, Felix G Fontaine to Hattie P, daughter of John Underwood.

Mrd: on Sep 30, in Meadville, Pa, by Rev A Varian, Mary E, eldest daughter of Hon John W Farrelly, of Meadville, to Dunbar S Dyson, of Wash City.

Died: on Sep 19, in St Mary's Co, Md, at the residence of her cousin, Mr Benj Pembroke, Miss Lizzie Frank, formerly a resident of Wash City.

Cleveland, Oct 8. Persons killed by an explosion in Delaware Co yesterday: Mrs A Walker, Thos Williams, Wm Finch, Henry Hommell, Lewis Powers, Mrs Shaw, Frank Smith, Hiram Nafus, Mr Tone, & a man & woman unknown.

MON OCT 6, 1856
Deserters massacred. News received at Granada that Capt Turley & his men, who originally came from New Orleans & subsequently deserted from Walker's army, have been killed by Indians in the mountains of Chontales. Their names are as follows: Capt Turley, Lt John J Rivra & Lt E F Russell. Privates: E R Fitzhugh, J F Butler, B F Boyle, Saml Browne, M Conrad, Geo Dunn, W O Earl, Jas A Gray, J A Gammon, J B Taylor, F R Welch, O P Lamton, A C Lewis, A Locke, W B Lofdin, M R Morrison, A N Moore, Saml Moore, Y B Smith, W R Shears, H Sphears, D F Klink, & M M Wells.

Mrd: on Oct 2, in Wash City, by Rev L I Gilliss, Leonidas C Campbell to Mary E, daughter of John C Kennedy, all of Wash City.

Died: on Oct 3, at **Weston**, the residence of his father, Dr Jas H Causten, eldest son of Jas H Causten, aged 38 years. His funeral will leave St John's Church at 1 o'clock on Oct 6.

Mrs B B Norris, Fashionable Dress Maker has removed from her late residence on 14th st, to 380 13th st, 4th door above N Y ave.

Wash City Ordinance: 1-Act for relief of John B Lord: sum of $22, & sum of $38.80, be paid to him for making fences at two precincts. 2-Act for the relief of Thos Welsh: to be paid $29.75 for injuries done to his horse by reason of a breakage in the floor of 14th st bridge over the Canal. 3-Act for relief of Ann Dunlop: fine imposed for selling groceries without license be remitted, provided she pay the cost of suit.

New Fall Millinery: Miss E E McDonald, 71 Bridge st, Gtwn, D C.

TUE OCT 7, 1856
Household & kitchen furniture at auction on: Oct 9, at the residence of Mrs Simpson, E st, between 9th & 10th sts. -Jas C McGuire, auct

Portland [Maine] Advertiser: Dr Wm H Allen, of Machias, was instantly killed on Sep 24, by the accidental discharge of a gun he was returning with from a hunting excursion. He was about 25 years old, of excellent habits, & leaves a wife.

Dr Branch T Archer, a native of Va, & well remembered as a leader in the Texas revolution, died at Galveston on Sep 22.

Obit-died: on Sat, at his residence in Balt, after a long illness, Hon John Johnson, brother of Hon Reverdy Johnson. He was a native of Annapolis, where his remains will be taken for interment. -Balt Sun of yesterday [Oct 9th newspaper: Chancellor Johnson was the son of John & Deborah Johnson, of Annapolis, born in that city on Aug 8, 1798; educated in St John's College; became a clerk in a commercial house in Balt; removed to New Orleans, with a small capital given him by his father, but was stricken down by the disease indigenious to a country possessing in all other particulars so many advantages, his life was imperiled & his means nearly exhausted. He returned to Md & commenced the study of law in his brother's ofc. He made Upper Marlborough, a village of his native State, & the county seat of PG Co, his home. When his judicial life ended, he removed to Balt to reside & resume the practice of his profession. He leaves a wife and children to mourn his loss.]

Manchester [N H] American announces the death of Rev John Milton Whitin, of Antrim, on Sep 28, at the age of 71 years. He was one of the most eminent divines of N H. He was born in Winchendon, Mass, Aug 1, 1785, graduated at Yale College in 1805, was ordained pastor of the church in Antrim Sep 28, 1808, & continued his pastoral labors for 45 years. In 1848 the honorary degree of doctor of divinity was conferred upon him by Princeton College, N J.

$5 reward for return of strayed white cow, to any person who will bring her home, or give information where she may be found. Eliz Wood, on the road leading from North Capitol st to Rock Creek Church.

Mrd: on Sep 25, in Wash City, by Rev Mr Greer, Mr Chas M Sanderson to Miss Georgiana Holroyd, all of Wash City.

WED OCT 8, 1856
Naval Academy at Annapolis-Appointment of Acting Midshipmen: the following candidates for admission into the Naval Academy have passed the preliminary examinations & received appointments as acting midshipmen:

Lyman B Foster, Maine
Chas S Whitman, Maine
Henry M Herman, N H
Sulivan D Ames, R I
Henry B Robeson, Conn
Chas S Hunt, Conn
John W Philip, N Y
Francis S Kinney, N Y
John Hesse, N Y
Francis S Brown, N Y
Sephen A McCarty, N Y
Silas Casey, NY
Wm W Smith, N Y
Ormus A Doolittle, N Y
E J W Raynsford, N Y
D S Hayward, N Y
H D Foote, N Y
Alfred T Mahan, N Y
Benj Gregory, N J
F A Shute, N J
Bruce Lambert, Pa
Saml W Knipe, Pa
J C Dowling, Pa
Robt H Porter, Pa

Wm Whitehead, Pa	J H Comstock, Ark
H DeHaven Manley, Pa	A D Wharton, Tenn
John Weidman, Pa	Wm W Carnes, Tenn
P S Sanderson, Pa	Chas Kean, Ky
W Scott Schley, Md	J C Watson, Ky
Wm H Barton, Md	Woodhull S Schenck, Ohio
J M Stevenson, Md	J D Marvin, Ohio
Julian M Spencer, Md	Saml B Paddock, Ohio
T E M Adams, Md	Harold Lewis, Ohio
Isaac P Webster, Md	T S Greiner, Ohio
Francis L Hoge, Va	Wm C Jacobs, Ohio
Thos L Dornin, Va	Moses S Stuyvesant, Ohio
R D B Sydnor, Va	Simeon P Gillet, Ind
Jno S McKinley, Va	Edwin R Devault, Ind
Roy M Hooe, Va	Jas O'Kane, Ind
Thos L Harrison, Va	Ernest D Cordell, Mo
John J Hunt, Ga	Antoine R McNair, Mo
Jas L Hoole, Ala	R P S Talbott, Mo
John W Allen, Ala	G R Griswold, Mich
Chas W Read, Miss	F A Davenport, Mich
Louis J Burt, Miss	Wm H Wall, Iowa
Geo P Harris, La	J O Bradford, Calif
Geo T Howard, Texas	C K Kirby, Dist of Col
Simeon B Reardon, Ark	Robt L Meade, Dist of Col

[Oct 9th newspaper-correction: C K Kirby, of Dist of Col should have been Chas Kirby King.]

Handsome one-horse pleasure carriage, superior family horse, & harness at auction: on Oct 11, in front of the auction rooms, being the property of the late Capt Williams. -Jas C McGuire, auct

A few days ago a little girl, daughter of Mr & Mrs Ernstein, of Columbia, S C, was strangled to death by the rope of a swing, which by some means became entangled around her neck.

Brvt Maj Geo W Rains, Capt in the 4th artl, has resigned his commission; the resignation to take effect on the 31st proximo.

At New Hampton Literary Institution, N H, on Monday, two lads, Jones, of Concord, & Carlos Bean, son of J M Bean, of Manchester, were rehearsing before school. A scene in the play required firearms. Carlos was impaled to the wall by the ramrod of a gun. He lived but 2 hours.

Wash Corp: 1-Cmte of Claims: bills passed-relief: of Henry S Davis; of Wilson M C Fairfax & John Costigan; of Jos Ruff; & of Dickinson Nailor, agent.

Balt Board of Trade annual meeting on Monday, Wm F Walter called to the chair, & G U Porter appointed Sec. Gentlemen elected ofcrs for the ensuing year: Pres, John C Brune; Vice Presidents: Enoch Pratt, Thos C Jenkins, Wm McKim, A Schumacher; Treasurer, E B Dallam; Sec, Geo U Porter; Dirs: Wm P Lemmon, J Hall Pleasants, Alex'r Rieman, Wm Bose, Thos W Levering, Hugh A Cooper, E S Courtney, Robt Leslie, Robt R Kirkland, Laurence Thompson, John Williams, Geo N Eaton, W T Young, H L Whitridge, Saml Fenby, Aaron Fenton, H G Rice, Wm E Hooper, Geo H Kyle, Wm Keighler, C D Slingluff, Wm Devries, H R Wilson, C D Hinks. -Clipper

Wash City school trustees elected on Monday:

Thos P Morgan	Josiah F Polk	A G Pendleton
Wm Wilson	J C Harkness	Theodore Wheeler
J P Dickinson	Chas W Davis	Peter M Pearson
T J Magruder	S A H McKim	Saml Yorke AtLee

Davenport, Iowa journal: new cemetery in that city is under the direction of our respected fellow-citizen of this District, Capt Geo F De la Roche. The name is *Oakdale Cemetery*. The carriageway is 5 miles long & the number of lots near 3,500.

The projected duel between Mr Pryor, Editor of the Richmond Enquirer, & Mr Botts, son of Mr John Minor Botts, was prevented yesterday by the interference of the police.

Orphans Court of Wash Co, D C. In the case of Jos Smith, adm of Catharine Brown, deceased: the administrator & Court have appointed Oct 28, for the final settlement of the personal estate of said deceased, of the assets in hand.
-Ed N Roach, Reg/o wills

Orphans Court of Wash Co, D C. In the case of Harriet Fischer & Geo J Fischer, excs of Wm Fischer, deceased, the executors & Court have appointed Oct 28, for the final settlement of the personal estate of said deceased, of the assets in hand.
-Ed N Roach, Reg/o wills

Mrd: on Oct 6, at St Patrick's Church, by Rev Fr O'Toole, Wm A Fenwick to Miss P M Johnson; & Walter Stewart to Miss S J Fenwick, all of Wash City.

THU OCT 9, 1856
Mrd: on Sep 25, at Natchez, Miss, by Rev Mr Watkins, Henry N Seibrecht, of New Orleans, to Mrs Anna E Fitzhugh, of Wash.

Died: on Oct 1, at the U S Hotel, in Wash City, of consumption, John Abner Young, eldest son of Coleby & Sarah Ann Young, in his 24th year.

Died: on Oct 6, in Wash City, Wm Dean, recently of Fredericksburg, Va, but formerly of the State of N Y, about 50 years of age.

Delaware [Ohio] Gaz of Oct 3. Yesterday a terrible tragedy occured at the Fair Grounds by the bursting of a steam engine on exhibition from the establishment of Bradley, Burnham, Lamb & Co. Killed were: Mrs A Walker; Thos Williams; F Smith; Louis Powers; Wm Finch; a son of Minor Tone, of Liberty; two Neffises, names not given; Mr Crook, residing on the plank road north of Columbus, [the person whose body lay for some time unrecognized in the Mayor's ofc;] & Mrs Shaw. Fatally wounded: Another son of Danl Stimel; Mrs Jeremiah Markle & child; [child since died.] Wounded: Blungluff, student, badly scalded; Benj Newberry, of Berkshire, leg & arm broken; Read & Kelley, students, each a leg broken; Mrs Jacob J Gross, of Troy, badley scalded; S S Stailey, student, of Waldo, scalded; son of Lewis Breeze; son of H P Havens; J P Slack; Mrs R Mickle; ___ Rawley; Miss Veley; ___ Bacheler; J Markle; B Hoss; J Nicholson; A Wells; H C Thomson; son of M L Griffin; ___ Wade; ___ Gavit.

U S Patent Ofc, Wash, Oct 7, 1856. Ptn of Jno P Sherwood, of **Fort Edward**, N Y, praying for the extension of a patent granted to him on Dec 17, 1842, for an improvement in door locks, for 7 years from the expiration of said patent, which takes place on Dec 17, 1856. -Chas Mason, Com'r of Patents

FRI OCT 10, 1856
The venerable Deacon Nathl Frothingham & his wife commemorated their golden wedding on Sat, in this city, having been married Oct 4, 1806. Deacon F was a widower & his wife a widow when they were united, & both had children. They have 5 sons & 4 daughters surviving, 4 of them in N Y, & all, except an invalid daughter, were present with their children on this joyous occasion. Rev Dr Emerson, whose golden wedding occurs on Oct 29, Thos Neeham, & others, were also invited. Deacon Frothingham is now 87 years of age & his wife 79 & his health is so vigorous that he is almost every day seen in our streets. He lived in Charlestown at the time of the battle of Bunker Hill, &, with an elder sister & her family, was compelled to flee from the flames of a happy home when the British burnt Charlestown.
-Salem Reg, Oct 6

$300 reward for runaways, belonging to the estate of the late Henry H Warring: negro men Charles, about 33; Sylvester, about 30; & Wm, about 28; & negro boy Washington, about 14; & negro woman Laura & 2 children, a girl about 5 & a boy about 2½ years. -Dionysius Sheriff, Exec of H H Warring, living in Bladensburg, PG Co, Md.

Municipal election in Balt on Wed last. List of the members of Council elect. Those in italics are Democrats & the balance Americans:

Fred S Turner	F Key Howard	Edw Horney
M A Daiger	Jas W Alnutt	Geo W Herring
Phillip H Muller	T Oswald Wilson	Saml Kirk
Fred'k Pinkney	John F McJilton	J B Seidenstricker
F H B Boyd	Henry Handy	Dr F B Hintze
Jacob Green	F C Crowley	Alex B Gordon
Henry Forrest	Henry Travers	John R Kelso
John B Tidy	Joshua H Hynes	Jos Simms
John K Carroll	Danl Harvey	B Bierbower
Benj F Nalls	Thos Sewell, jr	Robt Sullivan

Mrd: on Oct 8, in Phil, at her father's residence, by Rt Rev Thos Atkinson, D D, Bishop of N C, Lt Theodoric Lee, U S Navy, to Miss Fannie A, 2nd daughter of Jno Grigg.

Mrd: on Oct 9, at Orange Court House, Va, by Rev Philip Slaughter, Lt Thos Roney, U S Navy, to Miss Fannie P Robertson, of Culpeper Co, Va.

SAT OCT 11, 1856

Mrs Gadsden, the wife of Gen Gadsden, late Minister to Mexico, died on Oct 7. -Charleston News

I offer for sale the beautiful farm **Dresden**, upon which I reside. It is in Loudoun Co, Va, [on the **Snicker's Gap** turnpike,] 12 miles from Leesburg: contains 400 acres of land; a brick dwlg house & every necessary out-bldg; adjoins the lands of Jas F Ball & the heirs of Geo W McCarty. -Horace Luckett, Middleburg, Loudoun Co, Va

Real estate for sale in Montg Co, Md: the subscriber, as trustee, will offer at public sale, on Nov 3, the widow's dower in the real estate of which Thos Gittings, late of said county, died seized, in said county, on the road leading from Wash City to Colesville, containing 191 acres of land; with a dwlg house, kitchen, & other out-houses. -W Veirs Bouic, Trustee

Died: yesterday, at his residence, in PG Co, Md, Allen P Bowie. If the entire discharge of all the duties of a devoted husband, father, kind master, friend, & neighbor entitle him to the highest eulogy that society can bestow, he is richly entitled to it. He leaves a devoted wife & 12 children who are left to mourn his irreparable loss! His funeral will take place from his late residence at 11 o'clock today.

Died: on Oct 9, in Wash City, Nebraska, infant son of Wm A & Eliz P Elliott, aged 2 years & 9 months.

Real estate for sale in Montg Co: the subscriber, as trustee, will offer at public sale, on Nov 3 next, the following lots, of which the late Hanson Clarke died seized, in said county: lot 2, contiguous to lot 1, purchased by Oliver H P Clarke at a previous sale, on the one side, & on Bladensburg road on the other, & on the road from Colesville, by Bond's Mill, to Wash, on a third side: contains 180½ acres, more or less. Part of lot 3, adjoining lot 2, fronting on the Wash road from Colesville, containing 114 acres of land, more or less. Lot 7, formerly sold to Thos Riggles, will be resold at his risk. It lies nearly south of & adjoins lot 5, now owned by C H Clarke; contains 51½ acres of land. The property will be shown by the Messrs Clarke, residing in the neighborhood. -W Veirs Bouic, trustee

MON OCT 13, 1856
Geo W Johnston, one of the large sugar-planters on the Mississippi, below New Orleans, who died recently, has left an estate valued at not less than $700,000. He has by his will manumitted all his slaves, 200 in number. They are all to be sent to Liberia in 4 years from his death, & each is to be furnished with $50.
-Alexandria Gaz

Orphans Court of Wash Co, D C. Letters of administration with the will annexed on the personal estate of Jas H Causten, jr, late of Wash Co, deceased.
-Jas H Causten, adm w a

The neighborhood on 6th st, between G & H, was thrown into considerable excitement on Sat by the report of the death of Mrs McNaughton by violence on the part of her husband, Geo McNaughton. It was found to be true. He & his wife had lived unhappily for a long time, & their troubles were a matter of notoriety throughout the neighborhood. McNaughton dealt his wife a fatal blow. He tried to destroy himself, & was arrested. [Oct 14th newspaper: The hearing of Mr McNaughton yesterday, resulted in his dismissal.]
+
Died: on Oct 11, suddenly, Mrs Mary McNaughton, in her 60th year. Her funeral will take place from her late residence, on 6th st, between G & H sts, this morning at 10:30 o'clock.

Died: on Oct 11, after a long & painful illness, Eliz Henrietta, wife of Francis Lamb & daughter of the late Jas Sessford.

Died: on Oct 10, at Woodbury, N J, Mrs Margaret Pettibone, in her 74th year, after a long & severe illness. Her funeral will be from the residence of her son, John Pettibone, 14th st, [Island,] on Oct 18, at 2½ o'clock.

Died: on Oct 8, at Petersburg, Va, Mrs Maria Louisa, wife of B F Williamson, of that city, & daughter of Mrs Helen W Hungerford, of this place.

Died: on Oct 2, at Mobile, Ala, after a painful illness, Mrs Eliz Fonde, formerly of Wash.

Phil, Oct 12. Yesterday, while the Shiffler Hose Co was passing 9th & South sts, a man, Wm McIntyre, was shot through the heart & killed. He was a man of disreputable character, & was charged a few months since with having killed a woman with a porter bottle. The police immediately arrested the hose company, & others found in the hose house, making 33 persons in all. Among the prisoners is John English, said to be a constable in Balt. [Oct 21st newspaper: The inquest rendered a verdict of "Death from a wound inflicted by some person unknown."]

Orphans Court of Wash Co, D C. In the case of Richd H Willett, adm of Beniah Willett, deceased: the Court & administrator have appointed Nov 4 next, for the final settlement of the personal estate of said deceased, of the assets in hand. -Ed N Roach, Reg/o wills

Orphans Court of Wash Co, D C. In the case of Somerville Nicholson & Nicholas Callan, adms of Maj Augustus A Nicholson, deceased: the administrators & Court have appointed Nov 4 next for the final settlement of the personal estate of said deceased, of the assets in hand. -Ed N Roach, Reg/o wills

TUE OCT 14, 1856
Trustee's sale: by decree of the Circuit Court of Wash Co, D C, passed in a cause wherein Francis Wheatley & others are cmplnts & Chas H Winder & Wm H Winder are dfndnts: auction on Nov 10, in front of the premises: lots 1 thru 6 in square 170, in Wash City, according to Davidson's subdivision of original lots 9 & 10, in said square. -W Redin, trustee -A Green auct

Two young men, calling themselves Lewis Ahrens & Wm Paust, were arrested in N Y on Thu on suspicion of being counterfeiters. The prisoners were committed for examination.

C B Huntington, broker, of 52 Wall st, was arrested in N Y on Thu on a charge of forging a note for $6,500 on Phelps & Dodge. He says he received them from a street broker, Geo S Fitch, but Fitch denies it. Huntington had been arrested. [Dec 31st newspaper: The Jury in the Huntington case today found a verdict of guilty, & he was sentenced to the States prison for 4 years & 7 months.]

Public sale of a mill & 212 acres of land, the property known as ***Spence's Mill***, about 4½ miles from Annapolis, Md, heretofore advertised at private sale by the subscribers as trustees, under the will of the late Dr Saml Ridout. Public sale at the Court house in Annapolis, on Oct 29 next. There are tenements on this property.
-Jacob Winchester, John Ridout, trustees

Variety of ornamental & shade trees, at Jas Maher's Private Nursery on 16th st, Wash City. -Jas Maher, Public Gardner

On Tue last, at the hotel of the American Minister, Mr Jos M Heyward, of Charleston, S C, married Miss Maria Henrietta Magruder, daughter of Capt G A Magruder, of the U S Navy. Rev Dr Hall, chaplain of the British Embassy, was the officiating clergyman. -Paris Cor N Y Express

Drug Store for sale: the subscriber offers his Drug Store, 13th & G sts, on accommodating terms. -Robt L Teasdale

David Myerle, Underwriter & Ins Broker: ofc Todd's Marble Bldg, Wash.

Berkeley Springs, Va, invites the attention of capitalists & others to the great advantages which this place affords as a water-cure establishment. Address John Strother, at this place until Nov 1, & after that day to Martinsburg, Va.
-John Strother

Died: on Oct 4, at his residence, near Wash City, after a long & painful illness, Washington Berry, in his 67th year.

Died: on Oct 11, in Wash City, of congestion of the brain, Francis W Singleton, of Winchester, Va, aged 21 years.

Died: on Oct 13, Emily A Pennington, aged 7 years, daughter of Wm H & Emily A Faulkner. The friends of the family & the Wesley Chapel Sabbath School are invited to attend the funeral from the residence of her parents, 439 Pa ave, at 3 o'clock P M this day.

N Y, Oct 13. John L Durkee & Chas E Rand, indicted for piracy for taking the State arms from a schnr, have been tried & acquitted.

WED OCT 15, 1856
Household & kitchen furniture at auction on: Oct 22, at the residence of Thos White, on Indiana ave, between 1st & 2nd sts. -J C McGuire, auct

Burning of an old mansion. The house in which Gen Wm H Harrison lived when he was Govn'r of the Northwestern Territory, lit up the fimament above the city of Louisville on Fri night last. The Courier says it was perhaps the only bldg in Jefferson of historical interest in that vicinity. There he ruled the vast postion of our Confederacy known as the States of Indiana, Illinois, Iowa, Wisconsin, & the Territory of Minnesota.

Nicaragua. The ship **George Law** brought intelligence from Greytown to Sep 21, which reports that Col McDonald, one of Walker's ofcrs, with 63 men under his immediate command, in the province of Chontales, was attacked y the natives, & defeated with the loss of his ofcrs, Cole, Wiley, Marshal, & E H Laws.

Lindpainter, the well-known musical composer who died recently, was buried with great honors at Stuttgardt, where for 15 years he had honorably filled the important post of chapelmaster to the grand opera.

A powder-horn was discovered a few days since on one of the Hunting Islands, near the mouth of Morgan river, S C, marked 2 Rudolph. It is said to be the only trace ever discovered of the revenue-cutter **Hamilton**, Capt Rudolph, which was lost off the Charleston, S C bar in 1853 & never heard of.

Mr Saml Hoard, of Chicago, has raised a squash in his garden this season which weighs 186 pounds. Probably the largest squash ever grown in this country.

Young Throop, one of the 5 persons whose lives have been sacrificed to the fell spirit of lawless mobism as elicited by the Mayor's election in Balt on Wed last, died in that city on Monday. He died from a bullet from a gun or pistol in the hands of some person unknown. He went to Balt to take part in the election, & there seems to be no doubt of his active participation in some of its most violent scenes, for in one of such he received the fatal shot. His remains were brought to Wash City on Monday & buried yesterday.

Mrd: on Oct 14, in Wash City, at Trinity Church, by Rev Dr Cummins, N Clarendon McKnew, of Beltsville, Md, to Miranda E, daughter of Jno M Willson, of Wash City.

Milwaukee, Oct 11. H Miles More, of Leavenworth, was arrested on Oct 2, while at Kansas city enroute east, by Surveyor Gen Calhoun, & carried to Wyandotte city & imprisoned.

THU OCT 16, 1856

Extensive sale of boots, shoes, trunks, & carpet-bags, at public auction, on Oct 23, at the store of Mr L D Wall, Centre Market space, between 7th & 8th sts. We will sell his entire stock in trade, comprising one of the largest ever offered in Wash City.
-Wall, Barnard & Co, aucts

Mscl: When Col Monroe was President, & up to the period of his death, he owned a farm in Loudoun, Va, near Aldie, called *Oak Hill*. He spent a good deal of his time there, as did his son-in-law, Judge Geo Hay. The Judge was a gentleman of very fine talents, somewhat eccentric, but, when he chose to be, a most interesting & fascinating gentleman.

The farm of Lt Thos T Hunter, near Beltsville, PG Co, Md, recently advertised in this paper, has been sold to Nathan Tyson, of Balt, for $50.50 per acre, cash.

Rock Hill for sale: contains 30 acres, on the Va heights of the Potomac river, in front of Gtwn, where the bridge is contemplated to be constructed by Congress, a survey having been ordered to be made. Offered at public auction on Oct 28.
-J C McGuire, auct

Sale of dwlg houses & lots in Gtwn, D C, at auction, on Dec 17, by deed a certain deed recorded among the land records of Wash Co, in Liber J A S No 22, folio 454, by which I am substituted trustee in the place of John Kurtz, deceased, & authorized to execute the trust declared in 2 deeds to the said Kurtz, severally dated Nov 29, 1837, & Sep 15, 1842, duly recorded: sale of parts of lots 159 & 167 in Beall's addition to Gtwn, with a handome 2 story brick dwlg house, which fronts on the south side of Gay st, a few doors east of the residence of Judge Dunlop; the lot fronts 30 feet on Gay st, & runs through at that width to Olive st. Also, parts of lots 152, in said addition, & of 44 in Holmead's addition to Gtwn, lying at the northeast corner, formerly the intersection of Gay & Montg sts. This lot fronts 42 feet on the north side of Gay st, by 90 feet deep, with 2 very comfortable 2 story brick dwlg houses, in good repair. -John Marbury, trustee

Farm in Clarke Co, Va, at private sale. This farm is part of the old **Audley tract**, containing 400 acres, with a commodious dwlg & every necessary out-bldg. Address me at Berryville, Clarke Co, Va, Geo W Lewis.

Hot Springs, Bath Co, Va, for sale: this place, with the adjoining tract of land, containing some 1,200 acres, more or less. Improvements consist of a hotel & cottages, sufficient to accommodate 200 persons. -Th Goode, **Hot Springs**, Va

Law Notice. Chas Naylor, of Pa, will attend professionally to business in the Court of Claims, the Supreme Court of the U S, & to claims against the Gov't. Ofc: 23 4½ st.

Mrd: on Oct 14, at Christ Church, Gtwn, D C, by Rev Mr Hoff, Lt Wm P Craighill, U S Corps of Engineers, to Miss Mary A, eldest daughter of Hon Judge Morsell.

Mrd: on Oct 14, in Gtwn, D C, by Rev J R Eckard, of Wash, D C, Rev Danl Motzer, of Montg Co, Md, to Fannie L, daughter of the late Bushrod Washington, of Gtwn.

Died: on Oct 14, in Wash City, Mr Andrew Marks, in his 72nd year, father of Rev S A H Marks.

Died: on Oct 15, in Wash City, Vinal Luce, in his 74th year. His funeral is tomorrow at 10 o'clock, from his late residence, 14th & H sts.

FRI OCT 17, 1856
Household & kitchen furniture at auction on: Oct 23, at the rooms over Mr Redfern's store, 19th & Pa ave. -A Green auct

Administrator's sale, by order of the Orphans Court of Wash Co, D C. All the personal effects of A G Ridgley, deceased, at his late residence, 124 Pa ave, between 19th & 20th sts. -David Ridgley, adm -A Green auct

Trustee's sale of valuable improved real estate: by deed of trust from Thos P Venable & wife, dated Dec 17, 1851, recorded in Liber J A S No 33, folios 263 et seq, of the land records of Wash Co, D C: public auction on Nov 4 next, of lot N in square 93, with two 2 story frame dwlg houses. -John W McKim, trustee -A Green auct
[The purchaser will be required to make all payments to r H Laskey, atty-at-law.]

Mr A W Lee, one of the clerks in the Comptroller's Dept of the State Gov't, has within the past 8 or 10 days absconded from this city, & prior to his flight he stole from the Deputy Comptroller's desk a check for about $9,800, for which he obtained cash in N Y. -Albany Statesman, Oct 9

Mrd: on Oct 16, in Wash City, at the residence of the bride's uncle, Hon Robt J Walker, by Rev Smith Pyne, D D, John Duncan, of Yalobusha, to Lucy Duncan Howell, of Natchez, Miss.

Died: on Oct 16, after a painful illness, Mary Rosetta, the fourth daughter of Philip & Sarah Otterback, aged 20 years. Her funeral is on Sunday next at 3 o'clock, from the residence of her father, near the Navy Yard.

Wilmington, Del, Oct 16. On Tue night Geo M Townsend, the mail robber, & 2 other prisoners escaped from the jail in Newcastle. Townsend has been recaptured.
[Nov 11th newspaper: Townsend, the noted mail robber, has again broken out of the Newcastle jail. This is his third escape from prison.]

Information wanted. Within the last 3 years an advertisement appeared in a Wash, Balt, Phil, & N Y paper, calling upon the descendants of ___ Piggott, who came to this country about ___ year, to address ___. Should this meet the eye of the advertiser, he will please address Stephen M Crane, Cincinnati, Ohio.

SAT OCT 18, 1856
The son of Maj T Ambler, of Fauquier Co, Va, was found dead a few days since under the steps of the house of E C Marshall, near the Markham station, on the Manassas Gap railroad. He was some 13 or 14 years of age, & died of disease of the heart.

Herr Ahorn, the sculptor who executed the celebrated lion modeled by Thorwaldsen & carved out of solid rock at Lucerne, died recently at Constance. He was one of the most eminent artists of the day.

Mules, just arrived from Ky, 50 head fine large young Mules, for sale on accommodating terms. Apply to Jas Shreve, 7th st, between H & L sts.

Collision in the Chesapeake Bay on Tue, when the steamer **Monmouth**, Capt Dansay, bound to that port from York river, was run into off the Wolftrap Light by the brig **Windward**, thence fo New Orleans. Capt Russell, of the ship **Louisiana**, dispatched 2 of his boats to their rescue. The following are supposed to have been drowned: Jas Davidson, Mrs Davidson, & 2 children, passengers; Matthias Matthews, steward; Wm Woodland, cook; Chas Phillips, coal-heaver; & Perry Ridgway, deck hand. Capt Hewitt was last seen on a raft drifting toward the sea, &, though he was supplied with 4 blankets, it is feared that he perished. At the time of the collison the brig had no lights out, as required by law. The **Monmouth** belonged to a company of planters on the Pamunkey river, & is a total loss, there having been no insurance on her.

Died: on Oct 16, in Wash City, Gen Jas Thompson, in his 88th year. He was born on St Valentine's day, Feb 14, 1769, & for 50 years was a faithful servant of his country. He was a member of the Masonic Fraternity, & was probably the oldest Free Mason in the U S, having joined at the age of 21 years, & has been a Mason for nearly 67 years. His funeral will take place from his late residence, near the Circle, on Oct 18, at 4 o'clock. [Oct 31st newspaper: His mental faculties in full perfection remained with him to the last moment, his hearing as sensitive as a child; he was born in Gtwn, D C, then Md, & at an early age was taken into the accounting house of Robt Peter, a wealthy Scotch merchant, at the present time represented in his descendants by persons as respectable as any in this or any other community. About 1795 Gen Thompson commenced business in Gtwn on his own account; in 1798-99, when he was appointed by Pres John Adams a lt in the marine corps, the head of which was Col Burroughs, the father of the gallant Lt Burroughs, who, while in command of the American schnr **Enterprise**, fell in her action with the British brig **Boxer**, which he captured in the last war with Great Britain. One of the two daughters of Col Burroughs, Gen Thompson married about the year 1808; the other married Hon John Nelson, late Atty Gen of the U S. Gen Thompson was reputed the handsomest man of his day, height about 5 feet 11 inches, weight 165 pounds. Gen Thompson was buried in ***Oak Hill Cemetery***, Gtwn, by his Masonic brethren, with the ceremonies of the Episcopal Church, on Oct 18, 1856. May he rest in peace. {He stood close to Gen Washington when he laid the corner-stone of the old Capitol, with Masonic ceremonies, on Sep 18, 1793, & at the time of his death was one of the few living witnesses of that event.}]

Died: on Oct 17, in Wash City, in her 77th year, Mrs Catharine Smith, relict of the late Henry Smith. The deceased was a native of Hempstead, Long Island, N Y, & a resident of Wash City from the time it became the seat of gov't. Her funeral is tomorrow, Sunday, at 2½ o'clock, from the family residence, on 11th st, near F.

MON OCT 20, 1856
Wash City Ordinance: 1-Act for the relief of Mauris Holloran: the sum of $25.50 be paid to him for hauling 200 loads off earth on Ohio ave, & repairing 13th st west.

Obit-died: on Oct 4, 1856, at *Nemours*, on the Brandywine, Dela, Alfred Victor DuPont, in his 58th year. He was the eldest son of Mr Irene DuPont, who founded the great manufacturing establishments of gun-powder, wool, & cotton in the the State of Delaware. Alfred DuPont had an important agency in the futher progress & increase of these works. Like his noble-minded father, Irene DuPont, his heart was full of generous & liberal impulses. Compelled by ill-health to retire from active business, his later years, amid the suffering of protracted sickness, were devoted to study & literature.

One of the most worthy citizens of Balt, Col John Berry, died at his residence near that city on Oct 17. He was an active member of the Methodist Episcopal Church for 36 years. He commanded a company of artillery during the war of 1812-14, & was commanding ofcr on one of the days of the bombardment at *Fort McHenry*. He leaves a very large connexion to mourn his sudden demise, in his 65th year.

From El Nicaraguense of Sep 20. On Sep 19, 2nd Lt Jennings Estelle suffered the extreme penalty of the law by being shot on the Plaza for the murder of 2nd Lt Chas Gordon, in the guard house, in the city of Granada, while acting as ofcr of the guard. Estelle had been previously arrested for shooting Thos Edwards, & was, when he committed the unfortunate act for which he suffered death, a prisoner confined to his quarters. When he arrived at the spot where he was to breathe his last he requested that his hands might be untied, as he wished to address the crowd. This request being granted, he spoke in a fine unfaltering voice. He asked the forgiveness of the ofcrs & soldiers of the Nicaraguan army. Voices responded from the crowd, "God forgive you." While in prison he wrote that he was born in Marshall, Tenn, in 1833 & raised from infancy in Hinds Co, Miss. He started to Calif in 1852; on the road he had difficulty with a man by the name of Howard & shot him; he later shot a man named Hays, but the wound was not fatal. In the same year he stabbed Chas Robinson in 3 places. Estelle's body, as soon as life was extinct, was put in a good coffin & decently interred.

Mrd: on Oct 16, in Wash City, at St John's Church, by Rev Smith Pyne, Adna Anderson, of Nashville, Tenn, to Juliet C Van Wyck, of Wash City.

Died: on Oct 7, in Wash City, Lydia W, wife of Alfred Ray, & only surviving daughter of Mrs Harriet White, of Mount Pleasant, D C. She was a devoted wife, & leaves a large circle of friends to mourn her loss.

Died: on Sep 9, at San Francisco, Calif, Alexander Gideon, infant son of A T & R E Langton.

The Woodstock [Va] Tenth Legion publishes the death of Christian Dellinger, a Revolutionary soldier, at age 92 years. The Charleston [Va] Republican announces the death of David Thomas, aged 104 years, who served in the Revolution & the war of 1812.

Orphans Court of Wash Co, D C. In the case of Eliz Stillings, admx of John S Stillings, deceased, the administratrix & Court have appointed Nov 11 next, for the final settlement of the personal estate of said deceased, of the assets in hand.
-Ed N Roach, Reg/o wills

TUE OCT 21, 1856
Household & kitchen furniture at auction on Oct 29, at the residence of Wm P Howell, 9th & L sts. -Jas C McGuire, auct

A child, son of Allen McDonald, of Dodge Co, Wis, was killed by a bear which was chained to a post. The boy, 4 years old, inadvertently ran within reach of the bear, which had a range of about 20 feet.

The late Saml Rogers: on Dec 18, 1855, the Tithonus of living English poets, died in his own house, surrounded by the works of art which his fine taste had brought about him. He expired, wrote Dr Beattie, the physician who was with him, a tranquil & placid transition I never beheld. His devoted niece closed his eyes, & his faithful domestics stood weeping around his bed. In his 90th year his memory began to fail him; that was painful to his friends. His height was about 5 feet 5 inches; shy of praise, shy of censure. Sir Thos Lawrence & Mr Phillips have both very great merits as painters of female portraits. When Rogers was asked to distinguish their different excellencies, he replied, "Phillips shall paint my wife & Lawrence my mistress."

Gen Wm Hall died at his residence in Sumner Co, Tenn, a few days ago, in his 83rd year. His father & an older brother were killed by the Indians when he was a boy. During our last struggle with England he commanded a reg. under Gen Jackson, & acquired great reputation as a cool, skillful cmder; he served in the Legislature of the State as the Rep or Senator of Sumner Co, & as Speaker of the Senate succeeded to the ofc of Govn'r on the resignation of Gen Houston in 1828; & was chosen Rep of his district in Congress.

Jacksonport [Ark] Democrat of Oct 1: on Sat last the dwlg-house of Mr Henry S Durham, a mile from Jacksonport, was burnt, & Mr Durham, his wife, & a negro child perished in the flames. The skulls bore marks of being first murdered with an axe, & then the house set on fire. A negro man recently purchased by Mr Durham was suspected of the crime & is being pursued. He took the best horse & fled.

Mrd: on Oct 16, in Concord, N H, at St Paul's Church, by Rev Mr Hubbard, of Manchester, Seth Turner, of Randolph, Mass, to Ellen Montgomery, daughter of Capt Jos Manahan, of Wash City.

Mrd: on Oct 15, in Brooklyn, N Y, at the residence of Rosewell Woodward, by Rev Mr Lord, of Harlem, Hon Geo Landon to Miss Kate F Lay, both of Guilford, Conn.

Died: on Oct 18, in Wash City, Mrs Janet Cunningham, relict of Archibald Cunningham, in her 57th year. The deceased was a resident of Gtwn for the past 50 years.

Died: on Oct 19, in Wash City, after a painful illness, Sarah Eliz, wife of Jas Owner, in her 25th year. Her funeral is this afternoon at 3 o'clock, from the residence of her husband, on A st north, between 5th & 6th sts, Capitol Hill.

WED OCT 22, 1856
Thos Mackie Burgess, the 2nd Mayor of Pro---------, died on Fri last, in his 51st year.

Mr Hurdy Hitch, aged 81 years, assisted 64 years ago in making the sails of the barque **Maria**, of New Bedford, Mass, which was the first vessel that raised the American flag in the English Channel after a Revolution. A few days since Mr Hitch was at work in Fairhaven Village, Mass, on the sails of the same barque **Maria**.

Ex-Govn'r Sprague died at his residence in Providence, R I, on Oct 19. [Oct 24th newspaper: Wm Sprague died of typhoid fever, after an illness of little more than a fortnight. He was born in Cranston, in 1800, a son of Wm Sprague, who was one of the pioneers in the cotton manufacturing & printing business in his State. He had a fondness for politics, which continued all his life, & filled several ofcs. In 1848 he was chosen an Elector of Pres & Vice Pres of the U S, & at the time of his death was a candidate for the same ofc upon the Fillmore & Donelson ticket.]

Mr A J Moulder, the nominee for superintendent of public instruction in Calif, is from Washington, & the Democratic candidate there for clerk of the Supreme Court, Mr Chas Fairfax, is from the vicinity of Alexandria, Va.

For rent: a large brick house with furniture, adjoining Judge Dunlop's. Apply on the premises, 35 Gay st, between Montg & Greene sts, Gtwn, D C. -Letitia Humphreys

Obit-died: Judge J W Lesesne, of Alabama, & his son were drowned on Wed last by the upsetting of the yacht **Vesper** while crossing Mobile Bay on their way home. Among the lawyers of Alabama he was one of the first; a distinguished son of South Carolina. -Charleston Mercury

The Nashville [Tenn] Gaz notices the death of Hon John L Marling, American Minister to Guatamala, at Oakland, in the vicinity of that city, on Oct 16, in his 30th year. He was reared in a printing ofc, but studied law & connected himself with the Nashville bar. In 1854 he was appointed by the Pres as American resident Minister near Guatemala, Central America. He obtained leave of absence in May last & started for his native land, although the hand of disease was upon him. He reached home, & after 3 weeks of suffering, expired in the bosom of his family, leaving a wife & 2 children, a fond mother, & numerous relatives & friends to mourn his exit.

Mrd: on Oct 21, by Rev Mr Krebs, Mr Wm H Hage, of Wmsport, Md, to Miss Mary C McElwee, of Wash City.

Died: on Oct 15, at Unity, Montg Co, Md, Mrs Mary Frances, wife of Amos Lazenby, youngest daughter of the late Jas Darne, of Loudoun Co, Va.

THU OCT 23, 1856

Mrd: on Oct 10, in Columbus, Ohio, by Rev J W Waite, Mr Wm T Washington, of Prince Wm Co, Va, to Miss Fannie V Washington, of that city.

The Warrenton Whig states that the venerable Chief Justice Taney still remains at the Fauquier Springs, but expects to leave soon for Washington. His health continues to improve & by proper care he will soon be entirely restored.

Wm B Smith, convicted of killing his own son, has been convicted of manslaughter in the first degree by the Circuit Court of Tippah Co, Miss, & sentenced to 50 years in the State prison. Smith is now over 70 years of age, & will, according to the higher law of nature, be reprieved by death before the expiration of 50 years.

Mrd: on Oct 21, at St Stephen's Church, Phil, by Rev Chas W Dupuy, Rev Chas E Pleasants, of Wash City, to Anne Biscoe, daughter of the late John A Hamilton, of Phil.

Died: on Oct 22, at **Pomona**, near Wash City, Thos Bates, aged 73 years, a native of England, but for the last 38 years a resident of this District. His funeral will be on Sat at 3 o'clock, from his late residence.

FRI OCT 24, 1856
Trial on Tues last in the U S District Court at Balt, before Judge Giles, on a charge against Auguste L Baptista & Albert C Stabell of being engaged in the slave trade by owning & dispatching the schnr **C F A Cole**, of 92 tons burden, to the coast of Africa for a cargo of slaves. Capt Bush, of Alexandria, testified testified he went down to St George's creek, near Piney Point, & found the schnr in about 8 feet of water. Mr Edw A Slicer, a custom-house clerk, proved her manifest to have shown a freight of flour, whiskey, break, rice, potatoes, & lumber for Madeira, with which island, by the bye, very little trade is carried on from Balt. When the schnr left Cuba there were only 8 men on board: Capt Baker, Antonio Silva, mate, & 5 men, Capt Labradada, Antonio Pollens, a passenger named Lippold, Drummond, Frank Labradada, [a cousin of the Captain,] & the cook our of Cuba. At this stage of the examination the Court adjourned for the day.

Geo C Whiting, Chief Clerk in the Interior Dept, has been appointed Com'r of Pensions to succeed Judge Minot, resigned.

At the Essex Co Court of Common Pleas, at Lawrence, Mass, John H Driscoll, on a charge of cruel treatment of a cow, was sentenced to 10 months in the House of Correction.

Mrd: on Oct 21, in Wash City, at the Church of the Epiphany, by Rev J W Clark, J W Farrelly, jr, of Meadville, Pa, to Gertrude, daughter of Robt Widdicombe, of Wash City.

Mrd: on Oct 22, in Wash City, by Rev Mr Boyle, Hon P H Bell, of Texas, to Ella, only daughter of Gen Wm R Eaton, of North Carolina.

Mrd: on Oct 23, in Wash City, by Rev Geo Cummins, Isaac L Briceland, of Calif, to Emily Montoya, youngest daughter of the late S P Walker.

Died: on Oct 12, in Nanjemoy, Chas Co, Md, Edw Simms, aged 56 years.

Died: on Oct 14, at the **Convent of the Visitation**, Mobile, Ala, Sister Mary Filmena Martin, daughter of John B Martin, formerly of Wash City.

Wash City Ordinance: 1-Act for the relief of Wm G Deale: to be refunded $77.50, the amount of taxes he erroneously paid on part of lot 22 in square 454, Wash City.

SAT OCT 25, 1856
Mrd: on Oct 21, by Rev Mr Holmead, Mr Henry C Hepburn to Miss Harriet Cooper, daughter of Mr Wm Cooper, all of Wash City.

For rent: a fine 3 story brick house & basement, with a large brick stable attached to it, capable of holding 6 carriages & 4 horses, situated on 2nd st, Gtwn, the late residence of M de Bodisco, late Russian Minister. Possession given on Nov 15 next. Apply to Brooke B Williams, opposite Treasury Dept.

New Book. The Life of Mrs Eliza A Seton, Foundress & first superior of the Sisters, or Daughters of Charity in the U S, by Rev Chas J White, D D, a new & revised edition. Just received & for sale by R Farnham, Pa ave & 11th st.

Rockville Academy, Montg Co, Md: all branches of a classical education taught. -O W Treadwell, Principal

MON OCT 27, 1856

France has just lost two of her military notabilities. Baron Louis Doguereau is dead, in his 80th year. He made his debut under Napoleon. The other death is that of Baron Regnault, Genr'l of Brigade & Com of the Legion of Honor.

On Fri afternoon in the village of Evansburg, Upper Providence township, Montg Co, John Slough, an old gentleman & resident of that township, was burnt to death. He was out riding with his daughter on an errand in Evansburg. She left her father in the carriage for a short time, when he struck a match to light a cigar, but dropped it on the straw in the bottom of the carriage, which immediately caught fire. Before assistance could be rendered his body was entirely burnt. He lived but a short time afterwards.

Book Notice: Richmond by-gone Days; being Reminiscences of an Old Citizen. Richmond, Va. G M West, 1856.

A few months since the late Dr John C Warren dis-interred from the family tomb under St Paul's Church, Boston, the remains of his uncle, Gen Jos Warren, who fell in the fight of Bunker's Hill. The remains were placed in a stone urn, upon which an appropriate epitaph had been engraved. The skull was quite perfect, the chin still remaining. Behind one of the ears was seen an aperture, which indicated the place where the fatal ball entered which ended his brief but glorious career.

Died: on Oct 13, in Balt, Saml G, in his 22nd year, youngest son of Wm S & the late Mary Ann Espey.

Partial of a marriage notice: -Eliza Pumphrey, all of Wash City.

TUE OCT 28, 1856

First Lt Geo Adams, U S Marine Corps, died at Flushing, N Y, on Oct 21. -Star

Thos McGill has removed his Book & Job Printing Ofc to the new bldg on Pa ave & 11th st. Having added steam power & an additional large jobbing press, he is prepared better prepared than heretofore to execute all work entrusted to him.

Died: on Oct 25, at the residence of Raymond W Burche, in Montg Co, Md, of consumption, Annie Marcellotti, in her 18th year.

Richmond, Oct 27. The Grand Jury today found true bills against Robt G Scott, Hon J M Botts, Roger A Pryor, of the Enquirer, B B Botts, A D Banks, of the Petersburg Democrat, & others, for violation of the anti-duelling law of this State.

WED OCT 29, 1856
The London Times of Oct 11 contains an account of the death of Mr Chas Rowcroft, late British Consul at Cincinnati. He died & was buried at sea from on board the Amercian ship **Cherubim**, Capt Nelson Smith. The Captain said his death was certainly mysterious & sudden; that he was accompanied on board by his wife, 2 daughters, & 3 sons. The ship sailed from N Y for London on Aug 9; the decease took place on the evening of the 23rd.

In Balt a few evening since the wife & child of Mr Moses Roab were severely burnt by the explosion of an oil lamp. In the same city, on Sat, an ethereal oil lamp burst in the hands of Mrs John T Burns, but she was not injured, having the presence of mind to cast it from her.

On Thu last a lad named Chas O Jones, aged 17, was sentenced to the State prison for life, in Lawrence, Mass, for setting fire to a dwlg in the day time. This is the statute punishment, the judge having no discretion in the matter.

Distressing accident in the house of Andrew Moore, in Phil, on Sat. Mrs Moore was filling a camphene lamp, when one of the children bumped her arm & the can of fluid upset. It ignited, setting fire to Mrs Moore & the children in the room. Both Mr & Mrs Moore & 5 children were terribly burnt. One of the suffers, Eliza Jane Lawson, about 12, not a member of the family, died a few hours afterwards. Two children, Emma H Moore, aged 9 years, & Rachel D Moore, aged 4 years, died during the night. The two remaining children, Wilhelmina Moore, aged 6 years, & Elmira Moore, an infant, were still alive last night, but very little hopes that they would survive. Both parents are seriously burnt, but not so as to endanger their lives.

Mrd: on Oct 23, by Rev Geo L Machenheimer, of St Thomas' Parish, Wash Co, Md, Thos E Baden to Frances L, daughter of J L Henshaw, all of Wash City.

Mrd: on Oct 28, in Wash City, by Rev Dr Pyne, Geo Warner, jr, of Balt, to Mary Virginia, daughter of the late Prentiss Chubb.

We are informed that there is now in Washington an aged colored man, Rev Andrew Marshall, 100 years old, & a resident of Savannah, Ga. He is said to have served in the Revolutionary war under Govn'r Houston, of Ga, & was present at the battle of Savannah, where he saw Pulaski fall. He is pastor of the African Baptist Church in the city of his residence, & has been on a tour to the North for the purpose of collecting funds to rebuild the church edifice. He may be found for a few days at the house of Gustavus Brown, 362 21st st, between G & H sts.

Died: on Oct 28, in Wash City, Sallie Augustine, infant daughter of Anna & Colville Terrett, U S Navy, aged 5 months & 23 days. Her funeral will be from the residence of Mrs S T Mathews, n w corner of 8th & H sts, tomorrow at 3 o'clock.

Orphans Court of Wash Co, D C. Letters of administration on the personal estate of Andrew J McCoy, late of Wash Co, deceased. -Martha E McCoy, admx

Orphans Court of Wash Co, D C. Letters testamentary on the personal estate of Jas Thompson, late of Wash Co, deceased. -W H Y Taylor, J B H Smith, excs

THU OCT 30, 1856

Oregon. Capt Francis L Bowman, of the 9th infty U S Army had become insane, & escaped from his friends while they were taking him to the Dalles. His body was afterwards found nearly consumed by wild beasts.

Trustee's sale: by deed of trust to us from Richd Cruit, dated Jun 6, 1853: public auction on Dec 1, on the premises, all that piece of ground in Gtwn, bounded as follows, viz: beginning at the end of 32 feet & 6 inches on the first line of lot 9, in Holmead's addition to Gtwn, & running with the north side of Bridge st, east 23 feet to Robt Buller's brick house, it being the end of said first line; thence north & parallel to Montg st 120 feet; then south & parallel to Bridge st 23 feet; said piece of ground including part of said lot 9 & part of lot 181, in Beall's addition to Gtwn, with improvements. -Walter S Cox, Ferdinand W Risque, trustees
-Barnard & Buckey, aucts

Trustee's sale: by deed of trust to me from W R L Ward, dated Oct 15, 1852: public auction on Nov 14, on the premises, all those lots on the Chesapeake & Ohio canal, in Gtwn, known as lots 20 thru 22, on Niagara st, being part of a square formerly the property of Robt Peter, with the improvements. -Walter S Cox, trustee
-Barnard & Buckley, aucts

The Louisville Democrat announced the death of Hon Cyrus L Dunham, of Indiana, at his residence in that State on Oct 23. He represented for several terms the 3rd Congressional district of Indiana.

The late John Stevens, of Talbot Co, Md, left by his will a sum of money to the Md Colonization Society to be used in the construction of a vessel for the conveyance of emigrants to Liberia. The contract was given to the extensive builders, Messrs Abrahams & Ashcraft, & she is so far completed as to be able to be launched. -Balt Patriot

The oldest church in the U S is said to be at Hingham, Mass. It is a huge, square structure, the belfry rising out of the center of the roof. It is nearly 200 years old. In the adjoining burying ground stones may be seen dated as far back as 1619.

A paper in Birmingham, Ct, publishes the following: Residing within a stone's throw of our ofc is an old lady, Mrs Poll Beaman, a history of whose family presents the most striking instance of prolonged life that we ever knew of heard of. She is in her 92nd year; her partner, Tracy Beaman, died but a short time since; he was 2 years her senior; they lived together in the same farm house 69 years; they had a family of 9 children; the eldest of whom is 73, & she was married when she was 14. There are now 49 grandchildren, the oldest is 56. There are also 156 great-grandchildren & 18 great-great-grandchildren. A few are dead. This venerable mother can call 230 of her lineal pedigree around her thanksgiving table.

Boarding: Mrs Jane Taylor, 411 3rd st, between Pa ave & C st, on moderate terms.

Mrd: on Sep 18, 1856, at **Fort Vancouver**, Wash Territory, by Rev Mr Daly, Lt Philip A Owen, Adj of the 9th regt U S Infty, to Eliza Heron, daughter of Col Geo Wight, U S Army.

Mrd: on Oct 27, at Needwood, Fred'k Co, Md, the residence of her father, by Rev Mr Marbury, J Monroe Bibby, of N Y, to Eliz K Heiskell, of Wash City.

Public sale of valuable farm: at public auction, on the premises, on Nov 15 next, the Farm on which I now reside, 1 mile from Fairfax, Culpeper Co, Va: contains 156 acres of land, called **Rosenvick**; improvements are a comfortable dwlg house, kitchen, out-house, & ice-house. -Robt T Bowen

FRI OCT 31, 1856
Died: on Oct 27, in Wash City, Jas B T McNeir, eldest son of Col Wm McNeir, formerly of Annapolis, Md.

Mrd: on Oct 30, in Wash City, by Rev Geo D Cummins, Frederic Wippermann, of Hamburg, Germany, to Rosa Lee, daughter of the late Saml P Walker.

Mrd: on Oct 30, by Rev Mr Boyle, Mr Jas A Clark to Miss Jane E Lackey, both of Wash City.

Mrd: on Oct 1, in San Francisco, Calif, by Rev Mr Thrall, Capt H M Judah, 4th regt U S Infty, to Miss Maria B, daughter of John Ferguson, of that city, formerly of Wash.
+
Mrd: on Oct 1, in San Francisco, Calif, Jas L Trask to Miss Harriette B Judah, all of that city.

Died: on Oct 30, in Wash City, Mrs Mary Shussler, consort of Chas Shussler, in her 49th year, a native of Albige, Lincolnshire, England. Her funeral is this afternoon at 3 o'clock, from her late residence, Park Hotel, 7th st, near Boundary st.

The German Evangelical Lutheran Trinity Congregation, U A C, of Wash City, propose laying the corner stone for their church this afternoon, at 3 o'clock, at 4th & E sts. A collection will be taken in aid of the bldg fund. -Geo Willner & Fr Stutz, trustees

SAT NOV 1, 1856
Appointment by the Pres: Chas E Carr, Collector of the Customs at San Pedro, Calif, vice Isaac Williams, deceased.

Trustee's sale: by 2 deeds of trust to us, one from Patrick Kinney, dated Jul 7, 1853, & the other from Richd Cruit, dated Feb 7, 1854: public auction on Dec 2, on the premises: part of lot 6 in square 140, with a 2 story frame house. Part of lot 7 in square 481, with improvements. -Walter S Cox, Ferdinand W Risque, trustees -Jas C McGuire, auct

South Carolina Historical Society meeting in Charleston: J L Petigru, Pres, in the chair, reports the presentation to the society of the "<u>Lauren's Manuscripts</u>," a large & valuable donation.

The party recently formed in this city, under the direction of Col Wm H Noples, for the purpose of surveying an emigrant route to Calif, left yesterday. The company consists of 17 men, all thoroughly equipped. -St Paul's [Minnesota] Pioneer, Oct 23.

Kingston [C W[News tell of the death in Belleville on Fri, of a little girl aged 10 years, daughter of a Widow Brennan, while in a grave-yard, was killed by a grave-stone falling upon her.

Fall & Winter Millinery: W P Shedd, 502 11th st, Wash City.

Opening Winter Millinery: M Willian, Centre Market Space, between 7th & 8th sts.

I have this day acssociated with me in the Lumber & Coal business my son, H C Purdy. The business will be carried under the name of Jno Purdy & Son. -Jno Purdy

The death of Mr Wm McKenny *Osborne, of Gtwn, yesterday, of typhoid fever, will create a void in the family circle & the general society of the town not easy to fill. Mr Osborne has resided in the district within a year or two of 20 years, ever regarded as a gentleman of high moral worth, education & intelligence. He held a place in the Councils of the town for a series of election terms. Mrs *Osborne & several children are left to mourn this most weighty loss.
+
Died: on Oct 31, in Gtwn, of typhoid fever, Wm McK *Osborn, in his 45th year. His funeral will take place this afternoon at 4 o'clock, from his late residence on Beall st. [*Two spellings of Osborne/Osborn.]

Died: on Oct 21, in the city of Buffalo, Emily W Sibley, daughter of the late Hon Mark H Sibley, of Canandagua.

Died: on Oct 31, in Wash City, Thomas Oliver, only son of David R & Anna Lindsay, of Tuscumbia, Ala, aged 4 years, 4 months & 4 days. His funeral will be on Nov 2, at 3 o'clock, from the residence of his parents, 547 M st, between 8th & 9th sts.

Mrd: on Oct 30, in Wash City, by Rev Wm Krebs, Saml Stott to Miss Mary Lizzie Thompson, 2nd daughter of John Thompson, all of Wash City.

Mrd: on Oct 30, in Wash City, by Rev G W Samson, Geo F Henning to Jane Wall, both of Wash City.

Mrd: on Oct 30, in Wash City, by Rev Mr Boyle, Geo A Diggs to Sarah R, daughter of the late Maj Geo W Walker, U S Marine Corps.

Mrd: on Oct 28, at St Matthew's Church, by Rev Jas P Donelan, Mr Geo W Dant to Miss Mary Louisa Young, all of Wash City.

Mrd: on Oct 30, by Rev Dr Pyne, Wm B Webb to Emily Munroe, daughter of Henry K Randall, all of Wash City.

MON NOV 3, 1856
On Nov 7, we will sell, at the residence of Mrs A D Bodisco, on 2nd st, near Market, the entire household & kitchen furniture, china & glass ware. -Barnard & Buckey, aucts. The house, which is the one occupied for many years by A D Bodisco, the Russian Minister, is for rent. -Brooke B Williams, Banker, opposite the Treasury Dept.

Ancient Churches in Phil. The oldest Church in Phil is the Gloria Dei, which was erected in 1700, on the same site as its predecessor, which was built of logs, & served the double purpose of a place of worship & a defence against the Indians. Christ Church is where Washington & Franklin worshipped. It was also at first a log bldg. The present edifice was finished in 1753. Its chime of 8 bells was brought by Capt Budden from England free of freight, &, in compliment to him, rang out a joyous peal on his arrival. The good "Queen Anne" presented part of the communion service in 1708.

The St Louis [Mo] Evening news of Oct 24th states that Mr Wm Shoekendick had reached that city from Calif, &, while crossing the plains with his wife, 4 children, & a driver, was attacked about 80 miles east of **Fort Kearney** by a party of 50 or 60 Cheyennes, who killed his wife, one child, & the driver, & stole the mules. Mr Shoekendick with 3 of his children, managed to escape.

Near Rocky Point, Greenbrier Co, Va, on Thu week, at the residence of Wm T Mann, Geo Fox, about 15 years old, was instantly killed & partly eaten up by a large pet bear belonging to Mr Mann.

Mrs Ditty & Miss Lanphier will open Winter Millinery on Nov 5: 311 Pa ave, between 9th & 10th sts, upstairs.

Wash City Ordinance: 1-Act for the relief of M C Beth: the sum of $15 to be paid to him for damage done his hack, caused by the dilipadiated condition of a wooden trunk on K st south. 2-Act for the relief of G W Uttermuhle: the sum of $310.77 to be paid to him for casual repairs in the First Ward. 3-Act for the relief of Chas Wilson: the sum of $10 to be paid to him, for information given against Job Corson, master of the steamboat **George Washington**, for a violation of a city ordinance: Corson being fined $20, & afterwards sued out at the Circuit court & recovered by the Corp. -Approved, Oct 30, 1856.

Mrd: on Oct 16, by Rev W R DeWitt, Mr H C Fahnestock to Miss Maggie, eldest daughter of Isaac G McKinley, of Harrisburg, Pa.

Died: on Oct 25, in New Orleans, Margaret H Twiggs, eldest daughter of Maj Gen D E Twiggs, U S A, aged about 24 years.

Elmira, N Y, Nov 1. The Phil Express train of the Wmsport & Elmira railroad ran off the track near Crescent, killing Thos Fisk, the baggage master.

N Y, Nov 1. A daughter of Mr Blanchard, of Brooklyn, was killed, when the steamer **Bay State**, hence for Fall River, broke her walking beam & blew off her cylinder head. The steamer **Worcester** took the passengers to Norwich.

$200 reward for runaway negro woman Cornelia Diggs, about 25, belonging to the estate of Mrs Sophia H Perrie, deceased. -G Waters, adm w a

TUE NOV 4, 1856
Mrs Mary Bennett died on Wed, in Phil, at the advanced age of 102 years. She was a woman grown at the time of the Declaration of Independence.

Justin Ford, an Irish laborer working on the Alexandria & Lynchburg railroad in Ablemarle Co, Va, was tried last week in the Circuit Court, before Judge Field, for the murder of his wife in July. The jury condemned him to the penitentiary for 15 years.

Dr C S Goodman, Dentist, has removed to the magnificent rooms formerly occupied by the Gas Co, corner of 8th & Market Place: 21 years' experience in the various branches of his profession.

For rent: two 3 story brick store-houses on Bridge st, opposite Market Space, Gtwn. Apply to Mrs Ann Pickrell, 1st st Gtwn, or E Pickrell & Co, Water st, Gtwn.

W G Mezerott, successor to Geo Hilbus, Music Depot, corner of Pa ave & 11th sts, has on hand the largest selection of Musical Instruments in Wash City.

Boston, Nov 3. Hon Saml Hoar died yesterday at Concord, Mass.

Phil, Nov 3. Theodore Derringer was held to bail this afternoon on a charge of issuing fraudulent naturalization papers to parties that had never declared their intention to become citizens. Two parties exhibited Derringer's signature & the seal of the Court.

WED NOV 5, 1856
On Thu, near the Waltham depot, Luther Brooks, a Boston merchant, while attempting to cross the railroad track, was run over by the train & instantly killed.

A young man named Harvey Losee & his sister, Cynthia, aged 14, in Freeland, Ill, were returning from gathering nuts, when they were menaced by a bull. In the act of raising his gun one of the barrels accidentally discharged killing the unfortunate girl instantly.

Extensive stock of elegant fancy goods & plated ware at auction: on Nov 12, at the store of Messrs T Galligan & Co, under Brown's Hotel, Wash City, their entire stock. -Wall, Barnard & Co, aucts

Mrd: on Oct 21, at the residence of Alex G Davis, by Rev O A Kinsolving, Edmund A Tyler, of Aldie, Loudoun Co, Va, to Ellen T, daughter of Alex G Davis, of the same county.

Maine: Stephen Gomez was the first Spanish navigator who discovered [1525] & explored the coasts to the west & to the north of Cape Cod a little more particularly, & we therefore see on the Spanish maps these regions designated with the name of Tierra de Gomez, [Gomez's land.] so, for instance, at first on that of Ribeiro, [1529,] & afterwards on many others. The name of Maine was first introduced in 1639, when King Charles I granted to Sir Fernando Gorges all the land from Piscataqua river to Sagadahoc, to which tract of land he gave the name Province of Maine, in compliment to the Queen of Charles I, who was a daughter of France, & owned as her private estate the Province of Maine in France. Rhode Island: Roger Williams was the first settler in this territory. He & some other dissenters & refugees from Mass founded here the towns of Providence, Newport, & Portsmouth. Connecticut: The beautiful river from which the State of Connecticut derives its name was first discovered in 1614 by the Dutch Capt Adrian Block, who sailed into it as far up as the present site of Hartford, & who named it De Versche Rivier, the Fresh river.
New York: in 1664, when the English conquered the whole country it was named the Province of New York, in honor of James, Duke of York, brother of Charles II.
Maryland: in 1632 King Charles I gave a charter to Cecilius Calvert, Lord Baltimore, & granted to him a tract of land lying in that peninsula, between the ocean & the Chesapeake bay, & ordered this land to be called Maryland, in honor to the Queen Henrietta Maria, the consort of Charles I. She was of the Catholic religion, like Lord Baltimore himself, & likewise the greater part of the settlers which he carried out. The name appears for the first time in the charter of Maryland of Jun 20, 1632.

Mrd: Oct 23, at the residence of Mrs Mary K Tyler, by Rev Alex Compton, John S Ewell, of Prince Wm Co, Va, to Alice Jane, daughter of the late Edmund Tyler, of Loudoun Co, Va.

Mrd: Oct 23, in Charlotte, N C, by Rev A W Miller, J S M Davidson, of Quincy, Fla, to Miss Harriet Josephine Blake, of the former place, & daughter of Maj Jas H Blake, of Wash City.

Mrd: on Oct 29, near Winchester, by Rev C Walker, John T B Dorsey, of Elkridge, Md, to Miss Catharine C Mason, 2nd daughter of Hon Jas M Mason.

Died: on Nov 2, in Richmond, Va, Charles King, youngest child of Geo & the late Margaret Topham, in his 8th year.

Died: on Nov 4, Rosena Bryer, aged 30 years. Her funeral will be this afternoon at 3 o'clock, from the residence of her uncle, Gotleib Rau, on Ga ave, near 11th st, Navy Yard.

THU NOV 6, 1856

Household & kitchen furniture at auction on: Nov 10, at the residence of M S Roberts, [who is about to leave for Europe,] 83 Louisiana ave, between 9th & 10th sts. -Wall, Barnard & Co, aucts

Lost: the following notes: of Wm L Boak, Sep 18, 1854, 30 days, endorsed R B Hackney, for $100. Of R B Hackney, Nov 2, 1854, 30 days, endorsed by Chas E Sherman, for $300. Chas E Sherman, Nov 4, 1854, due bill for $250. D D Addison, Aug 29, 1854, 60 days, endorsed S A Pugh, for $150. D D Addison, Sep 23, 1854, 60 days, endorsed Richd Gott, for $200. The finder will be suitably rewarded on returning them to Geo T Massey, 13th st.

Balt elections: Affair yesterday resulted in the shooting & probable death of Richd Pryor, Pres of the American Ashland Club. The challenging of a supposed illegal vote led to a difficulty, in which Chas Harrigan, a member of the Empire Club, fired a pistol, the ball of which passed through the wrist of a young man named Wm Bright, & thence into the abdomen of Richd Pryor. He was carried home on a litter. Harrigan was arrested & released on $2,000 bail, Wm Byrnes, Pres of the Empire Club, becoming the bondsman. Mr Pryor was somewhat better last night, & it was hoped he would recover. [Nov 8th newspaper: there were 88 persons wounded in the late election riots in Balt, of whom 5 have died.]

Mrd: [Note-only legible part:] In Balt, ------------------daughter of Oliver W Treadwell, all of Rockville, Md.

New First Ward Restaurant: Pa ave, between 18th & 19th sts, Wash City, G E Divernois, proprietor; formerly proprietor of the Napoleon Hotel of Hoboken.

Mrs A Speir will open a new supply of Winter Millinery on Nov 5: 356 D st.

FRI NOV 7, 1856

Auction on Nov 18, of magnificent Grand Piano Forte, horses & carriages-built by Lawrence, of N Y, superior Paris made cabinet furniture, French plate-mirrors, French Clocks, splendid chandeliers, rich brocade & damask curtains, tables, parlor furniture, etc, at the residence of his Excellency, J Y Do Osmn, [Peruvian Minister,] on Indiana ave, between 3rd & 4½ sts. -Jas C McGuire, auct

Orphans Court of Wash Co, D C. Letters of administration on the personal estate of Eliz Braiden, late of Wash Co, deceased. -Margaret Lyons, admx

Virginia: the Spaniards, since 1520, included the land under the names of Terra de Ayllon & Florida, & the French, since 1568, under the name of Nouvelle France. The English invented the name Virginia at first [1588] for the country lying round Pamlico & Albemarle Sound. They composed this name, it is said, for 2 reasons: first, because it was discovered in the reign of their Virgin Queen, Elizabeth; &, secondly, because the country seemed still to retain the virgin purity & plenty of the first creation, & the people there the primitive innocence. Florida: Ponce de Leon, in the spring of 1512, discovered this coast & he gave to it the name of Florida, [the florid,] from 2 reasons, as Herrera says, at first because the country presented a very flourishing & pleasant aspect, & then because he saw the coast at that festival-day which the Spaniards call Pascua Florida, which corresponds to our Palm Sunday.

Sale by order of the Orphans Court of Wash Co, D, on Nov 13th, the household & kitchen furniture of Gen Jas Thompson, deceased, at his late residence, north M st, between 24th & 25th sts, near Gtwn. -A Green auct

Public Schools-Wash: Miss Kate McCarthy was promoted from assistant in primary No 4, to the principalship of primary No 3, to fill the vacancy caused by the resignation of Miss F L Henshaw. Miss Laura Reed was elected to fill the place made vacant by Miss McCarthy's promotion.

Mrd: on Nov 6, in Wash City, by Rev Wm Krebs, Geo A Bassett to Clorinda M Williams, all of Wash City.

Mrd: on Nov 6, in Wash City, by Rev Wm Krebs, Jas R Atwell to Lucy E Bullard, both of Va.

Mrd: on Nov 6, at St Mary's Church, Alexandria, Va, by Rev John B Blox, Francis Miller, of Wash, to Regina M, 2nd daughter of Wesley Summers, of Alexandria.

Mrd: on Nov 5, in Wash City, by Rev Mr Clarke, Lt Thos Scott Fillebrown, U S Navy, to Mary Eliza, daughter of S J Potts.

Died: Nov 5, in Gtwn, Mrs Ann D Dickson, wife of Mr John Dickson. Her funeral is be today at 3 P M, from her late residence, corner of Green & Stoddard sts, Gtwn.

Died: Nov 6, near the Navy Yard, Wash City, Patrick Callaghan, in his 79th year, a native of Galway Co, Ireland, & Parish of Moycullen. His funeral will take place at his son's residence, Dennis Callaghan, corner of 4½ & D sts east, at 2 P M.

SAT NOV 8, 1856
The Springfield [Mo] Advertiser mentions the death of Col Nathan Boone, youngest son of Danl Boone, week before last aged 7_ years.

Abner Hogg, who died in New Boston, N H, a few days ago at the age of 97 years, was a soldier of the Revolution, & fought at Bunker Hill & on several other fields. He felt a deep interest in the result of the present contest, & "stand by the Union" were among the last words he uttered.

Circuit Court of Wash Co, D C-in Equity. Whitney et al vs Dey et al. Nathl L Griswold & Wm Griswold, excs of Nathl L Griswold, sen, deceased, & the said Nathl Griswold & John L Griswold, excs of Geo Griswold, jr, deceased, having filed their respective petitions in said cause praying to be allowed & paid the dividend on the shares of their respective testators as stockholders in the Galveston Bay & Texas Land Co-that is to say, 7 shares to Nathl L Griswold, late senior, & 1 share to the said Geo Griswold, late junior-& it appearing by said petitions that the certificates of the said petitioners have been lost or mislaid: it is by the Court order that all persons who may claim any interest in said certificates or any of them adverse to the petitioners to produce the same & prove their right thereto on or before Dec 22 next. -Jno A Smith, clerk

Mrd: on Nov 5, in Wash City, by Rev G W Samson, Mr Jerome Elmore to Miss Barbara A Codrick, both of Wash City.

Mrd: on Nov 6, in Wash City, at Ryland Chapel, by Rev Mr Deale, Mr Saml Beall to Miss Margaret L Baggott, all of Wash City.

Mush Island for sale: by decree of the Court of Equity for Halifax Co, N C, Trent & others, vs parti, I will offer for sale at Weldon, on Dec 17, this well known & valuable plantation, on the Roanoke river, known as ***Trent land***, containing 856 acres. Also, adjoining, 325 acres, on the Wilmington & Weldon railroad. Mr J Fred Simmons, who resides at Weldon, will show the estate. -John H Ivey, C M E

MON NOV 10, 1856
Alex'r M Beebee, L L D, for 30 years past the editor of the Baptist Register, at Utica, N Y, died in that city on Thu last, at the age of 73 years. He has left a large circle of friends & admirers & his death is very generally regretted.

A correspondent of the Phil Inquirer confirms the death of Mr W A Babbitt, who was attacked by the Cheyenne Indians near ***Fort Kearney***, on Oct 25, while proceeding on his way to Salt Lake with his train, accompanied by 2 men & Mrs Wilson, of St Louis. On Sep 29 a train came in from Green river, a point some distance beyond Laramie. Mr Archambeau, the owner of it, informs that about 120 miles above this post, on the north side of the Platte, he found the place where the Indians came upon Mr Babbitt & killed him & all his party, & burnt or carried off his trunk, which contained his money, papers, & clothing. Some papers were scattered about & collected & delivered to me.

Winter Millinery: Mrs M A Hills will open Nov 12, 295 Pa ave, between 9th & 10th.

Circuit Court of Wash Co, D C-in Chancery, No 1090. Chas A Davis, Geo A Davis, & Alex McD Davis, vs Nathan Fales, Wm Fales, & others. The trustee in the above cause reported that on May 29, 1856, he, with Jas C McGuire, auctioneer, sold the west part of lot 4 in square 105, with the appurtenances, to Thos Berry, for the sum of $2,625, & the east part of said lot to Chas Gerecko, for $1,000; & on Oct 7, 1856, he sold lot 5 in square 377, with appurtenances, to Edw F Simpson, for $4,060; & that the said purchasers have since complied with the terms of the sale. -Jno A Smith, clerk [Nov 18th newspaper: Notice-statement of the account of the trustee & the shares of the several parties in the trust fund: on Dec 10 next, at my ofc, City Hall, Wash, 10 o'clock. -W Redin, aud]

Mrd: on Oct 30, at Farmer's Repose, near Arcola, Loudoun Co, Va, by Rev Saml Rogers, Mr John C Sprigg, of Wash City, to Miss Susan E Hutchinson, of the former place.

Mrd: on Nov 3, at Lexington, Va, by Rev Wm G White, D D, Rev John Miller, of Princeton, N J, to Mrs Sally C P McDuell, of the former place.

Mrd: on Nov 3, at St Louis, by Rev N L Rice, Mr W R Kibbey, of N Y, to Miss M Juliet, daughter of D Rokohl, of the former city.

Died: on Nov 7, in Wash City, Joanna S Deas, wife of Lt Chas Deas, U S Navy, & only daughter of F H Davidge.

Circuit Court of Wash Co, D C-in Chancery, No 860. Richd W Templeman & Annie W Templeman, vs John Miller & Chas A Comly, Hetty B Comly, Mary Templeman, & others, widow & heirs-at-law of Geo Templeman, deceased. Chas S Wallach, trustee, reported that on Oct 9, 1856, he, with Jas C McGuire, auctioneer, sold the lots of ground in the real estate in the above cause mentioned, to Thos T Mann for $4,925, & that the purchaser had complied with the terms of sale.
-Jno A Smith, clerk

TUE NOV 11, 1856
In the N Y Supreme Court the other day an action was decided against the Erie Railroad Company, brought by the widow of John Caffrey, who was killed by being run over by the train of cars in Jersey City. The plntf adduced that the deceased resided with his family in Jersey City, & on Jul 5, when returning home, he was tripped up by a rope which was used in hauling a locomotive into the depot, & was struck & killed. The defence was that the dfndnt lost his life by his own negligence. Verdict for the plntf $800.

Hon John Middleton Clayton, the veteran & distinguished Senator of the U S from the State of Delaware, died on Sunday at Dover. With his decease his immediate family & friends sustain a loss not greater than that which is suffered by the whole country. [Nov 14th newspaper: For several years Mr Clayton's health had been seriously threatened, his dangerous disease progressed. He was born in Sussex Co, Delaware on Jul 24, 1796, & but little more than 60 years old at the time of his death.] [Dec 6th newspaper: Mr Clayton died on Nov 9 last in his 61st year; his father, Jas Clayton, was a member of one of the oldest families in Pa, his ancestor having come to America with Wm Penn; his mother was a native of the Eastern Shore of Md; in Sep, 1822, he married the daughter of Dr Jas Fisher, of Delaware, an accomplished lady; after little more than 2 years of domestic happiness, she died in Feb, 1825, leaving him 2 sons; the youngest son died in Jan, 1849, in his 24th year, & the other two years afterwards.]

Thos Swann was yesterday inaugurated as Mayor of Balt, Md.

Lost, Land Warrant No 68,124, for 120 acres, issued in my name under the act of Mar 3, 1855. All persons are forewarned against the purchase of the same, as I intend to apply to the Com'r of Pensions for a duplicate. -Job Lewis

The battle-field of *Marengo*, with its palatial monuments, its rich museum of precious objects, & its richer historic souvenirs, in now offered at public auction in the streets of Paris. The domain of *Marengo* is near Alexandria, in Piedmont, on the line of the railroad between Genoa & Turin, & contains about 250 acres of ground. The palace was built in 1845 by Chevalier Delavo. It contains furniture, objects of art, paintings, & statues. -Correspondence of N Y Times

John Rosenburg, a citizen of Marshall Co, Va, was instantly killed at Wolf Run on Nov 1, by the falling of a huge oak, which also killed his horse. Mr R was highly esteemed in the neighborhood in which he lived.

A 13 year old boy named Mooney, while driving a mowing machine at Hamilton, N J, on Sat, dropped asleep & fell off amongst the machinery, which mutilated him so as to cause his death in about 3 hours.

Mrd: on Nov 9, in Wash City, by Rev A G Carothers, Mr Robt Warren to Miss Victoria Thorn, both of Wash City.

Died: on Nov 9, in Wash City, Georgiana, wife of John W Wade, in her 34th year. Her funeral will be today at 2 o'clock, from McKendry Church, Mass ave, between 9th & 10th.

Died: on Nov 9, in Wash City, Rachael Harrison, consort of the late Richd Harrison, of Anne Arundel Co, Md. Her funeral will be this morning at 10 o'clock, from St Matthew's Church.

Died: on Nov 10, in Wash City, Caroline Gilman, wife of John Gilman, of the Navy Dept, & daughter of Col Caleb Etheridge, deceased, of N C. Her funeral is this afternoon at 3 o'clock, from the residence of her husband, on N Y ave, between 12th & 13th sts.

Died: on Sep 13 last, at Liverpool, from accident, Wm Henry Harrod, in his 12th year.

WED NOV 12, 1856
Accident on Phil on Mon, by which 2 small children, Margaret & Mary Ann Mulcabey, lost their lives by being suffocated. Their mother had gone out to a day's work & left the girls locked in a back room. They played with matches & set the bed on fire, & before assistance could reach them they suffocated to death.

Old letter. Mr Wm S Mallicote recently picked up in one of the streets of Yorktown a letter written Aug 27, 1790, by Chas Lee, addressed to Wm Nelson, who was at that time Atty for the U S within the district of Virginia.

About 2 weeks ago 2 sons of Mr J S Wilhoite, of Monterey, Owen Co, Ky, one 10 years old & the other 8, rode their father's horse to the Ky river to water. The horse plunged into the water & the boys slipped off, the elder held onto the younger boy, & made it back to the shore.

Died: on Nov 9, in Wash City, after a brief illness, Richd M Heath, only son of Jas E Heath, of Va, late Com'r of Pensions. The deceased leaves aged parents & a devoted wife with 3 small children to mourn their sad bereavement. His remains were conveyed to Richmond to repose with those of his kindred in his native soil.

Died: on Nov 10, George Washington B., only child of Peter & Amelia A Gallant, aged 8 months & 19 days. His funeral is this afternoon at 3 o'clock, from the residence of his grandfather, Wm Gallant, on the corner of 5th & P sts.

Died: on Nov 6, in Brooklyn, Virginia Newton, youngest child of John C & Augusta Whitwell, aged 3 years.

THU NOV 13, 1856
Wash Corp: 1-Cmte of Claims: adverse reports on the ptn of Mary Shekell, & also on the ptn of Jas B Wood, & asked to be discharged from the consideration of the same: cmte was discharged accordingly.

Trustee's sale of frame house & lot: on Dec 22, on the premises, by deed of trust from Saml Curson & wife, dated Jun 8, 1853, recorded in Liber J A S No 39, folios 321 thru 324, of the land records for Wash Co, D C: sale of parts of lots 7 & 8 in square 419, with a neat 2 story frame dwlg house with back bldgs. -John W McKim, Richd H Clark, trustees -Jas C McGuire, auct

Brig Gen Jas Bankhead died at Balt on Nov 11, aged about [missing]-three, being at the time of his death in command of the Military Dept of the East. He entered the army as a captain of the 5th infty in 1808, & served with distinction through all our subsequent wars & brevetted brig genr'l for gallant conduct at the siege of Vera Cruz in 1847. He was a Virginian by birth, & spent some time in his youth in Europe in the family of President [missing] while that gentleman was Minister abroad. [Nov 11th newspaper: The funeral of the late Brvt Brig Gen Jas Bankhead, of the U S Army, took place Fri, from his late residence on Madison ave, Balt. The ceremonies were conducted by Rev Dr C C Coxe, of the Protestant Episcopal Church; burial was at **Greenmount Cemetery**.]

Hasty burial. Last week, in Sandusky Co, Danl Stearns, who had been ill with fever for some time, to all appearance died on Friday; all the arrangements were made, & the friends & clergyman were assembled to pay the last tribute of respect, when the body appeared warm to the touch. Restoratives were administered, & in a few minutes the man was setting up. He is now in a fair way of recovery.
-Cincinnati Columbian

Trustee's sale: by deed from Saml B Fowke & Ellen E T his wife, dated Apr 9, 1855, the subscriber will sell at auction, on Dec 15 next, lots 1 & 2 & southern part of lot 14 in square 439, with improvements thereon. -W Redin, trustee -A Green auct

Constable's sale: by 3 writs of fieri facias, issued by B K Morsell, a justice of the peace in & for Wash Co, D C, I have levied on & taken in execution one Longboat, as the property of Washington Browning, & will offer it for sale, at public auction, on Nov 18, for cash, at 7th st Bridge, on Wash Canal, to satisfy 3 judgments due Joshua Gibson. -John H Wise, Constable

Local Item: Messrs Coltman & Duncanson, well known & esteemed citizens of Washington, have invested some $30,000 in erecting & putting in operation a steam flouring mill near 12th St Bridge, in Wash City. Mr Jas Smith is the foreman.

Mrd: on Nov 11, in Balt, by Rev Mr Howard, John B Marchand, Cmder U S Navy, to Margaret D, daughter of Francis A Thornton, Purser U S Navy.

Died: Nov 11, in Wash City, Mrs Ann Mattingly, consort of Edw Mattingly, in her 73rd year. Her funeral will be on Oct 14 at 2 o'clock, from her late residence, 768 east 3rd st.

Died: on Nov 12, in Wash City, Mrs Eliz A K Schwartze, relict of the late Dr A J Schwartze, in her 52nd year. Her funeral will be on Friday evening, at 8 o'clock, from her late residence, on 3rd st, between East Capitol st & A st south.

Fourth Annual Ball of the Pres' Mounted Guard: to be held at Carusi's Saloon on Nov 13, 1856. Executive Cmte:

Capt Peck	Cpl Sanderson	Sgt King
Lt Teel	Lt Flint	W Cannon
Sgt McCutchon	Lt Owen	

Cmte on Refreshments:

Lt Owen	Sgt Seitz	
Cpl Jones	J T Essex	

Cmte of Reception:

Ensign J C Peck	Chas Thoma	H Hurley
Sgt Hayward	Saml Turner	R Laskey
Sgt Noer	Wm Wilson	J Murphy
Cpl Bein	John Yeabower	W Sauter
A Bohlayer	Surgeon Duhamel	Wm Thoma
A N Clements	Quartermaster Evans	G W Wall
M A Dubois	Cpl Augusterfer	Chas Wise
D A Harrover	Sgt Hamilton	P May
F A Lutz	R J Clements	H J Fisher
W H Langley	J W Cruitt	
A Schwartz	J F Hodgson	

Managers-Honoray Members:

W D Wallach	W H Birch	Jos Heard
John Pettibone	Wm Teel	Chas Miller
Clark Mills	John Alexander	H E Orr
Richd Wallach	S P Hoover	B Sothoron
J W Kelly	J Casparis	J S Robinson
W H Topping	John S Finch	G W Hinton
John Tretler	J S Kraft	Jas Thompson
Jacob Ashe	T Berry	Saml O'Brien
Jos Hamblin	Henry Otterback	
P O Donohue	L Pumphrey	

FRI NOV 14, 1856
$60 reward for runaway negro boy Robt Arnold, 21 years old. The informant can be notified by mail to the City Post Ofc. -Leonard Hilleary

Trustee's sale: by 2 deeds of trust from Reuben Daw, dated Mar 25 & Nov 14, 1853: public auction on Dec 18 next, on the premises, all that lot of ground in Gtwn: beginning at the n e corner of the 3 story brick house at the s e intersection of Bridge & Congress sts, running thence east on Bridge st 27 feet & 8 inches, more or less, to John Yerby's; thence south & parallel to Congress st 140 feet to a 12 foot alley; thence with said alley west 27 feet 8 inches; & thence north & parallel with Congress st 140 feet to Bridge st & the place of beginning, with improvements. -Walter S Cox, Ferdinand W Risque, trustees -Barnard & Buckey, aucts

A young Frenchman, Pierre Mathieu, about 20 years old, residing on Blache st, while out on a hunting excursion, a bull made after the party & gored young Mathieu. He shouted for his friends to shoot the bull; unfortunately they missed the bull & shot Mathieu. He was brought back to his residence, where he died on Tue.
-New Orleans Crescent

John G Taylor, sheriff of Winnebago Co, in endeavoring to arrest Alfred Countryman, charged with stealing, was shot dead by the prisoner, who fled to the woods. He was later captured & lodged in jail.

Mrd: on Nov 13, in Wash City, at the First Baptist Church, by Rev S P Hill, Wm J Rhees to Laura O Clarke, daughter of Isaac Clarke, all of Wash City.

Obit-died: on Oct 26, at the residence of his son-in-law, Gen John Miller, Wm Goodloe, sr, aged 87 years & 4 days. He was born in Granville Co, N C, on Oct 22, 1769; in 1790 he visited Ky with a view to a settlement; made the acquaintance of those early pioneers, Boone, Proctor, Warren, Kennedys, Hays, Estills, Irvines, & the Cradlebaughs. In Feb, 1795, he married Miss Susan Woods, the daughter of Capt Archibald Woods, late of Albemarle, Va, a lady of rare beauty of person & still rarer of powers of the mind, with whom he lived in the utmost harmony of conjugal affection until Oct 2, 1851, when she left him for a better world. In 1805 he was received into the fellowship of the old Baptist church, in which he was a pious member until he was summoned to his reward. He was the schoolmate of his distinguished kinsman, Gen Robt Goodloe Harper, of Balt, with whom he kept up a friendly correspondence until the close of the life of the latter. Wm Goodloe was a kind parent, an indulgent master, & a true friend. He retained his mental faculties to the moment of his death; losing in the last years of his life, in a great degree, his hearing. -Richmond [Ky] Messenger

Mrd: in Wash City, at St Peter's Church, by Rev Mr Knight, Dr Jos A Smith, of PG Co, Md, to Miss Mary E, daughter of Edw Fenwick, of the District of Columbia. [No date given-current item.]

Mrd: on Nov 11, in St Peter's Church, at Ellicott's Mills, Md, by Rev Alex'r J Berger, J Shaaff Stockett, of Balt, to Georgie Stockett, of Stockwood, Howard Co.

Mrd: on Nov 12, in Gtwn, D C, by Rev Dr Norwood, Robt B Bolling, of Petersburg, Va, to Margaret, daughter of Wm S Nichols, of the former place.

Died: on Nov 12, at the residence of her sister, Mrs Eliza Peyton, in Wash City, Mrs Priscilla B Wilkinson, relict of the late Geo Wilkinson, of Calvert Co, Md, aged 58 years. Her remains will be conveyed to her home for interment.

Died: on Nov 12, in Gtwn, D C, in his 80th year, Richd Horwell. His funeral is this morning at 9 o'clock, from the residence of his grandson-in-law, Thos J Adams, on Prospect st, Gtwn.

SAT NOV 15, 1856
Fatal election affray in the Snow Hill Shield, [Md] an account of the violent death of Bailey Hickman, an esteemed citizen of that county, at the hands of Mr John H Snead, formerly of Va, but recently a travelling dentist in Md. Words ensued outside between Hickman & Snead; & during a scuffle Snead stabbed Hickman, killing him. Snead was arrested & committed to jail. He was released on $4,000 bail on Sat last.

Mrd: on Oct 15, in Mound Prairie, Hempstead Co, Ark, by Rev J B Annis, Robt A Carrigan to Miss Mary F Moore, both of Hempstead Co, Ark.

Memphis [Tenn] Appeal says that Harris, alias Morgan, who murdered Mr Mosley, ex-sheriff of St Francis Co, Ark, on Oct 28, & had been committed to Marion jail, was taken out of prison by a mob on Oct 30, & was no doubt lynched by them.

Calif: 1-A notorious highwayman, Tom Bell, has been taken & executed in Tulare Co. Several reputed to be of his gang have also been arrested. 2-A man named Colebrook was hung by a mob at Andel's Camp for killing Dr Armstrong. 3-Two ruffians named Macauley & one Andy Carr, attacked a young man named Bond, with knives, at Whimtown, Tuolumne Co, when Carr drew his pistol & shot Bond, inflicting a mortal wound. One of the Macauleys then stabbed him in the back, killing him instantly. The ofcrs got him off to jail. 4-The jury in the trial of R P Hammond for embezzlement of the U S funds while Collector of this port failed to agree, & were discharged. A second trial commenced on Oct 27. 5-Martin Gallagher, one of the Vigilance Cmte exiles, returned from the Sandwich Islands on Nov 5 in the brig **Glencoe**. He was disguised, & passed under the assumed name of Wilson Hunt. The Vigilance Cmte are on the lookout for him, but as yet his whereabouts remain unknown.

The founder of the Icarain Community at Nauvoo, M Cabet, died at St Louis on Nov 9 of an attack of apoplexy. The community of Nauvoo was founded upon the ruins of the Mormon company of Joe Smith, & the bldgs occupied by the latter were devoted to the use of the Icarians. M Cabet was about 69 years old.

Circuit Court of Wash Co, D C. Wm Bird et al vs Hazel's heirs & administrator et al. The trustee in this case reported a sale of parts of lots 304, in square 784, to Wm Boss for $476.04, & that Boss has complied with the terms of sale. -Jno A Smith, clerk

Great exertions have been made to discover the whereabouts, dead or alive, of Mr John Claxton, son of Mr R W Claxton, of Gtwn, aged about 19 years. His family & friends are suffering from a suspense almost harder to bear than a knowledge of the worst. He left his home on Monday, &, on the authority of his cousin, named Luckett, in company with some other young man was present at a ball given at a house somewhere on the Island. The house was visited by a number of confederate persons, said to be chiefly from Balt, going under the name of Plug-Uglies. Luckett states that he & Claxton were chased until they were forced to separate, subsequently to which he heard firing. On Tue a young man with a shawl was seen lying on the ground, who was thought to be intoxicated. It is thought that it might have been Claxton. The shawl was found in the canal. Dragging was done till 3 p m, but without avail. [Nov 17th newspaper: It is with sorrowful satisfaction that we report the recovery of the body of John Claxton on Sat last from the canal. The jury brought in a verdict of accidental death by drowning. The body was removed to the residence of Mr Claxton, his father, in Gtwn, & will be buried this morning at 10 o'clock.]

Mrd: on Nov 13, in Wash City, by Rev Geo D Cummins, Saml P Richards, of N J, to Sarah, daughter of the late Wm Lippincott, of Phil.

Mrd: on Nov 13, in Wash City, by Rev Mr Tillinghast, Mr H A Cook, of Miss, to Miss Isabella A Humphreys, of Wash City.

Mrd: on Nov 11, in Wash City, by Rev Mr Finckel, Mr Herman M Snyder, of Phil, to Miss Anna Fertner, of Wash City.

Died: on Nov 13, in Wash City, Robt Manning Combs, son of Robt M Combs. His funeral will be on Nov 16, at 2 o'clock, from the residence of his father, on Garrison st, near the Navy Yard.

MON NOV 17, 1856
Peremptory sale of new carriages, buggies, & rockaways, at auction: on Nov 27, at the Carriage Factory of Messrs Haslup & Weeden, corner of La ave, & 9th st, their entire stock. Wall, Barnard & Co, aucts

The barque **Elise**, Capt Neilson, of & from Hamburg, arrived at N Y on Nov 14, & reports speaking on Nov 10 a Bremen barque having on board 16 passengers & the crew of the steamer **Lyonnaise**, hence for Havre on Nov 1, which was run into be a large ship on the night of Nov 2 & abandoned the next day. 16 persons were picked up in a boat on Nov 9, with 2 others who had died. There were 39 passengers on board the **Lyonnaise** in the cabin, making, with crew, ofcrs, & steerage passengers, about 150. Among the passengers was Mr Albert Sumner, a brother of Hon Chas Sumner. It is a melancholy coincidence that another brother of Mr Sumner, Horace, a young man of great promise, lost his life by drowning at the wreck of the ship **Elizabeth**, on Fire Island, in 1850.

The King of Denmark has conferred upon our distinguished countryman, Lt M F Maury, the cross of a Knight of the Order of Danneborg, as a mark of consideration for the eminent services he has rendered in that department of useful science to which he has devoted his talents.

The Carolina Times says: "Mr Wm Telfourd, aged 101 years, a native of Ireland, & for the past 75 years a resident of Richland district, in the neighborhood of Crane creek, departed this life on Monday last at his residence.

Orphans Court of Wash Co, D C. Letters of administration with the will annexed, on the personal estate of Mary E E Cutts, late of Wash Co, deceased. -J Madison Cutts, Richd D Cutts, adms with the will annexed.

Circuit Court of D C-in Equity, No 1,178. Nicholas W Gortuar & wife vs Wm Mechlin & others. Thos P Morgan, trustee, reported that on Jul 29th he sold lot 7 in square 118, in Wash City, & that part of lot 8, in same square, adjoining lot 7, & fronting on I st 25 feet 10 inches, with 3 story brick dwlg house & other improvements thereon, to Geo J Johnson for $2,955, & that the purchaser had complied with the terms of sale. -Jno A Smith, clerk

Mrd: on Nov 6, in Phil, by Rev Dr Furness, Capt Josiah Watson, U S Marine Corps, to Abbie Frances, daughter of Warren Murdock, of that city.

Mrd: at Aldie, Va, by Rev R L Dashiell, Jas S Oden to Julia, daughter of Jonas Hood. [No marriage date given-current item.]

Mrd: on Nov 12, at Canandaigua, by Rev Dr Ingersoll, John C Sibley to Mary Y, youngest daughter of Henry B Gibson.

Died: on Nov 15, in his 79th year, Mr Jos Brooks, of Gtwn, D C. His funeral will take place this afternoon at 3 o'clock, from the residence of his son, Lewis Brooks.

Died: on Nov 11, John Claxton, eldest son of Richd W & Catharine Ann Claxton, aged 20 years & 7 months. His funeral is this morning at 10 o'clock, from the residence of his aunt, Miss Claxton, Bridge st, Gtwn.

TUE NOV 18, 1856
A new method of copying pages of a printed work by transfer, invented by M Edw Boyer, in France, is called by the name of homoeagraphy. It is done accurately without injuring the original.

The court of inquiry, of which Brvt Brig Gen Churchill was president, not long since in session at Carlisle Barracks, Pa, has entirely exonerated Brvt Col Chas A May, major 2nd dragoons, of the allegation of unofficer-like conduct, brought against him by sundry citizens of Carlisle, in the circumstances growing out of a squabble between some recruits & persons belonging to that neighborhood. -Star

Wash City Ordinances: 1-Act for the relief of Steward & Eslin, for the use of Geo W Stewart: to pay Steward & Eslin, for the relief of Geo W Stewart, $28.50 for repairing gutters, pavement & alleys. 2-Act for the relief of Saml Payne: to pay him $5 for the removal of the dead body of a colored pauper. 3-Act for the relief of Alex'r Bradley: to pay him $18 for cleaning gutters, alleys & cartage.

The Lexington Gaz states that the ***Natural Bridge*** property, in Rockbridge Co, Va, including the hotel & 100 acres of land around it, has been sold to Mr Sheffield for $12,000.

Obit-died: on Nov 17, at his residence in Wash City, Hon John H Eaton, aged about 70 years. He commenced his public career in 1818 as one of the Senators from the State of Tenn, afterwards filling various offices of trust; he was Govn'r of Fla, & Sec of War under the administration of Gen Jackson. He closed his political career as Minister Plenipotentiary at the Court of Madrid. He was a kind & indulgent husband, & although not a member of any church, he practiced all the virtues which adorn the Christian & the gentleman. His funeral will take place today at 2 o'clock, from his late residence on I st. [Nov 20th newspaper: The funeral of Gen Jno H Eaton took place on Tue; attended by the Pres of the U S, members of the Cabinet, Foreign Ministers, ofcrs of the army & navy, & numerous citizens. The body was conveyed in procession to ***Oakhill Cemetery***, on Gtwn heights, where it was committed to the earth in the family burying ground. The religious services were conducted by Revs Dr Pyne Smith & Fielder Israel, the latter of Balt.]

Equity: No 1,178. Nicholas W Goertner & Lucretia Goertner against Wm Mechlin, Alex'r H Mechlin, Anna Maria Smith, Chas B More & Margaretta W his wife, Chas W Crebbs, & Fannie M Crebbs. Statement of the trustee's account in my ofc, in City Hall, Wash, on Dec 11 next. -W Redin, auditor

Equity: No 860. Richd W & Annie Templeman against John Miller & Chas A Comly & wife, Mary Templeman & others, widow & heirs of Geo Templeman. Statement of the trustee's account in my ofc, in City Hall, Wash, on Dec 12 next.
-W Redin, auditor

Equity: No 1,135. Guinilda Spencer, cmplnt, & Jos Spencer, Jas McKenney, Richd Smith, Eliz A W Riggin, Harriet McKenney, Saml D Donaldson, J M Campbell, & Hugh D Evans, dfndnts. By order of the Circuit Court of D C I am directed to state the account of the trustees with the fund; the debts due; the surplus, & the distribution thereof: on Dec 9, at my ofc, City Hall, Wash, 10 o'clock. -W Redin, auditor

Farm for sale at auction, in PG Co, Md, 3 miles south of Laurel station, formerly owned by Beale Duvall; adjoins the lands of Mrs Snowden & Dr Jenkins, & contains 300 acres of land; with a new frame dwlg, with 6 rooms. Public sale on Nov 27 at Mr Harrison's tavern, near the premises. Inquire of D Carter, 295 Caroline st, Balt.

Valuable property for sale: I will sell all my property lying on the west side of the Railroad at the Bladensburg Depot, containing about 12 acres, with a large 4 story brick bldg just finished, with modern improvements, containing 26 rooms. The house is well calculated for a hotel or a female boarding school. Apply to the subscriber at Bladensburg. -C C Hyatt

Mrd: on Nov 16, in Wash City, by Rev G W Samson, Mr Wm Starr to Miss Jane Keeck, both of Wash.

Intelligence received from Granada, Nicaragua, dated Oct 16, that our worthy young townsman, Mr Clement C Venable, son of Mr Geo Venable, of Wash, was one amongst the unfortunate victims of the wrath of the Guatemalans who assaulted & sacked that city in the absence of Gen Walker. At the time of the attack Mr Venable was confined to his bed by illness, & so stealthy was the approach of the enemy that 2 other occupants of the house, Stone & Dashields, were able to escape barely with their lives. This was on Oct 12. The savage assailants shot Mr Venable through the head & then the heart, & with their knives cut & mangled his person in a horrible manner. Shortly after Mr Venable's arrival in Granada he received a discharge from the army, & was appointed clerk of the first court of law established under Gen Walker's Gov't, a lucrative & responsible ofc.

Fireman's monument was laid yesterday in Alexandria. On Nov 16, 1856, & the morning of the 17th, a disastrous fire raged in our neighboring city of Alexandria, with the death of 7 by the falling of a wall. The deceased were: Geo Plain, Robt I Taylor, John A Roach, David Appich, jr, W S Evans, J Carson Green, & Jas W Keene.

Died: on Nov 1, at Mobile, Ala, Jos Gales Hellen, aged 24 years, a young gentleman of much promise, & of engaging & honorable qualities which had endeared him to all his family & acquaintances.

WED NOV 19, 1856
Geo W Johnson, one of the large sugar planters on the Missouri, below New Orleans, who died recently, has left an estate valued at not less than $7,000,000. He has by his will manumitted all his slaves, 200 in number. They are all to be sent to Liberia in 4 years from his death, & each one is to be furnished with $50.00.

Hon Johsua L Martin, an ex-Govn'r of Ala, died at his residence in Tuscaloosa on Nov 2.

John H McCutchen, Atty-at-Law, has removed his ofc & residence to 24 Missouri ave, between 4½ & 6th sts.

Mrd: on Nov 18, in Wash City, by Rev John C Smith, Thos Francis to Miss Lavinia C, daughter of Jos Bryan, all of Wash City.

Chancery Docket: 1,084. Oct Term, 1856. Circuit Court of Wash Co, D C. Richd Hirst, wife & others, vs Henry S Nelson. The trustee reported that he has sold the southeastern part of lot 16, in the original plan of Gtwn, with improvements thereon, the same fronting 25 feet on the north side of Bridge st, with a depth of 120 feet, with the privilege of a 10 foot wide alley, part of the real estate of W Nelson, deceased, & that Jas A Nelson was the purchaser of the same for $1,700, & hath complied.
-Jno A Smith, clerk

Orphans Court of Wash Co, D C. Letters of administration with the will annexed on the personal estate of Wm McK Osborn, late of Wash Co, deceased.
-Sam McKenney, adm w a

Circuit Court of Wash Co, D C-in Chancery, Oct Term, 1856. Edw M Linthicum & others vs Nicholas Gassaway & others, heirs at law of Hanson Gassaway, deceased. The trustee reported he has sold the real estate therein directed: E M Linthicum, Chas A Buckey, & John Marbury, jr, the cmplnts, were the purchasers of the following lots in Wash City, D C: lot 7 in square 367, for $294; lot 9 in same square for $249.90; lot 1, in Wilson & Callan's subdivision of part of the said square, for $179.07, & lot K in same subdivision, for $179.07; & lot 6 in square 72, in said city, for $164.80, making an aggregate sum of $1,066.84; that the said sum is less than the amount of debt by said decree ordered to be paid to the said cmplnts, & that the cmplnts propose to credit their said debt by proceeds of the said sales, after deducting the cost of suit & the expenses of executing the said trust. -Jno A Smith, clerk

St Timothy's Hall, Catonsville, Balt Co, Md: Classical & Commercial Institution of the Prostestant Episcopal Church, founded A D 1844 & incorporated 1847; terms $250 per session of 10 months. -Rev L Van Bokkelen, Rector

Mrd: on Nov 11, at Trinity Church, Staunton, Va, by Rev Philip Slaughter, Mr Nathl P Catlett to Miss Bettie T Breckenridge, both of Staunton.

Died: Nov 18, Mrs Rebecca Butt, after a brief illness, in her 85th year. Her funeral will be on Nov 20 at 11 o'clock, from the residence of her son, Richd Butt, Wash Co, D C.

Died: on Nov 17, in Wash City, of disease of the heart, Tobias Martin, of the War Dept, a native of Cornwall, England.

Died: on Nov 18, at Stamford, Conn, Truman Houston, eldest son of Hon Truman Smith, aged 4 years & 7½ months.

The friends of C Clement Venable, lately murdered in Granada, are requested to meet, at the chamber of the Board of Aldermen, this evening, at 7½ o'clock, to devise means for bringing home his remains to be interred in his native city. -Many Friends

Mrs Esther Moffett can accommodate 2 gentlemen & their wives or single gentlemen with board at 505 7th st, opposite Odd Fellow's Hall. Her rooms are comfortable, with fire-places in most of them.

THU NOV 20, 1856
Died: on Nov 18, after a brief illness, Mary E Murphy, aged 17 years & 4 months. Her funeral is this evening at 3 o'clock, from the residence of her mother.

Trustee's sale of the whole square No 125, fronting 133 feet one inch on 19th st west; by deed of trust from Emely Mallet to the subscriber, dated Oct 18, 1856, recorded in Liber J A S 86, folios 405 thru 408, of the land records of Wash Co, D C.
-Henry Naylor, trustee -Jas C McGuire, auct

Wash Corp: 1-Ptn from Nicholas Acker & Geo Krobb, asking permission to occupy 10 inches more of the pavement in front of their bldg than the law allows: referred. 2-Cmte on Finance: bill authorizing the refunding to Geo Miller certain taxes erroneously paid: passed. 3-Cmte of Claims: bills for the relief of Benj F Beers & Ann Smoot: passed. Same cmte: adverse report on the ptn of Thos Wilson.

SAT NOV 22, 1856
Mrs A E Young, Fashionable Dress Maker: 447 7th st, above the Patent Ofc.

Prof N M Hentz died at the residence of his son, Dr Chas A Hentz, at Mariana, Fla, on Nov 4. He was a French gentleman well known as a teacher in many seminaries of learning in different parts of our country. He was associated with the distinguished historian, Hon Geo Bancroft, as a teacher at Northampton, & at Cincinnati, & at Chapel Hill, N C, as Prof of Modern Languages & Belles Lettres. It is less than a year ago that the death of his accomplished wife, Mrs Caroline Lee Hentz, was announced.

At Paris lately the Contesse Charles Fitz James, in passing through a room when in full dress, stepped upon a Lucifer matcher lying upon the floor, by which her clothes were set on fire. She was so badly burnt that after several weeks of severe suffering she died.

Ofc of the Chief of Police, Wash, Nov 21, 1856. The undersigned has been directed by the Mayor to give notice that after this date, no bonfires will be permitted in any of the streets of avenues of the city; the law will be enforced against all persons who may be found firing cannons, guns, or pistols, contrary thereto, for the purpose of salute, or for any other object. -Jas W Baggott, Chief of Police

Three were arrested on Thu for disordery conduct: John Ennis, Richd T Jones, & Wm Sullivan, the last being the same who was tried & acquitted in Sep last on the charge of murdering a Germon on Jul 4 near the Park, on 7th st. They were sent to jail for trial.

Mrd: on Nov 20, at the residence of her father, in Wash, by Rev J B Byrne, Hon Stephen A Douglas, of Ill, to Adele Cutts, daughter of J Madison Cutts.

Mrd: on Nov 20, in Gtwn, by Rev T A Simpson, Chas A Buckey to Eliz L Shoemaker, daughter of Geo Shoemaker, all of Gtwn, D C.

Mrd: on Oct 30, at Demopolis, at the residence of Mrs G E Truehart, by Rev Mr Meneas, Wm D Prout to Miss Lizzie H Waugh, both of Mobile, Ala.

Mrd: on Nov 20, at the E st Baptist Church, by Rev G W Samson, Henry L Davison to Anna E Grigg, daughter of the late Jos Grigg, of Alexamdria, Va.

Mrd: on Oct 12 last, in the city of Oswego, N Y, by Rev A Schuyler, Lt Wm S Abert, of the U S Army, to Mary F, daughter of Benj Isaacs, of that city.

Died: on Nov 21, suddenly, John T Farrar, in his 45th year. His funeral is this afternoon at 3 o'clock, from his late father's residence, 6 Missouri ave.

Died: on Nov 21, at the residence of his father, Henry Naylor, son of Benj P & Matilda R Smith, in his 16th year.

Died: on Nov 19, at his residence, in Wash City, John Mason, [colored,] aged about 48 years. The death of this man should not go unnoticed. For many years he has been known & respected by citizens of Wash, not only by those of his own color, but by many of more exalted stations. He lived for a long time in the households of Mr Webster & Mr Everett, by whom he was always regarded with affectionate esteem.

Spring Grove for sale: contains 228 acres, located near Darnesville, Fairfax Co, Va; with a good & convenient dwlg, containing 9 rooms & all the necessary out-bldgs. Inquire on the premises, or to R W Bates, 154 Pa ave, between 17th & 18th sts. -Wm H Bates

Valuable fishing landing on the Potomac & other real estate at public auction: by decree of the Circuit Court for PG Co, sitting as a Court of Equity: public sale at Harbin's Hotel, in the village of Piscataway, on Dec 19 next, the Fishing Landing which belonged to the late Wm Bryan, [of Richd,] having attached to it about 4 acres of land. Also will be offered for sale at the same time a tract of wood land, containing about 136 acres, belonging also to the estate of the late Wm Bryan, [of Richd;] & a tract of land called **China**, supposed to contain about 200 acres, more or less. This property is sold clear of the widow's dower. -C C Magruder, trustee, Upper Marlboro, Nov 19, 1856.

PG Co Court: on Wed Judge Crain sentenced Robt Holbert, aged 16 years, to 2 years & 6 months' confinement in the penitentiary for breaking into a store at Laurel Factory. -Upper Marl Gaz

MON NOV 24, 1856
N Y, Nov 22. 1-A week ago the death of Miss Ann Jay, daughter of the late Chief Justice John Jay, was recorded, & yesterday her sister, Mrs Maria Banyer, the last of Mr Jay's daughters, also expired, having attained the age of 75 years. 2-Saml Swartwout, who formerly occupied a prominent position in the political world, & held the appointment of Collector at this port under Gen Jackson, died in this city yesterday in his 73rd year. He had lived in retirement since his unfortunate defalcation to the Gov't during his collectorship. [Nov 25th newspaper: Sam Swartwout in early life was connected for a short time with the navy; he was a steady & warm friend of Aaron Burr, though not implicated in the latter's political delinquencies.] [Nov 26th newspaper: Mrs Maria Banyer, was the widow of Goldsborough Banyer, & Miss Ann Jay, her sister. They lived together, one & inseparable, reflecting the purity & goodness of their illustrious father's character. -N Y Courier]

Household & kitchen furniture at auction on Nov 26, at the House Furnishing Establishment of A H Lee, 23 K st, between 7th & 8th sts. -A Green auct

Valuable business stand at auction: on Nov 27, the store & lot on 7th st, between G & H sts, at present occupied by Mr John Ball as a feed store.
-Wall, Barnard & Co, aucts

On Nov 19, whilst the Democrats of Dover, N H, were celebrating their victory in the late Presidential campaign, a premature explosion of a cannon took place, which caused the deaths of Geo S Clarke & John Foss.

Alex'r Falconer, late treasurer of the Petersburg & Roanoke railroad, has been indicted by the grand jury on 2 counts-on the charge of embezzlement & the other for making false entries on the books of the railroad company.

Among the slain at Granada, during the late attack by the troops under Gen Walker, was Rev D H Wheeler, the agent of the American Bible Society. Part of a letter to J C Brigham, Corr Sec American Bible Society, dated Granada, Oct 3, 1856. Should the enemy come & sack the city, I shall leave my books posted & money & effect in the hands of Col Jno H Wheeler, the American Minister. For reasons I need not name the U S flag will afford very little protection to American citizens here.
-David H Wheeler

Valuable cotton factory for sale: by 2 writs of fieri facias, issued from the Circuit Court for Allegany Co, at the suit of Alpheus Beall, Jos H Tucker, Thos J McKaig, Wm W McKaig, & Sam M Semmes, to me directed, against the goods & chattels, lands & tenements, of the corporation called "The Cumberland Cotton Factory," I shall sell, at public auction, on Dec 20, at the St Nicholas Hotel, in Cumberland, all that valuable property, with the land, factory bldgs & machinery, & all the appurtenances appertaining to the same. The above property has cost the original proprietors upwards of $40,000, & the factory has not been in operation for 2 years.
-John Everett, Sheriff

A small farm of Mr Chowning, in Louisa Co, Va, sold at public auction the other day at $62.50 per acre.

Florence Nightingale, it is said, will be married shortly to an English Earl who distinguished himself in the Crimean war.

Mr Valentine Austin was killed at Memphis on Nov 12 by the premature discharge of a cannon while firing a salute in honor of the election of Buchanan.

Orphans Court of Wash Co, D C. Letters of administration on the personal estate of Stephen McCrary, late a surgeon in the U S Navy, deceased. -W B Webb, adm

Circuit Court of Wash Co, D C-in Equity, No 918. Wm W Corcoran vs Richd W Griffeth et al. The trustess reported he has sold the south half of lot 6 in square 405, in Wash City, to Elias Travers for $610, & he hath complied with the terms of sale. -Jno A Smith, clerk

Notice to the heirs & legal reps of Lewis Urban, late of the city of Lancaster, deceased. You are to appear in the Orphans' Court of Lancaster Co, on the 3rd Monday of Dec next, at 10 o'clock, to accept or refuse to accept the real estate of said deceased at the valuation thereof, made by an inquest held thereon, & confirmed by said Court.
-Geo Martin, Sheriff. Sheriff's Ofc, Lancaster, Nov 19, 1856.

Orphans Court of Wash Co, D C. In the case of Neal Morgan, adm of Ann Morgan, deceased: the administrator & Court have appointed Dec 16 next, for the final settlement of the personal estate of said deceased, of the assets in hand. -Ed N Roach, Reg/o wills

TUE NOV 25, 1856
Gov Causey, of Dela, appointed Jos P Comegys, of Dover, to fill the vacancy in the U S Senate occasioned by the death of the late lamented Senator Clayton.

Washington Commercial Academy: over Sweeny, Rittenhouse, Fant & Co's Banking-house, 352, near Browns' Hotel, Pa ave. -Prof F Sherbrooke, Principal

New Orleans papers announce the awfully sudden death of Judge John C Larue, of that city. He remained home to be with his wife who had been indisposed to keep her company, & while laying on the sofa, with his wife & child very nearby, he told his wife he was dying. She called for the servants to get a Dr. When the Dr arrived all efforts of resucitation failed. Judge Larue was a native of N J. He came out to New Orleans about 22 or 23 years ago, & was engaged for some time as tutor in a family. He worked at one time as a printer, & early connected himself with the press in an editorial capacity. [No death date given-current item.]

The Boston papers state that Capt Hallett, of New Weston, who has been ill for a year or more, is proven to have been poisoned by a solution of lead in the water used in his family. His symptoms were colic & paralysis.

In Peekskill, N Y, a little boy, Chas Pickford, accidentally fell down & ran a splinter in one his eyes. It could not be removed & will remain in until thrown out in the gradual process of healing.

There was an artless manner of announcing marriages in the olden time which is quite refreshing to revert to occasionally. Wmsburg Gaz of 1776: On Sunday evening last, Mr Beverly Dixon to Miss Polly Saunders, a very agreeable young lady.

Mrs Catharine Burke, residing in 11th ave, learned that her husband Patrick has been killed at Tarrytown by a train of cars. She immediately started for that place, & seeing the body, recognized it as that of her husband. On the way to the *Calvary Cemetery*, with the body in a mahogany coffin, suddenly appeared Patrick Burke. He returned home in a carriage beside his wife. The corpse was taken to the Bellevue dead-house. -N Y Mirror

China: 1-Barbarous maltreatment, & murder of Rev Mr Chapdelaine, a French Catholic Missionary, by the Chinese authorities in the province of Kwangsi. So great is their hostility to Christianity that it is said a Chinese Christian, a widow of 23 years of age, employed by the missionary in teaching, was put to death after Mr Chapeldaine, & all those openly known in the neighborhood as Christians have had their property confiscated & have been thrown into prison. 2-The U S ship **Portsmouth**, Cmder Foote, arrived at Hong Kong from Batavia, via Macao, on Aug 29, all well. 3-The steamer **San Jacinto**, Cmdor Armstrong, had left for Japan a few days previous, & is now at Shanghai, with the sloop-of-war **Levant**, Cmder Smith. The **Levant** has also on board Hon Peter Parker, U S Com'r to China, & will probably proceed with him to Fuh-Choo. On the day previous to the arrival of the **Portsmouth**, Capt Avery, of the ship **Golden City**, shot himself through the head during a fit of temporary insanity. His funeral was on Aug 29 from the residence of the American Consul. Lt Avery was very highly esteemed as an ofcr & a gentleman by all who knew him.

Mrs Eliz Ruth Ridgely, relict of the late Gen Chas Sterrett Ridgely, of Md, died suddenly on Nov 17 at the residence of her son-in-law, Richd Grason, of Elkton. She was in her 74th year.

Letter from Morgan Co, Ill, to the St Louis [Mo] News says that a little girl, daughter of a widow named Ironmonger, was killed & partly eaten by a vicious sow near Jacksonville. The shock of the horrible spectacle killed the mother also, & on the next evening a camphene lamp exploded, whereby one child was burnt to death & another injured.

Circuit Court of Wash Co, D C. Yesterday the Court was occupied with a petition of freedom by certain negroes, the property of the late Thos Turner, of Gtwn. The ground of their prayer is the long time they have been to themselves without claim upon their services by their owner or his reps. Their petition is resisted by Mr Turner's heirs. Messrs Bradley & Carlisle for the petitioners; Mr Marbury for the other side.

Wash City Ordinances: 1-Act to reimburse John W Fitzhugh the sum of $81 for casual repairs in the Second Ward. 2-Act for the relief of Martin Bosse: to pay him $3.50 for the pump tax he erroneously paid.

WED NOV 26, 1856
Gtwn Custom House: the contract for this bldg, to be erected on Congress st, Gtwn, between Bridge & Gay sts, east side, has been awarded to Mr Saml C Wroe, his bid being the lowest, or $41,581, including all work & materials. The highest was $81,366 for the whole job.

Mrd: on Nov 18, in Wash City, by Rev Mr Stanley, Wm B Hall, of PG Co, Md, to Miss Sophia Wise, daughter of Chas Wise, of Va.

Mrd: on Nov 25, at Bethesda Church, Montg Co, Md, by Rev Wm T Eva, Jos H Bradley, jr, of Wash City, to Eliza M, only daughter of the late Dr John M Thomas, U S A.

Died: on Nov 24, in Wash City, Catherine W King, widow of the late Josias W King, of Wash. Her burial service will be from the residence of her son-in-law, D Higgins, 7th & H sts, this morning at 11 o'clock.

Died: on Nov 24, in Wash City, Mrs Ruth Cantine, wife of J J C Cantine, aged 48 years & 11 months. Her funeral is this morning at 10 o'clock, from the residence 421 I st.

Died: on Nov 14, in Wash City, after a long & painful illness, Eliza Jane, wife of Geo W Hopkins, in her 39th year. Her funeral will take place today at 11 o'clock, from his residence, on 20th st, near Holmead's burying ground.

St Andrew's Society of Wash, D C: meeting on Nov 27 at 7:30 P M.
-Jas MacWilliam, sec

THU NOV 27, 1856
John B Kindle was accidentally shot & instantly killed by Wm Walker, while hunting together on Thu. They both belonged to Wilmington, Del.

The earliest newspaper in the New World dates back to an earlier period than our annalists generally allow. In the Dictionary of Dates, by Putnam, it is stated, in accordance with the general belief, that the first American newspaper was the Boston News Letter, of 1704. In the State paper Ofc, at London, there is, however, a copy [perhaps the only one extant] of a folio newspaper sheet printed at Boston, & bearing the date of Sep 25, 1690.

Household & kitchen furniture at auction on: Dec 1, at the residence of Mr F Wheatley, on st, between Wash & Congress sts. -Barnard & Buckey, aucts

Lt John T Walker, of the Navy, committed suicide at the Mansion House, N Y, on Tue last. He was under orders to embark on the ship **Wabash**, to join the ship **St Mary's** on the Pacific coast.

Wash Corp: 1-Ptn from Cornelius Shaun, asking the use of Market Space: passed. 2-Cmte on Improvements: bill to authorize Nicholas Acker & Geo Kalb to use part of the pavement in front of their dwlg on North Capitol st: passed.

Nashville Patriot of Nov 22. Dr Boyd McNairy expired at his residence in this city yesterday, after a painful illness of several weeks. He was in his 74th year. With the exception, [the venerable Dr Robertson,] he was the oldest member of the medical profession in this city. He was assiduously attended during his last illness by his large family & many sympathizing friends.

Coshocton [Ohio] Democrat: Hon David Spangler, of Coshocton, died on Oct 18. He was twice Rep of his district in the U S House of Reps, & was Atty & Counsellor in the U S Supreme Court. In 1844 he received the nomination for the ofc of Govn'r by the Whigs, which he declined.

Mrd: on Oct 30, by Rev S A H Marks, Anthony Allen to Miss Vincentia Kelly.

Mrd: on Nov 18, by Rev S A H Marks, Thos T Allen to Miss Mary E Perkins.

Mrd: on Nov 20, by Rev S A H Marks, Thos Hooper to Mrs Eliz Botelor.

Mrd: on Nov 25, by Rev W Krebs, Saml T Crawford to Malinda V Brooks, all of Wash City.

Mrd: on Nov 25, by Rev Mr Morsell, Mr E A Ryther to Miss Margaret Spicer.

FRI NOV 28, 1856
W H Stanford, Merchant Tailor, 488 Pa ave, near 3rd st.

Dr Jas H Bogardus was married to Miss Isabella Hamilton at the Girard House, in N Y, on Sunday, & in 20 minutes afterwards was a corpse. The parties belonged in Kingston, Ulster Co, where Dr B was a highly respectable physician, with the best practice in the county. The marriage had been twice postponed on account of the death of relatives of the parties. The doctor was unwell, & was married in bed, but had just been pronounced so decidedly convalescent that further medical aid would be unnecessary.

Accident in St Louis on Nov 22: yesterday an omnibus was crushed by the wall of an old trunk factory, where a fire occurred some weeks ago. Miss Emily Bush was severely if not fatally injured.

Mrd: on Nov 25, by Rev Mr Whittle, Mr John J Riely, of Clarke Co, Va, to Miss Lucie O, daughter of John B Taylor, of Jefferson Co, Va.

Died: on Nov 27, in Wash City, Wm F Knight, aged 47 years. His funeral will take place from his late residence on 4½ st, between Mo & Pa aves, today at 10 o'clock.

Executor's sale of land & negroes: by authority vested in the undersigned by the last will & testament of Zephaniah Taylor, late of PG Co, deceased: public sale at T B, in said county, on Dec 22, all the real estate & negroes of which the said Taylor died seized & possessed: consisting of that valuable Tavern Stand at T B, with about 15 acres of land attached, on the new-cut road leading from Wash to Chas & St Mary's Counties, for many years occupied by said Taylor as a tavern. Also 2 lots of timber & wood land & 2 lots of arable land adjoining T B, containing in the whole 280 acres. At the same time will be offered for sale 12 young & valuable negroes, slaves for life, among which are several valuable house servants. -Saml H Berry, exc of Zephaniah Taylor, deceased.

SAT NOV 29, 1856

The Largest Piano Forte, Music & Musical Instrument Establishment in Wash: John F Ellis, 306 Pa ave, between 9th & 10th sts. Old pianos taken in part payment for new.

Newark Daily Advertiser of Nov 24. Roswell L Colt died yesterday at his own residence in the city of Patterson, at the age of 77 years. In early life he was in the extensive mercantile house of Leroy, Bayard & McKivers. He married the daughter of Mr Oliver, of Balt, a gentleman of very large fortune, & by this marriage had a large of family of children, most of whom are still living. Mrs Colt died within the last few months in Paris, where she had gone on a visit. The family of Colts are from Connecticut. The father, Peter Colt, was an ofcr of the Revolutionary war, being a colonel in the quartermaster's dept, & always sharing the confidence of Washington. Mr Colt's health has failed for the last few years, & it has been evident for some time past he could not last long.

Com'rs notice: to the heirs of David Beard, deceased, late of Rockingham Co, Va. By a decree of the Circuit Court of said county, rendered at its Oct term, 1856, in a suit pending in said court in the name of John C Baird vs David Beard's heirs, I will attend at my ofc in Harrisonburg, Va, on Jan 10, 1857, for purposes set forth in said decree; at which time & place you are required to report your names, places of residence, & proofs of heir-ship. -Wm McK Wartmann, M C C

The Staunton [Va] Spectator says that Mr R J Glandy, of that county, who deals largely in cattle in Pa, had $50,000 deposited in the Lancaster Bank. Being in Lancaster he heard a rumor that the bank was unsafe, & he proposed to withdraw his money; but the ofcrs assured him that there was no danger. He finally concluded to take it out, & the next morning the bank was closed.

Fatal accidents: 1-On Fri last, as the friends of Mr Buchanan in West Concord, N H, were manifesting their joy at the success of their party by firing a cannon, the gun burst & mortally wounded Mr Arthur Kimball, who died the next morning. 2-On Nov 15, whilst the Democrats of Knoxville, Tenn, were celebrating, a premature discharge of a cannon so seriously injured Mr Fuller Ryan, that he died in a few hours. 3-Chas M Patterson, of Naugatuck, Ct, was fatally injured on Sat last by the accidental discharge of his fire-arm whilst gunning.

Equity-No 1,221. John Van Reswick against Mary A Ayton, admx, & Mary V, Adeline C, Ellen S, Abram C, & Richd P Ayton, heirs of Richd Ayton. By an order of the Circuit Court of Wash Co, D C I am directed to state an account of the personal estate of Richd Ayton, deceased: parties above named & creditors are to meet at the Judge's room, City Hall, Wash, on Dec 23, at 10 o'clock.
-W Redin, auditor

Mrd: on Nov 27, in Wash City, by Rev Dr Cummins, Jos S Sessford to Sallie E, daughter of H A Weeden.

Mrd: on Nov 26, by Rev Harvey Stanley, Wm H Griffith, of Balt, to Laura V, daughter of Dr Chas Duvall, of PG Co, Md.

Mrd: on Nov 27, by Rev N R Young, Danl C Digges, of Upper Marlboro, to Bettie C, daughter of R W Glass, of Ill.

Mrd: on Nov 25, by Rev Mr Egleson, Mr Wm C Fowler, formerly of Wash, to Miss Alice G Jones, daughter of Maj Elisha Jones, of Clarksburg, Montg Co, Md.

Mrd: on Nov 11, at Smithfield, Jefferson Co, Va, by Rev Julius E Grammer, Mr Powhatan R Page, of Gloucester Co, to Miss Lizzie, daughter of Dr Saml Scollay, of the former place.

Died: on Nov 28, in Wash City, Anne Connor, aged 40 years, a native of County Tyrone, Ireland, & a resident of Wash for 20 years. Her funeral will take place on Nov 30th, from her late residence, corner of 9th st & Va ave, Island.
[No time was given.]

Died: on Nov 26, in Wash City, after a short & painful illness, Arthur Spring, in his 23rd year. His funeral will take place from the residence of his uncle, Thos Grady, on D, between 13th & 13½ sts, tomorrow at 2 o'clock.

Died: on Nov 27, in Wash City, after a prolonged illness, Obediah Feaster, in his 31st year. His funeral will be on Sunday at 2 o'clock, from his late residence, 8th st, between D & E sts.

Col Colt's Patent Pocket Pistol: New Model: just received the above beautiful Firearm & would invite an inspection of it. -E Tucker & Co, 353 Pa ave, near 6th st, south side.

MON DEC 1, 1856
Trustee's sale of bldg lots at 10th & O sts north, at auction, on Dec 22, by deed of trust from Estwick Evans & wife to the subscriber, dated Sep 4, 1854, recorded in Liber J A S No 83, folios 286 thru 289, of the land records for Wash Co, D C: sale in Wash City, D C, of lots 7 thru 9 in square 339-fronts on 10th st west 233 feet & 4 inches, & on north O st 99 feet & 10½ inches. Terms cash. -Hugh B Sweeny, trustee -A Green auct

From Calif: D L Wells, the Republican candidate for sheriff of Anador Co, was killed on Nov 2 by being thrown from his carriage.

N Y, Nov 29. A patent agent, John B Fairbank, who has also recently been on the editorial corps of the weekly journal called Life Illustrated, committed suicide this morning by jumping from a window in the 5th story of the Tremont House. Spiritualism, in which he was a believer, is supposed to have been the cause.

Mscl: Chief Justice Taney was a brother-in-law of Mr Francis S Key. In 1814 when the Star Spangled Banner was written, Taney resided in Frederick, & Mr Key in Gtwn. Key was a volunteer in the light artl commanded by Maj Peter, composed of citizens of D C; from the time the British fleet appeared in the Patuxent, Mrs Key refused to leave home while Mr Key was thus daily exposed to danger. Taney & his wife, & Key's father & mother, became very anxious about F S Key's family. When Taney reached Gtwn he found the English ships still at Alexandria & a body of militia encamped in Washington, which had been assembled to defend the city. Judge Nicholson & Mrs Key were nearly connected by marriage, Mrs Key & Mrs Nicholson being sisters.

The Boston papers announce the death of Rev Ephraim Peabody, D D, the minister of King's Chapel, in that city, aged 49 years, on Nov 28.

The Scottish people are about to erect in the Abbey Craig, near Stirling, a monument to Sir Wm Wallace, whose name will be ever honored by his countrymen, & by the admirers of courage & patriotism all over the world.

Mrs Jacob Fisher, of Newcastle, Ohio, on Nov 28, was severly injured when a lamp exploded. She died on the following day.

List of ofcrs of the U S flag ship **Savannah**, bearing the broad pennant of Cmdor Saml Mercer. G F Emmons commanding; Wm E Le Roy, flag lt; H S Newcomb, 1st lt; A F Warley, 2nd lt; Wm Mitchell, 3rd lt; C W Flusser, 4th lt & sailing master; B E Hand, 5th lt; J P K Mygatt, 6th lt; Danl Egbert, fleet surgeon; Chas Murray, purser; J T Doughty, capt of marines; Jos Stockbridge, chaplain; Wm Lowber, passed assist surgeon; J P Thom, passed assist surgeon; J W Jenkins, Cmdor's sec; J H Thatcher, Cmder's clerk; J Q Leckron, Purser's clerk; Robt Whittaker, boatswain; A F Thompson, gunner; Luther Manson, carpenter; R T Van Voorhis, sailmaker.

Yesterday fire was discovered in the unoccupied dwlg house on M st, between 17th & 18th sts, the property of the late Mr A Favier's heirs. It had been rented within a short period to 2 persons for the purpose of establishing there a lager-beer brewery, which they were on the point of doing. It was entirely consumed.

Miss Manning has her house fitted up for the reception of members of Congress & transients during the session: 452 13th st, between E & F sts.

Died: on Nov 30, at Gtwn, Mary Elizabeth, only daughter of Geo & Elizabeth Rhodes, in her 8th year. She leaves devoted parents to mourn her loss. Her funeral is this evening at 3 o'clock, at the residence of her father, Geo Rhodes, corner of Bridge & Market sts.

Wash United Fire Dept: meeting Dec 1 at 7½ P M. -Tyler Southall, sec

TUE DEC 2, 1856
Obit-died: on Nov 21, at his residence in the town of Newberne, N C, Hon Wm S Blackledge, in his 65th year. He married the daughter of one of our most respectable & enterprising farmers, who still survives him. He was for 20 years clerk of the Superior Court, & after the death of Gov Spaight in 1850 [the chairman of the county court for Craven] he was appointed to that place. He was a devoted friend, affectionate husband, fond father, & kind & indulgent master.

Serious accident on the Manassas Gap railroad on Sat, at River Station, Warren Co, Va, when the bridge across the Shenandoah river gave way, precipitating the engine & 5 cars a depth of 45 feet into the river. The engineer, fireman, & conductor were killed, & John G Buck, passenger, of Warren Co, was fatally injured.

The fall of the *Alamo*. On Feb 23, 1836, Gen Santa Anna entered San Antonio de Bexar & took possession of the town without firing a gun. As he advanced to the *Alamo*, the small garrison of 130 men, under the command of Wm Barret Travis, retired on the opposite side of the river, determined to offer such resistance to the progress of the tyrant as their energies & resources should permit. It is a dark & gloomy morning, devoted to a dark & unholy purpose. Santa Anna establishes his headquarters in a small stone building from which he may the more accurately perceive the progress of his designs, without exposing himself to his enemies. The signal is given before the sun has risen upon those hostile hosts, the roar of the Mexican battery awakens the echoes far & wide, & rouses from their slumbers the yet unconscious inhabitants. The defenders have not for a single moment lost sight of the movements of their wily & implacable foes. The siege continued for 10 days. Travis shows himself on the walls, cheering his cool, undaunted followers. Around him are Crockett, Evans, & Borham. Travis has fallen; Evans is no more; Bowie expires upon a bed of sickness, pierced in the heart by a Mexican bayonet; Borham falls directly before him, & he finds himself the only living warrior of the 163 who had been his companions. His foes assault him with blows from muskets, lances, & sabers. He dies, & the *Alamo* has fallen. -Putnam's Magazine

Supreme Court of the U S, Mon, Dec 1, 1856. Present:
Hon Roger B Taney, Chief Justice
<u>Assoc Justices:</u>

Hon John McLean	Hon Robt C Grier
Hon John Catron	Hon Benj R Curtis
Hon Peter V Daniel	Hon John A Campbell.

<u>Criminal Court-Wash: Grand Jurors sworn in yesterday.</u>

Benj F Middleton	Geo Mattingly	Geo McNeir
Thos Donohoo	Marinus Willett	Jonathan Prout
Judson Mitchell	Geo W Beall	Geo D Livingston
Wm Thompson	Henry C Matthews	Joshua Pearce
Eleazer Linsley	Wm Wilson	Nicholas Callan
Wm T Dove	Dr Benj S Bohrer	Benj S Jackson
Buckner Bayliss	Isaac Clark	Edw Hall
Wm J Stone, sr	John Purdy	Geo A Bohrer

<u>Petit Jurors:</u>

Thos D Larner		Peter Hepburn
John G Robinson	John W Burns	D A Gardiner
R H Harrison	P McKenna	Saml T Wall
Alfred Ray	R M Harrison	Wm A Wallace
Harrison Taylor	Saml S Noland	D A Oardwell
Wm E Spalding	Saml S Grubb	Walter Stewart
Jas Rhodes	Edgar H Bates	Danl Lightfoot
	Edw Brown	

John Cameron	John B Turton	Geo W Uttermuhle
R H Watkins	Wilson E Brown	Boyd Brooks
C F McCarty	John Murphy	Saml Phillips

The suit of Jacob Sanger vs the Central Railroad Co of Va, for damages for injuries received while traveling on the road in Jun last, was decided in the Superior Court of Stanton on Thu. The jury awarded the plntf $6,000. An appeal was filed.

Naval Academy: Midshipmen who have passed their final examination at the Naval Academy at Annapolis: Thos O Selkridge, Mass; Jos N Miller, Ill; John S Barnes, Mass; John M Stribling, Va. They constitute an advanced class, who have completed their studies in 3 instead of 4 years, the time usually required.

Jos Ferguson, Barber & Hair Dresser, Northern Liberties, 7th st, between L & M sts.

Died: on Dec 1, Susanna Ratrie, in her 63rd year. Her funeral will take place this day at 3 o'clock, from the residence of her brother-in-law, Richd Cruit, 34 Bridge st, Gtwn.

T Punington, M D, offers his professional services: 255 G st, opposite the State Dept.

Saml Chilton & Beverley Tucker have associated themselves for the prosecution of business before the Court of Claims. Chilton will continue to practice in the Court of D C & in the U S Supreme Court.

WED DEC 3, 1856
Trustee's sale of valuable real estate in Wash City: by decree of the Circuit Court of Wash Co, D C, passed in a cause in which Sarah B French & others are cmplnts, & Junius French & Rose French are dfndnts, the undersigned will sell at public auction, on Dec 27 next, part of lot 16 in square 457, in Wash City, fronting on E st north, between 6th & 7th sts; with a large & commodious dwlg-house. -Saml Chilton, Christopher Ingle, trustees -C W Boteler, auct

Elegant household & kitchen furniture at auction on: Dec 19, at the residence of Col Roberts, Gtwn Heights, intersection of High & Road sts. -Barnard & Buckey, aucts

A verdict of $2,500 has been obtained in the Court of Stark Co, Ohio, by E Reynold against W H Greek for slander. The plntf is a merchant in Waynesburg.

Orphans Court of Wash Co, D C. Letters of administration on the personal estate of John Mason, late of Wash Co, deceased. -Lewis H Brown, adm

Mrd: on Dec 2, by Rev W Krebs, Robt F Downes, of Balt, formerly of Lewistown, Pa, to Salena Gist, of Wash.

Mrd: on Dec 2, by Rev W Krebs, Horatio Tenley to Mary Jones.

Mrd: on Dec 2, in Wash City, by Rev G W Samson, Mr Jas B King, of Loudoun Co, Va, to Miss Anna Austin, of Balt, Md.

Died: on Dec 2, Mrs Frances D Lear, the widow of the late Col Tobias Lear, the private secretary of Gen Washington. Her funeral will take place from her residence on Pa ave, at 1 o'clock, on Thu, Dec 4.

THU DEC 4, 1856
The admission to probate of the wills of the 2 daughters of the late John Jay, recently deceased, shows bequests for charitable & religious purposes to the extent of over $34,000, amongst which is $1,000 devised by Mrs Banyer to Bishops Meade & Johns, of Va, for the benefit of the Episcopal Theological Semianry in Fairfax Co, Va, & $300 devised by Miss Ann Jay for the like purpose.

Criminal Court-Wash-Tue. 1-Wm Hickerson was found guilty for a cruel assault on a negro man, but his counsel moved for an arrest of judgment, with a view to a new trial. 2-John Nugent & Telemachus Harris, colored, were found guilty of rioting: sentenced to one month in jail.

Wash Corp: 1-The bill authorizing Nicholas Acker & Geo Kolb to use a part of the pavement in front of their dwlg on North Capitol was reconsidered & referred to the Cmte on Improvements. 2-Nominated by the Mayor [Dec 1] for:
Police Constable:
Wm H Fanning   Henry Yeatmen   Jos Mitchell
John H Reynolds   Hugh Dougherty   Jos H Gill
John R Queen: Intendant of the Wash Asylum. Geo H Fulmer: Com'r of the Wash Asylum. J Z Williams: Wood & Coal Measurer & Measurer of Grain & Bran.
R D Spencer: Clerk of the Northern Market.
R D Owens: Com'r of Improvements 3rd & 4th Wards.
T J Barrett: Com'r of Improvements 5th & 6th Wards.
John Codrick: Scavenger 7th Ward.
Mr Queen has been engaged in the discharge of the duties of that station for upwards of 5 months, & has evinced a most admirable fitness for it. Mr Fulmer has had large experience in the situation for which he is nominated, & has always evinced great zeal, capacity, & industry in the discharge of its duties. Dr Miller has been known to me for many years as a member of the City Council in which he lives, & I have never heard a word against him, either professionally or morally, to disqualify him for the place to which he is nominated.

Rufus Welsh, the well known theatrical & circus manager, died at Phil on Friday last.

Died: on Dec 3, Benj Oden West, in his 32nd year. His funeral will be from his late residence 330 K st. [No date or time given.]

Died: on Dec 3, Benj Oden West, in his 32nd year. His funeral will be from his late residence 330 K st. [No date or time given.]

Trustee's sale: by 3 several deeds of trust, executed to the subscribers [trustees] by John A Throckmorton & wife, dated Aug 17, 1852, Jun 17, 1853, & Mar 15, 1854, recorded in Liber J A S No 44, folios 76 thu 79; No 59, folios 89 to 93; & No 75, folios 101 thru 104, of the land records of Wash Co, D C: sale on Jan 5 of the east 20 feet front on north G st of lot 14 in square 455; improved by a brick tenement. -J B H Smith, Silas H Hill -A Green, auct

FRI DEC 5, 1856
Senate: 1-Ptn from the legal reps of Chas Peterfield, asking bounty land, commutation pay, & the reimbursement of advances made by their ancestor for the public service during the war of the Revolution: referred. 2-Ptn from Wm S Dearing, asking the reimbursement of expenses incurred by him in raising & equipping a company of mounted Tennessee volunteers for the Florida war in 1837: referred.

A farmer, Silas Gravel, died in Montg Co, Penn, a few days since, from handling guano with his hands when there were some slight sores upon them. He lingered in great agony for about a week, when death relieved him of his sufferings. -Rochester Democrat

The Gen Assembly in Arkansas, now in session recently elected the following State ofcrs: T B Hanly, Supreme Judge; D B Greer, Sec of State; Wm R Miller, Auditor of Public Accounts; John H Grease, State Treasurer; J W McConaughey, Land Atty & State Collector.

Wash City Ordinance: 1-Act granting certain privileges to Cornelius Shaun: to occupy a portion of Centre Market space, not exceeding 100 feet in diameter for exhibiting equestrian performances from Dec 24, 1856 to Mar 5, 1857. 2-Act to reimburse Jas Addison $7.09 for taxes erroneously paid. 3-Act for relief of Wm B Jackson, agent for Clement Hill: to pay him $6.62 for taxes erroneously paid. 4-Act for relief of Wealthy M Hanson: to pay him $3.15 for taxes erroneously paid. 5-Act for relief of Ann Smoot: to pay her $5.40 for taxes erroneously paid in 1855. Approved: Nov 20, 1856

Bill Blake was arrested lately in Angelina, Texas, for the murder of a whole family named Moore, & was immediately taken & executed by a mob. He made a full confession of his heinous crime, & said he was instigated to its commission by others.

The District Cmte of the House of Reps:
Orsamus B Matteson, of N Y
Wm O Goode, of Va
Edw Dodd, of N Y
Wm Cumback, of Ind
John Dick, of Pa
J Morrison Harris, of Mo
Hendley S Bennett, of Miss
Mark Trafton, of Mass
P H Bell, of Texas

Mrd: on Oct 26, at Perth Amboy, N J, by Rev Dr Odenheimer, Rector of St Peter's Church, Phil, P Radcliffe Hawley to Isabelle, daughter of Geo Merritt, of the former place.

Died: on Oct 28, in the city of Granada, Nicaragua, of fever, Mr Edw G Gary, in his 40th year, formerly of Louisville, Ky. The deceased leaves a family & a large circle of relations & friends to mourn his untimely loss. He was a kind & affectionate husband & father, & a warm & devoted friend.

I offer at private sale my property known as **Landon Academy**, in Fred'k Co, Md, 2½ miles from the Ijamsville depot, Balt & Ohio Railroad, & immediately on the road from Washington to Frederick. -J R Jones, Urbana, Md

SAT DEC 6. 1856
In Equity No 989. Geo McCullion & others vs Jos Peck, John Walker, & others. By order of the Circuit Court of Wash Co, D C I am directed to state the accounts of the trustees with the trust fund in the above cause; 2, to state the claims of the several creditors of the late Dorcas Walker; &, 3, the shares of the distributes or their assigns in the residue of the purchase money. Account to be stated on Dec 29, City Hall, Wash, D C. -John F Ennis, Special Auditor

Appropriations made during the first & second sessions of the 34th Congress:
1-Relief of the distributees of Col Wm Linn, an ofcr in the Revolutionary army, & to allow them 5 years' full pay as a colonel, which is the commutation of half-pay for life: indefinite.
2-Relief of Jacob Dodson: for pay as a private, during the war, in Capt Richd Owen's company of the Calif btln, & who was discharged on Apr 14, 1847, at Los Angeles, Calif, all the pay & allowances to which he would be entitled under the existing laws for such service, in the same manner as if he had been legally enlisted in, & honorably discharged from, the service of the U S, deducting the sum of $281, paid to him by Col J C Fremont for his services as a member of the exploring expedition, within the period named above: indefinite.

3-Act for the relief of Am M F Magraw: for increased expenses & difficulties of carrying the mails along route 8,911, from Independence to Salt Lake, for the year ending on Aug 18, 1856: $36,000. For full indemnity for his claim for property stolen & destroyed by the Indians, as included in his account filed with the Com'r of Indian Affairs: $17,750.

4-Act for the relief of John S Pendleton: for full compensation as Minister of the U S on special mission to the Oriental republic of Uruguay, in 1852, the sum of $9,000, deducting any amount which he may have received as compensation in said mission: indefinite. For full compensation for his services in same character to the Republic of Paraguay, in 1853, $9,000, deducting therefrom any amount of money he may have received as compensation in said mission to Paraguay: indefinite.

5-Act for the relief of Emma Bidamon: in full payment of the sum adjudged & decreed to her in lieu of dower by the circuit court of the U S for the district of Illinois, at the July term, 1852, in the case of the U S vs Jos Smith et al: indefinite.

6-To pay to Saml P Todd, a purser in the Navy, the amount of depreciation upon certain Treasury notes sold by him for the purpose of paying seamen & others employed in the U S Delaware flotilla, in 1814: $553.00

7-To pay to John Shaw, of Wisc, in full for his services, travel, & attendance, as an interpreter upon the trial of certain Winnebago Indians, in 1828, before Hon Jas Duane Doty, at Prairie du Chien: $1,000.00.

8-To pay Isadore D Beaugrand in full for expenses incurred & money expended by him for subsistence, quarters, & transportation furnished to Capt Bradley's company of Ohio volunteers, from the 1st to the 5th of Jun inclusive, 1846, prior to their being mustered into the service of the U S for the Mexican war: $257.12.

9-Act Authorizing a settlement of the accounts of Chas P Babcock, late Indian agent at Detroit, Mich: for expenses incurred for premiums in exchanging gold for silver coin, & also for one quarter's salary for his own services: $457.22.

10-Act for the relief of Eliz V Lomax, only surviving child of Capt Wm Lindsay, of the Revolution: for the arrears of pension due Capt Wm Lindsay, from Oct 1, 1778 to Sep 1, 1797: $5,675.00

11-Act for the relief of the legal reps of Zadock Thompson, of Vt: for his services in preparing a historical introduction to the returns of the 7th Census for the State of Vt: $300.00

12-Act for the relief of Levi Robinson: for fishing bounty for 1852, said schnr having complied with all the requisitions of law to entitle her to bounty, but was unable to present her papers, they having been consumed by fire: $216.00

13-Act for the relief of Bridget Maher: for boarding certain Cherokee Indians from the State of N C, disallowed by the Sec of the Interior on Jul 19, 1852: $293.00

14-Act for the relief of Chas Stearns: for losses sustained & expenses incurred in defending his title to certain lands claimed by the U S; & also in defending 2 criminal prosecutions brought against him by direction of the Sec of War: $5,000.00.

15-Act for the relief of Dempsey Pittman: for his military services in Florida, in 1838: indefinite.

16-Act for the relief of Norwood McClelland, master of the steamboat **New World**: for losses & expenses occasioned by the detention of the steamboat **New World**, in the Arkansas river, while engaged in transporting military stores belonging to the U S from New Orleans to *Fort Smith*, during 1855: $13,889.86.

17-Act for the relief of Thos H Baird: to pay to Thos H Baird, adm of the estate of Absalom Baird, a commissioned surgeon in the army of the Revolution, the sum of $10,074.84, with interest thereon from Oct 27, 1805, to Jun 1, 1856, deducting therefrom the sum of $2,400 paid under the act of Jun 23, 1836: $10,874.84.

18-Act for the relief of Abraham Kintzing: for the difference between his salary as special Examiner & that of Assist Appraiser, for 3 months & 25 days, the period during which he performed the duties of the latter ofc, in addition to his own, in consequence of the death of its incumbent: $319.50.

19-Act for the relief of Francis A Gibbons, & Francis X Kelly: for the balance due them, under their contract with the U S, for the bldg of light houses in Calif & Oregon: $31,190.54.

20-Act for the relief of the heirs of Jabez B Rooker, deceased: for the time he was actually employed in the ofc of the Com'r of Public Bldgs, subsequently to Mar 3, 1843: indefinite.

21-Act for the relief of John H Scranton & Jas M Hunt: for conveying the U S mail on Puget Sound, in 1854 & 1855: $7,333.33.

22-Act for the relief of Adam D Steuart, & of Alex'r Randall, exc of Danl Randall. To pay a commission of one percent, upon such amounts of money as were respectively collected by Adams Steuart & Danl Randall, & by them disbursed or paid into the U S Treasury, in virtue of the authority specially invested in them, by order of the commanding general of the U S Army, & arising from duties on imports, taxes, or other assessments in Mexico, during the late war with that Republic: indefinite.

23-Act for the relief of Brvt Brig Gen John B Walbach, of the U S Army: for the extra services performed by said Walbach, as aide-de-camp to Gen Wilkinson, com'r of the U S to treat with the western Indians, in 1801 & 1802: indefinite.

24-Act for the relief of Isaac Cook & others: for the use of the schnr **Tempest**, belonging to them & impressed by Maj J G Camp, in Sep, 1814: $200.00.

25-Act for the relief of Franck Taylor: for the amounts of duties paid by or for him to the collectors of the ports of N Y & Phil upon importations of quills, by or for him, during 1853, 1854, & 1855: indefinite.

26-Act for the relief of Anthony Rankin, of Tenn: for the amount paid by said Rankin in 1814, while engaged in the military service of the U S, for medical aid & attendance when confined by severe illness: $30.00.

27-Act for the relief of John Poe, of Louisville, Ky: for his services in purchasing horses & mules for the U S Army in 1846: $752.50.

28-Act for the relief of Josiah S Little: for a piece of land to which he lost title by the operation of the 4th article of the Treaty to settle & define the boundaries between the territories of the U S & the possessions of her British Majesty, of Aug 9, 1842: $1,000.00.

29-Act for the relief of Nathan M Lounsbury: for arrears of pension, from Mar 18, 1818, to Feb 4, 1826: $756.00.

30-Act for the relief of John H Scranton & Jas M Hunt, owners of the steamer **Major Tompkins**: for the services rendered, & for the risk, loss, & damages incurred in saving the U S mails & treasure, & in rescuing the passengers & crew which were on board the steamer **Southerner**, at the time of the wreck of that vessel on the uninhabited coast of Wash Territory, in Dec, 1854, & for the clothing & subsistence necessarily furnished to said passengers & crew: $9,600.00.

31-Act for the relief of John M McIntosh: for the amount of 2 accounts against the Gov't, duly certified to be correct, in favor of John Clutes & Jacob Hart, for $82 each; said accounts being on duplicate certificates, the originals having been lost & considered as canceled: $164.00.

32-By the joint resolution authorizing the Sec of the Interior to settle the accounts of Oliver M Wozencraft: for actual disbursements made by him: $7,000.00.

33-Joint resolution for the relief of Dr Wm P A Hall, late of Tenn volunteers in the Mexican war: for medical services rendered to the volunteers while serving in Mexico, upon the following principles, to wit: to allow said Dr Hall the pay of assist surgeon while engaged in professional services, with the consent of his commanding ofcr, deducting therefrom the amount paid to said Hall as a private in the 1st regt of Tenn volunteers, during the period he performed the duties of surgeon: indefinite.

34-Resolution for the settlement of the accounts of Chas M Strader & Ed P Johnson, mail contractors: for the discontinuance of that part of their aforesaid contract under the order of the Postmaster Genr'l, dated Feb 6, 1841, as may appear by the records of the Post Ofc Dept: indefinite.

35-Act for the relief of Henry L Robinson: for retained bounty, & for his services in the U S Army, from Apr, 1814, to the day of his discharge in Feb, 1815: $171.00.

36-Act for the relief of Wm B Cozzens: in full compensation for his store-house, taken from him for the use of the U S, in Jan, 1847, by Capt L H Webb, by order of Quartermaster Gen Jesup: $1,000.00.

37-Act for the relief of John Nash: for one moiety of the penalty collected of the master of the schnr **L J Bowden**, by the collector of the port of Fredericksburg, in 1853, for a breach of the revenue laws, it having been made to appear that the said penalty was incurred without any design to violate the law: $100.00.

38-Act for the relief of John Otis: in full compensation for services rendered in taking care of the sick & wounded at the battle of Sandy Creek, & for quarters & material furnished the wounded prisoners at said battle, in 1814: $917.50.

39-Act for the relief of Calvin Hall, assignee of Wm Jones: for the value of 302 sheep belonging to said Jones, & which were improperly seized & sold by the Govn't ofcrs, in 1851, for an alleged nonpayment of duties: indefinite.

40-Act for the relief of Capt Thos Ap Catesby Jones: for the moneys paid by him to Hall McAlister, as counsel on the trial of Black, & 5 others, for mutiny, before a general naval court martial on board the sloop-of-war **Warren**, in Oct, 1849: $900.00.

41-Act for the relief of the legal reps of Thos Gordon, deceased: for a certificate given by Timothy Pickering, quartermaster general, to the said Thos Gordon, deceased, for nineteen & eighteen-ninetieths dollars, & interest, & bearing date of Jul 29, 1782: indefinite.

Paul Delaroche, the painter, is dead, at the age of 59, having been born in Paris in 1797. He began to paint in childhood, his father's office of appraiser of works of art, at the Monte-de-Picte, throwing him in the way of studying both good & bad subjects. –News

Locomotive explosion near Sufferns, after leaving Jersey City: G W Vance, engineer, died 3 hours later; Jas Conly, a brakeman, was killed instantly; H Cary, fireman, badly scalded, but will probably recover. -N Y Mirror

At the recent session of the U S Circuit Court at Huntsville, Ala: Thos Cashions, of Marion Co, was sentenced to 10 years in the penitentiary, & John Montgomery for 15 years, for robbing the mail; the former as postmaster at Toll Gate & the latter as mail rider from Blountsville to Whitesburg. Cashions is 60 years of age & Montgomery not more than 18.

A pew in St John's Church & the elegant carriage belonging to the late Hon Danl Webster for sale. Apply to W P Williams, at Chubb Brothers' Banking house.

Detroit, Dec 5. Virgil McCormick, conviced of forging affidavits to procure bounty land warrants & pension papers, has been sentenced to 25 years' imprisonment in the penitentiary.

Boarding at 56 Missouri ave. -G G Lawrie

Disasters to steamers. The year about to close will present a fearful record of lives lost on passenger steamers, mostly navigating inland waters.
March, ferry boat **New Jersey**: 32 lost.
June, steamer **Longuil**: 38 lost.
July, steamer **Northern Indiana**, Lake Erie: 26 lost.
July, propeller **Tinto**: 18 lost.
July, steamer **John Jay**, Lake George: 15 lost.
July, steamer **Empire State**, 14 lost.
Aug, steamer **Nautilus**, Gulf of Mexico: 40 lost.
Sep, steamer **Niagara**, Lake Michigan: 66 lost.
Oct, steamer **Superior**, Lake Michigan: 35 lost.
October, propeller **J W Brooks**, Lake Ontario: 30 lost.
Nov, steamship **Le Lyonnaise**: 78 lost.
Nov, propeller **Toledo**: 41 lost.

Fancy Goods, Wash City: H J McLaughlin & Co, 20 Pa ave, between 8th & 9th sts. Our motto, quick sales & small profits, our terms cash; hence we can, we do, & we will sell cheap.

MON DEC 8, 1856
N Y Mirror of Dec 6. Miss Anna M Lachaise, daughter of Jas M Lachaise, of this city, died on board the ship **Arago** on Dec 3, after a short illness from brain fever, aged 19 years. This young lady was engaged to be married to a gentleman of this city immediately on her arrival, & the bridal wreath was bespoken. She was buried today in her wedding robes.

In Chancery-No 887. Hezekiah Clagett & others vs John Walker & others. By order of the Circuit Court of D C: statement of the account of the trustees of the fund, on Dec 30, at my ofc, City Hall, Wash, D C, at 10 o'clock. -Christopher Ingle, Special Auditor

We regret to hear of the failure of Saml Henshaw & Sons, an old & highly respectable banking firm of Boston. We are also informed of the failure of Jacob Little, one of the largest stock operators at the N Y Exchange. -Boston Journal

Balt, Dec 7. Henry George Kuper, the British Consul at this port, was suffocated last night in a house in the western part of this city, which was burnt. Other inmates escaped.

TUE DEC 9, 1856
Trustee's sale of drugs, medicines, soda apparatue, store fixtures, & gas fixtures, at auction, on Dec 15 next, by deed of trust dated Dec 11, 1855, recroded in the land records of Wash Co, D C, Liber J A S No 102, folios 423 to 426: all the stock & fixtures in the apothecary store of Wm T Evans, H & 7th sts. -John E Evans, trustee -A Green auct

N Y, Dec 7. The third trial of Lewis Baker, for the homicide of Wm Poole, was brought to a close yesterday at Nerburgh by the discharge of the jury, who were unable to agree upon a verdict, after 24 hours spent in consultation.

Criminal Court-Wash-Mon. Yesterday Wm Chase, colored, was found guilty of assault & battery with intent to kill Chas Hughes, also colored, on Sep 24 last. The same dfndnt & Jas Gardiner were then tried for riot at the same time & place. John Francis, colored, was found guilty of stealing a pair of shoes.

Mrd: on Dec 4, in Wash City, by Rev W Krebs, Christian Smith to Eliz Winegerg.

Mrd: on Dec 7, by Rev W Krebs, Geo W Ward to Julia A E St Clair.

Mr McClish, keeper of a variety store in Gtwn, left the District for the North some 3 weeks since to make purchases in his line of business, & was expected back on Dec 1, but has not returned. His friends are much concerned on account of his protracted & unexplained absence.

Senate: 1-Ptn from C S Todd, late Minister to Russia, asking to be allowed the amount of certain items which were disallowed in the settlement of his accounts. 2-Ptn from Eliza A Merchant, widow of Brvt Capt Chas G Merchant, on behalf of herself & children, asking to be allowed a pension. 3-Ptn from Wm L S Dearing, asking indemnification for losses sustained in consequence of furnishing a company of Tenn volunteers, raised by him at the request of Gen Jackson, Pres of the U S, for the Florida war, with horses & equipment. 4-Ptn from John Ryley, an Indian, who served in the war of 1812, asking to be allowed a pension. 5-Ptn from Roddpline Claxton, widow of the late Capt Alex'r Claxton, asking to be allowed arrears of pension. 6-Ptn from Alex'r J Atocha, asking the payment of his claims against Mexico under the treaty of Guadalupe Hidalgo of Feb 2, 1848. 7-Ptn from Wm Blake, a soldier in the war of 1812, asking to be allowed a pension. 8-Ptn from John Barney, on behalf of himself & others, heirs of John Barney, an ofcr of the navy during the Revolution, asking that the bill now before Congress for the settlement of the claims of ofcrs of the army of the Revolution may be so amended as to include those of the navy. 9-Ptn from the heirs of Jabez Rooker, asking compensation for his services as a clerk in the ofc of the Com'r of Public Bldgs. 10-Ptn from Adam D Steuart, asking the passage of an act explanatory of that of Aug 18, 1856, granting him a commission on certain disbursements. 11-Ptn from Mr McVicker, asking payment for supplies furnished to the U S troops during the war of 1812, at the request of Commissary John H Pratt. 12-Ptn from Robt H Gray, on behalf of Col Allen McLane & others, for half pay for life, in lieu of commutation under the resolves of the Continental Congress. 13-Ptn from Micajah Owen & Philip Williott, soldiers during the war of 1812, asking to be allowed a pension. 14-Ptn from Mary C Hamilton, widow of Fowler Hamilton, late a captain in the army, asking that the act of Mar, 1854, for her relief, may be extended. 15-Ptn from Jonas P Levy, asking that provision may be made for the appointment of schoolmasters to teach apprentices desirous of entering the navy, & also for their promotion in this service.

Oswego, Dec 6. Marine disasters on Lake Ontario in the recent gale: the schnr **Niagara** from Oswego bound to Bondhead went ashore at Port Hope. Capt Wood, of schnr **Anna**, & Robt Campbell, mate of another schnr, made an attempt to rescue them & were both drowned.

W J Bingham, assisted by his son, proposes re-opening his Select School at Oaks, Orange Co, N C, on Feb 11, 1857. Address W J Bingham, Oaks, Orange Co, N C.

Circuit Court of Wash Co, D C-in Equity. Hezekiah Clagett & others against John Walker & others. John A Linton & A Thos Bradley, trustee, reported that on Oct 11, 1856, they sold lots 1, 2, 5 thru 19, in square 555, & all the east half of square 554, with the dwlg house thereon, to Wm B Kibbey, for $12,500, & the purchaser has complied with the terms of sale. -Jno A Smith, clerk

WED DEC 10, 1856
Will case before the Rhode Island Supreme Court, at Providence, on Tue, the suit in equity of E H Derby, exc & trustee, vs various persons, devisees & legatees under the will of Richd C Derby, late of Newport, was in part heard. The necessity of recourse to the court by the executor results from the fact that the property & estate of testator fall short, by $30,000, of paying the legacies & bequests of the will & its 3 codicils. The cmplnt himself, of the Boston bar, is one party; the only son of the testator is another; the widow of the testator is a third, & a daughter of the testator is the fourth.

J A Gilligan, a young Irishman, arrived in N Y 3 years ago with $13,000, given to him by his father. A day or two since he drowned himself, & seventy-five cents of his last dollar was found on his person. The rest had been dissipated. It lasted pretty well.

Military movements: the U S steamer **Suwanee** arrived at New Orleans last week, from Brasos Santiago, with the following ofcrs & Gov't troops, destined for **Fort Myers**, Fla: Three companies 4th artl, D K, & M; 2 companies 5th Infty, D & H, under command of Capt J A Whitall, 5th Infty; Lt W A Weble, 5th Infty; Lt C J Lynde, 5th Infty; Lt J H Pelouye, 4th Artl; Lt L D Lee, 4th Artl; Lt S H Weed, 4th Artl; Surgeon Thos A McFarlan, U S Army. She brought also a detachment of 122 troops, under command of Lt J Updegraff, 5th Infty, & Surgeon L H Holden, U S Army. Capt Phelps, of the 4th Artl, came as a passenger. The transport ship **Julia**, Capt Tyler, sailed from the Brazos on Nov 23 with 8 companies of the 5th Infty, viz: Companies A, B, C, E, F, G, I, & K, under command of Capt C L Stevenson, accompanied by Surgeon J F Head, U S Army, destined for **Fort Myers**, Fla. Sailed also, on the same day, schnr **C B Knudson**, for New Orleans, with Capt Phelps' Light Battery Company B, 4th Artl; likewise, schnr **Chrysolite**, with camp equipages.

The Va Methodist Episcopal Conference closed its annual session at Richmond on Fri last: appointments announced for the Wash District: W W Bennett, P E; the city of Wash, D S Bogget, C A Davis, sup; Alexandria, J A Duncan; Rock Creek, J J Lumpkin; Howard, to be supplied; Fairfax, P F August; Fairfax Mission, to be supplied; Potomac, W B Twyman; Leesburg, Jno L Lark; Loudoun, T H Haynes, J H Creurd; Warrenton, Wm E Judkins, one to be supplied; Springfield, E A Gibb; Patterson's Creek, S V Hoyle; Manassas, R S Nash; Prince Wm, David Wallace.

Mrd: on Dec 9, in Wash City, by Rev G W Samson, Mr Robt B Bagby, of Richmond, Va, to Miss Eveline Keech, of Wash, D C.

Died: on Dec 8, Edw Quigley, in his 47th year. His funeral will be from the residence of his brother, Wm Quigley, East 10th st, Navy Yard, this afternoon at 2 o'clock.

Maj Louis Gally died yesterday, after a lingering & painful illness. He was a native of France, but had long been identified with Louisiana, her people & her institutions. He had been a veteran in military service, had fought under Napoleon, & was present at the final struggle at Waterloo. He died full of years & honors. New Orleans Bee of Dec 3.

Circuit Court of Wash Co, D C: yesterday the trial of Carroll's heirs vs Davis, in which, for the first time in the course of this series of suits, the plntfs lost their case. The jury found for dfndnt, on the ground that he had held the property in question, on Md ave, in quiet & peaceful possession for more than 20 years. Some other suits pending, involving the same circumstances, are thus also disposed of.

Senate: 1-Bills referred-relief: of Mary Reeside; of Amos B Corwine; of Geo H Giddings, contractor for carrying the U S mails on route 12,900; & of Dr Jas Morrow.

House of Reps: 1-Memorial of Sarah Wolf, widow of now in her 86th year, praying for a pension in consideration of her son's service in the U S Navy: referred. 2-Ptn of Louis N Bogy & another, excs of Antoine Soulard, deceased, for the satisfaction of a portion of a confirmed claim of 10,000 arpens: referred. 3-Bill for the relief of Henry T Mudd, of Missouri: introduced.

Jas M & Jeremiah L Taylor, exchange brokers at Chatham & Jas st, were arrested on Sat for passing counterfeit money: they gave bail in $5,000 each for trial. Augustus Kimberly, & another calling himself Williams, were detected passing the bills, & were also arrested & will be used as witnesses. -N Y Post

Pittsburg, Dec 9. The train from Cleveland for Pittsburg ran through the Pittsburg, **Fort Wayne**, & Chicago train at Alliance, smashing 2 passenger cars of the latter train. Killed were Jacob Rudy, John McIntyre, Dr Smith & lady, of Alliance; Wm Ritchie & Mr Jatterbidt, of New Garden, Ohio; & N G Taylor & John Brooks, of N J.

John H Buthmann, Importer & Dealer in Wines, Brandies, etc: Pa ave, between 4½ & 6th sts. Also, genuine Absinthe, Kirschwasser, & Havana Cigars.

THU DEC 11, 1856
Franklin Glason, of Sudbury, Vt, was instantly killed at a saw mill in that town on Nov 30, when he was caught in the belt & drawn between the pulley & drum.

Dr Snodgrass, lately arrested at Massilion, Ohio, on the charge of killing his wife, was subsequently found dead in jail.

Mrd: on Dec 9, in Wash City, by Rev Mr Samson, Thos G Holtzclaw, of Va, to Miss Emma Ford, of Wash.

Senate: 1-Ptn from John H Wheeler, late Minister to Nicaragua, asking to be reimbursed for moneys advanced for the relief of American citizens in distress in that county. [Certain Americans, en route from Calif to N Y, having been fired upon by the natives of Virgin Bay, by which some were killed & others wounded & robbed, & that the same party fired upon the passengers at *Fort St Carlos*, which guarded the passage, so that escape to either ocean was impossible. In this perilous condition the passengers were brought to Granada, the residence of the U S Legation; & claimed protection of the Minister.] 2-Ptn from Capt Thos Ap Catesby Jones, of the U S Navy, asking the restitution of the pay of which he was deprived by sentence of court martial, & setting forth that this severe sentence was passed, as the memorialist believes, & is well assured by several distinguished jurists familiar with the practice of courts martial, on testimony essentially defective, even to the admission of ex porte evidence, as the official record of the court asserts, & on which he claims that he was entitled to a full & honorable acquittal. 3-Ptn from Jos R Underwood, devisee of an ofcr of the Revolutionary army, asking that the bill now before the Senate for the settlement of the claims of Revolutionary ofcrs may be so amended as to include the devisees of ofcrs who died without issue. 4-Ptn from Jas Marks, asking relief on account of his son, Robt Marks, having been killed in the massacre at Panama in Apr last, on whom he was dependent for support, by the adoption of such measures as will enable him to get possession of the funds or other property his son was possessed of at the time of his death.

Died: on Dec 9, in Wash City, Jno Butler Purcell, in his 14th year, 2nd son of Hon Wm F & Mary F Purcell. The deceased was deprived by affliction from partaking of the joys & pleasures of youth during the past 5 years. His funeral is today at 11 o'clock, from the residence of his father, on L st, between 9th & 10th sts.

Orphans Court of Wash Co, D C. Letters testamentary on the personal estate of Frances D Lear, late of Wm Co, deceased. -Jas Dunlop, J B H Smith, excs

U S Patent Ofc, Wash, Dec 9, 1856. Ptn of Francis N Smith, of Kinderhook, N Y, praying for the extension of a patent granted to him on Jun 1, 1843, for an improvement in corn shellers, for 7 years from the expiration of said patent, which takes place on Jun 1, 1857. -Chas Mason, Com'r of Patents

FRI DEC 12, 1856
Judge Walsh, formerly a Judge of the Supreme Court of Missouri, to which State he emigrated from Louisa, Va, probably previous to 1815, died at his residence near St Louis on Nov 30. He was one of the old settlers, being 75 years of age at the time of his death, & much respected.

Trustee's sale of beautiful country seat: by deed of trust from Geo T Massey, as trustee, & Ann Brown, dated Dec 13, 1853, recorded in Liber J A S No 68, folios 505 thru 510, of the land records of Wash City, D C: public auction, on Jan 12, 1857, at the store of J C McGuire, all that piece of parcel of ground, in Wash Co & District, being a part of the land whereof Anthony Holmead, senior, died seized & part of the tract called **Pleasant Plains**, & part of the land which Anthony Holmead, jr, conveyed to Boltzell & Mayhew, which they conveyed to John Pickroll, the piece of land on the Washington & Rockville turnpike road, containing 5 acres & 1/16th, being lot 2 of Geo Taylor's subdivision, near the land owned by said Geo Taylor; & lot sold to J C Lewis; to the land conveyed to John Brown by John F Sharretts, by deed dated Apr 19, 1853, & duly recorded, with improvements. -Erasmus J Middleton, Richd H Clarke, trustees -A Green auct

Senate: 1-Memorial from Lt David W Porter, complaining of having been unjustly displaced from the active list of the navy, & asking that an act may be so altered or amended as to restore him to active service. 2-Ptn from Richd T Spotswood, for himself & the other heirs of John Spotswood, a captain in the Va line of the army of the Revolution, asking to be allowed commutation pay. 3-Ptn from T Kearney & others, watchmen employed in the Executive Depts in Wash, praying an increase of compensation. 4-Ptn from Michl Kinney, asking to be allowed a pension for a wound received while acting as a teamster in the public service. 5-Ordered that Danl Nipps have leave to withdraw his petition & papers. 6-Ordered that Wm De Buys have leave to withdraw his petition & papers.

The Nashville Banner announces the death on Dec 4 of Hon Thos L Williams, who suddenly died of an affection of the heart, at the residence in that vicinity of his brother-in-law, Mr John P Erwin. He had reached the patriarchal age of 70 years, & died full of years & usefulness.

Dr Francis T Stribling, the distinguished Superintendent of the Western Asylum for the Insane at Staunton, has withdrawn his resignation.

Wm Warren, the 12 year old son of Fitz Henry Warren, [formerly Assist Postmaster Gen,] is an attendant at the Academy of Rev Mr Woodbridge, at the village of Auburn Dale, Newton. Yesterday, with a young companion, named Lawson, they went up to the Charles river to skate on the ice. Wm Warren came upon a weak spot & went under the ice & drowned. -Boston Traveller of Wed.

Mrd: on Dec 9, by Rev Dr Sunderland, Walter M Ogilvie, of Edinburgh, Scotland, to Miss Emma J, youngest daughter of Robt Brown, of Wash City.

Died: on Dec 8, in Wash City, at the residence of her uncle, Fred'k Koones, after a short but painful illness, Viola Budd, only daughter of Wm & Phoebe A Budd, of Petersburg, aged 2 years & 3 months.

Died: on Dec 11, in Wash City, after a short but severe illness, Mrs Ann Dawson, in her 66th year. Her funeral will take place from the residence of her daughter, Mrs Norflet, G st, between 1st & 2nd sts, on Sat, at 2 o'clock.

House of Reps: 1-Ptn of Thos Duncan, of the U S Army, for permission to locate certain duplicate land warrants: referred. 2-Ptn of Henry T Mudd, of Missouri, in regard to a certain pre-emption claim purchased & held by him: referred.

Notice: by 4 writs of fieri facias, 3 issued by J H Birch & one by F J Murphey, 2 justices of the peace for Wash Co, D C, at the suit of Robt Rainy, use of Wm Bond & C W Boteler, against the goods, chattels, lands & tenements of Jas Crutchett, & to me directed, I have seized & taken in execution the all the right & claim of Crutchett in one sorrel horse & carriage & harness: public auction of the same on Dec 18, in front of the Bank of Wash. -J F Wollard, constable

SAT DEC 13, 1856
Gen John G Chapman, of Chas Co, Md, died on Wed of an attack of apoplexy, which terminated his life in a few hours. He was one of the most estimable citizens of Md, of the old & best school. -Alex Gaz

Mr David Burns, of Westminster, Md, has killed 2 hogs, one weighing 511 pounds, the other 424 pounds; & Mr Bazel Hayden one weighing 424 pounds.

Criminal Court-Wash-Fri: 1-The trial of Patrick Fagan, of Gtwn, on a charge of stealing coal from the Lonaconing Co's Coal Depot, in charge of Mr C M Cooke. Verdict, acquittal.

Nat'l Theater. This evening Mr Edwin Booth appears in the character of Richard III, in Shakspeare's play of that name.

House of Reps: 1-Cmte of Claims: discharged from the consideration of the ptns of John Veitch & of the legal reps of Whitmore Knaggs: referred to the Court of Claims. 2-Cmte of Commerce: bill for the relief of Shade Calloway: committed. 3-Cmte on Public Lands: bill to settle the claim of Wm Carey Jones for certain services: committed. 4-Cmte on Private Land Claims: bills for the relief of Capt Thos Duncan,

N Y, Dec 12. The ship **St Louis**, at this port from Liverpool, brings Capt Higgings, his wife, & 32 of the crew of the ship **Transport**, of Boston, wrecked during the hurricane about the middle of Nov.

U S Army; relief of the legal reps of Edmund H McCabe, assignee of Antoine Soulard; & for the relief of Henry P Mudd, of Missouri: committed. Same cmte: bill for the relief of the heirs & legal reps of Jeremiah Bryan: committed. 5-Cmte on Indian Affairs: bill for the relief of Mary Woodbury, Eliz Odell, & others: committed. 6-Cmte on Military Affairs: bill for the relief of Thos J Churchill, late a lt in the 1st Ky regt of volunteers: committed. Same cmte: joint resolution appropriating money to test Geo R Scriven's incendiary projecting shell, & also a joint resolution for the relief of Israel B Bigelow: committed. Same cmte: bill for the relief of Maj Jas Belger, U S Army: committed. 7-Cmte on Foreign Affairs: bills for the relief of Chas E Anderson, of J E Martin, & of Jos Graham: committed. Same cmte: bill for the relief of Donn Piatt: committed. 8-Cmte on Territories: bill for the relief of R G Elliott & others: committed. 9-Cmte on Revolutionary Pensions: bill to provide an increase of pension to Isaac Phillips, of N Y; also, bills for the relief of Gersham Van Vorst; of the children of Eliz Storrs; & for the relief of Eliz Martin: committed. Same cmte: bills for the relief of the children & heirs at law of Lt Danl Starr; & for the relief of the children & heirs of Levi & Mary Stone: committed. Same cmte: bill in favor of the children of Thos Giles; for the relief of Amos Oney, a Revolutionary soldier; relief of the children of Judah & Sarah B Mendigs; for the relief of the widow of Henry Walthall, a Revolutionary soldier; & for the relief of the grandchildren of Genevieve Victor: committed. 10-House to consider the bill for the relief of Mrs Agatha O'Brien, widow of Brvt Maj J P J O'Brien, late of the U S Army, the Senate having disagreed to the amendment of the House to said bill. 11-House bill to authorize the legal reps of Pascal L Cerre to enter certain lands in the State of Missouri, reported from the Senate with an amendment. 12-Mr Burnett, of Ky, introduced a bill for the relief of Richd B Alexander, late a major in the 1st Tenn regt in the Mexican war, & a bill for the relief of R D Gholson, late a captain in the Mexican war: each referred to the Cmte on Military Affairs. 13-Mr Ball, of Ohio, made an ineffectual attempt to obtain the consideration of the bill for the relief of Geo Cassady.

MON DEC 15, 1856

The New Orleans Picayune of Dec 7 announces the death, in that city, of Jos Saul, one of its oldest citizens. Mr Saul came to New Orleans the year after the cession of Louisiana, in 1803. He was the only cashier of the 1st branch bank of the U S, an office which he held until its affairs were wound up in 1810. He afterwards drafted the charter of the Bank of Orleans, & was its cashier until the second Bank of the U S was organized, of which he was appointed cashier of the branch in that city. He was president of the 1st insurance company chartered in the State of Louisiana.

Criminal Court-Wash-Sat. 1-Dr C H Van Patten on charge of forging the name of Michl O'Brien to a written instrument: acquitted. 2-John Monahan convicted of an assault & battery, & sentenced-1 month in the county jail. 3-Robt Cross, for keeping a disorderly house, sentenced-2 months in jail. 4-Wm Hickerson, convicted of cruel maltreatment of a negro man, fined $20 & 3 months' imprisonment in jail.

Wash, Dec 13, 1856: letter from John Barney to the Editors. Soliciting consideration to the memorial presented by him in behalf of the orphan children of my deceased brothers & sisters, heirs of the late Cmdor Joshua Barney, deceased; also, of the heirs of Cmdor Paul Jones; of Cmdor Thos Truxton; of Cmdor Sam, Ben, & Wm Nicholson, & 83 others, which embrace all the navy ofcrs of the Revolution, as per official register now on file in the State Dept, paying that the ofcrs of the navy may be embraced in the bill now before Congress to provide for the settlement of the half-pay promised the ofcrs of the Revolution. They certainly have equal claims to the justice of their country. The army ofcrs are ascertained to number 2,090, out of which the Gov't would have to provide for 1,045, requiring an appropriation of $2,000,000. The navy ofcrs number 89, requiring little over $100,000. The vote to take it up out of its turn at the last session of the Senate was 42 to 18; in the House 111 to 54. [Notice in the same paper: Reps of orphan children of his deceased sister & brothers, of the heirs of Com Paul Jones, Com Thos Truxton, Coms Jas, Saml, & Benj Nicholson, & 72 others, to meet this morning, at 9 o'clock, at 273 F st, to deliberate on combined action of army & navy ofcrs. -John Barney]

T Potentini, Confectioner: 279 Pa ave, south side, 4th door above 10th st, Wash City.

Mr Wm Herbert, who lives in the 1st Ward, was returning homewards from Gtwn on Sat night, when he was attacked by one of 4 persons, who, without the slightest provocation or a word spoken on either side, leveled blow after blow on him. Ofcrs Digges & May were not too far off & responded to Mr Herbert's calls. Stephen Dorsey, a very stout athletic Irishman, was captured & put in the watch-house; & held to bail for trial at court in the sum of $200. The other 3 persons who stood by, but took not part, have not been identified.

Fire on Sat in a shed adjoining the slaughter-house of Mr Philip Otterback, near the Navy Yard, was put out before the mischief extended very seriously.

Mrd: on Dec 3, in Balt, by Rev Dr Burnap, Wm E Mayhew to Miss Abby Eliz Poor.

Mrd: on Dec 11, in St John's Church, Gtwn, by Rev Halliday Johns, Capt Wm B Johns, U S Army, to Leonora R, daughter of Geo F de La Roche.

Died: on Dec 13, in Wash City, Clotilda Virginia, wife of Thos M Cassell, & daughter of Susan & the late Wm Dany, in her 22nd year. Her funeral will take place from M st south, Island, this day at 2 o'clock.

Died: on Dec 14, Margaret Rebecca, daughter of Jas H & Anna S Boss, aged 6 years, 2 months & 9 days. Her funeral is this day at 2 o'clock, from the residence of her parents, corner of H & 4th sts.

TUE DEC 16, 1856
Senate: 1-Ptn from Nathl P Swan, son & heir of Thos Swan, asking remuneration for the services of his father in the war of the Revolution. 2-Ptn from John W Chevis & others, asking the confirmation of their titles to a certain tract of land in the State of Louisiana. 3-Ptn from Atkins Eldridge, owner of the fishing schnr **Brilliant**, lost at sea, asking to be allowed fishing bounty. 4-Ptn from Benj Alvord, a paymaster in the U S army, asking remuneration for losses sustained by the wreck of the steamship **Southerner**, in Wash Territory. 5-Ptn from Anthony W Bayard, a soldier in the war of ___, asking arrears of pension. 6-Ptn from the widow of Peter Petery, asking compensation for the use of a wagon & team in the military service of the U S in the war of 1812. 7-Ptn from Geo Chipman & others, on behalf of themselves & others, clerks employed in the Executive Depts at Wash, asking an increase of compensation. 8-Ptn from Thos Fitman, asking the repayment of money expended by him for public use while warden of the penitentiary in the District of Columbia. 9-Ptn from Wm S Sullivant & others, asking the establishment of an overland communication from the Mississippi river to San Francisco, in Calif. 10-Cmte of Claims: act for the relief of Ransdell Pegg; & of ___ Schellinger: passed. 11-Cmte on Pensions: ptn of Mary C Hamilton, to continue pension heretofore paid to _ C Hamilton, widow of Capt Fowler Hamilton, deceased, late of the U S army.

The Artic Explorer. Dr Elisha Kent Kane was born in Phil on Feb 3, 1822, & graduated at the Univ of Pa in 1843; esteemed a good classical scholar, a good chemist, mineralogist, astronomer, & surgeon. He solicited & obtained an appointment in the navy as surgeon, & was attached to the first American embassy to China. He explored the Philippine Islands, mainly on foot. He was the first man who descended into the crater Tael, lowered more than 100 feet by a bamboo rope from the overhanging cliff. He traversed Greece on foot; had duty on the western coast of Africa; became ill with African fever & was sent home in a precarious state of health; recovered, & volunteered in the Mexican war; was employed in the Coast Survey Dept; transferred by the Sec of the Navy to the post of Surgeon on the Grinnell Arctic Expedition.

The Petersburg Intelligencer newspaper, bldg, fixtures, for sale: the subscriber, intending to remove from Petersburg, offers the above for sale, with all its presses, type, fixtures, & good will. The Intelligencer, with the exception of a single paper, is the oldest journal in Va, & one of the oldest in the U S. The site is the brick bldg on Bank st, one door east of the Exchange Bank. -John W Syme

Criminal Court-Wash: Christian Krouse, of Gtwn, was yesterday convicted of resisting ofcr Gross in the discharge of his duty on Oct 4 last, & sentenced to 6 weeks' imprisonment & fined $1. He was again put on trial & convicted of an assault & battery on Mrs Eliz Evans, for which he received a similar sentence. On a 3rd indictment of malicious mischief to the furniture of the house in which Mrs Evans lived he was also convicted & fined $5.

WED DEC 17, 1856
Household & kitchen furniture at auction on: Dec 19, at the house-furnishing store of A H Lee, 23 K, between 7th & 8th sts. -A Green auct

Senate: 1-Ptn from Miles Inderson, regarding certain money paid by him on account of the late Purser Andrew D Crosby, that he may be released from liability as one of his sureties. 2-Ptn from the legal reps of Roger Loisel, for confirmation to their title to a tract of land in Missouri. 3-Ptn from Mary Lisel, asking the confirmation of title to a tract of land claimed under a Spanish grant. 4-Ptn from the heir of Fulwer Skipwith, asking remuneration for diplomatic services & expenses incurred by his father while consul general of the U S in France in the years 1795-97. 5-Ptn from R R Kendall, from Thos Johnson, & from John Lunt, asking a modification of the pension laws. 6-Ptn from Thos Johnson, asking to be allowed arrears of pension. 7-Cmte on Patents & the Patent Ofc: bill for the relief of Chas Newbold & heirs.

House of Reps: 1-Ptn of Jas Marks, of Mercer Co, Pa, father of the late Robt Marks, who was killed at Panama, for relief.

Preacher married in his own pulpit: the congregation of the Cumberland Presbyterian Church, in Louisville, a few evenings ago, were startled by Rev Mr Newman, the pastor of the church, descending from the pulpit, & selecting a young lady, who had consented to become his help-meet, to whom he was immediately joined in the holy bonds of wedlock.

Criminal Court-Wash-Tue. Trial of 2 marines, Lorenzo G Burke & Geo Cromwell, charged with manslaughter, in having beaten a marine named Pasquaal de Falco, at the Navy Yard, on Sep 2 last, whereof he died in about 10 days after. A number of witnesses were examined. [Dec 18th newspaper: Burke & Cromwell were found guilty & sentenced to 5 years each in the penitentiary, to take effect from & after Dec 21.]

Mr Saml Walker, portrait painter, from London, has taken up his residence in Wash City, & has a collection of pictures now on free exhibition at the Iron Hall, Pa ave, to be sold at auction, today & Thu, by C W Boteler.

Died: on Dec 3, in Alexandria, Va, Mr Wm M Nalls, formerly of Prince Wm Co, Va, aged 64 years. His last painful illness was made peaceful by a Christian trust, amounting to rapture.

Died: on Dec 16, near Beltsville, PG Co, Md, Mary Anne, only daughter of Wm S & Anne T Clary, late of Wash, aged 12 years & 10 months. Her funeral is this day at 12 o'clock, from the Ninth St Protestant Methodist Church.

THU DEC 18, 1856
Hon R F W Allston was on Thu last inaugurated as Govn'r of the State of South Carolina. He has for some years past presided with ability ovet the Senate of the State.

Mrd: on Dec 17, by Rev W B Dutton, Mr Edw A Gallaher to Miss Sarah Newton Carter, eldest daughter of Isaac N Carter, all of Charlestown, Va.

Died: on Dec 16, in Wash City, John Mecklin, infant son of John G & Bertha M Clarke.

Senate: 1-Ptn from Saml McDougall, a lt in the army of the war of 1812, asking to be allowed a pension in consequence of injuries received while in service. 2-Ptn from the heirs of Thos Maddin, asking the confirmation of their title to a tract of land in Missouri. 3-Cmte on Pensions: asked to be discharged from the consideration of the ptn of the heirs of Richd Furber, on the ground that the law was already sufficient to cover the case.

Mr Gales C Walker, deputy warden, was killed in the chapel of the Massachusetts State Prison at Charlestown, on Monday, after a devotion, by a convict named Jas Magee, who plunged a knife into his neck, under the left ear, & severed the jugular vein. The chaplain of the prison, Rev Mr Hempstead, struck Magee with the Bible, & then seized him by the hair, confining him until the arrival of further aid, when Magee was put in irons and conveyed to a dungeon. Mr Walker died in a few moments. -Boston Courier

Criminal Court-Wash. Jacob *Brisbach was put on trial for stealing a horse worth $200 from Archibald White in Oct last, which he took off & sold in Balt. Owing to the absence of a witness material to the defence, the Court adjourned before the case could be given to the jury. [Dec 19th newspaper: Jacob *Briebach found guilty of stealing a horse.] *Two spellings.

Died: on Dec 16, in Wash City, Mr Isaac Searles, late of Newark, N J, aged 80 years.

An application of the provisions of the fugitive slave law was made in Wash City last evening in the case of the arrest of Mary Ann Williams, a colored woman claimed as the property of Mrs Mary Massey, of Alexandria, from whom the woman has successfully secreted herself for 5 or 6 years. She was duly identified as Mrs Massey's property, & taken from her place of service on Capitol Hill to her mistress in Alexandria.

The new **Wesley Chapel**, just finished, on the corner of 5th & F sts; will be dedicated on Sabbath next, at 2 o'clock; Rev J P Durbin, D D, Corr Sec of Missionary Society M E Church; Rev E S Janes, D D, Bishop M E Church, & other Ministers will officiate. [Dec 20th newspaper: the ornamentation which is found on the walls in the main body of the church was executed by Mr John D'Orsay, of N Y.]

In Equity-No 1,134. Aaron O Dayton vs John W Dick & Richd Cruit. Wm B Webb, the trustee, reported to the Court, that on Dec 3, 1856, he did sell lot 18 in square 453 in Wash City, to Aaron O Dayton for $660, & that he has complied with the terms of sale.

FRI DEC 19, 1856
Senate: 1-Cmte on Military Affairs: asked to be discharged from the consideration of the memorial of L A Latil, & that it be referred to the Cmte on Pensions: which was agreed to. Same cmte: adverse report on the memorial of Mrs Eliza E Ogen, widow of Capt E A Ogden.

Criminal Court-Wash-Thu. 1-Thos Johnson, convicted of stealing a cow, valued at $20: sentenced to 18 months' imprisonment. 2-Geo Stanley, colored, convicted of assault & battery: sentenced to 2 weeks' imprisonment. 3-Wm Johnson, guilty of stealing 12 hams & 4 pieces of pork, the property of Mr Peddicord. 4-Wm Nicholson, guilty of stealing a coat, valued at $2: sentenced to 6 months in jail. 5-Robt Cross, found guilty of 3 cases of assault on ofcrs in the Capitol yard: sentenced to 6 weeks' imprisonment & fined $3.

Mrd: on Dec 18, by Rev A F N Rolfe, Rector of Trinity Church, Upper Marlboro, Jeremiah Mullikin, of the above place, to Miss Eleanora Sherlock, of Wash City.

Mrd: on Dec 18, in Wash City, at the residence of C F Wood, by Rev P Light Wilson, John T Burke to Miss Virginia F Skinner, all of Fairfax Co, Va.

Died: on Dec 17, in Wash City, Miss Catharine C Smith, in her 26th year. Her funeral will be this day at 3 o'clock, from the residence of Dr Baum, 407 11th st.

Died: on Dec 17, aged 17 days, John Mechlin, 2nd son of John G & Bertha M Clarke.

Mourning Clothes. The subscriber has now on hand an assortment of Black Cloth Cloaks for deep mourning. -Frank A McGee, 244 Pa ave, between 12th & 13th sts.

Mr Jos Calhoun died in Dooley Co, Ga, at the age of 100 years & 10 months. He was a native of Edgecomb, N C; he saw both the beginning & close of the Revolutionary war, in which he participated; was under the command of Gen Gaster at the battle of Camden, & fought under Gen Greene at Guilford Court-house. [No death date given-current item.]

During a fracas on Friday at a tavern in Delaware, David Carr, the proprietor of the house, was killed by being beaten over the head. One of the perpetrators was arrested.

Dwlg house in Gtwn for rent or sale: the house is in Montg st, near Gay; contains 10 rooms. Apply next door, of Anthony Smith. Possession immediately.

In Equity-No 1,127. Circuit Court of Wash Co, D C. Christopher S O Hare & Washington Adams, against Mary M Prather, widow & admx, & Emily Prather, Sarah Ann Prather, Martha Prather, Geo Prather, & Henry Prather, heirs at law of Overton I Prather, deceased. The trustee reported that on Aug 14, 1856, he sold lot 60 in square 448, to John R McLeod for $466.35; & lot 12 in square 447, with improvements, to Theodore Mosher, for $374: purchasers have complied with the terms of sale. -Jno A Smith, clerk

SAT DEC 20, 1856
Senate: 1-Ptn from the heirs of John Allen, asking indemnity for property destroyed by the British during the war of the Revolution, setting forth that said Allen took an active part in sustaining the great principles of liberty, & that in consequence of his ceaseless exertions in the cause he incurred the hatred & vengeance of the enemy. 2-Ptn from John Mitchell, a soldier in the war with Mexico, who had lost both arms, asking an increase of his pension on account of his utter helplessness. 3-Bill for the relief of John Ferguson & others was taken up.

In Equity-No 1,127. Chris S O'Hare & Washington Adams against Mary M Prather, & Emily, Sarah Ann, Martha, George, & Henry Prather, widow & heirs at law of Overton J Prather: to meet on Jan 14 next, in City Hall, Wash, for statement of the account of the trustee in said cause. -W Redin, auditor

In Equity-No 1,134. Aaron O Dayton, cmplnt, against John W Dick & Richd Cruit, dfndnts. Statement of the account of the trustee, in my ofc, on Jan 15 next, in the City Hall, Wash. -W Redin, auditor

House of Reps: 1-Bill for the relief of Jason Wheeler: referred. 2-Bill for the relief of N Greene McDonald: referred. 3-Bill authorizing a settlement of the accounts of Frank S Holland, late postmaster at Oregon City, Oregon: referred. 3-Cmte of Claims: bill for the relief of Thos Rhodes & Jeremiah Anstill: committed. Same cmte: bill for the relief of Jos D Beers, of N Y C: committed. Same cmte: bill for the relief of Thos M Newell; & for the relief of Isaac Swain: committed. 4-Cmte on Military Affairs: bill increasing the pension of Danl Denver: committed. Same cmte: bill for the relief of Catharine M Hamer, widow of the late Gen Thos L Hamer: committed. Same cmte: bill for the relief of Benj W Smithson: committed. 5-Cmte on Invalid Pensions: bill for the relief of Eli Darling: committed. 6-Cmte on Accounts: adverse report in the case of John L Wirt. 7-Bill for the relief of Jos Richards, of Berks Co, Pa; & the bill for the relief of the heirs of the late Saml R Thurston, delegate from Oregon: recommended that they pass. 8-Bill for the relief of Mrs A W Angus, widow of the late Capt Saml Angus, U S Navy, was discussed.

In Equity-No 886. Wm Bird & others, cmplnts, against Horatio Maryman, exc, & John H, Richd A, Almira E, & Zachariah A Hazel, heirs at law of Zachariah Hazel, dfndnts. Funds in the hands of the trustee will be distributed among the creditors of said Hazel: on Jan 16 next, in the City Hall, Wash. -W Redin, auditor

In Equity-No 1,065. The U S, cmplnts, against Geo Schwartz & Maria his wife, Walter C Livingston & Mary L his wife, & Mgt A Dale, heirs at law of Jas Greenleaf; Robt Morris, John Cosgrove & Eliz his wife, Mary Vanderhennel, Henry W Morris, Caroline Stark, Harriet Morris, Emily Morris, Wm M Morris, Joshua L Husband & Mary M his wife, Henry Morris, Amelia S Morris, Robt Morris, Wm S Morris, Charlotte S Morris, Sallie Morris, Robt M Marshall, Jas Marshall, Henry M Marshall, Eliz Nixon, Hetty Nixon, John Moss & Emily H his wife, Edw N Waln & Ellen Cora his wife, heirs at law of Robt Morris; Wm S Cunningham, Jas Cunningham, Chas E Cunningham, Geo F Cunningham, Thos B Cunningham, & Rebecca Washington, heirs at law of Wm Campbell; Jas Dundass, & Clement S Miller, dfndnts. I am directed to audit & settle the accounts between the U S, through the late City Com'rs, & Morris, & Nicholson, & Greenleaf, & between the U S & said Greenleaf, & to take depositions in relation thereto for either party, & in relation to the claim of the U S upon the 6 squares of ground in Wash City, nos 465, 468, 469, 470, 495, & 498, released by Thos Law to Robt Morris, as stated in the cmplnt's bill. On Jan 19 next, at my ofc in the City Hall, Wash, I shall commence the taking of the said accounts. -W Redin, auditor

Richmond Despatch. Judge John Taylor Lomax, of the 8th judicial district of Va, has forwarded his resignation to the Govn'r, to take effect on Jan 20, 1857.

Mrd: on Dec 18, in Wash City, by Rev Andrew G Carothers, Col Wm Emmons, of Mass, to Mrs Mary A Weems, formerly of Raleigh, N C, but recently of Balt, Md.

Mrd: on Dec 17, in Wash City, by Rev Mr Samson, Noble J Thomas to Julia E McComb, all of Wash City.

Died: on Dec 17, in Wash City, in her 61st year, Miss Mary Ann King. Her funeral will take place today at 12 o'clock, from the Rev Dr Gurley's Church, on F st.

John C Stanford, assistant postmaster at Florence, N Y, was arrested on Sat last for robbing the mails at that place. -Albany Evening Journal

Trustee's sale of valuable farm: by decree of the Circuit Court for PG Co, Md, sitting as a Court of Equity: public sale, on the premises, on Jan 8 next: the estate belonging to the heirs of the late Richd Osborn, containing about 350 acres of land; located near Upper Marlborough, PG Co, Md; improvements consist of 3 new & large tobacco houses, quarters for servants, & stable. This land is sold clear of the widow's dower. Mr John T Osborn, who lives near the premises, will show it. -C C Magruder, trustee

MON DEC 22, 1856

Trustee's sale of handsome improved property on south B, between 13 & 13½ sts west at auction: on Dec 22, next, by deed of trust from Robt Cochran to the subscriber, dated Aug 14, 1855, recorded in Liber J A S No 102, folios 311 thru 312: sale of parts of lots 15, 16, & 18, in square 264, in Wash City, with a good dwlg house & other improvements: property fronts 24 feet on south B st. -Jos C Lewis, trustee -A Green auct

Bellona Arsenal, with 27½ acres of land attached thereto, in Chesterfield Co, on James river, 14 miles above Richmond, has been sold for $2,650. Dr Junius L Archer, of Powhatan, was the purchaser. This arsenal was established in 1816. It was formerly a depot for military stores, & was garrisoned by a company of U S soldiers, but of late years it has been abandoned on account of the unhealthiness of the location.

House of Reps: 1-Cmte on Invalid Pensions: bill for the relief of Lucy Fitzgerald & the children of Thos Fitzgerald: committed. 2-Bill for the relief of Jos Richards, of Berks Co, Pa: passed. 3-Bill for the relief of the heirs of the late Saml R Thurston, delegate from Oregon: recommendation that it pass. 4-Bills with recommendation that they pass-relief: of Mrs A W Angus, widow of the late Capt Saml Angus, U S Navy; & of Evelina Porter, widow of the late Cmdor David Porter, U S Navy.

Chester Jennings: no one who knew N Y 20 years since was unacquainted with him; he was a servant in the City Hotel, fire-maker & boot black; head-waiter, bar-keeper, chief manager, & finally lessee of that bldg. He died in N Y C on Tue, at the Astor House. -Phil Sun

Wash City Ordinance: 1-Act for the relief of Philip Kraft: the sum of $100 be paid to him for error in grade on 6th st west, in square 481.

Mrd: in Jefferson Co, Va, by Rev John S Deale, Mr Arthur E Wilson, of Portsmouth, Va, to Miss Anne T, daughter of Levi Moler, of said county. [No marriage death given-current item.]

Died: on Dec 20, in Wash City, after a short illness, Mrs Mary Coombe, relict of the late Griffith Combe, in her 84th year. Her funeral will be from the residence of her son, Dr Coombe, on 3rd st east, near the Eastern Branch, on Dec 22 at 1 o'clock.

Died: on Dec 6, at **Fort Brown**, Texas, Maj J Randall Hagner, Paymaster U S Army.

Died: on Nov 3 last, at Torquay, in Devonshire, England, Mrs Susan D Conner, relict of the late Cmdor David Conner. She left Phil in Sept in feeble health, &, after suffering with great severity, she resigned herself to her fate, & breathed her last away from her native land. Her two sons were with her at the time. Her body will be brought to Phil for interment.

Criminal Court-Wash-Sat. 1-Christian Krouse was acquitted of assault & battery. 2-Aquilla Allen submitted to the Court a case in which he was dfndnt for beating with a billey one O'Brien, at the Nat'l Theatre in Apr last, whilst acting in the capacity of a peace ofcr: fined $10. 3-Timothy D Sullivan was put on trial for an assault & battery with intent to kill his brother-in-law, Michl O'Brien, on Nov 8: shooting with a pistol 5 teeth right out of his upper row, but, as it appeared, without any other injury to his face or head. The pistol had nothing in it but powder. The jury found a verdict of simple assault & battery against Sullivan.

U S Patent Ofc, Wash, Dec 20, 1856. Ptn of Joel W Andrews, of Bridgeport, Pa, praying for the extension of a patent granted to him on Mar 21, 1843, for an improvement in burning bricks, for 7 years from the expiration of said patent, which takes place on Mar 21, 1857. -Chas Mason, Com'r of Patents

N Y, Dec 21. The President has issued an order for the arrest of Cornelius K Garrison, Chas Morgan, & Gen Walker, to answer for seizing the property of the Accessory Transit Co, valued at $1,000,000.

The Association of the Soldiers of the War of 1812 of D C, to meet at the residence of the Pres of the association tomorrow at 4 o'clock. By order R Burgess, sec

TUE DEC 23, 1856
Senate: 1-Memorial of Edw N Kent, chemist, melter, & refiner in the U S assay ofc at N Y, setting forth that he is the inventor & patentee of a new apparatur for separating gold, which is now in successful operation at the mint in Phil & at the assay ofc in N Y; he asks that Congress will appropriate such sum as may be deemed a suitable compensation for the invention & the perpetual use of his apparatus. 2-Ptn from the heirs of Capt Thos Hazard, an ofcr in the army of the Revolution, asking to be reimbursed for sums of money expended by him in raising & equipping a company of men to serve in said war. 3-Ptn from Thos W Ward, late U S consul at Panama, asking compensation for services & reimbursement of his expenses in procuring testimony in reference to the outrages committed on American citizens in the riot at Panama in Apr last. 4-Ordered that Chas Gratiot have leave to withdraw his memorials & papers. 5-Ptn from Thos Henderson, asking a confirmation of his title to a certain tract of land in the State of Michigan. 6-Ptn from Geo Phelps, a messenger in the ofc of the Quartermaster Genr'l, asking to be allowed compensation for the time he was employed after office hours. 7-Ptn from Wm Durell, asking compensation for fitting up the legislative ball at Detroit, in Michigan, for the use of the Territorial Legislature, by direction of the Govn't of the Territory. 8-Ptn from John Perry & other surviving heirs of Margaret Perry, asking to be allowed a pension. 9-Cmte on Naval Affairs: asked to be discharged from the consideration of the memorial of the widow of Capt Alex'r Claxton, of the U S navy, & that it be referred to the Cmte on Pensions. 10-Cmte on Military Affairs: asked to be discharged from the consideration of the memorial of A S Wright, & that it be referred to the Cmte of Claims.

Hon A S Lipscombe, one of the Justices of the Supreme Court of Texas, died in Austin on Dec 8 of typhoid pneumonia.

Died: The oldest man in Salem. The Salem [Mass] Gaz announces the decease of Mr Thos Norsworthy, of that city, who was nearly 100 years of age. He was born in Devonshire Co, England, May 7, 1758, & came to this country in 1816, previously to which he had served 20 years in the British army, under Lord Wellington & other ofcrs, in India, Russia, Prusia, Spain, & the West Indies, & for 11 years he was in the British navy, under Admiral Duckworth & other ofcrs. He was engaged in 65 battles during these 31 years, & escaped without the loss of a limb.

Died: on Dec 21, in Wash City, Miss Honora Sweeney, in her 16th year. Her funeral will be from the residence of her mother, Mrs Mary Sweeney, H st, between 4th & 5th sts, this afternoon at 2 o'clock.

Died: on Dec 22, at Portsmouth, N H, of African fever, contracted in the discharge of duty, Cmder Saml Larkin, of the U S Navy.

Died: on Dec 22, in Wash City, Geo Wilson Cole, son of John T & Eliz Ann Cole, aged 2 years, 8 months & 4 days. His funeral will be from the residence of his parents, on 5th st, between H & I sts, this evening, at 3½ o'clock.

Criminal Court-Wash. 1-John Donaldson, of Gtwn, was convicted of ann assault & battery & fined $10. 2-Wm Sullivan, John Ennis, & Richd Jones, found guilty of a riot, & sentenced to 9 months' imprisonment each & the usual fine of $1. 3-The Judge passed sentence on Timothy D Sullivan, convicted of an assault & battery on Michl O'Brien: fined $50. Because of his good character, the Court would not imprison him.

Right Hon Eliz Jerningham, widow of the 7th Baron Stafford in the peerage of Great Britain, died at Costessy Hall, in Norfolk Co, England, on Nov 19. Her ladyship was one of the 3 daughters of Richd Caton, of Balt, [grand-daughters of Chas Carroll, the last surviving signer of the Declaration of Independence,] who married English peers, viz, the late Dowager Marchioness of Wellesley & the Duchess of Leeds. Lady Stafford was married May 25, 1836, & became a widow Oct 4, 1851. The Lady Stafford whose death is noticed above was the wife of the present Lord Stafford & the daughter-in-law to the Dowager Lady Stafford, formerly Miss Caton, of the city of Balt. This information comes to us upon reliable authority. -Patriot

Northampton, England: on Nov 17th, Miss Ann Lynell, conductress of a boarding school, died of a broken heart caused by fright when she found her mother, who resided in the same house & had been ill, had expired. She died but a few seconds after her mother.

In Equity-No 934. Jas F Haliday & others, cmplnts, against Thos J Haliday, Saml Cockrell, & others, heirs at law of Thos, Anna, & Wm W Haliday, & of Lydia Hanlan, dfndnts. Trustee's account will be stated on Jan 17th, in the City Hall, Wash, at 11 o'clock. -W Redin, auditor

In Equity-No 1,040. Anthony Holmead, cmplnt, against John F Ennis, adm, & Messrs Wells, Sears, & Keane, heirs of Catharine E Dent, dfndnts. Trustee's account will be stated on Jan 17, in the City Hall, Wash, at 11 o'clock. -W Redin, auditor

WED DEC 24, 1856
From Europe: 1-Fr Mathew, the world-renowned advocate of temperance, died at Cork on Dec 9. 2-Count Lovatelli, an eminent liberal has been assassinated at Ravenna.

House of Reps: 1-Memorial of Francis D Leonard, praying for additional compensation for carrying the mail from Fred'k city to Wash: referred. 2-Ptn of the legal reps of Regis Loisel for the confirmation of & the privilege of locating a certain Spanish grant: referred. 3-Memorial of Jas Hall, formerly a private in the 6th Infty, U S Army, Co I, praying for an increase of pension in consequence of inability resulting from injuries received in the service of the U S. 4-Ptn of the heirs of Col Benj Wilson, deceased, of Harrison Co, Va, for a pension or other gratuity for services rendered in the Indian & Revolutionary wars.

Orphans Court of Wash Co, D C. Letters testamentary on the personal estate of Washington Berry, late of Wash Co, deceased. -Eliza T Berry, exc

Autobiography of Danl Webster: I was born Jan 18, 1782; my father, by 2 marriages, had 5 sons & 5 daughters. I am the youngest son, & the only surviving child. I have nephews & nieces, both of the whole & half blood; that is to say, sons & daughters of my brothers & sisters, of both my father's wives. In 1783 my father removed from his first residence, a log house on the hill, to the river side, in the same town. My father seemed to have no higher object in the world than to educate his children to the full extent of his very limited ability. I recollect no great changes happening to me till I was 14-a grest deal of the time I was sick, feeble system. On May 25, 1796, my father carried me to Exeter & placed me in Phillip's Academy, then & now under the care of that most excellent man, Dr Benj Abbott. My first exercises in Latin were recited to Jos Stevens Buckminster. At the winter vacation, Dec, 1796, or Jan, 1797, my father came for me & took me home. I formed in the few months there the long enduring friendship of J W Bracket, late of N Y, deceased; Wm Garland, late of Portsmouth, deceased; Gov Cass of Mich; Mr Saltonstall & Jas H Bingham, now of Claremont, N H, are of the number. In Feb, 1797, my father placed me under the tution of Rev Saml Wood, in Boscawen. I entered Dartmouth College as a freshman Aug, 1797. Some of my college friends who were Mr Bingham, before mentioned; Rev Mr Jewett, of Gloucester, [Sandy Bay;] Rev Mr Tenney, of Weathersfield; Rev Thos Abbott Merrill, of Middlebury; Judge Fuller, of Augusta; Mr Farrar, of Lancaster; Judge Kingsbury, of Gardiner. I was graduated in Aug, 1801. Owing to some difficulties, I took no part in the commencement exercises.
Mr Webster on the death of his wife. Wash, Mar 31, 1828. My Dear Nephew: Like an angel of God indeed I hope she is, in purity, in happiness, & immortaility. My dear nephew, I cannot pursue these thoughts, nor turn back to see what I have written. Adieu D W

Two brothers, aged 7 & 5, the only sons of John P & Lydia Worthington, of this village, were drowned in the Chenango river, near their father's residence, on Sat. They went down to the river & stepped on some ice, & in a few moments were floating into the currents. Before assistance could be given they were precipitated under the ice & were drowned. -Binghamton Republican

Senate: 1-Ptn from Richd L Long, asking to be allowed to locate certain pre-emption claims in Florida: referred. 2-Papers relating to the claim of Bud Higdon to a patent for land, under a warrant purchased by him of the administrator of the person to whom is was issued: referred. 3-Ptn from Danl Randall, asking the passage of an act supplemental to the act passed at the last session for his relief, to grant him such further allowances as in equity he is entitled to receive. 4-Cmte on Military Affairs: adverse report on the memorial of John S Vandyke. 5-Cmte of Claims: bill for the relief of Amos B Corwine: recommended its passage. Same cmte: bill for the relief of Elias Hall, of Rutland, Vt. 6-Ptn from the widow of Francis Jacobs, who served as a volunteer in the military family of Gen Geo Washington during the whole of the Revolutionary war, asking to be allowed a pension under the act of Feb 3, 1853. 7-Ptn from Thos C Nye & Geo Chorpenning, asking that a contract may be entered into with them for carrying the mail from some point in the Mississippi valley to San Francisco, Calif. 8-Resolved: that the Sec of War be directed to communicate to the Senate a copy of the survey & report of Lt Col Graham of the harbors, etc, in Wisc, Ill, Ind, & Mich.

The subscriber offers for sale his Farm, where he now resides, near Beltsville, on the Balt branch railroad, about 12 miles from Wash City, containing 167 acres; confortable dwlg-house, containing 4 rooms, a kitchen, & other necessary out bldgs, & a pump of excellent water; also, the stock, 2 horses, 2 milch cows, 1 yearling, 4 hogs, & about 60 chickens of the Dauphin breed, will be sold. -Wm S Clary

Mrd: on Dec 23, in Wash City, by Rev G W Samson, Mr Robt L Haynes, of Lynchburg, Va, to Miss Ann M Hutcheson, of Amherst Co, Va.

Mrd: on Dec 18, at Centreville, Ia, by Rev Dr Week, Mr W Wirt Tilley, of Lawrenceburg, Ia, to Miss Sue M Widup, of the former place.

Mrd: on Dec 16, at the *Valley Farm*, PG Co, Md, by Rev Mr Chew, Mr Thos F Bowie, jr, to Eliz Margaret, eldest daughter of the late Walter B C Worthington.
+
Mrd: at the same time & by the same, Mr Robt W Harper, of Little Rock, Ark, to Laura, 2nd daughter of the last W B C Worthington.

Mrd: on Dec 18, at Grace Church, Balt, by Rev A C Coxe, Chas Marshall to Emily R, daughter of Col T P Andrews, U S Army.

Died: on Dec 23, suddenly, Saml W Handy, aged 66. His funeral will be on Dec 26 at 11 o'clock, from his late residence, 227 Pa ave.

THU DEC 25, 1856
Mrd: on Dec 23, in Wash City, by Rev G W Samson, Mr Rufus Taylor to Miss Sarah E Cocke, both of Fauquier Co, Va.

Mrd: on Dec 23, in Wash City, by Rev G W Samson, Mr Robt C Fox, of Va, to Miss Fannie, daughter of Hon Amos Kendall.

Mr McCunnell, of Sangamon Co, Ill, has the largest flock of sheep in the U S: 21,000 of the choices merinos.

Died: on Dec 23, in Wash City, Mrs Eliza James, relict of the late Wm James, sen, in her 82nd year. Her funeral will be tomorrow at 3½ o'clock, from her late residence, 460 14 st.

Rev J M Henry, of the Presbyterian church, died in Pittsylvania Co, Va, where he had a church in charge, on Friday night week. Mr Henry was a few years since located in Washington. -Alex Gaz

N Y, Dec 22. Mr Jonathan L Coddington, an old merchant, & formerly a prominent Democratic politician & postmaster of this city under Gen Jackson & Mr Van Buren, died yesterday at the age of 73 years.

House of Reps: 1-Joint resolution in relation to the accounts of Calhoun Benham & David F Douglas: referred.

Winter Resort: Brock House, at Enterprize, on the St John's river, East Florida. Maj Babcock, of the Fayette Springs Hotel, in Pa, will have charge of the house during the winter. -Jacob Brock

SAT DEC 27, 1856
Senate: 1-Memorial from Neal Smith, adm of Arthur Gizemore & John Senie, Semenole or Semoice, asking indemnification for spoliations committed by the Creek Indians during the war of 1813-14: referred to the Cmte on Indian Affairs.

Yesterday morning the dead body of a man named McGinnis, by trade a tailor, was found on the ice at the edge of **Tiber creek**, about 30 years from the bridge on Pa ave. It appeared he was much intoxicated. Deceased was originally from Balt.

Died: on Dec 25, Martha Black, aged 27 years & 9 months. Her funeral will take place from her late residence, 6th & Mass ave, on Sunday afternoon, at 2 o'clock.

Died: on Dec 26, Cmdor Bladen Dulany, U S Navy. His funeral will be this day at 2 o'clock, from his residence, Seven Bldgs.

Died: at Frankford Arsenal, Pa, Marian, infant daughter of Mary C & Capt J L Reno, U S Army, aged 6 months. [No death date given-current item.]

Circuit Court of Wash Co, D C-in Chancery. John R Woods, cmplnt, against Robt W Latham, Matthew O'Brien, Geo W Graffin, & Geo P Frick, Robt Close, & Francis Dandelit, Jas, Geo, & Lawrence Sandston, & Isaac Pollard, Edw Pittman & Robt T Baldwin, Jos & Wm C Simms, & Walter M Clarke, & John Withers, Lawence P Bayne, Geo W Carlisle Whiting, & others, dfndnts. The bill states that said cmplnt, at the Oct term, 1852, of the Circuit Court of Wash Co, D C, recovered a judgment against Richd G Brisco & Jos S Clarke, for $573.26, with interest from Mar 19, 1849, & costs; that an execution was in due time issued on said judgment, & was returned by the marshal nulla bona; that said judgment is still unpaid; that said Brisco & Clarke have no property upon which an execution can be levied, but that each of them have a large real estate which they have conveyed, so that said cmplnt is hindered, delayed, & defeated in the recovery at law of his said debt; that among the property so conveyed by said Brisco is part of lot 9 in square 382, & lot 11 in square 408, in Wash City; that said Brisco, on Feb 22, 1849, conveyed said part of lot 9 in square 382 to said Robt W Latham & others in trust, to secure a certain debt as due to said O'Brien, Graffin, & Frick, & to said Close & Dandelit; that on Apr 25, 1853, he conveyed, with other property, said part of said lot 9 in square 382, & said lot 11 in square 408, to Thos Pursell, to secure certain debts as due to said Langston & Pollard, Pittman & Baldwin, Simms & Co, Selden, Withers & Co, & said cmplnts & others; that said deed to said Thos Pursell, though apparently for the benefit of cmplnt & others named therein, was really intended to hinder & delay the cmplnt & other creditors in the recovery of their said debts, as by the terms of said deed said Pursell could not sell any part of the property therein conveyed without the consent & concurrence of said Brisco, who, though often called on by said Pursell & the cmplnts to give his consent to sell, has evaded, delayed, & objected to the same; that the aggregate value of the property conveyed in trust by said Brisco & Clarke is much greater than the amount remaining unpaid of the debts mentioned in said deeds, even if the said debts or any of them were really due & owing; that said debts, if real, have been full paid off, & that, after discharging all valid encumbrances, the said property is of the value of $15,000; that no sales have been made of the property by the trustees, but that the same have been enjoyed by said Brisco, & the rents received by him; that cmplnt is entitled to have the property sold for the payment of his debts, & the object of the bill is to have the same sold under the direction of the court to pay all the claims due thereon by said Brisco & Clarke; & it appearing to the court that the said several dfndnts above named do not reside in this District, but in parts beyond: it therefore ordered, on the motion of Wm R Woodward, of counsel for the cmplnt, that said dfndnts appear in this court on or before the 1st Monday in May next.
-Jno A Smith, clerk

Col Thos F Hust, Assist Quartermaster Genrl U S Army, died at New Orleans on Dec 22nd.

Information wanted of Danl Pettibone. When heard from last he was in Chicago, Ill, late in the fall of 1854. He was a sheet iron worker by profession. Any information of him will be thankfully received by his brother, Wm Pettibone, Wash, D C.

Miss Catherine M Sedgewick, the authoress, did not die at her home in Stockbridge last Oct; she lives, & we trust has many a year before her.
-Springfield [Mass] Republican

Wash City Ordinance: 1-Act to authorize Nicholas Acker & Geo Kolb & others to use part of the pavement opposite their dwlgs on North Capitol st. With the consent of the President, they may use 10 inches of the pavement, in addition to the 7 feet allowed by law, in square 683, on North Capitol st, to enable them to erect steps by which they may enter the main stories of their respective houses, an error of 2 feet 10 inches having been made by the assistant of the late city Surveyor in furnishing the grade before the pavement was laid down. 2-Act for the relief of Henry S Davis: to pay him $3.12½ for taxes erroneously paid by him. 3-Act for the relief of Benj F Beers: to pay him $6, for erecting a platform & railing.

Yesterday at the Va hotel, E H Cleaveland, a traveler, was found lying upon the floor of his room dead. A deep wound was found on his breast & a large bowie knife lying upon him. He came to the hotel on Sat, in company with a man who registered as W T Alexander, & expressed his intention of leaving on Monday for St Charles. The deceased was to have left yesterday for Lafayette, Indiana, where he had a wife & 2 children. He paid his bill & went to his room to prepare to leave. His companion was with him. In the pocket of his overcoat were letters directed to him by the name Wm Sharp, from his mother, Pauline Sharp. He is a young man about 20 years of age, & the 2 had been traveling together, selling a drove of mules. In the pockets of the deceased was found $500 & a gold watch. The coroner's jury rendered a verdict that he was stabbed with a knife in the hands of W T Alexander alias Wm Sharp.
-St Louis Democrat, 22nd.

MON DEC 29, 1856
Household & kitchen furniture at auction on: Jan 5, at the residence of A J Bently, 368 8th st, between K & L sts. -Jas C McGuire, auct

Mrd: on Dec 27, in Wash City, by Rev G W Samson, Mr John Douglass Birch to Miss Mary Frances Birch, both of Wash.

Mrd: on Dec 16, in Wash City, by Rev A G Carothers, John Melson, jr, of Wash, to Miss Emila F Betker, of Cincinnati, Ohio.

Died: on Dec 25, in Wash City, William Thomas, the only child of John T & Emily Chancey, aged 5 months & 12 days.

The livery stable of Thos F Stephens, of Savannah, Ga, was destroyed by fire on Dec 22, together with between 30 & 40 horses, & a number of vehicles.

Orphans Court of Wash Co, D C. In the case of John McClellan, deceased, the administrator & Court have appointed Jan 20th next, for the settlement of the personal estate of said deceased, of the assets in hand. -Ed N Roach, Reg/o wills

Criminal Court-Wash. 1-Halbrook & others tried for rioting were acquitted. 2-John Donaldson, of Gtwn, acquitted of assault & battery. 3-Mark Thornberry, charged with assault & battery, fined $5 & costs. 4-John Moriarty charged with manslaughter upon his own son, aged about 7 years: found guilty, but recommended to the mercy of the Court.

Two weeks from Calif. Richd P Hammond, ex-collector of San Francisco, has been acquitted on the charge of defrauding the U S Gov't while in office.

TUE DEC 30, 1856
Piano Forte tuning & regulating: Mr B F Dennis. Orders left at the Music Store of Richd Davis, Pa ave, between 9th & 10th sts, will be attended to promptly.

Criminal Court-Wash: Mon. 1-Jos Dorsett was convicted of an assault & battery, & fined $10. The same, with Garcia & Moore, were acquitted. 2-John Ennis, last week sentenced to 9 months in jail, was again tried yesterday, with Washington Rollins, on a charge of assault & battery with intent to kill. The jury found for the assault, without the intent to kill. Ennis was sentenced to 6 months & Rollins to 4 months' imprisonment in the jail. 3-Jos Burney, Wm Mullin, & W L Delaney were tried for a riot, on which the first was acquitted & the latter two found guilty.

Mrd: on Dec 28, by Rev Andrew G Carothers, Mr Thos A Brown to Miss Margaret A Tenley, both of Wash City.

Mrd: on Dec 28, in Wash City, by Rev S A H Marks, Sgt Major John Robinson, of the U S Marine Corps, to Miss Sarah Virginia Windfield, of PG Co, Md.

Mrd: on Dec 24, at Boydville, near Martinsburg, Va, by Rev A H H Boyd, of Winchester, Hon John P Campbell, Rep in Congress from Ky, to Miss Mary Boyd, 3rd daughter of Hon Chas Jas Faulkner.

Mrd: on Dec 23, by Rev W Krebs, Andrew Baine to Martha Rebecca White, both of Wash City.

Mrd: on Dec 29, by Rev W Krebs, Jas H Beall to Eliz A E Morgan, both of Wash City.

Died: on Dec 20, Oliver S Wade, in his 27th year. His funeral will be from the residence of his mother, on 6th, between G & H sts, today at 3 o'clock P M.

Died: on Dec 24, at the <u>Convent of the Sacred Heart</u>, near N Y, Mary M Walsh, daughter of Lt Jos C & the late Mary Y Walsh.

Margaret Wittenouer, aged 6½ years, & living with her parents, at 7th & G sts, came to a painful death by burning. Death was due to playing with friction matches. Her dress was ignited & before help could arrive, she was enveloped in flames.

WED DEC 31, 1856
Senate: 1-Ptn from Henry Hubbard, asking compensation for service as agent for the preservation of public property at the harbor of Ashtabula, Ohio. 2-Ptn from John Shaw, asking indemnity for losses sustained by him in the destruction of his property by the Menominee Indians. 3-Ptn from Jos Haynes, a soldier in the war of 1812, asking to be allowed a pension. 4-Ptn from Geo H O'Brien, asking compensation for clerical services in the ofc of the 2nd Auditor. 5-Ptn from the widow of Robt T Ridley, asking permission to institute a suit in the U S Court for the northern district of Calif, to try the validity of her title to a certain tract of land. 6-Ptn from Thos Jenkins, asking to be allowed arrears of pension. 7-Ptn from David M Dryden, asking an appropriation for the improvement of the navigation of the falls of the Ohio river, according to a plan proposed by himself.

N Y, Dec 30. The ship **John Garrow**, from Savannah for Liverpool, foundered when 6 days out. Her crew & passengers wer brought here today.

Steamboat for sale. The owners of the steam boat **Augusta**, lately running between Port Walthall & Norfolk, Va, offer the boat & her furniture for sale at a low price; length 173 feet; breadth of beam [exclusive of guards] 19 feet 6 inches; was built in N Y in 1838. -Thos Dodamead, Supt Richmond & Petersburg R R.

Mrd: on Dec 29, in Wash City, by Rev Robt R S Hough, Mr Isaac C Hoeflick to Miss Rosina Barker, both of Richmond, Va.

Died: on Dec 30, in Wash City, David Koones, aged 72 years. His funeral will take place from his late residence, 450 D st, between 2nd & 3rd sts, on Jan 1, at 10 o'clock A M.

Died: on Dec 28, in Wash City, Mrs Sarah E Steuart, aged 26 years. Her funeral will be from her late residence, N st, between 14th & 15th sts, this morning at 10 o'clock.

Died: on Dec 30, in Wash City, at the Nat'l Hotel, Margaretta Hanson, infant daughter of Col Jas Reily, of Texas. Her funeral is this morning at 10 o'clock.

Died: on Dec 30, in Wash City, after a short & painful illness, James Buchanan, aged 6 months & 21 days, only son of David & Christiana Hines. His funeral will be tomorrow at 2 o'clock, from the residence of his parents, Pa ave & 20th st, 1st Ward.

Died: on Dec 29, in Wash City, Margaret, daughter of the late Alex'r & C Wittenaur, in her 7th year. Her funeral will take place this morning at 10 o'clock, from the residence of her mother, 7th & G sts.

Died: on Dec 30, in Phil, Ann Ingersoll Meigs, daughter of Chas J Ingersoll, & wife of John Forsyth Meigs.

Died: on Dec 26, in Phil, of scarlet fever, Guy Grayson Carleton, aged 3 years, 1 month & 9 days. He was the youngest son of Maj Jas Henry Carleton, U S A, & Sophia Wolfe Carleton.

Orphans Court of Wash Co, D C. Letters of administration on the personal estate of Verial Luce, late of Wash Co, deceased. -Charlotte Luce, admx

Fred'k Bowers, a young Frenchman, aged 21 years, was noticed the other day to take a letter from the St Louis post ofc, with which he walked off reading as we went. He was soon observed to be weeping, & finally tore the letter into fragments, took a pistol from his pocket, & shot himself dead.

Excessive smoking-the last number of the N Y Medical Gazette contains an article on the ill effects produced by the excessive smoking of tobacco.

A

A True wife, 28
Aaron, 348
Abbot, 305
Abbott, 90, 97, 163, 235, 296, 434
Abercrombie, 154
Abert, 328, 395
Abrahams, 373
Aby, 272
Academy of the Visitation, 63
Accardi, 261, 301, 307, 311, 316
Acker, 74, 96, 394, 401, 408, 438
Ackroyds, 266
Activity, 262
Acton, 304
Adams, 3, 12, 57, 59, 70, 82, 96, 97, 109, 155, 156, 197, 270, 271, 275, 282, 295, 304, 305, 306, 319, 323, 329, 354, 364, 370, 388, 428
Addington, 54
Addison, 13, 135, 156, 191, 215, 246, 322, 379, 409
Adington, 16
Adler, 99, 321
Adolphus the Great, 3
Ager, 287
Agg, 164
Agnew, 107
Agustofer, 61
Ahorn, 364
Ahrens, 144, 359
Aigler, 286
Aiken, 80
Aimun, 6
Ainsworth, 345
Alamo, 406
Albemarle Estate, 290
Alberti, 276
Albertson, 329
Albright, 30, 32, 211
Albriton, 289
Albritton, 97, 113, 136, 287
Alden, 272, 293
Alderson, 269
Aldorffer, 34
Aldrich, 281, 338
Aldroff, 17
Alexander, 47, 144, 149, 226, 235, 245, 282, 386, 422, 438
Alexander II, 346
Alexandria, 106, 417
Alig, 54, 139, 195
Allcock, 267
Allen, 36, 51, 54, 58, 62, 97, 118, 119, 131, 140, 159, 172, 173, 174, 182, 186, 208, 222, 260, 264, 266, 327, 345, 352, 354, 401, 428, 431
Allison, 269, 351
Allman, 110
Allmand, 273
Allnutt, 94
Allston, 426
Alnutt, 357
Altebury, 295
Altenburg, 287, 289
Alvarado, 85, 340
Alvarenga, 206
Alvord, 66, 424
Amaral, 75
Ambler, 363
Ames, 353
Ammen, 308
Andel, 388
Anderson, 3, 26, 38, 66, 82, 91, 96, 187, 214, 217, 232, 256, 290, 298, 313, 340, 365, 422
Anderton, 5
Andrew, 230, 318
Andrews, 18, 20, 54, 143, 146, 166, 431, 435
Andross, 317
Angney, 171
Angus, 148, 313, 429, 430

Anker, 137
Anneville, 76
Annis, 388
Anslem, 2
Anstill, 429
Apperson, 154
Appich, 392
Applebee, 227
Appleby, 255
Appleton, 99, 142
Aqueduct, 246
Archambeau, 381
Archer, 206, 265, 305, 324, 352, 430
Ardmillan, 15
Arguello, 130, 220, 242
Argyle Plantation, 28
Armbruster, 57
Armistead, 147, 197, 226
Armstrong, 9, 71, 78, 83, 137, 145, 150, 181, 193, 278, 296, 388, 399
Arnold, 20, 93, 163, 172, 173, 284, 322, 386
Arrison, 269, 351
Arthur, 13, 92, 205
Artic Explorer, 424
Ash, 61
Ashby, 9
Ashcraft, 373
Ashdown, 305
Ashe, 281, 323, 386
Ashford, 319
Ashland, 342
Ashland Farm, 342
Astor, 35
Atchison, 280
Atkins, 74, 170
Atkinson, 95, 112, 332, 357
AtLee, 355
Atocha, 416
Atwater, 48
Atwell, 380
Atwood, 345
Audley tract, 362

Audubon, 285
Aueroches, 187
August, 417
Augusterfer, 386
Auld, 181
Ault, 146
Austell, 307
Austin, 63, 397, 408
Averill, 298
Avery, 13, 89, 399
Avet, 315
Ayllon, 380
Ayre, 338
Ayton, 403

B

Babbin, 314
Babbitt, 343, 381
Babcock, 88, 115, 168, 205, 411, 436
Babina Plantation, 292
Bache, 156, 234
Bacheler, 356
Bacon, 95, 133, 254
Baden, 58, 61, 77, 146, 263, 319, 371
Badger, 273
Bagby, 234, 417
Baggott, 381, 395
Bagley, 261, 262, 284
Bagwell, 17
Bailey, 101, 142, 223, 226, 239, 292, 293, 297
Baily, 133, 137, 167
Bain, 26
Bainbridge, 226
Baine, 439
Baird, 145, 238, 267, 295, 319, 402, 412
Bakefish, 21
Baker, 17, 56, 100, 116, 138, 142, 143, 147, 185, 190, 196, 201, 206, 243, 273, 277, 305, 310, 323, 369, 415
Bakewell, 238

Balderston, 147
Baldwin, 8, 31, 134, 178, 190, 242, 294, 322, 437
Balentine, 5
Balestine, 249
Ball, 6, 28, 54, 133, 143, 331, 357, 397, 422
Ballard, 58, 129, 186, 266
Balmain, 156
Balsley, 105
Baltimore, 235
Baltzell, 277
Baltzer, 288
Bancroft, 395
Bangs, 73, 260
Bankhead, 50, 156, 385
Banks, 39, 143, 167, 371
Bannister, 35
Banyer, 396, 408
Baptista, 369
Barbarin, 113, 136, 259
Barber, 220
Barbour, 48, 183
Barboza, 187
Barclay, 140
Barcroft, 121
Bargy, 266
Barker, 119, 158, 227, 285, 296, 330, 440
Barkman, 174
Barloza, 75
Barnaby, 191
Barnaby Mansion House, 191
Barnaclo, 97
Barnard, 21, 191, 199, 262, 264, 274, 282, 338, 361
Barnes, 12, 58, 63, 80, 407
Barney, 56, 416, 423
Barnum, 57, 66, 102, 144
Barnun, 57
barque **Amazon**, 92
barque **Amelia**, 38, 92
barque **Archibald Gracie**, 227

barque **David Nickels**, 81
barque **Elise**, 390
barque **Gerhard**, 217
barque **Maria**, 151, 367
barque **Meridian**, 217
barque **Mississippi**, 217
barque **St Harlampy**, 43
Barr, 235
Barrand, 272
Barrett, 145, 272, 408
Barriger, 226
Barrington, 45
Barron, 73, 271
Barrows, 16
Barry, 88, 106, 227
Barth, 146
Barthlow, 55
Bartlett, 13, 161, 264, 270, 303
Bartolini, 71
Barton, 88, 354
Bartos, 75
Bassett, 12, 202, 252, 273, 380
Bate, 86
Batemen, 28
Batenahl, 21
Bates, 16, 110, 144, 170, 249, 304, 340, 349, 368, 396, 406
Baxter, 282
Bayard, 226, 267, 402, 424
Baylis, 270
Bayliss, 151, 406
Bayly, 21, 95, 123, 223, 236, 271
Bayly's Cross Roads, 21, 62
Bayne, 36, 222, 334, 437
Beach, 21, 89, 206, 300
Beacham, 137, 145
Beale, 306
Beall, 13, 30, 52, 73, 74, 76, 95, 116, 126, 223, 257, 287, 381, 397, 406, 440
Beam, 145
Beam Lot, 269
Beaman, 373

Bean, 107, 266, 317, 354
Beard, 402
Beardsley, 290, 298
Beattie, 366
Beatty, 146, 154, 176, 314
Beaugrand, 133, 411
Bechtel, 146
Beck, 17, 92
Beckert, 248
Becket, 259
Beckham, 258
Beckwith, 132, 243, 253
Beckwourth, 281
Bedford, 231
Bedinger, 137
Beebee, 381
Beechwood, 342
Beeman, 106
Beers, 54, 169, 276, 277, 394, 429, 438
Beeson, 111
Behavior Book, 75
Bein, 386
Beirnheim, 248
Belden, 52, 236
Belger, 151, 260, 422
Belknap, 273, 285
Bell, 6, 54, 61, 110, 113, 132, 133, 150, 151, 154, 174, 188, 225, 248, 251, 294, 302, 303, 320, 340, 369, 388, 410
Bellinger, 326
Bellona Arsenal, 233, 331, 430
Belt, 43
Belton, 101
Belvin, 346
Bendal, 208
Bender, 129, 200, 266
Benedict, 141
Benett, 98
Benge, 23, 133
Benham, 273, 323, 436
Benjamin, 145

Benlomond, 300
Bennet, 54
Bennett, 16, 18, 43, 44, 91, 133, 142, 146, 226, 272, 295, 377, 410, 417
Benson, 173, 250
Benteen, 145
Bently, 69, 438
Benton, 37, 270
Berard, 314
Berault, 169
Berger, 388
Bergman, 256
Berkeley Springs, 360
Berlin Female Seminary, 92
Berreditt, 314
Berrett, 125
Berridge, 48
Berrien, 2, 3, 25, 272
Berry, 17, 23, 58, 73, 74, 108, 135, 165, 178, 191, 192, 215, 249, 267, 309, 311, 325, 332, 343, 360, 365, 382, 386, 402, 434
Berryman, 202
Besancon, 192
Beth, 376
Betker, 438
Bettern, 165
Beuford, 300
Beuge, 63
Beverley, 257
Bevington, 39
Bevins, 26
Beyer, 347
Bibb, 259
Bibby, 373
Bickford, 245
Bidamon, 159, 168, 171, 180, 411
Biddle, 234, 306
Bien, 61
Bier, 273
Bierbower, 357
Bigelow, 57, 422
Biggs, 226, 295

Bigler, 325
Billing, 304
Bindon, 296
Bingham, 119, 416, 434
Binney, 165
Birch, 73, 137, 178, 179, 183, 254, 319, 386, 421, 438
Birchett, 277, 290
Birckhead, 320
Bird, 45, 116, 132, 143, 222, 302, 389, 429
Birnie, 132
Birth, 178, 320
Birth-place of Geo Washington, 53
Biscoe, 8, 9, 368
Bishel, 314
Bishop, 15, 179, 254
Bissell, 64
Bisselle, 258
Bittinger, 44, 271
Bixler, 16
Bizen, 65
Black, 133, 148, 413, 436
Blackford, 30, 76, 339
Blackledge, 405
Blackstone, 35
Blackwell, 31
Blades, 182
Blagden, 7, 127, 180, 322
Blain, 154
Blair, 104, 113
Blaisdell, 12
Blake, 4, 40, 271, 272, 273, 305, 378, 410, 416
Blakely Grove, 305
Blakemore, 19
Blanchard, 22, 71, 266, 376
Blanche, 170
Blanding, 179
Blasengame, 164
Blight, 206
Bliss, 164
Bloodygood, 134

Blount, 267, 309, 329
Blox, 380
Bloxam, 35
Blue, 288
Blue Plains, 260
Blungluff, 356
Blunt, 200, 218
Bly, 344
Blythe, 340
Boak, 379
Board, 234
Boarman, 23, 259
boat **Anna Maria**, 328
boat **Thomas Collyer**, 189
Bodine, 21
Bodisco, 117, 127, 370, 375
Boerum, 95
Bogardus, 401
Bogert, 12
Bogget, 417
Boggs, 272
Bogy, 418
Bohennon, 346
Bohlayer, 61, 386
Bohrer, 80, 204, 406
Boileau, 295
Bolling, 388
Bolton, 126
Boltzell, 420
Bond, 6, 100, 141, 142, 301, 318, 388, 421
Bonner, 258, 281
Bonney, 145, 286
Boomer, 301
Boon, 254
Boone, 110, 380, 387
Booth, 421
Borcke, 66
Borden, 165
Bordis, 314
Borham, 406
Boscom, 80
Bose, 355

446

Boss, 97, 167, 174, 319, 325, 330, 389, 424
Bosse, 61, 400
Bosworth, 4
Boteler, 10, 14, 42, 65, 108, 140, 157, 182, 191, 215, 230, 243, 407, 421, 426
Botelor, 401
Botts, 355, 371
Boudreau, 315
Boughter, 180
Bouic, 357
Boultbee, 288
Bounds, 184
Bouton, 277
Bouttbon, 314
Boutwell, 60
Bowden, 37
Bowen, 47, 48, 80, 87, 158, 167, 249, 267, 273, 309, 320, 337, 373
Bowens, 5
Bower, 170
Bowers, 18, 441
Bowie, 40, 126, 139, 147, 235, 237, 259, 281, 328, 357, 406, 435
Bowman, 111, 198, 372
Bowne, 64, 307
Bowyer, 99
Boyard, 60
Boyce, 14, 329
Boyd, 90, 105, 121, 146, 147, 150, 339, 357, 439
Boyer, 391
Boyle, 11, 41, 107, 127, 195, 349, 352, 369, 373, 375
Boyne, 253
Brace, 262, 284, 320, 322
Bracket, 434
Bradford, 124, 181, 184, 272, 279, 354
Bradley, 17, 115, 139, 140, 179, 208, 223, 235, 241, 242, 253, 254, 258,
286, 319, 349, 356, 391, 399, 400, 411, 417
Brady, 44, 80, 88, 166, 178, 191, 243, 264, 274
Braham, 83
Braiden, 341, 379
Brainard, 91
Braine, 6, 273
Branch, 6
Brand, 237
Brann, 233
Brant, 237
Brashear, 314
Braum, 321
Braun, 117
Brauns, 147
Brawner, 338
Breckenridge, 394
Breckinridge, 188
Breese, 273
Breeze, 356
Brennan, 374
Brent, 44, 117, 126, 151, 170, 201, 247, 272, 276, 279
Brenton, 144
Brereton, 97, 118
Bresente, 345
Brett, 213
Brewer, 5, 94, 117, 209, 254
Briceland, 369
Bride's row, 91
Bridges, 251
Bridgett, 254
Briding, 146
Briebach, 426
brig **Arctic**, 49, 63, 287, 300
brig **Boxer**, 364
brig **Constante**, 130
brig **Creole**, 125
brig **General Armstrong**, 103
brig **Gil Blas**, 242
brig **Glencoe**, 388
brig **Perry**, 75

brig **Victor of the Wave**, 213
brig **Washington**, 156
brig **Windward**, 364
Brigantine House, 60
Briggs, 21, 46, 52, 319
Brigham, 397
Bright, 110, 187, 379
Brisbach, 426
Brisco, 437
Briscoe, 258
Brittingham, 5
Broadwell, 12
Brochieri, 205
Brock, 253, 436
Brockenbrough, 96
Broderick, 254
Brodhead, 275
Brodie, 173
Bromwell, 201
Bronaugh, 40, 44, 267
Bronbert, 134
Bronson, 200, 232, 277
Brook, 30
Brooke, 31, 77, 85, 86, 106, 206, 231, 251, 272
Brooke Hall Female Academy, 210
Brooker, 255
Brooks, 75, 98, 143, 174, 198, 240, 334, 335, 377, 390, 401, 407, 418
Broughton, 5, 8, 297
Brouten, 311
Broutin, 287, 289, 294
Brown, 10, 15, 29, 31, 36, 42, 45, 50, 79, 80, 82, 97, 106, 116, 127, 133, 142, 144, 155, 162, 173, 174, 195, 220, 228, 238, 244, 247, 277, 286, 305, 310, 312, 315, 316, 326, 330, 331, 333, 338, 340, 346, 347, 353, 355, 372, 377, 406, 407, 420, 421, 439
Browne, 62, 131, 222, 352
Brownell, 11, 12, 219
Browning, 12, 148, 151, 188, 385

Brownlee, 248
Bruce, 4, 143, 260, 267, 340
Bruff, 71
Brumidi, 201
Brune, 146, 355
Brunell, 8
Brunet, 190
Brunett, 25, 254
Brunner, 236, 237
Bryan, 80, 95, 120, 178, 310, 340, 393, 396, 422
Bryant, 314
Bryer, 379
Bryson, 235
Buchanan, 41, 116, 215, 271, 276, 397, 403, 441
Buchly, 163
Buck, 405
Buck Lodge, 177
Buckery, 310
Buckey, 393, 395
Buckingham, 151
Buckland, 296
Buckler, 144
Buckley, 197, 204
Buckminster, 434
Buckner, 272
Budd, 421
Budden, 376
Budlong, 82
Buell, 216
Buellerdeick, 24
Buford, 110, 132, 217
Bulger, 206, 261, 262, 284
Bullard, 380
Buller, 372
Bullitt, 78
Bullock, 4, 323
Bulwer, 49
Bunting, 106
Burch, 56, 118
Burche, 232, 371
Burchell, 286

Burck, 348
Burdell, 205
Burdine, 318
Burgess, 9, 163, 199, 225, 367, 432
Burgher, 267
Burgoyne, 7
Burham, 192
Burke, 101, 262, 266, 324, 399, 425, 427
Burkhalter, 63, 133
Burks, 168
Burlingame, 289
Burnap, 423
Burnet, 97
Burnett, 422
Burney, 69, 164, 439
Burnham, 356
Burns, 2, 39, 45, 145, 274, 284, 314, 348, 371, 406, 421
Burr, 97, 307, 396
Burrall, 169
Burroughs, 364
Burrows, 11, 14, 25, 54, 177
Burt, 354
Burton, 168
Burwell, 113, 282
Busey, 106, 172
Bush, 369, 402
Bushell, 180
Busher, 97
Bushy, 218
Busick, 262
Buthmann, 418
Butler, 11, 29, 55, 61, 96, 110, 162, 165, 171, 187, 195, 198, 216, 257, 270, 279, 350, 352
Butt, 2, 80, 112, 143, 144, 394
Buzby, 96
Byers, 145
Byford, 23
Byington, 46, 93
Byrd, 33, 98, 142, 167, 196
Byrne, 195, 313, 395
Byrnes, 379
Byson, 223

C

Cabel, 46
Cabell, 240
Cabet, 389
Cabot, 58
Caffrey, 382
Cain, 329
Caldwell, 105, 167, 292
Calhoun, 157, 323, 361, 428
Callaghan, 380
Callahan, 155, 164
Callan, 81, 118, 124, 129, 245, 259, 285, 302, 334, 359, 393, 406
Callaway, 96
Callihan, 338
Callis, 191, 215
Calloway, 421
Calna-, 321
Calvary Cemetery, 399
Calvert, 43, 114, 268, 319
Calvin, 213
Calwell, 65, 147
Cameron, 73, 407
Camp, 277, 412
Camp Cooper, 327
Camp Holly, 61
Campau, 109
Campbell, 11, 12, 26, 27, 28, 75, 84, 93, 113, 163, 165, 181, 207, 238, 264, 265, 269, 270, 274, 279, 301, 340, 352, 392, 406, 416, 429, 439
canal boat **Anna Woodward**, 42
Canfield, 47, 144
Cannick, 306
Cannon, 135, 141, 142, 151, 259, 302, 386
Cantine, 400
Caperton, 128, 207, 348
Car, 262, 284
Cardwell, 80

Carey, 133, 186
Carl, 283
Carleton, 93, 441
Carlisle, 235, 399
Carlos, 312
Carlton, 148, 255
Carmady, 283, 302
Carman, 99, 133, 146
Carnes, 354
Carney, 264
Carother, 115
Carothers, 20, 86, 166, 193, 232, 236, 269, 287, 383, 430, 438, 439
Carpenter, 4, 73
Carr, 19, 178, 239, 261, 272, 374, 388, 428
Carrico, 90
Carrigan, 388
Carrillo, 142
Carrin, 188
Carrington, 130, 134, 187
Carriss, 144
Carroll, 101, 128, 144, 145, 226, 345, 350, 351, 357, 418, 433
Carson, 163
Carteer, 48
Carter, 32, 86, 127, 141, 180, 190, 238, 272, 273, 297, 317, 392, 426
Cartner, 204
Carusi, 122, 219
Cary, 109, 184, 266, 414
Casaris, 58
Case, 272
Casey, 173, 207, 219, 239, 262, 284, 348, 353
Cashions, 414
Casler, 12
Casparis, 181, 386
Cass, 44, 250, 434
Cassady, 105, 267, 422
Cassell, 5, 424
Casselly, 105
Castle, 117

Castro, 150
Cathcart, 291
Catlett, 394
Caton, 47, 433
Cator, 145
Catron, 406
Catts, 36
Causey, 398
Causten, 247, 280, 352, 358
Cavan, 121, 141, 151
Caves, 345
Cawthorn, 23
Cazelar, 200
Cecilius Calvert, 378
Cedar Hill, 203
Celler, 54
Ceran, 75
Cerre, 205, 268, 422
Cesanzon, 12
Cezar, 187
Chabere, 319
Chaffee, 73, 296, 298
Chalybeate Springs, 196
Chamberlin, 143
Chambers, 5, 34, 340
Champion, 59
Chancey, 439
Chandler, 208, 273
Channing, 50
Chapdelaine, 399
Chapin, 95, 271
Chapman, 168, 273, 340, 421
Chappel, 87
Charlant, 296
Charles II, 378
Charless, 340
Charlesworth, 48
Charrinaud, 48
Charter Oak, 317
Chase, 29, 56, 174, 190, 256, 301, 307, 311, 415
Chatard, 244, 272
Chauncey, 79, 155

Chauvenot, 291
Cheeseboro, 35
Cheevers, 17
Chegary, 169
Chellis, 12
Cheney, 333
Cherry, 1, 170, 291, 292
Chesapeake Bay, 268
Chesborough, 206
Chevallie, 138
Chevis, 424
Chew, 435
Chickering, 219
Childress, 155
Childrey, 112
Childs, 3, 21, 132, 232
Chillon Castle Manor Farm, 246
Chillum Castle, 215
Chilton, 212, 235, 291, 407
China, 396
Chinn, 54, 333
Chipman, 424
Chisholm, 224
Chisom, 236
Chorpenning, 435
Choules, 10
Chowning, 397
Christian, 75, 220
Christian VIII, 233
Chubb, 25, 107, 114, 118, 121, 182, 216, 371, 414
Chumascero, 232
Church, 81, 178
Churchill, 242, 244, 274, 283, 391, 422
Cilley, 267, 273
Clagett, 13, 28, 142, 243, 415, 417
Claiborne, 26, 299
Clampitt, 142
Clapp, 289
Clappsaddle, 325
Clare, 172, 348
Clarendon, 17

Clarens, 78
Clark, 39, 80, 116, 121, 128, 133, 154, 155, 171, 235, 257, 264, 266, 271, 274, 291, 294, 318, 333, 340, 345, 369, 373, 385, 406
Clarke, 9, 27, 122, 143, 211, 218, 236, 241, 242, 290, 304, 308, 326, 333, 334, 342, 358, 380, 387, 397, 420, 426, 428, 437
Clarkson, 195, 212
Clarkston, 298
Clarvoe, 347
Clary, 426, 435
Claxton, 47, 389, 391, 416, 432
Clay, 116, 141, 154, 155, 160, 200, 238, 258, 267, 333
Clayton, 316, 383, 398
Cleary, 215, 245
Cleaveland, 438
Cleghorn, 193
Clemens, 134
Clements, 33, 37, 61, 70, 103, 258, 259, 302, 386
Cleopatra, 156
Clephane, 327
Cleveland, 21, 62
Clifton, 321
Cline, 94, 146
Cline's Mill, 17
Clinton, 156, 195
Clisk, 231
Close, 296, 437
Cloud, 121
Clough, 102, 109
Clowes, 315
Cloyes, 135
Clubb, 89
Clutes, 413
Clutter, 43
Clymer, 181
Coad, 258
Coale, 144
Cobb, 170, 267, 301, 306, 311, 316

Cobham, 22
Cochran, 47, 154, 228, 252, 254, 430
Cocke, 162, 287, 436
Cockrell, 433
Coddington, 109, 436
Codrick, 381, 408
Coffroth, 15
Coggeshall, 14, 175
Cogswell, 237
Cohen, 120, 144, 254
Coke, 113, 128
Cokely, 274
Colburn, 178
Colby, 53, 141
Colclaser, 201
Cole, 6, 144, 146, 258, 259, 361, 433
Colebrook, 388
Colegate, 285
Coleman, 339, 340
Colfax, 343
Collier, 200, 288, 309, 331
Collingwood, 83, 228
Collins, 29, 49, 146, 154, 221, 224, 348
Colonization Society, 373
Colston, 76, 145
Colt, 219, 254, 402, 404
Coltman, 131, 385
Columbia Foundry, 26
Columbia Mills, 14
Columbus, 71
Colvin, 264, 275
Combs, 1, 8, 19, 51, 73, 119, 389
Comegys, 398
Comly, 382, 392
Commerford, 266
Como, 314, 315
Compton, 205, 378
Comstock, 142, 258, 354
Congdon, 274
Congress Cemetery, 138, 155
Congressional Cemetery, 155
Coningham, 149

Conkling, 111
Conlin, 274
Conly, 414
Connan, 166
Connecticut, 378
Connelly, 21, 149, 200, 256
Conner, 90, 106, 139, 161, 180, 431
Connolly, 109, 265, 306, 311, 316
Connoly, 299
Connor, 403
Conolly, 252
Conover, 19, 272
Conrad, 19, 352
Constable, 146
Constantine, 166
Contee, 271
Convent of the Sacred Heart, 440
Convent of the Visitation, 369
Conway, 91
Coo, 143, 146
Coogan, 21
Cook, 12, 13, 81, 119, 135, 155, 197, 204, 214, 227, 292, 301, 309, 389, 412
Cooke, 98, 421
Cooledge, 259
Coomb, 203
Coombe, 431
Coombs, 80, 106
Cooney, 239
Cooper, 5, 31, 69, 86, 105, 216, 301, 340, 355, 369
Coover, 143
Cooziere, 314
Cope, 18, 181
Cora, 219, 239, 262, 284
Corbin, 119, 322
Corby, 62
Corcoran, 56, 72, 114, 140, 149, 295, 310, 338, 398
Corcosa, 48
Cordell, 354
Core, 274

Corlin, 19
Cornelius, 205
Cornell, 146
Cornoyer, 54
Cornwell, 273
Corrie, 340
Corrigan, 94, 277
Corse, 78
Corson, 279, 376
Corwin, 25
Corwine, 309, 418, 435
Coryell, 347
Cosgrove, 348, 429
Coskery, 350
Costello, 158
Costigan, 184, 355
Cottle, 281
Cotton, 60, 348
Couch, 102, 269
Coues, 134
Coulter, 146
Coumbs, 290
Countess Danner, 233
Countryman, 387
Courcier, 109
Courtney, 147, 355
Covens, 246
Cover, 234
Coward, 119
Cowdy, 209
Cowen, 47
Cowling, 183
Cox, 30, 43, 50, 118, 123, 150, 176, 192, 221, 277, 278, 328, 348, 372, 374, 387
Cox's Row, 321
Coxe, 8, 385, 435
Coyle, 196, 240
Cozens, 286, 311
Cozzens, 278, 281, 413
Crabb, 273
Crabbe, 181
Crabtree, 16, 54

Cradlebaughs, 387
Cragen, 304
Craig, 233, 267, 331
Craighill, 362
Crain, 318, 396
Cramphin, 177
Crampton, 210
Cranch, 336
Crandall, 171, 200, 267
Crandell, 12
Crane, 8, 145, 233, 338, 363
Crawford, 29, 73, 125, 146, 168, 171, 183, 190, 204, 289, 401
Crawley, 96
Crease, 26
Crebbs, 391
Creurd, 417
Crightwell, 12
Crise, 145
Crittenden, 12, 301, 323
Crocker, 44
Crockett, 105, 406
Crogan, 223
Croggan, 137, 239
Croggin, 293, 297
Cromwell, 425
Cronan, 206
Crook, 137, 356
Cropley, 47, 73
Crosby, 110, 425
Cross, 239, 423, 427
Crossfield, 290
Croswell, 66
Crouch, 315
Crouse, 259
Crow, 16, 54
Crowe, 261, 262, 284
Crowell, 57
Crowley, 142, 206, 357
Crown, 20, 297
Cruikshank, 78, 177
Cruit, 61, 331, 372, 374, 407, 427, 429

Cruitt, 386
Crump, 40
Crutchett, 207, 421
Cruz, 75, 187
Cubitt, 116
Cuddy, 199
Culgers, 239
Cullen, 221, 227
Culverwell, 30, 48
Cumback, 410
Cummings, 21, 212, 273
Cummins, 55, 67, 98, 127, 178, 182, 190, 192, 194, 204, 213, 227, 306, 361, 369, 373, 389, 403
Cumminsky, 251
Cunningham, 47, 48, 70, 113, 131, 151, 260, 262, 267, 271, 284, 287, 298, 309, 367, 429
Curlett, 142, 143
Curran, 234, 265, 267
Curry, 62, 64, 307, 318
Curson, 385
Curtain, 190
Curtin, 283, 302
Curtis, 80, 240, 291, 327, 333, 345, 406
Cushing, 142, 147
Cushings, 142
Cushman, 147
Cusick, 261, 284, 338
Custis, 8
Custner, 252
Cutler, 219
Cutter, 48
cutter **Hamilton**, 361
cutter **Jefferson Davis**, 60
Cutting, 344
Cutts, 264, 390, 395
Cweos, 318

D

D'Orsay, 427
Daggy, 10
Dahlgren, 272
Daiger, 357
Daily, 271
Dainese, 296
Daisey, 252
Dale, 429
Dalhosie, 206
Dallam, 355
Dallas, 41, 234, 238, 273
Dallman, 180
Daly, 373
Dameron, 323
Dan, 12
Dana, 6, 141
Danby, 274
Dandelet, 142
Dandelion Coffee, 25
Dandelit, 437
Danels, 273
Danforth, 2
Daniel, 406
Dansay, 364
Dant, 375
Dany, 424
Darien, 204
Darling, 429
Darne, 368
Darnes, 118
Darrell, 77
Dart, 50, 66, 168, 278, 316
Dashields, 392
Dashiell, 10, 11, 136, 161, 390
Dashiells, 80
Daughters of Charity, 370
Daughtrey, 5
Davenport, 95, 354
David Crockett, 105
Davidge, 188, 235, 335, 382
Davidsohn, 143
Davidson, 8, 45, 109, 118, 119, 124, 158, 161, 184, 190, 273, 309, 359, 364, 378
Davies, 51

Davis, 12, 14, 16, 21, 27, 39, 47, 64, 76, 79, 97, 99, 104, 115, 127, 133, 184, 203, 214, 228, 233, 250, 258, 267, 270, 273, 291, 315, 319, 342, 355, 378, 382, 417, 418, 438, 439
Davison, 139, 145, 266, 395
Davy, 257
Daw, 387
Dawden, 76
Dawes, 120, 121
Dawson, 74, 163, 175, 266, 320, 328, 351, 421
Day, 5, 16, 343
Dayton, 248, 427, 429
de Ausoategui, 154
de Ayala, 342
de Berg, 346
de Boye, 328
De Bree, 237, 273
De Buys, 206, 420
De Camp, 88, 272
de Falco, 425
De Forrest, 1, 291
De Haven, 252, 273, 275
De Krafft, 273
de la Roche, 9
de La Roche, 423
de Moisille, 141
De Sabila, 165
De Saules, 216
de Silver, 90
de Sola, 130
De Stoeckl, 8
De Venois, 254
de Weissenfels, 138
de Wiessenfels, 17
Dea, 338
Deakins, 176
Deale, 106, 194, 233, 271, 325, 369, 381, 431
Dean, 7, 55, 134, 323, 356
Deardorff, 111
Dearing, 409, 416

Deas, 12, 219, 382
Deasy, 50
Deaver, 323
Debeet, 145
Decatur, 169, 204, 237, 238, 244, 255, 256, 288, 309
Degge, 204
DeHart, 226
DeKraft, 56
Delaigle, 259
Delaney, 227, 262, 439
Delaroche, 414
Delascule, 109
Delavo, 383
Delina, 311
Delino, 287, 289, 294
Dellinger, 366
Delso, 109
Demain, 293
Demaine, 137, 188, 297
DeMaine, 6
Dement, 196, 346
Demerest, 324
Denham, 87
Denin, 49
Denison, 18
Denman, 76, 301
Dennesson, 47
Dennis, 192, 439
Dennison, 18
Denniston, 272
Denny, 181
Densmore, 348
Dent, 40, 109, 433
Denver, 429
Derby, 417
Derrick, 151, 180, 202, 288
Derringer, 377
Detweiler, 47
Devault, 354
Devecmon, 209
Devers, 41
Devine, 79, 210

Devlin, 80, 106, 132, 274
Devries, 355
DeWitt, 376
Dey, 207, 381
Dick, 82, 265, 327, 410, 427, 429
Dickerson, 24, 281
Dickins, 123, 190, 256
Dickinson, 88, 315, 322, 355
Dickson, 299, 306, 311, 316, 322, 380
Diffenderfer, 12
Digges, 403, 423
Diggs, 215, 375, 377
Dillaye, 286
Dillon, 274, 288
Diman, 19
Dimick, 184
Dinge, 253
Dingel, 320
Dinkle, 34
Disasters to steamers, 414
Disharoon, 266, 277
Ditty, 376
Divernois, 379
Dix, 78, 144
Dixon, 154, 338, 399
Dobbin, 31, 325
Dobbins, 301
Dodamead, 440
Dodd, 410
Dodds, 90
Dodge, 14, 73, 145, 209, 225, 243, 359
Dodson, 66, 93, 141, 410
Dogan, 264
Doggett, 194
Doguereau, 370
Doherty, 50
Doland, 133, 151, 267
Dolly, 106
Donaldson, 67, 144, 189, 217, 263, 320, 392, 433, 439
Donavan, 190
Done, 284

Donelan, 3, 37, 96, 195, 348, 375
Donelly, 303
Donelson, 276, 367
Donin, 183
Donn, 64
Donoho, 131
Donohoo, 51, 80, 406
Donohue, 96, 386
Donovan, 320
Dooley, 13, 258
Doolittle, 353
Dooly, 66
Dorizano, 48
Dornin, 19, 76, 228, 271, 354
Doroty, 165
Dorr, 91
Dorsett, 48, 343, 439
Dorsey, 128, 146, 176, 259, 276, 320, 378, 423
Dortie, 340
Doty, 411
Dougal, 216
Dougherty, 83, 257, 408
Doughty, 278, 405
Douglas, 236, 395, 436
Douglass, 85, 200
Dousman, 267, 287, 289, 300, 308
Dove, 80, 95, 197, 272, 280, 283, 406
Dow, 156
Dowdale, 141
Dowling, 47, 127, 172, 310, 353
Downes, 408
Downey, 217
Downing, 290, 299, 302, 342
Downs, 182
Doyle, 6, 19, 290
Dr of Med-ladies, 213
Drake, 16
Drane, 3
Draper, 40, 43
Draub, 278
Dresden, 357
Drinker, 344

Drinkwater, 119, 190, 281, 282, 286
Driscoll, 290, 369
Driskill, 21
Drummond, 369
Drury, 288, 319
Dryden, 104, 143, 440
Du Pont, 271
Duane, 239, 261, 262, 284
Dubamel, 61
Dubois, 165, 253, 386
Duchess of Hamilton, 249
Duckett, 55
Duckworth, 432
Duddington, 151
Dudley, 154, 174, 317
Dudson, 274
Duer, 143
Duffey's Cottage, 295
Duffield, 245
Dugan, 144, 274
Dugas, 314
Duhamel, 58, 386
Duhurst, 144
Duke, 98
Duke de la Vittoria, 225
Duke Nicholas, 73, 82
Duke of Sotomayor, 22
Dukehart, 114, 143, 144
Dulaney, 55
Dulany, 36, 436
Dunbar, 12
Duncan, 92, 183, 235, 258, 289, 324, 340, 363, 417, 421
Duncanson, 131, 385
Dundass, 429
Dungan, 134, 142
Dunham, 12, 238, 372
Dunigan, 237
Dunlop, 188, 302, 319, 352, 362, 367, 419
Dunmead, 143
Dunn, 48, 158, 166, 215, 302, 352
Dunnington, 47, 62

Dunwell, 166
Dupont, 19, 179, 184
DuPont, 365
Dupuy, 368
Durban, 6
Durbin, 427
Durell, 432
Durfee, 210
Durham, 80, 100, 367
Durkee, 323, 348, 360
Duross, 145
Durrance, 255
Dusenbery, 236, 237
Dusenbury, 288
Dutton, 426
Duval, 16, 54, 133
Duvall, 47, 55, 144, 193, 210, 222, 273, 297, 392, 403
Dye, 287, 289
Dyer, 16, 43, 110, 184, 203, 295
Dyott, 55
Dyson, 108, 351

E

Eagle, 271
Eakin, 172
Earl, 230, 352
Earle, 114
earliest newspaper, 400
Easby, 241, 246, 253
Eastham, 50
Eastman, 46, 183, 184, 210
Easton, 64, 135
Eaton, 132, 135, 138, 301, 355, 369, 391
Eayres, 80
Echeveria, 20
Eckard, 193, 229, 362
Eckart, 92
Eckhardt, 218
Eckloff, 137
Edding, 59
Eddington, 237

Eddy, 12, 127, 237
Edelin, 40, 45, 254, 258, 259, 299
Edes, 73, 82
Edgar, 26, 173
Edge, 19
Edminster, 7
Edmondson, 289
Edmonston, 178, 277
Edmundson, 269
Edson, 190, 305
Edwards, 8, 13, 75, 78, 89, 111, 146, 162, 251, 306, 328, 365
Egbert, 405
Eggers, 239
Eggleston, 106, 248, 251, 273, 320, 339
Egleson, 403
Eide, 206
Eisenbrandt, 145
Eld, 132
Elder, 146, 185, 350
Eldon, 34
Eldredge, 11, 250, 276
Eldridge, 49, 237, 424
Eliason, 1
Eliot, 320
Ellery, 18
Ellicott, 144, 146
Elliot, 168, 250
Elliott, 1, 95, 109, 127, 137, 154, 160, 196, 245, 261, 266, 277, 279, 329, 357, 422
Ellis, 66, 93, 131, 155, 237, 294, 314, 323, 402
Ellsworth, 161, 347, 350
Elmore, 210, 381
Elsey, 173
Elvans, 304
Ely, 8, 17
Emerson, 356
Emery, 14, 75, 322, 330
Emmett, 64
Emmon, 11

Emmons, 238, 268, 405, 430
Emory, 184, 350
Empress Eugenia, 124
Empson, 301
Emrich, 215
England, 170, 236
Engle, 19, 271
English, 36, 73, 222, 252, 269, 272, 334, 359
Ennis, 40, 86, 163, 222, 223, 395, 410, 433, 439
Enos, 117, 226
Ensign, 13
Entwistle, 78
Enwright, 254
Erben, 38, 92, 109
Ereck, 147
Erick, 113
Ernest, 238
Ernstein, 354
Erving, 48, 307
Erwin, 20, 46, 197, 308, 420
Eskridge, 5
Eslin, 236, 391
Espey, 370
Espie, 48
Essex, 61, 210, 211, 297, 386
Estelle, 365
Estills, 387
Estlin, 199, 320
Etchison, 240, 302
Etheridge, 19, 236, 250, 384
Ette, 314
Eustis, 55, 175
Eutaw, 144
Eva, 140, 400
Evans, 8, 59, 61, 80, 86, 108, 142, 153, 154, 155, 169, 195, 207, 239, 246, 258, 325, 386, 392, 404, 406, 415, 425
Everett, 396, 397
Evergreen Park, 324, 330
Eversfield, 177

Ewbank, 1, 128, 181, 252
Ewell, 303, 378

F

Fabre, 55
Fabronius, 58
Fagan, 290, 421
Faherty, 6
Fahnestock, 376
Fahrenbaugh, 21
Fahs, 134
Fain, 318
Fairbank, 404
Fairfax, 272, 355, 367
Fairfield, 96, 141
Falconer, 10, 397
Fales, 211, 382
Fallard, 6
family of 16 children, 15
Fanning, 230, 290, 408
Fant, 253, 398
Farant, 346
Farelly, 293
Farish, 253
Farley, 253
Farmer, 270
Farnham, 167, 281, 327, 370
Farragut, 271
Farrall, 41
Farrar, 16, 395, 434
Farre, 266
Farrel, 260
Farrelly, 351, 369
Farribault, 196, 230
Farrow, 174
Faulk, 200, 288, 309
Faulkner, 360, 439
Faulkners, 339
Fauquier White Sulphur Springs, 196
Favier, 37, 259, 405
Feagens, 224
Feaster, 404
Fee, 105

Feeney, 307
Fellows, 146, 208
Fenby, 355
Fendall, 108, 114
Fenton, 67, 355
Fenwick, 32, 158, 193, 256, 355, 387
Ferguson, 46, 182, 234, 282, 286, 291, 322, 374, 407, 428
Fergusson, 306
Fern, 11
Ferribee, 5
Ferris, 78
ferry boat **New Jersey**, 414
ferryboat **New Jersey**, 99
Fertner, 389
Fetri, 145
Fidell, 99
Fidre, 314
Field, 39, 377
Fielden, 282
Fields, 165
Fill, 304
Fillebrown, 211, 380
Fillmore, 276, 287, 322, 344, 367
Finch, 5, 352, 356, 386
Finckel, 127, 389
Fink, 23
Finkle, 195
Finkman, 290
Finks, 210
Finney, 321, 340
Fischer, 32, 355
Fish, 100, 338
Fisher, 203, 236, 238, 277, 296, 315, 383, 386, 405
Fisk, 376
Fitch, 13, 163, 167, 359
Fitman, 424
Fitzgerald, 86, 107, 131, 159, 260, 286, 349, 350, 430
Fitzhugh, 226, 269, 352, 355, 400
Fitzpatrick, 8, 13, 99, 171, 209, 290, 292, 314

Fiuerias, 48
Flaherty, 110
Flanigan, 274
Flanner, 175
Flannigan, 137, 274
Flash, 314
Fleet, 285
Fleming, 16, 54, 186, 244
Fletcher, 32, 145, 327
Fleury, 274
Flint, 61, 386
Florence, 55
Florida, 380
Flournoy, 154
Floyd, 235
Flusser, 273, 405
Foertsch, 89
Foley, 143, 261, 314
Follansbee, 21
Foltz, 45
Fonde, 359
Fontaine, 351
Foot, 184, 230
Foote, 72, 95, 353, 399
Forbes, 126, 185
Force, 47, 88, 127
Ford, 35, 38, 62, 108, 147, 206, 281, 377, 419
Foreman, 234
Forney, 99
Forrest, 5, 18, 73, 109, 136, 137, 273, 301, 326, 344, 357
Forsyth, 226
Fort Brooke, 173
Fort Brown, 96, 431
Fort Carroll, 331
Fort Centre, 173
Fort Chadbourne, 92
Fort Craig, 208
Fort Dallas, 30, 41
Fort Edward, 356
Fort Fillmore, 174
Fort Frazier, 255

Fort Gibson, 40
Fort Gratiot, 111
Fort Griswold, 55
Fort Hamilton, 289, 338
Fort Henrietta, 54
Fort Jefferson, 56
Fort Kearney, 74, 291, 376, 381
Fort Laramie, 74
Fort Ligonier, 283
Fort Livingston, 323
Fort McHenry, 297, 365
Fort Meade, 255
Fort Montgomery, 152
Fort Morgan, 331
Fort Myers, 37, 173, 227, 417
Fort Niagara, 52
Fort Pierre, 251
Fort Scammel, 75
Fort Smith, 32, 412
Fort St Carlos, 419
Fort Taylor, 56, 297
Fort Ticonderoga, 138
Fort Vancouver, 373
Fort Walla-Walla, 54
Fort Washington, 189, 278, 345
Fort Wayne, 418
Fortune, 219
Fosnaught, 338
Foss, 397
Foster, 32, 34, 41, 59, 160, 273, 329, 353
Fouchee, 58
Foute, 340
Fow, 149
Fowke, 351, 385
Fowks, 269
Fowler, 88, 104, 129, 255, 259, 403
Fox, 155, 208, 246, 310, 324, 376, 436
Foxall, 149
Foy, 181, 199
France, 145, 146, 380
Francis, 12, 393, 415

Francisco, 123, 133
Frank, 351
Frankinberger, 320
Franklin, 8, 123, 223, 247, 272, 318, 376
Franklin Row, 41, 238, 337
Fraser, 297, 298
Frasier, 56, 104
Frazer, 167
Frazier, 223
Fred'k the Great, 138
Frederic VII, 233
Frederick, 258
Frederick the Great, 66
Free Branch, 293
Freeland, 40
Freeman, 3, 114, 136, 304
Fremont, 117, 276, 410
French, 44, 56, 75, 77, 83, 97, 161, 169, 194, 211, 267, 272, 278, 324, 407
Frere, 128, 311
Frick, 228, 437
Fricks, 330
Fried, 198
Friend, 216
Friendly Hall, 307
frig **Brandywine**, 66
frig **Colorado**, 228
frig **Constellation**, 225
frig **Euryalus**, 328
frig **Independence**, 325
frig **Merrimac**, 7
frig **Mississippi**, 55
frig **President**, 161, 169
frig **Seahorse**, 328
frig **St Lawrence**, 164, 344
Frimble, 144
Frisbee, 323
Fristoe, 289
Frothingham, 356
Frush, 310
Fry, 16, 54, 230, 269, 273

Frye, 2, 71
Fugitt, 88, 166, 247, 302
Fulkurt, 325
Fuller, 6, 13, 79, 337, 339, 434
Fullerson, 235
Fullerton, 212
Fulmer, 408
Fulvalle, 266
funeral car, 249
Funk, 191, 315, 321, 336
Funsten, 36
Furbee, 255
Furber, 426
Furness, 390
Furse, 286

G

Gable, 137
Gadberry, 174
Gadsby's Hotel, 230
Gadsby's Row, 130
Gadsden, 357
Gaehle, 145
Gaffney, 101
Gage, 12, 283
Gaines, 50, 158
Gale, 82, 167, 206
Gallagher, 167, 239, 261, 262, 274, 284, 388
Gallaher, 8, 47, 247, 332, 426
Gallant, 320, 321, 384
Gallaway, 319
Gallego, 138
Gallegos, 55
Galligan, 36, 44, 327, 377
Gally, 418
Galt, 82, 95, 99, 156, 208
Gamble, 273
Gammell, 285
Gammon, 301, 352
Gansevoort, 272
Ganton, 35
Gantt, 132, 288

Garcia, 439
Gardiner, 12, 15, 91, 106, 112, 179, 183, 254, 342, 406, 415
Gardner, 104, 163, 215, 260, 269, 271
Garesche, 29
Garey, 162
Garland, 434
Garlinger, 104
Garman, 300
Garner, 173, 187, 313
Garnett, 225
Garretson, 208
Garrett, 99, 121, 281
Garrettson, 254
Garris, 203
Garrison, 431
Garside, 42
Gary, 410
Gassaway, 93, 118, 321, 393
Gaster, 428
Gaston, 226
Gaszynski, 122
Gates, 32, 95, 237, 283
Gau, 75, 269
Gavit, 356
Gay, 301, 306, 323
<u>Gaz of 1776</u>, 399
Gedney, 23, 55, 75, 81, 189
Geer, 148
Geier, 320
Geiger, 10
Geisecking, 10
Geisell, 117
Geisinger, 252
Gelston, 145
Gennan, 314
Gentry, 226
George, 8, 428
Georgetown Cemetery, 31
Gerard, 314
Gerecko, 382
Gerhard, 234
Gerry, 156, 293

Gervais, 16
Gettings, 97
Getz, 48
Ghearity, 259
Ghequierc, 38
Ghequiere, 38
Gherardi, 273
Gholson, 422
Gibb, 417
Gibbons, 125, 275, 309, 412
Gibert, 267
Gibson, 133, 145, 153, 173, 225, 229, 263, 273, 289, 303, 308, 385, 390
Giddings, 275, 292, 309, 418
Gideon, 8, 9, 47, 156, 223
Gifford, 98
Gilbert, 62, 116, 135, 164, 177, 199
Gilchrist, 169, 265
Gildersleeve, 162, 332
Giles, 369, 422
Gill, 180, 287, 289, 408
Gillet, 12, 235, 354
Gillett, 61
Gilliam, 258
Gillies, 24
Gilligan, 417
Gillis, 207, 272, 273
Gilliss, 3, 55, 102, 247, 352
Gilman, 25, 108, 197, 226, 384
Gilmer, 157
Gilmor, 144
Gimble, 315
Ginn, 100, 135, 151
Girard, 113
Girardin, 171, 285
Gisboro, 279, 349
Gist, 408
Gittings, 29, 44, 142, 321, 357
Giverson, 99
Gizemore, 436
Gladmon, 165
Glanding, 267
Glandy, 403

Glason, 418
Glass, 149, 403
Glasscock, 328
Glassell, 273
Glen, 48
Glendy, 271
Glenn, 350
Glenroy, 47, 283
Glenwood Cemetery, 224
Gleson, 74
Glisson, 272
Gloria, 306
Gloria Dei, 376
Glossbrenner, 40
Glover, 170, 286
Goddard, 160, 197
Goddin, 69, 168
Godey, 73, 139
Godfrey, 176
Godfroy, 277
Godon, 272
Godwin, 105
Goertuer, 245
Goggin, 121, 171, 261
Golder, 145
Golding, 344
Goldsborough, 71, 167, 271, 272
Goldsby, 98
Gomez, 378
Gonng, 273
Gonzalez, 245
Good Hope Hill, 164
Goode, 79, 362, 410
Goodloe, 274, 387
Goodman, 377
Goodwin, 105, 119, 136, 283
Goodyear, 25
Gordon, 1, 12, 49, 58, 64, 67, 68, 122, 135, 167, 188, 256, 278, 281, 285, 286, 301, 306, 311, 316, 328, 357, 365, 414
Gorgas, 134
Gorges, 378

Gorman, 163, 222
Gorsuch, 85, 200
Gortuar, 390
Gossler, 134
Gott, 12, 379
Gotwalt, 106, 162
Gough, 71, 251
Gould, 141, 144
Goytre, 86
Grace, 17
Graddy, 237
Grady, 404
Graef, 21
Graff, 8, 30, 147
Graffin, 437
Graham, 19, 35, 128, 144, 162, 179, 200, 234, 254, 277, 340, 422, 435
Grammer, 9, 80, 403
Granger, 339
Grant, 155
Grantland, 11
Granville, 83
Grason, 399
Grassland, 198
Gratiot, 432
Gravel, 318, 409
Graves, 5, 235, 262, 282, 323
Gray, 23, 43, 69, 108, 147, 187, 259, 266, 273, 292, 352, 416
Grease, 409
Grebbens, 274
Greble, 100, 173
Greek, 407
Green, 2, 11, 12, 45, 59, 158, 182, 192, 220, 247, 272, 273, 274, 284, 339, 357, 392
Greene, 7, 45, 68, 122, 152, 182, 264, 428
Greenfield, 343
Greenlaw, 308
Greenleaf, 429
Greenmount Cemetery, 385
Greenough, 307

Greenup, 174
Greer, 39, 133, 194, 273, 353, 409
Greeves, 17
Grege, 166
Gregg, 85
Gregory, 7, 59, 207, 257, 353
Greiner, 354
Grevenburg, 314
Grey, 21, 173
Gribben, 348
Grice, 8
Grier, 406
Grierson, 140
Griffeth, 398
Griffin, 38, 47, 80, 254, 356
Griffith, 106, 145, 309, 403
Griffiths, 209
Grigg, 357, 395
Griggs, 267
Grigsby, 104
Grimes, 320
Grimsley, 340
Grinnell, 79, 424
Griscom, 6
Griswold, 293, 296, 300, 354, 381
Gross, 356, 425
Grounds, 282, 356
Grove, 146, 167, 209
Grover, 75, 119, 136, 256
Groves, 86
Grubb, 25, 333, 406
Grupy, 144
Guerra, 142
Guest, 119, 136, 156, 288
Guinand, 6
Guinard, 43
Guista, 335
Guliarrez, 150
Gum Spring, 246
Gum Spring Enlarged, 246
Gunn, 274
Gunnell, 110, 149, 254
Gunsally, 200, 267, 309

Gunsolly, 171
Gunton, 310, 338
Gurley, 58, 83, 103, 133, 193, 218, 430
Gurney, 230
Guthrie, 60, 128, 267
Guy, 56, 116, 238, 250
Gwin, 263, 273
Gwynn, 220

H

Habersham, 273
Hacker, 292
Hackney, 80, 379
Haddock's Hill Farm, 241
Haddock's Hills, 126, 241
Hadel, 8
Hagar, 200, 225
Hage, 368
Hager, 103, 176
Hagerman, 54
Hagerty, 147
Haggerty, 274
Hagner, 178, 431
Haig, 147
Haight, 48, 142, 277
Hail, 171, 187, 256
Haines, 173, 264
Halbrook, 439
Haldeman, 154
Hale, 269, 278
Haley, 19, 232
Haliday, 433
Hall, 9, 12, 30, 32, 45, 60, 79, 129, 146, 166, 168, 187, 192, 216, 264, 274, 278, 281, 286, 288, 290, 311, 316, 360, 366, 400, 406, 413, 434, 435
Halleck, 48
Hallett, 398
Halliday, 47
Halloren, 302
Halloway, 213

Hallowell, 245, 298
Halsey, 59, 109, 136, 163, 222, 309
Ham, 281
Hambleton, 104, 252
Hamblin, 386
Hamer, 286, 291, 429
Hamill, 114, 297
Hamilton, 61, 96, 132, 143, 157, 163, 167, 201, 205, 215, 261, 262, 273, 278, 284, 307, 308, 331, 332, 338, 340, 368, 386, 401, 416, 424
Hamlin, 350
Hammantree, 79
Hammett, 113
Hammond, 74, 111, 146, 314, 388, 439
Hampden, 116
Hampton, 103, 250
Hamtranck, 8
Hance, 143
Hancock, 158, 172, 173, 186
Hand, 260, 273, 405
Handley, 120
Hands, 228
Handy, 18, 97, 110, 138, 272, 357, 435
Handyside, 270
Hani, 15
Hanin, 233
Hanlan, 433
Hanly, 409
Hanna, 92
Hannay, 313
Hanoverian, 34
Hansell, 292
Hansen, 244
Hansford, 340
Hanson, 106, 119, 157, 202, 217, 227, 409, 441
Hanson Hill, 307
Hanson's Green, 174
Harbaugh, 10, 80, 103
Harbin's Hotel, 396

Hardcastle, 167
Harden, 274
Hardin, 141, 168, 171, 203, 260, 286, 301, 311
Harding, 7, 94, 144, 318
Hardy, 224, 288, 336
Hare, 273, 428
Hargrave, 138
Hargrove, 240
Harkness, 266, 355
Harlan, 139
Harmer, 3
Harmony, 273
Harper, 70, 95, 137, 160, 218, 387, 435
Harrell, 32
Harrigan, 379
Harrington, 12, 71, 80, 81, 93, 136, 244, 308
Harriott, 321
Harris, 5, 12, 70, 83, 119, 126, 136, 137, 143, 168, 179, 211, 254, 272, 273, 274, 298, 301, 354, 388, 408, 410
Harrison, 13, 26, 32, 60, 67, 216, 257, 258, 264, 265, 275, 324, 354, 360, 384, 392, 406
Harrod, 231, 234, 384
Harrover, 26, 61, 386
Hart, 42, 119, 136, 181, 256, 273, 315, 413
Harting, 86
Hartman, 96
Hartstene, 49, 63, 272, 326
Hartsuff, 37, 173
Hartzell, 145
Harve, 206
Harvey, 47, 70, 139, 146, 154, 157, 224, 263, 274, 357
Harvie, 46, 154
Harwood, 184, 271
Hasbrouch, 294
Hascall, 185, 200, 226, 277

Haskell, 77, 114, 143, 193, 263, 264
Haskins, 35
Haslup, 143, 389
Hassler, 185
Haste, 300
Hastings, 143, 180, 200
Hatch, 109, 141, 168, 171, 187, 199, 256
Hatfield, 208
Hathaway, 62
Hatt, 242
Haulbert, 93, 95
Haven, 318
Havens, 356
Haw, 223, 294
Hawes, 154
Hawkins, 123, 304, 314
Hawks, 222, 313
Hawley, 12, 106, 410
Hax, 125, 133, 171
Haxlitt, 147
Haxtum, 273
Hay, 215, 361
Haycraft, 70
Hayden, 133, 135, 265, 421
Hayes, 223
Hayne, 67
Haynes, 417, 435, 440
Haynie, 305
Hays, 17, 43, 147, 152, 233, 256, 258, 323, 331, 365, 387
Hayward, 61, 144, 256, 282, 301, 353, 386
Haywood, 143, 229
Hazard, 272, 313, 432
Hazel, 389
Hazlett, 120
Hazzard, 350
Head, 417
Head of Frazier, 260
Heald, 147
Healey, 332
Health Report, 104

Heard, 61, 78, 125, 218, 276, 386
Heath, 84, 124, 225, 267, 279, 323, 384
Hecht, 143
Heck, 48
Hedges, 229, 251
Hedgman, 162
Hedler, 295
Hedrick, 269
Hefflebower, 48
Heiderick, 117
Heileman, 273
Heim, 147
Heine, 255, 275
Heinhooldt, 21
Heining, 166
Heise, 61
Heiskell, 373
Heisman, 320
Heissler, 288
Helfrich, 228
Hellen, 393
Helm, 154
Helmer, 165
Hembert, 267, 306, 311
Hembree, 205
Hemenway, 207
Hemingway, 63
Hemkin, 287, 289, 294
Hempkin, 311
Hempstead, 426
Henderson, 31, 59, 95, 114, 190, 270, 272, 432
Hendricks, 122, 150, 183
Hening, 94
Henley, 153
Henly, 68
Hennesey, 38
Hennessey, 261, 262, 284
Henning, 3, 94, 375
Henrahan, 5
Henry, 21, 46, 90, 131, 180, 184, 209, 273, 295, 296, 324, 436

Henshaw, 304, 371, 380, 415
Hensley, 234
Hentz, 38, 64, 395
Hepburn, 74, 369, 406
Herbert, 23, 101, 178, 179, 183, 254, 423
Hereford, 217
Herman, 353
Herms, 148
Hernandez, 342
Herndon, 100, 125, 272, 316
Heron, 373
Herran, 326
Herrera, 380
Herries, 34
Herring, 143, 357
Herrington, 320
Herron, 259
Hersh, 290
Hess, 61
Hesse, 353
Hester, 273
Hetherington, 322
Heustis, 134
Heutis, 189
Hewes, 144
Hewitt, 336, 364
Heydon, 208
Heyward, 360
Hiawatha, 170
Hickerson, 408, 423
Hickey, 8, 126, 197, 258, 264, 274
Hickman, 388
Hicks, 12
Hieberger, 346
Higdon, 435
Higgings, 422
Higgins, 143, 229, 400
Highlands, 117, 170
Higinbothom, 147
Hilbus, 315, 377
Hildredth, 186
Hildreth, 267
Hildt, 39, 106, 114, 194, 201, 226, 305
Hill, 38, 72, 83, 88, 89, 95, 193, 194, 203, 236, 242, 260, 277, 289, 301, 311, 320, 346, 387, 409
Hilleary, 386
Hillen, 277
Hilliard, 182
Hills, 159, 382
Hilt, 13
Hilton, 197, 198, 212, 304
Hindes, 144
Hindman, 209
Hinds, 164
Hine, 188
Hineman, 5
Hines, 30, 147, 164, 288, 336, 441
Hinkle, 12, 182
Hinks, 143, 355
Hinson, 208
Hinton, 120, 137, 258, 259, 293, 386
Hintze, 357
Hirsch, 76
Hirst, 310, 393
Hiss, 144, 167
History of Immigration, 201
Hitaffer, 24
Hitch, 367
Hitchcock, 133, 140, 272, 349
Hoar, 377
Hoard, 361
Hobbie, 190, 192
Hobbs, 261
Hoboken, 159
Hobson, 11, 259
Hoburg, 320
Hocker, 288
Hodge, 132, 216, 297
Hodges, 3, 160, 257
Hodgson, 12, 386
Hoe, 85
Hoeflick, 440
Hoff, 325, 362

Hoffa, 293, 297
Hoffer, 137
Hoffman, 168, 169, 206, 220, 323, 341
Hog Island & the Main, 6
Hogan, 30, 42
Hoge, 354
Hoges, 155
Hogg, 145, 297, 381
Holbert, 396
Holbrook, 221, 340
Holden, 417
Holderness, 235
Holff, 323
Holiday, 12
Holker, 266
Holland, 217, 292, 429
Holliday, 90, 167
Hollin, 166
Hollingshead, 211, 319
Hollingswroth, 255
Hollins, 1, 271
Holloran, 266, 319, 330, 365
Holloway, 206
Holman, 278, 281
Holmead, 40, 74, 94, 96, 194, 201, 243, 268, 347, 369, 372, 400, 420, 433
Holmes, 12, 131, 142, 144, 198, 224, 245, 283, 292
Holroyd, 353
Holt, 23, 217, 340
Holton, 154
Holtzclaw, 419
Homans, 212
Homiller, 231
Hommell, 352
Honeyman, 93
Hood, 77, 131, 209, 320, 347, 390
Hooe, 128, 354
Hook, 62
Hooker, 255
Hoole, 354

Hoomes, 17, 322
Hooper, 131, 232, 355, 401
Hoops, 228
Hoover, 97, 106, 166, 174, 211, 223, 247, 386
Hope, 5, 158
Hopeton, 243
Hopewell Landing Farm, 311
Hopkins, 2, 210, 266, 281, 400
Hopkinson, 143
Hoppel, 278
Hopper, 162
Horf, 48
Horne, 66, 258
Horner, 85, 134, 147, 168, 171, 190, 256
Horney, 357
Hornsby, 155
Horsey, 267
Horstkamp, 234
Horwell, 388
Hoss, 356
Hot Springs, 362
Hotchkiss, 185
Hough, 106, 184, 194, 440
Houre, 252
House, 262
Houser, 278
Houston, 20, 160, 212, 226, 273, 366, 372, 394
Howard, 8, 47, 69, 99, 113, 122, 151, 198, 213, 223, 252, 256, 318, 333, 354, 357, 365, 385
Howe, 117, 118
Howell, 12, 77, 105, 145, 255, 363, 366
Howland, 112
Howle, 203
Hoxton, 86, 184
Hoye, 293
Hoyle, 417
Hoyt, 255
Hubard, 262

Hubbard, 367, 440
Hubert, 288
Huckelbury, 135
Huddleson, 163
Hudon, 262
Hudson, 24, 70, 271
Huey, 239, 288
Huffnerr, 43
Huggins, 98
Hugh, 337
Hughes, 140, 144, 146, 167, 188, 226, 227, 256, 351, 415
Hugo, 224
Hull, 11, 271
Hulse, 336
Humason, 54
Humble, 224
Humes, 47
Humphrey, 143, 166, 168, 205, 286
Humphreys, 65, 119, 311, 367, 389
Hunckel, 145
Hungerford, 358
Hunt, 6, 44, 81, 95, 136, 143, 187, 204, 242, 247, 272, 285, 288, 295, 309, 339, 353, 354, 388, 412, 413
Hunter, 45, 85, 89, 165, 218, 240, 301, 338, 343, 362
Huntingdon, 340
Huntington, 232, 339, 359
Huntsman, 252
Huntt, 87
Hurdle, 259
Hurlburt, 12
Hurley, 47, 97, 274, 386
Hurst, 296
Husband, 429
Hussey, 141, 185, 200, 277
Hust, 438
Huston, 239
Hutcheson, 435
Hutchins, 20, 90, 275
Hutchinson, 13, 382
Hutinack, 230

Hyatt, 392
Hyde, 42, 48, 68, 136, 241, 270, 295, 327
Hyland, 155
Hynes, 357
Hynson, 145

I

Iglehart, 144
Imperial child, 249
Impey, 34
Inderson, 425
Ingals, 12
Ingersoll, 205, 278, 390, 441
Ingle, 21, 89, 223, 335, 407, 415
Ingraham, 234, 271, 274, 323
Ingram, 35, 196
Iranistan, 102
Ironmonger, 399
Irvine, 96
Irvines, 387
Irving, 100, 322
Irwin, 90, 273, 280, 339
Isaacs, 395
Israel, 391
Iturbide, 247
Iverson, 178
Ives, 121, 226
Ivey, 381
Izard, 286

J

Jacksen, 109
Jackson, 2, 14, 20, 42, 119, 139, 141, 147, 155, 170, 226, 228, 245, 305, 330, 366, 391, 396, 406, 409, 416, 436
Jacob, 154
Jacobs, 9, 133, 354, 435
James, 190, 192, 206, 255, 395, 436
Jameson, 51
Jamieson, 258
Jamoo, 21

Janes, 209, 427
Janin, 171
Janney, 295
Jannie, 99
Jannings, 342
Jarboe, 39, 189, 197, 280
Jarrett, 143
Jarvaise, 54
Jarvis, 9, 52, 141, 219, 301, 307, 311
Jatterbidt, 418
Jay, 396, 408
Jeffers, 180
Jefferson, 7, 296, 350
Jeffroy, 14
Jemison, 204
Jenifer, 13
Jenkins, 4, 29, 103, 137, 144, 272, 355, 392, 405, 440
Jenning, 266
Jennings, 29, 53, 160, 200, 334, 340, 342, 431
Jerningham, 433
Jesup, 111, 413
Jewell, 27, 31, 65
Jewett, 38, 152, 434
Jillson, 269
Johmit, 166
Johns, 143, 206, 408, 423
Johnson, 9, 21, 23, 30, 35, 41, 52, 77, 80, 107, 113, 114, 115, 116, 125, 151, 158, 164, 181, 196, 197, 200, 213, 217, 251, 258, 273, 282, 309, 323, 353, 355, 390, 393, 413, 425, 427
Johnston, 7, 26, 131, 142, 145, 200, 273, 358
Johnstone, 35
Johsierder, 166
Jolly, 39
Jones, 5, 8, 9, 27, 48, 55, 60, 61, 73, 75, 80, 86, 96, 105, 107, 114, 130, 134, 141, 144, 148, 149, 152, 155, 162, 167, 168, 180, 181, 185, 187, 188, 195, 196, 198, 202, 209, 215, 218, 225, 237, 243, 250, 262, 267, 268, 272, 273, 278, 281, 286, 290, 296, 301, 302, 307, 311, 316, 338, 339, 340, 354, 371, 386, 395, 403, 408, 410, 413, 419, 421, 423, 433
Jordan, 48, 104, 113
Joseph's Park, 117
Joslin, 166, 242
Jost, 248, 320
Jouett, 273
Jourdan, 207
Joyner, 350
Joynes, 17
Judah, 374
Judge, 47, 48
Judkins, 417
Judson, 8, 123
Junkins, 100

K

Kaflinski, 143
Kalb, 401
Kamoikin, 205
Kanawha Salines, 269
Kane, 90, 132, 139, 149, 151, 252, 275, 316, 333, 424
Kavanaugh, 137
Kealy, 80
Kean, 354
Keane, 40, 433
Kearney, 19, 217, 239, 284, 420
Kearny, 261, 262
Kearon, 295
Keating, 84, 178, 179, 183, 240, 254
Keech, 191, 215, 278, 417
Keeck, 392
Keefer, 325, 337
Keen, 147
Keenan, 349
Keene, 392
Keese, 48, 237, 320
Keigan, 258, 259

Keighler, 355
Keilholtz, 51
Keith, 150, 189
Keleher, 140
Keliess, 39
Kell, 273
Keller, 232, 247
Kelley, 19, 262, 266, 275, 284, 320, 356
Kellogg, 300
Kelly, 16, 19, 54, 70, 110, 112, 235, 259, 261, 271, 274, 275, 281, 309, 348, 386, 401, 412
Kelsey, 54
Kelso, 16, 357
Kemble, 207
Kemf, 321
Kemp, 158
Kendall, 202, 267, 425, 436
Kengla, 259
Kenna, 231, 234
Kennedy, 9, 19, 126, 170, 187, 223, 235, 256, 272, 340, 345, 352
Kennedys, 387
Kennerly, 288
Kenney, 302
Kennon, 273
Kent, 271, 432
Kepler, 47
Kerman, 151
Kerr, 167, 196
Kershaw, 48
Kerwin, 101
Ketchum, 339
Key, 17, 108, 154, 179, 404
Keyer, 256
Keys, 17, 128, 230
Keyworth, 61, 106, 128, 209
Kibbey, 382, 417
Kidd, 234
Kidder, 57
Kidwell, 80, 98, 220
Kiger, 12

Kilburn, 173
Kilby, 3
Killmon, 50
Kilty, 62
Kimball, 267, 403
Kimberly, 273, 418
Kincaid, 270
Kincannon, 229
Kindle, 400
King, 16, 56, 61, 64, 80, 88, 91, 111, 119, 149, 160, 168, 206, 219, 236, 239, 241, 245, 247, 261, 279, 281, 286, 288, 302, 308, 310, 311, 321, 336, 346, 349, 354, 378, 386, 400, 408, 430
King Charles, 317
King Charles I, 378
King James, 317
King of Denmark, 390
King of the Netherlands, 148
Kingsbury, 59, 243, 267, 434
Kingsland, 91
Kinkead, 255
Kinney, 16, 17, 353, 374, 420
Kinsman, 232
Kinsolving, 378
Kintzing, 124, 151, 256, 309, 412
Kios, 12
Kirby, 33, 184, 193, 265, 278, 354
Kirk, 25, 145, 357
Kirkland, 118, 310, 355
Kirkpatrick, 183
Kirkwood, 171, 215
Kirwan, 191
Kirwin, 323
Kissel, 249
Kissell, 329
Klein, 69
Klinefelter, 146
Klinehause, 139
Klink, 352
Klopfer, 47
Klopp, 11

Knaggs, 421
Knapp, 201, 278
Knaube, 145
Knight, 145, 157, 161, 195, 250, 259, 290, 387, 402
Knipe, 353
Knotts, 106
Knowles, 159, 259
Knox, 39, 62, 123, 151, 265, 276
Koch, 166
Kohl, 268
Kohman, 248, 251
Kohrman, 320, 339
Kolb, 408, 438
Koones, 232, 421, 440
Koons, 143
Korsner, 274
Kraft, 386, 431
Kraus, 148
Krauter, 206
Krebbs, 127
Krebs, 106, 144, 162, 167, 182, 194, 243, 314, 368, 375, 380, 401, 408, 415, 439, 440
Kremer, 147
Krevals, 340
Krobb, 394
Krouse, 183, 425, 431
Kruman, 119
Kuhlman, 136
Kuhn, 145
Kunkel, 312
Kunston, 282
Kuper, 415
Kurtz, 362
Kussmane, 311
Kussmaul, 296, 316
Kyle, 355

L

La Fonte, 287, 289, 295
la Ronde, 287, 289, 294
La Ronde, 311
La Torry, 322
Labatt, 160
Labban, 240
Labradada, 369
Labranche, 113, 136, 287, 289
Lachaise, 415
Lackey, 373
Lackland, 70
Lacy, 219
Ladd, 110, 127, 158, 190
Ladies of Virginia, 107
Lafayette, 182, 294
Lafferty, 348
LaGrange, 113
Lagroue, 146
Laidley, 269
Laird, 239
Lakeman, 80
Laker, 184
Lamb, 5, 36, 356, 358
Lambel, 197
Lambert, 125, 266, 353
Lamborn, 47
Lambreth, 106
Lamden, 180
Lammond, 49
Lamont, 93
Lamothe, 119
Lamton, 352
Lanahan, 106
Lancaster, 258
Lance, 203
Landon, 367
Landon Academy, 410
Landry, 314
Lane, 73, 139, 273, 315, 318, 339, 340
Lanfear, 255, 260, 288, 309
Lanflant, 104
Lang, 148, 177, 208
Langdon, 13, 29, 66, 163
Langley, 267, 386
Langston, 437
Langton, 325, 337, 366

Lanman, 272, 347
Lanphier, 376
Lansdale, 89, 98, 171
Laporte, 34
Lappa, 48
Lara, 117
Larabee, 19, 144
Larcombe, 47
Lark, 417
Larkin, 272, 340, 433
Larned, 173, 188, 203
Larner, 406
Larrabee, 158, 267, 309
Larue, 398
Lary, 217
Lashhorn, 83, 218
Laskey, 40, 56, 61, 363, 386
Latham, 36, 197, 222, 267, 293, 297, 302, 308, 328, 337, 437
Latil, 288, 427
Latile, 306
Latimer, 62, 140, 313, 333
Laub, 81, 135, 259, 278
Laughlin, 110
Laurel Spring Farm, 206
Lauren's Manuscripts, 374
Laurie, 236
Lavalette, 19
Law, 29, 99, 272, 429
Lawder, 144
Lawler, 261, 262, 284, 302
Lawrence, 37, 45, 52, 195, 322, 351, 366
Lawrie, 414
Laws, 144, 318, 361
Lawson, 146, 371, 420
Lawton, 274
Lay, 367
Layton, 16, 54
Lazenby, 13, 368
Le Cerre, 125
Le Compte, 258
Le Croix, 111

Le Roy, 405
Lea, 158, 294
Leach, 57, 127
Leake, 29, 58
Leaman, 290
Lear, 182, 408, 419
Leatherbury, 17
Leavett, 131
LeBois, 270
Leckie, 87
Leckron, 405
LeCompte, 23
Lecompton, 315, 318
Ledyard, 266
Lee, 12, 21, 64, 149, 152, 220, 226, 264, 271, 272, 273, 278, 294, 305, 322, 323, 357, 363, 373, 384, 395, 397, 417, 425
Leef, 267
Leeke, 285
Leffler, 343
Leftwich, 12, 315
Legard, 157
Leggett, 206
Legrand, 167
Lelly, 264
Lemmon, 270, 355
Lemon, 154
Lenairs, 109
Lennairs, 199
Lenox, 25, 41, 95, 260
Leonard, 145, 173, 294, 434
Leroy, 402
Lesdernier, 170
Lesesne, 368
Lesh, 111
Leslie, 247, 355
Letters, 99
Levensworth, 169
Levering, 355
Leves, 47
Levy, 29, 64, 95, 109, 255, 416

Lewis, 11, 12, 16, 30, 81, 104, 144, 206, 208, 229, 234, 238, 243, 248, 260, 262, 273, 282, 284, 347, 352, 354, 362, 383, 420, 430
Libbey, 73, 271
Lidecker, 166
Lieden, 48
Liesburger, 299
Lightell, 80
Lighter, 215
Lightfoot, 168, 406
Lightner, 163
Lilly, 274
Limantour, 76
Lincoln, 228
Linden, 216, 307
Lindpainter, 361
Lindsay, 123, 133, 151, 198, 256, 301, 307, 311, 316, 375, 411
Linhart, 109
Linkins, 101
Linn, 17, 54, 63, 81, 85, 109, 410
Linsey, 1
Linsley, 406
Linthicum, 106, 118, 123, 147, 153, 168, 205, 214, 310, 393
Linton, 243, 328, 417
Linwood, 38
Lippincott, 389
Lippitt, 42
Lippold, 369
Lipscomb, 204, 346
Lipscombe, 432
Lipsey, 260
Lisel, 425
Littig, 145
Little, 9, 36, 97, 99, 136, 222, 256, 302, 309, 323, 325, 332, 349, 412, 415
Little Falls Bridge, 246
Littlefield, 135, 182
Livingston, 113, 136, 272, 287, 289, 308, 406, 429

Llangollen, 292
Lloyd, 139, 162, 199, 253
Locke, 11, 258, 345, 352
Lockett, 125
Lockwood, 9, 18, 110
Loder, 226
Lofdin, 352
Lofland, 162
Logan, 21, 133
Loisel, 425, 434
Lomax, 133, 151, 175, 198, 226, 411, 430
Lombard, 208
Lone Mountain Cemetery, 219
Lonehead, 215
Loney, 144
Long, 18, 78, 196, 259, 274, 288, 302, 435
Longfellow, 170
Longworth, 97
Loomis, 30
Lorain, 226
Lord, 12, 176, 226, 300, 349, 352, 367
Lord Baltimore, 378
Lore, 218
Lorell, 252
Loring, 128
Lorman, 13
Losee, 377
Loudon, 293, 312, 346
Loughborough, 198
Louis XVI, 182, 225
Loundsbury, 230
Lounsbury, 78, 278, 309, 413
Lovatelli, 433
Love, 69, 338
Lovejoy, 57, 63, 124, 144
Lovell, 273, 275
Lovett, 21, 48
Lowber, 405
Lowe, 16, 75, 304
Lowndes, 271
Lownsbury, 256

Lowrey, 47
Lowry, 89, 183, 272
Lubert, 259
Lucas, 45, 114, 200, 281
Luce, 273, 345, 362, 441
Luckauy, 21
Luckett, 104, 357, 389
Ludlow, 159, 242
Ludwig, 21
Luis, 130
Lukins, 132
Lumpkin, 51, 417
Lumsdon, 106
Lundberg, 294
Lunt, 137, 425
Lurty, 237
Luskey, 80
Lutz, 61, 162, 386
Lydoc, 40
Lyeth, 145
Lyles, 94, 333
Lyman, 33, 143
Lynah, 134
Lynch, 53, 60, 103, 125, 269, 324
Lynde, 417
Lynell, 433
Lynn, 105, 108
Lyon, 226
Lyond, 83
Lyons, 80, 284, 379

M

Mabee, 258
Macauley, 388
Macdonald, 122
Macdougal, 48
Mace, 148
Macfarland, 220
MacFarland, 65
Macgregor, 116
Machenheimer, 77, 371
Machette, 340
Mackall, 73, 321

Mackay, 61, 240
Mackenzie, 122
Mackey, 276
Macklin, 167
Macleod, 313
Macnamara, 294, 301
Macomb, 95, 155
Macpherson, 25
Macubbin, 339
MacWilliam, 77, 400
Macy, 206, 326, 345
Madden, 213
Maddin, 426
Maddox, 13, 213, 313
Maddux, 191, 215
Madison, 38, 238, 305
Madox, 39
Maent, 213
Maffit, 23
Maffitt, 6, 55
Magaw, 273
Magee, 112, 275, 304, 313, 349, 426
Mages, 282
Maglennen, 294
Magrath, 350
Magraw, 143, 190, 204, 411
Magruder, 73, 80, 91, 128, 130, 140, 142, 144, 178, 201, 210, 238, 256, 271, 322, 355, 360, 396, 430
Maguire, 65, 113, 128, 258
Mahan, 58, 353
Maher, 121, 287, 289, 292, 360, 411
Mahler, 78
Mahorney, 308
Maine, 378
Maitland, 35
Major, 226
Makepeace, 12
Malbon, 259
Malcolm, 144
Mallard, 337
Mallet, 394
Mallicote, 384

Mallory, 323
Malone, 113
Maloney, 281, 323, 339
Malonny, 2
Malony, 246
Maltby, 144
Mammack, 137
Manahan, 367
Manley, 354
Mann, 141, 376, 382
Manning, 9, 73, 174, 227, 405
Manny, 46
Mansell, 30
Manson, 405
Manvers, 56, 171
Manyett, 45
Marbury, 111, 128, 147, 153, 168, 205, 310, 331, 346, 362, 373, 393, 399
Marcellotti, 371
Marceron, 226
March, 256
Marchand, 270, 272, 385
Marcy, 125
Marden, 146, 162
Marengo, 383
Maria Antoinette, 225
Mariposa, 340
Markle, 8, 356
Markriter, 261
Marks, 44, 51, 67, 110, 165, 177, 187, 210, 235, 362, 401, 419, 425, 439
Marlang, 214
Marling, 368
Marlow, 135, 274
Marquand, 177
Marquez, 268
Marquis, 259
Marsden, 145
Marsellus, 276
Marselus, 204
Marsh, 11, 66, 82, 90, 260, 267, 314, 323

Marshal, 361
Marshall, 96, 122, 311, 363, 372, 429, 435
Marston, 181, 271
Martin, 13, 62, 87, 89, 94, 97, 140, 144, 157, 196, 197, 206, 211, 212, 216, 217, 254, 267, 277, 300, 312, 324, 326, 327, 344, 350, 369, 393, 394, 398, 422
Martinez, 22
Marvel, 81
Marvin, 9, 124, 151, 354
Maryland, 378
Maryman, 86, 429
Masi, 3
Maskell, 314
Mason, 4, 20, 72, 102, 121, 123, 142, 149, 220, 221, 251, 313, 378, 396, 407, 419
Massey, 379, 420, 427
Massie, 216
Masters, 246, 291, 292, 349
Mathais, 180
Matheny, 340
Mather, 286
Mathew, 433
Mathews, 155, 164, 372
Mathieu, 387
Mathiot, 142
Matteson, 410
Matthews, 4, 32, 33, 142, 144, 180, 200, 256, 309, 364, 406
Mattingly, 47, 80, 184, 386, 406
Mattocks, 199
Maull, 181
Maulsby, 209
Mauro, 127
Maury, 17, 23, 53, 88, 91, 102, 104, 123, 128, 129, 138, 148, 156, 275, 327, 390
Maxwell, 34, 35, 38, 145, 230, 233
Maxwells, 34

May, 21, 53, 58, 123, 271, 338, 386, 391, 423
Mayes, 318
Mayhew, 420, 423
Maynard, 93, 254
Mayo, 5, 19, 177, 200, 273
McAleer, 274
McAlister, 226, 413
McAllister, 323
McArthur, 309, 331
McAuley, 83
McAvoy, 146
McBeth, 174
McBlair, 259, 272
McBride, 231
McCabe, 422
McCain, 213, 274
McCallion, 119, 186
McCann, 72, 137, 142, 273
McCarthy, 304, 380
McCarty, 83, 353, 357, 407
McCarver, 16
McCathran, 304
McCauley, 152, 272, 296
McCausland, 233
McCay, 318
McCeney, 223
McChesney, 339
McCleary, 225
McClellan, 136, 439
McClelland, 32, 114, 166, 180, 412
McClery, 31, 103
McClish, 416
McCloud, 26
McCluney, 57
McClure, 266
McClusky, 117
McCollum, 273
McComas, 144
McComb, 430
McCombs, 165
McConaughey, 409
McConnell, 96, 266, 275
McConner, 261
McConvey, 348
McCoomb, 101
McCormack, 1
McCormick, 123, 141, 149, 184, 200, 250, 275, 278, 311, 414
McCoy, 13, 147, 372
McCrabb, 200, 309
McCrabbe, 185
McCrary, 398
McCreery, 143
McCullion, 410
McCulloch, 231
McCullough, 117
McCunne, 127
McCunnell, 436
McCutchen, 10, 18, 61, 393
McCutchon, 386
McDaniel, 8
McDelain, 264
McDermot, 272
McDermott, 190
McDonald, 41, 102, 123, 124, 187, 352, 361, 366, 429
McDonough, 27, 110
McDougall, 426
McDowell, 137
McDuell, 382
McElderry, 231, 278
McEldery, 236, 277
McElhalton, 93
McElmoth, 253
McElroy, 98
McElwee, 368
McEneany, 208
McErlain, 274
McEvoy, 320
McEwen, 313
McFarlan, 417
McFarland, 44, 52, 93, 146, 154, 189, 299, 340
McFee, 24
McFerran, 84, 93

McFittrick, 221
McGarvey, 172
McGary, 273
McGaw, 200
McGee, 106, 145, 147, 195, 274, 428
McGill, 258, 371
McGinnis, 436
McGirr, 264
McGowan, 34, 147, 262, 284
McGrath, 174
McGraw, 274
McGregor, 15
McGroarty, 154
McGrugan, 264
McGuigan, 274
McGuire, 3, 10, 45, 56, 82, 95, 116, 126, 261, 262, 264, 274, 284, 347, 382, 420
McGunnegle, 126, 247, 273, 301, 327
McGurk, 264, 274
McHenry, 26
McIntire, 264, 274
McIntosh, 19, 89, 180, 200, 256, 309, 413
McIntyre, 359, 418
McIver, 122
McJilton, 4, 357
McKaig, 279, 397
McKay, 179, 254
McKean, 22, 271
McKee, 267
McKeever, 122
McKel, 6
McKelden, 162, 322
McKenna, 319, 406
McKenney, 81, 247, 306, 317, 392, 393
McKenny, 375
McKesson, 161
McKim, 142, 197, 305, 308, 355, 363, 385
McKinleey, 181
McKinley, 68, 354, 376

McKinstry, 173, 272
McKivers, 402
McKnew, 191, 223, 361
McKnight, 76, 114, 119, 136, 235, 287, 289
McKorkle, 273
McLain, 287
McLane, 416
McLaughlin, 97, 156, 415
McLean, 48, 406
McLelland, 152
McLemore, 226
McLeod, 314, 428
McMahan, 17
McMillan, 226, 267
McMillen, 252, 270
McMurty, 60
McNair, 170, 354
McNairy, 401
McNamee, 177
McNaney, 197, 199
McNarey, 193
McNary, 265
McNaughton, 358
McNeil, 278
McNeill, 99, 220, 256, 309
McNeir, 8, 9, 80, 373, 406
McNerhany, 47
McNichols, 233
McNiel, 260
McPeak, 213
McPhail, 144
McPherson, 48
McQueen, 298
McRea, 204
McRoberts, 303
McScarlett, 136
McVey, 274
McVicker, 416
McWilliams, 106, 259
Meacham, 318, 324
Meachan, 143
Mead, 151, 159, 326

Meade, 185, 234, 242, 354, 408
Means, 6
Meany, 264
Mearis, 144
Mechlin, 245, 390, 391, 428
Mecklin, 426
Medary, 205
Medford, 228
Medley, 290
Megee, 301
Mehens, 147
Meigs, 441
Melcher, 307
Melnot, 49
Melson, 47, 438
Melvin, 216
Menard, 294
Mendigs, 422
Meneas, 395
Menendez, 268
Mercer, 106, 119, 136, 271, 302, 350, 351, 405
Merceret, 143
Merchant, 52, 416
Merrefield, 143
Merrick, 69
Merrill, 39, 111, 434
Merritt, 209, 410
Meschamp, 99
Metcalf, 81, 135, 285
Metsereau, 187
Metz, 120
Mezerott, 377
Michael, 145
Michelette, 301
Mickle, 356
Micodemus, 147
Middle Farm, 293
Middleton, 47, 72, 109, 164, 304, 406, 420
Middleton Square, 133
Milburn, 158, 230, 305, 318
Miles, 174, 202
Milineux, 268
Millandon, 164, 255
Mille, 314, 315
Miller, 3, 6, 8, 16, 42, 50, 54, 55, 66, 71, 83, 95, 96, 99, 114, 145, 181, 191, 192, 201, 207, 212, 213, 223, 226, 232, 236, 244, 247, 249, 254, 256, 258, 288, 298, 302, 310, 314, 329, 334, 347, 349, 378, 380, 382, 386, 387, 392, 394, 407, 408, 409, 429
Milligan, 22
Milliken, 79
Mills, 42, 64, 103, 174, 240, 386
Milstead, 197
Miltenberger, 9
Milton, 60, 282
Minard, 266
Miner, 74
Ming, 328
Minor, 272, 273, 303
Minot, 93, 369
Mirick, 167
Misroon, 272
Mitchel, 97, 185
Mitchell, 12, 13, 60, 70, 86, 95, 132, 135, 148, 159, 167, 170, 190, 236, 272, 278, 281, 294, 306, 307, 311, 349, 405, 406, 408, 428
Mix, 73, 222
Mizner, 226
Moast, 236, 238, 256
Mockabee, 137, 304
Moffett, 394
Mohnard, 173
Mohun, 65, 80, 232
Moler, 431
Monaghan, 233
Monahan, 423
Moncasis, 155
Moncton, 283
Moncure, 43
Monmouth, 43

Monroe, 26, 36, 205, 361
Monson, 54
Mont Alto, 204
Montell, 147
Montgomery, 19, 111, 164, 250, 282, 344, 348, 367, 414
Montoya, 369
Montsanet, 349
Moody, 78
Mooers, 52, 62
Mooney, 383
Moore, 11, 47, 48, 79, 87, 92, 119, 144, 149, 163, 173, 185, 193, 200, 208, 223, 231, 258, 259, 277, 301, 304, 326, 349, 351, 352, 371, 388, 410, 439
Mora, 150
Moran, 265
Moras, 306
Morcoe, 47
More, 81, 277, 361, 391
Moreland, 254, 319
Moreno, 259
Morfit, 334
Morgan, 7, 14, 23, 43, 86, 95, 106, 123, 218, 245, 283, 355, 388, 390, 398, 431, 440
Moriarty, 439
Mormon, 63, 231, 342, 389
Mormons, 78, 231
Moro, 125, 265, 301, 306, 311, 316
Moro, 59
Morong, 145
Morrill, 134, 226, 277
Morris, 31, 62, 66, 109, 121, 131, 137, 145, 229, 273, 429
Morrisey, 101
Morrison, 16, 30, 80, 100, 135, 151, 267, 278, 352
Morrow, 100, 111, 204, 301, 309, 418
Morse, 23, 100, 123, 136, 141, 147, 160

Morsell, 12, 16, 21, 53, 167, 194, 215, 319, 335, 341, 362, 385, 401
Morton, 118, 119, 206, 246, 254, 330
Moseley, 347
Mosely, 73, 82
Moses, 2, 174
Mosher, 7, 180, 428
Mosley, 388
Moss, 304, 429
Moss' Neck, 322
Mother Boston, 18
Mothershead, 22, 114, 136, 302
Motzer, 362
Moulder, 110, 367
Mount, 32, 67, 143, 340
Mount Alban, 247
Mount Custis, 236
Mount Hebron Cemetery, 150
Mount of Olives, 231
Mount Sharon, 238
Mount Vernon, 102, 107, 189, 206
Mount Vernon Ladies' Association, 102, 107
Mount Zephyr, 206
Mountz, 177
Mowrey, 90
Mowry, 171
Moxley, 259
Mudd, 217, 418, 421, 422
Mudge, 145
Muggah, 314
Muir, 323
Mulberry Grove, 13
Mulcabey, 384
Mulholland, 274
Mullen, 43
Muller, 163, 357
Mulligan, 239, 261, 262, 284
Mullikin, 191, 215, 231, 293, 427
Mullin, 439
Mullory, 260
Mulloy, 51, 223, 262, 284
Munday, 247

Munder, 26
Munford, 43
Munn, 12
Munroe, 58, 173, 198, 270, 375
Munson, 16
Muntz, 64
Murch, 102
Murdaugh, 180, 272
Murdock, 146, 390
Murillo, 312
Murphey, 421
Murphy, 61, 71, 96, 101, 106, 206, 211, 320, 348, 386, 394, 407
Murray, 52, 89, 105, 108, 191, 209, 211, 258, 262, 283, 284, 301, 311, 315, 319, 350, 405
Muse, 90, 272, 306
Musgrove, 348
Mush Island, 381
Myerle, 360
Myers, 9, 44, 73, 95, 143, 145, 147, 181, 228, 256, 304, 351
Mygatt, 273, 405
Myrick, 304

N

Nafus, 352
Nagle, 251
Nailor, 150, 205, 270, 322, 355
Nalley, 335
Nalls, 357, 426
Nally, 15, 189, 197, 280
Napoleon, 124, 332, 370, 418
Narvaez, 166, 312
Nash, 5, 79, 109, 136, 148, 224, 265, 278, 282, 291, 301, 311, 413, 417
Nason, 300
National Theatre, 270
Naylor, 25, 88, 137, 166, 200, 223, 225, 257, 260, 303, 329, 343, 362, 394, 396
Nazeraw, 246
Neale, 16, 42, 108, 143, 258, 316

Neale's Wharf, 108
Neeham, 356
Neffises, 356
Neil, 275
Neill, 15, 145
Neilson, 62, 75, 135, 390
Neller, 323
Nellis, 12
Nelms, 5
Nelson, 51, 111, 272, 282, 310, 331, 364, 384, 393
Nemours, 365
Nenning, 31
Nesby, 160
Neville, 128, 182
New, 230
New York, 378
Newall, 275
Newberry, 356
Newbold, 124, 425
Newcomb, 405
Newell, 59, 76, 277, 429
Newhall, 221
Newington, 278
Newkirk, 213
Newman, 145, 273, 290, 323, 425
Newton, 77, 80, 163, 384
Nicholas, 4
Nicholls, 128, 311
Nichols, 105, 132, 195, 343, 388
Nicholson, 19, 48, 146, 151, 261, 262, 271, 356, 359, 404, 423, 427, 429
Nichter, 206
Nicodemus, 146
Nicola, 93
Nicolassen, 143
Nighesdale, 34
Nightingale, 397
Nile, 267
Niles, 4, 124, 151, 209, 255
Nilis, 60
Nimmo, 106
Nims, 266

Nipps, 420
Nixon, 313, 429
Noble, 12, 238, 252, 256
Nock, 62, 267
Noel, 235
Noer, 386
Noerr, 61
Nolan, 17
Noland, 32, 274, 406
Noolan, 27
Noples, 374
Nordman, 195
Norflet, 421
Norfolk, 266
Noriega, 142
Norman, 30
Norment, 33, 160, 315
Norris, 60, 84, 142, 352
Norsworthy, 432
North, 120
Northrop, 111, 223
Northrup, 321
Northup, 147, 255
Norwood, 13, 263, 295, 324, 327, 388
Nott, 117
Nourse, 125, 159, 190, 256
Noyes, 2, 80, 278, 281
Nugent, 188, 198, 408
Nye, 112, 139, 198, 266, 435

O

O'Bannon, 174
O'Brian, 274
O'Brien, 18, 114, 136, 301, 303, 306, 386, 422, 423, 431, 433, 437, 440
O'Connell, 142, 259
O'Donnell, 312
O'Donnoghue, 259
O'Flanagan, 65
O'Hara, 312
O'Hare, 129, 238, 268, 428
O'Kane, 354
O'Keefe, 318

O'Reilly, 48, 147, 157, 293
O'Toole, 3, 120, 195, 355
Oak Hill, 206, 361
Oak Hill Cemetery, 91, 364
Oak Lawn, 245
Oakdale Cemetery, 355
Oakhill Cemetery, 391
Oakland, 349
Oardwell, 406
Ober, 33, 197
Occoquan Cotton Factory, 92
Ochiltree, 282, 338
Odel, 218
Odell, 422
Oden, 390
Odenheimer, 410
Offut, 333
Offutt, 38, 59, 203, 228, 270
Ogden, 11, 110, 113, 166, 185, 304, 321, 331
Ogen, 427
Ogilvie, 421
Ogle, 165
Old Ben Duke, 98
old ship **William Fane**, 101
oldest church, 373
Oldfield, 263
Oliver, 278, 402
Olmstead, 250
Olmsted, 79
Onan, 154
Onderdonk, 324, 330
One hundred & sixth ballot, 11
Oney, 422
Onnondaga, 8
Orgain, 299
Orloff, 346
Orme, 13, 47, 73, 80, 223, 338
Ormsbee, 43
Orr, 174, 386
Orso, 330
Osborn, 73, 299, 375, 393, 430
Osborne, 85, 375

Osbourn, 187, 319
Osmn, 379
Otero, 55
Otis, 134, 278, 281, 307, 311, 316, 413
Otterback, 363, 386, 423
Ottinger, 202
Otto, 12
Oudesluys, 146
Ould, 135
Overend, 230
Overton, 4, 99
Owen, 61, 107, 167, 273, 291, 373, 386, 410, 416
Owen's Mills, 167
Owens, 33, 40, 74, 84, 226, 349, 408
Owner, 367
Oxenham, 30
<u>Oysters for Families</u>, 113

P

Pablo, 142
Pacheco, 75
<u>Pacific Commercial</u>, 324
Packard, 298
packet-ship **Germania**, 112
Packwood, 218, 277
Paddock, 354
Padgett, 123, 305, 320
Page, 12, 68, 131, 180, 197, 207, 244, 272, 403
Paine, 23, 211
Pairo, 268
Palmer, 83, 91, 119, 136, 165, 174, 193, 227, 243, 258, 286, 302, 350
Palmerston, 332
Pannett, 60
Paramore, 243
Parcel, 77
Parish, 288
Parke, 86
Parker, 26, 32, 43, 66, 110, 114, 115, 127, 139, 147, 168, 186, 196, 206, 234, 255, 256, 262, 272, 273, 326, 328, 351, 399
Parkhurst, 105
Parks, 236
Parmalee, 101
Parmeter, 12
Parr, 143
Parris, 122, 134, 163, 232
Parrish, 343
Parry, 342
Parsons, 96, 304
Parton, 11
Partridge, 285, 291
Paskiewitch, 73
Pate, 217
Patten, 65, 423
Patterson, 57, 85, 102, 122, 133, 181, 223, 228, 234, 403
Patton, 202
Pauchette, 48
Paulding, 164, 272
Paust, 359
Paxton, 340
<u>Pay of Army Ofcrs</u>, 86
Payne, 16, 54, 78, 90, 258, 259, 290, 341, 349, 391
Peabody, 404
Peaco, 302
Peake, 217
Peale, 175, 200, 277
Pearce, 176, 246, 406
Pearson, 10, 172, 223, 271, 355
Pease, 60, 95, 351
Pecam, 314
Peck, 11, 12, 61, 79, 106, 119, 134, 186, 328, 386, 410
Peddicord, 427
Pedichord, 61
Pedro, 225
Pee Pee-Mox-Mox, 36
Peebles, 82
Peeples, 254
Peerce, 97

Peet, 277
Pegg, 301, 424
Pell, 28
Pelouye, 417
Pember, 29
Pemberton, 125
Pembroke, 272, 351
Pendergrast, 59, 161, 262, 271, 273
Pendleton, 75, 100, 146, 147, 161, 200, 222, 355, 411
Penet, 14
Penn, 283, 383
Penniger, 43
Pennington, 5, 187, 360
Pepper, 58, 89
Percival, 176, 272
Perkin, 166
Perkins, 45, 132, 143, 164, 181, 185, 260, 401
Perkinson, 145
Perrie, 377
Perrin, 56
Perry, 31, 55, 57, 62, 79, 81, 95, 187, 204, 249, 272, 293, 296, 328, 432
Perry Farm, 293
Peter, 8, 117, 118, 176, 364, 372, 404
Peter the Great, 3
Peter's Neck, 296
Peterfield, 409
Peterkin, 259
Peters, 6, 41, 111, 133, 155, 232, 327, 332
Petery, 424
Pether, 206
Petigru, 23, 374
Petre, 9
Petrie, 165
Petrona, 82
Pettibone, 358, 386, 438
Pettigru, 55
Pettit, 94
Petty, 21
Peu-peu-mox-mox, 16

pew in St John's Church, 414
Pews, 171
Peyton, 149, 290, 324, 388
Pfouts, 336
Pheillips, 287
Phelps, 17, 48, 106, 147, 272, 288, 359, 417, 432
Phenix, 273
Philaretes, 346
Philip, 272, 341, 353
Philips, 51, 53, 256, 267
Phillip, 341
Phillips, 51, 55, 83, 129, 143, 179, 185, 272, 330, 364, 366, 407, 422
Phipps, 30, 324
Physick, 161
Piatt, 29, 66, 129, 201, 264, 278, 422
Pickell, 263
Pickens, 174
Pickering, 272, 414
Pickett, 41
Pickford, 177, 398
Pickrell, 73, 80, 82, 259, 377
Pickroll, 420
Pierce, 1, 52, 63, 80, 131
Pierson, 61
Piggott, 301, 363
Pike, 59
Pinckney, 245
Pinkney, 119, 272, 357
Pise, 330
Piseros, 113, 136, 287, 289
Pitcher, 152
Piter, 104
Pittman, 93, 136, 301, 411, 437
Pitts, 129
Pizzini, 258
Plain, 392
Platts, 74
Pleasant Gardens, 20
Pleasant Plains, 420
Pleasanton, 163
Pleasants, 228, 355, 368

Pleasnt Plains, 347
Plowden, 258
Plug-Uglies, 389
Poe, 226, 258, 278, 281, 286, 308, 412
Poindexter, 155
Pointer, 105
Polack, 231
Poland, 117
Polk, 312, 355
Polkinhorn, 47, 161, 309
Pollard, 47, 437
Pollens, 369
Pollock, 13, 238, 298
Pombo, 326
Pomeroy, 12
Pomona, 368
Ponce de Leon, 380
Pond, 12
Pontier, 143
Pool, 186
Poole, 95, 143, 415
Poor, 172, 272, 423
Poore, 58
Pope, 104, 235, 249, 271
Poplar Point, 157
Popplein, 143
Pornu, 166
Porter, 6, 8, 62, 88, 119, 136, 144, 148, 174, 203, 226, 253, 328, 353, 355, 420, 430
Portman, 51
Posey, 63, 262
Post, 204
Posten, 193
Poster, 86
Poston, 165
Potentini, 423
Potter, 10, 21, 258, 259, 270
Pottinger, 139
Potts, 180, 310, 380
Poultney, 146
Powders, 201

Powell, 86, 101, 180, 244, 254, 260, 271, 272, 292, 296, 329
Powers, 68, 81, 119, 141, 302, 352, 356
Powhatan, 403
Prather, 129, 131, 268, 428
Pratt, 63, 173, 277, 355, 416
Prentiss, 272
Prescott, 265
Preston, 61, 73, 235, 318, 324, 337
Pretty Prospect, 247
Prettyman, 24
Prevost, 169
Price, 1, 79, 129, 141, 145, 154, 168, 171, 212, 256, 259, 272, 285
Prime, 117
Prince Aldabert, 337
Prince Frederick, 127
Prince Gortschakoff, 73
Prince Napoleon, 249
Prince Oscar, 249
Princess Royal of England, 127
Prine, 255
Pritchard, 60
privateer **Chasseur**, 119
Procter, 132
Proctor, 218, 387
propeller **J W Brooks**, 414
propeller **Republic**, 266
propeller **Tinto**, 265, 270, 414
Prospect Hill, 253
Prothro, 110
Prout, 80, 170, 395, 406
Prudhomme, 259
Pruett, 314
Pryor, 298, 355, 371, 379
Pucket, 278
Pugh, 59, 93, 314, 379
Pulaski, 372
Pumphrey, 39, 80, 94, 223, 287, 370, 386
Punhard, 130
Punington, 407

Purcell, 312, 419
Purchas, 268
Purdon, 298
Purdy, 80, 128, 375, 406
Purington, 122
Purnell, 87
Purple, 262, 284
Purrington, 305
Pursell, 437
Push-ma-ta ha, 156
Putnam, 80, 400
Pye, 311
Pyne, 50, 152, 165, 166, 194, 217, 350, 351, 363, 365, 371, 375

Q

Quackenbush, 272
Quail, 204
Quantrell, 262
Quartier, 326
Queen, 126, 223, 273, 408
Queen Isabella, 312
Queen of Spain, 198
Queen of Sweden, 249
Quigley, 210, 211, 297, 418
Quinn, 251, 253, 254
Quiros, 150

R

Race-course, 293
Radclif, 323
Radcliff, 269
Radford, 272
Ragan, 9, 82, 121
Raglan, 13
Ragon, 96
Railey, 108, 207
Rainey, 258, 259, 273
Rains, 354
Rainy, 421
Ralston, 75
Ramsay, 209, 261, 306
Ramsey, 336

Rand, 70, 134, 348, 360
Randall, 22, 137, 188, 256, 309, 322, 375, 412, 435
Randolph, 182, 271, 300, 304
Rankin, 168, 200, 234, 256, 309, 412
Ransom, 44, 183
Ranson, 9, 178
Rasmussen, 233
Ratcliff, 260, 318
Ratcliffe, 179
Ratler, 314
Ratrie, 407
Rau, 379
Raub, 240
Rawley, 356
Ray, 80, 137, 154, 223, 239, 261, 296, 366, 406
Raymond, 177
Rayner, 276
Raynsford, 353
Reach, 223
Read, 5, 51, 75, 183, 206, 230, 244, 247, 314, 354, 356
Reading, 98
Ready, 233, 280
Reardon, 254, 348, 354
Receding Gtwn, 226
Records, 12
Red Bud, 188
Redemptionist, 321
Redfern, 78, 363
Redfield, 201
Redin, 119, 186
Redman, 12, 350
Redmon, 11
Redwood, 302
Reed, 137, 143, 145, 238, 328, 340, 380
Reeder, 55
Reese, 105, 144, 281
Reeside, 286, 296, 309, 418
Regester, 106, 142, 194
Reggio, 287, 289, 294, 311

Regnault, 370
Reid, 26, 103, 147
Reigle, 8
Reiley, 131, 319
Reilly, 48, 146, 157
Reily, 41, 441
Reinhardt, 146
Reintzell, 149
Reiny, 286
Reip, 144
Relliena, 55
Relliend, 162
Renihen, 347
Renner, 267, 279
Reno, 437
Renshaw, 273, 285
Rentrop, 314
Resurvey on Lucky Discovery, 247
Revolutionary pensioners, 10
Revolutionary soldiers, 12
Revolutionary widows, 10
Rey, 274
Reynold, 407
Reynolds, 26, 179, 185, 228, 254, 275, 288, 408
Rhees, 175, 387
Rhett, 6, 332
Rhode Island, 378
Rhodes, 9, 51, 307, 405, 406, 429
Ricaud, 284
Rice, 16, 21, 59, 142, 168, 209, 355, 382
Rich, 45, 143, 164
Richard, 77
Richards, 5, 81, 125, 213, 389, 429, 430
Richardson, 9, 87, 93, 118, 143, 160, 184, 232, 244, 324
Richey, 3, 106, 172, 194
Richie, 304
Richmond, 171, 200, 267, 309
Rickels, 41
Rickets, 147

Ricketts, 37, 143, 144, 204
Rider, 336
Ridgate, 279
Ridgely, 61, 103, 168, 200, 258, 272, 399
Ridgeway, 112, 145
Ridgley, 9, 363
Ridgway, 48, 246, 364
Ridley, 440
Ridout, 359
Rieckelmann, 245
Riehle, 322
Riely, 402
Rieman, 355
Riggin, 392
Riggles, 182, 358
Riggs, 114, 197, 203, 223, 327, 339
Riker, 296
Riley, 73, 105, 254
Rind, 21, 231
Riners, 274
Ring, 302
Ringgold, 109, 167, 215
Riopell, 129
Riordan, 299
Ripley, 12, 152
Rise, 155
Risque, 372, 374, 387
Ritchie, 19, 43, 75, 140, 293, 418
Ritner, 8
Rittenhouse, 329, 398
Ritter, 226
Rivel, 274
Rivers, 264
Rives, 14, 184, 338
Rivra, 352
Rixey, 157
Roab, 371
Roach, 8, 82, 103, 137, 146, 208, 279, 348, 392
Roache, 208
Roane, 96
Robb, 190, 256

Robbinett, 314
Robbins, 142, 336
Robedeau, 111, 306, 311, 316
Roberts, 11, 12, 84, 120, 232, 278, 379, 407
Robertson, 6, 47, 100, 173, 210, 277, 340, 357, 401
Robeson, 353
Robidoux, 267
Robinson, 3, 11, 47, 64, 104, 113, 135, 144, 145, 147, 159, 167, 170, 178, 212, 252, 269, 278, 281, 286, 287, 290, 307, 308, 311, 315, 326, 334, 365, 386, 406, 411, 413, 439
Roby, 105
Roche, 69, 323, 355
Rochell, 314
Rochelle, 273
Rock, 184
Rock Creek Foundry, 216
Rock Hill, 86, 202, 362
Rockland Meadow, 300
Rockwell, 12, 292
Rodgers, 272, 328
Rodier, 47, 304
Rodman, 307
Rodrigo, 345
Roe, 272
Roemelley, 221
Roemle, 148
Rogers, 12, 99, 106, 111, 126, 161, 166, 187, 194, 224, 245, 255, 293, 306, 366, 382
Rogerson, 47, 72
Rojos, 150
Rokohl, 382
Rolando, 50, 55
Rolf, 63, 86
Rolfe, 427
Rollins, 162, 439
Rolph, 160
Roman, 183
Roney, 272, 357

Rooker, 175, 177, 256, 309, 412, 416
Roosevelt, 345
Root, 26, 142
Rootes, 272
Rose, 21, 115, 146, 149, 166
Roseberger, 101
Rosenburg, 383
Rosenvick, 373
Roslin, 283
Ross, 147, 298, 327, 328, 330, 342
Rotch, 307
Rothschild, 2, 28
Rothwell, 5, 34, 167, 192
Roumage, 314, 315
Rouse, 146
Rowan, 272
Rowcroft, 371
Rowland, 66, 243
Rowley, 333
Roy, 288
Royster, 314
Rudd, 19, 271
Rudolph, 361
Rudy, 418
Ruff, 355
Ruffin, 220
Ruffner, 269
Ruloff, 67
Rumery, 267
Ruse, 130
Rush, 26, 192, 305
Rusk, 160, 180
Russell, 81, 117, 119, 142, 204, 251, 261, 273, 352, 364
Ruth, 66, 303, 308
Rutherford, 240, 326
Rutledge, 245, 252
Ryan, 12, 77, 147, 302, 403
Ryland, 106, 194
Ryley, 416
Ryther, 401

S

Sackett, 178
Saddlier, 84
Sadleir, 84
Sadlier, 84
Saffell, 292
Sale, 219
sale of young negroes, 212
Salisbury, 123
Salomon, 166
Saltonstall, 434
Salyer, 270
Sampson, 39
Sams, 6
Samson, 5, 50, 128, 151, 194, 224, 257, 313, 321, 338, 347, 375, 381, 392, 395, 408, 417, 419, 430, 435, 436, 438
Samuels, 100
San Antonio, 74
Sandall, 320
Sanders, 74, 145, 147, 226
Sanderson, 13, 61, 340, 353, 354, 386
Sands, 18, 19, 22, 32, 73, 218, 272
Sandston, 437
Sanford, 4, 66, 234
Sanger, 204, 407
Sansenet, 15
Sansfacon, 111
Santa Anna, 406
Santa Rosa, 150, 166
Santa Ross, 150
Santos, 75, 187
Sappington, 312
Sareter, 61
Sargent, 115, 134
Sarten, 151
Sartori, 95
Saul, 82, 88, 192, 422
Saunders, 9, 56, 204, 399
Saurian, 135
Sauter, 386
Sauvan, 177

Savage, 166, 258, 280
Saviour, 15
Sawyer, 199, 217
Saxton, 237
Sayer, 294
Sayles, 298
Scaggs, 88, 132, 153, 166, 223, 322
Scarburgh, 51
Scearce, 1
Schaeffer, 144
Schaffieiter, 321
Schelatre, 314
Schelenvecker, 21
Schell, 47, 54, 166
Schellenger, 301
Schellinger, 424
Schellings, 229
Schenck, 49, 272, 354
Schlatre, 314, 315
Schleicker, 140
Schlesinger, 150
Schlessinger, 161
Schley, 339, 354
Schlosser, 106
Schmidt, 332
Schneider, 186
schnr **Anna**, 416
schnr **Bancroft**, 6
schnr **Brandywine**, 136
schnr **Brilliant**, 424
schnr **Brothers**, 136
schnr **C B Knudson**, 417
schnr **C F A Cole**, 369
schnr **Chrysolite**, 417
schnr **Enterprise**, 364
schnr **Essayons**, 323
schnr **Eudora Imogene**, 91, 279
schnr **Flying Cloud**, 270
schnr **Forrester**, 136
schnr **Glamorgan**, 151
schnr **Good Exchange**, 119, 168, 205, 311
schnr **Grampus**, 81, 136, 306

schnr **L J Bowden**, 413
schnr **Lapwing**, 119
schnr **Mary**, 136
schnr **Mary Adelaide**, 270
schnr **Mary Jane**, 11
schnr **Matthew Vassar**, 36
schnr **Niagara**, 416
schnr **Olive Branch**, 136
schnr **Onkahye**, 202
schnr **Searsville**, 154
schnr **Silver Ray**, 154
schnr **Stephen C Phillips**, 136
schnr **T W Levering**, 40
schnr **Tempest**, 412
schnr **Two Brothers**, 136
schnr **Union**, 136
schnr **Ursula**, 136
schnr **W Levering**, 33
schnr **Wanderer**, 136
schnr **Zadoc Pratt**, 79
schnrs **Wanderer, Mary, Olive Branch, Two Brothers**, & **Brothers**, 278
Scholfield, 268
Schonbork, 45
Schryver, 47
Schuermann, 327
Schumacher, 355
Schumacker, 147
Schussler, 320
Schuyler, 11, 283, 395
Schwartes, 61
Schwartz, 24, 386, 429
Schwartze, 386
Scollay, 403
Scott, 5, 34, 67, 70, 84, 131, 140, 151, 154, 188, 198, 223, 234, 246, 252, 273, 278, 323, 371
Scrantion, 309
Scranton, 95, 136, 187, 204, 242, 288, 309, 412, 413
Scriber, 200, 288, 309
Scribner, 254

Scriven, 422
Scrivner, 319
Scuddy, 314
Scwartz, 144
Seabrook, 288
Seabury, 276
Seagers, 145, 155
Seaman, 47, 51, 117
Searles, 427
Sears, 40, 84, 93, 119, 143, 433
Seaton, 8, 47, 225
Seaver, 71
Seawell, 79, 162
Sebastian, 308
Sedgewick, 438
Sedgwick, 300
Seefeld, 133
Seeley, 260
Seese, 29
Segelboum, 248
Seger, 146
Seibrecht, 355
Seidenstricker, 357
Seidenstrikcer, 144
Seitz, 20, 61, 386
Selby, 242
Selden, 26, 36, 41, 222, 223, 273, 334, 437
Selfridge, 271
Selkridge, 407
Selwood, 165
Semi, 288
Semken, 208
Semmes, 220, 258, 259, 272, 273, 275, 336, 343, 397
Semoice, 288
Semple, 105
Sengstack, 236
Senie, 436
Seroc, 117
Sessford, 47, 254, 358, 403
Seton, 370
Setton, 218

Seuzeneau, 72
Severance, 86
Sewall, 168, 200
Seward, 151
Sewell, 118, 357
Sexton, 282
Seymour, 52, 73, 141, 258, 259
Shackleford, 252
Shade, 99
Shafer, 324
Shakspeare, 421
Shankland, 44
Shanklin, 340
Shanks, 80
Shannahan, 38
Shannon, 315
Sharkey, 319, 323
Sharp, 146, 172, 273, 438
Sharretts, 347, 420
Shaun, 401, 409
Shaw, 11, 32, 47, 133, 136, 298, 324, 352, 356, 411, 440
Shealy, 297
Shears, 352
Shedd, 85, 374
Shedden, 197
Shee, 67, 69, 106
Sheelah, 264
Sheffey, 287
Sheffield, 391
Shei, 67
Shekell, 92, 384
Shelby, 217, 308
Sheldon, 48, 118, 134
Shelton, 166
Shepard, 183, 342
Shephard, 105
Shepherd, 54, 111
Shepperd, 95
Sherbrooke, 398
Sherer, 44
Sheridan, 264, 274
Sheriff, 167, 280, 356

Sherlock, 427
Sherman, 6, 88, 261, 334, 379
Shermhill, 12
Sherrod, 207
Sherwood, 254, 313, 356
Shield, 5
Shields, 229, 339
Shiles, 160
Shillington, 212
Shinn, 174, 226
ship **Africa**, 207
ship **Arago**, 415
ship **Ariel**, 80
ship **Asia**, 130
ship **Black Warrior**, 92
ship **Caledonia**, 188, 250
ship **Chariot of Fame**, 36
ship **Charles Morgan**, 161
ship **Cherubim**, 371
ship **Elizabeth**, 390
ship **Elvira Owen**, 235
ship **Emerald Isle**, 217
ship **Fashion**, 36
ship **George Law**, 361
ship **Golden Age**, 262, 284
ship **Golden City**, 399
ship **H M S Nankin**, 30
ship **H M S Pique**, 30
ship **James R Keeler**, 217
ship **Jamestown**, 181
ship **Johanna Elisa**, 217
ship **John Garrow**, 440
ship **John J Boyd**, 63
ship **John Rutledge**, 112
ship **Julia**, 417
ship **Louisiana**, 364
ship **Macedonia**, 235
ship **Macedonian**, 90
ship **Ohio**, 18
ship **Peruvian**, 149
ship **Plymouth**, 247
ship **Portsmouth**, 399
ship **Princeton**, 261

ship **Rattler**, 30
ship **Resolute**, 326
ship **Savannah**, 405
ship **Sierra Nevada**, 262, 284
ship **Sonora**, 262, 284
ship **St Denis**, 21
ship **St Louis**, 422
ship **St Mary's**, 401
ship **Thornton**, 224
ship **Transport**, 422
ship **Wabash**, 401
Shipley, 298
Shipp, 294
ships **Devastation, Aetna, Meteor, Erebus, & Fairy**, 328
Shoekendick, 376
Shoemaker, 395
Shorb, 95
Short, 323
Shreeve, 320
Shreve, 68, 174, 176, 364
Shryer, 257
Shryock, 165, 319, 330
Shubrick, 31
Shucking, 61
Shugert, 36, 222
Shulze, 293
Shussler, 374
Shute, 353
Shuttleworth, 181
Sibbern, 149
Sibley, 116, 127, 375, 390
Sigourney, 33
Sigur, 42
Silby, 105
Sill, 69
Silsbee, 29
Silva, 369
Silver Hills, 246
Simianer, 20
Simmance, 288
Simmons, 23, 235, 381

Simms, 73, 119, 163, 168, 171, 187, 223, 261, 275, 304, 313, 324, 330, 357, 369, 437
Simond, 97
Simonica, 314
Simons, 282, 291
Simpkins, 21
Simpson, 9, 33, 79, 95, 183, 240, 272, 352, 382, 395
Sims, 123, 267
Sina, 225
Sinclair, 272
Singer, 137
Singleton, 360
Sinon, 48
Sinton, 183
Sioussa, 332
Sis, 259
Sisson, 145
Sister Mary Angela, 110
Sister Mary Filmena Martin, 369
Sisterre, 318
Sizemore, 288
Skerrett, 273
Skidmore, 59, 65
Skinner, 9, 62, 225, 296, 427
Skipper, 255
Skipwith, 425
Skirving, 137
Skoote, 248
Slack, 356
Slater, 167
Slatford, 269
Slaughter, 14, 17, 100, 211, 357, 394
Slavin, 288
Sleder, 239
Slicer, 369
Slidell, 10
Slingluff, 355
Sloan, 145, 147, 199, 224, 274
Sloat, 52
Slocum, 14
sloop-of-war **Cyane**, 55, 79, 104

sloop-of-war **Germantown**, 188
sloop-of-war **John Adams**, 60
sloop-of-war **Levant**, 399
sloop-of-war **Macedonian**, 296
sloop-of-war **Portsmouth**, 95
sloop-of-war **Saratoga**, 38
sloop-of-war **Warren**, 413
Slough, 370
Sly, 342
Small, 173
Smallwood, 53, 228, 348
Smead, 303
Smith, 11, 12, 16, 21, 30, 31, 44, 47, 48, 54, 59, 60, 62, 64, 66, 71, 72, 78, 79, 80, 83, 87, 96, 99, 100, 105, 109, 113, 117, 119, 120, 125, 129, 136, 141, 143, 144, 145, 146, 149, 170, 178, 179, 181, 183, 186, 193, 204, 206, 207, 211, 214, 215, 217, 221, 222, 228, 229, 234, 241, 242, 247, 253, 254, 258, 259, 261, 264, 266, 267, 268, 272, 273, 276, 283, 284, 288, 290, 295, 301, 309, 315, 324, 330, 337, 341, 344, 346, 349, 352, 353, 355, 356, 365, 368, 371, 372, 381, 382, 385, 387, 389, 390, 391, 392, 393, 394, 396, 399, 409, 411, 415, 418, 419, 427, 428, 436
Smithson, 56, 107, 429
Smithwood, 261
smoking of tobacco, 441
Smoot, 27, 181, 186, 394, 409
Snead, 5, 303, 388
Sneed, 7
Snicker's Gap, 357
Snodgrass, 419
Snook, 16
Snooks, 54
Snowden, 143, 210, 392
Snyder, 226, 304, 314, 337, 389
Sola, 130, 142
Soldiers-1812, 8
Solze, 146

Somers, 245
Somerville, 330
Sorden, 167
Sothoron, 386
Sotomayor, 22
Soulard, 418, 422
Soule, 253
Soumarokhoff, 346
Southall, 405
Southard, 88, 169, 248
Southern, 259
Sowman, 143
Spa Spring, 319
Spaight, 405
Spalding, 13, 51, 406
Spangler, 401
Spaulding, 80
Spaulding's District, 246
Speake, 269
Spear, 39
Spedden, 273
Speed, 154, 300
Speiden, 95
Speir, 379
Spence, 147, 296
Spence's Mill, 359
Spencer, 45, 80, 247, 292, 354, 392, 408
Sperry, 4
Sphears, 352
Spicer, 347, 401
Spilcker, 145
Spineberg, 136
Spohn, 12
Spotswood, 183, 420
Spotts, 43
Sprague, 72, 142, 143, 271, 367
Sprigg, 344, 382
Spring, 276, 404
Spring Grove, 396
Spring Tavern, 217
Springer, 258, 259
Sproston, 273

Sproule, 110, 327
Spurr, 43
St Andrew's Society, 400
St Aubin, 231
St Clair, 19, 39, 138, 193, 256, 283, 288, 415
St Elizabeth, 157
St John, 304
St Mary's bay, 268
St Timothy's Hall, 394
Stabell, 369
Stadley, 227
Stafford, 433
Stailey, 356
Stallings, 208
Stanbraugh, 114
Stanford, 401, 430
Stanley, 55, 194, 251, 400, 403, 427
Stansbury, 144, 290
Stanton, 55, 119, 289
Staples, 202
Starbuck, 257
Stark, 429
Starr, 145, 392, 422
steam boat **Augusta**, 440
steamboat **Alabama**, 110
steamboat **Bellfair**, 155
steamboat **George Washington**, 376
steamboat **Henry Clay**, 300
steamboat **John Jay**, 285
steamboat **Metropolis**, 120
steamboat **New World**, 166, 412
steamboat **Star**, 314
steamer **Alabama**, 49
steamer **Bay State**, 376
steamer **Blue Hammack**, 315
steamer **Cambria**, 147, 157
steamer **Columbia**, 137
steamer **Elm City**, 15
steamer **Empire City**, 196
steamer **Empire State**, 300, 414
steamer **Fulton**, 38
steamer **Golden Age**, 261

steamer **Island Home**, 15
steamer **John Jay**, 414
steamer **Longuil**, 414
steamer **Lyonnaise**, 390
steamer **Major Hopkins**, 187
steamer **Major Tompkins**, 242, 288, 309, 413
steamer **Massachusetts**, 190
steamer **Merrimac**, 59
steamer **Michigan**, 231
steamer **Minnesota**, 252
steamer **Mississippi**, 266
steamer **Missouri**, 204
steamer **Monmouth**, 364
steamer **Nautilus**, 414
steamer **Niagara**, 345, 414
steamer **Northern Indiana**, 266, 414
steamer **Ohio Belle**, 105
steamer **Pacific**, 48, 49, 63, 147, 157, 220
steamer **Persia**, 49, 187
steamer **Prometheus**, 14
steamer **San Francisco**, 96
steamer **San Jacinto**, 399
steamer **Saranac**, 225
steamer **Southerner**, 413
steamer **Superior**, 414
steamer **Suwanee**, 417
steamer **Waterwitch**, 180
steamer **Water-Witch**, 68
steamer **Worcester**, 376
steam-frig **Powhatan**, 57
steamship **Asia**, 149
steamship **Charles Morgan**, 155
steamship **Daniel Webster**, 97
steamship **Le Lyonnaise**, 414
steamship **New World**, 180
steamship **Perseverance**, 323
steamship **San Francisco**, 32, 52
steamship **Southerner**, 81, 424
Stearns, 198, 277, 288, 385, 411
Stedman, 58
Steedman, 266, 272

Steel, 95
Steele, 3, 106, 256
Steer, 182
Steere, 48
Steers, 348
Steiger, 263, 264
Steil, 223
Stelle, 149
Stellwagen, 272
Stephens, 49, 51, 129, 439
Stephenson, 266
Stern, 186
Sterrett, 141, 399
Stetson, 83
Steuart, 114, 136, 256, 309, 412, 416, 440
Stevens, 51, 59, 64, 82, 84, 105, 140, 143, 159, 176, 204, 263, 267, 319, 323, 349, 373
Stevenson, 61, 154, 354, 417
Steward, 391
Stewardson, 234
Stewart, 19, 37, 50, 80, 110, 145, 147, 165, 178, 188, 192, 229, 244, 248, 266, 267, 273, 279, 315, 320, 343, 355, 391, 406
Stidham, 321
Stieff, 145
Stillings, 366
Stillwell, 273
Stiltz, 143
Stimel, 356
Stinchcomb, 143
Stinson, 289
Stirling, 144
Stisser, 192
Stivers, 226
Stockbridge, 405
Stockett, 388
Stocking, 21
Stockton, 276
Stockwell, 255
Stoddard, 97, 272
Stoddert, 149
Stokely, 299
Stokes, 165
Stone, 31, 80, 103, 111, 261, 273, 312, 392, 406, 422
Stonestreet, 311, 343
Storer, 19, 68
Storrow, 79, 135
Storrs, 422
Stott, 139, 336, 375
Stout, 272
Stow, 143
Stowe, 79
Stowell, 34, 144, 329
Strader, 282, 309, 413
Strain, 20, 204
Stran, 146
Strang, 231, 244
Stratton, 264, 340
Strausz, 67
Stribling, 77, 259, 407, 420
Strini, 14
Strobell, 163
Strong, 188, 340
Strother, 360
Stuart, 16, 24, 65, 162, 182, 255, 273, 317, 343
Stuarts, 34
Studivan, 54
Stump, 180
Sturdivant, 16
Sturgeon, 113
Sturgess, 171
Sturgis, 291
Stutz, 374
Stuyvesant, 206, 354
Styles, 43, 249
Suddards, 134
Sudders, 260
Suffield, 90
Suit, 259

Sullivan, 39, 74, 122, 174, 226, 233, 239, 248, 251, 261, 262, 284, 320, 357, 395, 431, 433
Sullivant, 81, 424
Summers, 79, 149, 380
Sumner, 9, 132, 178, 198, 238, 240, 390
Sunderland, 20, 44, 189, 193, 212, 252, 351, 421
Sunnyside, 101
Supplee, 294
Surratt, 303
Suter, 147, 270
Sutherland, 51, 105
Sutton, 5, 186
Suydam, 300
Swaim, 264
Swain, 188, 429
Swan, 424
Swann, 181, 278, 337, 383
Swanton, 81
Swartwout, 207, 272, 396
Sweeney, 15, 432
Sweeny, 26, 59, 67, 73, 83, 169, 207, 209, 239, 347, 398, 404
Sweet, 81, 128
Swift, 22, 76
Swinburn, 344
Sydnor, 354
Sylvester, 120
Syme, 425
Symmons, 48

T

Taber, 350
Taft, 15, 168
Taggart, 91
Talbird, 6
Talbot, 154, 242
Talbott, 354
Taliaferro, 238
Talley, 69
Tallhirst, 174
Tallmadge, 291
Tally, 298
Taney, 10, 368, 404, 406
Tasistro, 282
Tate, 37, 47, 49, 54, 131, 204, 252
Tatsapaugh, 18
Tavener, 328
Tayloe, 82, 165
Taylor, 4, 14, 20, 52, 62, 83, 91, 104, 110, 115, 141, 145, 151, 154, 155, 156, 180, 181, 204, 219, 226, 228, 244, 246, 263, 272, 277, 282, 288, 292, 309, 318, 327, 347, 352, 372, 373, 387, 392, 402, 406, 412, 418, 420, 436
Teachem, 129
Teale, 61
Teasdale, 13, 123, 194, 360
Tebbetts, 58
Teel, 386
Telfourd, 390
Temple, 154, 265, 272, 332
Templeman, 334, 382, 392
Tenley, 408, 439
Tenney, 434
Terrett, 121, 272, 372
Terry, 281, 295, 320, 322, 323, 337, 348
Tertrou, 77
Thatcher, 272, 405
the steamer **Nautilus**, 323
Thistle, 275, 277
Thom, 183, 295, 405
Thoma, 61, 386
Thomas, 9, 14, 15, 58, 106, 170, 175, 181, 223, 240, 266, 278, 290, 308, 316, 323, 346, 400, 430
Thompson, 6, 8, 10, 16, 20, 30, 58, 90, 143, 144, 146, 154, 172, 180, 191, 193, 200, 215, 262, 272, 278, 304, 305, 312, 323, 338, 355, 364, 372, 375, 380, 386, 405, 406, 411
Thomsen, 147

Thomson, 98, 304, 340, 356
Thorburn, 273
Thorington, 115, 259
Thorn, 159, 383
Thornberry, 321, 439
Thorne, 318
Thornley, 186
Thornton, 322, 385
Thorpe, 161
Thorwaldsen, 364
Thrall, 374
Thraves, 206
Three Brothers, 246
Threlkeld, 176
Thrift, 265
Throckmorton, 346, 409
Throop, 361
Thurston, 429, 430
Thwing, 285
Thyson, 176
Tiber, 240
Tiber creek, 436
Tiber river, 114
Tidball, 131, 150, 311
Tidy, 357
Tiernan, 147
Tierney, 259
Tiers, 306
Tiffany, 112
Tilghman, 124
Tilley, 435
Tillinghast, 156, 389
Tillis, 255
Tillman, 90, 148, 151
Tilton, 146
Tippett, 82, 158
Tipton, 226
Titus, 315, 318, 319, 326
Tobias, 278
Todd, 35, 95, 105, 114, 133, 154, 168, 237, 291, 301, 307, 311, 316, 360, 411, 416
Toffier, 315

Toland, 234
Toler, 155
Tolson, 80
Tone, 352, 356
Toombs, 151
Topham, 247, 378
Topling, 48
Topper, 202
Topping, 61, 386
Tormey, 142
Torrence, 301, 311
Totten, 31, 272, 303
Tourison, 105
towboat **F M Streck**, 323
Towers, 26, 27, 33, 47, 48, 150
Towles, 143
Townsend, 96, 140, 331, 340, 363
Towson, 144, 188, 250
Trabue, 233
Tracy, 145, 163, 274, 326
Trafton, 410
Trask, 374
Travers, 357, 398
Travis, 406
Treadway, 3
Treadwell, 171, 281, 309, 315, 370, 379
Treat, 119, 317
Trent land, 381
Tretler, 257, 386
Trigg, 217
Trimble, 57, 145, 340
Trimmer, 48
Trinity Church, 43
Triplette, 17
Tripp, 301
Trippe, 2, 42
Trocchia, 71
Trook, 104
Trosclair, 315
Trotter, 113, 136
Troup, 170, 175
Trout, 155

497

Truax, 12
Truehart, 395
Trueman, 25, 127
Trugien, 5
Truman, 40, 80, 346
Truro house, 14
Truton, 164
Truxton, 273, 423
Tschiffely, 112, 160
Tuaold, 346
Tubman, 117, 205
Tucker, 13, 22, 42, 44, 50, 77, 99, 109, 200, 203, 220, 256, 272, 309, 326, 330, 397, 404, 407
Tuckers, 22
Tudor, 124
Tudor Place, 124
Tuell, 319, 320
Tullus, 117
Turero, 315
Turk, 347
Turley, 352
Turnbull, 237, 299
Turner, 18, 21, 75, 106, 131, 144, 146, 154, 162, 171, 200, 204, 266, 267, 272, 309, 314, 315, 357, 367, 386, 399
Turton, 407
Tuthill, 175
Tweedy, 222
Twenty-bldg Hill, 93
Twichell, 323
Twiggs, 102, 376
Twyman, 417
Tyffe, 273
Tyler, 68, 73, 75, 157, 339, 378, 417
Tyrce, 240
Tysinger, 143
Tyson, 25, 280, 362

U

Umberfield, 4, 276
Underwood, 176, 292, 301, 351, 419

Union Farm, 206
Updegraff, 417
Upham, 186
Upshur, 157, 192, 272
Upson, 332, 337
Urban, 344, 398
Utterbach, 12
Uttermahle, 80
Uttermehle, 234
Uttermuhle, 221, 376, 407

V

Vail, 168
Valley Farm, 435
Valley View, 252
Valley View Farm, 236
Van Allen, 341
Van Bergen, 36
Van Bibber, 221
Van Bokkelen, 394
Van Brunt, 271
Van Buren, 212, 436
Van Buskirk, 59, 131
Van Fleet, 12
Van Hageriman, 16
Van Hook, 246
Van Ness, 102, 159, 247, 341
Van Nostwick, 147
Van Patten, 129, 203
Van Pelt, 296
Van Rensselaer, 8, 95, 278, 288
Van Reswick, 403
Van Riswick, 89, 93, 322
Van Voorhis, 405
Van Vorst, 422
Van Wyck, 365
Van Zandt, 34, 35, 273
Vance, 414
Vanderbilt, 281
Vanderhennel, 429
Vandivir, 294
Vandyke, 95, 435
Vanmeter, 212, 326

Vannerson, 281
Vansant, 95
Vantine, 109
Vanuxem, 255
Varian, 351
Vass, 124, 211, 286
Vasseurs, 60
Vattemare, 88
Vattier, 221, 277
Vaughan, 35
Vaughn, 141, 245, 301
Vault, 199
Vaustavern, 264
Vedder, 134
Veitch, 421
Veley, 356
Velplean, 39
Venable, 363, 392, 394
Vencinti, 201
Vermillion, 174
vessel **Mary St John**, 198
Vick, 284
Victor, 422
Vielmeyer, 80
Villiger, 215
Vincent, 173
Vineyard, 164
Vinson, 94
Vinton, 226
Virgin Queen, 380
Virginia, 380
Visser, 283, 302
Viti, 149, 150
Voisin, 314
Volcher, 135
Volcker, 151
Von Meschzisker, 145
Von Rothschild, 2, 28
Vonderlehu, 128
Voss, 16, 89
Vowell, 181
Vreeland, 52, 63
Vroom, 248

W

Waddell, 273
Wade, 189, 240, 286, 356, 383, 440
Wadington, 35
Wadsworth, 28, 317
Waesche, 142
Waggaman, 291
Wagner, 185
Wagnor, 117
Wailes, 112
Wainright, 11
Wainwright, 52
Wait, 146
Waite, 368
Walbach, 187, 277, 309, 412
Waldo, 66, 78, 267, 277, 299, 306, 311, 316
Walke, 32
Walker, 5, 22, 33, 70, 97, 113, 119, 143, 146, 150, 155, 157, 161, 165, 173, 178, 182, 186, 191, 193, 207, 215, 223, 226, 231, 243, 256, 271, 272, 273, 294, 305, 308, 328, 352, 356, 361, 363, 369, 373, 375, 378, 392, 397, 400, 401, 410, 415, 417, 426, 431
Wall, 95, 173, 338, 354, 361, 375, 386, 406
Wallace, 17, 111, 132, 136, 213, 301, 405, 406, 417
Wallach, 26, 33, 56, 93, 116, 119, 127, 132, 175, 186, 192, 250, 279, 328, 334, 382, 386
Wallach's Row, 277
Waller, 3
Wallis, 224
Walmsley, 93
Waln, 429
Walsh, 350, 420, 440
Walter, 143, 148, 355
Walters, 147
Walthall, 422
Walton, 206, 208, 217, 288

Wandestrand, 113, 136, 287, 289
Wankowiectz, 303
War of 1812, 432
Ward, 7, 33, 82, 99, 143, 144, 146, 159, 247, 259, 265, 267, 304, 320, 322, 338, 372, 415, 432
Warder, 80
Ware, 219
Warfield, 278, 312
Waring, 259
Warkman, 213
Warley, 272, 405
Warner, 117, 250, 252, 371
Warren, 146, 165, 172, 254, 370, 383, 387, 420
Warren Green Hotel, 78
Warring, 356
Warrington, 296
Warth, 269
Wartmann, 402
Warwick, 147
Wasco, 54
Wash City Ordinances, 27
Washbourne, 269
Washburne, 150, 267
Washington, 7, 9, 34, 53, 98, 101, 107, 133, 134, 152, 182, 206, 210, 228, 262, 263, 283, 303, 320, 323, 339, 349, 362, 364, 368, 376, 408, 429, 435
Washington House, 230
Washington Monument, 240
Waterbury, 234
Waterman, 196, 294, 343
Waters, 8, 26, 27, 47, 73, 80, 167, 195, 318, 377
Watkins, 9, 26, 142, 143, 163, 303, 355, 407
Watmough, 95, 255, 273
Watson, 26, 42, 64, 288, 290, 354, 390
Watt, 175, 231
Watt's Island, 33

Watters, 235, 273
Watts, 195, 318
Waugh, 395
Waveland, 276
Waverley, 168
Wayne, 204
Wayson, 330, 338
Weakley, 328
Weatherby, 146
Weatherford, 60, 171
Weaver, 70, 145, 273
Webb, 10, 81, 95, 103, 109, 146, 173, 213, 241, 242, 375, 398, 413, 427
Webber, 160, 185, 247
Weble, 417
Webster, 145, 157, 185, 325, 354, 396, 414, 434
Wechsler, 147
Weed, 417
Weeden, 389, 403
Week, 435
Weeks, 12
Weems, 92, 125, 136, 430
Wehrheim, 79
Weidman, 354
Weightman, 47, 56, 97, 267, 268
Weir, 140, 296, 308, 313
Weiss, 21
Weissenfels, 85, 138
Weit, 74
Welch, 73, 325, 352
Welchel, 239
Weller, 140, 179
Wellington, 306, 432
Wells, 39, 40, 116, 272, 274, 281, 290, 304, 352, 356, 404, 433
Welsh, 83, 253, 272, 302, 352, 409
Wendell, 47, 54
Werden, 92
Wesley Chapel, 427
West, 105, 166, 237, 250, 255, 265, 273, 293, 370, 409
Weston, 95, 146, 265, 352

Westwood, 106, 322
Westworth, 231
Wetenhall, 287
Wetherford, 237
Wethern, 257
Wetmore, 191
Weymouth, 260
Whales, 134
Wharton, 74, 354
Wheat, 240
Wheatley, 73, 158, 359, 401
Wheaton, 343
Wheelan, 258
Wheeler, 11, 52, 168, 183, 203, 243, 310, 319, 355, 397, 419, 429
Wheelwright, 145
Whidden, 255
Whipple, 119, 136, 141, 168, 171, 187, 221, 232, 256, 301
Whitaker, 287, 289, 311
Whitall, 417
Whitcomb, 229
White, 21, 42, 56, 73, 81, 106, 117, 124, 134, 180, 187, 195, 213, 214, 223, 238, 256, 262, 284, 293, 298, 314, 327, 338, 360, 366, 370, 382, 426, 439
White Cottage, 204
White House, 177
White Sulphur, 196
White Sulphur Springs, 65
Whiteford, 144
Whitehead, 12, 126, 354
Whitehurst, 281
Whitelock, 213
Whitfield, 14, 55, 217
Whitin, 353
Whiting, 36, 57, 61, 64, 85, 222, 230, 272, 369, 437
Whitman, 16, 142, 163, 353
Whitney, 12, 142, 150, 207, 324, 381
Whitridge, 355
Whittaker, 48, 240, 294, 316, 405

Whitten, 267
Whittington, 47, 87
Whittle, 402
Whittlesey, 22, 214, 285, 298
Whitwell, 384
Whitworth, 157
Whtflieth, 268
Wiadean, 248
Wiber, 47
Widdicombe, 369
Widup, 435
Wight, 373
Wightman, 262
Wigle, 300
Wilburn, 295
Wilcox, 51, 247
Wilds, 163
Wiley, 361
Wilhoite, 384
Wilkes, 75, 271
Wilkins, 227, 268
Wilkinson, 126, 171, 229, 291, 388, 412
Willard, 185, 254
Willcox, 272
Willett, 97, 197, 359, 406
Williams, 5, 8, 9, 10, 16, 23, 35, 57, 62, 77, 80, 89, 92, 93, 115, 128, 131, 142, 152, 154, 156, 159, 177, 180, 181, 186, 190, 192, 197, 212, 213, 225, 234, 238, 246, 273, 281, 295, 317, 319, 321, 327, 328, 348, 349, 352, 354, 355, 356, 370, 374, 375, 378, 380, 408, 414, 418, 420, 427
Williamson, 38, 40, 45, 275, 319, 330, 339, 358
Willian, 374
Williott, 416
Willis, 143, 232
Willison, 167
Williston, 33, 38
Willkings, 175

Willner, 374
Wills, 4, 288
Willson, 14, 361
Wilson, 5, 8, 9, 16, 21, 30, 45, 46, 48, 54, 61, 77, 91, 105, 108, 110, 118, 160, 174, 186, 189, 194, 195, 202, 211, 212, 218, 220, 227, 231, 234, 254, 256, 263, 264, 271, 273, 279, 297, 304, 310, 322, 333, 343, 349, 350, 355, 357, 376, 381, 386, 393, 394, 406, 427, 431, 433, 434
Wiltberger, 346
Wilton, 35
Wimberly, 302
Wimer, 47
Winchester, 145, 316, 359
Winder, 129, 158, 171, 255, 270, 359
Windfield, 439
Windle, 196
Windsor, 217, 243
Winegerg, 415
Winlock, 274
Winship, 301
Winslow, 253, 272, 305, 310
Winter, 26, 80, 207
Wippermann, 373
Wirt, 155, 429
Wise, 17, 29, 53, 61, 81, 97, 104, 132, 234, 259, 271, 385, 386, 400
Wisely, 229
Witherell, 129
Withers, 36, 208, 222, 328, 334, 437
Witman, 343
Wittenaur, 441
Wittenouer, 440
Wlodecki, 266
Wm & Mary College, 303
Woelpper, 93
Wolf, 106, 418
Wolfe, 101, 138, 283, 441
Wolfendyke, 22
Wolff, 223
Wollard, 421

Wollenham, 157
Wolsey, 208
Wood, 35, 69, 79, 82, 93, 112, 113, 121, 178, 210, 211, 247, 273, 283, 353, 384, 416, 427, 434
Woodbridge, 138
Woodburn, 50
Woodbury, 56, 220, 422
Woodhull, 35
Woodland, 21, 364
Woodley, 344
Woodroffe, 146
Woodruff, 90, 319
Woods, 387, 437
Woodward, 16, 47, 48, 161, 172, 220, 326, 367, 437
Woodworth, 90, 109, 141, 144, 172, 288
Wooldridge, 202
Wooster, 96, 133, 218
Woozencraft, 205
Worceser, 77
Worcester, 245
Worden, 38, 292
Woronzoff, 346
Worrell, 29, 68
Worster, 151, 267
Worth, 72
Worthington, 108, 157, 251, 319, 434, 435
Wozencraft, 141, 168, 413
Wright, 33, 47, 48, 56, 60, 83, 96, 111, 117, 207, 281, 432
Wroe, 308, 400
Wroth, 143
Wyatt, 22, 141, 311
Wyberd, 146
Wyett, 229
Wylie, 16, 222
Wyllys, 317
Wyman, 247
Wynn, 313
Wysong, 230

Y

yacht **America**, 348
yacht **Vesper**, 368
Yard, 272
Yates, 281
Yeabower, 61, 386
Yeakle, 136
Yeatman, 59, 146
Yeatmen, 408
Yerby, 73, 329, 387
York, 233

Young, 5, 9, 11, 33, 67, 89, 105, 160, 162, 174, 198, 204, 210, 212, 213, 225, 230, 239, 272, 273, 299, 303, 329, 355, 356, 375, 394, 403
Yuhl, 148

Z

Zantzinger, 32, 90, 112
Zeigler, 68
Zigler, 202
Zindell, 206

Other Heritage Books by Joan M. Dixon:

National Intelligencer *Newspaper Abstracts
Special Edition: The Civil War Years
Volume 1: January 1, 1861-June 30, 1863*

National Intelligencer *Newspaper Abstracts
Special Edition: The Civil War Years
Volume 2: July 1, 1863-December 31, 1865*

National Intelligencer *Newspaper Abstracts 1856*

National Intelligencer *Newspaper Abstracts 1855*

National Intelligencer *Newspaper Abstracts 1854*

National Intelligencer *Newspaper Abstracts 1853*

National Intelligencer *Newspaper Abstracts 1852*

National Intelligencer *Newspaper Abstracts 1851*

National Intelligencer *Newspaper Abstracts 1850*

National Intelligencer *Newspaper Abstracts 1849*

National Intelligencer *Newspaper Abstracts 1848*

National Intelligencer *Newspaper Abstracts 1847*

National Intelligencer *Newspaper Abstracts 1846*

National Intelligencer *Newspaper Abstracts 1845*

National Intelligencer *Newspaper Abstracts 1844*

National Intelligencer *Newspaper Abstracts 1843*

National Intelligencer *Newspaper Abstracts 1842*

National Intelligencer *Newspaper Abstracts 1841*

National Intelligencer *Newspaper Abstracts 1840*

National Intelligencer *Newspaper Abstracts, 1838-1839*

National Intelligencer *Newspaper Abstracts, 1836-1837*

National Intelligencer *Newspaper Abstracts, 1834-1835*

National Intelligencer *Newspaper Abstracts, 1832-1833*

National Intelligencer *Newspaper Abstracts, 1830-1831*

National Intelligencer *Newspaper Abstracts, 1827-1829*

National Intelligencer *Newspaper Abstracts, 1824-1826*

National Intelligencer *Newspaper Abstracts, 1821-1823*

National Intelligencer *Newspaper Abstracts, 1818-1820*

National Intelligencer *Newspaper Abstracts, 1814-1817*

National Intelligencer *Newspaper Abstracts, 1811-1813*

National Intelligencer *Newspaper Abstracts, 1806-1810*

National Intelligencer *Newspaper Abstracts, 1800-1805*

www.ingramcontent.com/pod-product-compliance
Lightning Source LLC
Chambersburg PA
CBHW071431300426
44114CB00013B/1396